Accounting Theory

An Information Content Perspective

Accounting Theory

An Information Content Perspective

John A. Christensen
University of Southern Denmark

Joel S. Demski
University of Florida

Boston   Burr Ridge, IL   Dubuque, IA   Madison, WI   New York   San Francisco   St. Louis
Bangkok   Bogotá   Caracas   Kuala Lumpur   Lisbon   London   Madrid   Mexico City
Milan   Montreal   New Delhi   Santiago   Seoul   Singapore   Sydney   Taipei   Toronto

McGraw-Hill Higher Education

A Division of The McGraw-Hill Companies

ACCOUNTING THEORY: AN INFORMATION CONTENT PERSPECTIVE
Published by McGraw-Hill/Irwin, a business unit of The McGraw-Hill Companies, Inc.,
1221 Avenue of the Americas, New York, NY, 10020. Copyright © 2003 by The
McGraw-Hill Companies, Inc. All rights reserved. No part of this publication may be
reproduced or distributed in any form or by any means, or stored in a database or retrieval
system, without the prior written consent of The McGraw-Hill Companies, Inc.,
including, but not limited to, in any network or other electronic storage or transmission,
or broadcast for distance learning.

Some ancillaries, including electronic and print components, may not be available to
customers outside the United States.

This book is printed on acid-free paper.

domestic   1 2 3 4 5 6 7 8 9 0 DOC/DOC 0 9 8 7 6 5 4 3 2
international   1 2 3 4 5 6 7 8 9 0 DOC/DOC 0 9 8 7 6 5 4 3 2

ISBN   0-07-229691-7

Publisher: *Brent Gordon*
Sponsoring editor: *Steve DeLancey*
Editorial coordinator: *Kelly Odom*
Marketing manager: *Richard Kolasa*
Project manager: *Natalie J. Ruffatto*
Production supervisor: *Gina Hangos*
Freelance design coordinator: *Laurie J. Entringer*
Supplement producer: *Susan Lombardi*
Cover design: *Leslie Nayman*
Typeface: *10/12 Palatino*
Compositor: *Interactive Composition Corporation*
Printer: *R. R. Donnelley & Sons Company*

Library of Congress Cataloging-in-Publication Data

Christensen, John Asmus.
    Accounting theory: an information content perspective / John A. Christensen,
    Joel S. Demski.
       p. cm.
    Includes index.
    ISBN 0-07-229691-7 (alk. paper) – ISBN 0-07-112327-X (international : alk. paper)
    1. Accounting. 2. Information theory. I. Demski, Joel S. II. Title.
    HF5625 .C578 2003
    657'.01–dc21

                                                                    2002022808

INTERNATIONAL EDITION ISBN 0-07-112327-X
Copyright © 2003. Exclusive rights by The McGraw-Hill Companies, Inc. for
manufacture and export. This book cannot be re-exported from the country to which it is
sold by McGraw-Hill.

The International Edition is not available in North America.

www.mhhe.com

To Mette and Millie

Table of Contents

About the Authors

John A. Christensen is professor of accounting at the University of Southern Denmark at Odense. Professor Christensen holds a M.Sc. degree in Mathematics and Economics from Aarhus University, Denmark, and a Ph.D. from Stanford University. His articles have appeared in such journals as the *European Accounting Review, Management Accounting Research, Journal of Accounting Research, Review of Accounting Studies, Bell Journal of Economics*, and *Management Science*. He is also the coauthor of several books, including *Virksomhedens årsregnskab (Financial Accounting)* and *Virksomhedens økonomistyring (Management Control)*. Professor Christensen is a Decorated Knight of the Order of Dannebrog. He serves as chairman of the PriceWaterhouseCoopers Doctoral Colloquium in Europe.

Joel S. Demski is the Frederick E. Fisher Eminent Scholar in Accounting at the University of Florida. Professor Demski holds B.S.E. and M.B.A. degrees from the University of Michigan and a Ph.D. from the University of Chicago. His articles have appeared in such journals as the *Accounting Review, Journal of Accounting & Economics, Journal of Accounting Research, Accounting, Organizations and Society, Contemporary Accounting Research, Journal of Economic Theory, Rand Journal of Economics, Management Science*, and *The Journal of Law, Economics and Organization*. He is also the author or coauthor of several books, including *Managerial Uses of Accounting Information* (Kluwer, 1994). Professor Demski was awarded the AAA Outstanding Educator Award in 1986 and the AAA Seminal Contribution Award (along with Jerry Feltham) in 1994 and was the recipient of an Honorary Doctorate from Odense University. He was inducted into the Accounting Hall of Fame in 2000 and served as president of the American Accounting Association, 2001–2002.

Preface

Accounting comes in an amazing variety of forms, including financial, managerial, governmental, national, and tax. Add to this the variety across firms and national boundaries, and we have a seemingly bewildering array of variations. With a modest amount of abstraction or theory, however, the essential details come into focus.

Of course offering such an exercise begs the question of why someone might want to identify the essential details. This reason is fairly simple. Accounting is not measurement for the sake of measurement. Significant resources and institutions are devoted to accounting, and judgment is essential to organizing, managing, and dynamically adjusting an organization's accounting system. Wise exercise of this judgment relies on understanding the essential details, on an appropriate, well-tuned abstraction.

Here we present such an abstraction. There are three keys to the abstraction. The first is to identify a substantive reason for "doing the accounting." To us, accounting is designed to convey information, so in the end we are dealing with some specific information source. We term this the information content perspective. The second key is to recognize, if you will, the structure that accounting places on its informational renderings: restrictive recognition and income as change in net assets adjusted for capital adjustments. The third key is to be thoughtful about the setting. If information is present, then uncertainty is present. If information is present, someone must be interested in acquiring that information. If the firm or reporting entity is confronted by some accounting issue, such as depreciating a long-lived asset, it must have had a reason for acquiring the asset in the first place.

That said, it is important to understand that being thoughtful and serious in this manner is not cost free. It is essential that we identify how the accounting information is or might be used. For this purpose, we will rely on individuals, firms, and markets behaving in economic fashion. So, an economic perspective, if you will, is present, but this is by no means an economics text.

It is also important to understand that our presentation uses a modest degree of formalism. This, it turns out, is essential if we are to be honest about the information content perspective. At the same time, however, this formalism is neither gratuitous nor highly technical. We purposely keep technical aspects at bay, and virtually every demonstration and exercise in the text can be approached with a spreadsheet.

A number of individuals have assisted in the preparation of this manuscript. First, numerous master's level students in Gainesville and Odense, worked through various iterations of our materials as we experimented with making these ideas both accessible and intellectually stimulating at the master's level. Second, Anil Arya, Tony Atkinson, Bill Beaver, Rebecca Carlisle, Peter Ove Christensen, Ron Dye, John Fellingham, Ole Friis, Hans Frimor, Frøystein Gjesdal, Karl Hackenbrack, Lene Holbæk, Eva Labro, Jytte Larsen, Paula Leary, Lin Nan, Mogens Nielsen, Barbara Pirchegger, Mort Pincus, Doug Schroeder, Mike Stein, Jannie Tholstrup, Alfred Wagenhofer, and Kristina Zvinakis all provided substantive comments on earlier versions of the manuscript. Third, the McGraw-Hill team was simply superb, especially Steve DeLancey, Rozi Harris, JaNoel Lowe, Kelly Odom, and Natalie Ruffatto. Finally, financial support from the FSR Research Foundation is also gratefully acknowledged.

John A. Christensen

Joel S. Demski

Fernandina Beach, FL

Chapter 1

Introduction

Accounting is a complex, highly varied, and far from static enterprise. At one level we are familiar with the multitude of options and choices by specific reporting entities: LIFO versus FIFO versus average cost inventory calculation; accelerated versus straight-line depreciation; cost pool and "cost driver" specification in an activity-based costing system; profit versus investment center reporting at the division level; when to recognize a problematic potential liability; and so on. At another level we are equally familiar with the fact that accounting comes in many forms: corporate, partnership, municipal, managerial, tax, not-for-profit, national income, and so forth. Here we see elaborate, ever-changing regulations, such as those of the Financial Accounting Standards Board (FASB), the Government Accounting Standards Board (GASB), the Securities and Exchange Commission (SEC), the Cost Accounting Standards Board (CASB), the International Accounting Standards Board (IASB), and the Internal Revenue Service (IRS). At a third level, we also know that auditing plays a crucial role in most settings; and here, too, we encounter a multitude of options and choices, as well as a set of elaborate, ever-changing regulations.

Notice the common theme of making choices. An individual reporting entity must specify its accounting method, presumably in accordance with applicable regulations. A regulatory agency must specify the set of admissible accounting methods for some set of activities, for example accounting for research and development activities. Equally clear, the auditor must settle on a particular audit strategy, again presumably in accordance with applicable regulations.

This is where accounting theory enters the picture. Accounting theory is all about understanding, making, and improving these choices. It is a guide to responsible, professional-quality decision making and responsible, professional-quality behavior in the accounting arena. We know that these choices are far from benign. For example, professional training in accounting is widespread, consultants are often hired to help design and install costing systems, the FASB is periodically threatened with Congressional intervention, and there is widespread concern over the financial reporting standards that accompany the globalization of financial markets.

Accounting theory, then, deals with accounting choices. Even here, though, the path to be taken is not unique, so it is imperative that we lay out our approach at the outset. We view accounting as a provider of information. Accounting theory, it then follows, deals with accounting choices from an information perspective.

The important terms are *accounting, information, uncertainty,* and *theory.* We take them up in turn.

ACCOUNTING

Ask yourself this: To what question is accounting the answer? In our view, this is straightforward: Accounting provides an answer, be it good or not so good, to this question: What is the temporal financial history of the organization or entity under consideration? *Accounting* seeks to answer such questions as how are we doing, what have we accomplished, what stocks of resources and obligations are before us, and so on.[1] (Be forewarned: This is not to say that historical cost is, or is not, an appropriate metric for this purpose.)

Next, we admit that history is not an easy subject. Individuals disagree over what to acknowledge, what to stress, and even what happened. Thomas Jefferson, the third president of the United States (and the face on a two-dollar bill), remains to this day a fascinating, active, and contentious subject among historians.[2]

Indeed, rendering the entity's financial history is unusually difficult because of the presence of accruals. *Cash basis accounting* simply tallies the cash flows, appropriately grouped; so we readily compile a systematic narrative of cash-based events. An *accrual system,* however, is forward looking. It relies on anticipated future activities. For example, listing receivables as an asset presumes that the customer will eventually pay, just as the *going concern concept* presumes that the entity will continue to be economically viable for the foreseeable future.

Now, if the organization's financial history were common knowledge to all, there would be little interest in accounting. We would all already

---

[1] We call this an *historical statement* because it is an attempt to assess where the organization has been and what its prospects are. It is, so to speak, a reckoning of the state of the firm as of some time. Naturally, this leads to questions such as what will the organization's history be if it does such and such? For example, what would this product cost to produce? The point is that we place a broad interpretation on what it means to report on the organization's financial history.

[2] The University of Florida's Smathers Library holds more than 100 books dealing with Jefferson.

know everything accounting might tell us. Of course, reality is a different story. We know very little about what most organizations have done or are doing, just as those inside the organization are less than fully informed about what is going on inside that organization or in its environment.

Reporting the organization's financial history, again as of some point in time, now has the possibility of telling us something we did not know. For example, are we ever surprised by a corporation's quarterly earnings announcement? Are we being sincere when we ask for an accounting report on the profitability of one of our products, or customers? Does the tax authority know our tax liability before we file our income tax return? Is the manager who forecasts unusually high earnings or claims product market success in any way influenced by the fact that an audited financial statement will follow this claim (or boast)?

Fundamentally, then, we view accounting as having the potential to tell us something, yes, something about the organization's financial history, that we did not know. This might be in a financial reporting context, in which the valuation of the reporting firm's common stock is the issue; it might be in a performance evaluation context, in which the management team's performance evaluation and compensation are the issue. The list is endless. An interest in the organization's history is not an interest in novelty or voyeurism, however. It is an interest in solving a resource allocation problem. The organization's history carries "information" to this as yet unspecified but broadly interpreted resource allocation exercise.

INFORMATION

This is critical: If the accounting system tells us something we did not know, then initially we were uncertain about something. In formal terms, being uncertain about something is expressed in terms of listing things that might happen coupled with a probability assessment over these possibilities. So the workhorse is a set of events, or a list of things that might happen, and a probabilistic description thereof. *Information,* in turn, is some observable that reveals something, leading to a change in the probability assessment. Examples are all around us: tomorrow's weather forecast, an analysts' consensus forecast of some firm's earnings, the latest consumer price index, or your score on the midterm examination. In each case we are initially uncertain about something (the weather, the firm's prospects, the inflation rate, or your performance) and in principle, in each case, we can think of the information release triggering a revision of our probabilistic assessment.

This will all be formalized in due course. For the moment we simply put forward the idea that information tells us something, reduces *uncertainty;* and in some way, by reporting an organization's financial history, the accounting system has the potential to tell us something we did not know about that organization.[3]

Our view, we should acknowledge, is not universal. Surely accounting is a formal financial measurement system. It uses a unit of account (e.g., dollars) and reports measures of accounting stocks on the balance sheet and accounting flows on the income statement. It also reports less aggregate measures such as revenue, the cost of some product, or the totality of some type of liability.

Viewed so, the formal financial measurement system is designed to record the organization's financial history as it marches through time—but in what manner? What particular details of this history are to be recorded?

A popular idiom is that accounting is, or should be, designed to measure value. Ideally, the argument goes, assets would be stated at fair value, income would be a fair and true measure of economic accomplishment relative to the net asset base employed, and so on. In this way, the organization's history is expressed in terms of a periodic stock—a stock of well-measured value—and associated flow—a flow of well-measured changes in value or income.

Once market structure departs from the textbook extreme of a perfect and complete set of markets, the very notion of a well-defined concept of value disappears. At that point, price guides are not available for all activities. Real estate, problematic liabilities, specialized capital equipment, and privately placed financial instruments are illustrative. In each case there is simply no well-functioning market whose current price can be relied upon as an indicator of value. Thus, the independent guideline for the accounting valuation has vanished. Moreover, we then see concern for, say, stakeholders in an organization simply because the imperfect market structure does not sort out the various demands on and conflicts over the organization's resources.

We hasten to add that if valuation is the purpose, accounting is an abject failure on a worldwide basis. Economic and accounting values, where we have data, are virtually never well aligned.

The information perspective, the notion that accounting is designed to provide information, views accounting as using the language and algebra of valuation but for the purpose of conveying information. The distinction between the two views is subtle but profound.

The "measure value" approach stresses the importance of a formal measurement system that well measures value. The "information content"

---

[3] We will learn that this casual description masks considerable, important subtlety. An important service provided by accounting is supplying a veracity check of other sources of information. For example, the management team's claim that demand has improved will be followed by an audited report of revenue. The larger story is modeled in equilibrium terms, and, you will come to appreciate, an important consideration in such a setting is what might be reported if the management team misbehaves, or plays, so to speak, off the equilibrium path.

approach stresses the importance of a formal measurement system that well conveys information.[4]

The value school, then, views the task as one of reasonably well approximating value, of designing a financial measurement system that will measure value. The information content school, by contrast, views the financial measures as measures of informative events, not of value. What is being measured, then, differs in a most fundamental sense for the two approaches.

For example, the value school would treat income as well measured if that measure corresponded well with some (vague) notion of fair, true, or economic income. The information school would treat income as well measured if that measure corresponded well with some underlying event structure we wished to communicate.

In the process, we routinely speak of assets, liabilities, cost, and income, for example, terminology that is rooted in economic valuation. Likewise, we think of income as change in value, adjusted for capital transactions, thereby using the algebra that underlies economic stocks and flows. This is the reason we say that the information content school views accounting as using the language and the algebra of valuation to convey the information.

The information perspective stops short, however, of claiming that the resulting accounting measures are explicit value, or value-related, measures. Sometimes they are (e.g., the cash balance), and sometimes they are not (e.g., fully expensed research and development). Rather, these measures are the result of specific calculations based on explicit procedures, explicit transactions by the reporting organization, and some, but only some, of what the reporting organization knows.

For example, suppose that the organization knows it faces a potential liability. At this point the liability's odds are low, and the eventual amount, should it materialize, is highly conjectural. The accounting system records nothing. Similarly, suppose that the organization invests heavily in product development and advertising and subsequently learns that its new product design has been market tested with spectacular results. The investment itself will be recorded, but none of the subsequent good news enters the accounting measures at this time. The organization routinely knows more than it discloses in its financial history.[5]

---

[4] In a deeper sense, to measure something means that we have a set of objects (e.g., sports cars) and some relationship among those objects (e.g., aesthetic appeal), and then assign numbers to those objects to represent the noted relationship. So one sports car has more aesthetic appeal than another if (and only if) its "aesthetic score" is higher than that of the other. *To measure* means, simply, to assign numbers to represent some underlying relationship. Although this is getting well ahead of the story, it is important to acknowledge that a measure might not exist but when it does, it may be far from unique. This latter issue is called *scaling* and will play an important role in subsequent chapters.

[5] It is also important to take a broad view of what we mean by *financial history*. The reporting organization, as we shall stress, conveys part of what it knows through its accounting system and supplements the formal rendering with, say, footnote disclosures.

Our task, then, is to construct a theoretical perspective, a "theory," that treats accounting as a source of information and that well explains these and many other institutional details, including its very survivorship.

THEORY

Theory refers to a set of knowledge that explains, or purports to explain, a set of phenomena. It is a coherent description or set of principles that illuminate or explain some particular set of phenomena. Newtonian physics, the efficient markets hypothesis, and Darwin's theory of evolution are ready examples.

The idea is to provide a coherent description, a coherent synthesis, without losing much accuracy in the process. Sims (1996, pp. 105–6) is particularly eloquent:

> Advances in the natural sciences are discoveries of ways to compress data concerning the natural world—both data that already exists and potential data—with minimal loss of information. For example, Tycho Brahe accumulated large amounts of reliable data on the movements of the planets. Kepler observed that they are all on elliptical orbits with the sun at a focus, thereby accomplishing a sharp data compression. Newton found the inverse-square law, allowing still further compression and also allowing the same formula to organize existing data and predict new experimental or practical data in areas remote from the study of planetary motion.

The idea of *parsimonious compression* is central to this view. This is what makes theory useful, it provides structure for organizing our thoughts about some set of phenomena. This structure, this parsimonious compression, though, is not, in general, without error. A theory is unlikely to be perfect, especially in the social sciences. This means that the theory with which we work is an approximation. If you like metaphors, theory comes with an error term.[6]

Newtonian physics is the classic illustration. It remains useful across a wide variety of applications but certainly not in subatomic matters. Closer to home, the efficient markets hypothesis has proven to be useful across a variety of settings, such as understanding the pricing of derivatives. It also has its limitations, such as the apparent anomalies in pricing initial public offerings. Classical price theory, with its emphasis on equating at the margin, is highly useful but not without its limitations. For example, we continue to struggle to understand the impact of increasing the minimum wage although classical price theory is quite compelling on this point.

---

[6] The *error term* metaphor is based on statistical analysis. Suppose that we have reason to think that crop production, y, is related to rainfall, x. In simple terms we think of a linear model, $y = \alpha + \beta x$, where α and β are constants. Looking at the data, we notice that they do not quite plot in a straight line, so we then get serious and write a linear model of the form $y = \alpha + \beta x + \epsilon$, where the additional term, ϵ, is an error term. It is a random variable that injects some slippage, some error, in the deterministic relationship of $y = \alpha + \beta x$. The model has an error term; it is not exact.

The FASB's *Conceptual Framework* is another illustration. Here the idea is to begin with qualitative characteristics of good or useful information, such as relevance and reliability, and proceed from there to a coherent view of financial accounting. As we shall see, however, when we focus on the choice of accounting method and use economic theory to model that choice, it turns out that these characteristics are not well-functioning guidelines. We cannot use economic theory to structure that choice and at the same time cling to relevance and reliability. Nevertheless, the *Framework* remains an important device for organizing regulatory matters. (We will revisit these cryptic comments in Chapter 19.)

In short, theory is an organizing device, one that is designed to illuminate without introducing too much error. We often phrase this in terms of the effects that are of major importance, called *first-order effects*, and effects that are of minor importance, called *second-order effects*. Theory focuses on first-order effects to highlight the central issues in understanding a set of phenomena. Parsimony is essential, and we must remember to allow for an error term, to allow for effects outside the formal theory with which we are working.[7]

Turning to the subject matter at hand, the set of phenomena with which we are concerned, what is it about accounting that we want to illuminate? The short answer is that we want to study, to illuminate, the choice of accounting method. Our focus is on the choice, not on how to do the accounting per se (not on "double entry matters").

Moreover, we view this choice in terms of the information that is subsequently provided and is consequential. It may, for example, affect activities within the organization, the financial market's perception of the organization, or the management team's compensation. This leads us to use economic theory, in particular the economic theory of choice under uncertainty, as the workhorse in studying this accounting choice. This allows us to treat accounting activity on a par with other activity. It has the additional advantage of treating financial market use, labor market use, and intraorganization use of the accounting product with the same perspective and tools. It has the disadvantage of relying on systematic, rational behavior by those who design and implement the accounting system, as well as by those who use that system's product.

Now you know why we stress the notion of theory as a parsimonious compression.

THE ROAD AHEAD

Our work is organized in the following fashion. Initially, in Part 1, we invest in building blocks that will be important in our work. First, it will be important to envision the organization or entity for which we account as explicitly making resource allocation decisions. For example, to study

[7] We even have colloquialisms to help sort these matters out. "True in theory and in fact" is an unusually strong statement; just as "it works only in theory" is an unusually weak statement.

depreciation, it is important to begin with a setting in which the organization finds it rational to acquire a long-lived asset in the first place. The same holds for, say, inventory or financial instruments. Likewise, to study the use of accounting measures in evaluating a manager, it is important to begin with an organization that finds it rational to acquire the services of a manager in the first place.

So we begin, in Chapter 2, with a sketch of a firm that combines factors of production, given its technology, to produce output. Three factors are highlighted: capital, labor, and management. This provides, as we shall see, a rich context in which to explore the usual variety of accounting issues coupled with the presence of a management that, itself, must be well motivated.[8]

From here we turn to the question of how this firm would be portrayed in a classical valuation exercise (Chapter 3) in which economic value and economic income are well defined. So equipped, we then contrast this portrayal with that of a classical accounting rendering (Chapter 4) in which accounting value and accounting income are highlighted. This provides an opportunity to formally define accounting and to link, in explicit form, the economic and accounting valuation renderings.

With the stage so set, we turn to the modeling of information (Chapter 5) and its use in a resource allocation context (Chapter 6). Importantly, information rests on the formal presence of uncertainty, and from this point forward, uncertainty plays a prominent role in our study. Moreover, information does not arrive in predigested, easily accessible format. It must be gleaned or extracted from the carrier, just as we interpret a newspaper story or a firm's financial statements. We model this interpretation, or information extraction, from the point of view of a sophisticated user, whose interpretation is described in terms of systematic probability revision. This focus on systematic probability revision places economic forces at the center of our modeling.[9]

The centerpiece of the information content perspective now comes into play (Chapter 7). If accounting uses the language and algebra of valuation to report the firm's financial history, what does it mean for the accounting system to be a source of information? Are the language and

---

[8] Accounting, of course, is not any old source of information; it is highly structured and uses the notions of asset, liability, equity, revenue, and expense. It also reports on the activities, so to speak, of a reporting entity. This entity might be an individual, a partnership, a corporation, a not-for-profit organization, a government entity, or even an entire economy—take your pick. Accounting reports about some reporting entity, tautologically. For convenience, we will emphasize a firm that acquires factors of production in factor markets, sells its output in product markets, and is organized as a corporation with identifiable residual claimants, or common shareholders.

[9] Sophisticated, systematic use, then, is the first-order effect we highlight. To quote the FASB's *Concepts Statement No. 1*, "The information should be comprehensible to those who have a reasonable understanding of business and economic activities and are willing to study the information with reasonable diligence." (FASB, 1978, paragraph 24). Cognitive and social considerations are considered in Chapter 20.

valuation algebra restrictive? Are degrees of freedom present in the historical rendering?

With these foundation items in place, we turn in Part 2 to the explicit information content perspective. This perspective requires a focus on the use of the information provided by the accounting system. Initially we focus on information that is used to value the firm in question (Chapters 8, 9, and 10). Following some initial setup work on highly stylized valuation settings under uncertainty and the role of information therein, we examine the case in which accounting is the only source of information for the "valuation machine." Following this we comingle accounting and non-accounting sources of information and review the empirical evidence on the relationship between security prices and accounting measures. This comingling of information sources is a theme that remains with us throughout the remainder of the study.

From here, we move (in Chapters 11 and 12) to a managerial evaluation setting in which information is potentially useful in contracting with a manager. In Chapter 13 we combine the evaluation and valuation themes, which is where inherent conflict between the two settings appears. We cannot confine our study to a setting in which information is being supplied solely for valuation purposes. We know that accounting information is used for valuation and evaluation purposes and that information content in the valuation setting does not imply information content in the evaluation setting and vice versa. In a deeper sense, this is as it should be. Information sources interact. What we learn from one source generally depends on what we have learned from other sources. So, we cannot hope to understand accounting as a source of information without putting on the table, so to speak, other sources of information. Similarly, what is useful in one setting is not necessarily useful in another. Indeed, it is possible to have information useful in a valuation setting while it is harmful in an evaluation system (intuitively because the presence of the information, although informative for valuation purposes, worsens the underlying control problem).

In Part 3 we explicitly deal with the theme of commingling sources of information by examining the comparative advantage of accounting as a source of information. We stress the feature that it is audited and is reasonably well protected against serious error and serious manipulation. We begin with an information content portrayal of recognition (Chapter 14). Here we stress the question of what subset of what the firm knows, or might know, should be admitted into the accounting system at any given point in time. The auditing connection is established in Chapter 15, where we mix self-reporting by the manager with an audited rendering of the firm's financial history.

This leads to conditional recognition (Chapter 16), where what information is produced and admitted into the accounting system depends on what the manager has self-reported. A picture of conservatism emerges here based on the simple idea that it is better to check "good news" rather than "bad news" when this news is being self-reported by the manager. Intertemporal issues (e.g., "income smoothing," Chapter 17) and intratemporal accruals (e.g., transfer pricing, Chapter 18) round out the picture.

Finally, in Part IV we connect this theoretical structure to institutional details. We begin, in Chapter 19, by sketching important institutional features of multiple reporting firms, coordinating institutions such as regulatory bodies, and the rhetoric of regulation. We also contrast the economic foundation on which we rely with the more macro view of accounting information being well described by qualitative characteristics such as relevance and reliability.

Chapter 20 concludes the odyssey with a discussion of the importance of judgment and professional responsibility. Detailing the firm's financial history is no easy matter, just as continual management of that recording and reporting exercise is no easy matter. Resources are at stake, both resources devoted to the recording and reporting enterprise and in terms of the consequences that follow from the reporting. Theory cannot tell us how to best manage this game. It can only structure the important choices. That is the reason we stress the ever-present theme of accounting choice and the importance of professional skill and judgment in that exercise. How could it be otherwise?[10]

Summary

To claim that accounting provides *information* is so commonplace as to be nearly colloquial, yet it is no easy matter to put substance on this claim, to think about accounting in a way that is logically consistent with the claim that information is being provided.

Putting *substance* on this claim requires us to be serious about what we mean by "information" and what we mean by "accounting information." We build a simple model for this purpose, one that allows us to well identify information, accounting information, the use of that information, and so on. The model, the *theoretical construction*, is designed to be clarifying and to sharpen our thinking. Three caveats should be understood before we proceed. First, any *model*, any theory of this sort, must focus on substantive details, on first-order effects, and leave the rest to chance. Otherwise, substance becomes lost in the details. We will revisit this theme at the end of our study. Second, the *information perspective* necessitates that we look to the users of that information. Studying accounting choice

---

[10] This hints at the issue of where we draw the line between where theory ends and judgment begins. In the information content school, theory structures the choices to be made, but the choices themselves require judgment and professional skill. Dieticians, even those equipped with state-of-the-art nutrition knowledge, do not prescribe precisely what one should eat (and when). The same holds for accounting. A contrary view, one associated with the value measurement school, holds that theory per se is nearly definitive with judgment being far less important. Universal application of fair value is illustrative.

without a focus on the users of the accounting product is devoid of substance. It blinds us to first-order effects and thus places far too much weight on the error term, so to speak. Third, *theory alone* cannot identify the most desirable accounting system or accounting treatment. Rather, the best choice is inherently contextual. No universal prescription is to be found, and there is no getting around the fact that professional judgment is an essential component of the exercise. Indeed, we hope that studying accounting theory will deepen and sharpen the reader's professional focus.

Selected References

Accounting thought has a long history. Luca Pacioli's 1494 publication, *Summa de Arithmetica, Geometria, Proportioni, et Proportionalita*, provided the first coherent description of double entry recording. The first half of the 20th century witnessed a deep interest in using classical economics to better understand and refine accounting measurements. Favorite examples are Paton (1922), Clark (1923), Canning (1929), Vatter (1947), and Edwards and Bell (1961). Hendriksen and Van Breda (1992) and Wolk and Tearney (1996) synthesize this tradition and its connection to U.S. GAAP.

More explicitly and more formally viewing and treating these measures as information then arrived on the scene. Examples are Feltham (1972), Ijiri (1975), Demski and Feltham (1976), Scott (1996), Sunder (1997), and Beaver (1998). Sorter's (1969) paper is particularly prescient, as is Watts and Zimmerman's (1986) stress on the reporting firm's choice of accounting method. Sterling (1970) offers an expansive view of the role of theory in accounting thought and helps place our reliance on Sims' (1996) view in perspective.

Key Terms

Our study of accounting rests on three ideas, expressed in three key terms. **Uncertainty** means not definitely ascertainable, or known, as tomorrow's weather or market success. **Information** is some observable that has the potential to lessen this uncertainty, as with a weather forecast or management's forecast of future market success. **Theory** is a coherent explanation of some set of phenomena, as the efficient markets theory. We stress the central idea of compressing the explanation into a parsimonious, coherent, and usable description that concentrates on the major issues, the first-order effects. Accounting, then, is an information source, one that uses the language and algebra of valuation to convey its essential message; and accounting theory is concerned with the choice of accounting method, with the design and management of this particular information source.

Exercises

1.1. What is the connection between *information* and *uncertainty*? Give several illustrations of this connection.

1.2. Provide three examples of accounting valuation, one in which accounting value is below "real" value, one in which it is above, and one in which the two are approximately equal. What, in your mind, explains the respective patterns?

1.3. Sims (1996) argues that a theory is a parsimonious, useful portrayal of some class of phenomena. Perfection is not the state of the art; rather, a useful model that explains "most" or "the first-order" portions of the class of phenomena is what is sought. Prepare a short paragraph that illustrates this argument. You should identify the class of phenomena you have in mind, the central idea of the theory or model in question, and, in general terms, what that theory or model explains or captures. Also provide a brief illustration of where it goes astray.

Part 1

Foundations

2

The Reporting Organization

Our study begins with some organization for which conveying something through its accounting system is a substantive issue. This "reporting organization," or firm, will always be present because it is essential to ground our study of accounting in a setting in which the particular accounting issue arises endogenously. The trick we use is to carry along a simple model of a firm, one that is simple enough to be tractable but flexible enough so the firm will find it rational to engage in behavior, such as the acquisition of a long-lived asset or contracting with a manager, that creates an accounting issue. Indeed, we will come to appreciate the fact that understanding why the firm is engaging in such behavior is the key to resolving the accounting issue associated with that behavior. This firm, you will also learn, uses factors of production and its technology to produce goods and services, which are, in turn, sold to customers. Patience is also in order, however; we must understand this simple firm before we move on to use it in our study of accounting.

We now introduce an explicit model of the reporting organization. Two themes are important here. First, what we mean by the *reporting organization* is purposely left vague. Accounting thought often refers to the reporting organization as the *entity*. Digging deeper we find, at times, an emphasis on personal stake (the proprietary view by which the organization is inherently identified with its owners), economic distinction (the entity view by which the organization is distinct from its owners), or a defined set of activities (the fund view by which assets and obligations are grouped together). Clearly, though, accounting practice includes financial reporting, divisional performance measurement, product line profitability assessment, not-for-profit reporting, municipal reporting, and national income reporting. So, we purposely leave open the question of what type of organization we are considering.[1]

Second, we typically and traditionally approach an accounting issue, such as how to depreciate a long-lived asset, by presuming that the asset is in place and then asking how best to report, or measure, the important consequences associated with that asset. From our standpoint, though, the beginning point should be a setting in which the reporting organization finds it rational, if you will, to acquire the long-lived asset in the first place. So, when we examine inventory reporting, we want to do so in a setting in which the organization finds it rational to hold inventory. When we examine derivatives, we want to do so in a setting in which the organization finds it useful to hold derivatives. When we confront the interactions inherent in a multiproduct firm, we want to do so in a setting in which the organization finds it useful to produce multiple products. Taken together, this concern for a proper beginning point compels us to begin with a model of the reporting organization.

This insistence on a reporting organization that finds it rational to engage in behavior that creates the accounting issue in the first place is not an academic nicety. A firm that produces multiple products is, presumably, driven by an *economy of scope;* but an economy of scope means that we cannot fully separate the income and assets associated with each of the products. A firm that holds inventory does so for a reason. To examine accounting for that inventory, we have to worry about why the firm is holding that inventory and why reporting, somehow, on that holding of inventory might be useful. Similarly, a firm that uses derivatives does so for a reason. To examine accounting for those derivatives, we have to worry about why the firm is using derivatives and why reporting, somehow, on that use of derivatives might be useful.

Having said that, we still face the problem of placing some structure on the activities and behavior of the prototypical organization whose accounting practice we will study. For this purpose we focus on an organization that acquires factors of production and, using some specified technology, transforms those factors into goods and services. To give the story context,

---

[1] The FASB, with its emphasis on corporate and not-for-profit financial reporting, uses the term "entity" in a nearly colloquial manner: Paragraph 24 of *Concepts Statement No. 6* (FASB, 1985) reads as follows: "All elements are defined in relation to a particular entity, which may be a business enterprise, an educational or charitable organization, a natural person, or the like. An item that qualifies under the definitions is a particular entity's asset, liability, revenue, expense, and so forth. An entity may comprise two or more affiliated entities and does not necessarily correspond to what is often described as a 'legal entity.' The definitions may also refer to 'other entity,' 'other entities,' or 'entities other than the enterprise,' which may include individuals, business enterprises, not-for-profit organizations, and the like. For example, employees, suppliers, customers or beneficiaries, lenders, stockholders, donors, and governments are all 'other entities' to a particular entity. A subsidiary company that is part of the same entity as its parent company in consolidated financial statements is an 'other entity' in the separate financial statements of its parent."

we interpret the organization as a profit-seeking firm, although this is done for expositional reasons, and you are encouraged to think in the broadest possible terms.

To build intuition and to ease the pain of assimilation, we begin with a single-product setting. We then move on to the important multiproduct setting. Keep in mind that we want a stylized, minimalist description of the reporting organization's activities and behavior, one rich enough to help train our intuition and to capture important first-order effects but not so complicated as to be unworkable, not to mention annoying and counterproductive.

SINGLE-PRODUCT CASE

Our organization, or firm, then, combines factors to produce and sell some product or service. Initially, there is only one product. Let $q(\geq 0)$ denote the quantity produced (and sold). Production requires that an appropriate combination of factors be available. Two factors are sufficient at this point; we call them *capital* in quantity $K (\geq 0)$, and *labor* in quantity $L (\geq 0)$.

The appropriate combination of factors is specified by the (exogenous) technology. We simply assume that it is given by the following restriction:

$$q \leq \sqrt{KL} \qquad\qquad \textbf{(2.1)}$$

The idea is that we require $K > 0$ and $L > 0$ to produce output $q(> 0)$. But capital and labor are substitutes. For example, both $K = 1$ and $L = 4$ and $K = 4$ and $L = 1$ can be used to produce $q = 2$ units. Indeed, any combination such that $KL = q^2$ can be used to produce output quantity $q (K > 0$ and $L > 0$, of course).

Naturally, the factor prices enter at this stage. If, for example, capital is unusually expensive, labor will be substituted for capital, and vice versa.[2] We do assume, however, that the technology is limited in the sense that no more capital than $K^{\max}$ units can be employed:

$$K \leq K^{\max} \qquad\qquad \textbf{(2.2)}$$

This upper bound limits the physical size of the capacity. The technology simply does not allow the firm to become arbitrarily large.

---

[2] This is a specific version of what economists call a *Cobb-Douglas technology.* More generally, for two factors, the restriction is written $q \leq K^{\alpha} L^{\beta}$, where the exponents are non-negative. (Our specific version, which is adequate for our purpose, rests on $\alpha = \beta = 0.5$.) Now, constant returns means that a proportionate increase in factors leads to a proportionate increase in output; and $\alpha + \beta = 1$ implies constant returns to scale. Likewise, $\alpha + \beta < 1$ implies decreasing returns to scale, and $\alpha + \beta > 1$ implies increasing returns to scale. Importantly, constant returns implies a linear cost curve, a cost curve with constant marginal cost.

Beyond this, the capital and labor mix depends on the factor prices. For simplicity we assume that the factors are acquired in perfect markets. Let p_K denote the price per unit of capital and p_L the (wage or) price per unit of labor. The total expenditure on factors, then, is simply $p_K K + p_L L$. If, now, q units are to be produced, the K and L are chosen to minimize this total expenditure, subject to feasibility. This gives us the cost of producing q units, defined as follows:

$$C(q) \equiv \underset{K,L \geq 0}{\text{Minimum}} \; p_K K + p_L L$$

$$\text{subject to (2.1) and (2.2)} \qquad \textbf{(2.3)}$$

In other words, the firm selects its capital (K) and labor (L) to minimize the total expenditure on factors (K and L here), subject to being able to produce the desired output. The minimum expenditure in Program (2.3) is often referred to as *economic cost* to distinguish it from the accounting construct accounting cost.

An Illustration

To illustrate, suppose that the factor prices are given by $p_K = 200$ and $p_L = 100$. So, capital is twice as expensive as labor. Furthermore, suppose that the capital limit is $K^{\max} = 125$, and $q = 150$ units are to be produced. Solving Program (2.3), using these specifications, gives us optimal choices of $K = 106.0660$ and $L = 212.1320$, along with a cost of $C(150) = 42{,}426.41$.

Varying, q and solving for the optimal K and L choices along the way, allows us to determine the firm's cost curve.[3] Exhibit 2.1 plots $C(q)$ for $0 \leq q \leq 300$. Notice that it is linear, with a slope of about 283 (282.8427, to be more precise), up to about $q = 175$ units (176.7767, to be more precise) and then increases at an increasing rate.

This is more evident in Exhibit 2.2, where we plot the corresponding marginal cost.[4] (*Marginal cost* is the rate of change of economic cost with respect to the product.) Notice that the marginal cost is constant, reflecting the underlying linear cost function, up to about $q = 175$; beyond that, it is increasing.

The culprit here is the capacity limitation of $K^{\max} = 125$. Given the factor prices of $p_K = 200 > p_L = 100$, the firm uses more labor than capital but naturally increases both as output expands. (In fact, the firm uses twice as much labor, L, as capital, K, in this case.) When $K^{\max}$ is reached,

---

[3] Notice that the solution for any q depends on the factor prices. So, technically, we should denote the cost by $C(q;$ factor prices). This dependency on the factor prices should be understood but will not be a formal part of our notational assault on your senses.

[4] We often think of marginal cost as being well approximated by the *incremental cost* of producing one additional unit at some particular point. Technically, however, it is the slope of the cost curve at a particular point. Literally, the marginal cost when output quantity q^* is being produced is the slope of $C(q)$ at the point $q = q^*$; it is the derivative of the cost function evaluated at point $q = q^*$.

EXHIBIT 2.1
C(q) for Numerical
Illustration

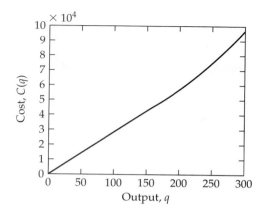

EXHIBIT 2.2
Marginal Cost for
Numerical
Illustration

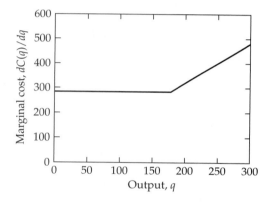

however, the firm can no longer use the optimal balance between the two factors. Hence, beyond that point, production becomes inefficient, marginal cost increases, and total cost increases at an increasing rate.

Additional details are developed in the Appendix.

Short-Run Cost Curve

From here we encounter the related notion of a *short-run cost curve*. The idea is straightforward. Suppose that one or more factors cannot be altered. Then the firm has limited freedom in finding the best mix of factors. In our simple two-factor story, we are in serious trouble if both factors are fixed. So, staying with our numerical story, suppose that the firm initially acquires $K' = 75$ units of capital. In the short run, this capital choice cannot be altered. Only labor can be altered, and the technology constraint forces $L = q^2/75$ if q units are to be produced. Clearly, then, with $K = K'$ frozen in place, producing q units will require labor [via (2.1)] of $L = q^2/K' = q^2/75$. So, the firm's short-run cost curve is simply:

$$C^{SR}(q) = p_K K' + (p_L q^2/K') = 200(75) + (100/75)q^2$$

EXHIBIT 2.3
Short-Run and
Long-Run Curves
for Numerical
Illustration

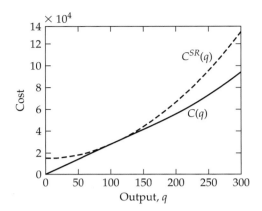

In Exhibit 2.3 we superimpose this particular short-run curve on the underlying long-run curve, $C(q)$.

The short-run versus long-run distinction surfaces in a variety of contexts.[5] For example, if we are trying to value inventory at replacement cost, it is essential to understand which, if any, factors are fixed at the point of the calculation. Similarly, if we are using a derivative instrument to hedge some type of exposure, it is likewise essential to understand which, if any, factors are fixed should the firm be called upon to deal with that exposure.

MULTIPRODUCT CASE

We next turn our attention to the important multiproduct case. The firm is now assumed to produce (and sell, of course) three products, with respective non-negative quantities denoted q_1, q_2, and q_3. The products will share a common capital base, K in our earlier story, but they will have dedicated labor inputs. Let L_1, L_2, and L_3 denote the non-negative quantities of the three labor inputs, where it is understood that labor quantity L_i is used in production of the ith product.

The original technology constraint, (2.1), is now replaced by the following family of constraints:

$$q_1 \leq \sqrt{KL_1} \qquad \textbf{(2.1a)}$$

$$q_2 \leq \sqrt{KL_2} \qquad \textbf{(2.1b)}$$

$$q_3 \leq \sqrt{KL_3} \qquad \textbf{(2.1c)}$$

---

[5] Notice the subtle terminology. *Long run* is the case when all factors can be varied. A particular (and emphatically, not the) *short run* is one in which some subset of factors is fixed at some specified point. Also, the K^{max} constraint is a statement about the long-run capabilities of the technology. The technology in the long run simply cannot use capital in excess of K^{max}.

Again, capital and labor are substitutes. In addition, capital is shared among the products, suggesting an economy of scope: It is less costly to produce the three products within the same firm. Beyond this we retain our earlier upper bound on the amount of capital that can be employed, constraint (2.2).

The firm operates in perfectly competitive factor markets. The price of labor type i is p_{Li} per unit, and the price of capital, as before, is p_K per unit.

The firm's cost curve is located in, hopefully, familiar fashion. Paraphrasing our earlier work, we have the following:

$$C(q_1, q_2, q_3) \equiv \underset{K, L_1, L_2, L_3 \geq 0}{\text{Minimum}} p_K K + p_{L1} L_1 + p_{L2} L_2 + p_{L3} L_3$$

$$\text{subject to (2.1a), (2.1b), (2.1c), and (2.2)} \qquad \textbf{(2.4)}$$

To illustrate, we expand our earlier setting to three products and assume that the labor prices are given by $p_{Li} = 100$ and continue to assume that $p_K = 200$. Again, $K^{\max} = 125$. Now suppose that $q_1 = 150$ while $q_2 = q_3 = 0$. We readily find $C(150, 0, 0) = 42{,}426.41$. You should recognize this as the same cost we had for producing 150 units in the single-product story. The reason is simple. If we produce only one of the three products, the technology reduces to the original technology, and we have, conveniently, assumed the same factor prices.

Also notice the built-in symmetry. With the labor prices identical, producing 150 of any one of the three products coupled with zero of the other two implies a cost of 42,426.41. Contrast this with the case where $q_1 = q_2 = 150$ and $q_3 = 0$. Solving (2.4), we find $K = K^{\max} = 125$, $L_1 = L_2 = 180$ ($L_3 = 0$, of course), and a cost of $C(150, 150, 0) = 61{,}000 < 2(42{,}426.41) = 84{,}852.82$. It is much less costly to simultaneously produce the products. This reflects the technological assumption that the products can share the capital.

This is further evident when we analytically construct the firm's cost curve. If the $K^{\max}$ constraint is not binding, we readily find[6]

$$C(q_1, q_2, q_3) = 2\sqrt{p_K\left(p_{L1}q_1^2 + p_{L2}q_2^2 + p_{L3}q_3^2\right)} \qquad \textbf{(2.5)}$$

---

[6] Deriving this expression is a simple extension of material developed in the Appendix. For any value of $K > 0$, producing q_i units of product i will lead the organization to acquire precisely $L_i = q_i^2/K$ units of labor. So, the expenditure calculation becomes

$$p_K K + p_{L1} q_1^2/K + p_{L2} q_2^2/K + p_{L3} q_3^2/K = p_K K + \theta/K$$

where $\theta = p_{L1} q_1^2 + p_{L2} q_2^2 + p_{L3} q_3^2$. Setting the derivative equal to zero allows us to identify the minimizing choice of K:

$$p_K - \theta/K^2 = 0$$

So $K^2 = \theta/p_K$, or $K = \sqrt{\theta/p_K}$. But then the overall expenditure is $p_K K + \theta/K = p_K\sqrt{\theta/p_K} + \theta/\sqrt{\theta/p_K} = 2\sqrt{\theta p_K}$. So we have $C(q_1, q_2, q_3) = 2\sqrt{\theta p_K}$ (where, again, $\theta = p_{L1} q_1^2 + p_{L2} q_2^2 + p_{L3} q_3^2$), as long as the chosen K does not violate the capacity constraint (2.2). In turn, (2.2) is not violated by unconstrained choice of K as long as $K = \sqrt{\theta/p_K} \leq K^{\max}$, or $\theta/p_K \leq (K^{\max})^2$. Outside this region, we resort to the use of the maximum feasible capital and have a cost expression of $p_K K^{\max} + p_{L1} q_1^2/K^{\max} + p_{L2} q_2^2/K^{\max} + p_{L3} q_3^2/K^{\max}$.

EXHIBIT 2.4
Marginal Cost of
First Product for
Three-Product Case

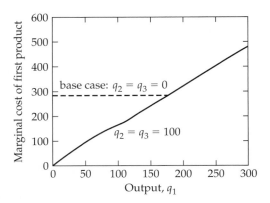

If two of the products are set to zero, we are back to our original, single-product setting.

Separability Concerns

We should also note the fact that this cost curve is not separable. We cannot separate it into three components, one for each of the three products. We cannot write the cost curve in the form $C(q_1, q_2, q_3) = F(q_1) + G(q_2) + H(q_3)$. While seemingly one more arcane point, it is important to understand that the multiproduct firm does not, in general, exhibit a *separable* cost curve, and this lack of separability means that we cannot unambiguously speak of the "cost of product *i*." In fact, this may be the very reason for having a multiproduct firm instead of having a series of single-product firms. Accounting costing procedures, however, lure us into thinking otherwise, but this is nothing other than a false impression created by approximation techniques used by the typical costing system.

One way to visualize this fact is to focus on marginal cost.[7] In Exhibit 2.4, we plot the marginal cost of the first product, assuming $q_2 = q_3 = 0$, as well as for the case where $q_2 = q_3 = 100$. The first case, of course, has no presence of the second and third products and thus reduces to our single-product story (and the marginal cost plot in Exhibit 2.2). The second has a substantive presence of the other two products, which results in $K = 100$ at the initial point of $q_1 = 0$. So, we have, for low values of q_1, a dramatically lower marginal cost of the first product simply because the large amount of capital, shared among the products, implies that very little labor is required to produce small amounts of the first product.

[7] Given cost curve $C(q_1, q_2, q_3)$, the marginal cost of the first product at some particular point is simply the partial derivative of the cost curve, $\partial C(q_1, q_2, q_3)/\partial q_1$, evaluated at the point in question. Carrying over the notation from Note 6, if the K^{max} constraint is not binding, we find $\partial C(q_1, q_2, q_3)/\partial q_1 = 2p_{L1}q_1/\sqrt{\theta/p_K}$. Conversely, if the K^{max} constraint is binding, we have $\partial C(q_1, q_2, q_3)/\partial q_1 = 2p_{L1}q_1/K^{max}$.

EXHIBIT 2.5
Total Cost Surface

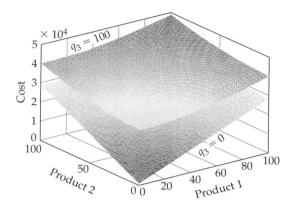

A second way to visualize this is to focus on the shape of the total cost curve. In Exhibit 2.5, we plot $C(q_1, q_2, q_3)$ for two different cases, one where $q_3 = 0$ and the other where $q_3 = 100$. Can you explain the qualitative shape of the two surfaces?

We could, with sufficient patience, continue on and examine short-run cost surfaces for our multiproduct firm.

Marginal versus Average Cost

The setting is a little more subtle, however, than merely adding a few extra products to the usual story. Return to our running example, and stay in the region in which the output is not so large that the $K^{\max}$ constraint is binding. This is expression (2.5) but now with the specific factor prices of $p_K = 200$ and $p_{Li} = 100$. Collecting terms gives us the following:

$$C(q_1, q_2, q_3) = 200\sqrt{2(q_1^2 + q_2^2 + q_3^2)}$$

Now use your intuition. We know that capital is shared across the products and that capital and labor are substitutes. Suppose that we are producing a large number of the second and third products but a small number of the first. The marginal cost of the first product will then be unusually low because considerable capital will be in place to support the production of the last two, and thus a small amount of extra labor is all that is necessary to produce slightly more of the first product. Intuitively, the marginal cost of a product depends on how many of each product is being produced. Remember that capital and labor are substitutes here and that capital is shared across the products.

This is, in fact, evident when we explicitly calculate the marginal cost. Product i's marginal cost is the (partial) derivative of the cost expression with respect to the ith product quantity. That is,

$$\partial C(q_1, q_2, q_3)/\partial q_i = 400q_i / \sqrt{2(q_1^2 + q_2^2 + q_3^2)}$$

If, then, q_2 and q_3 are large while q_1 is small, the denominator is large. For the first product, though, the numerator is small, so the marginal cost of the first product is small at that particular point. Exhibit 2.4 is illustrative.

The message, we hope, is clear. If the firm benefits from an economy of scope, if the firm finds it economical to produce a variety of products, we should expect the marginal cost of a product to depend on how many of the other products are being produced. We cannot, that is, view a product in isolation. The cost curve is simply not separable. This is the nature of the multiproduct firm.

We speak, then, without hesitation about a particular product's marginal cost in the multiproduct setting. The additional complication is that, in general, we expect a product's marginal cost to depend on the output of the other products.

Average cost, though, is another story. The idea is deceptive, of course: Divide the total cost associated with the product by the number of units of that product. This presumes that we know, unequivocally, how much of the total cost is due to each of the products. Glance back at our expression for the firm's cost, however; there is simply no way to separate that total into components that depend uniquely on each of the products, and that sum to the total cost in question. The cost curve is not separable. This means that average cost is not defined in this case. The simple, intuitive idea of average cost developed in the world of a one-product firm does not, in general, extend to the multiproduct firm. Marginal cost is a centerpiece concept in the world of multiproduct firms, but average cost is, in general, an oxymoron in that setting.[8]

The difficulty, again, is that we have no way of separating the total cost. In accounting, of course, we employ cost allocation procedures to provide such separation, but we must emphasize that this is an accounting procedure, a procedure quite capable of distorting the underlying reality. Average cost simply does not exist in the typical multiproduct firm![9]

It is important to dwell on Exhibits 2.4 and 2.5. In accounting our tendency is to treat groups of activities as more or less independent. We view the accounting income of a period as more or less independent of other periods, and we view the cost of a particular product as more or less independent of the other products. Indeed, in the product-costing arena, we almost always work with a linear approximation to the firm's cost curve. We should expect, however, that a firm lasts for many periods and produces

---

[8] With enough work and notation, we could extend this theme to a multiperiod setting in which the firm had multiple products as well and assets. We would also wind up having difficulty fully separating the assets, so each product was associated with a unique asset base.

[9] Once K^{max} is binding, the cost curve is $p_K K^{max} + p_{L1} q_1^2 / K^{max} + p_{L2} q_2^2 / K^{max} + p_{L3} q_3^2 / K^{max} = 200(125) + 100(q_1^2 + q_2^2 + q_3^2)/125$. Again, the concept of average cost is problematic because we must address how much of the 200(125) expenditure on capital should be associated with each of the products.

many products because grouping these activities is efficient. If so, if there is an economy of scope, we should not expect the activities to be independent. We should expect the marginal cost of one product to depend on the other products, and so on. Indeed, we should expect that the marginal cost of some product at time *t* will depend on products the firm anticipates producing in future periods. Enough!

VARIATIONS ON A THEME

This three-product story, the basis of (2.5), provides a platform for our exploration of accounting. To offer a glimpse of its versatility, we now briefly sketch three variations that will turn out to be useful in our work.[10]

Discounted Cash Flow

The first variation is a discounted cash flow story. To set the stage, stay with the running example, but also suppose that the three products are sold in perfectly competitive markets at respective prices of 120, 160, and 200 per unit. The firm seeks to maximize its profit, consisting of sales revenue less cost. That is, it wants to

$$\underset{q_1, q_2, q_3 \geq 0}{\text{maximize}}\, 120q_1 + 160q_2 + 200q_3 - C(q_1, q_2, q_3)$$

A solution has $q_1 = 75$, $q_2 = 100$, and $q_3 = 125$. This provides a total revenue of 50,000 and carries a total cost of 50,000. Merely breaking even

---

[10] Another variation, a fixed proportions story, provides an opportunity to deepen our understanding of the particular (square root) technology assumption. So, suppose the three products are produced in the fixed proportions of $\alpha : \beta : \gamma$. For example, the three products might be produced in the proportions 3 : 4 : 5. This means that any output profile can be written in the convenient form $q_1 = \alpha z$, $q_2 = \beta z$, and $q_3 = \gamma z$, for some number z. To illustrate, in the 3 : 4 : 5 case, we might have $q_1 = 3(10) = 30$, $q_2 = 4(10) = 40$, and $q_3 = 5(10) = 50$.

Now force this pattern into the cost curve. If K^{max} is not binding but the output is produced in fixed proportions, we can simplify our original expression for the cost surface in the following manner:

$$C(q_1, q_2, q_3) = 2\sqrt{p_K(p_{L1}q_1^2 + p_{L2}q_2^2 + p_{L3}q_3^2)} = 2\sqrt{p_K(p_{L1}[\alpha z]^2 + p_{L2}[\beta z]^2 + p_{L3}[\gamma z]^2)}$$
$$= 2z\sqrt{p_K(p_{L1}\alpha^2 + p_{L2}\beta^2 + p_{L3}\gamma^2)}$$

This is simply a constant, multiplied by the scale factor, z. In our running example, based on $p_K = 200$ and $p_{Li} = 100$, and assuming proportions of 3 : 4 : 5, we have a cost surface expression of $C(q_1, q_2, q_3) = 2{,}000z$. Cost is linear in the scale factor, z. Doubling output, while maintaining the noted proportions, doubles the cost. Now think back to the single-product story. There, when K^{max} was not binding, we had a linear cost curve. The same arises here, in the fixed proportions case. Intuitively, if output is always produced in fixed proportions, we de facto have a single-product story in which the product so to speak is the scale factor, z.

should come as no surprise; we presume perfectly competitive markets and any strictly positive profit prospects would be competed away. For later reference, the cost total is based on factor choices of $K = 125 (= K^{max})$, $L_1 = 45$, $L_2 = 80$, and $L_3 = 125$.[11]

Now alter the story in the following manner. Capital is acquired at time $t = 0$, and production immediately commences. The first product is sold (and customers pay) at the end of the first period, when the first product's labor factors are also paid. The second product is sold at the end of the second period when that product's labor factors are also paid. A parallel pattern applies to the third product. The interest rate is $r = 10$ percent.

Also suppose that the respective selling prices are $120(1.1) = 132$, $160(1.1)^2 = 193.60$, and $200(1.1)^3 = 266.20$. The respective labor prices follow the same pattern: $100(1.1) = 110$, $100(1.1)^2 = 121$, and $100(1.1)^3 = 133.10$. Now when the firm seeks to maximize the present value of receipts less expenditures, however, the prices all discount to precisely what we had before. For example, the present value of the time $t = 3$ selling price is $266.2(1.1)^{-3} = 200$. Our earlier solution thus reappears in full glory. (Of course, this exact replication depends on the judicious price assumptions, such as a spot labor price increasing at the rate of interest.)

We now have a story, however, in which the firm makes an up-front investment and then harvests that investment in later periods. This is evident in the tally of period-by-period cash flows, detailed in Exhibit 2.6. You should verify that the present value of the cash flow series calculated as of time $t = 0$ is precisely 0. In present value terms, the firm breaks even. Such is the power of perfect competition.

We will, in fact, make extensive use of this variation and this example in the next few chapters. To whet your appetite, notice that the firm now expends a total of $25,000 + 4,950 + 9,680 + 16,637.50 = 56,267.50$, and it receives revenues totaling $9,900 + 19,360 + 33,275 = 62,535$. So, it earns a

---

[11] This is a well-chosen razor's edge case in which the firm's behavior is identified by equating marginal revenue with marginal cost for each product, and in which, at such a solution, it earns zero rent, allowing us to interpret the story as one of perfect competition. To verify our solution, differentiate the profit expression for each q_i, and set the results equal to zero (that is, equate marginal revenue with marginal cost, for each product):

$$120 - \partial C(q_1, q_2, q_3)/\partial q_1 = 0$$

$$160 - \partial C(q_1, q_2, q_3)/\partial q_2 = 0$$

and

$$200 - \partial C(q_1, q_2, q_3)/\partial q_3 = 0$$

Now recall our earlier work on the marginal cost expressions. For product i, we have $\partial C(q_1, q_2, q_3)/\partial q_i = 2 p_{Li} q_i / \sqrt{\theta / p_K}$ if the K^{max} constraint is not binding and $2 p_{Li} q_i / K^{max}$ otherwise. (Recall $\theta = p_{L1} q_1^2 + p_{L2} q_2^2 + p_{L3} q_3^2$.) It is easy to verify that $q_1 = 75$, $q_2 = 100$, and $q_3 = 125$ satisfy these conditions, and put us right at the break point where any additional production encounters the K^{max} constraint. Indeed, any output in the proportion of $3 : 4 : 5$ that does not violate the K^{max} constraint satisfies these conditions, and we have merely taken from among these the largest possible output as our particular solution.

EXHIBIT 2.6
Cash Flow
Calculations for
Time Line Story,
$q_1 = 75$, $q_2 = 100$,
$q_3 = 125$

	$t = 0$	$t = 1$	$t = 2$	$t = 3$
Time t expenditures	200(125) =25,000	110(45) =4,950	121(80) = 9,680	133.1(125) =16,637.50
Time t receipts		132(75) =9,900	193.6(100) =19,360	266.2(125) =33,275
Net cash flow	−25,000	4,950	9,680	16,637.50

profit of 6,267.50 over the three periods. Typically, now, we ask how much of this profit is properly associated with each period. Here that boils down to asking how we should depreciate the initial investment of 25,000. We defer the answer but make the important point that the cash flows in Exhibit 2.6 arise from rational behavior by the firm. We begin, in other words, with a firm that finds it rational to engage in the behavior that creates our accounting concern.

Inventory

The second variation on our theme involves inventory. Stay with the time line sketched in the preceding section in which capital is acquired at time $t = 0$, the first product is delivered at time $t = 1$, and so on. Also retain the same factor prices and $K^{\max}$ setting. Now suppose, however, that we are dealing with the same product, say some subcomponent, that must be delivered at times $t = 1$, 2, and 3. The customer requires delivery of 75 units at time $t = 1$, 100 at time $t = 2$, and 125 at time $t = 3$.

One approach is to produce according to the customer's time schedule, thus setting $q_1 = 75$, $q_2 = 100$, and $q_3 = 125$. We know from our work immediately preceding that this policy will cost the firm (in present value terms) a total of $C(75, 100, 125) = 50,000$.

A second approach is to smooth production by setting $q_1 = q_2 = q_3 = 100$. Here the firm would build inventory in the first period and eventually deplete that inventory in the third period. This will cost the firm (again in present value terms) a total of $C(100, 100, 100) = 48,990 < 50,000$. It is less costly for the firm to smooth production and use inventory to absorb the differences between its output schedule and the customer's required delivery schedule. The reason is that, with shared capital and unchanging labor prices, it is less costly to produce a given total by equalizing the production across periods.[12] The firm rationally holds inventory at the interim stage, and this provides us a setting in which to examine proper accounting treatment of that inventory.

[12] In fact, producing 100 each period is the most efficient arrangement here. You can verify that this schedule equalizes the marginal cost of production across the three periods. Absent equalization, we would gain by shifting, at the margin, from the higher to the lower marginal cost setting. This does presume, however, that the only holding cost associated with inventory is the monetary cost of the investment in that inventory.

Managerial Activity

The final variation on our theme concerns managerial activity. We will eventually examine the use of accounting measures in evaluating the performance of the firm's management. Again, the approach we will follow rests on an endogenous perspective. Here we require that it be rational for the firm to hire the services of a manager and to subsequently worry about the services actually supplied to the extent that evaluating the performance of the manager is an important task.

The initial part of this, the rational use of a manager, is accomplished by expanding the list of factors from capital and labor, to capital (K), labor (L), and a manager (M). The specific technology setup simply expands what we have used to this point.

To avoid clutter, return to the single-product setting. Introducing the manager now alters the original technology constraint in (2.1) to (2.1'):

$$q \leq M\sqrt{KL} \qquad\qquad \textbf{(2.1')}$$

The idea is that the three factors are substitutes. More important, the new factor, M, can make the other two more, or less, productive. (No cynical comments, please.) For any positive K and L, the initial story was one in which output totaling $\sqrt{KL}$ could be produced. In the expanded setup, output totaling $M\sqrt{KL}$ can be produced. Implicitly, we used $M = 1$ in our earlier work.

The latter part, rational concern for evaluating the manager, is handled by presuming that the managerial factor is available in an imperfect market in which contracts for explicit services are not enforceable because the service actually supplied cannot be verified. For example, we can see whether the manager produced a new product plan but not the diligence, care, and strategic vision that went into producing that plan. Performance evaluation now enters the fray as an information device aimed at this lack of verifiability. For example, a more talented or focused manager is likely to provide a higher M, and a higher M makes the other factors more productive. Implicitly, then, the productivity of the other factors informs about the manager's talent and behavior. This establishes a connection between the cost or profit incurred and the manager's performance.

Several additional details must be added to the story to bring all of this alive; these details will be supplied in Chapter 11. For the moment, it is sufficient to see the flexibility of our model of the reporting organization.

Summary

Our study begins with a reporting organization, one in generic form that combines factors of production with its technology to produce goods and services. In its most extensive form, we identify three factors: capital (K), labor (L), and management (M). The discounted cash flow story stresses the investment aspects, the inventory story stresses substitution issues, and the managerial activity story stresses managerial behavior. We will move in and out of these variations throughout our study. The goal at each twist and turn is to exhibit the accounting issue in a natural setting with minimal distraction.

Appendix

An Analytic Aside for the Single-Product Case

It is possible to shed more light on the cost curve exercise in the text. It turns out that when the capital constraint is not binding, when the firm is free to select its mix of K and L, it does so in the following fashion:[13]

$$K/L = p_L/p_K$$

Intuitively, the higher the relative price of K, the more L is employed, and vice versa. In our specific story, we have $p_L/p_K = 100/200$, implying $L = 2K$, as noted.

Now, with this insight and using the specific prices in our illustration, we use the technology constraint (2.1) to tease out the factor choices:

$$q = \sqrt{KL} = \sqrt{K(2K)} = K\sqrt{2}$$

---

[13] To derive this, square both sides of (2.1): $q^2 \leq KL$. So, for any tentative choice of $K (> 0$, of course), the L choice must satisfy $q^2/K \leq L$. Naturally, we do not waste resources, so we match this tentative K with just the "right amount" of L: $q^2/K = L$. Now substitute this expression for the L into the overall expenditure calculation:

$$p_K K + p_L L = p_K K + p_L q^2/K$$

This expression, for any output q, depends only on K. Setting the derivative equal to zero allows us to identify the minimizing choice of K:

$$p_K - p_L q^2/K^2 = 0$$

This implies $K^2 = (p_L/p_K)q^2$, or $K = q\sqrt{p_L/p_K}$. But then $L = q^2/K = q^2/(q\sqrt{p_L/p_K}) = q\sqrt{p_K/p_L}$. We thus have $K/L = p_L/p_K$, as claimed.

Now, for the technically inclined, we have reduced this to a choice of K and then used the standard technique of setting the derivative to zero to find the optimal K (presuming, of course, the K^{max} condition is not violated). We should also check the second-order condition here, to convince ourselves we have located a minimum. (For example, setting the derivative to zero identifies the minimum point of the function if that function is convex, or "U-shaped.") We will not mention this issue again but assure the reader that throughout our work the optimization problems will remain well behaved, so these more technical considerations will not be an issue.

or

$$K = q/\sqrt{2} \quad \text{and} \quad L = 2K = q\sqrt{2}$$

Now, how large can q be before this delicate balancing of $L = 2K$ runs afoul of $K^{\max}$? Well, $K \le K^{\max}$ implies $K = q/\sqrt{2} \le K^{\max}$; or $q \le K^{\max}\sqrt{2} = 125\sqrt{2} = 176.7767$. Beyond this point, the best our firm can do is set $K = K^{\max} = 125$ and disproportionately use more and more labor, in effect solving $L = q^2/K^{\max} = q^2/125$.

Collecting these details, when q is not too large and the firm is free to balance its mix of K and L, it sets $L = 2K$ (which implies $K = q/\sqrt{2}$ and $L = q\sqrt{2}$). Beyond this point, the firm sets $K = K^{\max}$. So the cost curve is

$$C(q) = 200K + 100L = 200(q/\sqrt{2}) + 100q\sqrt{2} = 200\sqrt{2}q = 282.84q$$

if $q \le K^{\max}\sqrt{2} = 176.7767$, and

$$C(q) = 200K^{\max} + 100q^2/K^{\max} = 200(125) + (100/125)q^2 = 25{,}000 + 0.8q^2$$

otherwise. Notice that the marginal cost, defined as the derivative of $C(q)$ with respect to q, is 282.84 in the first region and $1.6q$ in the second. From here you should be able to replicate Exhibits 2.1 and 2.2.

Indeed, we can go further and derive the general structure of the cost curve here:[14]

$$C(q) = 2q\sqrt{p_K\, p_L} \quad \text{if } q \le K^{\max}\sqrt{p_K/p_L}$$

and

$$= p_K K^{\max} + p_L q^2/K^{\max}$$

otherwise. Notice in the first region, where $q \le K^{\max}\sqrt{p_K/p_L}$, the quantity is not too large, and the cost curve is linear; it is a constant multiplied by quantity q. Beyond this point, quantity is so large it leads to capital and labor choices that run afoul of the maximum capital size.

In this way we rationalize the firm's cost curve as an expenditure-minimizing choice of factor combinations, an efficient approach to production. From here we determine the firm's marginal cost curve, as in Exhibit 2.2. Its average cost curve, $C(q)/q$, provided $q > 0$, also falls into place. It is important to remember that the underlying concept is the efficient choice of factors. This is the essence of the minimization in (2.3).

---

[14] Recall in Note 13 that we derived factor choice expressions of $K = q\sqrt{p_L/p_K}$ and $L = q\sqrt{p_K/p_L}$. This provides an overall cost expression of

$$C(q) = p_K K + p_L L = p_K q\sqrt{p_L/p_K} + p_L q\sqrt{p_K/p_L} = 2q\sqrt{p_K\, p_L}$$

Of course, this all assumes that the chosen K satisfies $K \le K^{\max}$. If not, we set $K = K^{\max}$, and thus have

$$C(q) = p_K K^{\max} + p_L q^2/K^{\max}$$

Finally, $K \le K^{\max}$ requires $K = q\sqrt{p_L/p_K} \le K^{\max}$ or $q \le K^{\max}\sqrt{p_K/p_L}$.

Selected References

Because our firm is described in terms of selecting the best mix of factors for some specific purpose, we are dealing with economic cost. This is, in fact, an extensively developed line of thought. Your microeconomics textbook will contain the basics, though with an emphasis on a single-product firm. Chambers (1988) and Fare and Primont (1995) provide extensive treatments of the subject. Demski and Feltham (1976) and Demski (1994) provide connections to accounting. Clark (1923) is an important historical reference.

Key Terms

Economic cost is the minimum expenditure on factors that will allow the firm to produce whatever is to be produced. **Marginal cost** is the rate of change of economic cost with respect to the product in question; it is the derivative of economic cost with respect to the product in question. **Incremental cost** is the change in (economic) cost as output is changed by some specified amount. An **economy of scope** occurs when the economic cost of producing two or more products in the same firm is less than the economic cost of producing the products in separate firms. The firm's cost structure is not separable if it cannot be expressed as the sum of single-product cost functions, if the marginal cost of one product depends on how many of the other products are being produced.

Exercises

2.1. In what sense are capital and labor substitutes in the technology assumed in relation (2.1)? Give examples of factors that are substitutes.

2.2. When the story is expanded to include three products, as in relations (2.4) and (2.5), why does the cost curve turn out to be nonseparable? What is the importance of this lack of separability?

2.3. Verify the plot in Exhibit 2.1 using the same prices and K^{max}, of course, by solving for the optimal K and L choices for $q \in \{0, 25, 50, 75, 100, \ldots, 300\}$ and then plotting total expenditure on K and L versus output. Then repeat the exercise but using $K^{max} = 50$. Explain the difference in your two plots.

2.4. Exhibit 2.2 provides a plot of the firm's marginal cost as output varies. Using the same prices and K^{max} as in Exhibit 2.2, plot the incremental cost of one additional unit, defined as $C(q + 1) - C(q)$, for $q \in \{0, 25, 50, 75, 100, \ldots, 300\}$. Contrast your plot with that in Exhibit 2.2.

2.5. Suppose that, in our single-product firm, capital is priced at $p_K = 200$ while labor is priced at $p_L = 200$ per unit. Let $K^{max} = 125$. Solve for the firm's optimal factor choices and cost for outputs of $q \in \{0, 25, 50, 75, 100, \ldots, 300\}$. Plot the implied cost curve. Carefully explain its relationship to the cost curve plotted in Exhibit 2.1.

2.6. Using the prices in Exercise 2.5, suppose that capital is fixed at 75 units. Determine the firm's short-run cost curve. Also replicate the short-run and long-run cost curves displayed in Exhibit 2.3.

Carefully explain the difference between this display and that in Exhibit 2.3.

2.7. Return to the setting in Exhibit 2.4, which has three products present, along with $p_K = 200$, $p_{L1} = p_{L2} = p_{L3} = 100$, and $K^{max} = 125$. Suppose that the first product sells for $P_1 = 320$ per unit, and the second and third sell for zero. Determine the firm's optimal output and the associated profit. Provide an intuitive explanation.

2.8. This is a continuation of Exercise 2.7. Now change the second product's selling price from 0 to 50. Again determine the optimal output and the associated profit. Provide an intuitive explanation. What would the firm's optimal output be if the first and third products sold for zero while the second sold for 50?

2.9. This is a continuation of Exercise 2.8. Now change the respective selling prices to 320, 160, and 200. Determine the firm's optimal output and profit, and explain the difference between this output schedule and that in the text (where the selling prices are 120, 160, and 200).

2.10. Ralph's Firm (RF) uses three inputs to produce output. Let q denote the quantity of output and x_i the quantity of input i, $i = 1, 2,$ or 3. Respective factor prices are 100 per unit, 1 per unit, and 4 per unit. Output $q \geq 0$ requires the following inputs:

$$x_1 \geq q$$

and

$$\sqrt{x_2 x_3} \geq q(125 - 10q + q^2) \equiv f(q)$$

Determine RF's economic cost curve for $q \in \{0, 1, 2, 3, 4, 5, 6, 7, 8, 9, 10\}$. Plot total and average economic cost using your data points.

2.11. This is an extension of Ralph's Firm (RF) in Exercise 2.10. Here, we adopt a specific short-run setting and assume that factor x_3 is set at the value of $x_3 = 250$. Notice this is the x_3 amount that would have been chosen under $q = 5$ in the original problem. With this factor "fixed" in this manner, determine Ralph's short-run total cost and average cost for the original output series. Comment on the relationship with the original total cost and average cost constructions.

2.12. We now find Ralph managing a two-product firm. The technology mixes capital and labor to produce two products. Capital is shared, but labor is specific to each of the two products. Capital and labor are also substitutes. The technology is given by relations (2.1a), (2.1b), and (2.2) in the text. $K^{max} = 15$; $p_K = 100$ per unit; $p_{L1} = 50$ per unit; and $p_{L2} = 75$ per unit. (So we are dealing with a two-product version of the three-product illustration in the text.) Determine Ralph's cost, $C(q_1, q_2)$ for all combinations of $q_1, q_2 \in \{5, 10, 15, 20, 25\}$. Plot your data to provide a graphical depiction of

Ralph's cost surface. What patterns emerge? Finally, suppose that Ralph produces $q_1 = 15$ and $q_2 = 20$ units. What total cost would an accounting system report? What would the accounting system claim each unit of the first product cost? What would it claim each unit of the second product cost?

2.13. Redo Exhibit 2.6 for the case when all factor payments take place at the end of the third period while customer payments occur as originally assumed. Carefully explain your findings.

2.14. Suppose in the three-product setting (especially expressions (2.4) and (2.5)), the firm faces factor prices of $p_K = 300$ and $p_{L1} = p_{L2} = p_{L3} = 100$, along with $K^{\max} = 225$. First determine the firm's cost curve for the special case of $q_2 = q_3 = 0$. Second, suppose that each product sells for 200 per unit. Determine the firm's optimal output and factor choices, assuming that $K = K^{\max}$. Does the firm earn any rent at this point? Explain.

2.15. This is a variation on the discounted cash flow story in Exhibit 2.6. For convenience, only two periods are present (so, in a sense, $q_3 = 0$). Capital is purchased at time $t = 0$, at a price of $p_K = 500$. First-period labor, which is paid at $t = 1$, carries a spot price of $p_{L1} = 100$, and second-period labor, which is paid at $t = 2$, carries a spot price of $p_{L2} = 110$. As usual, the interest rate is $r = 10$ percent. $K^{\max} = 1,500$. Output in each of the two periods is really the same product, and the firm can produce to inventory in the first period. The firm has only one customer to which it must supply 100 units in the first period and 700 units in the second period. Determine and interpret the firm's optimal production schedule and factor choices. Repeat the exercise, assuming that $p_{L2} = 200$. Explain the differences in your two solutions.

Chapter 3

Classical Foundations

Accounting, we will learn, uses the language and algebra of valuation to convey information. Giving this curt phrase meaning requires care and study. The beginning point is "the language and algebra of valuation," the topic we now introduce. The difficulty is that terms such as *value* and *income* have taken on nearly colloquial status, as illustrated by the FASB's and IASB's fascination with fair value, yet their substantive meaning is to be found in a setting of certainty coupled with perfect and complete markets. This is the world of classical economics, and it is the source for our language and algebra. It is inevitable, then, that our study begin with a reporting organization that exists in a classical environment, one with well-functioning markets and foreknowledge.

Our study of accounting theory begins with a review of classical foundations, a setting in which the important notions of *economic value* and *economic income* are well defined. Here we presume that the reporting organization, or firm, operates in a world of certainty and perfect markets. Both assumptions are important. *Certainty* means that there are no surprises; everyone in the economy shares an unshakable confidence in their knowledge of what the future will bring. Of course, that future depends on how resources are allocated, so the setting is not entirely predestined. *Perfect markets* means that every resource is traded in a perfect market; everyone knows the price of every commodity and factor of production, and all trades take place in well-organized, *perfectly competitive markets* in which everyone acts as a price taker. (We are a bit casual here; we actually mean perfect *and* complete markets: There is a market in which every resource is traded, and that market is perfect.) These are daunting, unrealistic assumptions, but it is in this setting that the language and concepts of accounting are identifiable. Traditionally, accounting is thought of as a valuation process, and in the setting of this chapter, such valuation is well defined. Absent perfect markets, that is no longer the case.

It is also important to acknowledge that this classical setting of certainty and perfect markets carries a rich and deep intellectual tradition, covering such items as the existence and efficiency of competitive equilibrium in an economy. By necessity, we are highly selective in the formalisms and insights we highlight and examine.

Initially, we pose a simple cash flow setting and review the notions of present value and economic income associated with that setting. Next, we step back and identify the presumed cash flows as arising from profit-maximizing behavior on the part of the reporting organization. This leads us into the relationship between economic cost and economic income, an essential step if we are to understand accounting.

EXOGENOUS CASH FLOWS

Consider a setting in which the firm faces the cash flow prospects detailed in Exhibit 3.1. To avoid ambiguity, we presume throughout that the cash flow is denominated in dollars. Notice the cash flow is spread over three periods, with four distinct amounts. Also notice that the sum of these cash flows is $-25,000 + 4,950 + 9,680 + 16,637.50 = 6,267.50$.

This cash flow sequence is, in fact, the one we derived at the end of Chapter 2, in Exhibit 2.6. At this point, however, there is no derivation per se. We simply begin by assuming that this cash flow sequence is in place. It is exogenous. As you suspect, we will return to the earlier derivation at a later point, but first things first. For the moment, we simply have a cash flow sequence, and to reinforce this stark story, we display the sequence in the explicit time line format in Exhibit 3.1.

Now also suppose the periods are equally spaced, and interpret each period as a year. Let's also interpret the sequence of cash flows as the net cash flows between the firm and its owner or owners. We thus have a firm whose life history is described by an initial investment or cash flow from the owners of $CF_0 = -25,000$, followed by respective end-of-year cash flows distributed to the owners of $CF_1 = 4,950$, $CF_2 = 9,680$, and $CF_3 = 16,637.50$. *It is important to remember in what follows that the cash flows are between the firm and its owners.* Alternatively put, there is a claim to the firm's cash flows, and we will be economically valuing that claim.

EXHIBIT 3.1
Cash Flows for
$t = 0, 1, 2,$ **and** 3

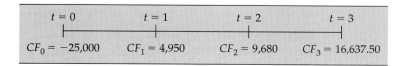

$t = 0$	$t = 1$	$t = 2$	$t = 3$
$CF_0 = -25{,}000$	$CF_1 = 4{,}950$	$CF_2 = 9{,}680$	$CF_3 = 16{,}637.50$

The firm lives for a short period of time, simply for our convenience. A more involved story would have the firm, among other things, growing and investing in a number of projects. This, however, would complicate the path ahead without offering any substantive additional insight. So we stick with the most simple of stories.

Continuing, we also assume that the interest rate is a constant $r = 10$ percent each period. Importantly, and emphatically, the interest rate is a market price. The market price in the current period of $(1 + r)^t$ dollars delivered t periods into the future is precisely \$1.00.[1] For example, the price of \$1.21 in the current period to be delivered in two periods is \$1.00. We can borrow \$1.00 today by paying the lender \$1.21 two periods from today. Stated differently, Z dollars today and $Z(1 + r)^t$ dollars t periods from today are economically equivalent. Likewise, $Z(1 + r)^{-t}$ dollars today and Z dollars in t periods are economically equivalent.

Present Values

This economic equivalence is often expressed in terms of present value.[2] The present value of Z dollars in t periods, at interest rate r, is, recall, simply $Z(1 + r)^{-t}$. In this setting, present value is merely a statement of equivalence based on market prices. With the presumed interest rate structure, holding Z dollars today gives one precisely the same command over resources as holding a claim to $Z(1 + r)^t$ dollars t periods from now. The one can be exchanged for the other. Perfect markets are awfully convenient.

Next, we introduce some useful notation. Suppose that we have a sequence of cash flows at times $t = 0, 1, \ldots, T$. Let CF_t denote the cash flow at time t. Also let $\mathbf{CF}$ denote the entire list or vector of cash flows:[3]

$$\mathbf{CF} = [CF_0, CF_1, CF_2, \ldots, CF_T]$$

Our example in Exhibit 3.1 has $T = 3$ and $\mathbf{CF} = [-25{,}000, 4{,}950, 9{,}680, 16{,}637.50]$.

Given a cash flow vector, we now define the *continuation present value* at time t, based on interest rate r, as the present value of the remaining cash flows, calculated as of time t. Denoting this calculation by PV_t, we have

$$PV_t = \sum_{j=t+1}^{T} CF_j (1 + r)^{t-j} \qquad \textbf{(3.1)}$$

---

[1] Note well that we are engaging in a partial equilibrium exploration. This particular set of prices, parameterized by the presumed constant interest rate, has not been derived from an equilibrium argument. We simply assume that this is the interest rate. Various additional price assumptions will be introduced as the example deepens.

[2] Recall that in Chapter 2 where we introduced the underlying details, we took the notion of present value for granted. Here we emphasize its roots in an explicit market structure.

[3] Square brackets are used to denote such a listing in vector format.

To illustrate, the data in Exhibit 3.1 provide the following, using $r = 10$ percent of course:

$$PV_0 = 4{,}950(1.1)^{-1} + 9{,}680(1.1)^{-2} + 16{,}637.50(1.1)^{-3} = 25{,}000$$

$$PV_1 = 9{,}680(1.1)^{-1} + 16{,}637.50(1.1)^{-2} = 22{,}550$$

$$PV_2 = 16{,}637.50(1.1)^{-1} = 15{,}125$$

$$PV_3 = 0$$

Notice that the calculation in period t ignores the cash flow in period t. The focus is on the future cash flows as of time t.

Economically, the continuation present value is simply the market value of the remaining cash flows in vector **CF**, as of time t. To appreciate this, suppose that we purchased the $t = 1, 2, 3$ sequence of cash flows in our example at time $t = 0$. Given the assumed interest rate, we should pay $4{,}950(1.1)^{-1} + 9{,}680(1.1)^{-2} + 16{,}637.50(1.1)^{-3} = 25{,}000$. This amount is, of course, the continuation present value at $t = 0$ that we calculated earlier. Suppose, however, that we paid 24,000. This means that we have a money pump: We pay 24,000 but can immediately sell the claim to the cash flow sequence for 25,000. We can do this until the sun sets and possibly beyond.

Surely something is wrong. Our mistake is assuming in the first place that we could buy something for 24,000 that could be immediately sold for 25,000. Intertemporal arbitrage is not possible in the perfect markets setting. So, at time t, the remaining future cash flows in vector **CF** must have a market value of PV_t.

Present value is market value, and market value is present value in the setting in this chapter. More precisely, for cash flow sequence **CF**, the market value at time t of the remaining cash flows is the continuation present value at that point, and the continuation present value at that point is the market value of the remaining cash flows at that point. Furthermore, this market value is unique and unambiguous. Consequently, the continuation present value is also called the *economic value*.

This valuation perspective turns out to be important in what follows, so we will embellish it with some notation. The firm's activities are summarized by cash flow series **CF**, and the interest rate is r. Valuation portrays this in terms of a sequence of economic values, here assumed to be the continuation present values in (3.1). Fundamentally, then, we have a valuation function, call it V, that assigns to any **CF** series in the presence of some interest rate r a series of temporal values. Formally, we have

$$V(\mathbf{CF}, r) = [PV_0, PV_1, \ldots, PV_T] \tag{3.2}$$

where PV_t is defined via expression (3.1). Literally, then, the present value apparatus is a mapping or rule that assigns a sequence of continuation present values to any such cash flow vector and interest rate specification.[4]

Economic Income

Closely associated is the notion of economic income. To set the stage, recall the Exhibit 3.1 story in which investors invested or "paid" 25,000 in exchange for the noted future cash flow series, one that has a continuation present value of $PV_0 = 25,000$. (After all, in a perfect market setting, competition ensures that no firm earns any rent.)

Nevertheless, we see that the owners have paid 25,000 and eventually will receive payments totaling $4,950 + 9,680 + 16,637.50 = 31,267.50$. How should we interpret the difference of $31,267.50 - 25,000 = 6,267.50$? Presumably, we, as accountants, would call it *income,* but this begs many questions, not to mention the issue of how much should be attributable to each of the three periods.

Economic income, though, is unambiguous in this setting. It is simply the increment in economic value over the period plus cash flow during the period. Cash flow, of course, is the cash that moves between the owners and the firm. Economic value, in turn, is our friend, the continuation present value [in (3.1)]. Let I_t denote the economic income for period t. We have the following algebraic definition of *economic income:*

$$I_t = PV_t - PV_{t-1} + CF_t \qquad \textbf{(3.3)}$$

Note well that economic income is simply the increment in value $(PV_t - PV_{t-1})$ plus the cash flow of the period (CF_t). Stated differently, it is the increment in value plus resources received if $CF_t > 0$ or the increment in value less additional resources provided if $CF_t < 0$. Economic value, in turn, is measured by present value, at interest rate r, in our setting.[5]

Moreover, just as the present value apparatus gave us a mapping from cash flow vectors and interest rates into a sequence of continuation present values, expression (3.2), the economic income apparatus gives us a mapping from cash flow vectors and interest rates into a sequence

---

[4] To develop this a bit more, a *function* is a rule that takes points from one set to points in a second set. The only requirements are that every point in the first set must be carried to some point in the second set and no point in the first set can be carried to more than one point in the second set. (We often find this idea of a function written as $f: X \rightarrow Y$, which reads "the function f maps set X into set Y.") We have, you should notice, not been this formal. To tighten things up, then, we should specify the set of **CF** vectors and interest rates we have in mind, and the mapping would be to some subset of $T + 1$ dimensional Euclidian space.

[5] By analogy, in a security price setting, we would think in terms of change in value of the underlying security plus dividends received (or additional investment made). Also notice that I_t depends on the underlying cash flow vector and the interest rate.

of income numbers. Specifically, we have an income function I defined via

$$I(\mathbf{CF}, r) = [I_1, \ldots, I_T] \qquad \textbf{(3.4)}$$

where, of course, I_t is defined in expression (3.3). The valuation function, (3.2), defines a sequence of stock measures while the income function, expression (3.4), defines a sequence of flow measures.

In this world of stringent market conditions, then, we readily identify (economic) stock and flow measures associated with cash flow sequence $\mathbf{CF}$ and interest rate (i.e., market price) r. An equivalent way to visualize the flow measure is to think in terms of "net receipts" less economic depreciation in period t. Net receipts, of course, corresponds to CF_t, and *economic depreciation* is the change in value, $PV_{t-1} - PV_t$. So

$$I_t = PV_t - PV_{t-1} + CF_t = CF_t - (PV_{t-1} - PV_t)$$

Returning to our numerical example in Exhibit 3.1, we have the following calculations:

$$I_1 = PV_1 - PV_0 + CF_1 = 22{,}550 - 25{,}000 + 4{,}950 = 2{,}500$$
$$I_2 = PV_2 - PV_1 + CF_2 = 15{,}125 - 22{,}550 + 9{,}680 = 2{,}255$$
$$I_3 = PV_3 - PV_2 + CF_3 = 0 - 15{,}125 + 16{,}637.50 = 1{,}512.50$$

These calculations are summarized in a more familiar income statement format of revenue less expenses in Exhibit 3.2. There we call the periodic cash inflows the *net receipts,* or *revenue.* And with an up-front investment of 25,000 and no other visible expenses, depreciation is the only expense, and here of course, it is *economic depreciation*. Also notice the implicit asset valuation here. It is simply the continuation present value.

The tight linkage between economic income and present value calculations allows us to demonstrate two implications of the definition of economic income. First, economic income in any period is simply the interest rate multiplied by the beginning-of-period value:

$$I_t = r \times PV_{t-1} \qquad \textbf{(3.5)}$$

You should convince yourself that this is indeed the case for our cash flow sequence (in Exhibit 3.1) and calculations (in Exhibit 3.2).

EXHIBIT 3.2
Income Statement Format for Economic Income Calculations

	$t = 1$	$t = 2$	$t = 3$	Total
"Net receipts" = "Revenue" (CF_t)	4,950	9,680	16,637.50	31,267.50
"Depreciation" = "Economic depreciation" ($PV_{t-1} - PV_t$)	2,450	7,425	15,125	25,000
"Income" (I_t)	2,500	2,255	1,512.50	6,267.50

To see the logic behind this important linkage, begin with the fact that adjacent continuation present values are intimately linked:[6]

$$PV_t = (1+r)PV_{t-1} - CF_t$$

From here apply the definition of economic income:

$$I_t = PV_t - PV_{t-1} + CF_t = (1+r)PV_{t-1} - CF_t - PV_{t-1} + CF_t = r \times PV_{t-1}$$

Second, the series of economic income calculations is "tidy" in the following sense:

$$\sum_{t=1}^{T} I_t = \sum_{t=1}^{T} CF_t - PV_0 \qquad \textbf{(3.6)}$$

That is, the total of the economic income assigned to the periods equals the total of the cash flows from $t = 1$ forward, less the initial continuation present value.[7] (This readily follows by using the definition of economic income and summing the terms from $t = 1$ to T.) Again, you should verify this in Exhibit 3.2.

Recall, now, that with our cash flow series in Exhibit 3.1, we also have $CF_0 = -PV_0$: the invested amount is the negative of the present value of the future cash flows. The tidiness property now explains why the sum of the economic incomes equals the sum of the cash flows in our simple story.[8]

To this point, we have identified the economic income, period by period as well as in total, associated with the cash flow story in Exhibit 3.1. We might even embellish our calculations with accompanying balance sheets, but more important is the question of interpretation. What does it mean, say, to claim that this firm's economic income was 2,255 in period $t = 2$? Fisher's (1906) stress on income as a flow of wealth or Hick's (1946) stress on how much can be consumed without diminishing the ability to

---

[6] Intuitively, we take the continuation present value at time $t - 1$ and move it forward in time one period. CF_t, however, must be subtracted as the time t calculation takes place after the cash flow occurs in period t. More precisely, it is routine to verify that

$$PV_{t-1} = (1+r)^{-1}(PV_t + CF_t)$$

which implies $(1 + r)PV_{t-1} = PV_t + CF_t$.

[7] Also recall that our firm faces a short life. Alternatively, suppose that T is unbounded large and the firm's growth rate is zero; it is neither growing nor declining. This implies that the continuation present value is constant, and (3.5) provides the familiar case of value being the capitalized income stream.

[8] Suppose we paid less than PV_0, implying that $PV_0 + CF_0 > 0$ for the claim to the cash flow sequence, a clear violation of our perfect market assumption. Now write the value up, at time $t = 0$, to PV_0, and label the gain of $PV_0 + CF_0$, economic rent. More broadly, then, the totality of economic income plus economic rent equals the sum of the cash flows, from $t = 0$ to $t = T$. We will return in due course to the issue of economic rent.

consume in the future come to mind. This is getting ahead of our story, however; it is time to retreat and dig into the background details of the story in Exhibit 3.1.

ENDOGENOUS CASH FLOWS

We now connect the cash flow sequence in Exhibit 3.1 to the richer story of a firm that purchases labor and capital in respective factor markets and uses its technology to produce products that are sold in the product markets. This exercise is important because it sheds light on the income interpretation question and exposes an important connection between economic cost and economic income.

To do this, we return to the prototypical firm presented in Chapter 2. The firm uses three types of labor and one type of capital to produce and sell three different products.[9] q_1, q_2, and q_3 denote the non-negative quantities of the three products. L_1, L_2, and L_3 denote the non-negative quantities of the three labor inputs, and K denotes the non-negative quantity of physical capital. The production technology, recall, is given by the following three technology constraints:

$$q_1 \leq \sqrt{KL_1} \qquad \textbf{(3.7a)}$$

$$q_2 \leq \sqrt{KL_2} \qquad \textbf{(3.7b)}$$

$$q_3 \leq \sqrt{KL_3} \qquad \textbf{(3.7c)}$$

along with an upper bound on the physical capital:

$$K \leq K^{\max} \qquad \textbf{(3.8)}$$

Timing Details

Now add an important time dimension. Suppose that the firm produces and sells product i in period i, implying we have a three-period story. Physical capital is acquired and paid for at the beginning of the story ($t = 0$), and output is delivered at the end of the respective periods ($t = 1, 2$, and 3). Customers pay upon delivery. Labor for each product is paid at the end of the respective product's period. That is, rather than everything taking place in the same period, the firm now operates in spot markets stretched across three periods. The interest rate is denoted r.

---

[9] We should also reflect on the economic meaning of a product. Naturally, the concept is expansive, covering goods and services. Moreover, the same good or service produced at different points in time will be treated as economically distinct products. So, for example, a specific type of refrigerator produced in year t is economically distinct from the same type of refrigerator produced in year $t + 1$.

EXHIBIT 3.3
Timing of the
Receipts and
Expenditures

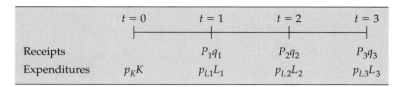

	$t = 0$	$t = 1$	$t = 2$	$t = 3$
Receipts		$P_1 q_1$	$P_2 q_2$	$P_3 q_3$
Expenditures	$p_K K$	$p_{L1} L_1$	$p_{L2} L_2$	$p_{L3} L_3$

Receipts and expenditures must now be identified by time. Let p_K denote the (time $t = 0$) price of physical capital. Similarly, let p_{L1} denote the (time $t = 1$) price of labor used in the first period, p_{L2} its counterpart in the second period, and p_{L3} its counterpart in the third period. Using parallel notation, let the (time $t = 1$) selling price of the first product be P_1; counterparts for the other two products are denoted P_2 and P_3.

Now, given these timing details, the firm's expenditures on factors and receipts from sales in the product markets are stretched out on the time line detailed in Exhibit 3.3.

From here, we assume that the firm selects its output and factor combination to maximize its *economic profit*, defined as the present value, at time $t = 0$, of the cash flows (i.e., the net gain to the owners). Conveniently, we approach this in stages.

First, for any output schedule, q_1, q_2, and q_3, the firm will select the efficient combination of factors. That is, among those combinations that support production of the noted output, it will select the one that minimizes the present value of factor expenditures. This is none other than our earlier definition of economic cost in Chapter 2.

Given the timing assumptions, the (time $t = 0$) present value of the firm's expenditures on factors is simply

$$p_K K + p_{L1} L_1 (1 + r)^{-1} + p_{L2} L_2 (1 + r)^{-2} + p_{L3} L_3 (1 + r)^{-3}$$

So, the firm's best choice of factors to produce q_1, q_2, and q_3 repeats our earlier development of economic cost:

$$C(q_1, q_2, q_3)$$

$$\equiv \underset{K, L_1, L_2, L_3 \geq 0}{\text{Minimum}} p_K K + p_{L1} L_1 (1 + r)^{-1}$$

$$+ p_{L2} L_2 (1 + r)^{-2} + p_{L3} L_3 (1 + r)^{-3}$$

subject to (3.7a), (3.7b), (3.7c), and (3.8)   **(3.9)**

The only difference is that cost expression $C(q_1, q_2, q_3)$ is now stated in economically equivalent present value terms. Spot prices, so to speak, are converted to economically equivalent present value expenditures. The cost expression, in other words, is now measured in (economically equivalent) present value terms. This insight is important in what follows.

With the cost expression identified, the second stage selects the profit-maximizing output schedule. Naturally, profit now takes on the convenient structure of the present value of receipts less the preceding determined cost.[10] Recall the timing convention that a unit of product i sells at time i for a price of P_i. The present value of the receipts from customers is

$$P_1 q_1 (1+r)^{-1} + P_2 q_2 (1+r)^{-2} + P_3 q_3 (1+r)^{-3}$$

So the profit-maximizing choice is described by

$$\underset{q_1, q_2, q_3 \geq 0}{\text{Maximize }} P_1 q_1 (1+r)^{-1} + P_2 q_2 (1+r)^{-2}$$
$$+ P_3 q_3 (1+r)^{-3} - C(q_1, q_2, q_3) \qquad \textbf{(3.10)}$$

The firm, in other words, makes its choices by maximizing the present value of the cash flows, or profit. Judiciously, we divide this exercise into stages of initially determining the optimal factor combination for arbitrary output choices, the economic cost expression in (3.9), followed by the optimal output combination, the profit maximization in (3.10).

Recycled Illustration

To illustrate, suppose the selling prices are $P_1 = 132$, $P_2 = 193.60$, and $P_3 = 266.20$; and the labor prices are $p_{L1} = 110$, $p_{L2} = 121$, and $p_{L3} = 133.10$. The capital price is $p_K = 200$. In addition, the capital limit is $K^{\max} = 125$. The interest rate, of course, is $r = 10$ percent.

Given the timing conventions, the (time $t = 0$) present value of expenditures on factors is

$$200K + 110 L_1 (1.1)^{-1} + 121 L_2 (1.1)^{-2} + 133.1 L_3 (1.1)^{-3}$$
$$= 200K + 100 L_1 + 100 L_2 + 100 L_3$$

So the firm's economic cost is defined by the following specific version of (3.9):

$$C(q_1, q_2, q_3) \equiv \underset{K, L_1, L_2, L_3 \geq 0}{\text{Minimum }} 200K + 100 L_1 + 100 L_2 + 100 L_3$$

$$\text{subject to (3.7a), (3.7b), (3.7c), and (3.8)}$$

---

[10] The use of the term "profit" here is purposely colloquial. In a literal sense, the firm seeks to maximize its economic rent (defined as the present value of the cash flows). With perfect markets, though, the solution entails zero rent. Also notice that the firm maximizing in this fashion is hardly gratuitous. With the perfect and *complete markets,* consumers and producers acting as price takers (in the sense that they optimize, taking the prices as given), and firms maximizing their profits, the resulting equilibrium is efficient. No one can be made better off without making someone worse off. The firm's behavior, in this setting, is therefore well directed by the market prices and is efficient. This is one of the celebrated theorems of welfare economics (i.e., efficiency of a competitive equilibrium). It is also called the *Fisher separation theorem,* reflecting the fact that market prices "separate" the firm's decision making from the tastes of the consumers. Firms maximize their profits, and consumers, the firms' owners, then take their largest possible consumption budgets to the consumption markets.

The solution, provided we stay in the region in which the output is not so large that the K^{max} constraint is binding, should be familiar. It is the very expression we derived in Chapter 2:[11]

$$C(q_1, q_2, q_3) = 200\sqrt{2(q_1^2 + q_2^2 + q_3^2)}$$

There we had a setting in which output was produced simultaneously, with a capital price of 200 and labor price of 100 for each labor type. This is economically equivalent to the present story in which the output is produced sequentially. (The reason is that we have the same technology, and we have rigged the factor prices so that their time $t = 0$ equivalent prices are the prices we used in the original setting.) But we linger.

Turning to the output choice, the present value of the receipts from customers is

$$132q_1(1.1)^{-1} + 193.6q_2(1.1)^{-2} + 266.2q_3(1.1)^{-3} = 120q_1 + 160q_2 + 200q_3$$

So the profit-maximizing choice is described by the following specific version of (3.10):

$$\underset{q_1, q_2, q_3 \geq 0}{\text{maximize}} \, 120q_1 + 160q_2 + 200q_3 - C(q_1, q_2, q_3)$$

A solution has $q_1 = 75$, $q_2 = 100$, and $q_3 = 125$. Moreover, the underlying factor choices are $K = 125 (= K^{max})$, $L_1 = 45$, $L_2 = 80$, and $L_3 = 125$.[12]

---

[11] Repeating the details, for any value of $K > 0$, the firm will acquire $L_i = q_i^2/K$ units of labor. So, the expenditure calculation becomes

$$200K + 100q_1^2/K + 100q_2^2/K + 100q_3^2/K = 200K + \theta/K$$

where $\theta = 100q_1^2 + 100q_2^2 + 100q_3^2$. Setting the derivative equal to zero gives us the minimizing choice of K:

$$200 - \theta/K^2 = 0$$

So $K^2 = \theta/200$, or $K = \sqrt{\theta/200}$. From here, the present value of the overall expenditure is $200K + \theta/K$. Working through the details gives us

$$C(q_1, q_2, q_3) = 2\sqrt{200\theta} = 200\sqrt{2(q_1^2 + q_2^2 + q_3^2)}$$

the expression in the text, again presuming the K^{max} constraint is not binding. Additional details were developed in Chapter 2.

[12] Again, we are revisiting the earlier example in Chapter 2. There we verified this solution by differentiating the profit expression for each output quantity and setting that derivative to zero:

$$120 - \partial C(q_1, q_2, q_3)/\partial q_1 = 0$$
$$160 - \partial C(q_1, q_2, q_3)/\partial q_2 = 0$$
$$200 - \partial C(q_1, q_2, q_3)/\partial q_3 = 0$$

Also from our earlier work, the marginal cost expression for project i is

$$\partial C(q_1, q_2, q_3)/\partial q_i = 2p_{Li}q_i/\sqrt{\theta/p_K}$$

if the K^{max} constraint is not binding and $2p_{Li}q_i/K^{max}$ otherwise. ($\theta = 100q_1^2 + 100q_2^2 + 100q_3^2$.) From here you can verify that $q_1 = 75$, $q_2 = 100$, and $q_3 = 125$ satisfy these conditions. As noted earlier, any output in the proportion of $3 : 4 : 5$ that does not violate the K^{max} constraint satisfies these conditions, and we have merely taken from among these the largest possible output as our particular solution.

EXHIBIT 3.4
Cash Outflows,
Inflows, and Net
Cash Flow

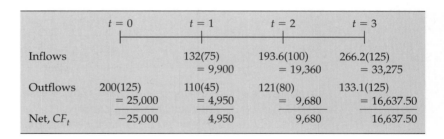

	$t = 0$	$t = 1$	$t = 2$	$t = 3$
Inflows		132(75) = 9,900	193.6(100) = 19,360	266.2(125) = 33,275
Outflows	200(125) = 25,000	110(45) = 4,950	121(80) = 9,680	133.1(125) = 16,637.50
Net, CF_t	−25,000	4,950	9,680	16,637.50

Now tally the cash inflows and outflows. Details are displayed in Exhibit 3.4. In addition, you should verify that the present value of the inflows is 50,000, just as the present value of the outflows is 50,000. The firm's profit is precisely zero.

Importantly, we have come full circle and are back to the cash flow series originally assumed in Exhibit 3.1. How is it we speak so casually, therefore, about our firm in a perfectly competitive setting having zero profit, yet having strictly positive economic income, as calculated in Exhibit 3.2 (or, for that matter, a lifetime income of 6,267.50)?

BACK TO ECONOMIC INCOME

The answer is in the timing. The best way to see this is to retell the story for the case in which all customers pay at the end of period $t = 3$ while all factor payments are made at time $t = 0$. We also adjust the various prices so their present value at time $t = 0$ remains the same. So the (time $t = 0$) factor prices are $p_K = 200$ and $p_{L1} = p_{L2} = p_{L3} = 100$. Similarly, the (time $t = 3$) product prices are $P_1 = 132(1.1)^2 = 159.72$, $P_2 = 193.6(1.1) = 212.96$ and $P_3 = 266.20$. Note well: We have preserved the present value of each and every price.

Revisiting the cost curve and profit maximization exercises, therefore, leaves the original choice of outputs and factors undisturbed. After all, the respective present value expressions are equivalent. The cash flows, though, are a different matter. Now the only cash outflows occur at $t = 0$. We have

$$CF_0 = -[200(125) + 100(45) + 100(80) + 100(125)] = -50,000$$

Likewise, the only cash inflows occur at $t = 3$:

$$CF_3 = 159.72(75) + 212.96(100) + 266.20(125) = 66,550$$

See Exhibit 3.5.

Exhibits 3.4 and 3.5 are, of course, economically equivalent stories. The present value of the factor payments in Exhibit 3.4 is 50,000, just as the $(t = 3)$ future value of all customer payments is 66,550. Moreover, the firm's profit remains at $66,550(1.1)^{-3} - 50,000 = 0$, yet its income over the

EXHIBIT 3.5
Equivalent Cash
Flows for Exhibit
3.4 Story

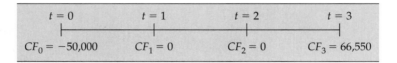

three periods has increased to $66{,}550 - 50{,}000 = 16{,}550$. Is this magic, or what? We seem to be maximizing income!

This is deceptive, however. The factor payments total 50,000 when converted to time $t = 0$ dollars. Clearly, the firm's economic cost is 50,000 stated in $t = 0$ dollars, but this cost tally is $50{,}000(1.1)^3 = 66{,}550$ when stated in time $t = 3$ dollars. If all factor purchases are paid at $t = 0$, the cost is 50,000 at that time. If all factors are paid at $t = 3$, the cost is 66,550 at that time. The latter is equivalent to borrowing 50,000 to purchase the factors up front and paying the loan, plus interest, at $t = 3$. Indeed, in this loan scenario, the firm's cash flow is precisely zero in each and every period, as it borrows everything up front (the 50,000 datum), then receives payments at time $t = 3$ totaling 66,550, and immediately pays off its loan (principal plus accumulated interest) for 66,550.

Now think back to the initial presentation of this four-factor, three-product firm in Chapter 2. There, production was timeless, and all cash transactions took place at the same point in time. If, then, all receipts and expenditures take place at the same instant of time, economic cost is the minimum expenditure on factors at that point in time. If production, factor acquisition, and output take place at various points in time, however, our usual formulation of economic cost prevails when we envision all factors as being paid for at time $t = 0$. Otherwise, we focus on the present value of all factor expenditures as of a particular point in time. Moving the time at which this present value is reckoned alters the magnitude of economic cost. If the calculation is centered on $t = 0$, the economic cost is 50,000, but if it is centered on $t = 3$, the economic cost is 66,550. The two are economically equivalent, of course.

For the record, we present the economic income calculations for the Exhibit 3.5 story in the same format as used in the original discussion. The continuation present value moves from 50,000 to 55,000, to 60,500. Be certain that you understand the calculations.[13]

Notice that the associated economic income calculations step the economic cost forward in time, to $t = 3$. Economic cost at time $t = 3$ (66,550)

---

[13] Also notice that, with our endogenous perspective, we continue with the format of "revenue" less expenses in the calculation, but "revenue" is "net receipts" in this case. Looking at the underlying details, we see that revenue consists of cash inflow from the customer less payment for the respective labor factor. Think of this as revenue less direct cost (in particular, direct labor). We continue with the net, the "revenue" format because that is how the exercise began—with exogenous cash flows. In Chapter 4, when we introduce the accountant's view of this story, we will have revenue measured as receipts from customers and expenses separately tallied for the labor and capital factors.

in this specialized case is economic cost at time $t = 0$ (50,000) plus the sum of the economic income over the three periods. Economic income is a component of economic cost.

This is no accident. Return to the features of economic income developed in expressions (3.5) and (3.6). In (3.6), we highlight the fact that total economic income equals the arithmetic sum of the cash flow series, given that we begin with zero economic profit. In (3.5), we highlight the fact that economic income is merely the interest rate multiplied by the beginning-of-period continuation present value. It is a "charge," so to speak, for monetary factors or investment.

Recall that markets are perfect and complete here. So at time t, when the remaining portion of the cash flow sequence has a value of PV_t, the continuation present value, it is actually possible to sell the claim to the remaining portion for precisely PV_t. Implicitly, then, the claimant is investing a monetary amount, totaling PV_t, at this time. It is as if *monetary capital*, in the amount PV_t, is invested. The market price of a one-period use of this amount is none other than $r \times PV_t$. After all, given perfect markets, this is what could be earned by investing this amount elsewhere.

The story in Exhibit 3.5 calls for acquiring all factors up front, at a total expenditure of 50,000. Three periods hence production is completed, and receipts totaling 66,550 are then in hand. The firm has therefore used labor, physical capital, *and monetary capital* in the process. The economic cost of the monetary capital is what we earlier termed *economic income*. Viewed from the firm's perspective, economic income arises only when transactions are spread out on the time line, and it is a component of economic cost. Then the income is equal to the rate of interest multiplied by the invested capital. This is what (3.5) says!

To be sure, the story in Exhibits 3.5 and 3.6 is unusual in that expenditures and receipts are completely separate. The Exhibit 3.4 story, the cash flow sequence with which we began this exploration, mixes receipts and expenditures on the time line. This means fewer monetary resources are required, the cost of monetary resources is therefore less, and overall economic income is less. Pure and simple, economic income is the period's cost of monetary resources. It is a component of economic cost. This is most vivid in the calculations of economic income in Exhibit 3.6.

EXHIBIT 3.6
Income Statement Format for Economic Income Calculations for Exhibit 3.5 Story

	$t = 1$	$t = 2$	$t = 3$	Total
"Net receipts" = "Revenue"(CF_t)	0	0	66,550	66,550
"Depreciation" = "Economic depreciation" $(PV_{t-1} - PV_t)$	−5,000	−5,500	60,500	50,000
"Income" (I_t)	5,000	5,500	6,050	16,550

EXHIBIT 3.7
Revised Income
Calculation
Including Monetary
Capital Charge

	$t = 1$	$t = 2$	$t = 3$
"Net receipts" = "Revenue" (CF_t)	4,950	9,680	16,637.50
"Depreciation" = "Economic depreciation" ($PV_{t-1} - PV_t$)	2,450	7,425	15,125
"Income" (I_t)	2,500	2,255	1,512.50
"Monetary capital charge" ($r \times PV_{t-1}$)	2,500	2,255	1,512.50
"Residual income" ($I_t - r \times PV_{t-1}$)	0	0	0

At this risk of beating a dead horse, this fact can be readily visualized by explicitly including the cost of the monetary factors in the periodic economic flow calculations. Using the original (Exhibit 3.4) cash flow series, we modify the original income calculation (in Exhibit 3.2) to include an explicit "charge" for the cost of the monetary factor employed. See Exhibit 3.7.

You should recognize the bottom line here, $I_t - r \times PV_{t-1}$, as residual income: income less a monetary capital charge. Others call it *abnormal earnings* or *economic value added*. It is precisely zero in each and every period here because the firm is facing zero economic profit. What would residual income look like for the story in Exhibit 3.6?

Economic profit in our world of certainty and perfect markets is the present value of receipts less the present value of expenditures. Economic income is the cost of monetary resources committed to the organization during the period in question. It is a component of economic cost that shows up when we reckon economic cost at a time other than $t = 0$.[14]

Does this reflect the familiar notion of how much can be consumed during the period while maintaining one's position? Yes is the short answer. The economic income in a period is the cost of monetary resources used during the period. It is akin to a rental charge. Consuming no more than the rental charge leaves the underlying asset undiminished.[15] It reflects the market rate for use of monetary assets, just as the labor wage rate reflects the market rate for use of labor services. The market price of labor used is a component of economic cost just as is the market price of monetary resources used.[16]

---

[14] The economic equivalence of the stories in Exhibits 3.6 and 3.7 is an illustration of the celebrated Modigliani–Miller theorem: Financial structure does not matter in a world of perfect markets.

[15] This, in turn, leads us to the notion of capital maintenance.

[16] Again reflecting on the fact financing does not matter in this world, notice that our organization could make its economic income arbitrarily large by issuing debt early on, investing the proceeds, and not making interest or principal payments until late in the time line. This would not affect its economic profit but would surely increase its reliance on monetary factors.

PRODUCT "PROFITABILITY" AND RENTS

We conclude this visit to the world of certainty and perfect markets with a brief look at two remaining issues, so-called product profitability and the distinction among *economic profit, economic income,* and *economic rent.*

Product "Profitability"

Return to our original cash flow sequence (Exhibit 3.4) and associated economic income calculations (Exhibit 3.2). Also recall the underlying story here is that a specific product is produced and sold during a specific period and that the labor uniquely associated with each product is acquired at the start of the respective period. So, we have product revenues separated by period, and we also have labor directly identified with each product. Moreover, economic depreciation appears to be identified by product as well. So, in this admittedly unusual circumstance, is economic income in period *t* attributable to the product produced and sold that period? Certainly, any reasonable accounting procedure would identify revenue, labor cost, and depreciation for each period and invite an interpretation that the income calculated that period was the income earned on that particular product line.

This movement from an income calculation to an assessment of product "profitability" is, in a word, fallacious. The economic cost curve is not separable here. The economic income we found is a charge for monetary resources that are not dedicated to a single product. Therefore, we cannot unambiguously speak of how much of the organization's total income is due to any one product. We can, of course, ask about *marginal* revenue and *marginal* cost of any product, given some output schedule (and product and factor price specification). Ascribing a portion of total (economic) income to any particular product, however, presumes separability in the sense that we can unambiguously treat each product as though it had no connection to other products. In short, we would have to assume that there was no reason in the first place for the firm to produce a variety of products. There is simply no connection between economic income and the product "profitability" assessments often associated with accounting-based calculations.[17] Indeed, economic income measures the cost of monetary factors employed during the period, and there is no reason to presume that those factors were

---

[17] Assigning total income in a period to the various products, then, is a troubling perspective. The same comment applies to assigning economic profit to the various products. On the other hand, it makes perfect sense to compare, say, economic profit with a product in place with economic profit when that product is not in the firm's portfolio.

employed exclusively for the product actually sold during the period in question.

Economic Rent

This interpretation of *economic income* should be carefully distinguished from the notion of *economic rent*. We have judiciously confined our stories to ones in which the firm's economic profit (the present value of its cash flows at inception, recall) was precisely zero. Suppose we now give in to temptation ever so slightly and admit that our firm has strictly positive economic profit (or a strictly positive NPV project). Without belaboring the details, suppose that we slightly lower the initial investment in the Exhibit 3.1 story from 25,000 to 24,000.

With this single change, the continuation present values remain exactly as before, $PV_0 = 25,000$, $PV_1 = 22,550$, and so on. The firm also has an economic profit of 1,000 since it just paid 24,000 for something worth 25,000.[18] Applying the economic income definition in (3.3), we have the same income numbers as before. Moreover, the three incomes sum to 6,267.50 (as before), but the cash flows sum to 7,267.50 (versus 6,267.50 in the original story).

The troublesome economic profit of 1,000 must be forced into the rendering. Under certainty, this is straightforward. We know at time $t = 0$ what the remaining cash flows will be. We know at that point we have exchanged 24,000 for something with a continuation present value of 25,000. The difference, the gain, is called an *economic rent*. It would be recorded at time $t = 0$ here, so to speak. The firm's asset, that is, would be immediately written up to 25,000. So, in this case, the firm has economic income totaling 6,267.50 over its lifetime, coupled with economic rent of 1,000 at its inception.

Economic rent, then, arises when the firm devises a production plan whose economic value is strictly positive, whose continuation present value at inception exceeds the associated investment (i.e., $PV_0 + CF_0 > 0$). Economic rent is synonymous with strictly positive economic profit. This notion is, of course, awfully important, but introducing it in a world of perfect markets is a little tongue in cheek. Competition would simply not allow for economic rent in such a setting.[19]

By analogy, though, and looking ahead, the accounting report reflects accounting revenues less accounting expenses. It is a residual amount reflecting, to a degree, a combination of economic income and economic rent.

---

[18] Recall (3.10); economic profit is the present value of customer payments less the present value of factor expenditures.

[19] Equally clear, relying on something less than perfect (and complete) markets would allow for rent but render the very meaning of value ambiguous. Market guides in such a setting, in the form of prices in well-functioning markets, would be absent. This is the reason we stress the importance of market structure in developing the notions of economic value and economic income. Be patient; our study is in the early stages.

Summary Accounting, as we shall emphasize, uses the language and algebra of valuation. Here, in a setting of certainty coupled with well-functioning markets, valuation is a present value exercise. For any conceivable project or firm, *certainty* means that its life can be described in terms of a sequence of cash flows, cash that flows between the firm and its owners. Valuation then enters via the continuation present value of the remaining cash flows as of each and every point in time. More broadly, valuation is simply a mapping from cash flow possibilities and interest rates into an implied sequence of temporal valuations.

From here we readily identify the associated notion of economic income, the change in value plus the cash flow delivered to the owners at that time. Indeed, economic income is simply the noted interest rate multiplied by the beginning-of-period value. We thus wind up with a pair of measures, the economic stock and the economic flow, so to speak. The stock measure is, of course, the value measure. It is the then economic equivalent of the remaining cash flow series. The flow measure, the economic income, is the implicit cost of resources tied up during the period. We stress its interpretation as a component of the firm's cost, an interpretation that becomes most vivid when we concentrate on the firm's *residual income,* which is its income adjusted for this capital charge.

Finally, while it makes perfect sense to identify, measure, and discuss the firm's economic income in this setting, asking the seemingly related question of the "profitability" of each of the firm's products is a different matter. The difficulty is that economic forces compel the firm to jointly produce a variety of products, so the firm's cost is not separable. We cannot divide or apportion its cost among the various products. We thus cannot well identify the profit associated with each of its products. Economic income, the cost of the monetary factor in the period in question, applies to the totality of the firm's products.

Appendix

Inventory "Valuation" and Nonseparability

The nonseparability theme is further illustrated by extending the setting to one in which the firm holds inventory as well as the capital asset. Traditionally, of course, we think of the firm's assets as individually valued and of the total of those individual values as reflecting the total value of the assets, yet nonseparability surfaces here as well.

To see this, stay with the setup in the (recycled) illustration in Exhibit 3.4, but change the story in one respect: The three products are identical, except for time, and the firm must supply 75 units in the first period, 100 in the second, and 125 in the third. So, if the firm produces according to this delivery schedule, it will behave precisely as portrayed in Exhibit 3.4.

Now for some fun. Might the firm smooth its production? If so, it would build inventory in the short run. The cost of producing (q_1, q_2, q_3) in the three periods is simply our friend, $C(q_1, q_2, q_3)$. This much is clear, but what quantities should be produced? The least costly way to meet these requirements is given by the following, where $\underline{C}(Q_1, Q_2, Q_3)$ is the cost, in present value terms, of supplying Q_1 units in the first period, Q_2 units in the second period, and Q_3 in the third.

$$\underline{C}(Q_1, Q_2, Q_3) \equiv \underset{q_1, q_2, q_3 \geq 0}{\text{Minimum}}\ C(q_1, q_2, q_3) \qquad \textbf{(3.11)}$$

subject to

$$q_1 \geq Q_1 \qquad \textbf{(3.12a)}$$

$$q_2 + q_1 - Q_1 \geq Q_2 \qquad \textbf{(3.12b)}$$

$$q_3 + q_2 + q_1 - Q_1 - Q_2 \geq Q_3 \qquad \textbf{(3.12c)}$$

The first constraint, (3.12a), requires that whatever is produced in the first period, q_1, be at least as large as the quantity required to be available in the first period, Q_1. Any amount above current requirements, any positive $q_1 - Q_1$, will be held as inventory and be available for meeting second-period requirements. Thus, the balance requirement in the second period, constraint (3.12b), requires that second-period production, q_2, plus any inventory accumulated in the first period, $q_1 - Q_1$, be at least as large as the quantity required to be available in the second period, Q_2; (3.12c) follows equivalently.[20]

The key here is to understand the economic forces that invite the accumulation of inventory. The technology allows physical capital to be shared across time periods. It also invites "well-balanced" production because this allows the most efficient combination of labor and capital in each period. *Well balanced*, in turn, means that we have exhausted any economic possibility of shifting production across the periods. Implicitly, then, if the balance constraints, (3.12a), (3.12b), and (3.12c), do not get in our way, we will arrange production across periods so that the marginal cost of production is equalized across the periods. Otherwise, intertemporal shifting is possible by moving some production from the high to the low marginal cost period.[21]

---

[20] Now glance back at the last exercise in Chapter 2.

[21] A more complicated story would also acknowledge explicit costs associated with inventory per se, as illustrated by obsolescence, taxes, and shrinkage. In our streamlined story, the only cost associated with inventory is the cost of the associated monetary capital, and this is properly treated in the underlying present value calculations.

EXHIBIT 3.8
Cash Flows, Given
$q_1 = q_2 = q_3 = 100$

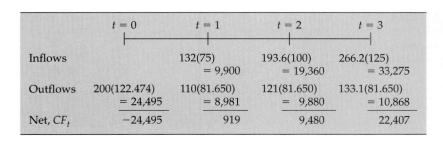

	$t = 0$	$t = 1$	$t = 2$	$t = 3$
Inflows		132(75) = 9,900	193.6(100) = 19,360	266.2(125) = 33,275
Outflows	200(122.474) = 24,495	110(81.650) = 8,981	121(81.650) = 9,880	133.1(81.650) = 10,868
Net, CF_t	−24,495	919	9,480	22,407

EXHIBIT 3.9
Cash Flows, Given
No Inventory at
$t = 1$ ($q_1 = 75$,
$q_2 = q_3 = 112.5$), and
$K = 122.474$

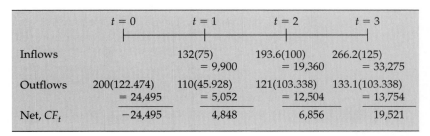

	$t = 0$	$t = 1$	$t = 2$	$t = 3$
Inflows		132(75) = 9,900	193.6(100) = 19,360	266.2(125) = 33,275
Outflows	200(122.474) = 24,495	110(45.928) = 5,052	121(103.338) = 12,504	133.1(103.338) = 13,754
Net, CF_t	−24,495	4,848	6,856	19,521

In our particular story, it turns out that the optimal production schedule is $(q_1, q_2, q_3) = (100, 100, 100)$. This relies on an initial capital choice of $K = 122.474$ and leaves us with an inventory of 25 at the end of period 1. The capital choice is less than in the original story in Exhibit 3.4 and reflects the fact that inventory is now being used to substitute for capital. This, in turn, leads to a nonseparability between capital and inventory.

Remaining details are summarized in Exhibit 3.8. At time $t = 1$, the continuation present value is $PV_1 = 9,480(1.1)^{-1} + 22,407(1.1)^{-2} = 27,136$. Moreover, the firm's assets consist of its capital stock and the inventory. The question is how to divide the total among the two assets.

One way to proceed is to compare this continuation present value with what it would be were the firm unable to hold inventory at time 1.[22] If, then, the firm could not hold inventory at time 1, it would find it optimal to produce 75 units in the first period followed by 112.5 in each of the remaining periods. Details are summarized in Exhibit 3.9, in which we retain the same capital choice as in Exhibit 3.8.

Here the $t = 1$ continuation present value is

$$PV_1 = 6,856(1.1)^{-1} + 19,521(1.1)^{-2} = 22,366 \text{[23]}$$

[22] Notice that we are treading on the *perfect and complete market assumption* here. There is no market for the inventory, and for that matter, the firm's customer has agreed to a specific delivery schedule that guarantees the firm strictly positive rent. Moreover, alternative approaches to valuing the inventory, such as net realizable value, will lead to the same conundrum.

[23] Capital is set at $K = 122.474$, so our comparison rests on the same physical capital. The efficient choice, however, is $K = 124.373$.

EXHIBIT 3.10
Cash Flows, Given
No Capital at $t = 1$
$(q_1 = q_2 = q_3 = 100)$

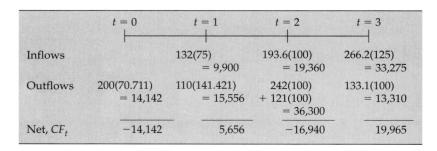

	$t = 0$	$t = 1$	$t = 2$	$t = 3$
Inflows		132(75) $= 9,900$	193.6(100) $= 19,360$	266.2(125) $= 33,275$
Outflows	200(70.711) $= 14,142$	110(141.421) $= 15,556$	242(100) $+ 121(100)$ $= 36,300$	133.1(100) $= 13,310$
Net, CF_t	$-14,142$	$5,656$	$-16,940$	$19,965$

So, with no inventory, capital is the only asset, and capital by itself has a value of 22,366 at $t = 1$. Similarly, the remaining cash flow series is worth an additional $27,136 - 22,366 = 4,770$ as a result of being able to carry inventory.[24] In other words, if the firm retained the same capital stock but could hold no inventory at $t = 1$, its value at that point would decrease by 4,770. It sounds like the inventory is worth 4,770.

With this success in hand, let's reverse the experiment and ask what the continuation present value would be were inventory the only asset on hand at $t = 1$. This requires some additional assumptions because production requires strictly positive amounts of capital and labor. Suppose, then, that the firm must abandon its capital at the end of the first period and, at the start of the second period, will acquire new capital, which will last for two periods. Furthermore, suppose this new capital is paid for at time $t = 2$, at a price of $200(1.1)^2 = 242$ per unit. Holding the production plan constant so that only the capital is varied leads to the details summarized in Exhibit 3.10.

Here the continuation present value at time 1 is $PV_1 = -16,940(1.1)^{-1} + 19,965(1.1)^{-2} = 1,103$. That is, if the firm is unable to carry capital between the first two periods, its time 1 value will be 1,103. So, its time 1 value declines from 27,136 to 1,103 if inventory is kept constant at 25 units, but its capital drops to zero. This suggests that the time 1 capital's value is $27,136 - 1,103 = 26,033$.

If, now, these calculations made sense, the time 1 value of 27,136 (via Exhibit 3.8) would be the amount contributed by the inventory (implied via Exhibit 3.9), or 4,770, plus the amount contributed by the capital (implied via Exhibit 3.10), or 26,033, but $4,770 + 26,033 > 27,136$. We simply cannot isolate the component of total time 1 value due to each of the assets.

This reflects the nonseparability of the firm's technology. It does not allow us to unambiguously identify how much of total value is attributable to its capital and how much to its inventory. The two assets interact. Thus, we cannot, even in this simple, deterministic setting, talk unambiguously about the value of a specific asset.

---

[24] This comparison presumes that the firm behaves optimally, which implies, for example, it adjusts its capital choice.

Selected References

The importance of perfect markets in classical valuation is well articulated by Beaver (1998), as well as by the typical microeconomics or finance textbook. Hirshlefier (1970) provides a deeper treatment, including the separation between production and consumption choices and the irrelevance of financial structure. In turn, the use of this setting to develop the notion of income and the pitfalls that ensue when we move beyond this setting leads to the works of Fisher, Lindahl, Hicks, Kaldor, and so on. An excellent primer is provided by Parker, Harcourt, and Whittington (1986).

Key Terms

Certainty is foreknowledge, a lack of ambiguity as to what will transpire. In our stylized setting, the firm's activities lead to a cash flow series, or vector, and this cash flow series is regarded as fact, as guaranteed to transpire. We then imagine the claim to this cash flow series as being traded in a perfectly competitive market, at each and every point in time. **Perfectly competitive market** means that there are no transactions costs of any sort; everyone knows the equilibrium price (the price at which supply equals demand), and everyone acts as a price taker. In turn, markets are **complete** if each and every conceivable trade is, indeed, available in a market. We then stylize the market price of the claim to the firm's remaining cash flow series, as of time t, as the **continuation present value** at time t, equation (3.1), where we assume a constant interest rate. **Economic value** is market value in a setting of perfect and complete markets. Economic value is the price at which supply equals demand in the presumed market setting. Given our stylization, it is given by the continuation present value. **Economic income** is change in economic value, adjusted for cash flow, equation (3.3). Given complete and perfect markets, economic income is the cost of monetary factors employed, the interest rate multiplied by the beginning-of-period continuation present value. The change in economic value is called **economic depreciation. Economic profit,** in this setting, is the present value of the firm's cash flow, the present value of the customers' payments less the present value of the payments to those who provide the factors of production. **Residual income** is economic income less the cost of the monetary capital employed. **Economic rent** is present when the firm's profit is strictly positive.

Exercises

3.1. What role is played by perfect markets in this chapter? What role is played by certainty?

3.2. Define *economic income, economic profit,* and *economic rent.* In what sense do your definitions rely on perfect markets?

3.3. Given the perfect markets assumption, is it correct to write the firm's cash flow vector as $CF = [-PV_0, CF_1, CF_2, \ldots, CF_T]$? Explain.

3.4. Examine expressions (3.3) and (3.5) more closely. Does it make sense to think of economic income as "all you can consume this period without affecting your ability to consume in the future" or as a "flow of wealth"?

3.5. Consider a two-period setting in which the cash flows are given by $CF = [-1,000, x, 1,210 - 1.1x]$, and the interest rate is $r = 10$ percent. Notice that for any value of x we have $PV_0 = 1,000 = x(1.1)^{-1} + (1,210 - 1.1x)(1.1)^{-2}$. Plot $PV_0 (= 1,000)$, $PV_2 (= 0)$, and PV_1 for $0 \leq x \leq 500$. Does your plot identify a valuation function V, as in expression (3.2), that maps cash flow vectors into sequences of value for the given interest rate? Explain.

3.6. Return to the setting in Exhibit 3.1, but now suppose that the firm retains all cash and distributes the total in a single liquidating dividend at time $t = 3$. Cash on hand is invested and earns at the rate $r = 10$ percent. (After all, markets are perfect.) Determine the firm's economic value and economic income sequences. Comment on the pattern that emerges. (*Hint:* The cash balance at $t = 2$ will be $9,680 + 4,950[1.1]$.)

3.7. Ralph's Enterprise displays the following annual cash flow series: $CF = [-2,000, 700, 600, 1,155]$ over its life of $T = 3$ periods. The cash flow at times $t = 1, 2,$ and 3 are paid out in a dividend just as the books are closed, so the end-of-period cash balance is always zero. Determine the value of Ralph's Enterprise at each and every period, as well as the economic income each period. Finally, how would these calculations differ if the dividend were declared and paid one instant after the books are closed?

3.8. Return to the setting in Exhibit 3.4, but now assume that labor is paid at the beginning of the respective periods. First determine the three wage rates so that we have the economically equivalent story. Then determine the economic income for each of the periods. Comment on your results.

3.9. This is a continuation of Exercise 2.14. Now assume the timing details in Exhibit 3.4 in which capital is acquired immediately, product i is delivered and paid for at the end of the ith period, and labor for product i is also paid at the end of the ith period. The interest rate is $r = 10$ percent. Product i customers therefore pay $200(1.1)^i$ per unit, at time i, and labor source i is paid $100(1.1)^i$ per unit, again at time i. Determine the firm's cash flow vector, sequence of economic valuations, and economic income for each period.

Chapter 4

Accounting Foundations

Accounting, as we have said, uses the language and algebra of valuation to convey information. In Chapter 3, we laid out the meaning of economic value and economic income and the algebra that connects them. We now highlight the same terminology and algebra in the world of accounting. In doing so, it is important to keep in mind that economic and accounting value are not coextensive, and there are strong, compelling reasons for which they should not be. For now, however, the important task is to become comfortable with this particular rendering of accounting.

Chapter 3 dealt with the notions of economic value and economic income. *Value* evokes the idea of some quantity of resources on hand, a stock concept. *Income* evokes the idea of some change in that stock, a flow concept. So, under appropriate market conditions, we speak of economic stock and flow measures. We now turn to a characterization of accounting as opposed to economic measures. Accounting, as we know, provides a listing of resources and obligations—the balance sheet—and a measure of accomplishment—the income statement. It is natural to think of these as accounting-based measures of stocks and flows.

A cautionary note must be given, however: It is natural, indeed tempting, to treat the accounting measures as pragmatic versions of their economic counterparts, and this is how we initially develop our abstract model of accounting measurement. In so doing, though, we stress the structure of accounting measurement. This is the structure that will eventually turn out to be the key to understanding what it means for accounting to be a source of information. Keep in mind that identifying and becoming comfortable with this structure is but a stepping stone on our path to modeling and understanding accounting as a source of information.

We continue the assumption of perfect (and complete) markets in a world of certainty, as in Chapter 3. This allows us to juxtapose accounting and economic measures in the most uncluttered of settings. As we shall remind ourselves, accounting uses structure and language that parallels that of the economist—but the reality is rather different.

Initially, we revisit the three-product, four-factor firm and retell its history with accounting values, or stocks, and accounting income, or flows. Then we turn to the issue of articulation along with dependent linkages between the accounting stocks and flows and the nature of accruals. Finally, we establish an important connection between "errors" in the stock measure being precisely balanced by "errors" in the flow measures. Throughout, the emphasis is on the parallel between economic and accounting measurement in this world of certainty and well-behaved markets.

ACCOUNTANT'S RENDERING

To begin, recall the cash flow series used in Chapter 3, $CF_0 = -25,000$, $CF_1 = 4,950$, and so on. The underlying story is based on a firm that acquires four factors and produces three products. An aggregate description of the important details is presented in Exhibit 4.1.[1] (We hope that Exhibit 4.1 is reminiscent of your study of accounting at the introductory level.)

We now apply the accountant's art to tell this story with a sequence of income statements and balance sheets. Revenue will be recognized when the respective products are sold (which is also the time the customers pay for the products). The labor cost, reflecting the fact that labor is readily identifiable with each product, will be traced and assigned to the respective products. Thus, in our particular rendering, labor cost will show up on the income statement when the associated product's revenue is recognized, which, conveniently, is the time the labor is paid. The substantive issue is how to assign the physical capital cost to the three periods, or products.

For now, we adopt a generic approach and let the depreciation in the first period be some unspecified amount, d_1. Likewise, let d_2 denote depreciation in the second period. Naturally, the remainder, $25,000 - d_1 - d_2$, is depreciated in the third period. Income statements now readily follow. See Exhibit 4.2. Notice that total income is $4,950 - d_1 + 9,680 - d_2 + d_1 + d_2 - 8,362.50 = 6,267.50$, regardless of the depreciation schedule.

In parallel fashion, any depreciation schedule implies a sequence of net book values for the capital asset. Since our firm has no work in process

---

[1] Notice that the labor payment is always half of the sales revenue. Our story rests on perfect competition in a setting in which factor prices and technology imply, at the margin, that half of the factor cost is labor cost.

EXHIBIT 4.1
Aggregate Transactions Supporting Cash Flow Series

$t = 0$	Owners invest, $CF_0 = -25,000$
	Purchase physical capital to be used by all three products, at cost 25,000
$t = 1$	Pay labor used for first set of products, at cost 4,950
	Sell first set of products, receiving 9,900
	Remit $CF_1 = 4,950 = 9,900 - 4,950$ to owners
$t = 2$	Pay labor used for second set of products, at cost 9,680
	Sell second set of products, receiving 19,360
	Remit $CF_2 = 9,680 = 19,360 - 9,680$ to owners
$t = 3$	Pay labor used for third set of products, at cost 16,637.50
	Sell third set of products, receiving 33,275
	Remit $CF_3 = 16,637.50 = 33,275 - 16,637.50$ to owners

EXHIBIT 4.2
Accounting Income Calculations for Transactions in Exhibit 4.1

	$t = 1$	$t = 2$	$t = 3$	Total
Revenue	9,900	19,360	33,275	62,535
Labor expense	4,950	9,680	16,637.50	31,267.50
Depreciation	d_1	d_2	$25,000 - d_1 - d_2$	25,000
Accounting income	$4,950 - d_1$	$9,680 - d_2$	$d_1 + d_2 - 8,362.50$	6,267.50

EXHIBIT 4.3
Balance Sheet Calculations for Transactions in Exhibit 4.1

	$t = 1$	$t = 2$	$t = 3$
Capital asset (net)	$25,000 - d_1$	$25,000 - d_1 - d_2$	0
Total assets (and equity)	$25,000 - d_1$	$25,000 - d_1 - d_2$	0

(conveniently) and always pays its cash balance out in a dividend at the end of the respective period (conveniently), its associated balance sheet is particularly simple: The only asset is the physical capital. Initially, at time $t = 0$, the acquired capital asset has an accounting value of 25,000. One period later, with the noted depreciation schedule, the net book value has declined to $25,000 - d_1$. It further declines to $25,000 - d_1 - d_2$ at the end of the second period and to zero at the end of the third. Exhibit 4.3 provides the (obvious) details.[2]

Think about this: Having specified the time of revenue recognition and the recording of the associated labor expense, the only free variable is the depreciation pattern, defined by d_1 and d_2. For reasons that will become clear, we prefer to leave the rendering with d_1 and d_2 as free variables at this point. After all, we are characterizing accounting in somewhat general

---

[2] Conversely, suppose that we tallied the assets just before the dividend was remitted to the investors. We would then have respective asset totals of $4,950 + 25,000 - d_1$, $9,680 + 25,000 - d_1 - d_2$, and 16,637.50.

fashion as opposed to offering a specific answer to how the accounting for the story in Exhibit 4.1 should be done.

You should apply your skill, nevertheless. If straight-line depreciation is used, $d_1 = 25,000/3 = 8,333.33$. So, first period book value would be $25,000 - 8,333.33 = 16,666.67$; likewise, first period income would be $4,950 - 8,333.33 = -3,383.33$. If economic depreciation is to be used, $d_1 = 2,450$ and $d_2 = 7,425$.[3]

Cash basis accounting is an extreme case. It rests on $d_1 = 25,000$ and $d_2 = 0$. In addition, the accompanying balance sheet would always show an asset value of zero because cash is the only recognized asset, and the firm always pays its cash balance out to the owners at the end of the period. Try it!

STOCK AND FLOW FUNCTIONS

We now step back slightly and place these characterizations into a more abstract context. The firm is described by the sequence of cash that flows from it to the owners, the series $CF = [CF_0, CF_1, CF_2, \ldots, CF_T]$. Underlying details will, of course, be used to implement any particular accounting treatment, but the economic fundamentals are CF and the interest rate r. To simplify our task ahead, we assume that this is an all-equity firm. It has a single class of shareholders and zero debt.

Accounting Valuation

Exhibit 4.3 provides a sequence of asset valuations for our illustrative cash flow series. At the risk of appearing cynical, the $t = 1$ and $t = 2$ valuations are whatever we might want them to be. Merely specify the d_1 and d_2 that will lead to the interim accounting values you desire. Though overly dramatic, this suggests that we think of accounting valuation as some procedure that leads to a sequence of asset values (or asset and equity values if we have a more complicated story).

Indeed, this is how you initially learned accounting. You were given a particular story and instructed to apply a particular accounting procedure to that story. In Exhibit 4.1, for example, the firm pays 25,000 for some asset with a useful life of three years. Now determine the periodic depreciation expense and track the asset's (accounting) value using, say, straight-line depreciation.

The idea, then, is that the firm's activities produce a cash flow series, and we apply accounting procedures to provide an accounting description

---

[3] See Exhibit 3.2. The continuation present value at time $t = 0$ is 25,000. So, economic income in the first period is 2,500, and this implies $d_1 = 2,450$. Also notice in Chapter 3, we termed the period's cash flow *revenue*, though here, with the benefit of added details, we term the customer payments *revenue* and the labor payments as *expense*. The net of these two cash flows is, of course, what we termed *revenue* in the earlier setting.

of these activities. Naturally, different procedures produce different accounting renderings.

To formalize this, to identify the essential features, think of the firm's activities as being well described by the cash flow series *CF* and interest rate *r*. Now let *A* be a function, for us a set of accounting procedures, that recharacterize the cash flow sequence as a sequence of accounting book values. If we are given a cash flow series, *CF*, and interest rate, *r*, and if we are given a well-defined set of accounting procedures to apply, the function *A*, the application of those procedures will give us an accounting book value at each point $t = 0, 1, \ldots, T$. We describe this formally as follows:

$$A(\mathbf{CF}, r) = [A_0, A_1, \ldots, A_T] \qquad \textbf{(4.1)}$$

A_t is the time t book value of the assets associated with the cash flow series. (We should write it as depending on *CF* and *r*, or $A_t[\mathbf{CF}, r]$.) Returning to our example, if straight-line depreciation is to be used, we have $A_0 = 25{,}000$, $A_1 = 16{,}666.67$, $A_2 = 8{,}333.33$, and $A_3 = 0$. Alternatively, we might set A_t equal to the continuation present value; we might use cash basis accounting; we might use some other depreciation policy. In each case, however, we apply a particular set of procedures, a particular *A* function, to the activities at hand.

In this fashion we conceptualize a set of accounting procedures, $A(\mathbf{CF}, r)$, as mapping the firm's economic history into an accounting history. That is the essence of (4.1). We must, however, specify the end points for this to be interesting, so we will regard the function $A(\mathbf{CF}, r)$ as essentially arbitrary except that it is required to start and stop at the obvious positions:

$$A_0(\mathbf{CF}, r) = -CF_0 \qquad \textbf{(4.1a)}$$

and

$$A_T(\mathbf{CF}, r) = 0 \qquad \textbf{(4.1b)}$$

Expression (4.1a) simply requires us to begin by recording the initial cash flow from the owners, and (4.1b) requires a liquidated organization to have zero *accounting value*. Expression (4.1), then, including (4.1a) and (4.1b), is what we mean by *accounting valuation,* a set of procedures that, when given *CF* and *r*, will give us back a sequence of book values.[4] Naturally, the accounting valuation apparatus, $A(\mathbf{CF}, r)$ in expression (4.1), is the accounting counterpart to our earlier characterization of economic valuation, expression (3.2) in Chapter 3.

To reinforce this theme, (and paralleling Exercise 3.5) consider a two-period setting in which 100 is invested at $t = 0$, $CF_1 = x$, so amount x is

---

[4] At this point, various approaches to accounting valuation should come to mind: replacement cost, service potentials, fair value. We are purposely abstract.

received at $t = 1$, and, finally, at $t = 2$, $CF_2 = 121 - 1.1x$ is received. The interest rate is $r = 10$ percent, and CF_2 is pegged so that the initial present value is a constant:

$$PV_0 = CF_1(1.1)^{-1} + CF_2(1.1)^{-2} = x(1.1)^{-1} + (121 - 1.1x)(1.1)^{-2} = 100$$

regardless of x. So we have a family of **CF** vectors, all with no rent (i.e., $PV_0 + CF_0 = 0$) and an initial value of 100.

With just two periods and all of this rigging, we have an initial economic value of $PV_0 = 100$ and an initial accounting value of $A_0 = 100$. At the end of the second period, when the economic life of the project is complete, we have corresponding values of $PV_2 = A_2 = 0$.

Time $t = 1$, of course, is the interesting case. With $CF_2 = 121 - 1.1x$, we have a $t = 1$ economic value of

$$PV_1 = CF_2(1.1)^{-1} = (121 - 1.1x)(1.1)^{-1} = 110 - x$$

We plot PV_1 in Exhibit 4.4 for $0 \leq x \leq 75$. Notice that PV_1 declines with x, simply because the remaining cash flow declines with x, and PV_0 is a constant 100 by construction. More broadly, this illustrates the idea of a mapping from cash flows and interest rates to a sequence of temporal values [Expression (3.2)]. That is, $PV_0 = 100$, $PV_1 = 110 - x$, and $PV_2 = 0$, as x ranges between 0 and 75.

In turn, the accounting value at time $t = 1$ depends on how we allocate the original cost ($A_0 = 100$) between the two periods. Straight-line amortization gives us $A_1 = 50$, regardless of x and therefore regardless of PV_1. Alternatively, we might use, say, a variation on physical units and set $A_1 = 100CF_2/(CF_1 + CF_2) = 100(121 - 1.1x)/(121 - 0.1x)$. This latter case is also plotted in Exhibit 4.4, again for $0 \leq x \leq 75$. In this scheme, the accounting value at $t = 1$ depends on x—indeed declines with x—but also strictly understates economic value.

EXHIBIT 4.4
Economic and Accounting Valuation Functions for $T = 2$ Illustration

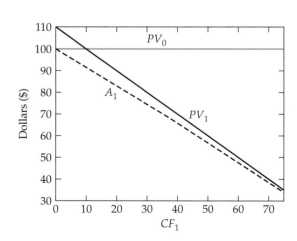

So, think of this firm's fundamentals as given by x. In accounting terms, straight-line amortization reports $A_1 = 50$ regardless of the fundamentals. In contrast, our equally ad hoc "units of production" scheme reports an A_1 that strictly declines with x. Depending on the choice of accounting method, we see different mappings from fundamentals to accounting numbers. In particular, straight line reports $A_0 = 100$, $A_1 = 50$ and $A_2 = 0$, while the units of production type scheme reports $A_0 = 100$, $A_1 = 100(121 - 1.1x)/(121 - 0.1x)$ and $A_2 = 0$, as x ranges between 0 and 75.

This notion or model of accounting valuation as a mapping from the fundamentals to the accounting stocks is central to the work before us. At this level of abstraction, our mapping is also highly simplified. For example, in our work in Exhibits 4.2 and 4.3, we grouped the transactions into revenue, labor, and physical capital components. We had only a single asset category. Suppose, however, that the labor was paid in advance. We would then record two assets, prepaid labor and the physical capital. Our stylization in (4.1) reflects only the total asset valuation. So, to be fair to the use of such grouping, we should specify our model in (4.1) as beginning with transactions aggregated into appropriate groupings rather than focusing on the net cash flow to or from the owners each period; we should also treat each A_t as depicting a list of asset values. This refinement adds more notation than insight, however, so we forge ahead with the simplified specification.

A more subtle timing issue should also be noted. Our model of accounting valuation envisions some particular set of procedures, some particular set of recognition and matching rules, as giving us a mapping from a given **CF** vector and interest rate r into a sequence of accounting values. As such, the accounting method, the $A(\textbf{CF}, r)$ function, is specified at the firm's inception. It is, so to speak, decided upon up front when the firm's fundamentals are identified.[5]

Accounting Income

Now consider a parallel sequence of accounting flow measures. That is, imagine an *accounting income measurement* procedure that will take cash flow series **CF** and interest rate r and tell this story with a sequence of accounting incomes:

$$\hat{I}(\textbf{CF}, r) = [\hat{I}_1, \hat{I}_2, \ldots, \hat{I}_T] \qquad \textbf{(4.2)}$$

[5] To reiterate, all of the accounting details are subsumed by this $A(\textbf{CF}, r)$ specification, presuming we do not use different rules for the balance sheet and for the income statement. (This caveat will be dealt with momentarily.) So, how the firm handles inventory valuation, what price index it uses to implement a lower-of-cost-or-market screen, how it estimates pension liability, and so on are all part of the $A(\textbf{CF}, r)$ specification, in principle. Likewise, if under particular circumstances the firm would change its accounting method, this too is built into the $A(\textbf{CF}, r)$ specification. It is simply the totality of accounting procedures, including the full double entry structure, that will be applied in the circumstance at hand.

Here $\hat{I}(CF, r)$ is the procedure, and $\hat{I}_t$ is the *accounting income* in period t.[6] Now the requirement we will place on any such rendering is that it get the total correct; otherwise, it is essentially arbitrary at this point:

$$\sum_{t=1}^{T} \hat{I}_t = \sum_{t=0}^{T} CF_t \qquad \textbf{(4.2a)}$$

That is, we require the accounting procedure to render a sequence of accounting incomes that recharacterizes the total cash flow as a sequence of accounting incomes. The total cash flow must equal the total accounting income over the firm's life.

This mapping is evident in Exhibit 4.2 in which the reported income series depends on the depreciation method chosen (d_1 and d_2) but reports the same lifetime income regardless of the depreciation method. It is also evident in the earlier $T = 2$ illustration (in Exhibit 4.4). There, with $CF = [-100, x, 121 - 1.1x]$, we had a lifetime income of $-100 + x + 121 - 1.1x = 21 - 0.1x$. Straight-line amortization reports $\hat{I}_1 = x - 50$ and $\hat{I}_2 = 71 - 1.1x$. This particular amortization method, then, provides a specific mapping from the firm's fundamentals into a sequence of accounting income, or flow, measures.

We also know from our study of economic income that lifetime economic income is the difference between $CF_1 + CF_2 + \cdots + CF_T$ and the $t = 0$ continuation present value, PV_0. Thus, when there is no economic rent, total accounting income and total economic income are identical over the lifetime of the firm. Conversely, if rent is present, it too will show up in the accounting income series, as implied by (4.2a).[7]

Articulation

You are probably wondering why we separately characterized accounting valuation and accounting income. Our motivation is driven by the fact that we observe somewhat different procedures affect the balance sheet and income statement. For example, the FASB advocates a foreign currency translation procedure under which translation gains bypass the usual income statement (although they are included in comprehensive income). Jumping back to Exhibits 4.2 and 4.3, then, this mixing of procedures would imply one d_1 and d_2 specification for the balance sheet series and another for the accounting income series.

---

[6] We should write the latter as $\hat{I}_t(CF, r)$ to reflect the functional relationship. To ease the notation, we just write $\hat{I}_t$ unless that would cause confusion.

[7] For example, in our $T = 2$ illustration, suppose that the initial cost was 80 instead of the originally assumed 100. This implies an economic rent of $100 - 80 = 20$. Straight-line amortization then provides incomes of $\hat{I}_1 = x - 40$ and $\hat{I}_2 = 81 - 1.1x$. In this sense, the accounting income series must also report any economic rent should it be present. Again, however, we emphasize that this is tongue in cheek because rent is inconsistent with perfect market conditions, and perfect markets are critical in understanding what we mean by *economic value* absent highly unusual conditions in the economy.

This leads to the notion of articulation. We say that valuation procedure A, the function displayed in (4.1), and income measurement procedure $\hat{I}$, the function displayed in (4.2), *articulate* if accounting income is change in accounting value plus cash flow (to or from the owners, again):[8]

$$\hat{I}_t = A_t - A_{t-1} + CF_t, \quad \text{for } t = 1, 2, \ldots, T \qquad \textbf{(4.3)}$$

The parallel to economic income as change in economic value plus cash flow should be apparent.

Expression (4.3) is often called a *clean surplus condition*. All accounting value changes flow through the income statement. The surplus section of the balance sheet does not contain any valuation adjustments that have not been passed through the income statement. With articulation, then, Exhibits 4.2 and 4.3 would use the same d_1 and d_2 numbers.[9] Indeed, our earlier definition of economic income in Chapter 3 relied on articulation!

Duality

Articulation also leads to a *duality* between accounting stocks and flows. If we specify CF_0 and the accounting income series, we have implicitly specified the book value series. Likewise, if we specify the book value series, we have implicitly specified the accounting income series. All we require for this duality is the presence of articulation. Merely apply expression (4.3).

With articulation, then, a so-called balance sheet perspective implies an accounting income series. Likewise, an income perspective implies a balance sheet perspective. As pithy as it sounds, it is important to remember that accounting valuation can be addressed directly or indirectly. For example, if we emphasize the selection of a depreciation pattern, we are emphasizing the flow of expenses or "service potentials" from the asset. We thus indirectly identify the accounting value of the asset. Conversely, when we adopt a lower-of-cost-or-market filter, we are directly identifying the asset's accounting value, and the attendant adjustment in value, if any, is an expense item.

Accruals

Articulation also gives us an unfettered entry (a good pun) to the notion of accruals. For example, in a cash flow statement, we begin with income from operations and adjust for noncash items in the income calculation, such as depreciation. We then go on from there to pick up financing and investment items. In the end, we have reconciled the change in the entity's cash balance to the entity's income, investment transactions, and financing

---

[8] More generally, think of A_t as net assets, or assets less liabilities at time t. Then, under articulation, income is change in net assets adjusted for capital transactions. Also notice that under articulation, the summation boundary condition for the income series, (4.2a), is implied by the boundary conditions for the valuation series.

[9] Notice that we have defined articulation in the presence of **CF** and r. More properly, the $A(\cdot,\cdot)$ and $\hat{I}(\cdot,\cdot)$ functions articulate if (4.3) holds for each possible **CF** and r combination over which the functions are defined or settings over which the procedures are applicable.

transactions. A major feature in this construction is the identification of the noncash components of the accounting procedures. These are the *accruals*.

Because accruals are central in what follows, it will be useful to expand our description of accounting stocks and flows to explicitly identify the accruals. On the stock, or accounting value, side, let cb_t denote the firm's cash balance as of time t. (Our example assumes that $cb_t = 0$.) Clearly, then, the firm's accounting value at time t consists of its cash balance plus all of the noncash items. Let $\hat{A}_t$ denote the total of these noncash items (receivables, capital equipment, etc.). We therefore have

$$A_t = cb_t + \hat{A}_t, \quad \text{for } t = 0, 1, \ldots, T \qquad \textbf{(4.4)}$$

Accounting valuation, defined by the function $A(\textbf{CF}, r)$, provides the total amount, and (4.4) expresses the fact that this total consists of cash and noncash items. The noncash items are, essentially, the time t stock of accounting accruals. Stated differently, at time t, the stock of accounting accruals is accounting value less the time t cash balance.

Presuming articulation between the accounting value and the income series, now rewrite the earlier expression for accounting income, (4.3), with this added detail:

$$\begin{aligned} \hat{I}_t &= A_t - A_{t-1} + CF_t \\ &= (cb_t + \hat{A}_t) - (cb_{t-1} + \hat{A}_{t-1}) + CF_t \\ &= [\hat{A}_t - \hat{A}_{t-1}] + [(cb_t - cb_{t-1}) + CF_t] \qquad \textbf{(4.3a)} \end{aligned}$$

That is, income is accruals plus cash flow *to the firm*, the latter being the net of the change in the firm's cash balance plus capital transactions (CF_t). The flow of accruals in the calculation, given articulation, is simply the change in the stock of accruals.[10] The accruals, of course, are central to accounting's reshaping of the **CF** series into a sequence of stock and flow measures. Accrual accounting, by definition, stresses such reshaping.

On the balance sheet, then, the accounting procedures display a current period stock of accruals; on the income statement, the procedures display a current period flow, or change, in that stock of accruals. Again, we could separate this into operations, investing, and financing components, but the detail is unimportant for what lies ahead.

The important point is to understand that the essence of any set of accounting procedures is to be found in the pattern of accruals. Cash basis accounting has, by definition, zero accruals. We also routinely report a cash flow statement, de facto reporting the results of cash basis accounting. All of the substantive work, then, shows up in the accrual-based rendering, which means that it shows up in the accruals themselves.[11]

---

[10] Now you should see why we claimed that exploring accruals was unfettered under articulation. Absent articulation, we would have to separately identify the accrual flows in the income calculation!

[11] To test your understanding, change the story in Exhibit 4.2 so that the firm retains all cash, investing it at $r = 10$ percent until time $t = 3$; at that point, it remits 33,275 to the owners. Can you identify asset values and income for each period? What are the accruals?

COUNTERBALANCING ERRORS

A final excursion links the accounting and economic valuations. Glance back at Exhibit 4.4 in which the particular accounting procedure resulted in $A_1 < PV_1$, a distinctly conservative treatment. Now we know that, say, recognizing as many expenses as possible at one point results in less expenses to recognize at a future point and thus increases future income (at the "expense" of today's income). Can we say anything of a general nature here? The answer is yes, given our valuation assumptions. In particular, if A_t and PV_t differ at some time t, this difference must show up, in a sense to be made precise, in the forthcoming income sequence. In this (albeit limited) sense, we say that errors in the stock measure imply offsetting errors in the future flow measures, where by *error* we mean the difference between economic and accounting measures in this setting.

To develop this, suppose that we have a **CF** series and interest rate r and are using accounting procedures A and $\hat{I}$ to give us balance sheet [via (4.1)] and accounting income renderings [via (4.2)]. Using these measures, we now mechanically calculate residual income, defined by

$$RI_t = \hat{I}_t - r \times A_{t-1} \qquad \textbf{(4.5)}$$

This calculation simply takes the accounting flow and adjusts it for an implicit monetary capital charge of r times the beginning-of-period accounting value. It goes by various names, including abnormal earnings (Feltham and Ohlson, 1995), excess realizable profit (Edwards and Bell, 1961) and, of course, residual income (Solomons, 1965). The idea is to remove the implicit capital charge from the calculated income. (And, you should recall, we calculated residual income for our economic income calculation in Chapter 3.)

Now do this for the accounting valuations and accounting income calculations developed for our running example, in Exhibits 4.2 and 4.3. We maintain the generic (i.e., d_1 and d_2) specification of the valuation procedure (or depreciation schedule), but using the same d_1 and d_2 in the stock and flow calculations also implies that our procedures articulate. Details are in Exhibit 4.5. For any d_1 and d_2, then, residual income is $2{,}450 - d_1$ in the first period, and so on.

Next calculate the present value at time t of all future residual incomes. This is a cousin to our earlier continuation present value. We term it the *continuation present value of the induced residual income series*. Formally,

EXHIBIT 4.5
Residual Income Calculations for Renderings in Exhibits 4.2 and 4.3

	$t = 1$	$t = 2$	$t = 3$
A_{t-1} (Exhibit 4.3)	25,000	$25{,}000 - d_1$	$25{,}000 - d_1 - d_2$
$\hat{I}_t$ (Exhibit 4.2)	$4{,}950 - d_1$	$9{,}680 - d_2$	$d_1 + d_2 - 8{,}362.5$
$r \times A_{t-1}$	2,500	$2{,}500 - 0.1 d_1$	$2{,}500 - 0.1 d_1 - 0.1 d_2$
$RI_t = \hat{I}_t - r \times A_{t-1}$	$2{,}450 - d_1$	$7{,}180 + 0.1 d_1 - d_2$	$-10{,}862.5 + 1.1 d_1 + 1.1 d_2$

we have:

$$PRI_t = \sum_{j=t+1}^{T} RI_j(1+r)^{t-j} \qquad \textbf{(4.6)}$$

Applying this to the calculations in Exhibit 4.5, we have the following:

$$PRI_0 = (2{,}450 - d_1)(1.1)^{-1} + (7{,}180 + 0.1d_1 - d_2)(1.1)^{-2}$$
$$+ (-10{,}862.5 + 1.1d_1 + 1.1d_2)(1.1)^{-3} = 0$$

$$PRI_1 = (7{,}180 + 0.1d_1 - d_2)(1.1)^{-1} + (-10{,}862.5 + 1.1d_1 + 1.1d_2)(1.1)^{-2}$$
$$= -2{,}450 + d_1$$

and

$$PRI_2 = (-10{,}862.5 + 1.1d_1 + 1.1d_2)(1.1)^{-1} = -9{,}875 + d_1 + d_2$$

Now examine the sum of each period's book value and continuation present value of the induced residual income series, $A_t + PRI_t$. This is presented in Exhibit 4.6. Notice that for any d_1 and d_2, this total never depends on d_1 and d_2 and is always equal to the continuation present value of the underlying **CF** series. Stated differently, for any accounting procedure in this example, the sum of the accounting value and the present value of the induced residual income series is always equal to economic value.

The interpretation is important. Accounting valuation procedure A results in a series of accounting values that may be near to or far from their economic counterparts. If, say, at $t = 1$ the accounting value is too low, we know that expenses in future periods will be too low and future income will be too high, all relative to their economic value and economic norms. At time t, errors in the stock measure, A_t, imply errors in the future flow measures, collapsed into the continuation present value of the induced residual income series, PRI_t. Stock errors imply future flow errors and vice versa. Focusing on one, say overly aggressive depreciation, is myopic. The error story has two related parts.

For example, suppose we immediately write off the physical capital in Exhibit 4.3. This implies that we set $d_1 = 25{,}000$ and $d_2 = 0$. Our scheme is certainly conservative, but notice what this does to the induced residual income series in Exhibit 4.5: Residual income would be $-22{,}550$ in the first period, 9,680 in the second, and 16,637.5 in the third period. Conversely, suppose we take the opposite tack and set $d_1 = d_2 = 0$, implying that we do not write any of the physical capital off until the final period. Now

EXHIBIT 4.6
Accounting Value plus Error Calculations

	$t = 0$	$t = 1$	$t = 2$
A_t (Exhibit 4.3)	25,000	$25{,}000 - d_1$	$25{,}000 - d_1 - d_2$
PRI_t (above)	0	$-2{,}450 + d_1$	$-9{,}875 + d_1 + d_2$
$A_t + PRI_t$	25,000	22,550	15,125
PV_t	25,000	22,550	15,125

residual income would be 2,450 in the first period, 7,180 in the second period, and −10,862.5 in the third, yet properly tallying the errors over the time horizon nets them to zero. This is the essence of the calculations in Exhibit 4.6.

How general is this? It is, in fact, a statement about the algebra that underlies present value calculations. So, it rests on economic value being represented by a present value calculation. It also requires that the accounting valuation and income measures, A and $\hat{I}$ in our notation, articulate. Otherwise, all valuation errors do not flow through the income statement and vice versa.

This is worth studying a little more closely. We begin by rewriting the expression in (4.6) for the continuation present value of the induced residual income series. Notice that we have substituted the definition of residual income (RI_t):

$$PRI_t = \sum_{j=t+1}^{T} (\hat{I}_j - r \times A_{j-1})(1+r)^{t-j}$$

Now recall that when procedures A and $\hat{I}$ articulate, accounting income is change in the accounting value plus the cash flow to or from the owners (expression (4.3)). This implies, given articulation, that we can write our expression for the continuation present value of the induced residual income series as follows:[12]

$$PRI_t = \sum_{j=t+1}^{T} (A_j - A_{j-1} + CF_j - r \times A_{j-1})(1+r)^{t-j}$$

$$= \sum_{j=t+1}^{T} A_j(1+r)^{t-j} - (1+r)\sum_{j=t+1}^{T} A_{j-1}(1+r)^{t-j} + \sum_{j=t+1}^{T} CF_j(1+r)^{t-j}$$

$$= \sum_{j=t+1}^{T} A_j(1+r)^{t-j} - \sum_{j=t+1}^{T} A_{j-1}(1+r)^{t-j+1} + \sum_{j=t+1}^{T} CF_j(1+r)^{t-j}$$

$$= A_T(1+r)^{t-T} - A_t + \sum_{j=t+1}^{T} CF_j(1+r)^{t-j}$$

Our valuation procedure A, however, must report zero value at liquidation [condition (4.1b) earlier]; so, the first term in our final expression must

---

[12] To verify the last step, notice

$$\sum_{j=t+1}^{T} A_j(1+r)^{t-j} = A_{t+1}(1+r)^{-1} + A_{t+2}(1+r)^{-2} + \cdots + A_T(1+r)^{t-T}$$

and

$$\sum_{j=t+1}^{T} A_{j-1}(1+r)^{t-j+1} = A_t + A_{t+1}(1+r)^{-1} + \cdots + A_{T-1}(1+r)^{t-T+1}$$

be zero. Moreover, the last term, the part dealing with the CF_t series, is simply the continuation present value of the **CF** series at time t. So we have

$$PRI_t = -A_t + PV_t$$

That is, given articulation of A and $\hat{I}$, the continuation present value of the **CF** series is equal to accounting value plus the continuation present value of the induced residual income series.[13] Stated differently, the difference between PV_t and A_t, the difference between the two stock measures, is equal to the continuation present value of the induced residual income series.

POSTSCRIPT

This completes our review of valuation and economic income in a perfect (and complete) market setting as well as our characterization of accounting procedures in that setting. It is important to understand that accounting uses the language and the algebra of the certainty, perfect market setting. This is most apparent when we look at the articulation idea in which the algebraic connection between stocks and flows is evident. It is the reason that we developed the parallel details for the economic valuation function, $V(CF, r)$ in expression (3.2), and the accounting valuation function $A(CF, r)$, in expression (4.1), not to mention their respective economic and accounting income counterparts. Do not lose sight of the fact that accounting uses the language (i.e., valuation and income) and the algebra of classical economic valuation.

It is also important to remember that today's balance sheet is related to tomorrow's income statement. This is forcefully pointed out by the fact that book value plus the continuation present value of the induced residual income series always equals the continuation present value of the cash flow series itself. (All we require for this is the usual boundary condition coupled with articulation.) In this sense, the errors are counterbalanced.

Our study has, to date, had a surreal quality. If we know **CF**, for certain, there surely is no reason to apply the A and $\hat{I}$ accounting procedures to that series. We know, by definition, all there is to know about the organization's economic condition and prospects.

This means that we must abandon our comfortable assumptions of certainty and well-behaved markets if we are to examine accounting in a setting in which one would consume resources to have the accounting done. This is our next step—but we must remember that the language and the algebra of this setting will be carried forward.

---

[13] A parallel derivation produces the same result for the case in which T is unbounded.

Summary

In broadest terms, the basic structure of accounting is derived from economic valuation and its algebra. This is brought into accounting by means of the boundary conditions (4.1a) and (4.1b) in conjunction with additivity. Additional structure is provided by articulation. This provides a duality between valuation and income as one then follows from the other. Moreover, the substance of accounting valuation is provided by the accruals, which are the building blocks leading from cash flows to accounting income and valuation. As we shall see, these are essential in making the accounting system a source of information.

Accounting, then, portrays the reporting firm's history in terms of a sequence of accounting values and a corresponding sequence of accounting income tallies. In the world of certainty and complete and perfect markets in which economic value and economic income are well defined, we see an almost haunting similarity as both accounting and economic valuation portray the firm's history with periodic stock and flow renderings.

Of course, these renderings need not be identical. If the accounting measures articulate, however, any difference between accounting and economic value at some point in time is systematically related to future differences between accounting and economic income. Stock "errors," so to speak, lead to future flow "errors" and vice versa. Of course, being able to make (and verify) this bold statement rests on a well-defined valuation function in the first place.

Our work is not finished. There is more to the story than a shared language and algebra.

Selected References

Any principles textbook, upon reflection, stresses the idea that a well-defined set of accounting procedures (e.g., some specific version of GAAP) results in a mapping that records the firm's history in terms of accounting values and income. Whittington (1992) and Butterworth (1972) are particularly eloquent. The connection between the present value of future cash flows and residual income has a long history, including Preinreich (1937), Edwards and Bell (1961), Peasnell (1982), and Feltham and Ohlson (1995).

Key Terms

Accounting valuation is a procedure that maps a cash flow series (cash that flows from the firm to the owners) and an interest rate assumption into a sequence of values subject to boundary conditions that the initial valuation is the invested amount and the terminal valuation is zero, equation (4.1) along with (4.1a) and (4.1b). In turn, **accounting value** is the result of applying a particular accounting procedure, *accounting valuation mapping,* to a specific setting. **Accounting income measurement** is a decomposition of a given cash flow series and interest rate assumption into period-by-period amounts that sum to the total of the given cash flow series, equation (4.2) along with (4.2a). **Accounting income** is the result of applying a particular procedure, *accounting income mapping,* to a specific setting. Accounting valuation and income measurement **articulate** if accounting income is change in accounting value plus cash flow, as in equation (4.3). This leads to **duality** between accounting income and value. If you know one, you also know the other. **Accruals** are central to accounting valuation because they include all noncash items. The accruals make it possible to derive the income series from the cash flow series. In the extreme, **cash basis accounting** restricts recognition to cash-based transactions, to no accruals whatever. The only asset is cash on hand, expenses are recognized as payments are made, and so on.

Exercises

4.1. What does it mean to claim that accounting uses the language and the algebra of valuation?

4.2. We often think of a firm's accounting system as reflecting a variety of recognition and matching rules, dealing with, say, when revenue is recognized, inventory valuation, and so forth. How does this procedural orientation relate to our use of the valuation function, $A(CF, r)$?

4.3. This is a continuation of Ralph's Enterprise, Exercise 3.7. The cash flow vector, recall, is $CF = [-2{,}000, 700, 600, 1{,}155]$ and $r = 10$ percent.

   a. Construct a balance sheet and an income statement for each period in the life of Ralph's Enterprise. Do this three different ways, using (1) straight-line depreciation, (2) SYD depreciation, and (3) economic depreciation.

   b. For each accounting method in part *a,* calculate the implied residual income and verify that economic value equals book value plus the present value of all future residual income.

   c. Suppose that Ralph wants the reported income in each of the first two periods to be the hat size of a favorite friend. Pick whatever number you like to represent the friend's hat size, and calculate the depreciation schedule that will result in income in each of the first two periods being equal in magnitude to the friend's hat size. [Naturally, the third period's income will be $700 + 600 + 1{,}155 - 2{,}000 - 2(hat\ size)$.] Repeat the residual income exercise you performed in part *b.*

   d. You now have four different inferred value calculations, one for each of the original measurement schemes and the fourth for your hat size scheme. What pattern do you observe among these various calculations? What is the explanation?

4.4. This is a continuation of Exercise 3.5. We now add accounting valuations to your original graph. Of course, with $T = 2$ we will always have $A_2 = 0$, just as we will always have $A_0 = 1{,}000$. Now you are asked to specify two accounting methods—your choice—and plot the value at $t = 1$ (i.e., A_1 for each, as x ranges between $x = 0$ and $x = 500$). Comment on your graph.

4.5. Return to Exercise 3.9. (You should have discovered heavy use of the number 225.) Now suppose that the accounting method applied to this story records depreciation expense of d_1 in the first period and of d_2 in the second period. Determine the sequence of balance sheets and income statements. Using these balance sheets and income statements, also verify that the continuation preset value at time t equals book value at time t plus the present value of the future residual income series, again at time t. Do this for $t = 0$, $t = 1$, and $t = 2$.

4.6. Answer the question in footnote 11.

4.7. Return to the setting in Exhibit 4.4, where $T = 2$. Verify that economic value at time $t = 1$ equals book value at time $t = 1$ plus the discounted value of the $t = 2$ residual income.

Chapter 5

Modeling Information

The information content perspective stresses the idea that accounting is a source of information; one, we hasten to add, that uses the language and algebra of valuation to convey its information. To this point we have dealt with the initial portion of this recurring phrase, the language and algebra of valuation and its centrality in the "accounting model." It is now time to tackle the term *information*. This turns out to take some care because the term has taken on near colloquial status, yet being even moderately serious about its nature requires considerable structure to describe what it is that we are uncertain about and how the information speaks to that uncertainty.

The *information content perspective* stresses accounting's role as a source of information. To provide information means it is possible to become better informed, to learn something we did not yet know. In turn, being able to become better informed means we were initially less informed, that uncertainty was present. The implication should be understood: To treat accounting as a source of information demands that we become facile with the notions of uncertainty and information.[1]

We begin with the notion of *uncertainty*. This notion entails how we represent resource allocation exercises when uncertainty is present. From here we move on to the question of how we represent information, both its source and its arrival. We conclude with the issues of comparing and combining information sources. In a subsequent chapter, once our skills are well practiced, we will extend the earlier treatment of accounting stock

---

[1] Ironically, we teach accounting by stressing certainty: Here is a set of events and here are the proper procedures; now practice until you can reproduce the correct answer.

and flow measures to an uncertain world. Then we will be in a position to study the information content perspective and our claim that accounting uses the language and algebra of valuation to convey information.

A word of caution: Being serious about information is no easy task. Developing the skill to understand and be facile with information issues requires patience and effort. The modeling device we emphasize for this purpose, that of a partition, is likely to appear excessively formal, if not needlessly awkward, at first blush, but it will pay considerable dividends in subsequent chapters.

MODELING UNCERTAINTY

Uncertainty is all around us: What will tomorrow's weather be? When will my hard disk fail? Will the driver in the other lane swerve as I attempt to pass? Is there a material error in this asset account? Take your pick. We are also familiar with the use of probability in describing the uncertainty. For example, the probability of precipitation tomorrow is 40 percent. The probability of heads on the toss of a fair coin is .5.

State-Act-Outcome Specification

It will, in fact, be useful to be formal, almost pedantic, about modeling uncertainty. We follow Savage (1954) and model a resource allocation exercise or decision in terms of states, acts, and outcomes. An *act* is a specific choice, for example, to attend some specific movie, invest in a specific combination of financial instruments, or launch a specific new product. The act is distinctly endogenous. An outcome is whatever of consequence follows from the choice of the act: enjoyment of the movie, profit from the investment, success from the new product (including not only profit but also reputation and self-fulfillment).

Certainty, of course, is the case when an act completely determines the outcome. Typically, though, we do not know the precise outcome that will follow from all available acts. This is where states enter. A *state* is a description of the world so comprehensive that if we know the state, we then know the *outcome* that will follow from any act.

Let S denote the set of possible or conceivable states, and $s \in S$ a particular state. Likewise, let X denote the set of possible outcomes, and $x \in X$ one such outcome. A, in turn, is the set of possible acts, and $a \in A$ is one such act.[2] From here we describe the connection among states, acts, and outcomes with a function $x = p(s, a)$. The function $p(s, a)$ catalogs the outcome that will follow if act $a \in A$ is chosen and state $s \in S$ "obtains."[3]

---

[2] In subsequent chapters we will employ a more mnemonic description of the acts.
[3] For a state to "obtain" is a hopelessly formal description, but it nicely connotes the idea of the realization of some exogenous variable.

EXHIBIT 5.1
State, Act, Outcome
Setup for Casual
Stroll

	s_1	s_2
$a_1 =$ No umbrella	Get wet	Stay dry
$a_2 =$ Umbrella	Stay dry	Stay dry

To illustrate, suppose an individual is planning to take a walk. The remaining issue is whether to carry an umbrella; the choices are to carry one or not, so $A = \{$*no umbrella, umbrella*$\}$. The individual cares only about whether he or she gets wet during the walk. This suggests the outcomes are "wet" or "dry." So $X = \{$*get wet, stay dry*$\}$. Notice there is no reason whatsoever to insist that the outcomes be monetary.

Also, in this setting, the set S would contain two events: It rains, s_1, or it does not rain, s_2, $S = \{s_1, s_2\}$. This leaves no important aspect of the decision problem out of the state description. The outcome in this example might then be described by the matrix, or $p(s, a)$ function, in Exhibit 5.1. Of course, if the decision maker is an airline pilot, this description of the state of the world in terms of rain or no rain is far from sufficient to describe the outcome of following one flight plan versus another.[4]

For a second illustration, one closer to our explicit concerns, suppose that a decision maker is facing two alternatives. Incremental cash flow is the important outcome. One act will result in a zero incremental cash flow; the other will result in a negative incremental cash flow of 100 or a positive incremental cash flow of 140. Then the complete description of the problem is contained in the matrix, or $p(s, a)$ function in Exhibit 5.2.

For a third illustration, suppose that a decision maker faces two investment alternatives, each lasting two periods. Incremental cash flow is again the important outcome, but now this incremental cash flow outcome is an issue in each of the periods. One of the alternatives will result in a zero outcome in both periods. The other will provide incremental cash flows as given in Exhibit 5.3, in which the first number in the ordered pair is the incremental cash flow in the first period, and the second is its counterpart in the second period.

As a final example, return to our model of the reporting entity in which capital (K) and labor (L) are combined to produce output (q) via the technology expression

$$q \leq \sqrt{KL}$$

Also suppose that the firm must supply either $q = 100$ or $q = 200$ units of output. The customer will announce the required amount after capital, K, has been acquired, but before labor, L, has been acquired. So, we basically

---

[4] Were we insisting on purity, we would admit to a single specification of the set of states, and then any specific decision problem would allow us to group states together into events whenever distinguishing among some finely detailed states was immaterial. For example, "rain a little" and "rain a lot" are grouped together in state s_1 in Exhibit 5.1.

EXHIBIT 5.2
Setup for Risky Investment

	s_1	s_2
a_1	0	0
a_2	−100	140

EXHIBIT 5.3
Setup for Two-Period Risky Investment

	s_1	s_2	s_3	s_4
a_1	0	0	0	0
a_2	(−100, 100)	(−100, 120)	(−140, 130)	(−140, 160)

EXHIBIT 5.4
Setup for Uncertain Customer Demand

	$s_1\,(q = 100)$	$s_2\,(q = 200)$
K	$p_K K + p_L (100)^2/K$	$p_K K + p_L (200)^2/K$

have two states, high or low demand for output, and for some initial (and feasible) capital choice of K, the necessary labor to produce q units is the solution to

$$q = \sqrt{KL}, \quad \text{or} \quad L = q^2/K$$

Also recall that the price of capital is p_K per unit and the price of labor is p_L per unit. With this in mind, the total expenditures to meet the customer's requirements, given the initial choice of K, would be as described in Exhibit 5.4.

Some common features of these illustrations should be noted. First, we will typically treat the states as finite in number. This means we can write the set of possible states as $S = \{s_1, s_2, \ldots, s_n\}$ for some number n. This simplifies what follows and does not cause any significant drop in insight. Second, the relevant description of states depends on available acts and important consequences. Rain or not, for instance, was adequate for the umbrella description but not for the pilot.[5] Third, each state represents one possible scenario that might occur. All conceivable scenarios are condensed in the state descriptions leaving out no aspects of importance. The notion of states is abstract and can be used in all circumstances when we do not know everything the future might bring (or, for that matter, that is hidden in the past).

Probability

It is also natural to attach the term *likelihood* to the states. Some states are more likely to occur than other states, just as others may be equally likely.

---

[5] In a deeper sense, once again we are dealing with a single specification of the set of states and then grouping irrelevant distinctions together into events or into what you will learn to call a *partition of the set of states*. This grouping phenomenon was coined the "payoff relevant description of events" by Marschak (1963), an important contributor to the development of the theory of information.

For example, cold weather is more likely than hot weather in the Northern Hemisphere during the month of January. The usual way of encoding this into an abstract description of an uncertain world is to attach probabilities to each of the states contained in S.

Recall that with a finite set of states, we write $S = \{s_1, s_2, \ldots, s_n\}$. In simplest terms, we think of probability in this context as the assignment of a number π_j for each $j = 1, \ldots, n$ such that

1.
$$\pi_j \geq 0 \quad \text{for } j = 1, \ldots, n$$

2.
$$\sum_{j=1}^{n} \pi_j = 1$$

The number π_j is the probability that state s_j obtains and will on occasion be written as $prob(s_j)$. The probability assignments, the numbers, are non-negative, and sum to unity.[6]

A remaining question before we proceed concerns the source of this probability measure. We will treat the measure as exogenous; it is just assumed to be present. The very meaning one might attach to the probability measure has been the subject of philosophical argument; for example, is this a long-run frequency notion, a completely subjective notion, or perhaps somewhere in between? Savage (1954) pioneered a subjective interpretation in which a person whose behavior in decision making is sufficiently consistent can be modeled as if subjective probability and subjective

---

[6] To add some perspective, we dig a bit further. Any subset of S is called an *event*. Thus, $\mathcal{E} \subseteq S$ is an event, and this holds for any subset of S. Now let $\mathcal{J}$ be the set of all events, the set of all subsets of S. For example, if $S = \{s_1, s_2\}$, the set of all events is $\mathcal{J} = \{\emptyset, \{s_1\}, \{s_2\}, \{s_1, s_2\}\}$. Yes, the set of all events is a set; and S itself is an event, just as the null set, $\emptyset$, the null event, is an event. Now, a probability measure on S is a real-valued function π defined on all subsets of S (i.e., defined on all events) such that:

1. $\quad \pi(\mathcal{E}) \geq 0 \quad$ for every $\mathcal{E} \subseteq S$
2. $\quad \pi(S) = 1$
3. $\quad \pi(\mathcal{E}_1 \cup \mathcal{E}_2) = \pi(\mathcal{E}_1) + \pi(\mathcal{E}_2) \quad$ when $\mathcal{E}_1, \mathcal{E}_2 \subseteq S$ and $\mathcal{E}_1 \cap \mathcal{E}_2 = \emptyset$

So, at this level, we speak of the probability of an event, the probability of a union of events, and so on. The probability is always non-negative and has a casual interpretation as the degree of likelihood. The expression $\pi(\mathcal{E}_1) > \pi(\mathcal{E}_2)$ means event $\mathcal{E}_1$ is more likely than event $\mathcal{E}_2$. (Parenthetically, it is also important to note our reliance on a finite S here. If S is a richer set, we must be careful to specify the collection of subsets of S, their complements, and so on. This leads us into things such as a σ-algebra, which is a set and collection of subsets thereof in which each subset's complement is present and in which the union of a countable number of subsets is also a subset. With a finite S, though, we work with all subsets of S without causing any ambiguities or measurement difficulties.)

Now $\{s_j\} \subseteq S$ is the event "state s_j" and $\{s_i, s_j\} \subseteq S$ is the event "state s_i or state s_j." (Don't miss the subtlety: s_j is an element of set S, but an event is a subset of the set S. Properly speaking, then, $\{s_j\} \subseteq S$ is the event "state s_j" and when we write the probability of state s_j as $prob(s_j)$, we should be writing $prob(\{s_j\})$.) And since the events "state s_i" and "state s_j" are distinct events, given $i \neq j$, the probability of any event in our setup is the sum of the "state probabilities" for each state contained in the event: $\pi(\mathcal{E}) = \sum_{s \in \mathcal{E}} prob(s)$.

utility assessments are made and decision theory calculus is invoked to identify the most preferred act. We treat the probability as a measure of likelihood in which likelihood might reflect "objective" events such as gambling encounters with known odds or "subjective" events such as new product introductions with anything but objective odds.[7]

This construct of probabilities assigned to state descriptions, then, captures the notion of the uncertainty. If we know which state will occur, we assign a probability of 1 to that state and a probability of 0 to all other states. If we find a state very likely to occur, we assign a probability close to 1 to that state; if a state is very unlikely, the probability assigned to that state will be close to 0.

Random Variables

States and probabilities, then, are our foundation for modeling uncertainty. In most cases, though, the state description is of little or no practical use. (No comment is necessary at this point.) We do not speak of the state of the weather but in terms of average temperatures, temperature range, precipitation expected, and so on. Similarly, we do not speak of the state of the enterprise but in terms of its earnings, growth prospects, book-to-market ratio, and so on.

The connection between this foundation and the things we so casually speak of is the concept of a *random variable*. Given state description $S = \{s_1, s_2, \ldots, s_n\}$, a random variable is a numerical valued function that assigns a real number $f(s)$ to every state $s \in S$. Technically, a random variable is a function that is defined on the state space and maps into the real line (perhaps an m-dimensional space).

Rainfall, temperature, accounting income, and your score on the final exam are all random variables. Likewise, in the state-act-outcome setup, if the outcome is a real number, such as cash flow, it too is a random variable.

To illustrate, consider the setting described in Exhibit 5.5 in which we have five possible states and two different random variables. Z is a

---

[7] Probability is a measure, a measure of likelihood. Suppose we have a set of events, as in our finite state setup. Further suppose we are able to rank all of the events in terms of likelihood. Let this ranking satisfy the following four properties: (1) it is complete and transitive; (2) any event is at least as likely as the null event; (3) S itself is strictly more likely than the null event; and (4) if $\mathcal{E}_1$ and $\mathcal{E}_3$ are disjoint events and if $\mathcal{E}_2$ and $\mathcal{E}_3$ are disjoint events, then $\mathcal{E}_1$ is strictly more likely than $\mathcal{E}_2$ if and only if $\mathcal{E}_1 \cup \mathcal{E}_3$ is strictly more likely than $\mathcal{E}_2 \cup \mathcal{E}_3$. Our noted definition of a probability measure satisfies all of these conditions. But is the opposite true? This was an open question for a long time, but the answer is no. (See Kraft, Pratt, and Seidenberg, 1959.) The point is that treating probability as a measure of likelihood is both natural and delicate. It requires considerable structure on what we mean by likelihood for this representation to be valid. Accounting theory is likewise concerned with measurement: what, how, and when should the accounting system measure? The idea, you will come to appreciate, is to use the measures to represent the underlying set of phenomena.

EXHIBIT 5.5
Illustrative Random
Variables

	s_1	s_2	s_3	s_4	s_5
$\pi_j = prob(s_j)$	.2	.2	.3	.2	.1
$Z = f(s)$	1	2	2	4	−1
$G = d(s)$	5	5	6	5	6

EXHIBIT 5.6
prob(z) **Specification**

	$Z = -1$	$Z = 1$	$Z = 2$	$Z = 4$
$prob(z)$	.1	.2	.5	.2

random variable, defined by the function $f(s)$. So is G, as defined by the function $d(s)$.

Notice that the probability measure is also specified.[8] This probability measure combined with the function, $f(s)$, allows us to identify a probability measure for the random variable (technically for the events associated with the random variable). Thus, $prob(Z = 1) = .2$, $prob(Z = 2) = .2 + .3 = .5$, and so on. We summarize the details in the matrix in Exhibit 5.6. Clearly, this leads to a probability measure defined on all subsets or events of the set $\{-1, 1, 2, 4\}$!

From here it is a short step to start talking about summary measures, such as the mean or expected value and variance of a random variable. For our random variable Z, we readily calculate the mean, $E[Z]$, and variance, $VAR(Z)$:

$$E[Z] = \sum_z z \times prob(z) = -1(.1) + 1(.2) + 2(.5) + 4(.2) = 1.9$$

and

$$VAR(Z) = \sum_z (z - E[Z])^2 \times prob(z)$$
$$= (-1 - 1.9)^2(.1) + (1 - 1.9)^2(.2) + (2 - 1.9)^2(.5) + (4 - 1.9)^2(.2)$$
$$= 1.89$$

The calculations, you will appreciate, rely on the fact that Z is numerical.

A more familiar specification occurs when we directly assess the random variable's probability measure. For example, the income of a firm for the forthcoming year is a random variable. It might be any conceivable real number. It might also be well described by a random variable, $\hat{I}$, which is normally distributed with mean $E[\hat{I}] = \mu$ and variance $VAR(\hat{I}) = \sigma^2$, which, for the notation connoisseur, is usually written as $\hat{I} \sim N(\mu, \sigma^2)$.

---

[8] You should have no difficulty moving from the given *prob(s)* specification to the probability of any event $\mathscr{E} \subseteq S = \{s_1, s_2, \ldots, s_5\}$. For example, the probability of "s_1 or s_2," that is, the probability of the event $\{s_1, s_2\}$ is simply $\pi_1 + \pi_2 = .4$.

The two parameters, mean μ and variance σ^2, are sufficient to describe the entire distribution.[9]

The final step is to introduce the notion of joint probabilities of the random variables Z and G. This is the probability that the pair Z, G takes on a specific value. For example $prob((Z, G) = (1, 5)) = .2$. The notion of joint probability conveys the dependency among the random variables. This becomes important once we skip the state space specification because the states that carry all uncertainty also keep track of the interrelationship among all random variables. In the random variable formulation, this is replaced by a joint probability measure. *Covariance* is a well-known summary measure of this dependency.

INFORMATION

Given that the state description contains every conceivable relevant aspect of the world, it is especially simple to define the notion of *information*. At one extreme, *perfect information* is equivalent to learning exactly which state will occur. At the other extreme is *null information* from which we learn nothing about which state will occur. The intermediate case occurs when we learn something but less than all there is to know.

To model this, recall that the state description in the state-act-outcome setup carries, so to speak, the uncertainty in the resource allocation exercise. Intuitively, then, information should "refine our knowledge" of the states.

For example, suppose that we have four states, $S = \{s_1, s_2, s_3, s_4\}$. Further suppose that an information source will reveal something about these states. In particular, it will reveal one of two possible reports: the state that will obtain, the true state, is either a member of $\{s_1, s_2\} = \delta_1$, or the state that will obtain is a member of $\{s_3, s_4\} = \delta_2$. So, the report will be either δ_1 or δ_2. Details, including $prob(s)$, are given in Exhibit 5.7.

Now, what do we learn if this source reports δ_1? We learn the true state is either s_1 or s_2 or formally that the state is a member of $\delta_1 = \{s_1, s_2\}$, and therefore not a member of $\{s_3, s_4\} = \delta_2$. Surely, then, the probability of either

---

[9] The normal density is completely described by the two parameters of mean and variance. In this example, now, income $\hat{\imath}$ can take on any value, so we are clearly outside our usual setup of a finite set of states. Our earlier warning about technical issues now resurfaces. We know that the mean and variance of a normally distributed random variable exist. In general, though, the event algebra has to be carefully specified to ensure, say, that the mean as a mathematical construction exists. This is far beyond any technical measurability issue we will encounter; but you should be aware we are not presenting a comprehensive treatment of the subject.

EXHIBIT 5.7
Probability Details
for Information
Example

	s_1	s_2	s_3	s_4
$\pi_j = prob(s_j)$	.1	.2	.3	.4
$prob(s \mid \delta_1)$	1/3	2/3	0	0
$prob(s \mid \delta_2)$	0	0	3/7	4/7

of the latter two states, given we have observed report δ_1 is zero. We write this in conditional probability format as $prob(s_3 \mid \delta_1) = prob(s_4 \mid \delta_1) = 0$. What about the other two states? Here we calculate

$$prob(s_1 \mid \delta_1) = \pi_1/(\pi_1 + \pi_2) = .1/(.1 + .2) = 1/3$$

and

$$prob(s_2 \mid \delta_1) = \pi_2/(\pi_1 + \pi_2) = .2/(.1 + .2) = 2/3$$

Note well: Observing report δ_1 or report δ_2 tells us something about the states. This, in turn, leads to a systematic revision of the probabilities. Begin with the noted probability assessment, $prob(s)$. If we subsequently learn that the source reports $\delta_1 = \{s_1, s_2\}$ (or $\delta_2 = \{s_3, s_4\}$), we use Bayes' rule to revise $prob(s)$ to the associated conditional probability, conditional on having observed report δ:[10]

$$prob(s \mid \delta) = \frac{prob(\{s\} \cap \delta)}{prob(\delta)}$$

You should verify the calculations for $prob(s \mid \delta_1)$ and $prob(s \mid \delta_2)$.

Partitions

An additional feature of the preceding example to notice is that each possible report is actually a subset of the set of states, S. Moreover, the two possible subsets, δ_1 and δ_2, share nothing in common (i.e., $\delta_1 \cap \delta_2 = \varnothing$) and collectively define S (i.e., $\delta_1 \cup \delta_2 = S$). In formal terms, δ_1 and δ_2 form a partition of the set S. This is a consequence of the comprehensiveness of the

---

[10] A more familiar expression for Bayes' rule relies on random variables. Suppose Z and W are random variables with joint probability $prob(Z, W)$. Having observed $W = w$, the probability that $Z = z$ is given by

$$prob(Z = z \mid W = w) = prob(Z = z, W = w)/prob(W = w)$$

or, in our shorthand notation, $prob(z \mid w) = prob(z, w)/prob(w)$. In our case, though, the probabilities are defined on subsets of S, and δ itself is a subset of S; so the joint occurrence of s and δ is the intersection: $\{s\} \cap \delta$. Likewise, $prob(\delta)$ is simply the sum of the underlying state probabilities for each state contained in δ. In particular, $\{s\} \cap \delta_1 = \{s\}$ for the first two states and is null for the last two. So, $prob(\{s_1\} \cap \delta_1) = prob(s_1) = .1$, along with $prob(\{s_2\} \cap \delta_1) = prob(s_2) = .2$; $prob(\{s_3\} \cap \delta_1) = prob(\varnothing) = 0$; and $prob(\{s_4\} \cap \delta_1) = prob(\varnothing) = 0$. In addition, with $\delta_1 = \{s_1, s_2\}$, $prob(\delta_1) = prob(s_1) + prob(s_2) = .1 + .2 = .3$. This provides $prob(s_1 \mid \delta_1) = .1/.3 = 1/3$, and so on.

state description. It includes all conceivable uncertainty, and that, of course, includes any information we might receive.

To illustrate, suppose the weather might be "wet" or "dry," and a weather forecast will predict "wet" or "dry." Naturally, this forecast might turn out to be correct or erroneous. We code this as four states: $S = \{wet$ *and forecast wet, wet and forecast dry, dry and forecast wet, dry and forecast dry*$\}$. So, a forecast of wet is a claim the first or the third state is true, and so on. In this fashion the state specification tautologically reflects all uncertainties, including those associated with the implications of what some information source reports. As a consequence, whatever that information source is, it defines a *partition* on the state space.

To go a bit further, let $\Delta = \{\delta_1, \delta_2, \ldots, \delta_m\}$ be a collection of sets. This collection of sets, Δ, forms a partition of $S = \{s_1, s_2, \ldots, s_n\}$ if

1. $\delta_i \subseteq S$, for every $\delta_i \in \Delta$

2. $\delta_1 \cup \delta_2 \cup \cdots \cup \delta_{m-1} \cup \delta_m = S$

3. $\delta_i \cap \delta_j = \varnothing$ for every $\delta_i, \delta_j \in \Delta$ and $i \neq j$

Think of Δ as defining a set of "holders." First, each holder, each δ must be a subset of S. Holder δ is not allowed to have any elements outside of S. Second, collectively, the holders must equal S. Every element of S must be placed in one of the holders. Finally, no ambiguity is allowed; the holders are mutually exclusive. The idea is classification: Every element of S belongs to exactly one element of Δ.

This is how we model information. It is a partition of the state space S. Suppose Δ contains a single set. This single set must be S itself (i.e., $\Delta = \{S\}$). Otherwise, we have not satisfied the definition of a partition. This is null information; it tells us nothing. After all, we already know $s \in S$! At the other extreme, suppose $\Delta = \{\{s_1\}, \{s_2\}, \ldots, \{s_n\}\}$. This is perfect information.

Two additional features of this modeling apparatus are important. First, as we observed earlier, revision of the state probabilities is particularly straightforward when information is modeled as a partition of the state space. If we know $\delta \in \Delta$ is true, we then know the true state is one of the elements of δ and, by implication, any state not in δ has now been ruled out. So, our earlier, surely awkward, statement of Bayes' rule simplifies to

$$prob(s \mid \delta) = \begin{cases} prob(s)/prob(\delta) & \text{if } s \in \delta; \text{ and} \\ 0 & \text{if } s \notin \delta \end{cases}$$

Second, an equivalent way to think about this construction of information as a partition of the state space is that the information source reports according to some function η that maps S into some set of possible signals, denoted $\hat{W}$. We formally state this as $\eta: S \rightarrow \hat{W}$, meaning "$\eta$ maps S

into $\hat{W}$." Alternatively, we write this as $m = \eta(s)$.[11] In this construction, we identify the information source, η, and the signal or message, $m \in \hat{W}$ it provides. Formal equivalence between the function and partition ideas should be evident by glancing back at our earlier example.

Indeed, we could go further here and think of this in terms of a random variable. Instead of reporting an element of the partition Δ (i.e., instead of reporting $\delta_j \in \Delta$), why not simply report the number "j"? Go back to our example, $\eta(s_1) = \eta(s_2) = 1$, and $\eta(s_3) = \eta(s_4) = 2$ defines a random variable that conveys the same information, the same underlying partition, as was used in the illustration. The substance of the information, though, is not whether the random variable's realization was 1 or 2; it is the underlying state partition, the underlying information content. For example, the substance of a firm that reports income of so many dollars is not that this amount of income was earned or recognized. The substance is what you learn about the firm given its accounting system has reported this income number.

Alternative Representations

Our partition (or function) formulation, although awkward at first encounter, is the simplest device on which to base our subsequent study of accounting as a source of information. Its (full) generality can be appreciated by briefly considering two alternative ways of representing the arrival of information. For this purpose, suppose that we are interested in a random variable $D \in \{0, 1\}$. We also have access to an information source that will report "good" (g) or "bad" (b) news. The joint probability is specified in Exhibit 5.8.

Notice that $prob(D = 0) = prob(D = 1) = .5$, and $E[D] = 0(.5) + 1(.5) = .5 = prob(D = 1)$. In addition, $prob(\text{signal } g) = .55$ and $prob(\text{signal } b) = .45$. Observing the noted signal is informative, it alters our opinion about the

---

[11] The Greek letter η (eta) is the traditional symbol for an information structure defined in this manner, just as ϵ is the traditional symbol for the error term in a regression equation, μ is the traditional symbol for the mean of a normal population, and so forth. Now, recall that a function is a mapping from one set to another with two properties: No element of the first set is left "unmapped," and no element of the first set is mapped into more than one element of the second set. Thus, if $\eta(s)$ is a function from S, it defines a partition of S. Suppose we observe $m = \eta(s)$. Then the inverse, $\eta^{-1}(m)$, identifies all elements of S that lead to m.

Treating information as a partition of S, then, is equivalent to treating the information source as providing a signal defined by the function $m = \eta(s)$. Subsequently, we will worry about information that is useful in monitoring an agent who selects the act a on behalf of someone else. We will then treat the monitor as reporting a signal defined by $\eta(s, a)$; that is, we will allow the agent's behavior to specify which partition of S we are observing. Stated differently, the information source will partition $S \times A$ in that setting. In similar fashion, an accounting procedure will take various activities of the entity (viewed as entity acts) and compile an accounting rendering based on other available information.

EXHIBIT 5.8
Binary Random Variable

	D = 0	D = 1
Signal g	.15	.40
Signal b	.35	.10

EXHIBIT 5.9
Partition Version of Exhibit 5.8 Setting

	s_1: D = 0 and Signal = g	s_2: D = 0 and Signal = b	s_3: D = 1 and Signal = g	s_4: D = 1 and Signal = b
$prob(s)$	.15	.35	.40	.10
$\eta(s)$	δ_1	δ_2	δ_1	δ_2
$prob(s \mid \delta_1)$	15/55	0	40/55	0
$prob(s \mid \delta_2)$	0	35/45	0	10/45

variable D. This becomes more apparent when we calculate the expected value of D, conditional on either of the signals:[12]

$$E[D \mid \text{Signal } g] = 0(15/55) + 1(40/55) = 40/55$$

$$E[D \mid \text{Signal } b] = 0(35/45) + 1(10/45) = 10/45$$

Can you represent this story in terms of a state space and the information itself as a partition Δ of this state space? See Exhibit 5.9 where we merely enrich the state description so it captures all of the noise in the information source as well.

Notice that $\delta_1 = \{s_1, s_3\}$ corresponds to signal g; and we readily have $prob(s_1 \mid \delta_1) = .15/(.15 + .40) = 15/55$ and $prob(s_3 \mid \delta_1) = 40/55$. Clearly, $E[D \mid \delta_1] = 40/55$. The remaining details should be transparent. We are telling the identical story.

Intuitively, this should be the case. After all, the state is specified so it carries all of the uncertainty. If there is uncertainty between the variable D and the signal, as in Exhibit 5.8, we merely "load" all of that uncertainty into an equivalent state specification.

Another way to model this story is to focus directly on the random variable D. Suppose that all we care about is the expected value of D. Well, absent any information, this is simply .50, but, if signal g (or partition element δ_1) is observed, we know the expected value increases to 40/55; and if signal b (or partition element δ_2) is observed, we know the expected value decreases to 10/45. So, let's represent the expected value as the random variable $\bar{D}$:

$$\bar{D} = .5 + \epsilon$$

Now, ϵ is a zero mean shock or disturbance term. Try the following: $\epsilon = 125/550$ (which is $40/55 - .50$) with probability .55, and $\epsilon = -125/450$

---

[12] Again, notice that because D can be only 0 or 1, its expected value is numerically equal to the probability that $D = 1$.

(which is $10/45 - .50$) with probability .45. So,

$$E[\bar{D}] = .50 + E[\epsilon] = .50 + .55(125/550) + .45(-125/450) = .50$$

That is, the revised expected value of D can be modeled as equal to its mean plus a random "innovation." In information terms, then, we observe the innovation or revision in the mean. Stated differently, information alters the expectation in this case.

Thus, we generally have alternative ways of modeling or representing information. The joint probability representation has the advantage of familiarity, but it becomes awkward when we compare information sources (as you will see). The innovation representation is intuitive, but it becomes awkward if not dysfunctional when we have multiple sources of information. The partition approach has the advantage of readily accommodating multiple sources of information and being particularly transparent on the subject of comparing information sources.

At times we will switch among these representations for expositional ease, but the more subtle issues will always lead us back to the partition formulation.

COMPARISON OF INFORMATION SOURCES

Next is the question of whether there is some way to order or compare information sources in terms of their "usefulness" or "value." For example, is it possible to say that one newspaper is better than another or to say that one accounting procedure is better than another? To explore this, let S have three elements $S = \{s_1, s_2, s_3\}$. We list all possible partitions of S in Exhibit 5.10.

Partition Δ_0 is, of course, null; it tells us nothing. Partition Δ_4 is perfect; it tells us exactly which state will obtain. The other three are in between; each distinguishes one of the three states and groups the other two.

Now suppose that we are given, say, partition Δ_1. Could we convert this into partitions Δ_4 by "splitting apart" or "subdividing" one or more of its elements? The answer is yes; simply take the second element of Δ_1, $\{s_2, s_3\}$, and split it into $\{s_2\}$ and $\{s_3\}$. This procedure goes by the name

EXHIBIT 5.10
Partitions of a Three-Element S

Label	Partition	Interpretation
Δ_0	$\{\{s_1, s_2, s_3\}\}$	Tells us nothing
Δ_1	$\{\{s_1\}, \{s_2, s_3\}\}$	Highlights s_1
Δ_2	$\{\{s_2\}, \{s_1, s_3\}\}$	Highlights s_2
Δ_3	$\{\{s_3\}, \{s_1, s_2\}\}$	Highlights s_3
Δ_4	$\{\{s_1\}, \{s_2\}, \{s_3\}\}$	Tells us everything

subpartition. We take a given partition and "subdivide" it. *Disaggregation* is an apt metaphor.

Here is the formal idea. Suppose $\Delta = \{\delta_1, \ldots, \delta_m\}$ and $\hat{\Delta} = \{\hat{\delta}_1, \ldots, \hat{\delta}_{m'}\}$ both partition state space S. Partition Δ is a subpartition of partition $\hat{\Delta}$ if for every $\delta \in \Delta$ there exists a $\hat{\delta} \in \hat{\Delta}$ such that $\delta \subseteq \hat{\delta}$. In words, if we can take any element of partition Δ and find a corresponding element in partition $\hat{\Delta}$ that contains that element, then Δ is a subpartition of $\hat{\Delta}$. Partition Δ_0 can be subpartitioned to create any of the other partitions. Being perfect information, Δ_4 is a subpartition of every other partition but cannot itself be subpartitioned. However, Δ_1 is not a subpartition of Δ_2 and vice versa. Any partition is naturally a subpartition of itself.

Think of a subpartition as providing more detail. If Δ is a subpartition of $\hat{\Delta}$, then anything $\hat{\Delta}$ might tell you will also be revealed by partition Δ, along with possible additional details. For example, consider Δ_1 and Δ_4 in Exhibit 5.11. The latter is simply the former, but with subset $\{s_2, s_3\}$ subdivided into subsets $\{s_1\}$ and $\{s_2\}$. That is, Δ_4 is a subpartition of Δ_1. Another way to see this is to begin with Δ_4. Notice we can now construct partition Δ_1 by combining subsets $\{s_2\}$ and $\{s_3\}$ into subset $\{s_2, s_3\}$.

A synonym for subpartition is "as fine as" (or, more emphatically, at least as fine as). Try it out; Δ_1 is as fine as Δ_0; Δ_4 is as fine as Δ_1 but not vice versa; Δ_1 is not as fine as Δ_2 and Δ_2 is not as fine as Δ_1; Δ_4 is the finest partition of S; Δ_0 is the least fine, or coarsest.

Two features of this odyssey should be noted. First, suppose we tell you that partition Δ is a subpartition of partition $\hat{\Delta}$, or equivalently partition Δ is as fine as partition $\hat{\Delta}$. Then everything you might learn from partition $\hat{\Delta}$ you can learn from partition Δ, and possibly more. Thus, partition Δ provides as much information as does partition $\hat{\Delta}$. In this limited sense, we can rank the information sources. If one is a subpartition of the other, we know that the first provides at least as much information as the second.

Second, this subpartition or *fineness* device provides a partial but not a complete ranking of partitions, or information sources. Compare partitions Δ_4 and Δ_3 in our three-state example. Partition Δ_4 is a subpartition of partition Δ_3, and Δ_4 is as fine as Δ_3, but not vice versa. Now try to compare partitions Δ_2 and Δ_3. Neither is a subpartition of the other. They

EXHIBIT 5.11
Subpartition
Relationships

Label	Partition	Subpartition of
Δ_0	$\{\{s_1, s_2, s_3\}\}$	Nothing but Δ_0
Δ_1	$\{\{s_1\}, \{s_2, s_3\}\}$	Δ_0, Δ_1
Δ_2	$\{\{s_2\}, \{s_1, s_3\}\}$	Δ_0, Δ_2
Δ_3	$\{\{s_3\}, \{s_1, s_2\}\}$	Δ_0, Δ_3
Δ_4	$\{\{s_1\}, \{s_2\}, \{s_3\}\}$	$\Delta_0, \Delta_1, \Delta_2, \Delta_3, \Delta_4$

cannot be compared via the subpartition or fineness device. The implication should not be missed: It is simply not always possible to compare two partitions or information sources and claim that, in terms of providing more information, one information system is superior to another.[13]

This fact turns out to be important in a variety ways, so we amplify a bit. Consider an ordering of a set of objects by some criterion (e.g., individuals by height or partitions of some state set using the subpartition idea). Now, this ordering is complete if for any two objects in the set, one is ordered above the other or vice versa. *Completeness* means that we can always compare the two objects using the noted criterion. Similarly, the ordering is transitive if when one object is ordered above a second and the second is ordered above a third, the first is ordered above the third. We call this ordering a ranking if it is both complete *and* transitive. Formally, these are the characteristics we use to define a ranking. The first makes sure that all objects are ordered and the second rules out circularity. Only then can we talk about the highest and the lowest ordered object.

The punch line is that the subpartition criterion provides an ordering that is transitive but not complete. Consequently, we find only a partial ranking of information sources using the subpartition or fineness criterion.

Equivalent Information Sources

Closely related to the notion of subpartition is the notion of equivalent information sources. Partitions Δ and $\hat{\Delta}$ are *equivalent* if they are identical, if $\Delta = \hat{\Delta}$. Equivalent information sources tell us the same thing. This amounts to (1) Δ is a subpartition of $\hat{\Delta}$ and (2) $\hat{\Delta}$ is a subpartition of Δ.

As obvious as this is, we should remember that information typically does not arrive in the form of an explicit state partition element. It is generally coded. Think of an important strategic report, written in both German and English. If nothing was missed in translation, this is the same information but in a different code, scale, or language.

Earlier we noted another way to represent the partition idea is to think in terms of a function that maps states into some set of admissible signals. For example, the function $\eta(s)$ might report a real number for each of the states. Let's concentrate on systems that do use real numbers to reveal what they know about S. So $\eta(s)$ is a real valued function. (Yes, it defines

---

[13] In the random variables setup, the notion of better information transforms to the condition that one random variable W is more informative than another random variable Z with respect to some random variable B if there exists a random variable ϵ, which is independent of B and has $E[\epsilon] = 0$ such that

$$Z = W + \epsilon$$

The interpretation is that random variable Z is equal to the random variable W plus a noise term that is totally unrelated to the variable of interest, B.

a random variable.) Now suppose we have two such functions, $\eta_1(s)$ and $\eta_2(s)$. Furthermore, suppose for at least one state, s_i, their reports differ: $\eta_1(s_i) \neq \eta_2(s_i)$. Are these different information systems? They surely are in the sense their reports will not always agree literally.

This is naive, however. Celsius and Fahrenheit scales tell us the same thing, but always with a different temperature reading except at negative 40 degrees. To deal with this, we must identify the partitions induced by the information systems in general.

The important aspect of an information system is what it tells about the underlying state space (i.e., what partition of the state space it induces). Thus, if the two information structures induce the same partition, the two information structures are equivalent. In that case, the two information systems carry the same information about the underlying state space. That will be the case whenever η_2 can be constructed from η_1 and vice versa.[14] In that case, there exists functions F and G such that for all states we have $\eta_1(s) = F(\eta_2(s))$ and $\eta_2(s) = G(\eta_1(s))$. Stated differently, in that case, the partitions of the state space induced by each of the systems are identical. The two systems have precisely the same information content but deliver it with a different code, measurement scale, or simply scale.

This equivalence of information structures leads to the observation that there might be many equivalent representations of an information source. The only difference among them is the labeling of the partition elements. The face value of an information system is not the source of its substance. It is the induced partition of the state space that matters.

Combining Information Sources

In many cases, more than one information structure is available. The mechanics are straightforward. Consider the case in which two information systems are jointly available, defined by partitions Δ and $\hat{\Delta}$ alone. Taken together, the two partitions provide a partition of the state space that is as fine as either Δ or $\hat{\Delta}$. The second source, so to speak, can only improve upon the first source.[15] To illustrate, let $S = \{s_1, s_2, s_3, s_4\}$. Also assume $\Delta = \{\{s_1, s_2\}, \{s_3, s_4\}\}$ and $\hat{\Delta} = \{\{s_1, s_3\}, \{s_2, s_4\}\}$. Combining the two partitions provides us the partition of $\{\{s_1\}, \{s_2\}, \{s_3\}, \{s_4\}\}$.

As we said, the mechanics of combining information sources are straightforward. What is far from straightforward is understanding the importance of one of the information sources. We will learn that studying one source by itself, say Δ, as though it were the only source of information tells us in general almost nothing about how important Δ might be in

---

[14] Let S have four elements $S = \{s_1, s_2, s_3, s_4\}$. Let $\eta_1(s_1) = \eta_1(s_3) = m_1$ and $\eta_1(s_2) = \eta_1(s_4) = m_2$. Let $\eta_2(s_1) = \eta_2(s_3) = m_3$ and $\eta_2(s_2) = \eta_2(s_4) = m_4$. Then the two information structures are equivalent because they both induce partition $\{\{s_1, s_3\}, \{s_2, s_4\}\}$. In turn, using $F(m_3) = m_1$ and $F(m_4) = m_2$ converts the second system into the first, and so on.

[15] Why, then, can we not have a situation in which the second source "destroys" the first?

the presence of information source $\hat{\Delta}$. Mixing or combining sources may make the source in question vastly more or vastly less important. As a hint of things to come, this is the reason that accounting theory cannot treat the accounting function in isolation. We must carry along other sources of information.

Summary

Surely accounting is a source of information, but carefully examining this colloquialism requires considerable setup. A major piece of this setup is modeling uncertainty and information. Our approach is to envision a state variable that tautologically carries all important uncertainty in whatever setting we find ourselves. We assign probabilities to the states to capture the notion of likelihood, both when it is objective and when it is subjective. *Uncertainty* is thus closely related to the calculus of probability.

Information is then modeled as a partition of this set of possible states. Eventually, we will learn to view an accounting system as providing a partition of some set of states, and, in this view, different "sets of books" are nothing other than different partitions.

The *partition* idea is at once conceptually useful and awkward. So at times, when this awkwardness becomes distracting, we will switch to *equivalent*, alternative specifications. Fundamentally, though, uncertainty is encoded in the state specification, and an information source is a partition of the set of states.

The partition idea also provides a partial comparison or ranking of information sources. This is based on the idea that if one source reports at least all that a second source might report, that first source provides "more" information than the second. In the state partition setup, this simply means the first partition is a *subpartition* of the second.

Accounting, of course, is not any old source of information, so we have yet to make clear what it means to say that accounting is a source of information and to address its comparative advantage as a source of some "type" of information (read that *partition*).

Selected References

Using the state idea to model uncertainty has its roots in Savage (1954), as mentioned. Marschak (1963) provides an excellent treatment. Information is treated in a variety of sources, including Demski and Feltham (1976), Demski (1980), Scott (1996), Beaver (1998), and Baye (1999). Marschak and Miyasawa (1968) and Feltham (1972) provide excellent, more formal treatments.

Key Terms

Uncertainty is the opposite of *certainty*, a lack of complete foreknowledge, a setting in which there is ambiguity as to what will transpire. This requires a specification of the "ambiguity as to what will transpire." For this we use the *state-act-outcome device* in which the outcome that will transpire, x, depends on the act chosen, a, and the state, s: $x = p(s, a)$. The state that "will obtain" is unknown, and this ambiguity is described by a *probability* measure on the set of possible states. **Information,** in turn, is something that provides insight into this ambiguity, something that revises the probability measure on the set of possible states. From a modeling perspective, we find it convenient to describe the information source as simply "shrinking" the set of possible states, in effect revealing something about states that are certain not to occur. This relies on an information source being a **partition** of the set of possible states, a collection of mutually disjoint subsets of the set of possible states whose union is the set of possible states. The information source then reveals which partition element contains the true state. In turn, one partition is a **subpartition** of a second partition if it "subdivides" the second, meaning each of its elements is a subset of an element of the second. Subpartition or **fineness** provides a partial ranking of information sources. Two information sources, two partitions, are **equivalent** if they reveal the same about the underlying state, if they are identical partitions.

Exercises

5.1. Accessing information presupposes uncertainty. Explain.

5.2. Suppose that you travel across time zones but do not reset your watch. Does your watch provide the same information in the new as opposed to the original time zone? Explain. Relate your answer to the notion of equivalent information structures.

5.3. Ralph's cash flow is uncertain; it will be either 100 or 400. In addition, Ralph will access an information source that will report signal "g" or signal "b." The joint probability of cash flow and signal are specified in the following table:

	CF = 100	CF = 400
Signal g	.10	.50
Signal b	.30	.10

Does the information source inform about Ralph's cash flow prospects? Carefully explain your answer. Next, calculate the mean and variance of Ralph's cash flow, conditional on each signal. Finally, provide an equivalent state-based description of this story. Be certain to identify the probabilities as well as the partition provided by the information source.

5.4. Consider the following setting in which D might be 10 or 20, and some information source might report "g" or "b":

	Signal g	Signal b
$D = 10$	.10	.40
$D = 20$	.40	.10

a. Determine the expected value of D, the expected value of D given signal g, and the expected value of D given signal b. What is the expected value of the conditional expected value of D?

b. Instead of revising the expected value of D in this fashion, think of the revised expected value of D as

$$\bar{D} = 15 + \epsilon$$

Specify the random variable ϵ: What values can it take on, and what is the probability of each? What is the expected value of ϵ?

c. Provide an equivalent state-based description of this story, including the information partition.

5.5. Suppose there are 10 possible, equally likely states: $S = \{s_1, \ldots, s_{10}\}$. Information source 1 will report signal "1" if the true state is one of the first five and "2" if it is one of the last five. Source 2 will report "odd" if the state index of the true state is an odd number (i.e., if the true state is one of $s_1, s_3, \ldots$) and "even" if the state index of the true state is an even number.

a. Specify the partitions of S that are provided by each source.

b. Then specify the partition provided by having access to both information sources.

c. In the latter case, suppose we have a single information source that maps S into the Greek letters $\{\alpha, \beta, \gamma, \delta\}$. Provide two such mappings that are informationally equivalent to observing the original sources 1 and 2.

5.6. Let $S = \{s_1, s_2, s_3, s_4, s_5\}$. Provide three partitions, one that is a subpartition of the second, which, in turn, is a subpartition of the third. Is the first a subpartition of the third? Finally, provide two partitions, neither of which is a subpartition of the other.

5.7. Repeat Exercise 5.4 using the following probability specification:

	Signal g	Signal b
$D = 10$	.10	.40
$D = 20$	.35	.15

5.8. We now find Ralph thinking about multiple sources of information. Consider the following matrix, concerning the cash flow random variable of $CF = 100$ or $CF = 200$, along with two information sources. One will report "g" or "b" while the other will report "g" or "b." Probabilities are given in the following table.

	$CF = 100$		$CF = 200$	
	g	b	g	b
g	.02	.16	.08	.04
b	.40	.02	.20	.08

a. Now suppose that we can observe both information sources. Determine the expected value of CF conditional on no information, on g only, on b only, on g only, on b only, and on g and g, g and b, b and g, and b and b. Also, can you express these changes in the expectation of CF as $140 + \epsilon_1 + \epsilon_2$, where the first "shock" term refers to that from the g/b observation and the second from the g/b observation? Explain.

b. Now suppose CF might be 300, 500, or 700. The only events with positive probability are the following four, and each has probability .25:

$g, g,$ and $CF = 700$

$g, b,$ and $CF = 500$

$b, g,$ and $CF = 500$

$b, b,$ and $CF = 300$

Again, we will track the expected value of CF as the g/b event is observed and then the g/b event is observed. Try to express this story as an expected value (of 500) that changes under additive innovations from the g/b event and from the g/b event. Explain.

Chapter 6

Information Use at the Individual Level

The information content theme stresses accounting as a source of information, but information and resource allocation go hand in hand. Information is useful to the extent that it improves the allocation of resources. This implies we must associate the information with specific resource allocation issues. Otherwise, we are unable to address even the most modest question of whether the information in question is likely to be useful. Eventually, we will stress the use of accounting information in the valuation of a firm and the evaluation of its management. The building block in these exercises is the use of information by a single individual, one facing an identified resource allocation issue under uncertainty. Having laid out the state partition device for modeling information, the natural next step is to develop this building block, the use of information by a single individual. In so doing, we emphasize the consistent use of information. Here rational behavior is essential. Later we want to compare information systems and, in most cases, the idiosyncratic details of the setting turn out to be important. Working with these details requires us to have facility with the tools of information use and, it turns out, risk aversion as well.

Having described uncertainty and information, we now turn to the use of that information by a single individual. This requires a model of resource allocation under uncertainty that is informed by the arrival of information. For this purpose we use an expected utility formulation. This formulation presumes uncertainty and captures the arrival of information through systematic probability revision. It is also the building block for our subsequent study of the use of accounting in various settings.

Initially, we review the economic notion of *rationality*. This requires, essentially, that an individual's choice behavior, or resource allocation behavior, be so consistent that it can be modeled as if that individual were behaving according to some overriding criterion or maximizing some objective function. We then specialize this notion of consistent behavior so that this "objective function" relies on tastes, encoded in a utility function, and beliefs, encoded in a probability assessment. From here we introduce the notions of *risk* and *risk aversion*, important concepts in our subsequent study. Finally, information is introduced, and its use in the resource allocation exercise is explored. Importantly, information content is fully described in this setting by systematic probability revision coupled with altered choice behavior based on that revision.

ECONOMIC RATIONALITY

The idea of *economic rationality* is rather simple. It is choice behavior so consistent that it can be described as though the choice maximized some objective function. Consistent profit and utility maximization are familiar examples.

Suppose an individual, here called a *decision maker*, is confronted with a set of alternative choices. These are listed or contained in the (nonempty) set $A = \{a_1, a_2, \ldots, a_n\}$. The decision maker must select one and only one of these possible choices. The set A is given, and one element from that set, one $a \in A$, must be chosen.

Consistency now enters in the following manner. Think of the set of alternative choices as coming from a large set, denoted $\underline{A}$. So, the available alternatives are $A \subseteq \underline{A}$. We now want to represent the selection of the preferred alternative by maximization of an objective function, denoted $F(a)$, no matter which subset of $\underline{A}$ is available in the decision problem at hand. This $F(a)$ is usually called a *utility function*. That is, we want to describe the decision maker to be acting *as if* the person were solving the following mathematical problem:

$$\text{maximize } F(a)$$
$$\text{subject to } a \in A \qquad\qquad \textbf{(6.1)}$$

where the objective or utility function, $F(a)$, does not depend on which (nonempty) subset, $A \subseteq \underline{A}$, of opportunities is available.

For this to be a valid characterization of a choice problem, independent of the specification of A, some regularity, some consistency, on the part of the decision maker is essential. This regularity is called *economic rationality*.

First, the decision maker's preferences must be complete. This means that whenever confronted with two alternatives, a_1 and a_2, belonging to the set $\underline{A}$, the decision maker must be willing and able to make a choice: The decision maker strictly prefers a_1, strictly prefers a_2, or is indifferent between the two choices. Our rational decision maker must never let us down by claiming or exhibiting an inability to make a choice. Of course, if the decision maker were confused in this sense, the desired $F(a)$ function could not exist. There would be no logical basis on which to define it at the point of confusion.

Second, these preferences must be transitive. Suppose that the decision maker prefers a_1 over a_2 and at the same time prefers a_2 over a_3. Then the decision maker must prefer a_1 over a_3. This requirement rules out circular preferences. If transitivity were violated, we would have a_1 preferred to a_2 and a_2 preferred to a_3 and, furthermore, a_3 preferred to a_1. Essentially, this is equivalent to the decision maker being unable to decide when confronted with a choice problem that contained just these three possible choices. When comparing any two of the alternatives, the decision maker would do fine but confronted with all three would be confused. Notice that if the decision maker were confused in this sense, were intransitive, then the desired $F(a)$ function would simply not exist because it would require $F(a_1) > F(a_2) > F(a_3) > F(a_1)$, which implies that $F(a_1) > F(a_1)$.[1]

Taken together, these two conditions are awfully strong. If the set $\underline{A}$ is finite, completeness and transitivity are equivalent to stating that a function, the $F(a)$ function, exists and that it captures the individual's preferences. *Completeness* ensures that a comparison can always be made, and *transitivity* ensures that all the elements of $\underline{A}$ are ranked. Then it is easy to define a function that describes the preferences. For example, the ranking of the elements will do.[2]

If the set of possible choices is infinite (technically, not countable), then complete and transitive preferences are not quite sufficient for a utility function to exist. The preference relation must also be smooth. This is a technical requirement and mainly rules out pathological cases.

Economic rationality, then, amounts to behavior so consistent that it can be modeled as though the individual were guided by a criterion or utility function.[3]

---

[1] Recall that we compared or ranked information partitions in Chapter 5 using the notion of *subpartition*. Our conclusion was that this ranking was transitive but hardly complete. The difficulty is that the subpartition idea stresses the information side of the coin, absent the intended use. This theme resurfaces in the present chapter once our preliminaries are in place.

[2] If set $\underline{A}$ is finite, and if the individual's preferences are complete and transitive, there exists a function, $F(a)$, such that $F(a_1) > F(a_2)$ if and only if the individual prefers a_1 to a_2; and this holds for all pairs of elements in set $\underline{A}$. The reverse is also true: If such a function exists, then the preferences must be complete and transitive. This important fact was discovered in the late nineteenth century by Cantor (a mathematician of Danish ancestry).

[3] Consistency is the hallmark. Random choice is not part of rational behavior in a single-person setting. Also notice that more colloquial use of the term *rationality* equates it with seeking wealth, personal consumption, or stark self-interest. If done consistently, this is rational behavior, but nothing in the theory confines the desideratum to wealth or to personal consumption. It is all about consistency.

EXPECTED UTILITY REPRESENTATION

We now move to a specialized version of rationality, one that forces the structure of uncertainty onto the $F(a)$ function. This requires us to enlarge the description of the alternatives so some notion of uncertainty is visible. From there we place additional restrictions on the decision maker's preferences so that this "visible uncertainty" shows up in the $F(a)$ function itself.

The first part is easy; we simply return to the setup in Chapter 5 when we sketched a state-act-outcome description of an uncertain world. There, recall, decisions are viewed in terms of uncertain consequences. We model this in terms of a consequence or outcome, denoted $x \in X$, that depends on the individual's choice, act $a \in A$ and the realization of some uncertain state, denoted $s \in S$. This is all encoded in the outcome function, $x = p(s, a)$. In addition, the state uncertainty is encoded in the probability specification, $\pi(s)$.

Now, in one sense, we might simply proceed as before and envision a utility function $F(a)$ measuring the decision maker's preferences, but we want the state-act-outcome description to show through in the $F(a)$ function in the following sense:

$$F(a) = \sum_{s \in S} U(p(s, a))\pi(s) = E[U \,|\, a] \qquad \textbf{(6.2)}$$

The structure is important. It begins with a (second) utility function defined on the outcomes, $U(p(s, a)) = U(x)$. The outcome is uncertain, however, so $U(x)$ is a random variable. We then calculate the expected value of $U(x)$, given the choice $a \in A$ and using the probability measure, $\pi(s)$. The utility of choice $a \in A$, then, is the expected value of $U(x)$, given $a \in A$ is chosen. In our ever-expanding notation, we write this as $F(a) = E[U \,|\, a]$. Note well: Tastes are encoded in the $U(x)$ function, beliefs are encoded in the $\pi(s)$ function, and the two components, tastes and beliefs, are combined using the expectation operator.

We thus arrive at an objective or criterion function that relies on the underlying uncertainty. Moreover, when we finally get around to information, we will see that information operates, so to speak, by revising the $\pi(s)$ specification.

Of course, this added structure in the $F(a)$ specification does not come without cost. We must now satisfy an independence requirement in addition to the completeness, transitivity, and smoothness conditions discussed earlier.

The independence requirement is a statement of independence among the consequences for which the individual has preferences and the uncertain events. It cannot be that some consequences are valued differently (more highly preferred) in conjunction with some random events compared to some other events. Only the *probability* of an event occurring must be relevant, not the *specifics* of the event. Otherwise, the consequence does not fully describe the person's preferences. So stated, then,

EXHIBIT 6.1
Setup for Risky
Choice

	s_1	s_2
$a_1: x = p(s, a_1)$	0	0
$a_2: x = p(s, a_2)$	-100	200

the individual's preferences factor into a taste component, the $U(x)$ function, and a belief component, the $\pi(s)$ component.

Parenthetically, an equivalent, and more familiar, formulation relies on the underlying random variable, $U(x)$. If $\pi(x \mid a)$ denotes the probability of outcome $x \in X$, given choice $a \in \underline{A}$, we then have the following transformation of (6.2):

$$F(a) = E[U \mid a] = \sum_{x \in X} U(x) \pi(x \mid a) \qquad \textbf{(6.3)}$$

Here we emphasize the decision maker's preference or utility function defined over consequences, and each possible choice is represented by the probability distribution of the consequences it produces.[4] This equivalence relies on two facts: The state realization does not enter the utility measure except through the probabilities of the outcomes, and the probability distribution for the outcome depends on the choice.

Either way, the *expected utility* representation is silent on what a consequence is or what mathematical form $U(x)$ takes. For the remainder of the chapter, though, we assume x is simply dollars and $U(x)$ is strictly increasing. The latter means that the decision maker prefers more to fewer dollars.

Example

Suppose a choice must be made between two acts. Choice a_1 offers zero for certain while choice a_2 offers a 50–50 possibility of a gain of 200 or a loss of 100. The full state-act-outcome description, utilizing two equally likely states, is given in Exhibit 6.1.

Furthermore, suppose that the decision maker's utility function is the following negative exponential function

$$U(x) = -\exp(-\rho x) + 3 \qquad \textbf{(6.4)}$$

where the parameter ρ is set at $\rho = .01$. Evaluation of the two alternatives provides the following:

$$F(a_1) = E[U \mid a_1] = -\exp(0\rho) + 3 = -1 + 3 = 2$$

$$F(a_2) = E[U \mid a_2] = -.5 \exp(100\rho) - .5 \exp(-200\rho) + 3$$

$$= -.5(2.7183) - .5(.1353) + 3 = 1.5732$$

The certain alternative is preferred because $F(a_1) > F(a_2)$.

[4] To complete the transformation, the probability $\pi(x \mid a)$ is given by the sum of $\pi(s)$ over all $s \in S$ such that $p(s, a) = x$.

Conversely, suppose the decision maker's utility function is the following square root function:

$$U(x) = \sqrt{10{,}000 + x} \qquad \textbf{(6.5)}$$

This leads to the following evaluation:

$$F(a_1) = E[U \mid a_1] = \sqrt{10{,}000 + 0} = 100$$

$$F(a_2) = E[U \mid a_2] = .5\sqrt{10{,}000 - 100} + .5\sqrt{10{,}000 + 200}$$

$$= .5(99.4987) + .5(100.9950) = 100.2469$$

And here we have the opposite preference, as $F(a_2) > F(a_1)$.

Importantly, varying the $U(x)$ specification, the "taste" component of the exercise, leads here to conflicting conclusions about the preferred choice. For that matter, using $\rho = .0001$ in the negative exponential function will lead to $F(a_2) > F(a_1)$, and the use of

$$U(x) = \sqrt{100 + x}$$

in the square root function will lead to $F(a_1) > F(a_2)$. Intuitively, the first choice, a_1, is riskless, the second is risky, and tweaking the utility function varies the attitude toward risk.

Because this "attitude toward risk" will be important in what follows, we develop it with some care. To begin, it is useful to calculate for each alternative the certain amount that makes the decision maker indifferent between the uncertain alternative and that certain amount. This is called a *certainty equivalent* and is denoted by CE_a. The algebra is simple. For act $a \in \underline{A}$ we solve the following:[5]

$$E[U \mid a] = U(CE_a) \qquad \textbf{(6.6)}$$

The left-hand side is our usual expression, and this is equated to the utility of receiving $x = CE_a$ for certain. By construction, then, the individual is indifferent between choice a and receiving CE_a for certain. Clearly, one act preferred to another means the expected utility of the first exceeds that of the second, and this is equivalent to the CE of the first being greater than the CE of the second.

Turning to the choice problem in Exhibit 6.1, let CE_1 and CE_2 denote the respective certainty equivalents. For the risky alternative, and using the negative exponential utility function, CE_2 is calculated as follows:

$$E[U \mid a_2] = -.5\exp(100\rho) - .5\exp(-200\rho) + 3 = -\exp(-\rho CE_2) + 3$$

We readily find[6] $CE_2 = -35.5440$. Likewise, the certainty equivalent of the riskless opportunity (that guarantees $x = 0$) is simply $CE_1 = 0$. Viewed

---

[5] Think of this as inventing a new act that provides $x = CE$ regardless of the state. We then set CE such that, for the act in question, we have $F(a) = F(\textit{new act})$.

[6] In particular, $E[U \mid a_2] = 1.5732 = -\exp(-\rho(-35.5440)) + 3$, given $\rho = .01$. The underlying algebra will be detailed shortly.

from this perspective, our decision maker views the risky choice as equivalent to losing a guaranteed 35.5440.

Conversely, for the (initial) square root story, we solve

$$E[U \mid a_2] = .5\sqrt{10,000 - 100} + .5\sqrt{10,000 + 200} = \sqrt{10,000 + CE_2}$$

We find that $CE_2 = 49.4403$; our decision maker views the risky choice as equivalent to receiving a guaranteed payment[7] of 49.4403.

Next, think of the utility function as defined on the individual's total wealth and suppose there is an initial amount, x_0, that will be supplemented with the outcome of the risky choice in Exhibit 6.1. So in the root utility case, we now have a utility function of

$$U(x) = \sqrt{10,000 + x_0 + x}$$

and in the negative exponential case, we have a utility function of $U(x) = -\exp(-\rho(x_0 + x)) + 3$, where $\rho = .01$. Now solve for the certainty equivalents as the initial amount ranges between $x_0 = -9,000$ (a clear debt) and $x_0 = 9,000$. Results are plotted in Exhibits 6.2 and 6.3. Notice in the root utility case that CE_2 increases as initial wealth increases but it is a constant, independent of initial wealth in the negative exponential case.

What are we to make of this? First, the algebra should be understood. For the root utility case, we solve the following expression. (The left-hand side is $E[U \mid a_2]$, and the right-hand side is $U(CE_2)$.)

$$.5\sqrt{10,000 + x_0 - 100} + .5\sqrt{10,000 + x_0 + 200} = \sqrt{10,000 + x_0 + CE_2}$$

Doing so (try squaring both sides) reveals that x_0 does not factor out, and, indeed, CE_2 increases as x_0 increases.[8] Conversely, for the negative exponential case we solve the following expression:

$$-.5\exp(-\rho(x_0 - 100)) - .5\exp(-\rho(x_0 + 200)) + 3$$
$$= -\exp(-\rho(x_0 + CE_2)) + 3$$

Here, x_0 factors out. To see this, subtract 3 from both sides to get rid of the constant; then factor out $\exp(-\rho x_0)$ on both sides (using the fact $\exp(x + z) = \exp(x)\exp(z)$):

$$\exp(-\rho x_0)[-.5\exp(-\rho(-100)) - .5\exp(-\rho(200))]$$
$$= -\exp(-\rho x_0)[\exp(-\rho CE_2)]$$

---

[7] Alternatively, using $\rho = .0001$ in the negative exponential case gives us $CE_2 = 48.8750$ while using

$$U(x) = \sqrt{100 + x}$$

in the root utility case gives us $CE_2 = -25$.

[8] In particular, we find that

$$CE_2 = [.5\sqrt{10,000 + x_0 - 100} + .5\sqrt{10,000 + x_0 + 200}]^2 - 10,000 - x_0$$

EXHIBIT 6.2
Root Utility
Certainty
Equivalent, $-9{,}000 \leq x_0 \leq 9{,}000$

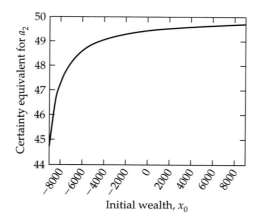

Initial wealth, x_0

EXHIBIT 6.3
Negative
Exponential
Certainty
Equivalent, $-9{,}000 \leq x_0 \leq 9{,}000$

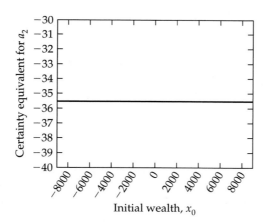

Initial wealth, x_0

That is, both sides are multiplied by the constant $\exp(-\rho x_0) > 0$. Once it is removed, we have

$$[-.5\exp(-\rho(-100)) - .5\exp(-\rho(200))] = -[\exp(-\rho CE_2)]$$

where we notice that x_0 has disappeared. CE_2 does not depend on initial wealth, x_0, in the negative exponential case.

Okay, that is the algebra, but what does it mean? In the root utility case, CE_2 varies with initial wealth, and this implies that choices will not, in general, be independent of the wealth of the decision maker. Just the opposite holds for the negative exponential case. The culprit is risk aversion: It varies with wealth in the root case but not in the negative exponential case.

Risk Aversion

A choice is *risky* if it has strictly positive probability on at least two outcomes (dollars in this case, recall). It is *riskless* if it delivers a specific

EXHIBIT 6.4
Setup for
Risk-Aversion
Illustration

	s_1	s_2
a_1: $x = p(s, a_1)$	100	100
a_2: $x = p(s, a_2)$	0	200

outcome with certainty (i.e., with probability one). In turn, an individual is *risk averse* if risk is regarded as noxious. What this means is, for any risky choice, the individual strictly prefers to receive the expected value of the outcome associated with that risky choice over the risky choice per se. If choice a is risky, in other words, a risk-averse person strictly prefers a choice that would guarantee $E[x \mid a]$ to choice a itself. Or, if you like to think in terms of certainty equivalents, *risk aversion* means that for any risky choice $a \in \underline{A}$, we have $E[x \mid a] > CE_a$.

Intuitively, risk aversion means insurance is a good thing provided it is not too expensive. $E[x \mid a]$ is simply the "fair insurance" value of choice a, and risk aversion simply means that fair insurance is strictly preferred to risky choice. Risk is noxious.[9]

Conversely, *risk neutrality* means that risk is a matter of indifference. This implies the individual is indifferent between fair insurance and the underlying risky choice, or $E[x \mid a] = CE_a$. This implies that the utility measure for an individual who is *risk neutral* is simply

$$U(x) = x \tag{6.7}$$

Now consider the two alternatives in Exhibit 6.4 in which the states are equally likely. The first is riskless; it guarantees $x = 100$. The second, of course, is risky, but it also has an expected value of $E[x \mid a_2] = .5(0) + .5(200) = 100$. A risk-neutral individual would be indifferent between the two, and a risk-averse individual would strictly prefer the first to the second.[10]

Risk aversion is present in our earlier utility functions. With $\rho = .01$ in the negative exponential function, (6.4), we have $E[U \mid a_1] = -\exp(-100\rho) + 3 = 2.6321$, which exceeds

$$E[U \mid a_2] = -.5\exp(0\rho) - .5\exp(-200\rho) + 3 = 2.4323$$

The respective certainty equivalents are $100 > 56.6219$. Likewise, the respective certainty equivalents in the root utility case, (6.5), are $100 > 99.7525$. Moreover, we know that initial wealth does not influence the certainty equivalent in the negative exponential case, but it does in the root utility case.

Now our intuition suggests that as the individual becomes "more risk averse," the certainty equivalent of risky choice a_2 should decline. Stay with the negative exponential case, and solve for the certainty equivalent in this case:

$$-.5\exp(0\rho) - .5\exp(-200\rho) + 3 = -\exp(-\rho CE_2) + 3$$

[9] In turn, $E[x \mid a] - CE_a$ is called the *risk premium*.
[10] For the risk-neutral case, (6.7), we have $E[U \mid a_1] = E[U \mid a_2] = 100$.

EXHIBIT 6.5
CE₂ as Function of Risk-Aversion Parameter, ρ

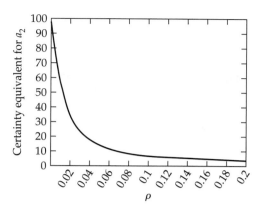

or

$$.5\exp(0\rho) + .5\exp(-200\rho) = \exp(-\rho CE_2)$$

Take the natural logarithm (i.e., ln) of both sides (the logarithm to the base $e = \exp(1) = 2.71828$) and remember that $\ln(\exp(z)) = z$. This gives us

$$\ln[.5\exp(0\rho) + .5\exp(-200\rho)] = \ln[\exp(-\rho CE_2)] = -\rho CE_2$$

or

$$CE_2 = (-1/\rho)\ln[.5\exp(0\rho) + .5\exp(-200\rho)]$$

Stare at this for awhile. The only thing CE_2 can depend on is the parameter ρ. In Exhibit 6.5 we plot CE_2 as ρ varies between 0 and .2.

Notice that the certainty equivalent declines as ρ increases and that as ρ approaches zero, the certainty equivalent approaches a value of 100 (the certainty equivalent for a risk-neutral individual). Larger ρ is tantamount to more risk aversion.[11]

Risk aversion, then, is just what it says, an aversion to risk. When it does not detract from the main message in our work ahead, we will use the more convenient case of risk neutrality, and when it is important, we

---

[11] Although we do not want to turn this into a treatise on risk aversion, an important fact underlies this demonstration. Suppose that the utility function, $U(x)$, is twice differentiable; examine the negative of the ratio of the second derivative over the first derivative. This ratio is called the *Arrow-Pratt measure of absolute risk aversion.* For our negative exponential utility function, this ratio is a constant:

$$-U''(x)/U'(x) = \rho$$

The ratio does not depend on "scale" so to speak. Indeed, we can turn this around and ask what utility function is implied by the Arrow-Pratt measure being a (positive) constant. The answer is a negative exponential function (of the form $U(x) = \alpha - \beta\exp(-\rho x)$, where α is an arbitrary constant and β is an arbitrary positive constant).

Conversely, for the original root utility measure, we find an Arrow-Pratt measure of

$$-U''(x)/U'(x) = .5/(10{,}000 + x)$$

This clearly depends on x. Indeed, it declines with x, a case of decreasing absolute risk aversion. (Here, you also see that strict risk aversion is equivalent to $U''(x) < 0$.)

will use a negative exponential formulation. The reason is that the negative exponential utility function exhibits risk preferences that are constant, so to speak, that are independent of the wealth of the decision maker, and we do not believe that wealth effects are a first-order effect when studying accounting theory.

Another item to note here concerns *scaling*. The utility function in the expected utility setup is not unique. It can be transformed by adding an arbitrary constant, say α, or by multiplying by an arbitrary positive constant, say β. A claim that $E[U \mid a_1] > E[U \mid a_2]$ is surely equivalent to a claim that $E[\alpha + \beta U \mid a_1] > E[\alpha + \beta U \mid a_2]$, for arbitrary α and arbitrary, though strictly positive, β.[12]

Subjective Probability

A final point in this discussion of expected utility concerns the probabilities. The decision maker's tastes, encoded in the $U(x)$ function, are inherently personal—but what about the beliefs encoded in the $\pi(s)$ function? To this point, we have simply relied on given, or exogenous, probabilities. These are called *objective probabilities*. This description is adequate in a number of cases. Flipping a coin, rolling a dice, or spinning a wheel of fortune will result in probabilities of this nature, provided an absence of fraud, but this is hardly descriptive of all real-life decision problems.

In those cases we rely on our judgment of the likelihood of the possible future events. This, of course, carries over to decision making. We would rather select an alternative with what we perceive to be high odds at succeeding than pick an alternative for which the odds are more modest but based upon objective probabilities. The point is that more generally we use personal beliefs to guide our decision making.[13]

IMPACT OF INFORMATION

Acquiring information before finalizing an important decision is a familiar exercise. We often search for a lower price, just as prior to acquiring an automobile we study consumer guides, interrogate our friends, and visit competing dealers. Similarly, it would be unusual to launch a new product

---

[12] So the constant, 3, in the negative exponential case, (6.4), is superfluous. Also notice that the Arrow-Pratt measure of risk aversion, discussed in Note 11, is the same regardless of which scaling option is invoked.

[13] Savage (1954) pioneered the work in this field. He developed a set of axioms leading to an expected utility representation of the individual's preferences including beliefs that are personal to the decision maker. Importantly, the notion of expected utility representation is not tied to objective probabilities. Our beliefs about tomorrow's weather or economy might very well enter our decision problem, despite the fact we might not agree with the forecasts of others. The conditions for personal beliefs that Savage developed mainly require rational betting behavior (i.e., complete and transitive coupled with a smoothness condition) along with a rich state description.

EXHIBIT 6.6
Details for Information Example

	s_1	s_2	s_3	s_4
$\pi_j = \pi(s_j)$	.15	.35	.40	.10
$a_1: x = p(s, a_1)$	0	0	0	0
$a_2: x = p(s, a_2)$	−100	−100	200	200
$y = \eta(s)$	g	b	g	b
$\pi(s \mid g)$	15/55	0	40/55	0
$\pi(s \mid b)$	0	35/45	0	10/45

without some form of market research.[14] Supposedly more information leads to an improved decision. This intuition also carries over to our abstract setting.

Basics

Recall that in Chapter 5, we utilized the state-act-outcome setup to model information as providing a partition of the set of states. We now combine this theme with expected utility analysis. An example is given in Exhibit 6.6 in which we have four states along with an information source. That source, labeled η, will report signal $y = g$ or $y = b$. Signal g is the revelation that the true state is in $\{s_1, s_3\}$, and signal b is the revelation that it is in $\{s_2, s_4\}$. To get the notation straight, system η maps states into the two signals, $y = g$ or $y = b$ in this case. This mapping, in turn, defines some partition of S, here given by $\Delta = \{\{s_1, s_3\}, \{s_2, s_4\}\}$. The partition is, of course, the substance of the information, and system or source η is simply some convenient scaling of that substance.

Initially suppose there is no access to this information. Choice a_1 guarantees an outcome of $x = 0$. Choice a_2 provides an outcome of $x = -100$ or $x = 200$ with 50–50 odds. This is the setting we originally used in Exhibit 6.1. All we have done here is to expand the state description to accommodate the identified information story.

Continuing, and using the negative exponential utility function, (6.4) (with $\rho = .01$), we know from our earlier work (surrounding Exhibit 6.1) that absent any information, the decision maker prefers the safe choice, a_1. Now suppose that signal $y = g$ is observed before this choice is finalized. This means $s \in \{s_1, s_3\}$ and leads to revised probabilities of $\pi(s_1 \mid g) = 15/55$, $\pi(s_3 \mid g) = 40/55$ and $\pi(s_2 \mid g) = \pi(s_4 \mid g) = 0$, as noted in Exhibit 6.1. The expected utility expressions, now conditioned on the observation of signal g and denoted $E[U \mid g, a]$, follow immediately:

$$E[U \mid g, a_1] = -\exp(0\rho) + 3 = 2$$

and

$$E[U \mid g, a_2] = -(15/55) \exp(100\rho) - (40/55) \exp(-200\rho) + 3 = 2.1602$$

[14] In another venue, we often see an elaborate evaluation of, say, a manager's performance. This will be taken up in subsequent chapters. For now, notice that the evaluation story has two or more explicit players in the game, and this alters in a fundamental way how we think about and use information.

The risky choice, a_2, is now preferred. Naturally, this is driven by the fact that signal g implies the risky choice is less risky than it was originally perceived to be.

In parallel fashion, observing signal b implies that $s \in \{s_2, s_4\}$ and leads to revised probabilities of $\pi(s_2 \mid b) = 35/45$, $\pi(s_4 \mid b) = 10/45$, and $\pi(s_1 \mid b) = \pi(s_3 \mid b) = 0$. The expected utility expressions, now denoted $E[U \mid b, a]$, are

$$E[U \mid b, a_1] = -\exp(0\rho) + 3 = 2$$

and

$$E[U \mid b, a_2] = -(35/45)\exp(100\rho) - (10/45)\exp(-200\rho) + 3 = .8557$$

No surprise here. Signal $y = b$ implies the risky choice, a_2, is even more risky and a_1 is preferred.

Now, signal $y = g$ will be observed with probability $\pi(g) = .55$, and $y = b$ will be observed with probability $\pi(b) = .45$. So the expected utility of observing the signal and acting appropriately is[15]

$$E[U \mid \eta] = \pi(g)E[U \mid g, a_2] + \pi(b)E[U \mid b, a_1]$$
$$= .55(2.1602) + .45(2) = 2.0881$$

Do not miss the notation: $E[U \mid \eta]$ is the individual's expected utility if the signal from information source η can be observed before acting and the individual then acts appropriately (i.e., selects the conditionally best act upon observing that signal). Moreover, our individual in this case is quite happy to access this information because $E[U \mid \eta] = 2.0881 > E[U \mid a_1] = 2 > E[U \mid a_2] = 1.5732$.

It is important, however, to take a larger view of this analysis. Before the information arrives but knowing it is about to arrive, the decision maker has four options: (1) select a_1 regardless of the signal, (2) select a_2 regardless of the signal, (3) select a_1 if signal g is observed and a_2 otherwise, and (4) select a_2 if signal g is observed and a_1 otherwise. Think of each such option as a policy, strategy, or function that assigns a particular choice, a_1 or a_2, to each signal, y. These "policy alternatives" or strategies are laid out in Exhibit 6.7 in an expanded version of our original state-act-outcome display in which the policy or strategy function is denoted $\hat{a}(y)$.

Evaluating these four strategies returns us to familiar ground:

$$E[U \mid \hat{a}(g) = a_1, \hat{a}(b) = a_1] = -\exp(0\rho) + 3 = 2$$

$$E[U \mid \hat{a}(g) = a_2, \hat{a}(b) = a_2]$$
$$= -.50\exp(100\rho) - .50\exp(-200\rho)] + 3 = 1.5732$$

$$E[U \mid \hat{a}(g) = a_1, \hat{a}(b) = a_2]$$
$$= -.35\exp(100\rho) - .55\exp(0\rho) - .10\exp(-200\rho)] + 3 = 1.4851$$

---

[15] It is often helpful to formally draw the individual's decision tree.

EXHIBIT 6.7
State-Policy-Outcome Summary for Information Example

	s_1	s_2	s_3	s_4
$\pi_j = \pi(s_j)$	.15	.35	.40	.10
$y = \eta(s)$	g	b	g	b
(1): $\hat{a}(g) = a_1$, $\hat{a}(b) = a_1$	0	0	0	0
(2): $\hat{a}(g) = a_2$, $\hat{a}(b) = a_2$	−100	−100	200	200
(3): $\hat{a}(g) = a_1$, $\hat{a}(b) = a_2$	0	−100	0	200
(4): $\hat{a}(g) = a_2$, $\hat{a}(b) = a_1$	−100	0	200	0

and

$$E[U \mid \hat{a}(g) = a_2, \hat{a}(b) = a_1]$$
$$= -.15 \exp(100\rho) - .45 \exp(0\rho) - .40 \exp(-200\rho)] + 3 = 2.0881$$

The first two strategies ignore the information and return us to the original setting. The latter two use the information, and the best choice—strategy 4—is to select a_2 if g is observed and a_1 if b is observed, with an expected utility evaluation of $E[U \mid \hat{a}(g) = a_2, \hat{a}(b) = a_1] = 2.0881$.

This policy, of course, is precisely what we discovered earlier: $E[U \mid \hat{a}(g) = a_2, \hat{a}(b) = a_1] = E[U \mid \eta]$. Now you know what we meant when we labeled $E[U \mid \eta]$ the expected utility of observing the signal from information source η and "acting appropriately" once that signal was observed.

Also notice the increased possibilities displayed in Exhibit 6.7. Originally, without any information, the individual was confined to the first two policies, but access to the information makes the latter two policies feasible as well. Information can be empowering!

More Notation

To connect explicitly to the partition theme in Chapter 5, complete with lots of notation, let the information source, again denoted η, provide a partition of the set of states, say $\Delta = \{\delta_1, \delta_2, \ldots, \delta_m\}$. Signal y corresponds to some particular element of this partition, and for the sake of argument, let's assume it directly reports that partition element without any additional scaling. A specific policy corresponds to one choice of $a \in A$ for $y = \delta_1$, one choice of $a \in A$ for $y = \delta_2$, and so on. In condensed format, this policy is denoted by $\hat{a}(y)$, a function that specifies precisely one choice of $a \in A$ for each possible signal.

Essentially, when we focus on the best policy to use in some information environment, we are "rolling the decision tree back" to the point at which the information is to be acquired. Viewed in this manner, we readily see that the impact of introducing additional information in a decision problem is equivalent to expanding the set of possible choices. The original choices continue to be available. Consequently, the decision maker is always weakly better off getting additional information, presuming it is costless,[16] but new possibilities that depend on switching the choice as a function of what information is reported are also introduced. This expansion is apparent in Exhibit 6.7 and in the following formalization:

$$E[U \mid \eta] = \max_{\hat{a}(y)} \sum_{y = \delta \in \Delta} \sum_{s \in y} U(p(s, \hat{a}(y)))\pi(s)$$

$$= \sum_{y = \delta \in \Delta} \pi(y) \max_{a_y \in A} \sum_{s \in y} U(p(s, a_y))\pi(s)/\pi(y)$$

$$= \sum_{y = \delta \in \Delta} \pi(y) E[U \mid y, a_y^*)] \qquad\qquad \textbf{(6.8)}$$

The first line is simply the activity of selecting the best policy as we did in Exhibit 6.7. The second line multiplies and then divides by the signal probability, $\pi(y)$, and moves the policy choice to a signal-by-signal format of selecting the best $a_y \in A$ to match with each signal y. The third line merely reports that the resulting inner maximization is what we did originally, with a_y^* being the optimal choice in the presence of signal y.

The point here is that we view the impact of information either as an expansion of the feasible choices (because the choice set now consists of all functions from the possible signals into the original opportunity set, A) or as a sequential decision problem such that after signal y is observed, the corresponding optimal act, a_y^*, is chosen. The two views are equivalent.

Information Content

The other feature to notice in (6.8) is that either way, the information is processed by revising the probabilities in consistent (Bayesian) fashion. Use rests here on the updated beliefs, that is, $\pi(s \mid y) = \pi(s)/prob(y)$. Information, we have stressed, has the power to tell us something that we do not know, and what we do not know is, under expected utility representation at the individual level, encoded in the probabilities. Information, pure and simple, affects the probabilities, in systematic fashion, in this setup.

Now glance back at the illustration in Exhibits 6.6 and 6.7. The information source reported one of two signals, $y \in \{g, b\}$, and it turned out that the optimal policy set $a_g^* = a_2$ and $a_b^* = a_1$. The individual's choice depends on the signal received. This is what we mean by *information content* in this setting: The individual finds it advantageous to act on the information. Source η has information content in this setting if the individual's choice is affected by that information, if a_y^* is not identical for all possible signals. It is as simple as that.

---

[16] Remember that we are presently working with a single individual. This individual's decision outcome depends on the act chosen and the state realization. It does not depend in any way on what others might do. Once this latter possibility is introduced, it is possible that acquiring even free information is a bad idea because of the reaction on the part of these other players.

COMPARISON OF INFORMATION SOURCES

From here it is a short step to compare two information sources. Suppose the individual must select between sources η_1 and η_2. The first is as good a choice as the second source whenever $E[U \mid \eta_1] \geq E[U \mid \eta_2]$. Naturally, the evaluation is forward looking; it depends on what the individual anticipates doing with the information.[17]

This, of course, hints at the issue of selecting from among a set of potential information sources. As noted, with the machinery in place, this is a conceptually straightforward exercise. It is also an elaborate exercise, however, because it relies on intimate knowledge of how the information will be used. This leads to the question of what can be said without digging into the details of the $E[U \mid \eta]$ evaluation.[18]

It turns out that pursuing this question of streamlined evaluation leads us back to the subpartition idea developed in Chapter 5. Remember that the substance of any information source, our η, is the partition of the state set it provides. Now glance back at Exhibit 6.7, where we moved from no information to the $y = g$ or $y = b$ story, which was, in fact, the partition $\Delta = \{\{s_1, s_3\}, \{s_2, s_4\}\}$. This partition, this Δ, is also surely a subpartition of the no-information case partition. Also recall that, as in Exhibit 6.7, the effect of information is to expand the set of possible decisions because a decision can be interpreted as a strategy with one choice for each possible information signal.

This suggests that *comparison of two information sources*, which amounts to comparing two partitions, is easy when the first is a subpartition of the second. In that case, the set of strategies that is feasible for the second information system is also feasible for the first. (Again, in Exhibit 6.7, only the first two of the four strategies are feasible in the no-information case.) Therefore, absent cost differences, the decision maker is at least as well off having access to the first as opposed to the second system.

To explore this further, we return to the illustration in Chapter 5 where S had three elements: $S = \{s_1, s_2, s_3\}$. In Exhibit 6.8, we list, in a repeat of Exhibit 5.10, all possible partitions of S, and the associated subpartition relationships.

Next, suppose that we face a decision problem in this setting in which choice must be made between acts a_1 and a_2. All possible act and state

---

[17] Likewise, if cost is a consideration that, too, is factored into the consequences or outcome.

[18] Accounting thought, for example, has long taken a more distant view in which accounting principles are articulated or information is analyzed in terms of qualitative characteristics such as relevance and reliability. The FASB, for example, guides its decisions without explicit reference to or perhaps even without intimate knowledge of the precise context in which the information is or might be used. In so doing, it relies on more broad brush interpretations, coupled with the use of qualitative characteristics such as relevance and reliability. We will return to this theme in Chapter 19.

EXHIBIT 6.8
Subpartition
Relationships

Label	Partition	Subpartition of
Δ_0	$\{\{s_1, s_2, s_3\}\}$	Nothing but Δ_0
Δ_1	$\{\{s_1\}, \{s_2, s_3\}\}$	Δ_0, Δ_1
Δ_2	$\{\{s_2\}, \{s_1, s_3\}\}$	Δ_0, Δ_2
Δ_3	$\{\{s_3\}, \{s_1, s_2\}\}$	Δ_0, Δ_3
Δ_4	$\{\{s_1\}, \{s_2\}, \{s_3\}\}$	$\Delta_0, \Delta_1, \Delta_2, \Delta_3, \Delta_4$

EXHIBIT 6.9
Feasible Strategies
for Two-Act Setting

	$a = \hat{a}(s)$			
	s_1	s_2	s_3	**Enabling Partitions**
1	a_1	a_1	a_1	$\Delta_4, \Delta_3, \Delta_2, \Delta_1, \Delta_0$
2	a_1	a_1	a_2	Δ_4, Δ_3
3	a_1	a_2	a_1	Δ_4, Δ_2
4	a_1	a_2	a_2	Δ_4, Δ_1
5	a_2	a_1	a_1	Δ_4, Δ_1
6	a_2	a_1	a_2	Δ_4, Δ_2
7	a_2	a_2	a_1	Δ_4, Δ_3
8	a_2	a_2	a_2	$\Delta_4, \Delta_3, \Delta_2, \Delta_1, \Delta_0$

combinations are listed in Exhibit 6.9. Notice that always selecting a_1 or always selecting a_2 is feasible regardless of the information partition. In all other cases, the "switching" among states requires the underlying state identification to be provided by the information at hand. So, for example, the second strategy requires us to know when state s_3 is present, which means we must be accessing partition Δ_4 or partition Δ_3. Furthermore, notice that for all the substantive strategies—those for which switching does take place—the enabling partitions are ranked by the subpartition relationship. We are on to something! Any strategy that is feasible with partition Δ_3, say, is also feasible with partition Δ_4, and partition Δ_4 is a subpartition of partition Δ_3. Partition Δ_4 tells us all that Δ_3 tells us and more.

The reverse is also true. If all decision makers prefer one partition, Δ, to another, $\hat{\Delta}$, then partition Δ is a subpartition of (or is as fine as) partition $\hat{\Delta}$. To see this, consider the two examples in Exhibits 6.10 and 6.11 using our three-state world. The three states are equally likely.

Notice that the best you could do in either case is a prize of $x = 200$, but to guarantee this, you must distinguish state s_1 in the first case and state s_2 in the second case. Further suppose, however, that the only information possibilities are partitions Δ_1 and Δ_2 in Exhibit 6.8, so Δ_1 distinguishes state s_1 and Δ_2 distinguishes state s_2. Clearly, Δ_1 is preferred in the first case, just as Δ_2 is preferred in the second case. Equally clear, neither partition is a subpartition of, or as fine as, the other.

EXHIBIT 6.10
Setup for Risky
Choice I

	s_1	s_2	s_3
a_1	200	−100	−100
a_2	−100	200	200

EXHIBIT 6.11
Setup for Risky
Choice II

	s_1	s_2	s_3
a_1	−100	200	−100
a_2	200	−100	200

The idea is that when two information sources are not ranked by the subpartition relationship—by fineness—we can find a pair of decision problems such that one partition is preferred in one case whereas the other partition is preferred in the other case. This proves for the specific case that only when the information sources are ranked by the subpartition idea—by fineness—can we expect all decision makers to prefer one over the other. However, the line of proof (by contradiction) is easily generalized to include all possible settings.

The conclusion from this meandering is awfully important. Let S be a given set of states. A choice problem defined on S consists of some choice possibilities, set A; the outcomes, $x = p(s, a)$; the preferences, $U(x)$; and the beliefs, $\pi(s)$. Also suppose that, for this choice problem, we must also select between two information sources, denoted η_1 and η_2. Naturally, the first is as good as the second only when $E[U \mid \eta_1] \geq E[U \mid \eta_2]$. The following fact now emerges:[19]

> Let η_1 and η_2 be two (equally costly) information sources that induce partitions of state set S. Then $E[U \mid \eta_1] \geq E[U \mid \eta_2]$ for all choice problems defined on S if and only if the partition induced by η_1 is a subpartition of (is as fine as) the partition induced by η_2.

To illustrate, suppose we are forced to choose between two partitions, two information sources. Without getting into the specifics of precisely how that information will be used, we cannot say which partition is preferred unless we are in the happy circumstance that one is a subpartition

---

[19] This is the partition version of what is called the *Blackwell theorem*. A formal proof is available in a variety of places (e.g., Marschak and Miyasawa, 1968). The intuitive idea is that one information source is better than another, regardless of circumstance, if it reports all that the other source reports and something else (i.e., if it retains all of the original options and adds some more). Moreover, the basic idea extends to information sources that are not modeled with the formal state partition setup. (See note 13 in Chapter 5.) In addition, it is important to remember that this is a single-person setting. In a strategic setting, it is quite possible that obtaining better information can be harmful simply because of the competitor reaction it induces. We will see this phenomenon at play in subsequent chapters.

of another. If one is a subpartition of the other, we know it provides at least as much information as the second and then all decision makers prefer the finer information source, or system. As noted in Chapter 5, this ranking is incomplete.

SEPARABILITY CONCERNS

A final topic here is the issue of separability. Can we, in general, concentrate on a single information source when multiple sources are present? This is a close cousin to the question in Chapter 2 of whether the multiproduct firm's cost function separates. There the answer was not very reassuring, and the same is true here. In general, our analysis of a particular information source depends on what other information is present.

This seemingly simple observation has a profound effect on the way we study accounting. It is the exception, not the general rule, that accounting-based information can be studied in the absence of other sources of information.

This lack of separability is more apparent when we frame the analysis of a particular information source in terms of the "value" of the information that source provides. This is explored in the Appendix to this chapter.

Summary

The key to understanding accounting issues is to look ahead to how the renderings by the accounting system might be used. In putting this theme to work, we stress the role of accounting as a provider of information. This requires us to envision someone using that information.

The building block for this purpose is an economically rational individual, someone so consistent that an *expected utility* view of that individual's choice behavior is possible. This means the individual is equipped with preferences, encoded in $U(x)$, and beliefs, encoded in $\pi(s)$, and acts as if choice were driven by the expected value of $U(x)$ that is induced by the choice. In corollary terms, when confronted with information, our individual systematically revises those beliefs but not $U(x)$ itself. In this respect, our individual is far from a casual or naive consumer of information. To the contrary, our individual is a sophisticated consumer of information, in effect using Bayesian revision to wring every bit of insight out of an information release.

Why, you might ask, do we invoke such powerful machinery at this point? One reason is that we want to stress, as a first-order effect, the use of accounting information in a *consistent manner*; this implies systematic (i.e., Bayesian) revision of probabilities. A second reason is signaled by our work *comparing information sources*: If one source's partition is not a subpartition of the other source, we must look to the idiosyncratic details of the setting to sort out which information source is to be preferred. This requires a coherent way of dealing with the idiosyncratic details. A third reason is that the value of information depends on the *presence of other information sources*. Finally, risk aversion plays an important role in our work ahead, and the very notion and measurement of risk aversion are straightforward exercises in the world of expected utility analysis.

We close with two cautionary observations. First, this chapter focuses on a *single individual*. Once we introduce *multiple individuals*, we will learn that the consequences of information being available are not a simple, straightforward extension of what we see in the single-person case. Second, *expected utility analysis* places a premium on sophistication, and people routinely fall short of this level of sophistication when confronted with elementary experimental tasks. They tend to be oversensitive to small probability effects, to fall prey to overreliance on prototypes or experience, to extract "less" than is present via Bayesian revision, and to be influenced by the manner in which a decision or choice opportunity is presented. As a first-order effect, however, the building block of sophisticated, consistent use of information will provide a compelling, insightful basis for our study of accounting.

Appendix

Value of Information

Analysis of a particular information source depends on what the individual might learn from that source as well as the cost of obtaining the information in question. We have, for expositional reasons, ignored the cost of information, yet, as is the case with most commodities and services, information is hardly costless. This implies a trade-off between giving up resources in exchange for the information and the improved decision that is the consequence of having the information.

This leads to a commonplace colloquialism, the "value of information." One way to place structure on this phrase is to claim the information has value if the decision maker's expected utility is higher with than it is without the information. While certainly true to the theme, this merely restates the obvious and does so using the particular scaling of the decision maker's utility measure.

With the decision's consequence, x, measured in dollars, a more natural approach would be to seek a measure in dollars. The most commonly used measure is to ask how much would the decision maker be willing to pay for the information.

Some streamlined notation (What else?) will help. Let η again denote the information system, or source, in question, and η^0 the absence of that information source. Also let $E[U \mid \eta^0]$ denote the decision maker's maximum expected utility in the absence of the information. Now, the most that the decision maker would be willing to pay for information source η is that amount V that, if paid, would drive the decision maker to indifference between acquiring that information, at price V, and proceeding in its absence (meaning settling for an expected utility of $E[U \mid \eta^0]$). Naturally, paying V for the information leads to a net outcome or consequence of $x = p(s, a) - V$. Identifying this maximum price also entails solving the following for V in this slight extension of the notation in (6.8):

$$E[U \mid \eta^0] = \sum_{y=\delta \in \Delta} \pi(y) \max_{a_y \in A} \sum_{s \in y} U(p(s, a_y) - V)\pi(s)/\pi(y) \quad \textbf{(6.9)}$$

The left-hand side is the expected utility without the information, and the right-hand side is the expected utility with the information, given it has a price of V.

To illustrate, we found in the previous example that the expected utility in the absence of any information was $E[U \mid \eta^0] = 2$ (which implies a certainty equivalent of $CE = 0$). Conversely, with the noted information, we found that $E[U \mid \eta] = 2.0881$ (which implies a certainty equivalent of 9.2251). Solving (6.9), we find (1) $V = 9.2251$; (2) the optimal choice under signal $y = g$ is $a_g^* = a_2$; and (3) the optimal choice under signal $y = b$ is $a_b^* = a_1$. Indeed, we also see that V is the difference between these noted certainty equivalents.

Lest you begin to think life is simple, however, this algebraic connection depends on the decision maker exhibiting a constant attitude toward risk. Intuitively, when we subtract V from the consequence of $p(s, a)$, we have to be careful that this "shifting" does not carry with it a change in attitude toward risk. For example, if the decision maker's attitude toward risk led to increasing risk aversion as the *net* x declined, the way that the information was used would, in principle, depend on how much was paid for that information. So, be wary; this value calculation, this V, places an upper bound on how much the decision maker would be willing to pay, but one source's V exceeding another's does not imply that the decision maker would select the first over the other.[20]

---

[20] This important but subtle point revolves around the difference between the most you would pay for something if you did not have it versus the least you would accept, if you had it, in trade. The two prices are identical under constant absolute risk aversion (i.e., risk neutrality or the negative exponential function) but not otherwise in general.

Another caveat concerns multiple sources of information. For example, the typical financial report contains accrual and cash basis renderings, two different partitions so to speak. In addition, some data do not pass the test for inclusion in the accrual accounting system yet are likely relevant for a given decision maker. Examples are order books, forecasted future sales, and the pricing of a competitor's product line. The important issues here are how to treat the arrival of multiple information sources and when an additional information source is of value.

The first issue, combining multiple information sources, was dealt with in Chapter 5. In the state partition format, the two sources simply define a new, refined state partition, and all proceeds as before. Thus, the use of multiple information sources is straightforward and, indeed, follows basically the rule of a single information source.

The "value" issue proceeds in equally transparent fashion except for interaction effects. Let η_1 be the original information system and η_{12} be the combined sources when we use η_1 along with a second source, η_2. Now consider the options of no information, only the first source, only the second source, or the two sources combined. Using our earlier notation and the implied optimal strategy or policy with each information environment, we envision respective expected utilities of $E[U \mid \eta^0]$, $E[U \mid \eta_1]$, $E[U \mid \eta_2]$, and $E[U \mid \eta_{12}]$.

From here, suppose that we calculate the most we would pay for the first (V_1), the second (V_2), or the combined (V_{12}) sources. To keep things simple, also suppose that we are dealing with a risk-neutral or negative exponential utility function. This way, the value of information is well defined by the preceding maximum buying prices. Now, what is the relationship among V_1, V_2, and V_{12}? It is routine to exhibit settings where (1) $V_{12} = V_1 + V_2$; (2) $V_{12} > V_1 + V_2$; and (3) $V_{12} < V_1 + V_2$. The first case is one in which no interaction is present, where separability is present. The second and third cases are a lack of separability: The second is when the two sources complement one another, and the third is when they are at least partial substitutes.

Selected References

Decision making and judgment is a deep, well-studied, and unsettled topic. Some personal favorites of your authors follow. For expected utility itself, introductory treatments are available in a typical economics text, such as Baye (1999); Demski (1980) also provides an introductory treatment. Formal treatments are available in, say, Kreps (1988) and, of course, Savage (1954). Kreps (1988) also deals with risk aversion, as does Pratt (1964). Difficulties with expected utility are studied in Nisbett and Ross (1980), Machina (1987), Bell, Raiffa, and Tversky (1988), Dawes (1988), Bazerman (1997), Plous (1999), and Starmer (2000). Finally, Maor (1994) is a delightful reference on the number e.

Key Terms

Economic rationality is behavior that is so consistent that it can be modeled as though the individual (or institution, for that matter) maximizes some objective function, that the choice behavior can be described in terms of maximizing behavior, as in expression (6.1). A specific version is **expected utility** representation, in which the objective function is the expected value of the utility associated with the various possible outcomes, as in expressions (6.2) and (6.3). A **certainty equivalent** is a guaranteed outcome that the individual views as equal in preference to some contemplated choice, the certain amount the individual views as equivalent to going forward with the contemplated choice, expression (6.6). An act, or choice, is **risky** if its outcome is not certain. The individual is **risk neutral** if risk is a matter of indifference—expression (6.7)—and **risk averse** if risk is regarded as noxious. In turn, the individual displays constant (absolute) risk aversion if the attitude toward risk is independent of scale or wealth, expression (6.5). **Information content** of an information source is tied to the use of the information. If the decision is a nonconstant function of the possible signals, the information source has information content. **Comparison of information sources** in turn depends on the use of the information, the very essence of expression (6.8).

Exercises

6.1. What is meant by the word *rationality*? What role is played by completeness? What role is played by transitivity?

6.2. In what sense is it rational to revise probabilities using Bayes' rule?

6.3. In constructing the expected utility evaluation associated with an information source, we used the phrase "selects appropriately upon observing that signal." Carefully explain the meaning of that phrase and its significance in our study of information.

6.4. Consider a risky choice, say one that provides $x = 100$ or $x = 400$ with equal odds. Determine the certainty equivalent for this choice, using $U(x)$ specified in (6.4), (6.5), and (6.7). Why is the certainty equivalent for a risky choice always less for a risk-averse individual than it would be were that individual risk neutral?

6.5. Consider the following variation on the story in Exhibit 6.1,

	s_1	s_2
$a_1: x = p(s, a_1)$	0	0
$a_2: x = p(s, a_2)$	$-100 - z$	$200 + z$

where $z \geq 0$. The riskless choice remains as before, but the risky choice now leads to $-100 - z$ or $200 + z$, with equal odds, of course.

However, the expected value of the outcome under the risky choice remains as before: $E[x \mid a_2] = .5(-100 - z) + .5(200 + z) = 50$.

a. Using the negative exponential utility function in (6.4) (along with $\rho = .01$), solve for the certainty equivalent of the risky choice for $z \in \{0, 25, 50, 75\}$. Interpret your findings.

b. Repeat for the risk-neutral case (in (6.7)).

6.6. Suppose that we rescale the utility functions identified in the text, in (6.4), (6.5), and (6.7). In particular, suppose we replace each $U(x)$ by $55 + 4U(x)$. (So, for example, the utility function in the risk-neutral case is now given by $55 + 4x$.) Repeat Exercise 6.5 using these three rescaled utility functions. Comment on your findings.

6.7. Ralph is now a game show contestant. The prize depends on Ralph's "guess" and which of four equally likely states materializes. So $S = \{s_1, s_2, s_3, s_4\}$. Ralph is risk neutral. Depending on the exact game, Ralph will also select from among a set of information partitions before making the all-important "guess." We concentrate on three possible partitions, or information structures. One, called "low/high," will tell whether the state will be one of $\{s_1, s_2\}$ or one of $\{s_3, s_4\}$. The second, called "odd/even," will tell whether the state will be one of $\{s_1, s_3\}$ or one of $\{s_2, s_4\}$. Finally, the third will tell whether the state will be $\{s_1\}$, $\{s_2\}$ or one of $\{s_3, s_4\}$. Call this last information source "low/high/plus."

a. Ralph initially participates in a game show that gives a prize if the contestant correctly predicts the state. The prize structure is as follows.

	s_1	s_2	s_3	s_4
Guess s_1	999	0	0	0
Guess s_2	0	999	0	0
Guess s_3	0	0	999	0
Guess s_4	0	0	0	999

Before making a guess, Ralph has the option to receive the signal from one of the three information sources. Which source should Ralph select? Why?

b. Ralph is popular and is invited to return to the game show. Now, however, all Ralph knows is the game will entail some choice from among alternatives whose prizes depend on which of the four states materializes. Before seeing the exact game to be played, though, Ralph must now select between information source low/high and information source low/high/plus. What is Ralph's best choice? Why?

c. Ralph returns one more time to the game show. A third appearance is reserved for clever participants. (No comment, please.) Initially, Ralph is told the game is the following:

	s_1	s_2	s_3	s_4
Guess odd	999	0	999	0
Guess even	0	999	0	999

Before playing, Ralph is also able to observe the signal from information source low/high or information source odd/even. Which information source should Ralph elect? Why?

d. Following this, Ralph is offered the following, concluding game.

	s_1	s_2	s_3	s_4
Guess low	999	999	0	0
Guess high	0	0	999	999

And again, before playing, Ralph is able to observe the signal from information source low/high or information source odd/even. Which information source should Ralph elect? Why?

6.8. Return to the setting in Exhibit 6.6, but now assume the individual is risk neutral. Determine the value of the information. Similarly, suppose the individual is risk averse with the utility function in (6.4) but now with $\rho = .1$. Determine the value of the information in this case. Comment on any pattern in the respective values.

6.9. Ralph is faced with one of life's tough choices, selecting a risk-free option that will net (cash flow of) $x = 410$ or a risky option that will result in $x = 100, 400,$ or 700, with respective probabilities of .15, .60, and .25. Ralph is risk neutral. Determine Ralph's best choice.

Now suppose Ralph will receive, at no cost, some information prior to making this choice. This information source will deliver one of two messages, coded y_1 or y_2. The joint probabilities, given the risky choice, follow.

	$x = 100$	$x = 400$	$x = 700$
y_1	.10	.20	.20
y_2	.05	.40	.05

(Thus, for example, the joint probability of cash flow of $x = 100$ and message y_1 is .10.) Initially, restate this setup in terms of six states, acts and, outcomes, and an information source that maps states into signals. Then provide an expanded version, parallel to Exhibit 6.7, that includes all of the policies Ralph might use were this information available. How much would Ralph pay for this information? If Ralph were very, very risk averse, what do you think would happen here?

6.10. Ralph faces a decision in which the (cash) outcome depends on choice and which of four equally likely states will materialize; so we have $S = \{s_1, s_2, s_3, s_4\}$. Two information sources are available. One, called "low/high," reveals the partition $\{\{s_1, s_2\}, \{s_3, s_4\}\}$. The second, called "odd/even," reveals $\{\{s_1, s_3\}, \{s_2, s_4\}\}$. Ralph is risk neutral. The outcome structure is given below, where we notice that the selection must be made from among four distinct acts.

	s_1	s_2	s_3	s_4
a_1	100	0	0	0
a_2	0	100	0	0
a_3	0	0	100	0
a_4	0	0	0	100

a. Determine the value to Ralph of (1) observing only low/high before acting, (2) observing only odd/even before acting, and (3) observing both information sources before acting. Are the values additive?

b. Repeat your analysis for the following structure of outcomes.

	s_1	s_2	s_3	s_4
a_1	100	0	0	-100
a_2	0	100	-100	0
a_3	0	-100	100	0
a_4	-100	0	0	100

6.11. Ralph, who is once again risk neutral, must select between a risky and a safe project. The safe project will net Ralph 140. The risky project will net Ralph $x = 100$ or $x = 200$. Odds are 50–50. Before deciding, Ralph also has the option to listen to information source 1 or to information source 2. Ralph cannot contact both sources; (for convenience) each source is free (or costless). So, at the start Ralph can (1) be dogmatic and proceed, (2) listen to source 1 and then proceed, or (3) listen to source 2 and then proceed. Either source will have one of two things to say, coded y_1 and y_2. If Ralph selects the risky alternative and the first information source, the joint probabilities are as follows.

	y_1	y_2
$x = 100$	.10	.40
$x = 200$	.40	.10

Conversely, the joint probabilities for the risky alternative and second information source are given by

	y_1	y_2
$x = 100$	.11	.39
$x = 200$	.29	.21

Determine the value of each information system to Ralph. What explains the implied preference?

6.12. Repeat Exercise 6.11, but assuming $U(x)$ given in (6.4), using $\rho = .0001$.

Chapter 7

The Accounting System as an Information Channel

We now deliver on our oft-repeated claim that accounting uses the language and algebra of valuation to convey information. The key step is to revisit our earlier depiction of accounting but now to formally add uncertainty to the story. The resulting accounting stock (or value) and flow (or income) functions become mappings from states into signals, precisely how we have modeled information. Two important themes follow. First, any substantive information delivered in this fashion is conveyed by the accruals. Second, using the structure of "the language and algebra of valuation" is without loss of generality; it imposes no significant restriction on the accounting apparatus. It is a wonderfully flexible information channel.

To this point we have put a model of a reporting firm in place, reviewed the classical approach to economic and accounting-based measures of stocks and flows, introduced the conceptual notion of information as a partition of some underlying set of states, and reviewed the essentials of consistent decision making in the presence of uncertainty and information. It is now time to expand our thinking, to formally, not metaphorically, treat accounting as a source of information. The immediate issue is how to go about doing this. Subsequent chapters deal with the question of what information is to be conveyed in this fashion.

We begin with the example of the three-period firm used in our earlier exploration of economic and accounting measurement. Expanding it to include uncertain cash flows and paying careful attention to the accounting system in place provide an illustration of what it means for an accounting system to serve as a source of information. We then provide an enlarged interpretation of this example and discuss two important questions: What information is conveyed by a particular accounting system? What, if any, are the limits, in principle, to an accounting system's ability to convey information? We then examine the difference between the information content and the valuation themes that are used to describe accounting measurement.

Keep in mind the fact that theory focuses on essential details, on important features or first-order effects in its role of putting structure on a class of phenomena. We now formally treat accounting as a source of information. This is accomplished by retaining the accounting structure of Chapter 4, the stock and flow functions, and adding uncertainty to the story. We continue in streamlined fashion with an asset total being reported along with a "bottom-line" income number; as before, this focus on essential details means that we continue to assume, for convenience, we are dealing with an all-equity firm.

AN OLD FRIEND

In Chapters 3 and 4 we relied on an illustration in which distinct products were produced and sold in each of three periods. The technology and prices were such that a profit-maximizing choice by the firm had $q_1 = 75$ being sold at $t = 1$ (at unit price 132), $q_2 = 100$ sold at $t = 2$ (at unit price 193.6), and $q_3 = 125$ sold at $t = 3$ (at unit price 266.2). Remaining details included a sequence of labor expenditures and physical capital with an initial cost of 25,000.

Exhibit 3.4 summarizes the various details, and we repeat it as Exhibit 7.1. Remember that the inflows are payments from customers, the initial outflow is the payment for the physical capital, and the subsequent outflows are the payments for the labor in the respective periods.

EXHIBIT 7.1
Cash Inflows and Outflows for Continuing Illustration

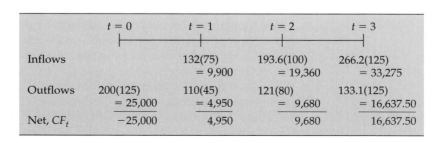

	$t = 0$	$t = 1$	$t = 2$	$t = 3$
Inflows		132(75) = 9,900	193.6(100) = 19,360	266.2(125) = 33,275
Outflows	200(125) = 25,000	110(45) = 4,950	121(80) = 9,680	133.1(125) = 16,637.50
Net, CF_t	−25,000	4,950	9,680	16,637.50

Now, to provide a setting in which information is present, we must introduce some uncertainty. To keep things uncluttered, suppose the selling price of the first product will be 132 ± 10 per unit and the selling price of the third product will be 266.2 ± 10 per unit. In each case $+10$ and -10 are equally likely events, and the two price events are also independent. This implies that we have four equally likely combinations to worry about: first up and third down, first up and third up, first down and third down, and first down and third up.

Further suppose the setting is otherwise identical to that assumed before (e.g., the interest rate is 10 percent, capital is limited to $K^{\max} = 125$, the spot price of first period labor is $p_{L1} = 110$ and so on) and the firm behaves in risk-neutral fashion. In addition, to keep the story as simple as possible, the firm must commit to its production schedule at time $t = 0$. This means that the firm will design its activities to maximize the expected value of the present value of its cash flows.

If you lay all of this out, you will notice the expected value of each selling price is equal to the assumed known price in the original story. So, the firm will settle on precisely the same input and output schedules as before. The only difference is that the inflows will depend on which prices prevail, and two of these prices are uncertain.[1]

Naturally, we model the four price combinations as associated with four (equally likely) states, denoted $S = \{s_1, s_2, s_3, s_4\}$. With our many assumptions, then, the firm's cash flow will depend on which prices prevail (i.e., on which state prevails). The calculations, for each state, are displayed in Exhibit 7.2.

In turn, we summarize these calculations with the state-dependent cash flow specification, **CF**(s), in Exhibit 7.3. Notice the expected value of each period's cash flow, denoted $E[CF_t]$, is, given our various assumptions, the cash flow amount we earlier assumed to be present with certainty.

---

[1] At the risk of being overbearing, remember that the first and third selling prices are uncertain, and that all other prices and the technology are both known and identical to what was initially assumed. With technology and factor prices all known, we arrive at the cost curve as originally derived. For example, staying in the region where the $K \leq K^{\max}$ constraint is not binding, the cost curve is what we derived earlier:

$$C(q_1, q_2, q_3) = 200\sqrt{2(q_1^2 + q_2^2 + q_3^2)}$$

In turn, the expected value of the present value of the receipts is

$$E[P_1(1.1)^{-1}]q_1 + P_2(1.1)^{-2}q_2 + E[P_3(1.1)^{-3}]q_3$$
$$= 132q_1(1.1)^{-1} + 193.6q_2(1.1)^{-2} + 266.2q_3(1.1)^{-3} = 120q_1 + 160q_2 + 200q_3$$

And we wind up with the maximizing exercise of

$$\underset{q_1,q_2,q_3 \geq 0}{\text{maximize}} \; 120q_1 + 160q_2 + 200q_3 - C(q_1, q_2, q_3)$$

which is what we had in the initial example.

EXHIBIT 7.2 **Cash Flow Calculations**

	$t = 0$	$t = 1$	$t = 2$	$t = 3$
State $s_1 - (P_1, P_3) = (142, 256.2)$				
Inflows		142(75) = 10,650	193.6(100) = 19,360	256.2(125) = 32,025
Outflows	200(125) = 25,000	110(45) = 4,950	121(80) = 9,680	133.1(125) = 16,637.50
Net, CF_t	−25,000	5,700	9,680	15,387.50
State $s_2 - (P_1, P_3) = (142, 276.2)$				
Inflows		142(75) = 10,650	193.6(100) = 19,360	276.2(125) = 34,525
Outflows	200(125) = 25,000	110(45) = 4,950	121(80) = 9,680	133.1(125) = 16,637.50
Net, CF_t	−25,000	5,700	9,680	17,887.50
State $s_3 - (P_1, P_3) = (122, 256.2)$				
Inflows		122(75) = 9,150	193.6(100) = 19,360	256.2(125) = 32,025
Outflows	200(125) = 25,000	110(45) = 4,950	121(80) = 9,680	133.1(125) = 16,637.50
Net, CF_t	−25,000	4,200	9,680	15,387.50
State $s_4 - (P_1, P_3) = (122, 276.2)$				
Inflows		122(75) = 9,150	193.6(100) = 19,360	276.2(125) = 34,525
Outflows	200(125) = 25,000	110(45) = 4,950	121(80) = 9,680	133.1(125) = 16,637.50
Net, CF_t	−25,000	4,200	9,680	17,887.50

EXHIBIT 7.3
Cash Flow Vector as a Function of State

$CF_t(s)$	s_1	s_2	s_3	s_4	$E[CF_t]$
$CF_0(s)$	−25,000	−25,000	−25,000	−25,000	−25,000
$CF_1(s)$	5,700	5,700	4,200	4,200	4,950
$CF_2(s)$	9,680	9,680	9,680	9,680	9,680
$CF_3(s)$	15,387.50	17,887.50	15,387.50	17,887.50	16,637.50
$\sum_t CF_t(s)$	5,767.50	8,267.50	4,267.50	6,767.50	

Do not miss the larger picture. The firm must decide, in the face of uncertainty, which combination of products, quantities, and factors is best.[2] Having so decided, it faces an uncertain cash flow sequence. As we see in Exhibit 7.3, one of four such sequences will materialize. Earlier, in the certainty world, we specified the economic facts with a cash flow vector, **CF**, and an interest rate, r. Here the cash flow vector depends on the state. Naturally, the interest rate might also depend on the state, but we will forgo that refinement.[3] So, the economic facts now take the form of a state-dependent cash flow vector and an interest rate.

[2] Just beneath the surface, then, is some outcome structure, described via $x = p(s, a)$ in Chapter 6. Here that outcome is a sequence of cash flows, and any given choice or decision implies some cash flow sequence that depends on the state.
[3] Interest rates would, presumably, reflect macro forces in the economy as well as a market-based synthesis of all available information in the economy.

Importantly, our original story has now expanded to include an uncertain cash flow sequence. We model this uncertainty using a state descriptor, $s \in S$. So, the firm's cash flow now depends on the state, and we write it $CF(s)$. Moreover, this $CF(s)$ specification reflects underlying choices by the firm.

Cash Flow Is a Source of Information

Initially, we remind ourselves that cash flow itself may and often does tell us something.[4] Would it, for example, be good news if a start-up company's cash flow from operations was unexpectedly large (and positive)? Would it be bad news if an established firm's cash flow from operations was unexpectedly low (and negative)?

This simple idea is also present in our example. We know that the selling prices of the first and third periods might be high or low. Observing the $t = 1$ cash flow, given our knowledge of the firm's environment and activities, allows us to figure out whether the first period's selling price was, indeed, high or low. A parallel comment applies to the third price and the $t = 3$ cash flow.

It will, however, be useful to address this in a more formal matter. Closely examine Exhibit 7.3. Each $CF_t(s)$ is a mapping from states, from S, into possible cash flows. For example, $CF_0(s)$ is constant across the states, while $CF_1(s)$ is 5,700 for the first two states but 4,200 for the last two. Thus, observing $t = 1$ cash flow of 5,700 tells us that $s \in \{s_1, s_2\}$. Likewise, observing $t = 1$ cash flow of 4,200 tells us that $s \in \{s_3, s_4\}$. Observing the $CF_1(s)$ realization at time $t = 1$ is equivalent to observing the partition $\{\{s_1, s_2\}, \{s_3, s_4\}\}$ at time $t = 1$. Cash flow is a source of information!

This follows, in a formal sense, simply because $CF_t(s)$ is, literally, a function of the state. So, all we do is interpret the realization of period t cash flow as a signal. At time $t = 1$, that signal is either 5,700 or 4,200. It is as simple as that.

Continuing, $CF_2(s)$ is constant across s, but $CF_3(s)$ is another story. Observing $t = 3$ cash flow of 15,387.50 tells us that $s \in \{s_1, s_3\}$. Likewise, observing $t = 3$ cash flow of 17,887.50 tells us that $s \in \{s_2, s_4\}$. Observing the $CF_3(s)$ realization at time $t = 3$ is equivalent to observing the partition $\{\{s_1, s_3\}, \{s_2, s_4\}\}$ at $t = 3$.

Of course, observing partition $\{\{s_1, s_3\}, \{s_2, s_4\}\}$ at $t = 3$ having already observed partition $\{\{s_1, s_2\}, \{s_3, s_4\}\}$ tells us exactly which state was present. For example, knowing that $s \in \{s_1, s_2\}$ and subsequently learning that

---

[4] Remember that our story began in a perfect market setting with no uncertainty. There was, therefore, no reason to hold cash on hand, so cash flow to and from the owners was stressed. Now treating this cash flow as a source of information is akin to treating dividends as a source of information. Enlarging the story to distinguish cash flow from operations would allow us to treat that construction as a source of information, but the expanded detail would not bring additional insight.

$s \in \{s_1, s_3\}$ implies $s = s_1$. In temporal terms, then, the story in Exhibit 7.3 is equivalent to the following sequence of partitions, or information sources:

$t = 0$: null.

$t = 1$: $\{\{s_1, s_2\}, \{s_3, s_4\}\}$.

$t = 2$: $\{\{s_1, s_2\}, \{s_3, s_4\}\}$.

$t = 3$: $\{\{s_1\}, \{s_2\}, \{s_3\}, \{s_4\}\}$.

Our story gradually grows in information from null to perfect. Given the underlying details, this gradual refinement to perfect information is no surprise. The only uncertainty is the selling price of the first and third period's products. With known quantities, observing cash flow as we march through time inevitably reveals all there is to know, but this reflects our particularly simple story. The important point is that the cash flow series is a source of information.

In a more subtle sense, we are working with a great deal of structure. We know the structure of the firm's decision problem, and we know or anticipate that its decisions will culminate in the cash flow possibilities, literally, the cash flow functions in Exhibit 7.3. Subsequently observing the cash flow realizations, knowing the mapping from states to cash flows, reveals something about the states. We begin, in other words, with a sound understanding of the firm's fundamentals. We therefore know the partition before us; we know Exhibit 7.3. We simply do not know which element of that partition is about to be revealed.[5]

Accrual Accounting Is a Source of Information

Now turn to the accrual reporting of this story. Initially recall the way we calculated accounting income for these transactions in the world of certainty. Revenue was recorded at the time of delivery to the customer (and payment from the customer). Labor cost was easily matched to revenue, thanks to the technology and payment timing assumptions. In addition, the physical capital was depreciated over the three-year horizon, using a generic depreciation schedule of d_1, d_2 and $25{,}000 - d_1 - d_2$. This earlier rendering, originally displayed in Exhibit 4.2, is repeated in Exhibit 7.4.

Suppose we adopt the same tack here. Revenue will be recognized at the time of delivery. Labor cost is matched, as noted, and depreciation is again identified in generic terms. This accounting system is installed at

---

[5] Return to the underlying story. We know the firm's technology, the factor prices it faces, and the uncertain product prices it faces. We know it behaves in risk-neutral fashion. We infer from all of this that its decisions lead to the cash flow possibilities in Exhibit 7.3, possibilities that turn on what the uncertain prices turn out to be.

EXHIBIT 7.4
Accounting Income Calculations for Transactions in Exhibit 7.1

	$t = 1$	$t = 2$	$t = 3$
Revenue	9,900	19,360	33,275
Labor expense	4,950	9,680	16,637.50
Depreciation	d_1	d_2	$25,000 - d_1 - d_2$
Accounting income	$4,950 - d_1$	$9,680 - d_2$	$d_1 + d_2 - 8,362.50$

EXHIBIT 7.5   **Possible Accounting Income Calculations for Data in Exhibit 7.3**

$\hat{I}_t$	s_1	s_2	s_3	s_4	$E[\hat{I}_t]$
$\hat{I}_1$	$5,700 - d_1$	$5,700 - d_1$	$4,200 - d_1$	$4,200 - d_1$	$4,950 - d_1$
$\hat{I}_2$	$9,680 - d_2$	$9,680 - d_2$	$9,680 - d_2$	$9,680 - d_2$	$9,680 - d_2$
$\hat{I}_3$	$d_1 + d_2 - 9,612.50$	$d_1 + d_2 - 7,112.50$	$d_1 + d_2 - 9,612.50$	$d_1 + d_2 - 7,112.50$	$d_1 + d_2 - 8,362.50$
$\sum \hat{I}_t$	5,767.50	8,267.50	4,267.50	6,767.50	6,267.50

time $t = 0$ and from that point on merely records transactions (and depreciation) as they occur. Of course, selling prices and, therefore, revenue depend on which state materializes. So, the income sequence will depend on the state. You should be able to replicate the accounting income calculations summarized in Exhibit 7.5. (To check our work and your intuition, notice the total income in each state equals the total cash flow in that state and the expected value of the income in each period equals the income for that period in Exhibit 7.4.)

For example, under state s_1, it is learned at $t = 1$, when the first product's revenue is recognized, that the product's selling price is 10 above expectation, resulting in first period income (i.e., $5,700 - d_1$) that exceeds what was expected by 75 units at 10 extra per unit, or 750. Likewise, at time $t = 3$ when the third product's revenue is recognized, a price of 10 below expectation per unit is recorded, resulting in a third period income that falls short of expectation by 125 units at 10 per unit, or 1,250. Naturally, with no price uncertainty associated with the second product, we have no surprise in the second period's income. Also, just as the cash flow each period is a mapping from states to possible cash flows, we see in Exhibit 7.5 that income each period, given a specific accounting method, is a mapping from states to possible income realizations.

Now turn to the information side of our work. Given the specified accounting treatment (i.e., the depreciation pattern of d_1 and d_2) and given our understanding of the firm's fundamentals (i.e., Exhibit 7.3), we know the details of Exhibit 7.5. We know, for example, first period income will be $5,700 - d_1$ or $4,200 - d_1$. Think of this as a mapping from states to signals. When we see a signal, an income, of $5,700 - d_1$, we know, since we know Exhibit 7.5, that $s \in \{s_1, s_2\}$. Likewise, when we see a signal, an income, of

$4,200 - d_1$, we know that $s \in \{s_3, s_4\}$. Thus, observing accounting income at time $t = 1$ is equivalent to observing the partition $\{\{s_1, s_2\}, \{s_3, s_4\}\}$. Simply working through Exhibit 7.5 should convince you that regardless of the choice of d_1 and d_2, observing accounting income as calculated in that exhibit is equivalent to observing the following partition sequence:[6]

$t = 0$: null.

$t = 1$: $\{\{s_1, s_2\}, \{s_3, s_4\}\}$.

$t = 2$: $\{\{s_1, s_2\}, \{s_3, s_4\}\}$.

$t = 3$: $\{\{s_1\}, \{s_2\}, \{s_3\}, \{s_4\}\}$.

Accounting measurement, then, provides in this case a mapping from states into accounting flows, or income. This mapping induces a partition on the set of states, and we thus have an information source, a partition. Cash and accrual basis measurement, that is, are simply two different ways of doing the accounting, and both, in principle, are sources of information.

Euphoria, though, needs to be checked; we have a slight problem with our example. The sequence of partitions induced by the accrual method in Exhibit 7.5 is identical to that induced by the cash basis (or cash flow) reporting in Exhibit 7.3. This is hardly surprising, though, because the depreciation pattern is confined to the constants d_1 and d_2. There is no way that such constants can carry any information to the accrual process. If accounting accruals reveal nothing, information wise, that is not discernible from the cash flow series itself, we have arrived at a particularly embarrassing, nebulous view of accounting.

RICHER REPORTING STRUCTURE

There are two keys to moving forward. One is to endow the accrual process with the ability to reveal more than simply tracking the cash flow. The accruals must access some underlying information and carry it forward into the accounts. For example, when a troubled receivable is written off, this write-off is based on additional information suggesting that the receivable will not be collected. Likewise, the usual accrual story based on the going concern assumption is actually a story based on the lack of

---

[6] We are focusing on the income measure because it strikes us as most intuitive in this particular setting. The same approach could be used by focusing on the balance sheet, although in this case we would want to focus on the point in time just before the cash balance is distributed to the firm's owners. Shortly, however, we will combine cash basis and accrual basis reporting, and this concern over the time at which the balance sheet is reckoned will be moot.

EXHIBIT 7.6   **Revised Accounting Income Calculations**

$\hat{I}_t$	s_1	s_2	s_3	s_4	$E[\hat{I}_t]$
$\hat{I}_1$	$5{,}700 - d_1 - d$	$5{,}700 - d_1$	$4{,}200 - d_1$	$4{,}200 - d_1$	$4{,}950 - d_1 - .25d$
$\hat{I}_2$	$9{,}680 - d_2$	$9{,}680 - d_2$	$9{,}680 - d_2$	$9{,}680 - d_2$	$9{,}680 - d_2$
$\hat{I}_3$	$d_1 + d_2 + d$	$d_1 + d_2$	$d_1 + d_2$	$d_1 + d_2$	$d_1 + d_2 + .25d$
	$-\,9{,}612.50$	$-\,7{,}112.50$	$-\,9{,}612.50$	$-\,7{,}112.50$	$-\,8{,}362.50$
$\sum \hat{I}_t$	$5{,}767.50$	$8{,}267.50$	$4{,}267.50$	$6{,}767.50$	$6{,}267.50$

information, suggesting that the going concern assumption is problematic. Our accrual rendering, then, cannot be as mechanical as that depicted in Exhibit 7.5 if we are to capture this essential feature of the accrual process.

The second key is to remember that we typically report cash and accrual-based measures. Treating both as information sources, then, requires us to carry along the substance and the fabric of multiple information sources.

Return to our example but further suppose the accrual system can record a restructuring charge at time $t = 1$, in the amount d, if the first period selling price is high but the third period price will be low.[7] Intuitively, the firm is experiencing good times (a high selling price) in the first period but also has learned that those good times will not continue (a low selling price will be forthcoming in the third period). So, the asset is written down via the additional charge of d. Glancing back at Exhibits 7.2 and 7.3, you should notice that this combination of high initial price followed by low subsequent price is the state s_1 story. We further assume, simply for convenience, that the firm cannot act on this foreknowledge of the third price. This means we stay with the original production plan and the cash flow details in Exhibits 7.2 and 7.3, but the accrual story is affected by this possibility. Details are in Exhibit 7.6.

Note well: Everything is as before, with the single exception that an additional expense, in the amount ($d \neq 1{,}500$) is recorded in state s_1. For *any* non-zero restructuring charge d and any depreciation pattern (d_1 and d_2), at time $t = 1$, we have three distinct income reports: $5{,}700 - d_1 - d$, $5{,}700 - d_1$, and $4{,}200 - d_1$. These three possible reports correspond, respectively, to $\{s_1\}$, $\{s_2\}$, and $\{s_3, s_4\}$. Just as before, the second period's income is constant across the states, and the third period's report will be one of three distinct reports (again, for any nonzero $d \neq 1{,}500$ and completely arbitrary d_1 and d_2). Overall, then, the proposed accounting system

[7] Remember that this illustration is purposely kept simple. The only uncertainty is the selling price in the first and third periods. With everything else kept constant, merely observing the cash flows will reveal what prices actually prevailed. So, if the accounting system is to tell us more than can be gleaned by observing cash flow, it must somehow be observing and acting upon something over and above the cash flows themselves.

is equivalent to the following sequence of partitions:[8]

$t = 0$: null.

$t = 1$: $\{\{s_1\}, \{s_2\}, \{s_3, s_4\}\}$.

$t = 2$: $\{\{s_1\}, \{s_2\}, \{s_3, s_4\}\}$.

$t = 3$: $\{\{s_1\}, \{s_2\}, \{s_3\}, \{s_4\}\}$.

The $t = 0$ and $t = 3$ partitions are identical to those provided by the cash flow itself, but the $t = 1$ partition is a subpartition of that provided by the cash flow measure. (That is, partition $\{\{s_1\}, \{s_2\}, \{s_3, s_4\}\}$ is a subpartition of $\{\{s_1, s_2\}, \{s_3, s_4\}\}$.) The same holds for the $t = 2$ position. Moreover, the $t = 2$ partition is identical to that of $t = 1$; as we accumulate information over time, we never forget. Initially, we know the depreciation and restructuring charge patterns. Given that, we interpret the observed accounting income by translating it into an element of the partition that is induced by the underlying process. We thereby learn more about which state of the world we are facing. This illustrates the idea of an accrual-based system carrying more information than a cash-based system.

Several points are in order. First, the movement from the accounting income report to the underlying partition is, as usual, a decoding exercise. It presumes we understand the firm's fundamentals and its choice of accounting method. The typical financial report, recall, details in the first note which accounting policies (e.g., depreciation and inventory valuation) are being used. In parallel fashion, we would never use an accounting system's measurement of product cost without knowledge of the costing procedures used to produce that datum. So the decoding begins with knowledge of the firm's fundamentals and knowledge of what accounting procedures the firm is employing. With this in place, the details in Exhibit 7.6 are rationalized, and we have a mapping from states to signals, an information source in our language.[9]

Second, and closely related, is the issue of *scaling*. The task assigned to the accrual process here is to report the previously noted sequence of

---

[8] Indeed, cash flow itself is redundant here in the presence of accounting income, but that need not necessarily be the case. This is the reason that we craft the exercise in terms of cash flow and accounting accruals being informationally equivalent to cash flow and whatever else the accounting system is able to access in its calculations. To appreciate this, suppose we set $t = 1$ depreciation at $d_1 = 2{,}400$ in the first two states, but at $d_1 = 900$ in the second two states. This equalizes accounting income across the four states except for the restructuring charge in state s_1. In this case, we would combine the cash flow and accounting income reports to de facto observe the noted partition at time $t = 1$.

[9] In turn, the firm's fundamentals are determined at its inception, and any change in fundamentals is a random event that is captured by a well-specified state description. Similarly, the firm's accounting methods are chosen, or specified, at inception. Any change in those methods is, again, captured by a well-specified state description. So far, of course, we have not explicitly dealt with selecting the accounting method. That will be addressed in due course. For the moment, we concern ourselves with how to model the notion that accounting is, indeed, a source of information.

EXHIBIT 7.7   **Companion Asset Values for Story in Exhibit 7.6**

$A_t(s)$	s_1	s_2	s_3	s_4
$A_1(s)$	$25{,}000 - d_1 - d$	$25{,}000 - d_1$	$25{,}000 - d_1$	$25{,}000 - d_1$
$A_2(s)$	$25{,}000 - d_1 - d_2 - d$	$25{,}000 - d_1 - d_2$	$25{,}000 - d_1 - d_2$	$25{,}000 - d_1 - d_2$
$A_3(s)$	0	0	0	0

partitions. We are accustomed, say, to Celsius and Fahrenheit temperature scales, essentially different scales used to measure the same phenomenon. Scaling options are present here as well. As we have stressed, in Exhibit 7.6, d_1 and d_2 are arbitrary constants, and d can be any number other than 1,500 or zero.[10] Such enormous freedom in the scaling is driven by the simplicity of the example, but scaling is an important issue that will remain throughout our study. It is also an important issue in the world of affairs. From an information perspective, it makes no difference whether goodwill is written off immediately or is amortized over 10, 20, or 50 years. It makes no difference whether all depreciation schedules are straight line or accelerated as long as an utterly mechanical approach is taken. It makes no difference what percentage of sales we accrue as uncollectible as long as that percentage is a constant. In all of these cases, we would see through the particular imposed regularity in the recording.[11]

Third, the essence of the story in Exhibit 7.6 is that the accrual process is reporting something that cannot be discerned by merely observing the cash flow. The critical addition, of course, occurs at time $t = 1$. There, cash flow reveals the partition $\{\{s_1, s_2\}, \{s_3, s_4\}\}$, but the income measure reveals the subpartition $\{\{s_1\}, \{s_2\}, \{s_3, s_4\}\}$. The accrual process is able here to report some type of "forward-looking" information. Implicitly, then, the firm is somehow observing the partition $\{\{s_1\}, \{s_2, s_3, s_4\}\}$ because this is essential if the firm is going to know enough to make the advertised restructuring entry or adjustment. In other words, if the accrual process is to report something over and above what is reported by the cash flow itself at that point in time, the firm must have access, somehow, to that additional underlying information.

Finally, the corresponding asset balances directly follow, given the cash balance is immediately distributed to the owners and given we insist on articulation. See Exhibit 7.7. (For example, at time $t = 1$, no restructuring

---

[10] This is not a cynical comment. In our example, the depreciation schedule itself is not called upon to carry any information. It is essentially arbitrary. The restructuring charge is merely an indicator simply because the price revelation it is reporting can be but one of two values.

[11] A subtle point is also present here. In, say, the goodwill case, if we write it off immediately, we have destroyed the option to write it off later. Conversely, if we write it off over, say, 20 years but prior to the end of that horizon, it turns out that this venture has gone sour, we have the option of accelerating the remaining write-off. Again, this is letting the accounting system access an underlying information source and report accordingly.

charge is recorded under states s_2, s_3, or s_4, and the depreciation expense totals d_1, so the net asset value is $25,000 - d_1$.)

ACCOUNTING STOCKS AND FLOWS

We use the device of an unknown state variable to model uncertainty, and we use the idea of observing a partition (technically, an element of a partition) of the set of possible states as our model of information. In turn, this information partition can be thought of as being produced by some mapping from states into signals. Cash flow, we have stressed, is such a mapping. It is a source of information, as is accrual accounting, formally understood. Understanding Exhibits 7.6 and 7.7 is important.

Earlier, in Chapter 4, we introduced accounting stock and flow measures as cousins, so to speak, of their economic counterparts. There, *accounting valuation*, the accounting stock measure, was depicted as a mapping that took some specific cash flow vector, **CF**, and interest rate, r, and converted those fundamentals into a sequence of book value or stock reports. We wrote this as follows:

$$A(\textbf{CF}, r) = [A_0, A_1, \ldots, A_T] \qquad \textbf{(7.1)}$$

The only restriction we placed on this mapping was the boundary conditions at the birth and death of the firm: $A_0(\textbf{CF}, r) = -CF_0$ and $A_T(\textbf{CF}, r) = 0$. In parallel fashion, we depicted accounting income measurement, the accounting flow measure, as a mapping that took this **CF** and r into a sequence of income or flow reports:

$$\hat{I}(\textbf{CF}, r) = [\hat{I}_1, \hat{I}_2, \ldots, \hat{I}_T] \qquad \textbf{(7.2)}$$

The only restriction here was that everything add up in the end,[12] but this adding up, in turn, became superfluous when we imposed articulation:

$$\hat{I}_t = A_t - A_{t-1} + CF_t, \quad \text{for } t = 1, 2, \ldots, T \qquad \textbf{(7.3)}$$

This, of course, all depends on certainty, the very antithesis of an information perspective. It is vital we understand how this characterization extends to our uncertain setting.

The trick, quite simply, is to carry along the state variable. Glance back at Exhibit 7.7 where we have the restructuring charge of d if state s_1 prevails. The net asset balance clearly depends on the state. So, depending on the firm's business plan or strategy (Exhibits 7.2 and 7.3) and accounting method (here choice of d, d_1, and d_2 along with the noted recognition and matching conventions), the time t accounting value or stock report further

---

[12] That is,

$$\sum_{t=1}^{T} \hat{I}_t = \sum_{t=0}^{T} CF_t$$

depends on the realization of $s \in S$. This is the $A_t(s)$ series given in Exhibit 7.7.

So we now express accounting valuation, the accounting stock measure, as some function that maps the firm's fundamentals, $CF(s)$, the interest rate r, and the state $s \in S$ into a sequence of reported values:

$$A(CF, r, s) = [A_0(s), A_1(s), \ldots, A_T(s)] \qquad \textbf{(7.4)}$$

We naturally continue to respect the boundary conditions, now written as $A_0(CF, r, s) = -CF_0(s)$ and $A_T(CF, r, s) = 0$, for each $s \in S$. Exhibit 7.7 is illustrative.

Likewise, accounting income measurement, the accounting income or flow measure is now depicted in state-dependent fashion as

$$\hat{I}(CF, r, s) = [\hat{I}_1(s), \hat{I}_2(s), \ldots, \hat{I}_T(s)] \qquad \textbf{(7.5)}$$

Articulation naturally requires

$$\hat{I}_t(s) = A_t(s) - A_{t-1}(s) + CF_t(s), \quad \text{for } t = 1, 2, \ldots, T \quad \textbf{(7.6)}$$

which, again, ensures the previously noted "adding up" requirement, now on a state-by-state basis. (See Exhibit 7.6.)

This "visualization" in (7.5), (7.6), and (7.7), this extension of the certainty setting of Chapter 4 to a setting that includes uncertainty, is central to our information content approach. At time t, cash basis reporting reveals the realization of $CF_t(s)$, and the accounting system reveals the realization of its stock, $A_t(s)$, and flow, $\hat{I}_t(s)$, calculations. We have three mappings from states to signals, three information sources, $CF_t(s)$, $A_t(s)$, and $\hat{I}_t(s)$. (Although given the duality imposed by articulation, one of the accounting measures is redundant, given the other and given the cash flow observation.)

LANGUAGE AND ALGEBRA OF VALUATION

Conceptually, then, we view accounting stock and flow measures as reporting, at each instance, some partition of the underlying state. Clearly, if the accounting system is indeed reporting some partition, the firm must be observing that partition. Otherwise, it would not know enough to "do the accounting" in the desired fashion. For example, using a lower-of-cost-or-market rule presumes the firm is observing a reliable market price in the first place. Likewise, recording a problematic liability presumes the firm knows about that liability.

What about the reverse question? The apparatus, the language of stocks and flows and the underlying algebra, has its roots in the classical theory of value and income measurement. We periodically hear concerns that the accounting model is inadequate or somehow deeply flawed. For example, as of this writing, we are told that the accounting model, not to mention economic theory in general, simply could not cope with so-called dot coms (firms that display an unusual combination of possible future prospects and a nearly empty current balance sheet) and the inherent option nature of their fundamentals.

To bring this concern into focus, suppose the firm's fundamentals result in the state-dependent cash flows of $CF(s) = [CF_0(s), CF_1(s), \ldots, CF_T(s)]$, a vector of time-dated cash flows (to and from the owners, of course) that depends on state $s \in S$. Further assume the firm has access to, and wants to convey via the accounting system, whatever it observes from the following sequence of information sources:

$$\eta(s) = [\eta_0(s), \eta_1(s), \ldots, \eta_T(s)]$$

At period t, then, the firm learns the realizations of these two information sources; denote them by $c_t = CF_t(s)$ and $y_t = \eta_t(s)$, for $t = 0, 1, \ldots, T$. Of course, c_t is the cash flow at time t, which, for convenience, we assume is distributed to the owners. In turn, y_t might be additional information dealing with product development activities, product market issues, and so on.

The accounting system has access to, can observe, and can process these additional pieces of information, as well as what was observed in prior periods. As of time t, then, write this string of observations as

$$h_t \equiv (c_0, y_0; c_1, y_1; \ldots; c_t, y_t)$$

We interpret h_t as the accounting system's historical documentation (or audit trail) as of time t. It is the full history of whatever the accounting system has archived.[13] Notice h_t is, in reality, a function of the state. It describes an ever-refining partition of S, or a sequence of subpartitions of S. Conveniently, we have a recursive expression of $h_t = (h_{t-1}; c_t, y_t)$.

Now, since the accounting stock measure at time t can only use this history of realizations, it cannot rely on additional details beyond this history, we can reexpress the stock measurement at time t as

$$A_t(h_t) = A_t(h_{t-1}; c_t, y_t) \qquad \textbf{(7.4a)}$$

That is, the valuation at time t depends on what the accounting system "knows" or processes at time t. What it knows at time t is what it knew at time $t - 1$ coupled with the new observations (the cash flow and additional information realizations) in period t.

---

[13] A natural interpretation here is that the accounting system maintain a library of observations. Examples are recent monthly statistics on a division's performance, the profile of the firm's physical assets, and the compensation records for its various employees. Naturally, we expect a great deal of aggregation as well. It is also important to understand h_t is not meant to catalog everything the firm has learned or observed through time t—hardly. It catalogs only those observations that are allowed to enter or influence the accounting statements. For example, a major R&D breakthrough will be awfully important but will not be immediately recognized in the accounting system.

In parallel fashion, imagine an accounting income series that articulates with this accounting stock series:

$$\hat{I}_t(h_{t-1}; c_t, y_t) = \hat{I}_t(h_t) = c_t + A_t(h_{t-1}; c_t, y_t) - A_{t-1}(h_{t-1}) \quad \textbf{(7.6a)}$$

(Notice how we carry the history forward, making certain that the change in accounting value is consistent with the underlying history.)

Given duality between the stock and flow measures, it is sufficient to focus on one of these series. The accounting value series is more transparent in what follows, so that is our focus. Now the underlying information structures are the partitions defined by $CF(s)$ and $\eta(s)$. Under what conditions, then, would this sequence of information structures be informationally equivalent to reporting cash flow and accounting value each period? Cash flow in period t, c_t, is reported each period under either regime. That part is easy.

The real question, then, is whether we can decode the accounting value calculation to infer the underlying additional information event conveyed by $\eta(s)$. Suppose the two regimes are informationally equivalent up to time t. Then when the time t report is observed, we know the prior history h_{t-1}, current cash flow, c_t, and current accounting value, $A_t(h_{t-1}; c_t, y_t)$.

Do we therefore know, or can we infer, the underlying additional information signal, y_t? The answer is yes if the accounting valuation function at this point reports a distinct value for each possible realization of y_t. Stated differently, we can decode the observables at this point to learn y_t if the valuation function $A_t(h_{t-1}; c_t, y_t)$ is invertible in y_t for each possible partial history, consisting of h_{t-1} and c_t.

Return to Exhibit 7.7. Our use of a nonzero restructuring charge (i.e., d) when $\eta_1(s)$ reports that s_1 is true accomplishes precisely this. If we observe the restructuring charge, we know that the information event is $\{s_1\}$, just as we know it is $\{s_2, s_3, s_4\}$ if we do not observe the charge. Any $d \neq 0$ ensures that we can decode the accounting series, in the presence of the cash flow series, to discern the underlying information. (Thus, our earlier concern for $d = 1,500$ in Exhibit 7.6 turns out to be superfluous.)

The point, now, is that the language and algebra of classical valuation that the accounting system uses do not preclude it from being an information source. How onerous is the invertibility condition? Somewhat casually, we merely must guarantee the valuation function has enough flexibility to respond to the underlying information. Then what type of restrictions did we place upon the accounting series? The answer is next to none. We imposed a set of boundary conditions in our valuation series that requires only $A_T(h_T) = 0$. Consequently, it is important that $\eta_T(s)$ be null for the invertibility condition to hold. Otherwise, it is of no importance.

We identified accruals early on as the centerpiece of the accounting product. Notice here that, if cash basis recognition is used, the accounting system reports only cash flow and has no ability to convey anything else. Moreover, if serious accrual accounting is engaged, any information conveyed beyond that conveyed by the cash flow itself is embedded in the accruals. Deciphering the accruals in $A_t(h_{t-1}; c_t, y_t)$ is precisely how the additional information is conveyed.[14] Thus, the accounting system's ability to convey information depends on its ability to distinguish and signal different elements of a partition. The variation of the accounting report across different states carries the information. It is not the value in one particular state that matters.

The conclusion should not be missed. The concern over the accounting system's ability, in principle, to convey information is without merit. The accounting system's use of the language and algebra of valuation is, from an information perspective, a simple choice of scale with which to report some underlying information base. This means we must look elsewhere to understand why we see some things, such as sales and depreciation, routinely reported while other things, such as order books or growth prospects associated with successful R&D, are not routinely reported.

VALUATION VERSUS INFORMATION CONTENT THEMES

One schooled in the valuation view of accounting measurement will, no doubt, find the construction in Exhibit 7.6 baffling if not misdirected. A valuation perspective implores us to conceptually view the accounting system as reporting stocks and flows of economic value. We could not, then, offer an allegedly well-functioning construction, as in Exhibits 7.6 and 7.7, where for any nonzero restructuring charge and any depreciation schedule we are perfectly content with the accounting. The valuation theme implores us to report value without ambiguity. Of course, there is always the issue of which currency to use and how to peg it to some purchasing power base. These are regarded as minor annoyances, however, within the larger theme of reporting value, or fair value in today's vernacular. There is also the problematic and hardly minor issue of what we mean by *value* when markets are not perfect and complete.

The information content theme, on the other hand, identifies the substance of the accounting report with the information it conveys.

---

[14] A number of more subtle issues also arise here. First, in our simple example, d nonzero and completely arbitrary d_1 and d_2 convey the noted information. In this sense, the measurement apparatus offers a wide variety of equivalent scales. We see the same in practice. Various stock depreciation patterns are illustrative. Second, the invertibility argument has the flavor of accounting using a specific code, and the user must be able to decode the report. This decoding is most simple when no other information sources are available, but the same argument extends to a setting of multiple information sources. Finally, many look for a simple linear processing of the (coded) report, for example, value is equal to the capitalized income stream. This is, however, as we shall see, a rather simplistic view of the world of affairs, not to mention theory.

Conceptually, information is a partition of the underlying state space at some moment in time.[15] The precise language used to convey this information is, while clearly important in the world of affairs, strictly speaking, outside the theory. It is the underlying partition that matters. We often think of temperature as a source of information and are accustomed to different temperature scales. The same holds for information sources in general. Varying d (as long as it is not zero) and the depreciation pattern in Exhibit 7.7 merely rescale the measurement scale, so to speak. Celsius and Fahrenheit scales tell us the same thing, as do various combinations of d, d_1, and d_2 in Exhibit 7.7.

We do, to be sure, rely on various conventions here. U.S. GAAP, for example, codifies many of the scaling conventions a firm might employ, and, for that matter, the International Accounting Standards Board offers a competing codification. We also require the organization to disclose its accounting policies (here, the state partition and scaling convention in place), and any changes therein. Knowledge of this is important when the information that is contained in the accounting report is interpreted and translated into a useful format. This is the *invertibility condition* at work.

It is also important to acknowledge that the valuation and information content themes numerically converge. In the long run, total accounting income will approach total economic income (plus rent) simply because the two calculations converge to the total cash flow over the long horizon.[16]

The two perspectives remain fundamentally different, however. The valuation school emphasizes stocks and flows of values, yet in practice it steps away from problematic valuations. Examples are R&D findings, human capital, and national highway systems. These items are surely not valued in any typical accounting system. The information content school emphasizes information conveyed by the accounting system. The invertibility requirement discussed here is sufficiently general that the substantive issue becomes what information to convey. Surely, again taking our cue from practice, the answer is not all information. In practice, the accounting system steps away from problematic information. Examples are new product plans, order books, and market values of various assets. Moreover, the

---

[15] Subsequently, when we introduce labor-contracting issues, we will expand the domain of the information story to include states and "acts" taken by managers, or agents.

[16] This statement is a bit tongue in cheek. Under perfect and complete markets, economic value and economic income are well defined. Adding uncertainty to the stew—our state descriptor—expands the notion of complete and perfect markets to include a full set of insurance markets. Ex ante, then, the firm's plans would have a unique, fully insured, valuation, but insurance markets are surely not so rich. (Can you, for example, purchase career insurance?) Less than complete markets imply that economic value is not in general well defined.

information content theme confronts us with an array of scaling options (taking us back to the d, d_1, and d_2 parameters in Exhibits 7.6 and 7.7 again).

For now, though, the important point is to understand what it means to treat the accounting system as an information channel. Viewed so, the accounting system uses the language and algebra of valuation to convey its information. This structure, this tie to valuation mechanics, is not constraining. The comparative advantage of the accounting channel, then, is not to be found in its use of valuation algebra and language. To explore this further, however, we must turn to the users of the accounting product.

Summary

Accounting valuation was described in Chapter 4 as a procedure that maps a cash flow series (cash that flows from the firm to the owners) and an interest rate assumption into a sequence of values subject to boundary conditions that the initial valuation is the invested amount and the terminal valuation is zero. We now extend this description to include uncertainty: a procedure that maps a cash flow series (cash that flows from the firm to the owners), interest rate assumption, and states into a sequence of values (or signals) subject to the noted boundary conditions. This is the essence of (7.4) and (7.4a). Likewise, our earlier, certainty-assuming description of accounting income measurement is now extended to a mapping (or decomposition) of a cash flow series, interest rate assumption, and states into period-by-period amounts (or signals) that sum to the total of the given cash flow series. This is the essence of (7.6) and (7.6a), presuming articulation. Thus, with the CF(s) and interest rate specified, accounting valuation and income measurement provide mappings from states into signals, the very essence of an information source. Under uncertainty, then, accounting value is the result of applying a particular accounting procedure, accounting valuation mapping, to a specific setting, a specific signal realization; and accounting income is the result of applying a particular procedure, accounting income mapping, to a specific setting, a specific signal realization. Furthermore, recall that two distinct mappings that induce the same state partition are informationally equivalent. They merely do so with different scales, different numerical assignments that convey the same underlying information.

Of course, accounting is a highly structured language with the underlying stock and flow calculations tightly connected (through articulation). This raises the question of what limits are imposed by this reliance on the language and algebra of valuation. The answer is virtually none. The structure of accounting is not limited in its ability to convey information. This means we must look elsewhere to identify and understand what information is conveyed by the typical accounting system.

Selected References

The modeling of accounting as an explicit information source, one that must be decoded or inverted to discern the underlying state partition, is developed in Demski and Sappington (1990) and Antle, Demski, and Ryan (1994). Butterworth (1972) is an important precursor. In turn, this inversion theme is extended in Arya, Fellingham, and Schroeder (2000) and Arya, Fellingham, Glover, Schroeder, and Strang (2000) to focus on identifying the set of transactions the firm might have engaged in, given the financial reports. Beaver and Demski (1979) highlight the valuation versus information content themes in a setting where the market structure is not too accommodating.

Key Terms

We have learned to conceptualize information as a partition of some set of states and an information system as a mapping from states to signals. This mapping is merely the language that is used to convey the underlying partition. Turning to accounting, **accounting valuation,** the **accounting stock measure,** provides an explicit mapping from states into signals, taking the realized cash flows and the interest rate and mapping them into **accounting values.** Equivalently, **accounting income measurement,** the accounting flow measure, specifies a mapping of states into **accounting incomes.** Then particular accounting value and accounting income realizations become signal realizations from information systems. The mappings provide the language with which the underlying state partition is conveyed. Here **scaling** is important because different mappings that induce the same state partition are informationally equivalent and thus convey the same information.

Exercises

7.1. What is the connection between information and uncertainty? Give several illustrations of this connection.

7.2. Return to the illustration in Exhibit 7.4 in which reported income depends on the depreciation schedule (d_1 and d_2). We claim the choice of depreciation schedule here is arbitrary, that regardless of the specific schedule chosen, the same partition of S will be revealed, through time. Why is this so? Why do we refer to this as an issue of scaling?

7.3. This is a continuation of Exercise 7.2. Why, in the illustration in Exhibits 7.6 and 7.7, do we require the restructuring charge, d, be nonzero? Is $d = 1,500$ problematic?

7.4. The illustration in Exhibit 7.6 is one in which accrual reporting is able to convey strictly more information than is cash basis accounting. Even so, the precise accruals (i.e., d, d_1, and d_2) are far from unique. This illustrates an old Danish design adage: Form follows function. Explain.

7.5. Consider the fuel gauge in your automobile. What do you know about its peculiarities? Is it "late" to report? For example, does it take a while to register full after the tank has been filled? Is it well calibrated? For example, when it reports a reading of "half," does that mean the stock of gasoline equals one-half of the tank's capacity? Is its reading useful? What, then, does the fuel gauge purport to measure? Do you see an analogy to the information content perspective in accounting?

7.6. Return to the three-product firm and story in Exhibits 7.2 through 7.7 in which the firm observes the partition $\{\{s_1\}, \{s_2\}, \{s_3, s_4\}\}$ at time $t = 1$. Contrary to the example, however, now assume the firm can adjust its third period output based on this information at time $t = 1$. Determine the firm's optimal production plan, assuming that all of the details of the setting, such as the prices and random structure of the selling prices of the first and third periods, remain. Display your findings in exhibits that parallel Exhibits 7.3 and 7.6.

7.7. This is a continuation of Exercise 4.5. Now assume that the selling prices of the first and third periods are uncertain. The first will be 220 ± 40, and the third will be 266.20 ± 50. The price possibilities are equally likely and are independent. The firm is risk neutral and must commit to its production schedule at the start prior to learning the prices. (This implies that the optimal factor choices and output schedules remain as determined in the original exercise.) Determine the firm's cash flow prospects, as a function of the state, following the pattern in Exhibit 7.3. Then, for an arbitrary depreciation schedule, determine the firm's income in each period and state, following the pattern in Exhibit 7.5. What state partition is induced, at each point in time, by your method of calculating the firm's income?

7.8. Ralph is now dealing with a two-period cash flow story in which there are six equally likely states. The periodic cash flows, as a function of the state, are displayed in the following table. Notice the expected cash flow in the first period is 110 and that its counterpart in the second period is 121. Naturally, the interest rate is 10 percent. Also notice the information source that will provide one of three signals. This information is privately observed by Ralph, just as the first period cash flow is also privately observed by Ralph.

	s_1	s_2	s_3	s_4	s_5	s_6
CF_0	-200	-200	-200	-200	-200	-200
CF_1	100	100	100	120	120	120
CF_2	101	101	141	141	141	101
Signal y	y_1	y_2	y_2	y_3	y_2	y_2

a. What partition of the set of states is identified (for Ralph) at time $t = 1$ by the combination of observing CF_1 and the noted signal? (Notice that prior observation of CF_0 is superfluous.)

b. Now suppose Ralph wants to convey all of this information by issuing a report at time $t = 1$, a report consisting of CF_1 and accounting income for the first period. Accounting income, of course, is linked to the accounting valuation series. This series has $A_0 = 200$ and $A_2 = 0$. Assume that A_1 is defined by straight-line depreciation, nothing else. Will the report convey all that Ralph knows? Be specific.

c. Repeat part b for the case $A_1 = E[CF_2/1.1 \mid CF_1]$.

d. Repeat part b for the case $A_1 = E[CF_2/1.1 \mid y]$.

e. Repeat part b for the case $A_1 = E[CF_2/1.1 \mid CF_1$ and $y]$.

f. Repeat part b for the case $A_1 = \text{minimum}\{120, E[CF_2 \mid CF_1 \text{ and } y]\}$.

g. Repeat part b for the case
   $A_1 = \text{minimum}\{120, E[CF_2/1.1 \mid CF_1 \text{ and } y]\}$.

h. Write a short paragraph summarizing your observations on the various ways to measure accounting value at time $t = 1$.

7.9. This is a continuation of Exercise 7.8. As before, Ralph wants to convey all that is known at time $t = 1$ by issuing a report consisting of CF_1 and accounting income for the first period. In what sense are the measurement schemes explored in Exercise 7.8 alternative scalings of what Ralph is seeking to disclose? Likewise, we know Fahrenheit and Celsius convey the same information but with a different scale. Carefully contrast this notion of scaling with what you have identified here.

7.10. This is a continuation of Exercise 7.7. Now suppose there are two firms, identical in all respects. Initially assume that the price realizations are independent, so, one firm's price tells us nothing about the other's price. Provide a state specification, common to both firms, and verify that each firm's accounting system is indeed a mapping from states into signals. What happens if the two firms face the same price realizations?

Part 2

Information Content

Chapter 8

Information in a Valuation Setting

We now know what it means to say accounting uses the language and algebra of valuation to convey information, and we also know information content is present when that information is actually used or is acted upon. The next step involves multiperson settings in which the information is acted upon. Here we focus on trading arrangements in which we use the terms at which individuals trade as an *observable assessment of value.* Information then enters the story by affecting these terms of trade, the valuation. Hence, the title—information in a valuation setting. It is, however, important to understand that the terms under which trade takes place—the observable assessment of value—depend not only on what the individuals know but also on how their trading is organized. We examine two such organizational arrangements: the classical perfectly competitive setting in which we emphasize risk-neutral, market-based trade with public information, and a small numbers auction setting in which we emphasize a nonmarket arrangement with private information.

The *information content* perspective requires us not only to formally treat accounting as a source of information but also to formally identify someone who uses that information. Absent a use, we are reduced to speculating about what difference one or another information structure might make, and that is hardly the grist for a useful theory.

We will emphasize valuation and contracting uses. The natural starting point is valuation, specifically, trade-based valuation. Emphasizing trade allows us to identify and define *valuation* as reflecting the terms of trade between (or among) economically rational individuals. Moreover, trade involves more than one individual, so we explicitly enter the world of multiperson resource allocation at this point. Our interest, of course, is tracking the use of information in the trade or valuation exercise. Indeed, fair value, mark-to-market, and historical cost approaches to accounting measurement all have their roots in trade-based valuation.[1]

Two caveats should be noted at the outset. First, we adopt a minimalist approach and use settings that are adequate to support our study of information, but we hardly cover the theory and practice of trade-based valuation. Second, the information itself is in generic format. Explicit accounting structure and issues must await our mastering the basics.

Initially, we revisit the ubiquitous classical setting, here extended to risk-neutral valuation in a pure exchange, competitive market. This is a natural extension of our earlier work in Chapter 3, is particularly intuitive, and provides a transparent window into the use of information. The idea is to track the value of some asset or claim, through time, as information arrives. Risk neutrality allows us to do this in a particularly transparent and intuitive fashion.

Unfortunately, this is also a setting in which there is no explicit reason to produce the information in the first place. The reason is that risk-neutral valuation places no premium on early resolution of uncertainty, and our setting is too simplified to offer any explicitly productive use of the information. Nevertheless, risk-neutral valuation is responsive to new information in a transparent fashion. So, when transparency is called for, we will use this vehicle. Be forewarned: Mixing of information sources is hardly transparent, even in this minimalist setting. One information source might have no impact on price, on the risk-neutral valuation, on its own yet have an impact when combined with another source, just as it might have a natural good-versus-bad-news interpretation on its own but lack or even reverse that interpretation when combined with another source. Separability issues are universal.

The second setting we examine is a small numbers story in which the trade mechanism is an auction. The central issue here is modeling trade among individuals who possess different information, and the terms of trade explicitly depend on the traders' behavior, in contrast to the price-taking behavior in a perfectly competitive market under equilibrium conditions. This setting offers a setting in which public and private information can be valuable (at least to some) and can mix in subtle ways.[2] It has the further advantage of taking us into the world of information use in a trade-based setting that differs from the classical competitive market.

---

[1] This perspective of valuation being manifest in observable, equilibrium trades is a fundamental perspective in economic theory. This explains the title of Debreu's famous monograph, *The Theory of Value.*

[2] Combining these themes leads to rational expectations modeling at the competitive level when traders are privately informed and the equilibrium price reveals some of what they know, to other traders, in aggregate. Noise traders or unobservable supply shocks are used to mask the informed traders' actions. The models presented here are adequate for our purpose and have the advantage of not relying on unmodeled activities of some "players."

Here we find differences between value and observed price because the price only imperfectly reflects the information available to those engaged in trade.

Combining these themes, we might think of the setting in two related phases. Initially, a risk-averse individual, in possession of a risky asset, trades this asset via auction to a risk-neutral individual, one clearly better equipped to carry the risk. This second individual, then, eventually enters the noted (risk-neutral) valuation market and tracks the value of the asset as information subsequently arrives. Of course, this begs the question of why the trade mechanisms are not combined into a single rich market setting, but we warned you that our approach would be minimalist by design!

RISK-NEUTRAL VALUATION

The story begins with a firm whose factor and output choices result in an uncertain cash flow between it and its owners. As usual, we describe the cash flow uncertainty with a state descriptor, $s \in S$. We write the cash flow vector, in state-dependent fashion, as $CF(s) = [CF_0(s), CF_1(s), \ldots, CF_T(s)]$.

From here we want to say something about the value of the remaining portion of this sequence, as of time t. That is, we want to focus on the value, at time t, of the claim to $[CF_{t+1}(s), CF_{t+2}(s), \ldots, CF_T(s)]$, and we want to employ risk-neutral valuation. We must remember, however, that information is present. We have, presumably, learned something by time t about the remaining cash flows. After all, merely observing the cash flows up to and including time t is itself a source of information!

A convenient way to keep track of the unfolding information is to use the history device introduced in Chapter 7. There we were concerned about what we learned from the sequence of cash flow realizations (c_0, c_1, etc.) and a sequence of information signals (y_0, y_1, etc.). So at time t, we knew the (partial) history $h_t = (c_0, y_0; c_1, y_1; \ldots; c_t, y_t)$.

Now, however, we treat this history of information releases or observations as being known by "the market." Exactly what is being released or observed will be clear from the context, but whatever it is, this history of releases and observations, or equivalently the underlying state partition, as of time t will be denoted h_t.

Next, let $E[CF_j \mid h_t]$ denote the expected value of cash flow $CF_j(s)$ given we know history h_t. Similarly, let $E[PV_t \mid h_t]$ denote the expected value of the continuation present value, as of time t and conditional on history h_t. Using interest rate r, we have the immediate extension of the continuation present value calculation introduced in Chapter 3.

$$E[PV_t \mid h_t] = \sum_{j=t+1}^{T} E[CF_j \mid h_t](1 + r)^{t-j} \qquad \textbf{(8.1)}$$

Now comes the important assumption. We assume that the claim to this cash flow series is traded in a perfectly organized market, that history h_t is available to all market participants, that the interest rate, r, is constant, and that the price at which the claim trades is none other than $E[PV_t \mid h_t]$ in expression (8.1). Under risk neutrality, risk is a matter of indifference, so we focus on the expected value of each of the cash flows.

In more suggestive notation, think of the price at time t as a function of what is known at time t, or $P_t(h_t)$. Our pricing assumption, then, is simply

$$P_t(h_t) \equiv E[PV_t \mid h_t] \qquad \textbf{(8.2a)}$$

given that we are pricing the claim to the remaining cash flow series at time t after CF_t has been remitted. Likewise, suppose that we are pricing the claim just before CF_t is remitted and the totality of what is known at that point is the history $\hat{h}_t$. The pricing assumption then becomes

$$P_t(\hat{h}_t) \equiv E[CF_t \mid \hat{h}_t] + E[PV_t \mid \hat{h}_t] \qquad \textbf{(8.2b)}$$

Given that we know history $\hat{h}_t$ the market's best estimate of the immediately forthcoming cash receipt is $E[CF_t \mid \hat{h}_t]$, and its valuation of the more distant receipts is $E[PV_t \mid \hat{h}_t]$. Either way, we assume a perfectly competitive market with the noted equilibrium pricing functions.

Implicitly, then, the assumption is that risk does not matter in valuing the claim to **CF** as we march through time. Only the passage of time and the arrival of new information matter. This is sufficient for our purpose. (In Appendix 1 we sketch an equilibrium argument that leads to the assumed pricing behavior in (8.2).)

Extended Illustration

Now consider the setup in Exhibit 8.1 in which we have four equally likely states.[3] The unconditional expected values of the cash flows should be familiar:

$$E[CF_1] = .5(2,950) + .5(6,950) = 4,950$$

$$E[CF_2] = .5(6,680) + .5(12,680) = 9,680$$

$$E[CF_3] = .25(17,637.50) + .25(15,637.50) + .25(26,637.50)$$
$$+ .25(6,637.50) = 16,637.50$$

We also identify two explicit information sources, imaginatively denoted η and $\hat{\eta}$. Each will report one of two signals. The first, η, provides

---

[3] We forgo the temptation to provide surely elaborate details in terms of factor and product price changes and technology effects that would produce this particular **CF** specification.

EXHIBIT 8.1
Setup for Extended
Illustration

	State			
	s_1	s_2	s_3	s_4
$prob(s_i)$	.25	.25	.25	.25
CF_0	−25,000	−25,000	−25,000	−25,000
CF_1	2,950	2,950	6,950	6,950
CF_2	6,680	12,680	6,680	12,680
CF_3	17,637.50	15,637.50	26,637.50	6,637.50
Information source η	y_1'	y_1'	y_1''	y_1''
Information source $\hat{\eta}$	y_2'	y_2''	y_2'	y_2''

the partition $\{\{s_1, s_2\}, \{s_3, s_4\}\}$, and the second, $\hat{\eta}$, provides the partition $\{\{s_1, s_3\}, \{s_2, s_4\}\}$. Cash flow, itself, is also potentially a source of information. Here, CF_1 provides partition $\{\{s_1, s_2\}, \{s_3, s_4\}\}$ while CF_2 provides $\{\{s_1, s_3\}, \{s_2, s_4\}\}$. CF_3 provides perfect information.

So, observing CF_1 at time $t = 1$ is informationally equivalent to observing information source η's report at time $t = 1$. Observing source η's report at time $t = 0$, however, is not informationally equivalent to observing CF_1 at time $t = 1$. *Information equivalence*, recall, refers to the same information, the same state partition, at the same time.

We now examine a variety of information stories associated with this setup. Naturally, the interest rate is $r = 10$ percent.

Cash Flow Only

As mentioned, the valuation assumption in (8.2) implies the price, or value, of the claim to cash flow **CF** will vary with the passage of time and with the information at hand. Initially, we assume that the only information is the cash flow realization itself. So at time $t = 0$, no information is available. At time $t = 1$, however, we know $CF_1 = 2,950$ or $CF_1 = 6,950$; equivalently, we know the partition $\{\{s_1, s_2\}, \{s_3, s_4\}\}$. In terms of the history variable, at time $t = 0$, h_0 is null, but at time $t = 1$, it is $h_1 = \{s_1, s_2\}$ or $h_1 = \{s_3, s_4\}$. (Notice that we associate the history here with the underlying state partition rather than carry along the coded signal itself, such as the cash flow realization.)

Using the preceding unconditional cash flow expectations, the initial, time $t = 0$, value would be

$$P_0(h_0 = \text{null}) = 4,950(1.1)^{-1} + 9,680(1.1)^{-2} + 16,637.50(1.1)^{-3} = 25,000$$

Again, we encounter an old friend!

Moving to time $t = 1$, we will have observed $CF_1 = 2,950$ (implying that $h_1 = \{s_1, s_2\}$) or $CF_1 = 6,950$ (implying that $h_1 = \{s_3, s_4\}$). The revised, remaining cash flow expectations are calculated as follows:

$$E[CF_2 \mid h_1 = \{s_1, s_2\}] = .5(6{,}680) + .5(12{,}680) = 9{,}680$$

and

$$E[CF_3 \mid h_1 = \{s_1, s_2\}] = .5(17{,}637.50) + .5(15{,}637.50) = 16{,}637.50$$

or

$$E[CF_2 \mid h_1 = \{s_3, s_4\}] = .5(6{,}680) + .5(12{,}680) = 9{,}680$$

and

$$E[CF_3 \mid h_1 = \{s_3, s_4\}] = .5(26{,}637.50) + .5(6{,}637.50) = 16{,}637.50$$

Here knowledge of CF_1 does not alter the expected values of the remaining cash flows. So, our valuation expression is unaffected by knowing the partition $\{\{s_1, s_2\}, \{s_3, s_4\}\}$ at time $t = 1$:

$$P_1(h_1 = \{s_1, s_2\}) = 9{,}680(1.1)^{-1} + 16{,}637.50(1.1)^{-2} = 22{,}550$$

and

$$P_1(h_1 = \{s_3, s_4\}) = 9{,}680(1.1)^{-1} + 16{,}637.50(1.1)^{-2} = 22{,}550$$

Of course, this reflects the fact that the assumed event structure in Exhibit 8.1 provides for revised expected values of CF_2 and CF_3 that are uninformed by whether $CF_1 = 2{,}950$ or $6{,}950$.

Cash Flow Coupled with Information Source $\hat{\eta}$ at Time $t = 1$

Now consider the case when cash flow and information source $\hat{\eta}$ are jointly present, with the latter also reporting at time $t = 1$. At that time, then, observing $\hat{\eta}$'s report is equivalent to observing partition $\{\{s_1, s_3\}, \{s_2, s_4\}\}$, and with CF_1 imparting knowledge of $\{\{s_1, s_2\}, \{s_3, s_4\}\}$, the two partitions together amount to perfect information: $\{\{s_1\}, \{s_2\}, \{s_3\}, \{s_4\}\}$. You should verify that the history-dependent time $t = 1$ valuations are now

$$P_1(h_1 = \{s_1\}) = 6{,}680(1.1)^{-1} + 17{,}637.50(1.1)^{-2} = 20{,}649.17$$

$$P_1(h_1 = \{s_2\}) = 12{,}680(1.1)^{-1} + 15{,}637.50(1.1)^{-2} = 24{,}450.83$$

$$P_1(h_1 = \{s_3\}) = 6{,}680(1.1)^{-1} + 26{,}637.50(1.1)^{-2} = 28{,}087.19$$

$$P_1(h_1 = \{s_4\}) = 12{,}680(1.1)^{-1} + 6{,}637.50(1.1)^{-2} = 17{,}012.81$$

Notice for each distinct history (h_1), for each distinct combination of CF_1 and report from source $\hat{\eta}$, the valuation of the remaining cash flows is distinct. For each possible report from source $\hat{\eta}$, the valuation varies, depending on the CF_1 realization. Thus, while knowing CF_1 by itself does not inform us (at time $t = 1$), knowing CF_1 in the presence of source $\hat{\eta}$ does inform us.[4] Once again, combining multiple information sources is not a simple matter because we find that separability is absent.

Value of Information

We could, at this point, examine the valuation at time $t = 1$ under alternative information assumptions, just as we could move on to time $t = 2$. The mechanics should be clear, however, and we have other matters to pursue.

As an aside, though, notice that we can express, for example, the initial price or value as reflecting the time $t = 1$ cash flow coupled with the value of the claim at time $t = 1$:

$$P_0(h_0) = E[CF_1 \mid h_0](1 + r)^{-1} + E[P_1(h_1) \mid h_0](1 + r)^{-1}$$

For the preceding case when cash flow and source $\hat{\eta}$ are observed at $t = 1$ (and h_0 is null), we have

$$P_0(h_0) = 4{,}950(1.1)^{-1} + (.25(20{,}649.17) + .25(24{,}450.83) + .25(28{,}087.19)$$

$$+.25(17{,}012.81))(1.1)^{-1} = 25{,}000$$

Conversely, for the initial case when only the cash flow is observed, the comparable calculation provides

$$P_0(h_0) = 4{,}950(1.1)^{-1} + 22{,}550(1.1)^{-1} = 25{,}000$$

The two stories have the same underlying randomness, but one has this randomness revealed sooner than the other. Yet their initial valuations are identical. The reason is that risk-neutral valuation is strictly indifferent to when the uncertainty is resolved. Be it sooner or be it later, the initial ($h_0 = $ null) prices will be the same.

The valuation is, as the name states, risk neutral. There is no premium associated with a risk-free series of cash flows compared to a risky series whose period-by-period expected cash flows match their counterparts in the risk-free series. Furthermore, the series of risky cash flows is valued, priced, on the basis of the underlying expected values. At time $t = 0$, these initial expectations are not affected by the anticipated arrival of information at a future date. Consequently, risk-neutral valuation per se places no value on information and no premium on early resolution of uncertainty.

Information Content in the Risk-Neutral Valuation Setting

The valuation expression in (8.2), then, is our basic model for tracking information in a valuation setting. Now, what about information content

---

[4] In turn, source $\hat{\eta}$ reporting at time $t = 1$ is simply foreknowledge of what the CF_2 realization will be. You should also notice that source $\hat{\eta}$ by itself at time $t = 1$ will inform about the expected value of the continuation present value.

in this setting? Recall in the single-person setting of Chapter 6 that we identified information content with the individual's choice being affected by that information. Here, in the valuation setting, we identify information content with the observed valuation, the market price, being affected by that information.

To stress essentials, let's momentarily focus on time $t = 1$ and assume we have at most two information sources reporting at that time. Call them sources η and $\hat{\eta}$. Viewed in isolation, source η will report some signal (partition element) denoted y_1, and source $\hat{\eta}$ will report some signal (again, partition element) denoted y_2. For example, source η might be the CF_1 source, and $\hat{\eta}$ might be the second source in Exhibit 8.1.

If no other information is present and, in particular, if we have no information being provided at time $t = 0$, the history at time $t = 1$ is whatever we have learned from whatever sources are reporting at time $t = 1$. Thus, *if* there is no information at time $t = 0$ and *if* source η is the only source present at time $t = 1$, the history at time $t = 1$ is simply signal y_1. We then say source η has information content in the risk-neutral valuation setting (of (8.2)) at time $t = 1$ *if* value as defined by $P_1(h_1 = y_1)$ varies in nontrivial fashion as a function of y_1.[5] The source has information content if it will affect the valuation. As before, information content is associated with the source but cannot be ascertained without reference to some well-defined setting. Here that well-defined setting is some particular risk-neutral valuation machine, as defined by (8.2).

Now what about adding a second source to the reporting stew? Here we must be careful to keep track of the other information. Suppose we are already observing the output of information source η, which reports signal y_1. Does information source $\hat{\eta}$, which reports signal y_2, now have information content? If there is no information at time $t = 0$, the history at time $t = 1$ will consist of a pair of reports, one from each source: $h_1 = (y_1, y_2)$. So, *if* there is no information at time $t = 0$ and *if* sources η and $\hat{\eta}$ are the only sources present at time $t = 1$, we then say that source $\hat{\eta}$ has information content *in the presence of source η* in the risk-neutral setting (of (8.2)) at time $t = 1$ *if* $P_1(h_1 = (y_1, y_2))$ varies in nontrivial fashion as a function of y_2 for some y_1.

Before concluding this exploration, though, we should apply our deepening understanding to the story in Exhibit 8.1. Concentrate on the post-dividend valuation expression of (8.2). Suppose there is no information source observed at time $t = 0$, and concentrate on time $t = 1$. Is observing CF_1 an information source? (Surely it is.) Does this source have information content at time $t = 1$ if it is the only source? (No!) Does it have information content at time $t = 1$ if it is observed in the presence of source $\hat{\eta}$? (Yes.) This reminds us that information content is a delicate issue; it

---

[5] The phrase *varies in nontrivial fashion as a function of* y_1 means that $P_1(h_1 = y_1')$ differs from $P_1(h_1 = y_1'')$ for some distinct pair of signals, y_1' and y_1''.

depends on what other information is present.[6] We always have to think about separability.

You should be starting to worry that we will belabor this point still further. Instead, we delegate that task to you, but with the admonition to remember information content in this setting boils down to the source in question being able to alter the valuation. Of course, this requires us to keep track of what we are learning from other sources as well as specify the time period in which we are searching for information content.[7]

SMALL NUMBERS TRADE

Although we have merely sketched the implications of risk-neutral valuation, relying on the structure in the pricing model of (8.2), it is important to understand that the underlying details are a perfectly competitive market, one in which price-taking behavior is paramount and in which the price of risk is zero. Although adequate for studying a variety of information issues, it is also important to understand the use of information in alternative trade-based settings. Here we turn our attention to a small numbers setting.[8]

One individual owns an asset but has no ability to turn this asset into a productive opportunity. It is worth precisely zero to this individual. If it is placed in the hands of someone with the requisite ability, however, the asset can indeed be productive. There are two such individuals; both are risk neutral and equally capable. Trade should take place, but to whom and at what price?

Think of this as a cash flow vector. If placed in the hands of one of the other individuals, if trade takes place, the cash flow prospects are favorable

[6] For the moment, at least, we sidestep the question of whether the information has value. This is far from transparent. If the information arrives after an efficient asset allocation has been achieved, it is of no importance. This follows from the joint assumptions of risk neutrality and no production. Conversely, if the information arrives before an efficient allocation is achieved, it is potentially harmful. The reason is that it arrives before risk is efficiently allocated in the economy and thus negatively impacts those who prefer to reduce their risk exposure. For example, it is a little late to buy flood insurance once the weather report predicts a flood is imminent. Just to make matters worse, we should also note that the information content associated with an information source reporting at time t might show up only at a later point in time. This is illustrated by the noted pair of sources in the Exhibit 8.1 illustration.

[7] Just to drive this a little deeper, imagine a source that, when it reports, has no immediate effect on the valuation calculation but has one in a subsequent period when it is combined with another source. To illustrate, with a touch of the apocryphal, imagine receiving the secret code at time $t = 1$ and the coded message at time $t = 3$! A source with no information content at the time of release may, that is, have information content at a later date. Content is setting and time dependent.

[8] This setting is based on Myerson's (1991) analysis of the auction of an object of equal but unknown value to two bidders.

although random. If trade does not take place, however, the cash flow is simply zero at each point. Alternatively, think of the first individual as risk averse and of the cash flow as so risky it has zero certainty equivalent to the first individual. Again, trade should take place. Those for whom risk is a matter of indifference should be carrying that risk.

The trade mechanism is a sealed bid auction. The seller solicits bids and sells the asset to the high bidder, who pays the seller the amount of the winning bid. The object is worth zero to the seller. To either buyer, though, it is worth the expected value of the present value of the cash flow vector. (What else?)

The value of the cash flows, if the asset is placed in the hands of one of the other individuals, if it is placed in the hands of someone with appropriate management skills or risk preferences, is given by

$$PV_0 = \alpha y_1 + \beta y_2 \qquad\qquad \textbf{(8.3)}$$

where $\alpha \geq 0$ and $\beta \geq 0$ are known constants and y_1 and y_2 are potentially observable random variables, or information sources.[9] For example, αy_1 might be the current book value of that claim, and βy_2 might be the present value of the future abnormal earnings associated with the cash flow series and whatever accounting procedures are in place.

To keep things within bounds, y_1 and y_2 are independently distributed and described by a uniform distribution on the $[0, 1]$ interval. So, the expected value of the object's value is simply[10]

$$E[PV_0] = \alpha E[y_1] + \beta E[y_2] = \tfrac{1}{2}(\alpha + \beta)$$

All three players know this value expression, although they may differ as to their respective knowledge of the two random variables. Stated differently, all three parties agree on the fundamentals of the object's value: It is nil to the seller and given by expression (8.3) for both potential buyers.

The auction rules are straightforward. The seller is committed to sell the object. Each bidder submits a bid without knowledge of the other's bid. The higher bid wins, and the winning bidder then pays the seller the amount of the winning bid and claims the asset. In the event of a tie, a coin is flipped to determine the winner.

Remember, now, that the value of the object is $PV_0 = \alpha y_1 + \beta y_2$ if trade takes place and zero if it remains in the hands of the seller. Total gains to trade, then, are simply $\alpha y_1 + \beta y_2$, and expected total gains to trade are $\tfrac{1}{2}(\alpha + \beta)$. Who captures these potential gains to trade depends on the information structures in place at the time the auction takes place.

---

[9] At least one of α and β is strictly positive. Otherwise, our story is trivial.
[10] Recall that a uniform density on $y \in [0, 1]$ is defined by $f(y) = 1$ for $y \in [0, 1]$ and 0 otherwise. In turn, $E[y|y < z] = \tfrac{1}{2}z$ for any $0 \leq z \leq 1$. Likewise, $E[y] = \tfrac{1}{2}$. With this setup, then, we might think of the object's value as depending on the state, where state is a point in the unit square defined by y_1 and y_2.

The key to sorting this out is the bidders' behavior. They will behave strategically, and therefore it is important to think in *equilibrium* terms because either bidder's success depends on what both bid.

The idea is mutual best response. Abstractly (no comments, please), suppose we have two players, each selecting some action, say $a_i \in A_i$. Furthermore, suppose the utility from player i's perspective if the two actions are a_1 and a_2 is $F_i(a_1, a_2)$, so each player is concerned about both players' behavior. Now the pair of actions (a_1^*, a_2^*) is an equilibrium if a_1^* is the solution to

$$\max_{a_1 \in A_1} F_1(a_1, a_2^*)$$

and a_2^* is the solution to

$$\max_{a_2 \in A_2} F_2(a_1^*, a_2)$$

That is, player 1's choice is best for player 1, against player 2's choice, and player 2's choice is best for player 2, against player 1's choice.[11]

No Information Equilibrium

The analysis is transparent when no information is available to any of the parties. Suppose the bidders employ pure strategies (i.e., do not randomize in setting their bids) and bidder 1 intends to bid $b_1 < E[PV_0]$. What is bidder 2's best response to such a strategy? Surely it is to bid $b_2 = b_1 + \epsilon$, with ϵ arbitrarily small but greater than zero. Continuing, it should be clear that equilibrium bids are $b_1 = b_2 = E[PV_0] = \frac{1}{2}(\alpha + \beta)$. (Apply the definition of an equilibrium: If one bidder bids in this fashion, what is the best response of the other?) Having two competitors equally informed and valuing the object in identical fashion results in the object being traded at a price, a bid, equal to this common value. Competition is a strong force in this setting![12]

Hence, in the absence of information, the buyer pays $E[PV_0]$, the object's value. The seller captures fully the gains to trade because the winning bid is equal to the buyers' valuation of the object. The price at which the asset trades perfectly reflects the underlying value, defined by (8.3).

---

[11] Delicacies now arise; an equilibrium might not exist, or multiple equilibria might exist. Randomization may be in order. Our use here and in subsequent chapters when we study contracting between the firm and its manager is in settings in which these more technical issues are not of concern.

[12] *Equilibrium,* then, refers to market-clearing conditions (or supply equal to demand) in the usual market setting but is a reactive concept in a strategic setting. A cautionary note is also in order in our particular strategic setting. We are presuming the use of a pure strategy by both parties. Mutually supporting randomization provides an entire family of equilibria in this case. For simplicity, we concentrate on the pure strategy case.

Perfect Public Information Equilibrium

Equally transparent is the case in which all parties know the exact cash flow ($y_1 \in [0, 1]$ and $y_2 \in [0, 1]$) at the time of bidding. Arguing in parallel fashion, it should be clear that equilibrium bids are for each buyer to bid the object's value (in this case $\alpha y_1 + \beta y_2$). Again, the observed price at which the asset trades is equal to the underlying value in (8.3), now in the presence of full revelation of both information variables.

Also notice, in passing, that with the buyers being risk neutral, it is a matter of indifference to them whether they trade with null information or acquire perfect information prior to trading because the uninformed price equals the expected value of the informed price. This is not the case for a risk-averse seller, however. In the no-information case, the seller will receive $\frac{1}{2}(\alpha + \beta)$. In the perfect public information case, however, the seller will realize the random amount $\alpha y_1 + \beta y_2$, whose expected value is $\frac{1}{2}(\alpha + \beta)$. The risk-averse seller is strictly worse off. Early arrival of the information destroys any insurance opportunity by revealing the full force of the uncertainty before the risk-averse individual can trade with a risk-neutral individual. Indeed, in our specialized case in which the seller's certainty equivalent is precisely zero, the information completely wipes out any gains to trade!

Private Information Equilibrium

Now change the story in an important way. Assume bidder 1 privately knows $y_1 \in [0, 1]$ while bidder 2 privately knows $y_2 \in [0, 1]$. It is also common knowledge what each party is observing.[13] So bidder 1's bid, say, is now informed by the actual realization of $y_1 \in [0, 1]$ and by the fact that bidder 2 is bidding with knowledge of $y_2 \in [0, 1]$ as well as the fact that bidder 1 is so informed. The story, then, is two bidders who agree on the valuation fundamentals but are asymmetrically informed.

It turns out a pair of equilibrium bidding strategies is given by

$$b_1(y_1) = \tfrac{1}{2}(\alpha + \beta)y_1$$

and

$$b_2(y_2) = \tfrac{1}{2}(\alpha + \beta)y_2$$

That is, each bidder submits a bid that is linearly increasing in the privately observed information variable. The bid, though, is below the privately informed best estimate of the object's value. In particular, notice that upon observing $y_1 \in [0, 1]$ but knowing nothing about y_2, bidder 1's best esti-

[13] Something is *common knowledge* if everyone knows it, knows that everyone knows it, knows that everyone knows that everyone knows it, and so on.

mate of the object's value is $E[PV_0 \mid y_1] = \alpha y_1 + \beta E[y_2 \mid y_1] = \alpha y_1 + \frac{1}{2}\beta$. The equilibrium bid is below this estimate, however:

$$E[PV_0 \mid y_1] - b_1(y_1) = \alpha y_1 + \frac{1}{2}\beta - \frac{1}{2}(\alpha + \beta)y_1 = \frac{1}{2}\alpha y_1 + \frac{1}{2}\beta(1 - y_1) \geq 0$$

and

$$E[PV_0 \mid y_2] - b_2(y_2) = \frac{1}{2}\alpha + \beta y_2 - \frac{1}{2}(\alpha + \beta)y_2 = \frac{1}{2}\alpha(1 - y_2) + \frac{1}{2}\beta y_2 \geq 0$$

This "shading" below the estimate reflects the fact that the bidders each want to maximize their respective shares of the expected gains to trade, as well as the fact that winning the auction tells the winner his bid was the higher. This, in turn, reveals something about what the other bidder knew and therefore something about the object's value. The expected value of the future cash flows conditional on y_1 and winning is below the expected value only conditional on y_1. Details are worked out in Appendix 2.

Two observations emerge. First, the private information allows the bidders to extract some of the gains to trade, and the seller suffers accordingly. To see this, notice from the bidding strategies that $b_1(y_1) = \frac{1}{2}(\alpha + \beta)y_1 > b_2(y_2) = \frac{1}{2}(\alpha + \beta)y_2$ if and only if $y_1 > y_2$. So, looking at the expected gains before the information is received, the seller's expected receipt is $E[\text{winning bid}] = \frac{1}{2}(\alpha + \beta)E[\max(y_1, y_2)]$. This reduces to $(\alpha + \beta)/3$.[14] Similarly, the expected gain to bidder 1 reduces to $\alpha/6$.[15] Likewise, bidder 2's expected gain is $\beta/6$. Naturally, the sum of the three expected gains is $\frac{1}{2}(\alpha + \beta)$ because trade always takes place in this setting.

Second, the bids are designed to protect the bidders from the so-called winner's curse. Upon placing a bid (of $\frac{1}{2}(\alpha + \beta)y_1$), bidder 1 knows y_1 but also knows that the bid wins only when $y_1 > y_2$. Winning carries information to the winner, information here that the winner's information was more favorable than the loser's. So, in this sense, there is a "curse" associated with winning. The winner learns that his view was most favorable. Protecting against this "curse," the bids are downward biased.

---

[14] In particular, we have

$$\frac{1}{2}(\alpha + \beta)E[\max(y_1, y_2)] = \frac{1}{2}(\alpha + \beta)\int_{y_1=0}^{1}\left[\int_{y_2=0}^{y_1} y_1 \, dy_2 + \int_{y_2=y_1}^{1} y_2 \, dy_2\right] dy_1$$

$$= \frac{1}{2}(\alpha + \beta)\int_{y_1=0}^{1}\left[y_1^2 + \frac{1}{2}(1 - y_1^2)\right] dy_1 = (\alpha + \beta)/3$$

[15] To verify this, recall that for any $y_1 \in [0, 1]$ and $y_2 \in [0, 1]$ the object's value is $\alpha y_1 + \beta y_2$; and if $y_1 > y_2$, bidder 1 wins this prize by paying $b_1(y_1) = \frac{1}{2}(\alpha + \beta)y_1$. The net gain is $\alpha y_1 + \beta y_2 - \frac{1}{2}(\alpha + \beta)y_1 = \frac{1}{2}\alpha y_1 + \beta(y_2 - \frac{1}{2}y_1)$. Overall, then, the expected gain to bidder 1 is given by

$$\int_{y_1=0}^{1}\int_{y_2=0}^{y_1}\left[\frac{1}{2}\alpha y_1 + \beta\left(y_2 - \frac{1}{2}y_1\right)\right] dy_2 \, dy_1 = \int_{y_1=0}^{1}\left[\frac{1}{2}\alpha y_1^2\right] dy_1 = \alpha/6$$

EXHIBIT 8.2
*PV$_0$ and Winning
Bid as Functions
of Information
Variables*

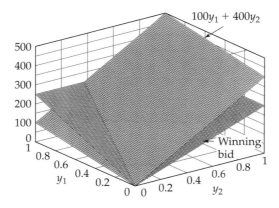

In sum, the close connection between value, as defined in (8.3), and the observed price at which the asset trades, is removed. According to (8.3), there should be a linear connection between the two pieces of information (y_1, y_2) and the value of the object. Yet the winning bid is $\frac{1}{2}(\alpha + \beta) \times$ $\max(y_1, y_2)$, which is somewhat removed from (8.3) and hardly linear in (y_1, y_2). The reason is that the bidders are taking their information advantage and the winner's "curse" into account when forming their bid. This is why we lose the close connection between the asset's value and the price at which it trades.

To illustrate, let $\alpha = 100$ and $\beta = 400$, giving us an underlying value of $PV_0 = 100y_1 + 400y_2$. In Exhibit 8.2 we plot PV_0 along with the winning bid, of $250\max(y_1, y_2)$. For small values of y_2, the observed price, the winning bid, tends to exceed the underlying value, while just the opposite occurs for large values of y_2; price equaling value is the exceptional case. Private information and a thin market, so to speak, disrupt the price versus value relationship.

One-Sided Information Equilibrium

A final story that will be useful occurs when one, but only one, of the bidders is informed. To illustrate, suppose bidder 1 privately observes $y_1 \in [0, 1]$ before bidding while bidder 2 knows only that bidder 1 is so informed. It turns out that an equilibrium here is for bidder 1 to bid $\frac{1}{2}(\alpha y_1 + \beta)$ and for bidder 2 to submit a random bid determined by $\frac{1}{2}(\alpha z + \beta)$, where z is drawn from a uniform density on the $[0, 1]$ interval.[16] Working through the details, Exhibit 8.3, notice that the uninformed

---

[16] That this is an equilibrium is readily verified. Just remember that bidder 1's bid winning the auction carries no additional information about the value of the object because the other bidder has no value-related private information. You will also notice that bidder 2 is indifferent and that is the key to bidder 2 being willing to randomize in the noted fashion.

EXHIBIT 8.3 **Expected Gains to Trade in Auction-Based Trade and Valuation Setting**

	Seller*	Bidder 1	Bidder 2	Total	Winning Bid
No information	$\frac{1}{2}(\alpha + \beta)$	0	0	$\frac{1}{2}(\alpha + \beta)$	$\frac{1}{2}(\alpha + \beta)$
Perfect public information	$\frac{1}{2}(\alpha + \beta)$	0	0	$\frac{1}{2}(\alpha + \beta)$	$\alpha y_1 + \beta y_2$
Private information	$(\alpha + \beta)/3$	$\alpha/6$	$\beta/6$	$\frac{1}{2}(\alpha + \beta)$	$\frac{1}{2}(\alpha + \beta)\max(y_1, y_2)$
One-sided information	$\alpha/3 + \beta/2$	$\alpha/6$	0	$\frac{1}{2}(\alpha + \beta)$	$\frac{1}{2}\beta + \frac{1}{2}\alpha\max(y_1, z)$

*This is the expected payment to the seller. The risk premium is not accounted for.

bidder here plays a nuisance role that keeps the informed bidder from extracting additional rent and thus helps the seller.

Valuation in the Small Numbers Auction Setting

In sum, the value expression in (8.3) and auction summarizations in Exhibit 8.3 provide our basic model of auction-based valuation and pretrade information. Recall that the setting is designed so the asset always trades. The only question is how the trading gain is divided among the parties who trade. Perfect or null information guarantees the bidders bid the price as high as reasonable, leaving the gain to the seller. With private information, however, the bidders are advantaged and capture some of the gain.

Also remember the seller is risk averse, so trading with perfectly informed bidders ensures that they capture none of the gain, but this is a moot victory because the seller now absorbs all of the risk associated with the project.

This setting has the convenience of explicitly accommodating private information and serves as a useful antidote to the usual classical market setting of perfect competition. Exhibit 8.3, in particular, demonstrates the slippage between value and the observed terms of trade that can occur in a private information setting. While we have kept the valuation fundamentals constant, the winning bid, the price, varies with the information setting. The distribution and the timing of the information matter.

It is also important, however, to stress that we provide the most simple of settings to allow the information usage question to be most transparent. Seemingly beneficial trade is not even guaranteed in more complex settings.[17]

---

[17] For example, we might have multiple units at auction, and the seller might value the object in nontrivial fashion and have private information as well. In the latter case, it would then no longer be guaranteed that the object would wind up in the hands of the party that valued it the most. Likewise, we assume here the individual retains the object won at auction, unlike, say, an IPO auction in which the winner has the option to resell the object at some later date.

Information Content in the Small Numbers Auction Setting

From here it is a short step to revisit our earlier information content theme. As before, imagine two information sources denoted η and $\hat{\eta}$. Here source η will report $y_1 \in [0, 1]$ and source $\hat{\eta}$ will report $y_2 \in [0, 1]$. Because our auction setting is essentially a single-period story, we will not worry explicitly about whatever prior information history is present or about the time at which the information becomes available. In particular, the only information is some combination of η and $\hat{\eta}$, and whatever combination is present, the signals are observed before the buyers' bids are submitted. We must, however, pay attention to what information is publically as opposed to privately observed.

Now, *if* source η, be it public or private, is the only source present, we then say source η has information content in the auction valuation setting (of (8.3)) *if* the winning bid varies in nontrivial fashion as a function of $y_1 \in [0, 1]$. The source has information content if it will affect the equilibrium valuation. With $\alpha > 0$, source η has information content, although the particulars depend on whether the information is public or private. Conversely, with $\alpha = 0$ (and $\beta > 0$), for example, source η has no information content regardless of whether it is publically or privately employed.

In parallel fashion, *if* sources η and $\hat{\eta}$ are the only sources present, we then say source $\hat{\eta}$ has information content *in the presence of source η* in the auction valuation setting (of (8.3)) *if* the winning bid varies in nontrivial fashion as a function of $y_2 \in [0, 1]$ for some $y_1 \in [0, 1]$.[18] Indeed, as suggested by Exhibit 8.3, we find $\hat{\eta}$ has information content in the presence of source η but also that, in this setting, the specifics depend on whether the information is private or public. Also note the subtlety when both information sources are private. There the winning bid, the price, reflects both pieces of information even though only one is winning. Winning carries information of the losing party's private information!

We emphasize that information content is a nominal concept: It is present or absent.[19] Moreover, information content is a conditional concept. It depends on the context, the auction-based trade and valuation setting here, and on what other information is present. Content does not imply that the individual or society, for that matter, is better off with the information being produced.

---

[18] With independence between the two random variables and the assumed valuation expression, source $\hat{\eta}$ having information content does not depend on the presence of source η. More broadly, though, the importance of conditioning on the presence of other information remains in this type of setting as well.

[19] We sidestep the issue of "social value" or a cost-benefit perspective at this point and stress the nominal notion that information content is present or absent. This will be revisited in Chapter 19.

THE LARGER STORY

What about the value of information in this setting in general? We have left many dimensions of trade, valuation, and resource allocation out of the story. The temptation, now—at least on our part—is to move on to a larger, more inclusive story. We give in to the temptation on one issue: the ambiguous link between information content in a trade-based valuation setting and the "social value" of producing the information in question.

The easiest way to see this ambiguity is to ponder the fact that information can hinder potential trading arrangements. Lottery players rely on no one knowing the winning number in advance. Fear of acquiring a lemon haunts the used auto market. After all, who would be prone to sell their autos: those who are pleased with its performance or those who are displeased? Insider trading is deeply frowned upon. Disclosure requirements are commonplace in real estate markets.

To dramatize the possibilities, return to the risk-neutral valuation setting and suppose risk-neutral players own the claim to the cash flow series, at time $t = 1$ after information structure η has reported. Next suppose those who hold the claim now privately receive the signal from information structure $\hat{\eta}$, say signal y_2, where source $\hat{\eta}$ has information content in the presence of source η. It is common knowledge the claim holders are now privately informed. What happens if they now try to sell their claim? Presumably, they would accept a price that only equals or exceeds their updated value of $E[PV_1 \mid h_1, y_2]$. Yet if someone would accept this price—which depends on the seller's private information—this person would implicitly be admitting to a willingness to knowingly pay for the proverbial overpriced security. The fact that the risk-neutral holder of the claim has private information and is willing to trade at some price de facto signals that the proposed trade is bad news to the other party. No trade takes place because of the private information.[20] The information, then, affects the risk-neutral claim holder's private valuation, but without advantageous trade this is a matter of indifference to that individual. No trade takes place. Here information content is present, but the information is of no use whatever.

This hints more deeply at the subtle side of information production and allocation in an economy. Trade, for example, is neither helped nor hindered by the production of public information in the risk-neutral valuation setting, with an important caveat. Suppose the risky claim is

---

[20] Similarly, in our auction-based setting, suppose only bidder 1 is informed. Furthermore, suppose bidder 1 wins the bid, subsequently privately learns $y_2 \in [0, 1]$, and then offers to sell the object to bidder 2 (or even to offer bidder 2 a share of the object). If bidder 2 knows the winning bidder has acquired additional information, any trade that is strictly profitable to the winning bidder is a loser to the would-be buyer. No thank you is bidder 2's appropriate response.

presently owned by risk-averse individuals. Further suppose information with nontrivial information content is released before trade takes place. This is harmful to the initial owners because they are forced to bear fully the risk of information-induced revaluation on the initial claims. It is important that any such information arrive after the market has cleared. Otherwise, risk-averse owners of risky claims are inefficiently exposed to risk. Such information, then, surely has information content, but society is worse off for the information having been produced. Moreover, once the market has cleared and the risk-neutral individuals hold the risky claim, there is no interest on their part in producing additional information. They are, literally, indifferent about such a prospect.

On the buyers' side, private information allows the bidders to extract some of the gains to trade from the seller. At this point the seller has an interest in becoming informed because that neutralizes the information-based advantage of the bidders. So, here information redistributes the gains to trade, and in a more complicated setting (e.g., when the seller also had private information), information would affect whether trade takes place.

Now step back from these details and imagine a complex, productive economy marching through time. Production, investment, and consumption take place at each point in time. What can we say about information's effect in the financial markets sector of this economy? Presumably, information is useful in directing investment and production as well as in timing consumption, and this will presumably be visible in the financial markets sector as valuations move in response to the arrival of new information.

Moving beyond the obvious, however, is a tall order. A possible way to proceed is to use the capital asset pricing model (CAPM) to provide a more structured view of valuation activity in the financial markets. This allows us to think in terms of risk and return, with risk well defined and priced (contrary to our risk-neutral model in (8.2)). Recall, however, that the CAPM stresses the idea of individual investors selecting their preferred location on the efficient risk-return frontier. This implies investors have well-diversified portfolios and if the economy is sufficiently large, the idiosyncratic risk of any given instrument simply does not matter. That risk is diversifiable. Only the systematic risk is central to the valuation.

In information terms, then, the important issues focus on well-diversified portfolios. Reporting by a single entity has no major effect if it concerns the diversifiable portion of the entity's risky return stream. It is difficult to imagine under these circumstances that as a matter of routine, each solitary reporting entity carries profoundly important information to the financial market. That is, the information side of the CAPM stresses economywide valuation while accounting issues tend to surface at the single reporting entity level. This suggests that valuation effects associated with accounting-based information take on a different hue when thought of as coordinated behavior by a large array of reporting entities because no single entity is being endowed with "market power." Suppose, through some regulatory intervention, additional accounting-based disclosures of some type are mandated. Do these new disclosures have information content? Presumably, by affecting "all" reporting entities, they may speak to economywide events that would be of significant interest to well-diversified investors.

Moreover, the story is significantly more subtle than even this perfunctory observation suggests. We also know that we must condition on other information in order to conceptually make such an assessment. It is also possible other information sources will adjust in light of the new disclosure mandate. For example, analysts might decide to chase this forthcoming disclosure to get a leg up, so to speak. They also might decide to back away from some information sources they are presently using. The point is that a regulatory intervention does not necessarily leave the other information sources as they were.

Trade-based valuation is our avenue for identifying information content in a valuation setting. In addition to the various subtleties, we also acknowledge that the link from information content to "social value" of the information is problematic. Risk-neutral valuation, with no production effects, removes any concern for information as long as the claims are in the hands of risk-neutral individuals. Introducing information before risk-averse individuals have traded with risk-neutral individuals is harmful, however, to the risk-averse individuals. More broadly, with risk aversion there is concern for early resolution of uncertainty and, hence, an interest in public information, just as there would be such an interest were production plans sensitive to that information. Looking to a more involved setting with multiple securities and balanced portfolios, the demand for information concentrates on economywide as opposed to firm-specific information. Thus, "social value" is ambiguous in these settings; and strategic use of private information further clouds the picture and leads to divergence between price and value of the underlying claims. It is important to remember that information's impact depends on other information sources and how imaginatively we view the valuation setting. The link between information content and whether production of that information is desirable, even if it is cost free, is ambiguous. This is the inherent nature of information in a multiperson setting.

Summary

Accounting is often thought of as being closely connected to valuation, in part because it uses the language and algebra of valuation in its own measurement apparatus and in part because it is often an important information source for firms with actively traded shares. Here we begin our exploration of how this connection might be made. The essential detail is individuals trading, or offering to trade, claims to uncertain cash flows.

The more familiar of the two regimes explored is a setting of risk neutrality and competitive pricing, such that the value, or market price, of the claim to any future cash flows is simply the expected value of the underlying continuation present value. Equivalently, we might think of this as a setting in which the value, or market price, is the continuation present value of the remaining cash flows' expected values. Naturally, these expectations are informed by whatever information is available, and that information is assumed equally available to all market participants. This gives us a valuation function that is a direct extension of that used in Chapter 3 that incorporates uncertainty and the arrival of information. It also gives us a valuation function in which information's effect is particularly transparent via its systematic revision of the expected value of each of the remaining cash flows.

Even so, information content is not a particularly transparent topic in this setting. The reason is the interaction among multiple sources of information. If the price at time t is affected by the release of information at time t, we have an unequivocal display of information content. The nature of this effect may well depend on what information was released in prior periods, just as the full importance of what was released in prior periods may not be discernible until additional information arrives at a later point in time. The troublesome part of this risk-neutral story is that there is no demand for early resolution of uncertainty and, consequently, no demand for accounting to convey any information about what cash flows will eventually materialize.

A second trade regime introduced is that of an auction. In contrast to the direct extension of valuation under certainty, the auction allows us to introduce potential traders with private information. Here information content becomes more subtle as does the use of that information. More important, it serves as a warning not to build our intuition by exclusive reliance on the risk-neutral, public information trading story. For example, in the auction setting, we lose the tight connection between the price at which an object trades and the underlying "value" of that object, simply because of the presence of private information and the players jockeying over the rent, or gains to trade.

These two regimes represent two extremes, and combining them allows us to make inferences in more involved settings. There is limited comfort in this, however, because we have no direct connection between information content and the "social value" of information. The emerging picture is one in which content and value of information are closely tied to the individual and the detailed setting, including the allocation of information and the organization of markets. It is essential for us never to forget that the individuals will use their private information strategically and that information sources interact.

Appendix 1

Market Equilibrium

Both of our explorations of valuation rely on trade to render an observable assessment of value. This is explicit in the auction setting but is merely presumed in the risk-neutral valuation setting. In this Appendix, we expand on this theme of value in a market setting.

Generically, value stems from individual consumption and is tied closely to personal tastes and consumption opportunities in the economy. In a market economy, these individual preferences are aggregated into a market valuation. None of this is explicitly present in the model we presumed, (8.2). In what sense is this value calculation faithful to this aggregate personal taste characteristic of a well-functioning global market?

To provide a sketch, imagine an economy in which markets are used to allocate a given supply of commodities. (This is called a *pure exchange economy*.) Our highly simplified version will have three representative actors. One owns the claim to the risky "cash" flow series described earlier in Exhibit 8.1. The others each own "cash" totaling W_i at time $t = 0$ but nothing else. (W_i is sufficiently large that bankruptcy is of no concern.) "Cash" in this story is shorthand for other consumption goods. Cash is the only good available, and it cannot be stored. Whatever the economywide endowment in period t is, this amount and only this amount can be consumed, economywide, in period t.[21] Consumption might go negative for some individuals in some periods. The endowed amounts, cataloged by the initial owner, are displayed in Exhibit 8.4. The $t = 0$ amount is known while the amounts in the remaining periods are uncertain.

How much of the total available in any given period that each type will consume depends on their respective preferences and the nature of the resource allocation mechanism. We assume time-additive preferences for each type, strict risk aversion for individual 1 and risk neutrality for the other individuals.

In particular, with the economy lasting through period $T = 3$, we envision consumption taking place at times $t = 0$, 1, 2, and 3. Let $x = [x_0, x_1, x_2, x_3]$ denote some generic consumption plan. The utility for individual 1 for x is given by

$$U_1(x) = u(x_0) + u(x_1)(1 + r)^{-1} + u(x_2)(1 + r)^{-2} + u(x_3)(1 + r)^{-3}$$

---

[21] The reason for assuming that "cash" cannot be stored or saved from one period to the next is that we want to rule out production of any sort. Naturally, storage is a form of production as it moves goods from one period to the next. We want to rule out production at this point because it dramatically complicates the story, although in this case without any added insight.

EXHIBIT 8.4
Endowed
Quantities in
Market Equilibrium
Illustration

	Period-by-Period Endowed Consumption Claims			
Individual	$t = 0$	$t = 1$	$t = 2$	$t = 3$
1	CF_0	CF_1	CF_2	CF_3
2	W_2	0	0	0
3	W_3	0	0	0
4	$CF_0 + W_2 + W_3$	CF_1	CF_2	CF_3

We want consumption to matter, so utility function $u(\cdot)$ is strictly increasing; risk aversion implies $u(\cdot)$ is a strictly concave function. This implies, among other things, that individual 1 has a keen interest in appropriately "smoothing" consumption through time. Otherwise, the individual has not intertemporally balanced consumption by equating marginal utility across the time periods.

The two other individuals, recall, are assumed to be risk neutral. Each such person's utility for generic consumption plan $x = [x_0, x_1, x_2, x_3]$ is given by

$$U_i(x) = x_0 + x_1(1+r)^{-1} + x_2(1+r)^{-2} + x_3(1+r)^{-3}$$

These individuals do not care about the timing of consumption per se but only about the total "discounted" consumption. Conveniently, all individuals share the same time discount factor, $r > 0$. Moreover, the risk-neutral types' preferences mimic our valuation model in (8.2).

Now individual 1 is strictly risk averse and owns a risky cash flow series. The others are risk neutral. Risk is noxious to individual 1 but is a matter of indifference to the others. Gains to trade are clearly available. Individual 1 would gain by exchanging the uncertain cash flows for their expected values at each point in time. The others are indifferent between these two alternatives. How the gains to trade are allocated among the three individuals depends upon a number of factors, including the distribution of information and the trade mechanism itself. (Think back to our auction setting, for example.)

From here, let's assume an exchange market meets at time $t = 0$. All individuals are strict price takers, and no information is present. Consumption quantities for any of the time periods can be bought and sold, as can the claim to the noted **CF** series described in Exhibit 8.4. Let Φ_t denote the current market price of a unit of the consumption good to be received at time $t = 0, 1, 2,$ or 3. Let's also normalize the prices with $\Phi_0 = 1$.

The key is to identify competition among the risk-neutral types. Consider exchange of period 0 consumption versus period 1 consumption. With $\Phi_0 = 1$, suppose $\Phi_1 < (1+r)^{-1}$. That is, suppose a unit of $t = 1$ consumption can be purchased for less than it is worth to a type 2 individual.

This implies excess demand for $t = 1$ consumption. In particular, consider any tentative consumption plan for a risk-neutral type. What if θ of the $t = 0$ consumption amount is sold and the proceeds are used to buy additional units of the $t = 1$ amount? The gain to this individual is $-\theta + (\theta/\Phi_1)(1+r)^{-1}$, which is strictly positive as $\Phi_1 < (1+r)^{-1}$. Parallel comments apply to the possibility of $\Phi_1 > (1+r)^{-1}$. So, market equilibrium requires us to have $\Phi_1 = (1+r)^{-1}$. Repeating the argument gives us $\Phi_t = (1+r)^{-t}$, for $t = 2, 3$.

From here we use the same observation to convince ourselves that the risk-neutral person will evaluate the risky asset or stream of cash flows as

$$E[CF_1]\Phi_1 + E[CF_2]\Phi_2 + E[CF_3]\Phi_3$$

$$= E[CF_1](1+r)^{-1} + E[CF_2](1+r)^{-2} + E[CF_3](1+r)^{-3}$$

$$= E[PV_0 \mid h_0 = \text{null}] = P_0(h_0 = \text{null})$$

our assumed valuation expression in (8.2). The present owner (individual 2 or 3) would not sell it for anything less, and nobody would buy it at a higher price either. Thus, the market valuation is the price $P_0(h_0 = \text{null})$.[22]

In brief, then, this is how we might rationalize the risk-neutral valuation expression in (8.2). It reflects market equilibrium in a trading economy in which risk-neutral participants carry all the risk, and thus risk itself is "priced at zero." This is, of course, not the only such argument, but it does provide the flavor for the manner in which we model market behavior in a classically competitive setting.[23]

From here it is a straightforward extension to track the arrival of public information. Suppose we are at time $t = 1$ and new public information has arrived, updating the history variable from h_0 to h_1. (The new information might be the CF_1 realization itself or that supplemented with other information.) We now reapply the earlier argument. Renormalizing the current prices, via $\Phi_1 = 1$, we now must have $\Phi_2 = (1+r)^{-1}$. Present value calculations remain central. At time $t = 1$, then, with information history h_1, we find the value, the market price, of the remaining elements of the **CF** series to be $E[PV_1 \mid h_1] = P_1(h_1)$, as assumed in (8.2).

---

[22] Now roll forward from this equilibrium to time $t = 1$. Suppose the markets reopen. Will trade take place? The answer is no because the risk-averse type 1 individual is now sitting on fully insured consumption claims, and the risk-neutral counterparts have nothing to offer that is mutually agreeable.

[23] Another approach is to admit we are offering a partial equilibrium view and to recast the equilibrium market value of the claim to some cash flow series by adjusting the probabilities, so it is as if the claim were priced in risk-neutral fashion. These adjusted probabilities are called *risk-neutral probabilities*. Although technically feasible, this does not seem to do justice to the issues that concern us at this juncture.

Appendix **2**

Equilibrium in the Private Information Auction

We now verify our claim in the private information auction setting that the pair of bidding strategies given by $b_1(y_1) = \frac{1}{2}(\alpha + \beta)y_1$ and $b_2(y_2) = \frac{1}{2}(\alpha + \beta)y_2$ is indeed equilibrium behavior. Suppose bidder 2 uses the noted $b_2(y_2) = \frac{1}{2}(\alpha + \beta)y_2$ strategy and, upon privately observing $y_1 \in [0, 1]$, bidder 1 proffers a bid of b. What is bidder 1's optimal bid? If $b > \frac{1}{2}(\alpha + \beta)y_2$, bidder 1 wins outright. If $b < \frac{1}{2}(\alpha + \beta)y_2$, bidder 2 wins outright. Under a tie, recall, a coin is flipped, but for any bid b, the probability that $b = \frac{1}{2}(\alpha + \beta)y_2$ is zero because y_2 is a continuously distributed random variable. So, the bid of b wins when $b > \frac{1}{2}(\alpha + \beta)y_2$, or $2b/(\alpha + \beta) > y_2$. The uniform density is convenient at this point because $prob(b \text{ wins}) = prob(y_2 < 2b/(\alpha + \beta)) = 2b/(\alpha + \beta)$. That is, 1's bid of b will win with probability $2b/(\alpha + \beta)$.[24]

Next, what is the expected value of the prize if the bid of b wins? With $PV_0 = \alpha y_1 + \beta y_2$, winning implies $2b/(\alpha + \beta) > y_2$, so $E[y_2 \mid 2b/(\alpha + \beta) > y_2] = b/(\alpha + \beta)$.[25] And $E[PV_0 \mid y_1$ and b wins$] = \alpha y_1 + \beta E[y_2 \mid 2b/(\alpha + \beta) > y_2] = \alpha y_1 + \beta b/(\alpha + \beta)$.

Now bidder 1 wants to select b to maximize expected net gain, given the presumed bidding behavior of bidder 2 and given knowledge of $y_1 \in [0, 1]$. So, the bidder selects bid b to

$$\text{maximize } prob(b \text{ wins}) \times (E[PV_0 \mid y_1 \text{ and } b \text{ wins}] - b)$$

$$+ prob(b \text{ does notwin}) \times 0$$

$$= (2b/(\alpha + \beta))(\alpha y_1 + \beta b/(\alpha + \beta) - b)$$

Notice the probability of winning is $prob(b \text{ wins}) = 2b/(\alpha + \beta)$, the value of the object conditional on knowing y_1 and on winning the bid is $E[y_2 \mid 2b/(\alpha + \beta) > y_2] = \alpha y_1 + \beta b/(\alpha + \beta)$, and the price paid for the object is b.

To locate the maximum, we differentiate with respect to b and set the derivative to zero.

$$(2/(\alpha + \beta))(\alpha y_1 + \beta b/(\alpha + \beta) - b) + (2b/(\alpha + \beta))(\beta/(\alpha + \beta) - 1) = 0$$

or

$$\alpha y_1 + \beta b/(\alpha + \beta) - b + b(\beta/(\alpha + \beta) - 1) = 0$$

---

[24] This assumes $0 \leq 2b/(\alpha + \beta) \leq 1$. As we shall see, this turns out to be the case.
[25] Once again, we see the convenience of assuming a uniform density.

or

$$\alpha y_1 - 2\alpha b/(\alpha + \beta) = 0$$

So, the best response having observed y_1 is to bid $b = \frac{1}{2}(\alpha + \beta)y_1$. Now assume $b_1(y_1) = \frac{1}{2}(\alpha + \beta)y_1$ and perform the companion analysis for bidder 2. You will find $b_2(y_2) = \frac{1}{2}(\alpha + \beta)y_2$, as claimed.[26]

---

[26] Two loose ends should be checked. We assumed $0 \leq 2b/(\alpha + \beta) \leq 1$. This is now readily verified. Also, when we differentiated to locate the maximum, we presumed we were locating a maximum, not a minimum. This is verified by checking that the second derivative is negative. (It is as we presume, $\alpha \geq 0$ and $\beta \geq 0$, with at least one strictly positive, and $\alpha = 0$ is a trivial story.)

Selected References

A rich literature exists here. To illustrate, Penman (2000) stresses sophisticated investor valuation; Radner (1968) analyzes economywide equilibrium issues in the presence of uncertainty and information; also see Hirshleifer (1970; 1971), Hakannson, Kunkel, and Ohlson (1982), Ohlson (1987), and Schlee (2001). Grossman and Stiglitz (1980) study the ability of equilibrium prices to convey some of the information privately held in the economy, and Demski and Feltham (1994) examine reactive responses in the private information sector when public disclosure is increased; also see Dye (2001) and Verrecchia (2001). Sargent (1999) offers a macro perspective. Strategic considerations are explored in Milgrom and Stokey's (1982) no trade setting (also see Ingersoll, 1987) as well as in Gibbons (1992), Milgrom and Roberts (1992) and Rasmusen (2000). Auctions are also the subject of considerable work and application; in addition to Gibbons (1992) and Rasmusen (2000), favorites include Boyes and Happel (1989), McMillan (1994), and Milgrom (1989; 1998). Myerson (1991) is an excellent reference on the winners' curse.

Key Terms

An information source has **information content** if it affects behavior. In a single-person setting, Chapter 6, this reduces to whether the individual's choice is affected by, literally varies with, the arrival of the information. In a risk-neutral valuation setting, when expression (8.2) describes the price or valuation process, information content boils down to whether price, or value, is affected by the information's arrival. Of course, we must be careful to control for other sources of information. Likewise, in the bidding setting, when expression (8.3) describes the asset's value but the trade arrangements depend on an auction, information content is present when the price, the winning bid, at which the asset trades depends on what the information sources report. In addition, the way the information is used depends on equilibrium behavior. In the perfect market setting, **equilibrium** refers to the market-clearing price, but in the strategic setting, it refers to strategic behavior, to mutual best response.

Exercises

8.1. The pricing functions in (8.2a) and (8.2b) depend on the expected value of the future cash flows, conditional on whatever information is available at the time the price is quoted, so to speak. Why does this presumed pricing function depend on only these conditional expected values and the interest rate?

8.2. Suppose a regulator seeks to regulate the time at which one of the information sources in Exhibit 8.1 conveys its signal (e.g., "early" versus "late" reporting). What are the potential consequences of the regulator myopically focusing exclusively on this one information source, given other sources are or may be present?

8.3. Suppose a strictly risk-averse individual owns a risky cash flow series and seeks to sell it in a world in which prices are well explained by the pricing functions in (8.2a) and (8.2b). Information will also be arriving. Does the seller care whether the information arrives before or after the sale? What about the buyer? Carefully explain.

8.4. Alter the cash flow possibilities in the story in Exhibit 8.1 as given in the following table. (Notice that the expected value of each cash flow remains as before, as do the information sources.) The interest rate remains at 10 percent. Further assume information source η reports at time $t = 1$ while information source $\hat{\eta}$ reports at time $t = 2$. Does the first source have information content at time $t = 1$? Does it have information content at time $t = 2$? Carefully explain.

	State			
	s_1	s_2	s_3	s_4
$prob(s_i)$	.25	.25	.25	.25
$CF_0(s)$	−25,000	−25,000	−25,000	−25,000
$CF_1(s)$	4,950	4,950	4,950	4,950
$CF_2(s)$	9,680	9,680	9,680	9,680
$CF_3(s)$	17,637.50	15,637.50	26,637.50	6,637.50
Information source η	y_1'	y_1'	y_1''	y_1''
Information source $\hat{\eta}$	y_2'	y_2''	y_2'	y_2''

8.5. Consider the cash flow, $CF(s)$, and information sources in the following table. The interest rate is 10 percent.

	State			
	s_1	s_2	s_3	s_4
$prob(s_i)$	.25	.25	.25	.25
$CF_0(s)$	−200	−200	−200	−200
$CF_1(s)$	20	20	20	20
$CF_2(s)$	0	0	220	220
$CF_3(s)$	0	242	0	242
Information source η	y_1'	y_1'	y_1''	y_1''
Information source $\hat{\eta}$	y_2'	y_2''	y_2'	y_2''

Initially suppose the only information present is that provided by the cash flows themselves. Determine the price, or value, of the claim to the remaining cash flow series, at each point in time, and for each state. Do this for valuation immediately following the distribution of the period's cash flow. Use the following table to record your calculations.

	State			
	s_1	s_2	s_3	s_4
$P_0(h_0) \equiv E[PV_0 \mid h_0]$				
$P_1(h_1) \equiv E[PV_1 \mid h_1]$				
$P_2(h_2) \equiv E[PV_2 \mid h_2]$				
$P_3(h_3) \equiv E[PV_3 \mid h_3]$				

Now repeat the pricing calculations in the above table for the case in which we price the claim at time t just before the time t cash flow is observed, that is, $P_t(\hat{h}_t) \equiv E[CF_t \mid \hat{h}_t] + E[PV_t \mid \hat{h}_t]$.

8.6. Repeat Exercise 8.5, assuming that information structure η reports at time $t = 1$, just before the value calculation takes place.

8.7. Repeat Exercise 8.5, now assuming that both information structures report at time $t = 1$, just before the value calculation takes place.

8.8. You should have discovered in Exercises 8.5, 8.6, and 8.7 that the price, or value, at time $t = 0$ does not depend on which information story we tell. Carefully explain.

8.9. Ralph is holding an auction for an asset whose value is given by $v(y_1, y_2) = 100y_1 + 200y_2$. y_1 and y_2 are independently distributed and described by a uniform distribution on the $[0, 1]$ interval. So, the expected value of the asset's value is simply $100E[y_1] + 200E[y_2] = \frac{1}{2}(100 + 200) = 150$. There are two bidders. High bid wins the auction and the winner pays the winning bid to Ralph. Bidder 1 privately observes variable y_1 before bidding, and bidder 2 privately observes y_2 before bidding. A pair of equilibrium bidding strategies is given by $b_1(y_1) = 150y_1$ and $b_2(y_2) = 150y_2$.

Now suppose that we, as outsiders, observe the sale of this asset to the winning bidder, and record the magnitude of the sale as equal to the winning bid. Plot the winning bid, and, hence, recorded value, for each realization of y_1 and y_2. Also plot, on the same graph, the actual value of the asset for each realization of y_1 and y_2. Carefully explain the pattern that emerges.

8.10. This is a continuation of Exercise 8.9. By way of contrast, now suppose both bidders observe y_1 and y_2 before bidding. Repeat the plotting exercise in Exercise 8.9 for this case. Interpret and contrast your results. (Be careful here; the pure strategy equilibrium bidding strategies are now to bid $b_1(y_1, y_2) = b_2(y_1, y_2) = 100y_1 + 200y_2$.)

Chapter

9

Accounting Information in a Valuation Setting

We now introduce accounting as an explicit information source in a valuation setting. This allows us to juxtapose accounting and trade-based valuations while treating accounting as the source of information in the valuation exercise. Doing so, however, is devoid of intuition unless we place some structure on the firm's fundamentals. For this reason, we proceed with a heavily stylized firm whose fundamentals are affected by transient and permanent shocks. What is learned about these shocks is learned from the accounting-based information release. In turn, risk-neutral, competitive market valuation is used to identify the valuation implications of these accounting-based information releases. Scaling, you will see, plays an important role in the exercise.

It is time to combine the themes of accounting as a source of information and that information being used in a valuation setting. Here we assume the accounting system is the sole supplier of information to the valuation market. This means the accounting measures and the market valuation are based upon the same underlying source of information about the reporting entity. In Chapter 10, we mix accounting and nonaccounting sources, thereby allowing the market valuation to be informed by nonaccounting as well as by accounting information.

The point of the present analysis is to contrast accounting and market-based valuation in a setting in which both "valuation processes" are carrying or accessing the same information. The important difference, then, involves the different structures that are hidden in the two valuation processes. The market valuation, here, is a risk-neutral valuation of the discounted (expected) cash flows. As such, it is an aggressive user of all available information, processing the information in Bayesian fashion to update the expected values of the remaining cash flows. It is informationally efficient; whatever information is available is available to all market participants, and the market valuation, the market price, fully reflects that information.

The accounting side, though, is another story. It is wedded to accounting as opposed to economic structure. Its predominant characteristics are found in the recognition rules and the calculus of accounting. This structure restrains the processing of information in the accounting system and typically results in a lack of alignment between accounting and market valuation.

Recognition rules, of course, specify when an event is recorded in the accounting system. Conventional wisdom, for example, states that significant uncertainty implies income will be recognized late in the process, only after the bulk of the uncertainty has been resolved. For the moment, though, we neutralize this issue by assuming that whatever information is available is used by both the accounting and market processes.

On the calculus side, linearity permeates accounting. The primary means of aggregating the information that is included in the accounting system is the addition or subtraction of numbers. The asset total of a company is found by adding the value of the individual assets. Individual asset values, in turn, are often calculated as initial amounts coupled with an additive adjustment, such as receivables less an allowance or capital assets less accumulated depreciation. Allocation itself is inherently linear. Income is calculated as revenue less cost of goods sold and period expenses. This linear approach to processing is highlighted in what follows.

We focus on a single-asset setting and track its value through time. Injecting accounting as the information source allows us to contrast the (risk-neutral) valuation path with the corresponding accounting measures associated with that asset. In the process we identify connections between the two series that depend on the accounting treatment, or policy, as well as what information is conveyed by the accounting measures.

Our work is extended in the Appendix to a dynamic setting in which the firm replenishes its supply of assets through time. This allows for, among other things, a steady-state perspective in which we are able to exhibit a more or less constant connection between temporal value and the related accounting measures.

Though surely straining reality, it is important to work through the details of linking market value to accounting variables. For example, we often compare market (value) to book (value), or divide market (value) by earnings (a price-earnings ratio). Here a similar tack is taken but by explicitly treating the accounting variables as carriers of information.

Literally, the accounting variables are not measures of value but are carriers of information that inform the value assessment.

EXOGENOUS CASH FLOWS

We begin with the usual setting, a single investment or asset. Cash is invested at time $t = 0$, and cash inflow is received at times $t = 1, 2, \ldots, T$. We concentrate on the $T = 3$ case for expositional purposes. This sequence of cash flows is exogenous; at this juncture, it is simply a given. Presumably, an investor or group of investors initially invests $-CF_0$ at $t = 0$ and subsequently receives dividends of CF_t, at $t = 1, 2$, and 3. As usual, any cash on hand at time t is always paid out to the investors.[1]

The inflows, of course, are random variables. In Chapter 8, we modeled the uncertainty by carrying along a state descriptor and modeled the information as providing a sequence of partitions of the underlying state set. This general description is an important starting point, but its generality removes any notion of context. For example, other than identifying a depreciation schedule, there is little fodder on which to identify accounting structure.

For this reason, we now (purposely) switch to an alternative specification of the uncertainty. This is, as you will see, a highly stylized specification. It has the advantage of being intuitive and providing a window into important institutional details that will be explored in Chapter 10. Nonetheless, the specification is a special case of the risk-neutral valuation setting developed in Chapter 8.

Stylized Cash Flow Structure

Assume, then, that the initial (investment) amount is known with certainty and, as usual, is denoted $CF_0 < 0$. The three inflows are now treated simply as random variables and denoted, respectively, CF_1, CF_2, and CF_3. Also denote the expected value of the respective cash inflows by $E[CF_1] = \bar{c}_1$, $E[CF_2] = \bar{c}_2$, and $E[CF_3] = \bar{c}_3$.

From here we model the uncertainty in terms of four independent shock terms, denoted ϵ, ϵ_1, ϵ_2, and ϵ_3:

$$CF_1 = \bar{c}_1 + \epsilon + \epsilon_1 \qquad \textbf{(9.1a)}$$

$$CF_2 = \bar{c}_2 + \theta\epsilon + \epsilon_2 \qquad \textbf{(9.1b)}$$

$$CF_3 = \bar{c}_3 + \gamma\epsilon + \epsilon_3 \qquad \textbf{(9.1c)}$$

[1] This reduced form treats the reporting entity as a one-asset firm. We purposely suppress underlying details of factor choices, production, sales, customer receipts, and factor payments.

EXHIBIT 9.1
Cash Flows for
$t = 0, 1, 2,$ and 3

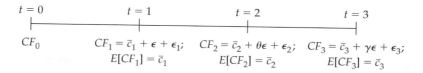

Tautologically, each shock term has an expected value of zero, $E[\epsilon] = E[\epsilon_1] = E[\epsilon_2] = E[\epsilon_3] = 0$. See Exhibit 9.1.

The feature to note here is that in each period we have a shock term but that an additional shock term in the first period, term ϵ, affects all three cash inflows. It affects the first period cash inflow directly, but ϵ carries over to add the amount $\theta\epsilon$ to the second period inflow and $\gamma\epsilon$ to the third period inflow. θ and γ are known constants. With these constants both positive, good news (i.e., $\epsilon > 0$) in the first period persists, just as does bad news (i.e., $\epsilon < 0$). Importantly, then, the valuation at time $t = 1$ will be affected by what is known about the common shock term, ϵ. Conversely, with $\theta = \gamma = 0$, there is no future effect, and the $t = 1$ valuation is unaffected by what is known about the common shock term.

Intuitively, the cash flow of each period is affected by a transitory component (the ϵ_ts), and if the θ and γ parameters are nonzero, the cash flow of each period is also affected by the noted persistence effect. For example, think of both parameters as strictly positive. Then good news in the first period persists. In a casual sense, then, an earnings measure that well identifies the persistence effect, the ϵ, provides a case in which the first period earnings would be "quality earnings" in that the news they signal via the reported earnings can be anticipated to continue. (A second period persistence effect might also be introduced, but we have limited patience.)

To better appreciate the persistence effect, notice that at time $t = 0$, and in the absence of any information, all we know about the shock terms is they are zero mean (i.e., $E[\epsilon] = E[\epsilon_t] = 0$). Conversely, at time $t = 1$, when we have observed the first period cash inflow, we de facto have observed the combined first period shock of $\epsilon + \epsilon_1$. This tells us nothing about ϵ_2 or ϵ_3 because of the assumed independence among the shock terms, but it tells us something about the persistence term. For example, if both ϵ and ϵ_1 are normally distributed[2] (with zero means, of course) with identical variances, the assumed independence implies $E[\epsilon \mid \epsilon + \epsilon_1] = (\epsilon + \epsilon_1)/2$.

In this way, knowledge of the first period cash flow explicitly helps us predict the remaining cash flows. So, having observed that $CF_1 = \bar{c}_1 + \epsilon + \epsilon_1$, we know $\epsilon + \epsilon_1$. The resulting conditional expectations are

---

[2] More generally, assume ϵ is normally distributed with a variance of σ^2 and ϵ_1 is normally distributed with a variance of σ_1^2. Given the assumed independence between the two shock terms, we then know $\epsilon + \epsilon_1$ is normally distributed with a variance of $\sigma^2 + \sigma_1^2$. From here, applying Bayes' rule, we readily conclude that conditional on observing $\epsilon + \epsilon_1 = x$, shock term ϵ is normally distributed with a mean of $\sigma^2 x/(\sigma^2 + \sigma_1^2)$. That is, $E[\epsilon \mid \epsilon + \epsilon_1 = x] = \sigma^2 x/(\sigma^2 + \sigma_1^2)$.

EXHIBIT 9.2   **State-Based Illustration of Cash Flow Structure in (9.1)**

	s_1	s_2	s_3	s_4	s_5	s_6	s_7	s_8	s_9
$prob(s_i)$	1/9	1/9	1/9	1/9	1/9	1/9	1/9	1/9	1/9
ϵ	−500	−500	−500	0	0	0	500	500	500
ϵ_1	−500	0	500	−500	0	500	−500	0	500
$\epsilon + \epsilon_1$	−1,000	−500	0	−500	0	500	0	500	1,000
$E[\epsilon \mid \epsilon + \epsilon_1]$	−500	−250	0	−250	0	250	0	250	500

written as follows:

$$E[CF_2 \mid CF_1 = \bar{c}_1 + \epsilon + \epsilon_1]$$
$$= E[CF_2 \mid \epsilon + \epsilon_1] = \bar{c}_2 + \theta E[\epsilon \mid \epsilon + \epsilon_1] \quad \textbf{(9.2a)}$$

$$E[CF_3 \mid CF_1 = \bar{c}_1 + \epsilon + \epsilon_1]$$
$$= E[CF_3 \mid \epsilon + \epsilon_1] = \bar{c}_3 + \gamma E[\epsilon \mid \epsilon + \epsilon_1] \quad \textbf{(9.2b)}$$

Stated differently, observing the first cash inflow reveals the shock total of $\epsilon + \epsilon_1$, and knowledge of that total tells us something about the persistence term, in effect altering its expected value from zero to $E[\epsilon \mid \epsilon + \epsilon_1]$. This, in turn, tells us something about the remaining cash inflows (assuming we do not have $\theta = \gamma = 0$). For example, first period cash sales may tell us something about future period cash sales. Our modeling device based on the four shock terms is simply a convenient way to tell this story.

To illustrate, and to demonstrate the connection to the underlying state descriptor, assume the ϵ_2 and ϵ_3 terms are guaranteed to be zero, so the only concern is the persistence shock, ϵ, and the first period transitory shock, ϵ_1. Additional details are given in Exhibit 9.2.

Notice that either shock term (i.e., ϵ or ϵ_1) can take on a value of −500, 0, or 500 with equal probability. Now suppose that we observe only the total of the two shock terms, $\epsilon + \epsilon_1$. This total can be −1,000, −500, 0, 500, or 1,000, and observing the total induces the partition $\{\{s_1\}, \{s_2, s_4\}, \{s_3, s_5, s_7\}, \{s_6, s_8\}, \{s_9\}\}$. Naturally, we find that the total shock, the $\epsilon + \epsilon_1$ term, is informative about ϵ. From here the associated updated expected values, that is, $E[\epsilon \mid \epsilon + \epsilon_1]$, follow in straightforward fashion.

Temporal Valuation

Now consider the value, the market price, of the claim to the cash flow series as we march through time. We rely on risk-neutral pricing, or valuation, with a constant interest rate, r. As usual, PV_t denotes the present value of the remaining cash flows as of time t (and using interest rate r). As used in Chapter 8, h_t denotes the totality of all information received up to time t. So, our valuation assumption (equation (8.2)) is simply a history-dependent price at time t, $P_t(h_t)$, of

$$P_t(h_t) = E[PV_t \mid h_t] = \sum_{j=t+1}^{T} E[CF_j \mid h_t](1+r)^{t-j} \quad \textbf{(9.3a)}$$

if we are pricing the claim to the remaining cash flow series at time t in the presence of information history h_t. Likewise, if we are pricing that claim moments before the receipt of dividend CF_t and if at the time of pricing we know information history $\hat{h}_t$, we have[3]

$$P_t(\hat{h}_t) \equiv E[CF_t \mid \hat{h}_t] + E[PV_t \mid \hat{h}_t] \qquad \textbf{(9.3b)}$$

The central feature of the calculation, of course, is the impact of the information on the underlying cash flow assessments. For example, suppose that in (9.3a) the only available information at time $t = 1$ is the first period cash flow itself, CF_1. This implies the information available at that time is simply $h_1 = \epsilon + \epsilon_1$, the sum of the persistent and transitory shocks. With the revised cash inflow expectations, noted in (9.2), we have a value at this point based on

$$\begin{aligned}
E[PV_1 \mid \epsilon + \epsilon_1] &= \bar{c}_2(1+r)^{-1} + \bar{c}_3(1+r)^{-2} + \theta E[\epsilon \mid \epsilon + \epsilon_1](1+r)^{-1} \\
&\quad + \gamma E[\epsilon \mid \epsilon + \epsilon_1](1+r)^{-2} \\
&= E[PV_1] + \alpha E[\epsilon \mid \epsilon + \epsilon_1] \\
&= E[PV_0] + [rE[PV_0] - c_1] + \alpha E[\epsilon \mid \epsilon + \epsilon_1] \\
&= E[PV_0] + [E[PV_1] - E[PV_0]] \\
&\quad + [E[PV_1 \mid \epsilon + \epsilon_1] - E[PV_1]] \qquad \textbf{(9.4)}
\end{aligned}$$

where the constant $\alpha = \theta(1+r)^{-1} + \gamma(1+r)^{-2}$. In other words, beginning with the $t = 0$ value expression of $E[PV_0]$, that expression is updated to reflect both the passage of time (i.e., $E[PV_1]$ versus $E[PV_0]$) and the updated assessment of the persistence effect (i.e., $\alpha E[\epsilon] = 0$ versus $\alpha E[\epsilon \mid \epsilon + \epsilon_1]$). Time and information are interacting here, so to speak.

Accounting Valuation at $t = 1$, with $h_1 = \epsilon + \epsilon_1$

It is, of course, natural to associate this information with an accounting report. To lay this out, we take a particularly simple case and assume the initial investment is depreciated some amount, d_1, in the first period, followed by some amount, d_2, in the second, and the remaining amount, $d_3 = -CF_0 - d_1 - d_2$, in the third period. With this accounting policy choice, we have the rendering in Exhibit 9.3, where we treat cash inflow as (net) revenue and mechanically depreciate the initial investment.[4] This is our recognition rule because we recognize only the realized part of the

---

[3] In (9.3a), the cash flow CF_t is included in the information history h_t because it has just been received and is therefore known. That might not be the case, however, in (9.3b), and, consequently, we use a different information history, $\hat{h}_t$, and value the immediately forthcoming cash flow at its expected value conditioned on whatever we know at that point.
[4] Remember that the cash flow sequence is exogenous, merely as a matter of convenience. A more detailed story would identify factor acquisition, use, and payment as well as customer payments. For now, we proceed with the exogenous version of the story and label the cash inflow as revenue.

EXHIBIT 9.3   **Accounting Calculations for Cash Flows in Exhibit 9.1**

	$t = 1$	$t = 2$	$t = 3$
Revenue (CF_t)	$CF_1 = \bar{c}_1 + \epsilon + \epsilon_1$	$CF_2 = \bar{c}_2 + \theta\epsilon + \epsilon_2$	$CF_3 = \bar{c}_3 + \gamma\epsilon + \epsilon_3$
Depreciation (d_t)	d_1	d_2	d_3
Accounting income ($\hat{I}_t$)	$CF_1 - d_1 =$	$CF_2 - d_2 =$	$CF_3 - d_3 =$
	$\bar{c}_1 + \epsilon + \epsilon_1 - d_1$	$\bar{c}_2 + \theta\epsilon + \epsilon_2 - d_2$	$\bar{c}_3 + \gamma\epsilon + \epsilon_3 - d_3$
Beginning book value (A_{t-1})	$-CF_0$	$-CF_0 - d_1$	$-CF_0 - d_1 - d_2$
Ending book value (A_t)	$-CF_0 - d_1$	$-CF_0 - d_1 - d_2$	0
Residual income ($\hat{I}_t - rA_{t-1}$)	$\bar{c}_1 + \epsilon + \epsilon_1 - d_1$	$\bar{c}_2 + \theta\epsilon + \epsilon_2 - d_2$	$\bar{c}_3 + \gamma\epsilon + \epsilon_3 - d_3$
	$+ rCF_0$	$- r(-CF_0 - d_1)$	$- r(-CF_0 - d_1 - d_2)$

shock term and mechanically apportion the historical cost over the periods. Moreover, the construction is additive and thus allows us to illustrate the accounting system's inherent structure. Notice that we also "close the books" and calculate the asset total after the period t dividend has been remitted.

With this setup, the first period accounting income measure reveals $\epsilon + \epsilon_1$, the second reveals $\theta\epsilon + \epsilon_2$, and the third reveals $\gamma\epsilon + \epsilon_3$. Thus, as we march through time, we gather more information and are thus able to update our beliefs about the persistence term, ϵ.[5] The book value, though, is deterministic in this case. This occurs for two reasons. First, we assume the cash inflow is paid out in a dividend before the books are closed. Second, we also assume that the depreciation schedule is utterly mechanical, it is set at the time of the investment and is not altered thereafter (e.g., straight line). This implies, of course, that our modest accounting policy is informationally equivalent to merely reporting the cash flow. (Indeed, you can verify this by setting $d_1 = -CF_0$.) We are purposely working with a transparent setting at this juncture.[6]

STOCK AND FLOW "ERRORS"

Since the valuation equation is a present value calculation, we can revisit the Chapter 4 theme of juxtaposing economic and accounting values. Indeed, the connection between economic and accounting value in this setting parallels that developed in the case of certain cash flows. The added twist is that we must remember to acknowledge the information available at each point in time. We have the following extension of our

---

[5] You should recognize this as the decoding or invertibility trick introduced in Chapter 7.
[6] Were the books closed, so to speak, before the cash was paid out, the book value at time t would simply be $A_t + CF_t$. We might also have a deprecation schedule that reflects some of the underlying information, say via a write-down when bad news occurs. Either variation, though, needlessly complicates our analysis at this point.

earlier work, based on book value and the "error" therein:

$$P(h_t) = E[PV_t \mid h_t] = \sum_{j=t+1}^{T} E[CF_j \mid h_t](1+r)^{t-j}$$

$$= A_t + \sum_{j=t+1}^{T} E[\hat{I}_j - rA_{j-1} \mid h_t](1+r)^{t-j} \quad \textbf{(9.5)}$$

Value, at time t, is simply the expected value of the present value of the remaining cash inflows conditioned on whatever information is available, as assumed.[7] In turn, this value calculation can be equivalently expressed as accounting value at time t, that is, A_t, plus the expected value of the present value of the remaining residual income series, conditioned on whatever information is available.[8]

The structure should not be missed. We literally know A_t, the accounting value or stock. The "error" in this value measure will show up in subsequent periods in the accounting income or the flow measure. This future pattern of errors is then informed by the information at time t. Information potentially tells us something about the future income, and this

---

[7] $P(h_t)$, of course, is the price expression in (9.3a). The (9.3b) case is equally clear. We simply must remember to condition the expected value of the continuation present value on the information available at the time of the price calculation, that is on $\hat{h}_t$ instead of on h_t.

[8] Although the proof of this claim proceeds just as was exposited in the earlier case of certain cash flows, it is instructive to examine the argument in this setting. For this purpose, consider the time $t = 1$ valuation expression for the three-period case of Exhibit 9.1. Using the noted expression, the accounting value plus expected present value of the remaining residual income series is

$$A_1 + E[\hat{I}_2 - rA_1 \mid h_1](1+r)^{-1} + E[\hat{I}_3 - rA_2 \mid h_1](1+r)^{-2}$$

Substituting the expressions for accounting income and accounting value, as noted in Exhibit 9.3, gives us the following equivalent expression:

$$(-CF_0 - d_1) + (E[CF_2 \mid h_1] - d_2 - r(-CF_0 - d_1))(1+r)^{-1}$$
$$+ (E[CF_3 \mid h_1] - d_3 - r(-CF_0 - d_1 - d_2))(1+r)^{-2}$$

Now combine the terms in suggestive fashion:

$$E[CF_2 \mid h_1](1+r)^{-1} + E[CF_3 \mid h_1](1+r)^{-2} + (-CF_0 - d_1)$$
$$+ (-d_2 - r(-CF_0 - d_1))(1+r)^{-1} + (-d_3 - r(-CF_0 - d_1 - d_2))(1+r)^{-2}$$

Next, remember how value is defined and that $d_3 = -CF_0 - d_1 - d_2$. This allows us to express our calculation as

$$E[PV_1 \mid h_1] + (-CF_0 - d_1) + (-d_2 - r(-CF_0 - d_1))(1+r)^{-1} + (-(-CF_0 - d_1 - d_2)$$
$$-r(-CF_0 - d_1 - d_2))(1+r)^{-2}$$

$$= E[PV_1 \mid h_1] - CF_0 - d_1 + CF_0 + d_1 = E[PV_1 \mid h_1]$$

(The latter follows from straightforward algebraic manipulation.)

knowledge about future income is used to revise our assessment of the "error" in book value.

In short, the fundamental ingredients in the economic valuation are the uncertain future cash flows. These also enter the accounting-based valuation as part of the future residual income. Furthermore, the information bases are identical for the two types of valuation. The error that is introduced in the accounting valuation is countered in the remaining residual income series.

The only caveats are that we assume (1) economic value is as defined, (2) accounting income is change in accounting value plus cash transactions with the shareholders (i.e., articulation or clean surplus accounting), and (3) the same information base is used for the two valuations.

EXAMPLE

It is time for a numerical example. Assume an expected cash flow sequence of $\bar{c}_1 = 4{,}950$, $\bar{c}_2 = 9{,}680$, and $\bar{c}_3 = 16{,}637.50$, along with $CF_0 = -25{,}000$. The interest rate is $r = 10$ percent. Also, with $E[PV_0] = 4{,}950(1.1)^{-1} + 9{,}680(1.21)^{-2} + 16{,}637.50(1.331)^{-3} = 25{,}000$ and an initial cost of $CF_0 = -25{,}000$, we have a project with no economic rent. (The expected values should be familiar.)

On the accounting side, we initially use straight-line depreciation. Following the rendering in Exhibit 9.3, this particular depreciation policy provides the accounting treatment displayed in Exhibit 9.4.

Now focus on time $t = 1$ and examine the effect of information on the market value, the price, of the remaining cash flow series. The only information available at this point is the time $t = 1$ accounting report; and the first period accounting income is $\hat{I}_1 = -3{,}383 + \epsilon + \epsilon_1$. So, what we know at time $t = 1$ is the initial shock total of $\epsilon + \epsilon_1$. This is our information

EXHIBIT 9.4 **Accounting Calculations for Specific Cash Flows Using Straight-Line Depreciation**

	$t = 1$	$t = 2$	$t = 3$
Revenue (CF_t)	$CF_1 = 4{,}950 + \epsilon + \epsilon_1$	$CF_2 = 9{,}680 + \theta\epsilon + \epsilon_2$	$CF_3 = 16{,}637.50 + \gamma\epsilon + \epsilon_3$
Depreciation (d_t)	8,333	8,333	8,334
Accounting income ($\hat{I}_t$)	$-3{,}383 + \epsilon + \epsilon_1$	$1{,}347 + \theta\epsilon + \epsilon_2$	$8{,}303.50 + \gamma\epsilon + \epsilon_3$
Beginning book value (A_{t-1})	25,000	16,667	8,334
Ending book value (A_t)	16,667	8,334	0
Residual income ($\hat{I}_t - rA_{t-1}$)	$-5{,}883 + \epsilon + \epsilon_1$	$-319.70 + \theta\epsilon + \epsilon_2$	$7{,}470.10 + \gamma\epsilon + \epsilon_3$

history $(h_1 = \epsilon + \epsilon_1)$.[9] Importantly, the information tells us nothing about the forthcoming ϵ_2 and ϵ_3 shocks, but it does tell us something about the persistence term. This is reflected in the revised expectation, $E[\epsilon \mid \epsilon + \epsilon_1]$. With this, we have $E[CF_2 \mid h_1] = 9{,}680 + \theta E[\epsilon \mid \epsilon + \epsilon_1]$ and $E[CF_3 \mid h_1] = 16{,}637.50 + \gamma E[\epsilon \mid \epsilon + \epsilon_1]$. Mirroring (9.4), this leads to a time $t = 1$ price or value of

$$\begin{aligned}
P(h_1) &= E[PV_1 \mid h_1] \\
&= (9{,}680 + \theta E[\epsilon \mid \epsilon + \epsilon_1])(1.1)^{-1} \\
&\quad + (16{,}637.50 + \gamma E[\epsilon \mid \epsilon + \epsilon_1])(1.21)^{-2} \\
&= 22{,}550 + \theta E[\epsilon \mid \epsilon + \epsilon_1](1.1)^{-1} + \gamma E[\epsilon \mid \epsilon + \epsilon_1](1.21)^{-2} \\
&= 22{,}550 + \alpha E[\epsilon \mid \epsilon + \epsilon_1]
\end{aligned}$$

where, recall, the constant $\alpha = \theta(1.1)^{-1} + \gamma(1.1)^{-2}$.

Now turn to the accounting valuation. The book value at this point is 16,667. It does not, given our assumption of straight-line depreciation, vary with the information at hand. Expressing value as the sum of book value and the expected value of the present value of the remaining residual income series, then, implies the entire information effect must show up in the latter half of the calculation.

Glancing back at Exhibit 9.4, notice that, with knowledge of the first period shock term, we have revised residual income expectations of $E[\hat{I}_2 - rA_1 \mid h_1] = -319.70 + \theta E[\epsilon \mid \epsilon + \epsilon_1]$ and $E[\hat{I}_3 - rA_2 \mid h_1] = 7{,}470.10 + \gamma E[\epsilon \mid \epsilon + \epsilon_1]$. This gives us, following (9.5), a market value calculation of

$$\begin{aligned}
E[PV_1 \mid h_1] &= 16{,}667 + (-319.70 + \theta E[\epsilon \mid \epsilon + \epsilon_1])(1.1)^{-1} \\
&\quad + (7{,}470.10 + \gamma E[\epsilon \mid \epsilon + \epsilon_1])(1.1)^{-2} \\
&= 22{,}550 + \alpha E[\epsilon \mid \epsilon + \epsilon_1]
\end{aligned}$$

Surprise! The accounting-based valuation, appropriately adjusted for what is known about the remaining future residual income series, winds up being identical to the market's valuation. It is important to understand that the details of this calculation, or expression, depend on the accounting treatment. Both sides of the equation, not to mention the accounting per se, are fed the same information. The structure of the accounting system, however, handicaps the accounting valuation, and an adjustment in terms of the expected residual income for the two future periods is used to counter this "error." The accounting system underutilizes the provided information from the perspective of the market's approach to valuation.

To dramatize this, suppose we use a depreciation schedule that results in a time t book value equal to economic value in the absence of all information, that is, $A_t = E[PV_t]$. Were there no uncertainty, this would

---

[9] At this point, the income calculation is redundant if we also know the cash flow. In general, accounting reports both cash and accrual-based measures, and we must be careful to identify the information conveyed over and above that conveyed by the cash measure itself—but that is getting ahead of our story.

EXHIBIT 9.5 **Accounting Calculations for Specific Cash Flows in Exhibit 9.3 Based on "Economic Depreciation"**

	$t = 1$	$t = 2$	$t = 3$
Revenue (CF_t)	$CF_1 = 4{,}950 + \epsilon + \epsilon_1$	$CF_2 = 9{,}680 + \theta\epsilon + \epsilon_2$	$CF_3 = 16{,}637.50 + \gamma\epsilon + \epsilon_3$
Depreciation (d_t)	2,450	7,425	15,125
Accounting income ($\hat{I}_t$)	$2{,}500 + \epsilon + \epsilon_1$	$2{,}255 + \theta\epsilon + \epsilon_2$	$1{,}512.50 + \gamma\epsilon + \epsilon_3$
Beginning book value (A_{t-1})	25,000	22,550	15,125
Ending book value (A_t)	22,550	15,125	0
Residual income ($\hat{I}_t - rA_{t-1}$)	$\epsilon + \epsilon_1$	$\theta\epsilon + \epsilon_2$	$\gamma\epsilon + \epsilon_3$

amount to fully aligning economic and accounting values, accounting income equal to economic income, and, of course, accounting depreciation equal to economic depreciation.

In any event, this leads to a depreciation policy of $d_1 = 2{,}450$, $d_2 = 7{,}425$, and $d_3 = 15{,}125$. It streamlines the residual income series because no accounting "errors" other than the shock terms themselves are now present. See Exhibit 9.5.

Of course we still have a time $t = 1$ value of $22{,}550 + \alpha E[\epsilon \mid \epsilon + \epsilon_1]$. Moreover, the difference between the market and accounting valuations persists. The accounting system continues to underutilize the information relative to how it is used by the market.[10] Once more the expected residual income carries the "error" between accounting value and market value. Fundamentally, though, the settings in Exhibits 9.4 and 9.5 are informationally equivalent. Precisely the same information is conveyed by the accounting measures in each case. The depreciation schedule here is merely a choice of scale, so to speak.

Finally, with additional structure, we can now express this value as book value plus a multiple (α) of period 1 residual income. This might have an intuitive appeal. For example, and as mentioned earlier, if all the shock terms are normally distributed with the same variance, we have $E[\epsilon \mid \epsilon + \epsilon_1] = (\epsilon + \epsilon_1)/2$, so we have value at this point equal to book value plus $\alpha/2$ times the residual income of the period. This convenience stems from the particular depreciation schedule in Exhibit 9.5, the persistence structure of the shock terms, and the assumed probability distributions, to be sure.

[10] In particular, notice that the accruals, the depreciation amounts, are completely uninformed by the information, but if we rigged the accounting so that it mimicked the market's value, so that it reported market value, the accruals would, of necessity, depend on the information.

Parsimonious Information Processing

This leads to the questions of whether we can develop a parsimonious connection between market value and the accounting measures and of whether we can neutralize the passage of time. The latter requires us to look at a portfolio of projects through time and will be deferred to the Appendix. Here we concentrate on the parsimonious connection question.

One way to further examine the relationship between market value and accounting information is to focus on the "surprise" in the accounting report, along with the associated "surprise" in the market value series. For example: Did the firm's earnings exceed analysts' expectations? Relatedly, how are we to interpret the magnitude of the unexpected earnings?

To develop this, we continue to focus on time $t = 1$. Initially, at time $t = 0$ and before any information has arrived, we expected to be in possession, at time $t = 1$, of a dividend in the amount $E[CF_1] = \bar{c}_1$, and a claim to the remaining cash flow series, with a value of $E[PV_1]$. With the cash flow being observed, a history variable of $h_1 = \epsilon + \epsilon_1$, the actual dividend is $\bar{c}_1 + \epsilon + \epsilon_1$. Likewise, the actual market value of the claim to the remaining series, using our work in (9.4), is $E[PV_1 \mid h_1] = E[PV_1] + \alpha E[\epsilon \mid \epsilon + \epsilon_1]$. The *value "shock,"* now, is simply the difference between what was expected and what was realized. Call this difference $\tilde{V}_t$:

$$\tilde{V}_1 = CF_1 + E[PV_1 \mid h_1] - E[CF_1] - E[PV_1]$$
$$= \epsilon + \epsilon_1 + \alpha E[\epsilon \mid \epsilon + \epsilon_1] \qquad \textbf{(9.6)}$$

Notice that time is neutralized here because we are comparing time $t = 1$ assessments with and without the available information. Thus, by design, $\tilde{V}_1$ depends only on the information; and absent any information, $\tilde{V}_1$ is zero. (Indeed, $E[\tilde{V}_1] = 0$.) $\tilde{V}_1$ is a measure of "surprise" in the sense that it compares the actual value with the no-information benchmark case. Notice that this surprise includes the $t = 1$ dividend, and it clearly reflects the information available at time $t = 1$, $h_1 = \epsilon + \epsilon_1$. Also, the benchmark is the no-information market value because we are dealing with the first period in a single-asset story.

In parallel fashion, the *accounting income "shock"* is the difference between first period income and what that income was originally expected to be. Call this difference $\tilde{I}_1$. Drawing on Exhibit 9.3, we have

$$\tilde{I}_1 = \hat{I}_1 - E[\hat{I}_1] = \bar{c}_1 + \epsilon + \epsilon_1 - d_1 - (\bar{c}_1 - d_1) = \epsilon + \epsilon_1 \quad \textbf{(9.7)}$$

The income shock contains exactly the information that was used in (9.6). We have information equivalence. Connecting the magnitude of these two expressions boils down to what is learned about the persistence variable, ϵ, given we know only the sum of the persistent and transitory shocks (i.e., $\epsilon + \epsilon_1$).

For example, as noted earlier, if both shock terms are normally distributed with the same variance, we have $E[\epsilon \mid \epsilon + \epsilon_1] = (\epsilon + \epsilon_1)/2$. In this special case, then, we have a proportional relationship:

$$\tilde{V}_1 = \epsilon + \epsilon_1 + \alpha E[\epsilon \mid \epsilon + \epsilon_1] = \epsilon + \epsilon_1 + \alpha(\epsilon + \epsilon_1)/2$$
$$= (1 + \alpha/2)(\epsilon + \epsilon_1) = (1 + \alpha/2)\tilde{I}_1 \qquad \textbf{(9.8)}$$

The economic shock is proportional to the accounting income shock. Unless $\alpha = 0$, however, the two are not identical. The reason is that our presumed accounting treatment (in Exhibit 9.3) treats CF_1 as net revenue of the period and employs a mechanical depreciation policy. Inevitably, then, the accounting system does not recognize the persistence effects of the first period shock term. Rather, the accounting system defers recognition until the cash itself is realized. For example, if $\alpha(\epsilon + \epsilon_1)/2 > 0$, the accounting system does not capitalize or aggressively recognize this windfall gain in the first period. The market, on the other hand, is not reticent to look into the future and immediately pick up the entire windfall gain.

Nevertheless, value shocks and accounting shocks are intimately connected in this setting. Indeed, we can express this by saying (1) new information, in the form of the current period cash flow realization, is an immediate source of value revision and causes a revision in the value of the remaining cash flow series and (2) this new information is perfectly conveyed by the surprise in the first period earnings. The two measures, however, are identical only when $\alpha = 0$ because the respective scalings of the two shocks are fundamentally different.

This tight connection has, of course, been manufactured. It relies heavily on our persistence device, and the structure of the revised expectation, $E[\epsilon \mid \epsilon + \epsilon_1]$. More important is the assumption that cash flow is the only source of information. Substantively, we have no hope of tightly connecting economic and accounting variables once we allow the former to be based on more information than the latter or once we allow for a variety of information sources.[11]

Accounting Income at $t = 1$, with $h_1 = (\epsilon, \epsilon_1)$

A glimpse into these complexities is provided by the case in which, again, the accounting system is the sole source of information but that system

---

[11] To appreciate the role of the information assumption, suppose instead that at time $t = 1$ the cash flow is observed, along with the second shock term, ϵ_2. Further suppose that the foreknowledge of ϵ_2 is not recognized by the accounting system. Now the valuation calculation has more information than the accounting calculation. The accounting income shock at $t = 1$ remains as before, as calculated in (9.7). The value shock, however, will now be

$$\tilde{V}_1 = \epsilon + \epsilon_1 + \alpha E[\epsilon \mid \epsilon + \epsilon_1] + \hat{\alpha}\epsilon_2$$

where $\hat{\alpha} = (1 + r)^{-1}$. With foreknowledge of ϵ_2, the information base has expanded, and we know more about CF_2. This severs the tight connection between value and accounting surprise simply because the underlying information "sets" are no longer coextensive. (Moreover, the additive representation is clearly driven by our independence assumption.)

EXHIBIT 9.6   **Accounting Calculations for Specific Cash Flows Using Straight-Line Depreciation but Separating ϵ and ϵ_1 Shock Terms**

	$t = 1$	$t = 2$	$t = 3$
Revenue (CF_t)	$CF_1 = 4,950 + \epsilon + \epsilon_1$	$CF_2 = 9,680 + \theta\epsilon + \epsilon_2$	$CF_3 = 16,637.50 + \gamma\epsilon + \epsilon_3$
Depreciation (d_t)	$8,333 - d\epsilon$	$8,333$	$8,334 + d\epsilon$
Accounting income ($\hat{I}_t$)	$-3,383 + \epsilon + \epsilon_1 + d\epsilon$	$1,347 + \theta\epsilon + \epsilon_2$	$8,303.50 + \gamma\epsilon + \epsilon_3 - d\epsilon$
Beginning book value (A_{t-1})	$25,000$	$16,667 + d\epsilon$	$8,334 + d\epsilon$
Ending book value (A_t)	$16,667 + d\epsilon$	$8,334 + d\epsilon$	0
Residual income ($\hat{I}_t - rA_{t-1}$)	$-5,883 + \epsilon + \epsilon_1 + d\epsilon$	$-319.70 + \theta\epsilon + \epsilon_2 - .1d\epsilon$	$7,470.10 + \gamma\epsilon + \epsilon_3 - 1.1d\epsilon$

now separately identifies the persistence (ϵ) and transitory (ϵ_1) shocks. This, quite naturally, provides precise identification of the persistence term, and the information updating in (9.4) in which we relied on knowing only $h_1 = \epsilon + \epsilon_1$, now simplifies to $E[PV_1 \mid \epsilon, \epsilon_1] = E[PV_1] + \alpha\epsilon$.

The accounting side, though, hardly simplifies. First period accounting income must now somehow reflect the effects of both shock terms without merely adding them together. Suppose, in the earlier example, we now use a depreciation policy of $d_1 = 8,333 - d\epsilon$, $d_2 = 8,333$, and $d_3 = 8,334 + d\epsilon$, where d is some nonzero constant. Details are in Exhibit 9.6.

If $d = 0$, this is our original straight-line policy, worked out in Exhibit 9.4. But suppose $d > 0$. If the persistence shock, ϵ, is positive, we depreciate less in the first period, reflecting the future good news, and more in the last period. (Naturally, we could spread this over both periods.) So the intuitive idea is to "revalue" the asset upward if good news is present ($\epsilon > 0$) and revalue it downward otherwise.[12] The accounting system can do this programmed adjusting because it is observing both ϵ and ϵ_1 at time $t = 1$.

Moreover, the recipient of the accounting report can decode that report to infer both shock terms. Ending first period book value will be $A_1 = 16,667 + d\epsilon$, and this implies $\epsilon = (A_1 - 16,667)/d$. In turn, first period income will be $\hat{I}_1 = -3,383 + \epsilon + \epsilon_1 + d\epsilon$, and this, coupled with knowledge of ϵ, reveals ϵ_1.

Now juxtapose surprise in the valuation and accounting domains, again at time $t = 1$. With the market observing $h_1 = (\epsilon, \epsilon_1)$, we have a

---

[12] Alternatively, we might think of this as testing the asset for impairment.

value shock of

$$\tilde{V}_1 = CF_1 + E[PV_1 \mid h_1] - E[CF_1] - E[PV_1]$$
$$= \epsilon + \epsilon_1 + \alpha\epsilon = \epsilon_1 + (1 + \alpha)\epsilon \qquad (9.9)$$

but the corresponding income shock is

$$\tilde{I}_1 = \hat{I}_1 - E[\hat{I}_1] = \bar{c}_1 + \epsilon + \epsilon_1 - d_1 - (\bar{c}_1 - E[d_1])$$
$$= \epsilon + \epsilon_1 + d\epsilon = \epsilon_1 + (1 + d)\epsilon \qquad (9.10)$$

The point is that the overall value shock is a linear combination of the two shocks, as is the overall income shock; but the weights are different unless the accounting system uses the precise accrual adjustment of $d = \alpha$. The market, in other words, processes the information in one fashion, and the accounting measurement apparatus processes it in another fashion. Juxtaposing the two, even though they use the same language and underlying algebra, requires considerable care.[13]

It is possible, of course, in this highly stylized setting to set the accounting system's scaling choice so the two valuation processes report the same valuation numbers. This is more a comment on how stylized the setting is, however, than a comment on general possibility. Accounting systems simply do not recognize all information in the economy (e.g., order books or anticipated rents from a breakthrough patent), although here we presume that all information pertinent to the reporting firm is indeed recognized by the accounting system. Likewise, when recognized, accounting exhibits a strong preference for linear processing. Here, too, our stylized setting leads to linear processing (at least in the first period). Even in this case, however, from an information content perspective, there simply is no reason for the two processes to be identical. Rather, we require only that the chosen processing be capable of being decoded, be invertible in the language of Chapter 7.

Summary

We have repeatedly stressed the fact that accounting uses the language and algebra of valuation. This is the very substance of the current exploration in which we assume the market price, or value, of a financial claim reflects risk-neutral pricing, conditional on all available information, and all available information arrives exclusively in the form of accounting stock and flow measures. Juxtaposing price, or value, and accounting measures then allows us to identify the information with accounting measures, to identify the connections and disparities between the market-based and accounting-based "processing" of the underlying information

---

[13] Following our earlier path, it is also possible to express price as equal to book value plus "error." For example, at $t = 1$ along with $h_1 = (\epsilon, \epsilon_1)$ and, using, Exhibit 9.6, the "error" is $E[-319.70 + \theta\epsilon + \epsilon_2 - .1d\epsilon \mid \epsilon, \epsilon_1](1.1)^{-1} + E[7,470.10 + \gamma\epsilon + \epsilon_3 - 1.1d\epsilon \mid \epsilon, \epsilon_1](1.1)^{-2}$, which simplifies to $5,883 + \alpha\epsilon - d\epsilon$ (as the $t = 1$ shocks tell us nothing about ϵ_2 or ϵ_3).

variables, and to see, once again, the importance of scaling options in the accounting domain.

This juxtaposition is well aided by the assumption that both sides of the comparison rely on, and process, the same information base, yet we see repeatedly that the connection is not one-to-one. The accounting information source codes or "preprocesses" the information in a manner that generally differs from the market's processing. Information content allows for scaling alternatives!

Placing structure on this juxtaposition naturally requires us to salt some type of structure into the firm's fundamentals. Otherwise, the comparison is more mechanical than intuitive. For this purpose, we assume a setting in which persistent and transitory shocks are mixed, giving us the prospect of tracking a persistent shock through time.

The accounting system's approach to measurement is also at work here. Its general characteristics are governed by the recognition rule and linear processing of information. Here, though, we neutralize the recognition issue by presuming the accounting system is the sole supplier of information to the valuation market. We also work with a setting that lends itself to linear processing of the underlying information. Even here, though, it is the unusual case in which accounting and market valuations agree. The information question is not agreement per se but whether the accounting system is carrying the information to the valuation market. Scaling options in the accounting domain are far from trivial.

Given risk-neutral pricing, with its underlying present value structure, we naturally return to the earlier theme of expressing value, or market price, as equal to book value plus "error." This "error," in turn, is now the expected value of the present value of the future residual income flows, conditional on all available information at the time of the pricing. Details inevitably depend on the firm's fundamentals and on the accounting method it adopts, but a constant refrain is the use of all available information to ferret out the "error" in the accounting valuation.

A more modest approach to juxtaposing market-based and accounting-based measures is to look at the surprise in the accounting measure and contrast it with the surprise in the market value. Even here, though, complexity is an issue, and we have yet to mix accounting and nonaccounting sources.

Either comparison naturally extends to a dynamic setting in which we encounter additional complexity in associating market- and accounting-based calculations. It is also important to remember that the development in this chapter relies on risk-neutral valuation. This provides a particularly transparent processing of information by the market-based valuation mechanism. Dropping risk-neutral valuation leads to information processing that depends on the allocation of information in the economy as well as on the organization of markets, as hinted at in the auction exploration in Chapter 8.

Dynamics

In this Appendix, we expand the basic setting by assuming one of these assets, or projects, is acquired in each period and this process of renewal goes on forever. Everything else remains as before, with one exception. To simplify, we assume that the only shock term in the first period is the persistent shock. The second shock term in the first period (the ϵ_1 term) is no longer present. In this way, observing the first period cash inflow fully identifies the persistent shock and considerably reduces the pain in what follows.

In steady state, now, the firm will have a brand new asset, a one-year-old asset and a two-year-old asset at each and every period. This offers the possibility, if not the fantasy, of a more or less time-invariant connection between the value and accounting measures.

STEADY-STATE VALUATION

We begin with an overdose of notation. It will be important to keep track of the shock terms. To do this, we specify the cash inflows associated with the asset acquired at time $\bar{t}$ in the following manner:

$$CF_{1,\bar{t}} = \bar{c}_1 + \epsilon_{\bar{t}} \qquad \textbf{(9.1a')}$$
$$CF_{2,\bar{t}} = \bar{c}_2 + \theta\epsilon_{\bar{t}} + \epsilon_{2,\bar{t}} \qquad \textbf{(9.1b')}$$
$$CF_{3,\bar{t}} = \bar{c}_3 + \gamma\epsilon_{\bar{t}} + \epsilon_{3,\bar{t}} \qquad \textbf{(9.1c')}$$

So, $CF_{1,\bar{t}}$ is the cash inflow one period later from the asset purchased at time $\bar{t}$; $CF_{2,\bar{t}}$ is the cash inflow two periods later from the asset purchased at time $\bar{t}$; and so on. Again, the second shock term has been dropped from the first expression, so observing $CF_{1,\bar{t}}$ now fully reveals the persistence term, $\epsilon_{\bar{t}}$.

Now, at time t (where $t > 2$), we will have cash outflow for a new asset coupled with cash inflow from a one-year-old asset, a two-year-old asset, and a three-year-old asset. Let C_t denote the net cash flow at time t. We then have

$$\begin{aligned} C_t &= CF_0 + CF_{1,t-1} + CF_{2,t-2} + CF_{3,t-3} \\ &= CF_0 + \bar{c}_1 + \epsilon_{t-1} + \bar{c}_2 + \theta\epsilon_{t-2} + \epsilon_{2,t-2} + \bar{c}_3 + \gamma\epsilon_{t-3} + \epsilon_{3,t-3} \\ &= \bar{c} + \epsilon_{t-1} + \theta\epsilon_{t-2} + \epsilon_{2,t-2} + \gamma\epsilon_{t-3} + \epsilon_{3,t-3} \end{aligned}$$

Here, $\bar{c}$ is the expected cash flow each and every period in the absence of any information (i.e., $\bar{c} = CF_0 + \bar{c}_1 + \bar{c}_2 + \bar{c}_3$). Absent uncertainty, we would then, in steady state, have a perpetuity with a constant value of $PV_t = \bar{c}/r$.

Next, suppose that we observe the disaggregate cash flows each period but nothing else. So each period t, we observe CF_0, $CF_{1,t-1}$, $CF_{2,t-2}$, and $CF_{3,t-3}$. This allows us to fully identify the persistence effect for in-place, older projects but nothing else because the shock terms are independent. We thus have the following future cash flow expectations as of time t and conditional on the available information:[14]

$$E[C_{t+1} \mid h_t] = \bar{c} + \theta\epsilon_{t-1} + \gamma\epsilon_{t-2}$$
$$E[C_{t+2} \mid h_t] = \bar{c} + \gamma\epsilon_{t-1}$$
$$E[C_{t+3} \mid h_t] = \bar{c}$$
$$E[C_{t+4} \mid h_t] = \bar{c}$$

and so on.

Intuitively, it is as if we have a perpetuity of $\bar{c}$ coupled with two persistence effects, one from a one-year-old asset (the ϵ_{t-1} terms in periods $t+1$ and $t+2$) and the other from the two-year-old asset (the ϵ_{t-2} term in period $t+1$). In turn, the initial shock from the one-year-old asset now conveniently fully identifies the related persistence effect, ϵ_{t-1}. With the perpetuity effect valued at $\bar{c}/r$, we have an overall value at time t of

$$E[PV_t \mid h_t]$$
$$= \bar{c}/r + (\theta\epsilon_{t-1} + \gamma\epsilon_{t-2})(1+r)^{-1} + \gamma\epsilon_{t-1}(1+r)^{-2}$$
$$= \bar{c}/r + \alpha\epsilon_{t-1} + \grave{\alpha}\epsilon_{t-2} \qquad \textbf{(9.11)}$$

where $\alpha = \theta(1+r)^{-1} + \gamma(1+r)^{-2}$ is our earlier multiplier from the single asset case, and $\grave{\alpha} = \gamma(1+r)^{-1}$.

BACK TO ACCOUNTING

Next recall that any such asset is, by assumption, expensed via the depreciation policy of d_1, d_2, and d_3. This policy implies in steady state that we have a book value each period of a new asset, a one-year-old asset, and a two-year-old asset: $A_t = -CF_0 - CF_0 - d_1 - CF_0 - d_1 - d_2 = -3CF_0 - 2d_1 - d_2 = A$. That is, in steady state the book value is a constant, denoted A. (Again, this reflects the assumption that net cash flow C_t is paid out as a dividend just before the books are closed, and the firm is simply renewing its asset base period by period.)

Accounting income in period t, in turn, is simply the three revenue streams, $CF_{1,t-1} + CF_{2,t-2} + CF_{3,t-3}$, less the sum of the three depreciation amounts, or (since $d_1 + d_2 + d_3 = -CF_0$)

$$\hat{I}_t = CF_{1,t-1} + CF_{2,t-2} + CF_{3,t-3} + CF_0$$
$$= (\bar{c}_1 + \epsilon_{t-1} - d_1) + (\bar{c}_2 + \theta\epsilon_{t-2} + \epsilon_{2,t-2} - d_2)$$
$$\quad + (\bar{c}_3 + \gamma\epsilon_{t-3} + \epsilon_{3,t-3} - d_3)$$
$$= \hat{I}_{t,t-1} + \hat{I}_{t,t-2} + \hat{I}_{t,t-3} \qquad \textbf{(9.12)}$$

---

[14] Again, the available information is the history of cash flow realizations on an asset-by-asset basis.

Notice, in the last line, that we have grouped the components of the income calculation that are attributable to each of the assets in place at the start of period t; $\hat{I}_{t,t-1}$ refers to the income component in period t that is attributable to the asset acquired at time $t-1$, and so on.

Can we now connect the accounting and value measures? One way to proceed parallels our earlier comparison of value and income shocks. At time t, the new persistence revelation is the shock term ϵ_{t-1} because the older ϵ_{t-2} term was observed in the prior period. So, the time t value shock reduces to[15]

$$\begin{aligned}
\tilde{V}_t &= C_t + E[PV_t \mid h_t] - E[C_t \mid h_{t-1}] - E[PV_t \mid h_{t-1}] \\
&= \epsilon_{t-1} + \epsilon_{2,t-2} + \epsilon_{3,t-3} + \theta\epsilon_{t-1}(1+r)^{-1} \\
&\quad + \gamma\epsilon_{t-1}(1+r)^{-2} \\
&= (1+\alpha)\epsilon_{t-1} + \epsilon_{2,t-2} + \epsilon_{3,t-3}
\end{aligned} \qquad (9.13)$$

As you should suspect, the shock, or surprise, in the related $\hat{I}_t$ component of income is simply the fresh supply of shocks, or $\epsilon_{t-1} + \epsilon_{2,t-2} + \epsilon_{3,t-3}$. We are pretty much back to where we started in the one asset case. The information about the shock terms is imbedded in the accounting income report, but as usual, the weights that are attached to the shock terms in the accounting measure differ from their counterparts in the market's valuation. The reason, of course, is that each asset has a persistence effect that shows up in the first period of its life, and all other randomness is, well, utterly random. The accounting system, however, acknowledges only the part of the persistence term that materializes in the first period whereas the market incorporates the entire effect immediately.

More interesting is the book value plus residual income approach explored earlier in the single-asset case (9.5). Glance back at Exhibit 9.3. Keeping track of the timing details and remembering the initial asset value is $-CF_0$, in period t, the one-year-old asset will have a residual income of

$$\hat{I}_{t,t-1} + rCF_0 = \bar{c}_1 + \epsilon_{t-1} - d_1 + rCF_0 = \omega + \epsilon_{t-1}$$

That is, given the stated depreciation policy, the one-year-old asset's residual income in period t will simply be a constant ($\bar{c}_1 - d_1 + rCF_0 = \omega$) plus the "first period" shock term, ϵ_{t-1}.

Now recall the time t value calculation (9.5). You can guess what is coming. Time t residual income from the one-year-old asset equals $\omega + \epsilon_{t-1}$, just as time $t-1$ residual income from the then one-year-old asset was $\omega + \epsilon_{t-2}$. Moreover, book value is the constant A. So, we can surely express the value of the remaining cash flow sequence as

$$E[PV_t \mid h_t] = \beta A + \alpha(\hat{I}_{t,t-1} + rCF_0) + \grave{\alpha}(\hat{I}_{t-1,t-2} + rCF_0) \qquad (9.14)$$

---

[15] For any information history at time $t-1$, h_{t-1}, the history at time t is $h_t = (h_{t-1}, \epsilon_{t-1}, \epsilon_{2,t-2}, \epsilon_{3,t-3})$.

where the constant β, an obvious plug, depends on the particular depreciation policy.[16]

Importantly, we now have a case in which the market price, or value, at time t is a constant (the constant βA) plus constant weights on current and lagged residual income components (the constants α and $\grave{\alpha}$).[17] This, of course, serves as a warning that simply focusing on a single accounting number is a simplified view of the connection between the market price, or value, and the accounting measures. In this case, two accounting income components are essential to identify the market value. Each of the two residual income measures carries one piece of information (ϵ_{t-1} and ϵ_{t-2}) to the table, and both are important to move from the accounting to the aggregation that is used in the market valuation.

Note the subtle influence of the accounting system. Recognition rules govern the inclusion or exclusion of information about the error terms. Here the system recognizes only the error terms that are part of, are revealed by, the realized cash flows. Any potential information about the other error terms is simply excluded, and since accounting is the sole source of information, this other—potential—information is also not used by the market.

EXAMPLE

To illustrate, return to the numerical setting used earlier (Exhibit 9.4, for example). We now, in steady state, have three of these assets at each point in time. Periodic expected cash flow is $\bar{c} = -25{,}000 + 4{,}950 + 9{,}680 + 16{,}637.50 = 6{,}267.50$. Income calculations, presuming straight-line depreciation, are tallied in Exhibit 9.7.

---

[16] For the record, notice that $\alpha(\hat{I}_{t,t-1} + rCF_0) + \grave{\alpha}(\hat{I}_{t-1,t-2} + rCF_0) = \alpha(\omega + \epsilon_{t-1}) + \grave{\alpha}(\omega + \epsilon_{t-2}) = \omega(\alpha + \grave{\alpha}) + \alpha\epsilon_{t-1} + \grave{\alpha}\epsilon_{t-2}$. Time t value, from (9.11), is $E[PV_t \mid h_t] = \bar{c}/r + \alpha\epsilon_{t-1} + \grave{\alpha}\epsilon_{t-2}$. Equating this with our expression in (9.14) now requires $\beta A = \bar{c}/r - \omega(\alpha + \grave{\alpha})$. So, $\beta = (\bar{c}/r - \omega(\alpha + \grave{\alpha}))/A$, where $\omega = \bar{c}_1 - d_1 + rCF_0$ and $A = -3CF_0 - 2d_1 - d_2$. Clearly, the plug, β, depends on the accounting policy, or depreciation schedule. From here you should guess, correctly, that setting that policy as we did in Exhibit 9.5 implies that $\beta = 1$. This follows from the fact that ω would then be zero and A would equal $\bar{c}/r$.

[17] Notice that the same pattern could be achieved in our simple setting by merely "pricing" the noted income components and book value as opposed to the residual income components and book value. Another subtle point concerns the mixing of cash flow and accrual measures. Here, for example, we might think in terms of cash flow being reported as cash flow from operations (i.e., $CF_{1,t-1} + CF_{2,t-2} + CF_{3,t-3}$), coupled with the new investment. Commingling the three operating streams, though, precludes the valuation analysis we have relied on because we could then no longer identify the critical persistence shock in period t. So, now imagine line-of-business reporting in the accrual section of the financial statements. This decomposes the aggregate operating cash flow measure, so to speak, and allows us to identify the critical persistence shock in period t. That is precisely what we are relying on in the valuation calculation.

EXHIBIT 9.7 **Accounting Income Calculations for Steady-State Case Based on Straight-Line Depreciation**

	One-Year-Old Asset	Two-Year-Old Asset	Three-Year-Old Asset
Revenue $(CF_{j,\tilde{t}})$	$CF_{1,t-1} = 4,950 + \epsilon_{t-1}$	$CF_{2,t-2} = 9,680 + \theta\epsilon_{t-2}$ $+ \epsilon_{2,t-2}$	$CF_{3,t-3} = 16,637.50$ $+ \gamma\epsilon_{t-3} + \epsilon_{3,t-3}$
Depreciation (d_t)	8,333	8,333	8,334
Accounting income	$\hat{I}_{t,t-1} = -3,383 + \epsilon_{t-1}$	$\hat{I}_{t,t-2} = 1,347 + \theta\epsilon_{t-2}$ $+ \epsilon_{2,t-2}$	$\hat{I}_{t,t-3} = 8,303.50$ $+ \gamma\epsilon_{t-3} + \epsilon_{3,t-3}$

Market value at time t reflects the expected perpetuity effect of $\bar{c}/r = 62,675$ plus the two identified persistence effects of $\alpha\epsilon_{t-1}$ and $\grave{\alpha}\epsilon_{t-1}$. The first of these persistence effects is, of course, revealed by the current period income of a one-year-old asset, and the second by the prior period income of a then one-year-old asset. These two revelations constitute our minimal, relevant information history at time t. (Remember that the persistence effect shows up in the first year of the asset's life, by assumption.) Now further assume that $\alpha = 3$ and $\grave{\alpha} = 2$ (or rather $\theta = 1.3$ and $\gamma = 2.2$). This implies the time t value of the remaining cash flow series, using (9.11), is given by $E[PV_t \mid h_t] = \bar{c}/r + \alpha\epsilon_{t-1} + \grave{\alpha}\epsilon_{t-2} = 62,675 + 3\epsilon_{t-1} + 2\epsilon_{t-2}$.

To reexpress this calculation in terms of accounting variables, we next follow the calculation in (9.12). With straight-line depreciation, residual income from a one-year-old asset at time t is $\hat{I}_{t,t-1} + rCF_0 = -3,383 + \epsilon_{t-1} - .1(25,000) = -5,883 + \epsilon_{t-1}$. Likewise, residual income in the prior year for a then one-year-old asset is $\hat{I}_{t-1,t-2} + rCF_0 = -5,883 + \epsilon_{t-2}$. That is, the important residual income calculation is $\omega = -5,883$ plus the shock term that carries the persistence effect.

In turn, book value at each and every period in steady state is $A = 25,000 + 25,000 - d_1 + 25,000 - d_1 - d_2 = 50,001$. (As in Exhibit 9.7, we are rounding the straight-line depreciation calculation.) Equating market value and the accounting-based calculations now leads to

$$E[PV_t \mid h_t] = 62,675 + 3\epsilon_{t-1} + 2\epsilon_{t-2}$$
$$= \beta A + \alpha(\hat{I}_{t,t-1} + rCF_0) + \grave{\alpha}(\hat{I}_{t-1,t-2} + rCF_0)$$
$$= \beta A + 3(\hat{I}_{t,t-1} + rCF_0) + 2(\hat{I}_{t-1,t-2} + rCF_0)$$
$$= \beta(50,001) + 3(-5,883 + \epsilon_{t-1}) + 2(-5,883 + \epsilon_{t-2})$$

Equality requires $\beta \approx 1.8418$. That is, in this highly structured setting, we can express market value as 1.8418 times book value plus respective weights of 3 and 2 on the noted current and lagged residual income components. *Value*, so to speak, can be thought of as a weighted combination of accounting stock and flow measures.

The weight on the flow measures is explained by the persistence effect. The weight on the stock measure is explained by the depreciation policy.

Here, for example, straight-line depreciation is unusually conservative. Indeed, using the deprecation schedule in Exhibit 9.5 based on economic value in the absence of any information implies that book value will be an unbiased estimate of economic value. Working through the details, with $d_1 = 2{,}450$, $d_2 = 7{,}425$, and $d_3 = 15{,}125$ implies a steady-state book value of $A = 62{,}675$, $\omega = 0$, and $\beta = 1$.

We have worked hard, of course, and strained credulity to construct this stable relationship between value and contemporaneous accounting measures. We began with a convenient representation of the uncertainty, the persistence effect in the cash flows; we coupled this with an equally convenient steady-state dynamic story in which the firm is continuously renewing itself while earning no rent in the process.

Nevertheless, whenever we group firms, for example, in an industry analysis or in a statistical test of the connection between value and earnings surprise, we are presuming some type of first-order connection between the value and information variables. Here, for example, we have market value as a weighted combination of the accounting stock and flow measures. So, if we look at a market to book ratio, we are ignoring the flow component of this connection; if we look at a price-earnings ratio, we are ignoring the stock component of this connection.

VARIATIONS

To reinforce this theme of weighting stock and flow measures, we close by briefly sketching a related approach developed by Feltham and Ohlson (1996).[18] The idea is to exploit the algebraic connection between present value and the sum of book plus the present value of the remaining residual income series, presuming clean surplus accounting (articulation). In turn, searching for a parsimonious relationship between accounting variables and value then boils down to placing some type of structure on the residual income series.

Staying close in spirit to our stylized persistence setup assumes we invest $-CF_0$ in each and every period, just as before. Cash inflows, or receipts, are now denoted CR_t and are described by the following autoregressive structure:

$$CR_t = \lambda CR_{t-1} - kCF_0 + \mu_t \qquad \textbf{(9.15)}$$

The constant λ, $0 \le \lambda < 1$ is a persistence parameter, modeling how cash receipts in one period persist into the next and beyond. The constant $k > 0$ identifies the addition to current receipts due to investment (in the prior period, to be exact); and μ_t is our inevitable random shock term with $E[\mu_t] = 0$. Net cash flow in period t, of course, is $CR_t + CF_0$. As usual, we assume this net amount is "paid out" at the end of each period.

---

[18] Indeed, our three-period, steady-state exercise is inspired by their work.

We furthermore assume no economic rent. So, in expectation, the investment of each period has an expected present value, absent any information, equal to the investment amount of $-CF_0$. This requires[19] $k = 1 + r - \lambda$.

Turning to the value calculation, we know $-CF_0$ is invested every period. We also know the constants δ, λ, and k and the fact that new investment carries no economic rent. The latter implies that value at time t depends only on the asset stock at time t and what we know about that stock. (Since future asset acquisitions have no rent, we anticipate paying out $-CF_0$ for something worth $-CF_0$ in each future period.)

Further suppose that the only information is observation of the cash receipts, CR_t, in each and every period. With this setup, then, glancing back at (9.15), at time t, our assessment of time $t + 1$ cash receipts is given by $E[CR_{t+1} \mid h_t] = \lambda CR_t - kCF_0 = v$. Two periods out, it is $E[CR_{t+2} \mid h_t] = \lambda(\lambda CR_t - kCF_0) = \lambda v$, and n periods out, it is $E[CR_{t+n} \mid h_t] = \lambda^{n-1}(\lambda CR_t - kCF_0) = \lambda^{n-1}v$. The usual algebra gives us our value calculation at time t:[20]

$$E[PV_t \mid h_t] = \sum_{j=t+1}^{\infty} \lambda^{j-t-1}(\lambda CR_t - kCF_0)(1 + r)^{t-j}$$

$$= \frac{\lambda CR_t - kCF_0}{1 + r - \lambda} = \frac{\lambda CR_t}{1 + r - \lambda} - CF_0 \qquad \textbf{(9.16)}$$

To conclude the odyssey, we link this expression to the contemporaneous accounting variables. The asset stock in period t, A_t, must be depreciated. We adopt a declining balance formulation in which depreciation in period t is equal to $(1 - \delta)A_{t-1} = d_t$. So the time t asset balance is simply the remaining asset stock, δA_{t-1}, coupled with the new acquisition, $-CF_0$, $0 < \delta < 1$ is a known constant, and this gives us income in period t of $\hat{I}_t = CR_t - d_t$.

---

[19] Suppose, for convenience, that $-CF_0 = 1$, a \$1 investment. This provides, in expectation, that cash receipts of k one period later, λk two periods later, $\lambda^2 k$ three periods later, and so on. The present value of this series is $k(1 + r)^{-1} + \lambda k(1 + r)^{-2} + \lambda^2 k(1 + r)^{-3} + \cdots$. This, in turn, equals $(k/\lambda)[\lambda(1 + r)^{-1} + \lambda^2(1 + r)^{-2} + \lambda^3(1 + r)^{-3} + \cdots] = (k/\lambda)[((1 + r)/\lambda)^{-1} + ((1 + r)/\lambda)^{-2} + ((1 + r)/\lambda)^{-3} + \cdots] = (k/\lambda)[(1 + R)^{-1} + (1 + R)^{-2} + (1 + R)^{-3} + \cdots]$, where R is defined by $1 + R = (1 + r)/\lambda$, or $R = (1 + r - \lambda)/\lambda$. Using the usual perpetuity formula, \$1 per period, at interest R has a value of $1/R$, implies that we have a present value of $(k/\lambda)[\lambda/(1 + r - \lambda)] = k/(1 + r - \lambda)$. With no rent, however, this must equal our original investment of \$1, so $k = 1 + r - \lambda$. (Recall that we also assume $0 \leq \lambda < 1$.)

[20] $E[PV_t \mid h_t] = v(1 + r)^{-1} + \lambda v(1 + r)^{-2} + \lambda^2 v(1 + r)^{-3} + \cdots = (v/\lambda)[\lambda(1 + r)^{-1} + \lambda^2(1 + r)^{-2} + \lambda^3(1 + r)^{-3} + \cdots] = (v/\lambda)[((1 + r)/\lambda)^{-1} + ((1 + r)/\lambda)^{-2} + ((1 + r)/\lambda)^{-3} + \cdots] = (v/\lambda)[(1 + R)^{-1} + (1 + R)^{-2} + (1 + R)^{-3} + \cdots]$, where R is defined by $1 + R = (1 + r)/\lambda$, or $R = (1 + r - \lambda)/\lambda$. Using the usual perpetuity formula, we have a summation of $(v/\lambda)[\lambda/(1 + r - \lambda)] = v/(1 + r - \lambda)$.

Now, it turns out that value at time t can be expressed in terms of the contemporaneous accounting stock and flow measures:[21]

$$E[PV_t \mid h_t] = A_t + \frac{\lambda}{1+r-\lambda}(\hat{I}_t - rA_{t-1})$$

$$+ \frac{(1+r)(\lambda-\delta)}{1+r-\lambda} A_{t-1} \qquad \textbf{(9.17)}$$

That is, value at time t is equal to book value at time t plus a constant multiple of residual income in period t plus a constant multiple of lagged book value. Moreover, if the depreciation and persistence rates are equated, if we set the depreciation parameter to $\delta = \lambda$, the latter term disappears, and we have a straightforward book value plus persistence of residual income effect that determines value.

From this point, the story can be embellished to have investments with rent, growth (as opposed to a purely steady-state structure), and investment opportunities with a shock term. One can also add additional information that provides foreknowledge of the next cash receipt and investment opportunity shock term, so long as it arrives as an additive shock. The picture should be clear: It is possible to construct dynamics at this level of abstraction such that value can be expressed as a parsimonious calculation based on underlying information variables. More important, we see in (9.17) that the depreciation parameter is more or less a free parameter in this case. The same information can be carried by a wide class of accounting treatments. There is simply no demand in our analysis to remove this degree of freedom from the accounting system. The accounting system conveys the information without noise, and the market is able to process it to set the market value.

---

[21] This is easily verified. Take the expression in (9.16) and substitute $-CF_0 = A_t - \delta A_{t-1}$ and $CR_t = \hat{I}_t + (1-\delta)A_{t-1}$. Now combine all the terms that contain the lagged asset measure, A_{t-1}.

Selected References

Beaver (1998) and Watts and Zimmerman (1986) are excellent references on accounting versus economic valuation in a financial market setting. Penman (2000) emphasizes valuation fundamentals in moving from the accounting to the market side. The primary reference in the dynamic setting used here is Feltham and Ohlson (1996), which builds on work begun in the early part of the twentieth century (e.g., Preinreich, 1937). In a related paper, Feltham and Ohlson (1995) place the shock term directly on the residual income series, which has the advantage of simplicity but the disadvantage of removing the ability to think of a class of accounting treatments as being informationally equivalent. Anyway, to sketch the idea, suppose that residual income in period t is given by $RI_t = \lambda RI_{t-1} + \mu_t$. Working through parallel details, one can establish that value at time t can then be expressed as book value at time t plus $\lambda/(1 + r - \lambda)$ times the current period's residual income.[22]

Key Terms

The valuation implications of an information release in the setting here are identified by the **value shock,** or price surprise, in relation (9.6), the difference between the actual price of the claim to the remaining cash flow series following the information release less what that price was expected to be just prior to the information release. The accounting versus market juxtaposition is then based on the value shock compared to the **accounting income "shock"** in (9.7), the difference between the accounting income actually reported and what that income report was expected to be just prior to its release.

Exercises

9.1. Exhibits 9.4 and 9.5 illustrate a setting in which the financial statements are distinctly different, yet the two accounting systems are informationally equivalent. Explain.

9.2. Return to the setting of Exhibits 9.4 and 9.5, but now set $d_1 = 25,000$. Verify the book value plus "error" expression here. Is this cash basis accounting? Is it informationally equivalent to the stories in Exhibits 9.4 and 9.5? Explain.

9.3. In (9.6) and (9.7), we compare market- and accounting-based measures, yet the comparison does not depend on the firm's accounting policy. Explain.

9.4. The value shock expression in (9.8) is a story in which the price reaction associated with an earnings release is proportional to the surprise in the earnings release. Relate this to the notion of "quality" of earnings, where supposedly high quality earnings are valued differently than low quality earnings.

9.5. In Note 10, we claim the depreciation schedule must depend on the information if the accounting system is to report economic or market value. Return to this setting, Exhibits 9.5 and 9.6, and determine the depreciation schedule such that book and market values are equated. Does this accounting treatment still reveal the underlying information to the market? What happens to the residual income series?

9.6. Assume, in the setting of Exhibit 9.2, that $\bar{c}_1 = 1,100$, $\bar{c}_2 = 1,210$, and $\bar{c}_3 = 1,331$. Also set $CF_0 = -3,000$ and the interest rate at 10 percent. (Also remember that ϵ_2 and ϵ_3 are always zero in this simplified setting.) The only source of information is the accounting report, and that report reveals only the total or sum of the persistence and

[22] Emphatically, our work here focuses on a stylized juxtaposition. It is not directed at financial analysis per se, as in, for example, Penman (2000). Doing so would require a far more detailed specification of the dynamics, the accounting structure, and so on, not to mention the nonaccounting information.

transitory shock terms. Prepare the appropriate variation on Exhibit 9.4 using straight-line depreciation. Next, assume the probability specification in Exhibit 9.2 and fill in the following table. Notice this asks you to determine the price path of the claim to the cash flows as a function of time and state. It also asks you to determine the reported accounting income path.

	s_1	s_2	s_3	s_4	s_5	s_6	s_7	s_8	s_9
$prob(s_i)$	1/9	1/9	1/9	1/9	1/9	1/9	1/9	1/9	1/9
ϵ	−500	−500	−500	0	0	0	500	500	500
ϵ_1	−500	0	500	−500	0	500	−500	0	500
$\epsilon + \epsilon_1$	−1,000	−500	0	−500	0	500	0	500	1,000
$E[\epsilon \mid \epsilon + \epsilon_1]$	−500	−250	0	−250	0	250	0	250	500
$P_0(h_0)$									
$P_1(h_1)$									
$P_2(h_2)$									
$P_3(h_3)$									
$\hat{I}_1$									
$\hat{I}_2$									

9.7. In the setting of Exercise 9.6, verify that at each point in time, the market value you calculated is equal to the book value plus the expected value of the present value of the remaining residual income series. Explain why, in your calculations, the conditioning information affects the "error" portion of the calculation but not the book value calculation.

9.8. Again in the setting of Exercise 9.6, concentrate on $t = 1$, and compare the surprise in the price domain, that is, (9.6), with the surprise in the accounting domain, that is, (9.7).

9.9. Assume in the setting of Exercise 9.6 that the end-of-period dividend is distributed just after the books are closed and the financial statements are released. Repeat your price calculations, and explain the noted differences.

9.10. Repeat Exercises 9.6 and 9.8 for the case in which the first period shocks, ϵ and ϵ_1, are separately revealed at time $t = 1$. Consistent with the theme of the chapter, the two shocks are revealed by the accounting system. (*Hint:* You should record an additional accrual based on the persistence term.)

9.11. Return to the setting of Exhibit 9.6. First determine the value, or price, at each time as a function of the information history variable. Then verify that this value, or price, is equal to the contemporaneous book value plus "error" term where the latter is the expected value of the present value of the future residual income flows, conditional on the information history. You might want to use the hint in Note 10.

9.12. Return to the setting of Exhibit 9.7, but now use a depreciation policy of $d_1 = 2,450$, $d_2 = 7,425$, and $d_3 = 15,125$. Determine the appropriate weights for expressing the market price as a weighted combination of the accounting stock and flow measures. Repeat for a depreciation policy of $d_1 = 25,000$, $d_2 = 0$, and $d_3 = 0$. Provide an intuitive explanation for your findings.

9.13. Exercise 9.6 is a one-asset story. You are now asked to expand this story, parallel to Exhibit 9.7, to a steady-state setting. Can you express the time t (steady-state) market value as a weighted sum of the accounting stock and flow measures? Be specific. What does this tell you about market-to-book or price-earnings ratios? Use $\epsilon_1 \equiv 0$ to simplify.

9.14. In what sense does your analysis in Exercise 9.13 depend on a specific depreciation schedule (such as straight line that is used in Exhibit 9.7)?

9.15. Ralph's Venture has paid $50 for a "coin flip" in which with probability .5, the eventual cash flow and liquidating dividend will be $D = 0$; with probability .5, it will be $D = 100$. Risk-neutral valuation prevails, and the interest rate is zero. The dividend will be delivered at the end of the second period. In addition, the firm acquires private information at time $t = 1$. This can be one of three signals characterized by the following joint probability structure:

	$D = 0$	$D = 100$
y_1	.30	.10
y_2	.10	.10
y_3	.10	.30

Determine $E[D \mid y]$ for each possible signal. Next, suppose the firm's accountant adopts a lower-of-cost-or-market rule. The underlying asset will be valued at $t = 1$ at $A_1 = 50$ unless, based on the private information, it is calculated that $E[D \mid y] < 50$; in that event, the asset will be written down to the revised expected value. What asset value will the firm report at time $t = 1$ as a function of what it learns (y), given this accounting rule? In turn, the only source of information for the valuation market is whatever is reported by the accounting system. Determine the market price, or value, that will be observed at time $t = 1$ following the accounting report.

9.16. The dynamic setting in the Appendix relies on pricing the financial claim just after the dividend has been remitted. Suppose, instead, the claim is priced just before the dividend is to be remitted. The accounting report, then, is made just before the dividend is paid and, importantly, a nonzero cash balance is also present. What happens to the pricing in, for example, equation (9.14) and our ability to express price as a linear function of the accounting stock and flow measures?

Chapter 10

Accounting and Nonaccounting Information in a Valuation Setting

The final stop in our look at accounting information in a valuation setting is mixing accounting and nonaccounting sources of information. We retain the stylized cash flow story of permanent and transient shocks but now introduce a second, distinctly nonaccounting source of information. This reminds us of the importance of identifying all information sources if information content is to be understood. It also provides an opportunity to sample the large body of empirical evidence on the linkages between accounting measures and security prices. In so doing we emphasize the importance of multiple sources of information and scaling in the accounting domain.

We now mix accounting and nonaccounting sources of information in our (continuing risk-neutral) valuation setting. Analysis of this is important for three reasons in addition to the institutional fact that this is the way the world works. First, interactions among multiple sources can be important and subtle. For example, if an earlier reporting source reports all that accounting has to report, then the accounting source surely lacks information content. So, in documenting empirical regularities associated with the accounting source, we must be careful to factor in the presence of these other sources. Otherwise, we run the risk of attributing information content to the uninformative source. Similarly, we often work with analysts' forecasts of a firm's future earnings simply because we suspect multiple information sources are present and we rely on the analysts to be aware of this and to be adept at combining these sources to form a well-informed forecast.

Second, information is presented in scaled format, a fact we have seen repeatedly. However, the scaling options increase with the presence of multiple sources of information simply because the scale can incorporate some, if not all, of what the other sources report. Third, one information source might have a disciplining effect on other sources of information. For example, we will eventually (in later chapters) treat the accounting source as one that helps ensure the reporting integrity of other sources. Were these other sources not present and were their integrity not potentially open to question, this important theme would be missing.

We begin with an anecdote, a comparison of accounting and market values for a large U.S. corporation. From here we survey the systematic evidence on the relationship between market and accounting measures. This survey carries along a simulation based on the stylized cash flow setup developed in Chapter 9. Here, however, we use a mixture of accounting and nonaccounting sources. As we shall see, the simulation well illustrates much, but not all, of the documented empirical regularities.

The major theme we emphasize is the joint influence of multiple sources of information, including the accounting source, and scaling in the accounting domain.

ANECDOTE

We begin with an illustration. In Exhibit 10.1 we plot the end-of-year closing market price for a share of General Electric common (adjusted for splits) over the most recent decade, along with the corresponding book

EXHIBIT 10.1
Market and Book Value

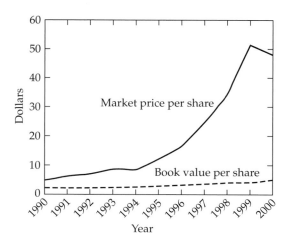

value per share (again adjusted for splits). Think of this as a portrait of the contrast between economic and accounting value.

What are we to make of this? To be sure, it is but a single reporting firm and, hence, an anecdote. We also know this is a period in which "the market" has risen dramatically, and no adjustment for economywide forces is being made. Similarly, price-level changes are ignored, as is the fact that General Electric has made a number of acquisitions during this period. In addition, this is a time period when reporting regulations were changed, and no adjustment for constant accounting treatment across the periods is being made.

Nonetheless, it is clear that the economic measure is more volatile than its accounting counterpart. This is more apparent in Exhibit 10.2 where we plot the corresponding ratio of price, or market value, to book value. This ratio is trending up because the market price itself rises dramatically during the decade, but the trend is hardly uniform, or monotonic. Volatility is evident.

At this point the usual suspects come to mind. Accounting is, well, "conservative" and thus is slow if not reticent to recognize growth prospects. Likewise, accounting procedures themselves tend to smooth over the good and bad times, perhaps aided and abetted by managements' actions.

For our purpose, though, a straightforward observation comes into view. If we envision the market price as being determined by some process that is approximated by our valuation model and if the accounting value is likewise determined by some process that is approximated by our accounting model, this anecdote suggests that the economic side of the comparison uses information either more aggressively than or, more to the point, accesses information that is unavailable to the accounting system.

EXHIBIT 10.2
Market to Book Ratio

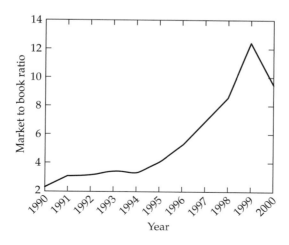

EVIDENCE

This pattern of multiple sources of information and accounting structure is evident in the systematic evidence. Here we present a brief survey of some of this evidence. Throughout we contrast the evidence with simulations of an analytical model of the reporting firm.

Stylized Illustration

To deepen intuition, then, we carry along the stylized description of the reporting entity used in Chapter 9. That firm, recall, lives for three periods and, following investment of CF_0, the cash flow uncertainty is described by:

$$CF_1 = \bar{c}_1 + \epsilon + \epsilon_1 \qquad \textbf{(10.1a)}$$

$$CF_2 = \bar{c}_2 + \theta\epsilon + \epsilon_2 \qquad \textbf{(10.1b)}$$

$$CF_3 = \bar{c}_3 + \gamma\epsilon + \epsilon_3 \qquad \textbf{(10.1c)}$$

The shock terms are mutually independent, and ϵ has a persistence feature in that it affects the cash flow in each period. Now θ and γ are strictly positive, so $\epsilon > 0$ implies a strictly positive persistence effect in each period, just as $\epsilon < 0$ implies the opposite.

We concentrate on the relationship between price and the accounting stock and flow measures at time $t = 1$. The presumed timing, however, is slightly altered from Chapter 9 in order to attenuate the effect of working with a three-period firm that does not continue to invest.[1] Specifically, we assume all information arrives, including the accounting report, just before the dividend is paid. Importantly, then, market price at time $t = 1$ reflects the immediately forthcoming dividend. Likewise, the accounting stock measure now includes the corresponding cash balance.

On the market side, however, two sources of information are now present: the accounting report and an additional source that reports the first period transitory shock, ϵ_1. This implies the market value calculation benefits from full identification of the persistence effect. With the accounting source revealing $\epsilon + \epsilon_1$ and with ϵ_1 revealed by the second source, the persistence effect of ϵ is fully identified. So, with the information history at time $t = 1$ of $h_1 = (\epsilon, \epsilon_1)$, the remaining cash prospects are valued as

$$\begin{aligned}
E[PV_1 \mid \epsilon, \epsilon_1] &= (\bar{c}_2 + \theta\epsilon)(1+r)^{-1} + (\bar{c}_3 + \gamma\epsilon)(1+r)^{-2} \\
&= \bar{c}_2(1+r)^{-1} + \bar{c}_3(1+r)^{-2} + \theta\epsilon(1+r)^{-1} + \gamma\epsilon(1+r)^{-2} \\
&= E[PV_1] + \theta\epsilon(1+r)^{-1} + \gamma\epsilon(1+r)^{-2} \\
&= E[PV_1] + \alpha\epsilon
\end{aligned}$$

---

[1] Recall that in Chapter 9 we also sketched a steady-state version in which the firm continues to invest in each and every period.

EXHIBIT 10.3 **Accounting Calculations**

	$t = 1$	$t = 2$	$t = 3$
Panel A Accounting Calculations When $\epsilon \geq 0$			
Revenue (CF_t)	$CF_1 = \bar{c}_1 + \epsilon + \epsilon_1$	$CF_2 = \bar{c}_2 + \theta\epsilon + \epsilon_2$	$CF_3 = \bar{c}_3 + \gamma\epsilon + \epsilon_3$
Depreciation (d_t)	d_1	d_2	d_3
Accounting income (I_t)	$CF_1 - d_1 =$ $\bar{c}_1 + \epsilon + \epsilon_1 - d_1$	$CF_2 - d_2 =$ $\bar{c}_2 + \theta\epsilon + \epsilon_2 - d_2$	$CF_3 - d_3 =$ $\bar{c}_3 + \gamma\epsilon + \epsilon_3 - d_3$
Ending book value (A_t)	$CF_1 - CF_0 - d_1$	$CF_2 - CF_0 - d_1 - d_2$	$CF_3 + 0$
Panel B Accounting Calculations When $\epsilon < 0$			
Revenue (CF_t)	$CF_1 = \bar{c}_1 + \epsilon + \epsilon_1$	$CF_2 = \bar{c}_2 + \theta\epsilon + \epsilon_2$	$CF_3 = \bar{c}_3 + \gamma\epsilon + \epsilon_3$
Depreciation (d_t)	d_1	$d_2 - \theta|\epsilon|$	$d_3 - \gamma|\epsilon|$
Restructuring charge	$(\theta + \gamma)|\epsilon|$		
Accounting income (I_t)	$CF_1 - d_1 - (\theta + \gamma)|\epsilon|$	$\bar{c}_2 + \epsilon_2 - d_2$	$\bar{c}_3 + \epsilon_3 - d_3$
Ending book value (A_t)	$CF_1 - CF_0 - d_1$ $- (\theta + \gamma)|\epsilon|$	$CF_2 - CF_0 - d_1 - d_2$ $- \gamma|\epsilon|$	$CF_3 + 0$

where, again, the constant $\alpha = \theta(1 + r)^{-1} + \gamma(1 + r)^{-2}$. To this we add the dividend, in the amount CF_1, that is both known, thanks to the information, and imminent. So, with this timing convention and with the information history of $h_1 = (\epsilon, \epsilon_1)$, we have the following price expression at time $t = 1$:[2]

$$P_1(h_1) = CF_1 + E[PV_1 \mid \epsilon, \epsilon_1] = \bar{c}_1 + \epsilon + \epsilon_1 + E[PV_1] + \alpha\epsilon \quad \textbf{(10.2)}$$

The accounting side follows in familiar fashion with one exception. We now assume that, if the persistence effect is negative, the accounting system will record an "appropriate restructuring charge" during the first period, one that books the entire nominal effect of the persistent, negative effect. This gives the accounting source a conservative bias because it selectively reports the other information when it is bad news. Details are displayed in Exhibit 10.3 for the case in which the persistence effect is positive (Panel A) and for the case in which it is negative (Panel B). Recall that the initial investment is denoted $CF_0 < 0$, so the initial balance sheet description of the asset will be the amount $-CF_0$. At time $t = 1$, the ending

[2] It is important to remember that the simulation deals with a market setting in which all market actors have the same information; there is no private information in the valuation market. Expression (10.2), then, is a statement of "market efficiency" in the sense the market price fully reflects (via Bayesian updating) all information that is available to the market participants.

book value is the cash balance (of CF_1) plus the long-lived asset's value of $-CF_0 - d_1$, if the persistence effect is positive; but if it is negative, the long-lived asset is written down to $-CF_0 - d_1 - (\theta + \gamma)|\epsilon|$. Subsequent depreciation in the write-down case, then, will be $d_2 - \theta|\epsilon|$ in the second period followed by $d_3 - \gamma|\epsilon|$ in the third period. For later reference, this implies that the first period income is simply $\hat{I}_1 = \bar{c}_1 + \epsilon + \epsilon_1 - d_1 + (\theta + \gamma)\min(0, \epsilon)$.[3]

Information Content

With this in place, we turn to the question of whether there is evidence that the accounting report has information content. In the most simple case, this boils down to asking whether the accounting release is associated with price movements at the time of that release.[4]

In our stylized setting of Exhibit 10.3, suppose we set the respective expected cash flows at 4,950, 9,680, and 16,637.50 (as in the illustration in Chapters 8 and 9). Also set the two persistence parameters at $\theta = \gamma = 1.5$, and the interest rate at $r = 10$ percent. The initial cost is 25,000, and straight-line depreciation will be used. Further suppose each shock term follows a normal distribution with (mean zero, of course), and a standard deviation of 1,500. We now simulate this setting with a sample of 100 draws. The resulting time $t = 1$ prices are summarized in Exhibit 10.4.

The intuition should be clear. We have 100 initially identical firms. Each experiences random cash flows and random variation in future cash flow prospects. The underlying revelation takes place, simultaneously, with accounting and nonaccounting sources of information. We have rigged the story so the accounting source is essential to fully identifying the persistence effect. Quite naturally, then, we see in the simulation that price dispersion is present. The prices are, by construction, responding to both of the underlying information releases. What a surprise![5]

Now turn to the real data. Beaver (1968) examines price variability for a sample of firms at the time of an accounting release, or so-called earnings announcement. The firms, of course, are heterogeneous, so it makes no sense to simply plot the corresponding price dispersion. Instead, we

---

[3] The accruals, in other words, are designed to book the entire nominal effect of a negative persistence term at $t = 1$ and subsequently report an income figure purged of this already recognized bad news.

[4] Recall, however, that content so defined does not imply the information is valuable, or vice versa; it is also possible that the essential price movement does not take place at the time the accounting report is released. For example, it might be the case that the accounting information confirms an anticipated large capital expansion, but the consequences of that expansion remain largely unclear until subsequent readings on the firm's order book are released.

[5] With the setup in the simulation, the value, or market price, at $t = 1$ is a normally distributed random variable with a mean of 27,500 and a standard deviation of $1,500\sqrt{1 + (1 + \alpha)^2}$, or about 5,600. This follows from the price expression in (10.2), the assumed cash flow means, and independence among the shock terms.

EXHIBIT 10.4
Price Dispersion at
Time $t = 1$

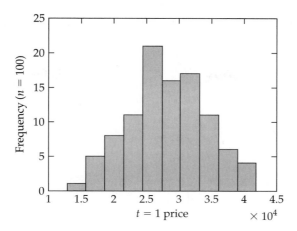

EXHIBIT 10.5
Beaver's
Information
Content
Demonstration

Source: Beaver, 1968, p. 91.

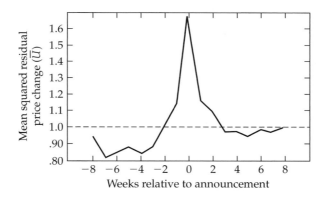

focus on the return (change in price plus dividend received over initial price). This is analyzed during the announcement period, the period of time during which the accounting report is released. Moreover, economy-wide forces are at work, as in our earlier anecdote, so, the return is also normalized to adjust for marketwide effects. Although we gloss over details, Beaver (see Exhibit 10.5.) plots the normalized square of the unexplained return as we pass through the announcement period. (This is a measure of the variability of the returns.) The resulting graph "spikes" during the announcement period. Importantly, the announcement is associated with otherwise unexplained price movement, just as in our simulation.[6] The noted pattern is consistent with the release of information at the time of the accounting announcement.

---

[6] A number of subtle issues arise here. For example, economywide effects are absent in our simulation, just as is the issue of firm-by-firm heterogeneity. The time at which a firm makes an announcement can also be a factor, but here we rely on the fact that firms make periodic accounting releases at more or less predictable times.

Next, instead of merely looking for some evidence of price movement during the accounting release, consider the relationship between the market and accounting variables. Here we relate the unexpected component of the price change to the unexpected component of the income report, or *earnings release.* This is easy to do in our simulation, especially at time $t = 1$. The unexpected component of the price change is simply the actual price, detailed in (10.2), less the time $t = 0$ expected value of that price:[7]

$$P_1(h_1) - E[P_1(h_1)] = \bar{c}_1 + \epsilon + \epsilon_1 + E[PV_1] + \alpha\epsilon - (\bar{c}_1 + E[PV_1])$$
$$= \epsilon + \epsilon_1 + \alpha\epsilon$$

Likewise, the unexpected component of the income measure, or earnings release, is the actual income less the $t = 0$ expected value of that income:[8]

$$\hat{I}_1 - E[\hat{I}_1] = \bar{c}_1 + \epsilon + \epsilon_1 - d_1 + (\theta + \gamma)\min(0, \epsilon)$$
$$- (\bar{c}_1 - d_1 + E[(\theta + \gamma)\min(0, \epsilon)])$$
$$= \epsilon + \epsilon_1 + (\theta + \gamma)\min(0, \epsilon) - E[(\theta + \gamma)\min(0, \epsilon)]$$

We display the resulting simulation results in Exhibit 10.6. Notice the pattern: The two surprises tend to move together, but not in one-to-one fashion and not even in linear fashion. This particular pattern, of course, is driven by the persistence effect and the conservative accounting approach of booking a negative persistence effect but delaying recognition of the full force of a positive persistence effect. The market valuation, of course, has access to finer information, and well processes that information relative to the accounting construction.[9]

Turning to real data, researchers have found a positive, but slight, relationship between earnings and price surprise. Again glossing over the details, the idea is to relate unexpected return, as in the Beaver study, to unexpected earnings. The latter are usually measured as the difference between actual and analysts' forecasts or between actual and a historical trended forecast. In turn, the return calculation might be based on a narrow time span centered on the time of the earnings release, a short

[7] This is none other than Equation (9.9).
[8] The unusual feature here is the one-sided recognition of the persistence effect. If $\epsilon < 0$, the accounting value is immediately written down in the amount $(\theta + \gamma)\epsilon = (\theta + \gamma)\min(0, \epsilon)$. Because this write down is asymmetric, so to speak, its expected value is not zero. In fact, with the noted values in our simulation, we find $E[(\theta + \gamma)\min(0, \epsilon)] \approx -1,800$. Think of this as a conservative approach in which we expect a "lower" first period income because any unanticipated bad news is fully booked at the time it is discovered.
[9] For that matter, we should remember the scaling effect built into the simulation. Glance back at the presumed price expression in (10.2) where we see that price, thanks to our assumptions, processes the two shocks in additive fashion. It does not process the accounting report in additive fashion, however, simply because of the scaling. Naturally, this level of specificity is unavailable in empirical work where we often rely on additive processing. Accruals versus cash flow, as studied by, say, Sloan (1996) and Collins and Hribar (2000), is illustrative.

EXHIBIT 10.6
Price versus Income
Surprise at $t = 1$

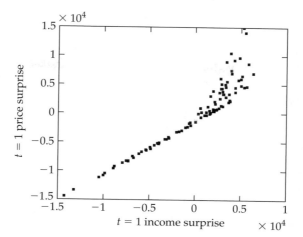

window, so to speak, or it might be based on a longer time span, or wide window. While our simulated data show a correlation of about .9 (or an R^2 of about .8), the real data are another story. Summarizing a variety of such studies, Lev (1989, pp. 172–73) observes:

> The evidence on the returns/earnings relation cumulated over the past 20 years provides a consistent picture. Earnings and earnings-related information (e.g., cash flows) explain 2–5% of the cross-sectional or time-series variability of stock returns for relatively narrow windows, and up to perhaps 7% for very wide windows. Accordingly, an earnings explanatory power of about 5%, on the average, for large, heterogeneous samples appears representative. The parameters of the returns/earnings relation are subject to considerable instability over time, which has yet to be explained. These findings appear robust to the time periods examined and to the various methodologies used.

It is also clear this relationship is far from linear. Freeman and Tse (1992), for example, document an "S-shaped," or transcendental, pattern. The idea is that the surprise in the price domain, measured by the unexpected return, levels off as the surprise in the earnings release becomes larger and larger in magnitude.[10] The "earnings response coefficient," so to speak, is hardly a constant. Indeed, other studies have identified effects

---

[10] In qualitative terms, the statistically identified relationship between earnings surprise and return surprise looks as follows.

of persistence estimates, risk, and market to book as important explanatory variables in understanding the "earnings response coefficient."

Why, then, does our modest simulation in Exhibit 10.6 reflect the basic directional pattern in the real data but not the wide dispersion in the data or the more pronounced nonlinear effects? First, our modest specification of the fundamentals in (10.1) is far removed from reality. At any point in time, we suspect the typical firm is displaying a variety of transitory and persistent effects, not to mention ever-changing growth prospects. Second, our simulation employs an extremely modest information structure while the typical firm is valued on the basis of a large variety of information sources. Third, our simulation presumes that all market actors are equally informed.[11]

Multiple Information Sources

The data are also highly consistent with the presence of multiple sources of information. One approach to documentation is to notice that if the market valuation reflects information beyond that on which the accounting calculations rely, we should be able to use the market valuation, the price, to predict the future accounting report.[12]

Returning to our simulation, we plot first period price against second period income in Exhibit 10.7. If $P_1(h_1)$ is high, it is likely the persistence effect, which is fully identified by the information sources available to the market, is large and positive; since a large, positive persistence effect affects accounting income in the future periods, we expect the next period income to be high. Of course, the connection is not tight because the transitory effect is also present. Real data exhibit the same phenomenon (e.g., Beaver, Lambert and Ryan, 1987).

More dramatic is the famous Ball and Brown (1968) study. Using monthly data over a 20-year period, they explore a hypothetical experiment. Suppose we could (privately) learn, with perfect foresight, a firm's time t income one year in advance (i.e., at time $t - 1$). Take all of the firms whose income will be above expectations, will be a positive surprise, and track their corresponding price surprise (measured via marketwide adjusted return surprise) over the time $t - 1$ to time t interval. Do the same for all firms whose forthcoming income will be a negative surprise. Call these two groupings the good news and bad news portfolios.

Their diagram is reproduced in Exhibit 10.8. Three slightly different ways of measuring the surprise in income are used (variables 1, 2, and 3).

---

[11] We should also mention difficulties in measuring both the surprise in the information variable and the surprise in the valuation variable.

[12] The market valuation reflects what is known about future dividends, which depend on future cash flows. This implies that nonaccounting information used in that valuation speaks to those future cash flows and thus indirectly speaks to forthcoming accounting measures because they too reflect the forthcoming cash flows.

EXHIBIT 10.7
Current Price versus
Future Income

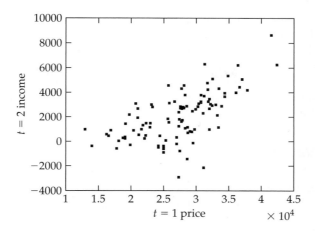

EXHIBIT 10.8
Ball and Brown's
"Fan" Diagram

Source: Ball and Brown,
1968, p. 169.

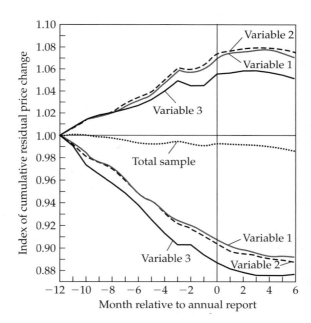

Importantly, foreknowledge of good news is associated with marketwide adjusted positive returns, just as foreknowledge of bad news is associated with negative returns.

Several aspects of this pattern should be noted. Income surprise and price surprise, so to speak, are clearly correlated.[13] Most of the price

[13] It is important to remember we are detailing the average relationship in Exhibit 10.8. Positive income surprise does not guarantee positive price surprise in each and every case. More about this later.

surprise occurs, however, well before the accounting report is released. This is consistent with other sources of information being present and, on the surface, being far more important in the valuation process than the accounting measures per se. Also, at the time of the accounting report's release, the price surprise is relatively minor, just as noted in our earlier documentation. In the Appendix we explore this consistency in another simulation.

Value Relevance

Closely related to the theme of multiple sources of information in the typical valuation market is so-called value relevance. The idea here is to ask whether some particular accounting measure, such as fair value of financial instruments or banks' loan loss provisions, is useful in statistically identifying prices. If some such item is statistically important, it is said to have *value relevance:* It is as if the market finds that measure relevant in setting prices.

Return to our modest simulation. The first period price depends on both the transitory and permanent shock terms because both are known by the market at time $t = 1$. Moreover, first period price is statistically related to the firm's cash balance (because that balance will be paid out in a dividend) and to the noncash balance on the balance sheet. Indeed, if we ask whether both the cash and the noncash components of the balance sheet are useful in statistically identifying prices, the answer will be affirmative.

Intuitively, then, we might begin with the cash balance as the first variable and then ask whether the accrual component, the noncash balance, has value relevance. The answer would be affirmative, but the noncash balance hardly has information content. It reflects the asset write-down when the persistence term is negative, but this is learned from observing the cash flow (or the cash balance) and combining that with the nonaccounting source's identification of the transitory component of the cash balance.

The difficulty, of course, is failing to control for other sources of information.[14] This other information is transmitted to the valuation through the nonaccounting source, and it incidentally informs about the noncash balance recorded by the accounting system. Alternatively, then, suppose the accounting system is the only source of information and it operates as described earlier. Lack of an asset write-down then signals that the persistence shock is positive, just as an explicit write-down completely identifies

---

[14] Once labor contracting is introduced, we will see an additional difficulty with the value relevance theme based on its sidestepping the potential importance of what might be reported were the management team to engage in one activity as opposed to another.

the negative shock. Here, with a single information source, we would find both value relevance and information content.

The larger point, of course, is the importance of understanding the information environment. Absent such understanding, statistical association between prices and some potential information variable is hardly an error-free identifier of information content. Accounting and non-accounting information interact in subtle ways. When both carry the same information, timing becomes important. The most timely source is the carrier of the information. Myopically focusing only on the accounting variable runs the risk of missing this basic point.

Stock Association

Another view of the connection between economic and accounting measures comes into focus when we concentrate on the association between accounting stock and flow measures and market value. The Ball and Brown diagram, for example, suggests that while accounting income is a late reporting source, overall it is associated with market value. Similarly, our earlier work in Chapter 9 points out that a present value–based valuation can be algebraically expressed as book value plus error, where the error is the expected value of the present value of the future residual income series. From here, it is a short step to thinking of current income as providing a proxy for the residual income series.

Returning a final time to our simulation, we plot, in Exhibit 10.9, $t = 1$ price less book value, the error, versus accounting income. Naturally, this reflects the policy of immediately writing off a negative persistence effect, but it also suggests linking market value to accounting value and to

EXHIBIT 10.9
Price-Book Value versus Income at $t = 1$

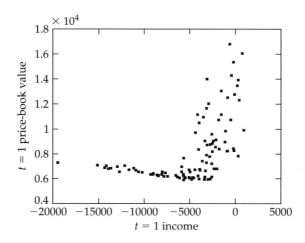

accounting income.[15] For example, Collins, Maydew, and Weiss (1997) report market value is positively related to both accounting value and accounting income as well as a slight shifting of relative weight from the flow to the stock measure through time.[16]

Self-Selection

Another issue is the fact that firms are not automata. Real choices matter. Accounting choices are made by managers, professional judgment is routinely exercised in measuring and cataloging various events, and opportunism opportunities naturally arise. For example, should a large sale late in the reporting cycle be booked during the current or next cycle?[17] Accounting estimates also matter; for example, when should an admittedly subjective write-off take place, and in what amount? Likewise, when should a new reporting requirement be adopted?

Burgstahler and Dichev (1997) provide evidence consistent with these possibilities. They plot the change in annual accounting income $(\hat{I}_t - \hat{I}_{t-1})$ scaled by (beginning of the specific year) market value for a large sample of firms over a nearly 20-year period. Their histogram is displayed in Exhibit 10.10.

The histogram is basically smooth and single peaked, as would be expected from such a set of data. Unusually, however, slight declines in accounting income occur in an uncommonly low proportion of the sample, just as slight positive increases occur in an uncommonly high proportion of the sample. A parallel pattern occurs for losses, per se. Apparently, real data are not as mechanically produced as implied by our modest simulation. There is an element of self-selection by the reporting firm.

---

[15] The simulated data also display a difference in the relationship depending on whether accounting income is negative. Real data display a similar connection, though in the opposite direction. Returns seem to be more sensitive to negative than to positive income. (This is documented by Basu, 1997, although we must, again, be careful to control for other information sources.) The simulation, remember, is of a short-lived firm, and negative income is associated with a negative persistence effect that is immediately recognized. This produces a more aggressive reaction to positive income.

[16] Dechow, Hutton, and Sloan (1999) and Myers (1999) illustrate the use of additional structure in attempting to tease out the error between market and accounting (book) value, the expected present value of the residual incomes term. It is also possible, as in Easton, Taylor, Shroff, and Sougiannis (2001), to use analysts' forecasts and a parametric specification of the residual income term to focus on the implied expected rate of return. Frankel and Lee (1998; 1998a) also use analysts' forecasts to identify the residual income term. Moving across a large number of countries and different reporting regimes (e.g., U.S. versus German reporting regulations), they report that the noted abnormal earnings term is important, that value differences are well explained by the "fundamentals" expressed in this fashion, and that neither international nor domestic accounting differences are a major issue, yet another illustration of our scaling theme.

[17] We should also not be naive and assume that the time at which this order arrives is completely exogenous.

EXHIBIT 10.10
Burgstahler and Dichev's Change in Income Histogram

Source: Burgstahler and Dichev, 1997, p. 105.

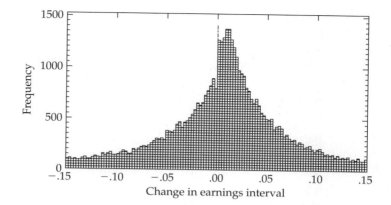

Another illustration of the self-selection theme is provided by Liu, Ryan, and Wahlen (1997). They focus on loan loss provisions reported by banks. It turns out that market reaction to an unanticipated loan loss provision is positive if the provision is booked in the fourth quarter and the bank is at risk but is negative otherwise. In other words, depending on other information (indicating whether the bank is in a more or less risky position) and depending on the quarter in which the bank elects to book the provision, the overall interpretation is "good news" or "bad news."[18]

Taken together, this suggests an element of self-serving behavior, of "earnings management." Stated differently, incentive issues appear to be present, and this leads us to conclude that these incentives properly play an important role in accounting theory. After all, accounting rules are not iron clad or free of interpretation, nor do they prescribe a completely inflexible approach to reporting choices. We must, however, defer this important topic to a later chapter because we have yet to introduce an explicit management function complete with incentive issues. For the moment we are limited to pointing out the issue of self-selection.[19]

Scaling

A final stop on our selective sample is the long-standing question of whether "the market" sees through accounting artifacts. Is the evidence consistent with the claim accounting measures are processed in sophisticated fashion by "the market"? Stated differently, we know the

---

[18] For that matter, the digits in reported income are not random, just as a retail price of 9.99 is far more likely than one of 10.00 (Thomas,1989 and Niskanen and Keloharju, 2000), nor is the availability of supplementary disclosures random (Schrand and Walther, 2000).

[19] It is not sufficient to presume that management has and acts upon an incentive to intertemporally manage its accounting renderings. Rather, this incentive should and will be derived and analyzed in a later chapter. This is one of the reasons we examine the use of accounting information in both valuation and evaluation, or contracting, contexts.

information conveyed by a measurement system, such as accounting, can be conveyed with a wide variety of (informationally equivalent) scaling alternatives. For example, the depreciation schedule in our simulation is essentially arbitrary; the simulation results are unaffected by the choice of depreciation schedule in Exhibit 10.3. (This is the invertibility argument developed earlier in Chapter 7.) However, are the real data equally transparent in this regard?

Lev and Sougiannis (1996) focus on the U.S. GAAP requirement that R&D expenditures be expensed (excepting some software development costs). Presuming that these expenditures lead, on average, to important long-term investments, this procedure surely amounts to conservative reporting. Using only public data sources, they statistically estimate R&D amortization rates by identifying the time series connection between operating income and prior and current R&D expenditures. The importance of prior, lagged, expenditures identifies the presumed amortization schedule. For example, in the scientific instruments industry, the average relationship is amortization over five years, at respective rates of 14, 21, 24, 24, and 17 percent. They go on to "correct" reported stock and flow measures, using these estimated schedules, and document much closer association between economic and adjusted measures than between economic and unadjusted measures. (Notice the value relevance theme.)

Clearly, however, the derived amortization rates and subsequent adjustments are all based on publicly available information. So, the nonaccounting information structure coupled with extant reporting is informationally equivalent to the nonaccounting information structure coupled with the adjusted reporting structure. No new information has been introduced. The adjustment amounts to a rescaling of the accounting measures chosen so they more closely correspond to their market-based counterparts.

Beaver and Dukes (1973) illustrate another version of the scaling phenomenon. They contrast price-earnings ratios for a group of firms using accelerated depreciation with another group using straight-line depreciation. The average price-earnings ratio is higher for the accelerated group, but adjusting the straight-line firms to an accelerated pattern dramatically reduces the difference between the two groups' average price-earnings ratios. This mechanical adjustment between straight-line and accelerated depreciation has not altered the underlying information content. It has only recast it with an alternative scale.[20]

---

[20] Some of the more subtle side of scaling is explored in the Appendix. It is also important to remember we are dealing with information structure equivalence, and this means, in the end, we have to worry about what is being reported by other sources. One might, for example, think that LIFO and FIFO are simply scale differences, but this is not the case because they operate in the vein of index numbers with different weights. In addition, a LIFO implementation will footnote disclose the LIFO reserve while a FIFO implementation offers no such conversion option.

The evidence, then, is not consistent with the view that market participants are using a naive model to move from the accounting reports to market value. Rather, the evidence is consistent with the view that they are mixing the accounting reports with knowledge of the accounting methods used and with nonaccounting information to set the market value.

Summary

Our survey of the relationship between accounting and market-based value measures was designed to build intuition for the reason that accounting and economic measures move together but less than perfectly. Viewed as an information source, accounting conveys its information by engaging in various accounting calculations, or procedures. Thus, the information comes coded in a particular measurement scale. Moreover, we know there are multiple sources of information, and at any given point in time, the accounting system does not capture all available information. So, the metaphor is one of restrictive recognition, but this implies that accounting and market values cannot possibly be identical because the latter have access, presumably, to much more information. So, the slippage between the two sets of measures increases, but the connection remains because the typical accounting procedure, or measurement scale, records the "news" it processes in a way roughly—we emphasize *roughly*—comparable to that of the economic calculation. Accounting, we have repeatedly stressed, uses the language and algebra of valuation to convey its information, but accounting is by no means an aggressive user of the information at hand. Scaling and timing issues are present in the financial reporting environment.

We conclude with three cautions. First, once we admit to market frictions, the concept of economic value becomes ill defined if not vacuous. So, extension of this theme into more complex settings moves us into uncharted territory.

Second, the same phenomenon exists in other settings in which we worry about the connection between accounting and economic assessments. For example, a multiproduct firm whose economic cost curve is not linear cannot in general be well described for all products by an accounting costing procedure that imposes a linear structure on the product costing apparatus (as, for example, is almost always the case, even with an ABC procedure). Presumably, the marginal costs of some products will be reasonably well approximated by the accounting calculations, while those of others will not. From an information perspective, though, we have to understand the procedures as providing a particular measurement scale to convey information, not to convey unadorned, predigested economic assessments.

Third, the survey juxtaposes valuation market and accounting measures. It has a distinct "valuation usefulness" orientation, but information content in this domain is not coextensive with information content in a contracting domain, a topic to which we turn in the next chapter.

A Closer Look at Scaling

In this appendix we provide a closer examination of the scaling phenomenon. To keep things simple, we streamline the story so that the firm experiences only a single cash inflow and assume that this eventual cash inflow can take one of only two values. Denote it $D \in \{0, 1\}$, with 50–50 odds. (So, in usual notation, $\pi(D = 1) = \pi(D = 0) = .50$.) Also let the interest rate be zero. The latter allows us to keep discounting calculations from cluttering the analysis. It also implies, presuming risk neutrality, that the initial value of the firm is simply the expected value of D, or (conveniently)

$$E[D] = 1 \times \pi(D = 1) + 0 \times \pi(D = 0) = \pi(D = 1) = .50$$

This is also its cost.

SEQUENCE OF INFORMATION RELEASES

We also want to introduce a sequence of informative signals, or information sources. The easiest way to do this is to stretch out the time line and assume the cash inflow of D occurs at some distant point, say at time $T = 8$. So, the cash flows are $CF_0 = -.50$, $CF_8 = D$, and zero otherwise.

Turning to the information story, simplicity is again in order. Let y denote a report. Each report will be "good news" ($y = g$) or "bad news" ($y = b$), according to the following probability structure: $\pi(y = g \mid D = 1) = \pi(y = b \mid D = 0) = \beta$. When multiple sources are present, they all operate in this fashion and are conditionally independent. β, then, is simply the probability that any such source is "correct." (Of course, $\beta > .5$.) Examine Exhibit 10.11 where we portray an informative observation, denoted y_t, each period. Additional details are given in Exhibit 10.12 where we display the joint probabilities, $\pi(D$ and $y)$, for $t = 3$ periods. A full information history here, then, is the time $t = 3$ history of

EXHIBIT 10.11   Information Sequence for Single Project with Uncertain Cash Inflow

$t = 0$	$t = 1$	$t = 2$	$t = 3$	$t = 4$
$CF_0 = -.50$	$CF_1 = 0;$ $y_1 \in \{g, b\}$	$CF_2 = 0;$ $y_2 \in \{g, b\}$	$CF_3 = 0;$ $y_3 \in \{g, b\}$	$CF_4 = 0;$ $y_4 \in \{g, b\}$

EXHIBIT 10.12
$\pi(D$ and $h_t)$ for $t = 3$ and $\beta = .9$

$h_3 = (y_1, y_2, y_3)$	$D = 1$	$D = 0$	$\pi(h_3)$
(g, g, g)	$.5\beta^3 = .3645$	$.5(1 - \beta)^3 = .0005$	.3650
(g, g, b)	$.5\beta^2(1 - \beta) = .0405$	$.5\beta(1 - \beta)^2 = .0045$	.0450
(g, b, g)	$.5\beta^2(1 - \beta) = .0405$	$.5\beta(1 - \beta)^2 = .0045$	.0450
(g, b, b)	$.5\beta(1 - \beta)^2 = .0045$	$.5\beta^2(1 - \beta) = .0405$	.0450
(b, g, g)	$.5\beta^2(1 - \beta) = .0405$	$.5\beta(1 - \beta)^2 = .0045$	.0450
(b, g, b)	$.5\beta(1 - \beta)^2 = .0045$	$.5\beta^2(1 - \beta) = .0405$	.0450
(b, b, g)	$.5\beta(1 - \beta)^2 = .0045$	$.5\beta^2(1 - \beta) = .0405$	.0450
(b, b, b)	$.5(1 - \beta)^3 = .0005$	$.5\beta^3 = .3645$	.3650
$\pi(D)$	.5000	.5000	

EXHIBIT 10.13
$E[D \mid h_t] = \pi$
$(D = 1 \mid h_t)$ for $t = 1, 2,$ and 3

$h_3 = (y_1, y_2, y_3)$	$P(h_t) = E[D \mid h_t]$		
	$t = 1$	$t = 2$	$t = 3$
(g, g, g)	.9000	.9878	.9986
(g, g, b)	.9000	.9878	.9000
(g, b, g)	.9000	.5000	.9000
(g, b, b)	.9000	.5000	.1000
(b, g, g)	.1000	.5000	.9000
(b, g, b)	.1000	.5000	.1000
(b, b, g)	.1000	.0122	.1000
(b, b, b)	.1000	.0122	.0014

$h_3 = (y_1, y_2, y_3)$. We also use $\beta = .9$. Notice that over the three periods, we have eight possible information histories.[21]

With this in place, what is the expected value of D, the market value of the claim, or asset, conditional on all available information at time t? In mechanical terms, having observed history h_t, we calculate this[22] as

$$P(h_t) = E[D \mid h_t] = 1 \times \pi(D = 1 \mid h_t) + 0 \times \pi(D = 0 \mid h_t) = \pi(D = 1 \mid h_t)$$

We tally these revised assessments for this information story in Exhibit 10.13 where we present distinct calculations for $t = 1, 2,$ and 3. For

---

[21] Some additional features of the stochastic setup should be noted. If $t = 1$ and $y_1 = g$, we have $\pi(D = 1 \mid h_1 = g) = \beta$. If $t = 2$ and $h_t = (g, b)$ or (b, g), we have $\pi(D = 1 \mid h_2) = .50$. In addition, if you recall your study of statistics, you will recognize that the informative signal is a binary random variable. To illustrate, suppose $D = 1$; now what is the probability of precisely $\hat{g}$ observations of signal g over t periods? This probability is given by

$$\binom{t}{\hat{g}} \beta^{\hat{g}} (1 - \beta)^{t - \hat{g}}$$

the number of $\hat{g}$ successes in t trials (given $D = 1$).

[22] The conditional probability, in turn, follows from Bayes' rule:

$$\pi(D = 1 \mid h_t) = \pi(D = 1 \text{ and } h_t) / \pi(h_t).$$

EXHIBIT 10.14
Change in Market Value Calculations (Δ_t) for $t = 1, 2,$ and 3

$h_3 = (y_1, y_2, y_3)$	Δ_1	Δ_2	Δ_3	$\pi(h_3)$
(g, g, g)	.4000	.0878	.0108	.3650
(g, g, b)	.4000	.0878	−.0878	.0450
(g, b, g)	.4000	−.4000	.4000	.0450
(g, b, b)	.4000	−.4000	−.4000	.0450
(b, g, g)	−.4000	.4000	.4000	.0450
(b, g, b)	−.4000	.4000	−.4000	.0450
(b, b, g)	−.4000	−.0878	.0878	.0450
(b, b, b)	−.4000	−.0878	−.0108	.3650

EXHIBIT 10.15
Summary Effects of Information Release

Time t	$E|\Delta_t|$	$VAR(\Delta_t)$
1	.4000	.1600
2	.1440	.0351
3	.0878	.0296

example, using the data in Exhibit 10.12, we calculate:

$$E[D \mid h_2 = (g, g)] = \pi(D = 1 \mid h_2 = (g, g))$$
$$= \frac{.3645 + .0405}{.3645 + .0405 + .0005 + .0045} = \frac{.4050}{.4100} = .9878$$

Now consider the change in price, in market value, as we move through time. At time $t = 1$, prior to observing the information, the change in market value is a random variable: $\Delta_1 = E[D \mid y_1] - .50$. At time $t = 2$ it is the random variable $\Delta_2 = E[D \mid (h_1, y_2)] - E[D \mid h_1]$, and so on. Details are provided in Exhibit 10.14.

Notice that the expected value of the change in market value is zero:[23] $E[\Delta_1] = E[\Delta_2] = E[\Delta_3] = 0$. Moreover, at any point in time, we face a fair game with respect to the next information release. That is, the expected value of the time t expected value of D, given we know history realization h_{t-1}, is $E[E[D \mid h_{t-1}, y_t] \mid h_{t-1}] = E[D \mid h_{t-1}]$ for any history of signals h_{t-1}. Volatility, though, will systematically decline because the assumed probability structure implies that each additional piece of information is, on average, less informative. This is reflected in Exhibit 10.15 where we provide the mean absolute value and variance of Δ_t, for $t = 1, 2,$ and 3. Be aware that this particular pattern of declining information content is driven by the binary random variable (and *iid*) characterization of the information sources. Nevertheless, it leads to important insight into the impact of multiple sources of information.

[23] Recall we have neutralized risk by assuming risk neutrality. So, changes in risk are moot. We also have neutralized time by assuming a zero interest rate. So, change in market value, in price, as we step through time is due solely to the arrival of new information and its impact on the expected value of D.

ACCOUNTING SOURCE

Now suppose one, but only one, of these information sources is the accounting system. In particular, across the first four information releases, assume that one, but only one, comes from the accounting system. Let τ denote the index in the sequence where the accounting source is operative. If, then, $\tau = 3$, the information at times $t = 1, 2,$ and 4 comes from nonaccounting sources while the information at time $t = 3$ comes from the accounting source. This provides a simple, intuitive way of mixing accounting and nonaccounting sources of information. We have a sequence of informative observations, and one in the sequence is the accounting source.

Accounting, though, does not report some abstract signal. It conveys its information through the application of accounting procedures to underlying events. We examine two such procedures. Both, naturally, begin by recording historical cost (at time $t = 0$ of .50), and both report the realization of D at time $T = 8$. The intermediate point of time τ is where they differ. One method is a fair value method, in which accounting and economic value are equated at the time of the accounting release. So, for any history of nonaccounting information up to the time of the accounting report, $h_{\tau-1}$, and period τ signal realization, y_τ, the accounting system will record a time τ accounting value of $A_\tau = E[D \mid (h_{\tau-1}, y_\tau)]$ and associated accounting income of $\hat{I}_\tau = E[D \mid (h_{\tau-1}, y_\tau)] - .50$. The asset, so to speak, is marked to market; and any change in accounting value is reflected in the accounting income measure.

The second method is a myopic, or highly restricted, version of fair value. For any history of nonaccounting information, $h_{\tau-1}$, it simply records a time τ accounting value of $A_\tau = E[D \mid y_\tau]$ and associated accounting income of $\hat{I}_\tau = E[D \mid y_\tau] - .50$. This procedure ignores, or does not recognize, the earlier nonaccounting information, summarized in history $h_{\tau-1}$. It uses the same valuation formula as in the market value calculation but with a restrictive recognition rule.

Nevertheless, both methods reveal the time τ realization of y_τ. The fair value method, for example, reports an income of $E[D \mid (h_{\tau-1}, y_\tau)] - .50$. Prior to the report, other sources have reported in cumulative terms the history of $h_{\tau-1}$, and the market value of the asset just prior to the accounting report is known to be $E[D \mid h_{\tau-1}]$. Decoding the accounting report, then, we see that reported accounting income is surprisingly large (given $h_{\tau-1}$) if and only if the reported accounting value is surprisingly large. In turn, this value is surprisingly large if and only if $y_\tau = g$. So, a "positive surprise" conveys the fact $y_\tau = g$, just as a "negative surprise" conveys the fact $y_\tau = b$.

Similarly, at time τ the myopic method reports an income of $E[D \mid y_\tau] - .50$. This is positive if and only if $y_\tau = g$. The two methods use different measurement scales but are informationally equivalent in the

EXHIBIT 10.16
Accounting Income
versus Market
Value Change for
Fair Value System

$h_3 = (y_1, y_2, y_3)$	Accounting Income: $\hat{I}_3 = E[D\,|\,h_3] - .5$	Expected Income: $E[\hat{I}_3\,|\,h_2]$	Difference (Surprise)	Price Change at $t = 3$: Δ_3
(g, g, g)	.4986	.4878	.0108	.0108
(g, g, b)	.4000	.4878	−.0878	−.0878
(g, b, g)	.4000	.0000	.4000	.4000
(g, b, b)	−.4000	.0000	−.4000	−.4000
(b, g, g)	.4000	.0000	.4000	.4000
(b, g, b)	−.4000	.0000	−.4000	−.4000
(b, b, g)	−.4000	−.4878	.0878	.0878
(b, b, b)	−.4986	−.4878	−.0108	−.0108

presence of the nonaccounting information. Understanding this is critical to what follows.[24]

Now suppose the accounting report takes place at time $\tau = 3$. What can we say about the relationship between the accounting and economic measures? We concentrate on the accounting income measure. Recall, for the fair value system, reporting at time $\tau = 3$ results in an income measure of $\hat{I}_3 = E[D\,|\,(h_2, y_3)] - .50$. In turn, the expected value of the income measure just before its release depends on the information releases up to that point, so we write it as $E[\hat{I}_3\,|\,h_2]$. We tabulate the possibilities in Exhibit 10.16. (The last column, Δ_3, is taken from Exhibit 10.14.)

Study the last two columns: The change in market value at the time of the accounting report coincides with the surprise in the accounting income measure. This is intuitive. With the fair value system, the accounting stock measure is identical to its market counterpart at the time of the report (time τ). The market measure, though, receives some information at an earlier time. We control for this by focusing on the surprise in accounting income, the income less what we expected that income to be, based on all available information just prior to the accounting report.

Contrast this with the myopic system. Since the two systems are informationally equivalent, given the nonaccounting information, the change in market value at the time of the accounting report will be the same. The accounting income number, though, is no longer so closely aligned to the change in market value. Details are presented in Exhibit 10.17.[25]

---

[24] In Exhibits 10.16 and 10.17 we identify the accounting income measures for a time $\tau = 3$ report for each possible realization of the sequence of information variables. For the myopic system, Exhibit 10.17, notice that positive income is equivalent to $y_3 = g$. Similarly, for the fair value system, Exhibit 10.16, notice that, for each possible history of signals, the accounting report differs between $y_3 = g$ and $y_3 = b$.

[25] To verify these calculations, notice that the income report is .4 if $y_3 = g$; so, the key is to identify $\pi(y_3 = g\,|\,h_2)$. Go back to Exhibit 10.12. Suppose $h_2 = (g, g)$. We then have $\pi(y_3 = g\,|\,h_2 = (g, g)) = .365/.410$. Thus, the expected value of the forthcoming income report, having observed $h_2 = (g, g)$ is $.4(.365/.410) - .4(.045/.410) = .3122$.

EXHIBIT 10.17
Accounting Income versus Market Value Change for Myopic System

$h_3 = (y_1, y_2, y_3)$	Accounting Income: $\hat{I}_3 = E[D \mid y_3] - .5$	Expected Income: $E[\hat{I}_3 \mid h_2]$	Difference (Surprise)	Price Change at $t = 3$: Δ_3
(g, g, g)	.4000	.3122	.0878	.0108
(g, g, b)	−.4000	.3122	−.7122	−.0878
(g, b, g)	.4000	.0000	.4000	.4000
(g, b, b)	−.4000	.0000	−.4000	−.4000
(b, g, g)	.4000	.0000	.4000	.4000
(b, g, b)	−.4000	.0000	−.4000	−.4000
(b, b, g)	.4000	−.3122	.7122	.0878
(b, b, b)	−.4000	−.3122	−.0878	−.0108

We clearly have a positive relationship between the accounting and market measures. Accounting income is positive only when the change in market value is positive. Controlling for earlier information preserves the connection between positive surprise and positive market value change, but the connection is hardly one to one.[26] Intuitively, this must be the case. The change in market value reflects the totality of all available information while the accounting calculation is restricted in its access to this information. The two systems bring the same new information forward but wrapped, so to speak, in different measurement scales.

MORE SCALING

Another view of this scaling phenomenon surfaces when we mimic the Ball and Brown experiment (Exhibit 10.8). Assume that at time $t = 0$ we privately learn what the accounting report at time $\tau = 3$ will be. This report can be either "good news" or "bad news." For the myopic method, this boils down to knowing in advance whether $y_\tau = g$ or b. Suppose we do this for a large, large number of assets of this type.

In Exhibit 10.18 we plot, again using $\beta = .9$, the average change in market value of the asset (Δ_t recall), conditional on knowing in advance whether the time τ report was good or bad news. The upper solid line in the graph is the case in which we know $y_3 = g$. Notice that it begins at zero and systematically increases to .4. Beyond that point we have no information, so the expected value of the price is simply $E[D \mid y_3 = g] = .9$,

---

[26] Even this degree of connection is critically dependent on our information setup. Observing a report of g is always good news here; information complementarities are well under control.

EXHIBIT 10.18
Market Value
Calculations
Presuming Advance
Knowledge of Time
$\tau = 3$ Report

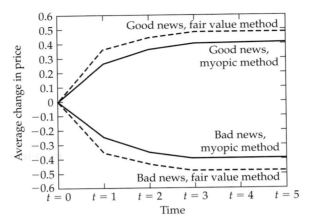

implying a change in market value of $.9 - .5 = .4$. The lower solid line is the companion case of advance knowledge that $y_3 = b$.[27]

Indeed, we have chosen the parameters in the simulation so the calculations lead to an appearance qualitatively similar to that in the Ball and Brown experiment. (We have the luxury, however, of being able to precisely identify the market's expectation of the forthcoming accounting release.) Further notice in Exhibit 10.18 that the average change in market value at the time of the accounting release (the value at $t = 3$ versus at $t = 2$) is positive for the upper graph and negative for the lower graph, although hardly one to one. Accounting value and market value tend to move together but less than perfectly, as we saw in Exhibit 10.17.

Now consider the fair value procedure. It reports income in period $\tau = 3$ of $\hat{I}_3 = E[D \,|\, (h_{\tau-1}, y_\tau)] - .5$. The upper dashed line in Exhibit 10.18 reports the corresponding expected value of the change in market price, conditional on knowing $E[D \,|\, (h_{\tau-1}, y_\tau)] - .5 \geq 0$. It is strictly above its counterpart for the myopic accounting procedure. The reason is that this procedure employs strictly more historical information in conveying its report at time $\tau = 3$. So, advance knowledge of that report implies we are conditioning on strictly more information. The good news filter, so to

[27] To remove some of the mystery here, consider the upper solid line in Exhibit 10.18, the case in which we know $y_3 = g$. Using the calculations in Exhibits 10.12 and 10.13, the expected value of the asset's market value at time $t = 1$, when we know $y_3 = g$, is simply

$$E[P(h_1) \,|\, y_3 = g]$$
$$= \sum_{h_1} E[D \,|\, h_1]\, \pi(h_1 \,|\, y_3 = g)$$
$$= [.9(.365) + .9(.045) + .1(.045) + .1(.045)]/[.365 + .045 + .045 + .045]$$
$$= .756$$

So, the expected value of the change in value, as of time $t = 1$, is simply $.756 - .5 = .256$.

speak, is a stronger filter here. Of course, this means the companion bad news graph, the lower dashed line where the expectation is conditional on knowing that $E[D \mid (h_{\tau-1}, y_\tau)] - .5 < 0$, is strictly below the myopic graph. Moreover, we now tighten the connection between the accounting and market measures.

What happens, now, when we move the release point earlier or later? This is sketched in Exhibits 10.19 and 10.20. The pattern should be taking on a familiar appearance. In particular, the slope of each graph in the region between times $\tau - 1$ and τ is flatter the larger is τ. With a later report time, a larger τ, more information has been released in front of the accounting report. In our particular setup, each additional piece of information, each additional observation, is less informative. Diminishing returns to information, so to speak, are built into the simulation. A large τ, then,

EXHIBIT 10.19

Market Value Calculations Presuming Advance Knowledge of Time $\tau = 2$ Report

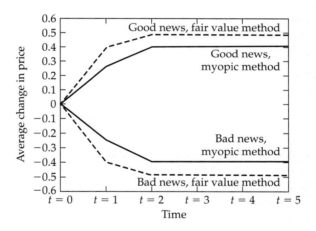

EXHIBIT 10.20

Market Value Calculations Presuming Advance Knowledge of Time $\tau = 4$ Report

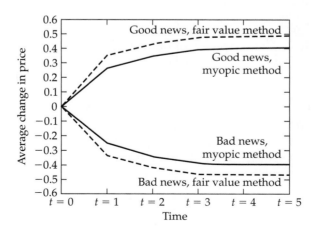

corresponds here to an accounting system whose information is largely overshadowed by the reports of earlier reporting sources.[28]

[28] What would these exhibits look like if we instead had the accounting report at time τ merely report the information provided by the $\tau - 1$ earlier reports? This corresponds to the case in which we use the delayed accounting report to check on the veracity of the earlier reports. Assuming, then, that these earlier reports are, in equilibrium, correctly reporting, the accounting report would appear to be completely redundant.

Selected References

Beaver (1998) is a favorite reference on the topic of juxtaposing market-based and accounting-based measures. Watts and Zimmerman (1986) is also highly recommended. Penman (2000) and White, Sondhi, and Fried (1997) provide a more pragmatic perspective. Lev (1989) provides a review and critique of the work that documents the market price versus accounting income connection, and Holthausen and Watts (2001)[29] review and critique the value relevance theme. Dechow and Skinner (2000) expand on the earnings management theme; and Antle, Demski, and Ryan (1994) examine multiple sources of information and the scaling theme, especially as treated in the Appendix. Analysts' forecasts and their tendency to be optimistic, is examined in Das, Levine, and Sivaramakrishnan (1998), and a parallel tendency toward optimism by movie critics is reported in Eliashberg and Shugan (1997). Ryan (1995) examines book to market ratios; Wilson (1986) and Bernard and Stober (1989) treat cash flow and accrual measures as distinct information sources; and Barth, Cram, and Nelson (2001) focus on using accruals to predict cash flows.

Key Terms

An **earnings release** is simply the accounting income that is reported, at the time of the "release," of course. **Value relevance** of an information variable, such as an earnings release, is a claim that the variable in question is statistically important in explaining observed values or prices. If the statistical test is well specified, including controls for all other sources of information, value relevance is the statistical demonstration of information content.

Exercises

10.1. The chapter emphasizes information content, in particular the question of whether accounting has information content in a valuation setting. Define *information content* in this setting. Are the simulations and summarized studies consistent with the claim that accounting has information content in this setting? Explain.

10.2. In juxtaposing accounting and market-based measures, we take as given the underlying theme that the accounting measures are a source of information. Is it essential, then, that the accounting measures reflect "economic value?" Explain.

[29] The Holthausen and Watts critique is contained in a compendium of critiques, reported in the 2001 *Journal of Accounting & Economics.*

10.3. Exhibits 10.1 and 10.2 contrast market and accounting values for a diversified, successful enterprise. What would these exhibits look like for a dot-com startup or for a mutual fund specializing in treasury bills? (Rather than speculating, collecting and plotting the data make an excellent exercise.)

10.4. *Market efficiency* in this context refers to the market's ability to well use all available information. (This is most apparent in the price expression for our simulations.) What do we mean here by the phrase "all available information," and how is market efficiency relied on in both the simulations and the summarized studies?

10.5. In Exhibit 10.4 we depict a situation in which the price of a financial claim varies at the time of an information release. Is this consistent with the information sources having information content? Explain.

10.6. Using the same setup as in Exhibit 10.4, construct a sample of 100 information events and plot the resulting price dispersion. Contrast your plot with that in Exhibit 10.4. Then construct a companion plot for which the rate of return on the investment rather than the time $t = 1$ price is plotted. Explain the connection between your two plots.

10.7. The relationship between price and earnings surprise, as in the simulation results in Exhibit 10.6, provides a glimpse into the impact of an accounting report in an organized security market. Here you are asked to construct a sample of five such events. In particular, locate five public corporations whose common stock is traded on an organized exchange. Then, for each firm, determine the date on which that firm released a quarterly earnings measure, the earnings per share that was announced for the quarter in question, and the earnings per share that was announced for the year earlier quarter in question. Also determine the closing price of a share of the firm's common stock on the date of the announcement as well as one week before the earnings announcement. This gives you four data points for each firm. Plot the earnings surprise (measured as the difference in the two earnings per share) versus price surprise (measured as the difference in the two prices). Comment on your plot.

10.8. The Ball and Brown (1968) study, summarized in Exhibit 10.8, provides a classic, enduring pattern of the relationship between financial reporting and security price behavior. Write a brief essay answering the following two questions.

   a. Suppose you were asked to collect data on five firms and replicate the experiment; carefully explain what data you would collect and how you would construct the graph that parallels theirs.

b. What does the "fan diagram" appearance of their graph tell you about financial reporting for entities whose residual claims are traded in an organized financial market?

10.9. Return to Exercise 9.6, but now assume that a nonaccounting source reports the transitory shock at time $t = 1$. Determine the resulting price paths. Also, what happens to the income measures identified in the initial exercise? Explain.

10.10. Binary Ralph[30] has just paid $50 for a cash flow that will be realized at the end of period $t = 3$. This cash flow, denoted CF, will be either 0, 1, 99, or 100. Ralph is risk neutral, and the interest rate is $r = 0$. At the end of the first period, that is, at $t = 1$, a nonaccounting information source will issue a signal, denoted $y_1 = g$ or b. At the end of the second period, that is, at $t = 2$, the accounting system will de facto report a signal, denoted $y_2 = g^a$ or b^a. The joint probabilities are given in the following table.

a. Compute the expected value of CF based on no information, at $t = 1$ if g is observed, and at $t = 1$ if b is observed.

	(b, g^a)	(b, b^a)	(g, g^a)	(g, b^a)
$CF = 0$	.005	0	0	0
$CF = 1$	0	.495	0	0
$CF = 99$	0	0	.495	0
$CF = 100$	0	0	0	.005

b. Now suppose the accounting system can use only the y_2 realization to update its value. In particular, suppose that at $t = 2$ it reports the asset's value as the expected value of CF conditional on y_2. Determine these valuations. Does reporting the value calculated in this manner de facto reveal the underlying signal that was observed by the accounting system?

c. Finally, at $t = 1$, is g versus b a "good news" versus "bad news" story? If the $t = 1$ information is available at $t = 2$, is g^a versus b^a a "good news" versus "bad news" story? Does this still make sense when the initial information, $t = 1$, is not available? How does this relate to the Ball and Brown diagram (Exhibit 10.8)?

10.11. Ralph pays 100 at time $t = 0$ for a cash flow series that will deliver 30 at time $t = 1$ and $88 + \epsilon$ at time $t = 2$. ϵ is a random shock term. Thus, initially, the cash flow at time $t = 2$ is uncertain. The interest rate is 10 percent. The expected value of the shock term is zero, and risk-neutral pricing prevails. Initially, suppose ϵ is observed by both the market and the accounting system at time $t = 2$.

[30] Based on Antle, Demski, and Ryan (1994).

a. Determine book value, accounting income, abnormal earnings, and market value for times $t = 1$ and $t = 2$ using an arbitrary depreciation schedule. Does market value equal book value plus the *expected* value of the present value of future abnormal earnings at each point in time?

b. Now change the story so the accounting system recognizes ϵ at time $t = 2$, as in part a, but the market observes ϵ at time $t = 1$. Repeat your various calculations.

c. Finally, change the story again so that both the accounting system and the market observe ϵ at time $t = 1$. Repeat your various calculations.

10.12. Ralph's Entity will last three periods. The projected cash flows are given by

$$CF_1 = 1{,}300 + \epsilon + \epsilon_1$$

$$CF_2 = 1{,}200 + 10\epsilon$$

$$CF_3 = 1{,}100 + 12\epsilon$$

where ϵ and ϵ_1 are random shock terms. These shock terms are described, using our usual state specification, in the following table. In addition, the initial investment to purchase this "asset" was 2,400, and the interest rate is $r = 10$ percent.

	s_1	s_2	s_3	s_4	s_5	s_6	s_7	s_8	s_9
$\pi(s_i)$	1/9	1/9	1/9	1/9	1/9	1/9	1/9	1/9	1/9
ϵ	−20	−20	−20	0	0	0	20	20	20
ϵ_1	−20	0	20	−20	0	20	−20	0	20
$\epsilon + \epsilon_1$	−40	−20	0	−20	0	20	0	20	40

a. The accounting system observes only the cash flow in each period, so it observes the total of the two shock terms in the first period and the persistent shock term by itself in the second period. Straight-line depreciation is used. Determine accounting income in each period as a function of the state.

b. The dividend is paid just after the books are closed and the financial report is released. However, the market, from a nonaccounting source, observes the persistent component of the shock term at time $t = 1$. So, the market knows both shock terms at time $t = 1$. Determine the time- and state-based sequence of prices for the claim to the remaining portion of the cash flow sequence. What connection do you see between market price and accounting income at time $t = 1$? What role is played by scaling here?

10.13. Return to the characterization of expected present value that equals book value plus the expected present value of the future residual income stream. This characterization is, of course, applicable to both accounting methods in Exhibit 10.18. What is implied about the abnormal or residual income stream in this setting? In particular, how do you use the nonaccounting information in this calculation? Be explicit.

10.14. Construct companions to Exhibits 10.14 through 10.17 on the assumption $\beta = .7$. Comment on the differences between your exhibits and those in the text.

Chapter 11

Information in a Managerial Contracting Setting

Our study now switches from a valuation to an evaluation setting, to the use of accounting information in evaluating the firm's management team. The building block here is contracting between two parties when compensation is exchanged for service or "labor" and evaluation provides the information glue in the exchange. The first step is to expand our prototypical firm so managerial input is an important factor of production. The second step is to characterize the market in which this factor is acquired. Initially, we examine a perfect market but then introduce a friction-laden variant, which leads us to the noted contracting exercise. The parallel with the valuation setting should not be missed. There we fed information to a valuation setting and used the model (risk-neutral valuation) to tell us how the information would be used. Here, you will see, we feed information to a contracting exercise and ask the model to tell us how the information would be used. Eventually, we will see that information content in a valuation setting does not imply information content in an evaluation setting and vice versa. The two settings are similar on the surface but remarkably different in reality.

Our earlier focus on valuation can be interpreted in terms of trading goods, or commodities, in an organized, informationally efficient market. Trading in a labor market where "compensation" is exchanged for "services" generally exhibits different characteristics than trading in ordinary commodities. A key difference is that the supplier of the product in a labor market exchange might take actions on its own. After all, the supplier is able to think for itself.[1] Consequently, the buyer of the services is not in total control over what is presumably being acquired. This might be an advantage, but it might also be a disadvantage. In addition, it might be impossible to observe the act or the precise service the supplier actually provides.

In some sense, labor services are bought blindfolded. One response is clever design of the employment contract (e.g., pay for performance). Another is clever design of the organization structure that governs the working conditions of the hiring organization (e.g., decision rights). We stress the first alternative because we will study contracting in a small organization called an *agency*.

An additional complication in labor contracting is the possibility the employee is or becomes better informed than the employer. In fact, that might be the very reason for hiring the individual in question. It might also increase the control problem because the employee might use the private information to promote his own interests at the expense of the employer. The response is even more clever design of the compensation contract (and organization structure), as we shall see in Chapter 12.[2]

Another difficulty is the buyer's side of the relationship. Can, for example, the employer be relied upon to provide the stated working conditions, to faithfully perform the promised evaluation, to honor the explicit and implicit understandings between the two parties? The response is still more clever design of the employment relationship, including job design, hierarchies, and perhaps even extending to additional independent services such as those of an auditor, compensation consultant, or strategic consultant.

Initially, we return to our prototypical firm and expand it so managerial input is substantive, both in terms of productivity and contracting arrangements. We then examine a benchmark case of a perfect managerial labor market. From here we turn to efficient contracting in the face of market imperfections. Our focus, quite naturally, is on the information side of the trade or contracting arrangement.

MANAGERIAL INPUT

Assume that our firm now uses three factors of production and produces a single product. The three factors are, of course, capital (K), labor (L), and management (M). Capital and labor combine as in previous chapters. Both are available in perfect factor markets at respective unit prices of p_K and p_L. The added feature is inclusion of a third input, labeled *managerial input*. This managerial factor, as sketched in Chapter 2, has a multiplicative impact on output.

---

[1] We may also be uncertain about the supplier's skill, talent, and what have you. Similarly, we may be uncertain about the quality of a particular item, for example, an automobile or menu item at a restaurant.

[2] Not all such tendencies will necessarily be controlled. Some may be "allowed" to continue simply because the alternative is too expensive.

The production function has the following form:

$$q \leq M\sqrt{KL} \qquad \textbf{(11.1)}$$

where, again, K is capital, L is labor, and M is managerial input or service; q is the output quantity the firm is committed to producing. The intuitive idea is that capital and labor are substitutes, as before, and the managerial input, M, can make those factors more ($M > 1$) or less ($M < 1$) productive.

The added twist is that M is a random variable. It can take on one of two values, $M = M_H$ or $M = M_L$ with $M_H > M_L$. Since q units must be produced, we handle this additional complexity by assuming that the choice of labor (L) but not capital (K) can be deferred until the actual value of M is observed or known.

If, then, the firm seeks output q, capital K has been chosen, and managerial input M_H has been observed, labor must be chosen to satisfy

$$q \leq M_H\sqrt{KL}$$

(or $q^2/KM_H^2 \leq L$). If $M_L < M_H$ has been observed, however, more labor is required and must be chosen to satisfy

$$q \leq M_L\sqrt{K(L + L')}$$

(or $q^2/KM_L^2 \leq L + L'$). Notice that this second, larger quantity is depicted as the original amount, L, plus a supplemental amount, L'. Also notice we rule out the possibility that the firm produces a different amount depending on the realization of M. (As we have cautioned you in the past, we too have a limited supply of patience, and nothing of importance is lost by proceeding in this fashion.)

As noted, both K and L are available in perfect markets, and the impact of the two factors through the production function is certain. That is not necessarily the case for the managerial input.

The manager supplies managerial service or action, or "effort"; the action supplied determines the odds on whether $M = M_H$ or $M = M_L$. This action supply is modeled as a choice by the manager. Think of the manager as selecting some element a from among those available in set $\hat{A}$. So, the choice amounts to selecting some $a \in \hat{A}$. In most cases set $\hat{A}$ is restricted to be binary. That reduces complexity in what follows, and the loss of generality is limited. Thus, we assume the manager's *action* is $a = a_H$ or $a = a_L$, and the ultimate choice between the two is under the control of the manager.

The connection between managerial action and managerial input M is detailed in Exhibit 11.1. In the more general setup of the model, the generic probabilities of π_H and π_L are used. However, in most illustrations the numerical values are used.

If the manager provides high action, a_H, high managerial input, M_H, will materialize with probability π_H, and low managerial input, M_L, will materialize with probability $1 - \pi_H$. The interpretation of a_H as high action is connected to the probabilities. If $\pi_H > \pi_L$ (which we assume), there is a

EXHIBIT 11.1
Action-Induced
Managerial Input
Lotteries

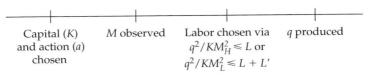

	M_H	M_L
a_H	$\pi_H = 0.5$	$1 - \pi_H = 0.5$
a_L	$\pi_L = 0.3$	$1 - \pi_L = 0.7$

EXHIBIT 11.2
Time Line for Factor
and Action Choices

Capital (K) M observed   Labor chosen via q produced
and action (a) $q^2/KM_H^2 \leq L$ or
chosen $q^2/KM_L^2 \leq L + L'$

higher probability that a_H leads to high managerial input M_H. Thus, given that high productivity is preferred (provides more output for any combination of labor and capital), it follows that a_H is preferred by the firm if the two action supplies are equally costly. This justifies the label of high action on the managerial choice a_H.

The timing details are summarized in Exhibit 11.2. Action is chosen by the manager while the capital and labor choices are made by the firm.[3]

The next part of the setup deals with the cost of providing managerial action. The firm desires a particular action profile from the manager. The manager, however, may be more interested in allocating his time and talents in a different way. He may be more interested in building his own human capital or his personal reputation; he may have an unusual affection for one of the firm's products or divisions; he may prefer the social atmosphere of an unusually large staff. Take your pick. The idea is that the firm and the manager are unlikely to agree over how best to allocate the manager's time and talents.[4]

Now, in our stylized setup, we generally work with a reduced-form, single-dimension description of the manager's "effort." This leads to the simple, perhaps overly simple, presumption the firm desires input a_H, but other things equal, the manager desires input a_L. The easiest way to tie this story together is to assume that the manager experiences a personal cost of action supply and that a_H is more personally costly than a_L.[5]

More precisely, we assume the personal cost of supplying the high-action level, a_H, is c_H and the personal cost of supplying the low action, a_L, is c_L. These costs enter the manager's utility function because they are

---

[3] Equivalently, we might think of the labor choice as made by the manager as well, but this issue is moot, as we shall see.

[4] Consumption at work, something much broader than the usual notion of pay plus benefits, is the generic idea.

[5] For example, think of the manager as having various activities and of this particular one as draining time from others. So, activity on the firm's tasks affects these other activities, resulting in the noted personal cost. More broadly, this is a simple device that we use to guarantee there is a contracting friction. Read on!

considered strictly personal. They are reflections of the manager's underlying preferences.

Separate from this is the cost of contracting for a specific level of managerial action to the firm. For now, let ι_H denote the expenditure or cost (or price) to purchase a_H and ι_L denote the corresponding magnitude to purchase a_L. The linkages between c_H and ι_H and between c_L and ι_L will be discussed shortly.

We next turn to the firm and the question of how best to combine the K, L, and M factors to produce the desired output (q). The firm is risk neutral and therefore selects factors to minimize the expected value of its expenditure on those factors, subject to being able to produce the desired output.

So, suppose the firm tentatively decides on managerial action a_H and must pay the manager some amount ι_H in exchange for this action. Its best choice of capital, K, and subsequent labor supply are located by the following minimization exercise:

$$C(q; a_H) \equiv \underset{K,L,L' \geq 0}{\text{minimum}} \ p_K K + p_L(L + (1 - \pi_H)L') + \iota_H$$
$$\text{subject to: } q \leq M_H \sqrt{KL}$$
$$q \leq M_L \sqrt{K(L + L')}$$
$$K \leq K^{\max} \qquad\qquad \textbf{(11.2a)}$$

$C(q; a_H)$, then, is the firm's cost of supplying q units, presuming it contracts for action supply a_H from the manager. The first constraint ensures K and L are adequate to produce output q should M_H materialize. (And with high action being supplied, M_H materializes with probability π_H.) The second constraint ensures that K plus the supplement L' coupled with L are adequate to produce output q should M_L materialize. The third constraint ensures that the choice of K respects the capital limit of $K^{\max}$. Overall, then, the firm expends $p_K K$ on capital, ι_H on managerial input, and $p_L L$ on labor. In addition, with high action supplied, low managerial input will materialize with probability $(1 - \pi_H)$, and thus supplemental labor expenditure of $p_L L'$ will emerge with probability $(1 - \pi_H)$.[6]

A companion calculation for the low managerial action case follows. Here the probability that supplemental labor must be acquired increases to $(1 - \pi_L)$, but the expenditure for managerial action presumably reduces to ι_L:

$$C(q; a_L) \equiv \underset{K,L,L' \geq 0}{\text{minimum}} \ p_K K + p_L(L + (1 - \pi_L)L') + \iota_L$$
$$\text{subject to: } q \leq M_H \sqrt{KL}$$
$$q \leq M_L \sqrt{K(L + L')}$$
$$K \leq K^{\max} \qquad\qquad \textbf{(11.2b)}$$

---

[6] Notice that we assume L and the supplement L' are both acquired at a price of p_L per unit. Naturally, we could make the story more complicated by assuming a different price for supplemental labor—but to what end?

Naturally, $C(q; a_H) < C(q; a_L)$ implies that high managerial action is preferred given q units are to be produced.[7]

Before proceeding, you should reflect on the modeling choices we have sketched. Our overriding interest is injecting a control problem into the story. We do this by sketching a model of trade or compensation for managerial action in which there is an inherent conflict of interest between the buyer and the seller. This conflict, salted into the model in most direct fashion, is an assumption concerning the manager's preferences. Moreover, our earlier labor factor, factor L, is acquired in a perfect market, obviating any concern over control issues at that point. We are selective, and we are hopefully being parsimonious, but you are warned not to take the collection of assumptions as literal.[8] Rather, take them as an efficient combination that will exhibit a useful platform for our continued study of accounting.

Manager's Preferences

As implied, the manager's preferences, including the personal cost expression, play an important role in the story. Specifically, the manager is assumed to be strictly risk averse with preferences well described by a negative exponential utility function defined on "net compensation." Thus, the manager's utility measure is given by $-\exp(-\rho z)$ where $\rho > 0$ is a constant and z is net compensation. The negative exponential assumption means the manager is characterized by constant absolute risk aversion.[9] This removes a wealth effect from the analysis. The idea is that

---

[7] These cost expressions are not very friendly in appearance. Clearly, we will never acquire factors to excess, so for any choice of capital, K, the corresponding labor choices will be made to drive the technology constraints to equality. Conveniently, then, the first constraint is

$$q = M_H \sqrt{KL}$$

Rearranging, we have $L = q^2/KM_H^2$. Doing the same for the second constraint gives us $L + L' = q^2/KM_L^2$. Now substitute these expressions into the overall expenditure expression. For example, for the high-action case, we have the following:

$$C(q; a_H) = \min p_K K + p_L q^2 \left[\frac{1}{KM_H^2} + (1 - \pi_H)\left(\frac{1}{KM_L^2} - \frac{1}{KM_H^2} \right) \right]$$

subject to $K \leq K^{\max}$

Notice that, having substituted the implied L and L' choices into the expression, the minimization is with respect to capital choice, K. Also, for the notationally obsessive, our cost expression will reflect the best choice of managerial action as well, so we have an overall cost expression of $C(q) = \min\{C(q; a_H); C(q; a_L)\}$.

[8] Indeed, we have worked hard to construct the smallest model that contains that conflict of interest without losing generality.

[9] ρ, you should recall, is a measure of risk aversion with larger ρ implying more risk aversion.

changing risk aversion is regarded as a second-order effect and is therefore formally suppressed in our model.

Net compensation, in turn, is simply the manager's compensation less personal cost of action. Suppose the manager supplies action level a, which carries personal cost c_a, and receives compensation ι. Net compensation is then $\iota - c_a$. We denote the manager's utility measure for compensation ι and action supply a (which implies net compensation of $\iota - c_a$) by

$$U(\iota, a) = -\exp(-\rho(\iota - c_a))$$

This sets the stage for understanding the trade of compensation for service or action. A conflict of interest is present, a conflict stylized with the idea the manager incurs a personal cost not incurred by the buyer. In addition, the firm, the buyer, has an inherent advantage at carrying risk because it (literally, its owner) is risk neutral while the supplier of managerial action is strictly risk averse.[10]

Market Discipline

Next is the subject of market discipline. The agent is willing to work in this firm only if the offered trade of compensation for services is personally attractive. Attractiveness, of course, is measured by the manager's expected utility. So, tautologically, the manager will find the arrangement attractive only if its expected utility weakly exceeds the expected utility of what she could otherwise command in the labor market. In that labor market, there is presumably some sort of equilibrium setting the standard for the minimally acceptable trade arrangement with the manager. Here we assume that equilibrium is in place and concentrate on the bilateral relationship between the manager and the firm. Thus, the level of "attractiveness" in the outside market is assumed to be given and is used only implicitly in the model because it enters as a constraint in the contracting problem. This constraint is called the agent's *individual rationality* constraint: After all, it would hardly be rational for the manager to accept an employment offer she finds less attractive than her next-best alternative.

This "next-best alternative" is expressed in monetary terms. Let $\hat{\iota}$ be the certainty equivalent of the arrangement the manager is able to obtain by seeking employment at another firm. So, the manager's expected utility from laboring under the employment arrangement must (weakly) exceed

---

[10] Again, you are cautioned not to be literal. We seek a convenient device to impart a conflict of interest. This leads to the noted *personal cost term.* Think of this as a convenient expression of the more general idea that the manager does not always agree with the firm on precisely how to allocate personal time, talent, and energies. The manager might be subtly inclined to protect career interests or gamble excessively in hopes of developing a major new product line, or might be too prone to monitoring day-to-day activities at the expense of critical strategic planning. The list is endless. (Schefter, 1997, provides a fascinating portrayal of corporate intrigue and infighting in the development of a new product.)

$-\exp(-\rho\hat{\imath})$. This puts the following restriction on the feasible compensation contracts:[11]

$$E[U \mid \iota, a] \geq -\exp(-\rho\hat{\imath})$$

where $E[U \mid \iota, a]$ denotes the manager's expected utility under the offered arrangement.

The compensation is not restricted to a fixed payment and can depend on whatever contracting variables, or performance measures, are present. This will be developed shortly. For now, it is sufficient to think of $E[U \mid \iota, a]$ as the manager's utility score for the proffered arrangement, whatever it is.[12]

This provides a prototype, if not a caricature, of the following problem. The firm seeks the services of a manager. The firm is good at carrying risk but the manager is not; however, the manager is good at supplying managerial services but the firm is not. Trade of compensation for managerial service is efficient given the circumstances. A friction, the noted personal cost term, is also present. The importance, indeed the mere presence, of this friction depends on the nature of the managerial labor market. If the friction is not controlling, we have what is called *first-best* efficiency when no grains to trade are left unexploited. In contrast, if the friction is controlling, if it affects the equilibrium trading arrangements, we are confined to what is called *second-best* efficiency.

PERFECT MANAGERIAL LABOR MARKET

Given a perfect labor market in which all parties at all times honor any agreement, this friction is absent.[13] The trade arrangement is now quite simple because the firm is indifferent toward risk while the manager regards risk as noxious. This implies that the optimal trade will be risk-free compensation (i.e., fixed remuneration) in exchange for managerial

---

[11] An alternative explanation is that we are seeking an efficient way to organize the trade. Parametrically, we do this by maximizing one's gains to trade, so to speak, subject to the constraint that the other's position is defined by the noted parameter, here $\hat{\imath}$. Then varying that parameter, $\hat{\imath}$, allows us to identify the set of efficient trades. The labor market story strikes us as a more natural interpretation. Note well, however: Built into the story is efficient trade in the light of whatever frictions are present.

[12] Indeed, pay itself could and does take a variety of forms: cash now, cash later, various insurance arrangements, parking, countless accoutrements, colleagues at work, or advancement opportunities at work. Are you surprised by the streamlined focus on a single dimension, cash?

[13] Literally, the perfect market arrangement is one in which there is a known price for an explicit service; no trade friction of any sort is present. The parties behave cooperatively, and both sides abide by their arrangement. Thus, we stress the notion of agreements that are honored. Shortly we will have the parties to the trade playing noncooperatively, and then, with sufficient information, we will be able to replicate this cooperative, ideal solution.

service. Any other arrangement will result in an efficiency loss. (If given a stake in the risky asset, the manager will have his compensation at risk, and be called upon to bear risk needlessly. The firm, in contrast, is indifferent toward risk.)

The level of compensation as opposed to its form is explained by the manager's personal cost and opportunities. Suppose that the firm wants high action and offers the manager fixed amount ι_H. To be attractive to the manager, net compensation must exceed the manager's opportunity certainty equivalent, $\hat{\iota}$. Stated in utility units, the offered compensation, ι_H, must satisfy

$$E[U \mid \iota_H, a_H] = -\exp(-\rho(\iota_H - c_H)) \geq -\exp(-\rho\hat{\iota})$$

The left-hand side is the manager's utility measure for accepting the trade, and the right-hand side is the corresponding measure for rejecting the trade. Naturally, with a fixed salary, the compensation is certain and the expectation operator is gratuitous. So, we restate the condition for trade to take place as

$$\iota_H - c_H \geq \hat{\iota}$$

The firm is not foolish in these matters and will set $\iota_H = \hat{\iota} + c_H$. In parallel fashion, it will set $\iota_L = \hat{\iota} + c_L$ for low action. This clarity should come as no surprise. By assuming a perfect market, we have constructed a setting in which it is natural to speak of a specific price, here ι_a, for a specific service, here a_L or a_H.

Thus, in this case, the connection between the personal cost of action on one hand and the price of action is simple and essentially one to one. The perfect market forces ensure that personal cost is directly transferred to the firm. As a result, the optimal action level can be characterized by a straightforward "cost-benefit" test. High action is preferred if the expected decrease in capital and labor expenditures exceeds the corresponding increase in personal cost.[14]

We now turn to a numerical illustration. Details are displayed in Exhibit 11.3. The factor prices on capital and labor are set to $p_K = p_L = 100$, and $K^{\max} = 1,500$. The productivity variable resulting from managerial action will be $M_H = 1.1$ or $M_L = .9$, with equal probability under high action. So, under high action, the expected value of the managerial input is unity. The action-induced probabilities are taken from Exhibit 11.1, and we focus on the case when output is $q = 1,000$ units.

Under perfect market conditions, the efficient contracting arrangement with the manager is a fixed compensation amount in exchange for the desired action supply. The "price" of high action is the sum of what the

---

[14] In a more elaborate setup, the feasible set of possible action choices would be some region, say $0 \leq a \leq a'$, and presuming suitable regularity, the cost-benefit test would reduce to equating the marginal reduction in the expected expenditure on capital and labor to the marginal increase in c_a.

EXHIBIT 11.3
Details for
Numerical
Illustration

Firm details	
Output quantity	$q = 1,000$
Managerial input	$M_H = 1.1$ and $M_L = .9$
Managerial input odds (Exhibit 11.1)	$\pi_H = .5$ and $\pi_L = .3$
Manager details	
Risk-aversion coefficient	$\rho = .0001$
Opportunity certainty equivalent	$\hat{\imath} = 5,000$
Personal costs	$c_H = 5,000$ and $c_L = 3,000$
Market prices	
Capital	$p_K = 100$
Labor	$p_L = 100$
High managerial action	$\iota_H = 10,000$
Low managerial action	$\iota_L = 8,000$

manager could earn elsewhere (the opportunity certainty equivalent of $\hat{\imath} = 5,000$) plus the personal cost (of $c_H = 5,000$). That is, $\iota_H = 10,000$. Similarly, $\iota_L = \hat{\imath} + c_L = 8,000$. From here we sort out the remaining factor details.

Consider the case of high action. Using the program in (11.2a), optimal capital and labor choices, given $q = 1,000$, are found to be $K = 1,015.14$, $L = 814.12$, and $L' = 402.04$. This implies an overall cost of producing $q = 1,000$ units of

$$C(q; a_H) = p_K K + p_L(L + (1 - \pi_H)L') + \iota_H = 213,027.79$$

Conversely, in the case of low action, using the program in (11.2b), we find $K = 1,054.58$, $L = 783.68$, and $L' = 387.00$. The overall cost is

$$C(q; a_L) = p_K K + p_L(L + (1 - \pi_L)L') + \iota_L = 218,915.28$$

Thus, the trade-off makes it optimal to demand the high level of managerial action. The incremental productivity gain, allowing for lower use of capital and offering lower odds of having to acquire supplemental labor, is well worth the price difference between high and low managerial action.[15]

It is worth highlighting the assumptions that drive this analysis. The firm (or literally, its owner) is risk neutral and is consequently willing to absorb all risk.[16] The principal determinants of the salary, or price, are the

[15] Do not be fooled into thinking that the choice between high and low action is obvious. If we are producing $q = 100$ units, for example, $C(q; a_H) = 31,091.53 > C(q; a_L) = 28,302.78$.

[16] At present, that is not considered a major issue because the introduction of risk aversion on the part of the firm would only introduce mutual insurance policies to be included in the contract. The reason for not considering this a major point is that insurance for the firm is not a prime concern in employment contracting, and the inclusion of insurance does not change the conclusion dramatically.

managerial labor market and personal cost. Furthermore, the incremental price for higher action is independent of the manager's market alternative, $\hat{\imath}$. From here, strong assumptions are placed on the contracting infrastructure. It is assumed that all agreements are honored by all involved parties. That means that salary is paid as promised and work is performed as agreed. The importance of this latter assumption is analyzed next.

MARKET IMPERFECTIONS

If all agreements are honored, there is absolutely no demand for a control system. The manager would perform exactly as agreed without question or ambiguity. Unfortunately, life is not that simple. Most people are a little selfish. In other cases, managers have objectives that differ from those of the organization. In both situations managers may be tempted to act in accordance with their personal interests, and one begins to worry that agreements will be honored only if they are enforceable. This puts pressure on the organization's control system to produce information that can be used to help render the agreement enforceable.[17]

The key to exhibiting significant control issues is to relax the presumption the manager will dutifully honor any agreement down to the most minute instructions. So, we now adopt the opposite tack and assume that both parties will behave, or play the game, in noncooperative fashion.

Given this, the contract providing the manager with a fixed payment, or flat salary, of 10,000 places the manager in a position of severe temptation. One alternative, having accepted the terms of the contract, is to provide high action, as stipulated, and collect that 10,000 payment. Net compensation would be $\iota_H - c_H = 10,000 - 5,000 = 5,000$. A second alternative is to provide low action and collect the 10,000 payment on the presumption that the firm thought high action was indeed supplied. Net compensation would then be $\iota_H - c_L = 10,000 - 3,000 = 7,000$.[18]

The choice is easy. If the contract described is in place, the manager is fully insured and is paid the same amount regardless of the realization of M. As a result, the manager will be tempted to renege and provide low action (presuming, of course, that such behavior would go undetected). To be more pointed, we have assumed the manager is motivated by net

---

[17] It is a short step from here to using the court system. Indeed, courts have a long history of adjudicating performance in contractual matters. An important issue involves contractual arrangements that are based on verifiable information, information that is accessible to the contracting parties and to the court. More about this later.

[18] In utility terms we have

$$\text{supply } H\colon E[U \mid \iota_H, a_H] = U(\iota_H, a_H) = -\exp(-5000\rho) = -0.6065$$

and

$$\text{supply } L\colon E[U \mid \iota_H, a_L] = U(\iota_H, a_L) = -\exp(-7000\rho) = -0.4966.$$

compensation in this "game." Net compensation is strictly higher if the manager reneges on the promise to supply high action in exchange for payment of 10,000.

This is not a flattering view of either the manager or the human condition. On the other hand, we routinely engage internal and external auditing, supervision, monitoring, and quality control. (Columbus carried an auditor on his famous voyage!) Indeed, the insurance industry has long recognized that insurance dulls incentives and has given us the phrase *moral hazard* for this phenomenon.[19]

Moral Hazard Concerns

We model these concerns with a streamlined trading game. Instead of trading a stated amount for a stated service, which is our perfect market stylization, we now invoke a more elaborate employment contract based on contingent compensation. The centerpiece of this arrangement is a public information source that will report signal $y \in Y$. The nature of this information will be made clear in the specific contexts that follow. The important point is that this information, when observed, is public; both the firm and the manager observe the information.[20] For example, both would observe the cash flow or the audited accounting report.

In turn, the manager's salary or fixed compensation is replaced by a contingent arrangement. Compensation now depends on what information is observed. For example, the manager might receive a base salary plus 3 percent of sales (so total sales is the public information). Alternatively, the manager might receive a base salary plus a bonus if accounting income exceeds some stated amount as well as possess a number of stock options (so accounting income and the firm's security price on an organized exchange are the public information sources). Notice that any such arrangement can be thought of as a function defined on Y. Let $I(y)$ denote some such function. Then, in our ever-expanding notation, the manager's compensation is given by $\iota = I(y)$.

---

[19] Do you think driving behavior is influenced by the existence of collision insurance; do you think theft protection activities are affected by the existence of comprehensive coverage? In a related vein, the insurance industry gives us the companion phrase of *adverse selection,* a story in which people use private knowledge of their characteristics to self-select among advantageous offers, thereby leading to groupings of individuals that are not representative of the population as a whole. Are young, healthy individuals likely to purchase health insurance? Similarly, do different driving types elect different deductibles in the auto insurance market? Might we combine both phenomena in our model of contracting for managerial services? Again, we stick with the simple story. Also, moral hazard is sometimes called a *hidden action problem* because the substance of the friction is the manager and only the manager knows what action was supplied; adverse selection is sometimes called a *hidden knowledge problem* because the noted characteristics are known privately.

[20] Implicitly, being public, a court could also observe this information.

EXHIBIT 11.4
Time Line for
Contracting Game

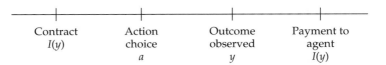

Contract	Action	Outcome	Payment to
$I(y)$	choice	observed	agent
	a	y	$I(y)$

The presumed trading game proceeds as follows. Initially, the firm makes the manager an offer that consists of an instruction and a payment arrangement. The instruction is simply the firm's requested supply of managerial services. In our simple case, it is a request that some particular action level be supplied. The payment arrangement is a contingent arrangement or function, $I(y)$. Notice that this arrangement includes a specification of both the public information and the function defined thereon.

Once this offer has been made, the manager accepts or rejects the offer. If the offer is rejected, the game ends; no trade takes place. If the offer is accepted, the manager then supplies managerial services, that is, selects action $a \in \hat{A}$. We hope that the action supplied will be the action desired or instructed, but managers are on their own at this point. Finally, the public information is observed, and the manager is paid according to the terms of the noted function or contract.[21] The time line is displayed in Exhibit 11.4 where we highlight the contracting arrangements, or game, to the exclusion of the capital and labor factors (in Exhibit 11.2).

The manager thus faces a sequence of choices: whether to accept the offer and, if so, what action to select. Here we rely on the manager's preferences, and this reliance should explain why we were so obsessive in describing those preferences. Let $\pi(y \mid a)$ denote the probability signal $y \in Y$ will be observed; this probability is parameterized by the manager's action choice, $a \in \hat{A}$. For example, the odds of exceptional sales are higher if the manager allocates sales action in a wise and aggressive fashion. Given contract $I(y)$, then, the manager will receive compensation of $I(y)$ with probability $\pi(y \mid a)$ when action a is supplied. So, the manager's expected utility is

$$E[U \mid I, a] = \sum_{y \in Y} U(I(y), a) \, \pi(y \mid a)$$
$$= -\sum_{y \in Y} \exp(-\rho(I(y) - c_a)) \, \pi(y \mid a) \quad \textbf{(11.3)}$$

The utility score, denoted $E[U \mid I, a]$, depends on both the compensation function, I, and the action choice, a. Importantly, the compensation does not directly depend on the action choice. Rather, action choice affects the

[21] Notice that we assume the contingent compensation is in fact paid. A deeper analysis doubles up the story by allowing the firm some additional room to maneuver at this point, perhaps by having to supply some of the public information. This is called *double moral hazard*.

probability of the various signals, and through this indirect mechanism we achieve a connection between pay and performance. The compensation lottery, so to speak, is affected by the action choice. The resulting information asymmetry is important. At the end of the game when payment is delivered, both parties know the signal realization, y, but the manager also knows which action was actually supplied.

In our simple setting in which the action choice is high or low (i.e., a_H or a_L), suppose the firm wants high action. This requires the employment arrangement to make high action an attractive choice for the manager. So, the following must be satisfied; otherwise, the manager is actually motivated to act in a contrary manner:

$$E[U \mid I, a_H] \geq E[U \mid I, a_L] \qquad\qquad \textbf{(11.4)}$$

This is called an *incentive compatibility* constraint. The offered arrangement must make it in the manager's best self-interest to obey the instruction.[22]

The offer must also be sufficiently attractive to the manager; it is our old individual rationality concern

$$E[U \mid I, a_H] \geq -\exp(-\rho \hat{\imath}) \qquad\qquad \textbf{(11.5)}$$

Now consider an easy case. Suppose the information source will report the manager's action choice. The possible signals, then, are $Y = \{H, L\}$ and $\pi(H \mid a_H) = \pi(L \mid a_L) = 1$. Returning to our numerical illustration, consider the contract $I(H) = 10{,}000$ and $I(L) = 0$: The manager is paid if and only if high action is observed. So, the manager nets $I(H) - c_H = 5{,}000$ for "good behavior" and $I(L) - c_L = -3{,}000$ for opportunistic behavior. Equivalently, in utility terms, we have

$$H: E[U \mid I, a_H] = U(I(H), a_H) = -\exp(-\rho(I(H) - c_H))$$
$$= -\exp(-.5) = -0.6065$$
$$L: E[U \mid I, a_L] = U(I(L), a_L) = -\exp(-\rho(I(L) - c_L))$$
$$= -\exp(.3) = -1.3499$$

In equilibrium, then, an outside observer would see an exchange of 10,000 for the supply of high action. Hidden from view is the fact that the supply of low action would be reported by the information source and (un)rewarded accordingly. The manager never finds it rational to challenge the control system, and an outside observer never sees the substantive strength of the control system because of this lack of challenge.

---

[22] Literally, once the offer is accepted, there is one remaining move in the game, the manager's action choice, and that move is made noncooperatively. Furthermore, notice the reliance on the "mutual best response" equilibrium notion first used in Chapter 8. Here the manager's response to the contract offer is maximizing for the manager, just as the firm's contract offer is maximizing from its perspective, given anticipation of the manager's subsequent maximizing behavior.

Of course, this is rendered obvious by the all-powerful information assumption that the manager's behavior is in full public view. So what if the information is not so powerful? Here we recall that the first move in the trading game is an offer put forward by the firm. Suppose, for the sake of argument, the firm wants a supply of high action. Remembering that it is risk neutral, the firm will construct an offer that has minimal expected payment to the manager but is still acceptable to the manager (i.e., satisfies the individual rationality constraint (11.5)) and is "incentive compatible" (i.e., satisfies the incentive compatibility constraint (11.4)). This gives rise to the following generic design program:[23]

$$\ddot{I}_H = \min_{I(y)} E[I \mid a_H] = \sum_{y \in Y} I(y) \, \pi(y \mid a_H)$$

subject to (11.4) and (11.5) **(11.6)**

where the minimization is over the contingent payments, $I(y)$, and the expected value of the manager's compensation is denoted $\ddot{I}_H$.

To illustrate, return to our earlier numerical illustration, Exhibit 11.3, but now assume that the only public observables are output, capital (K), and labor (L and L') choices. Furthermore, suppose, for the moment, high action is desired. We know from our earlier work that the optimal mix when high action is supplied by the manager is $K = 1,015.14$, $L = 814.12$, and $L' = 402.04$. We also know the supplemental labor of L' will be required with probability $(1 - \pi_H) = .5$ if high action is supplied but will be required with probability $(1 - \pi_L) = .7$ if low action is supplied.

Importantly, then, $q = 1,000$ units will be produced, using the noted K, L, and L' quantities.[24] What is at issue is whether the manager follows

[23] Several additional points are in order. First, this is a noncooperative game in which the firm moves first (by offering a contract and instruction) and the manager moves second and with knowledge of the firm's offer. Second, once the firm's offer has been made, the manager's choice is well illustrated by the resulting decision tree. This tree, in our simple case, has three choices: accept and supply a_H, accept and supply a_L, or reject. So, the essence of the program in (11.6), the firm's choice of offer, is to make the most advantageous offer subject to the constraints that the manager's induced decision tree "rolls back" as desired, meaning that constraints (11.4) and (11.5) are satisfied. Finally, this game may and, in our case usually does, have multiple equilibria. The constraints are stated as weak inequalities, not strict equalities. This is for convenience of illustration but also reflects a presumption that, if indifferent to a set of moves in the game, the manager will take the one among those most preferred by the firm.

[24] Recall we presume, for convenience, that the firm selects the capital and labor (as in Exhibit 11.2), although these could be delegated to the manager. The reason is that the public information source will reveal an improper output or mix of factors. It is therefore immaterial who selects these quantities since their choice, by whomever, is public knowledge. So, the contractual arrangement would include a penalty if an improper output or mix of factors were ever observed. In turn, this is a variation on our earlier illustration of a penalty contract that relied on public observation of the manager's action supply. We treat this aspect of the story informally to highlight the important contracting details.

instructions and supplies high action, or, to the contrary, selects low action. This choice will influence the odds with which the supplemental labor, L', is acquired; that is the important information source for contracting purposes.

Think of the public information, then, in reduced form format. It reports $y = 0$ if no supplemental labor is acquired ($L' = 0$), and it reports $y = 1$ if supplemental labor is acquired ($L' = 402.04$). Glancing back at Exhibit 11.2, you will see that this is informationally equivalent to reporting $M = M_H$ ($y = 0$) or $M = M_L$ ($y = 1$). Equivalently, the information source reports $y = 0 < 1$ if total expenditures on capital and labor are "low" and $y = 1 > 0$ if they are "high."

We thus have $\pi(y = 0 \,|\, a_H) = .5$ and $\pi(y = 0 \,|\, a_L) = .3$. A contract contingent on observation of $y \in \{0, 1\}$ pays $I(0)$ under $y = 0$ and $I(1)$ under $y = 1$. Following program (11.6), the firm's best contract offer to accompany an instruction to supply high action, then, is the solution to the following:

$$\ddot{I}_H = \min E[I \,|\, a_H] = .5I(0) + .5I(1)$$

$$\text{subject to: } E[U \,|\, I, a_H] = -.5\exp(-\rho(I(0) - 5,000))$$
$$-.5\exp(-\rho(I(1) - 5,000))$$
$$\geq -\exp(-\rho\hat{\imath}) = -\exp(-\rho(5,000)); \text{ and}$$

$$E[U \,|\, I, a_H] \geq E[U \,|\, I, a_L] = -.3\exp(-\rho(I(0) - 3,000))$$
$$-.7\exp(-\rho(I(1) - 3,000))$$

where the manager's expected utility calculations follow from (11.3).

The solution is to pay $I(0) = 18{,}063$ when $y = 0$ and to pay $I(1) = 5{,}595$ when $y = 1$ is observed.[25] Stated differently, the overall cost of producing $q = 1{,}000$ units can be "low" (no supplemental labor, $y = 0$) or "high" (supplemental labor, $y = 1$). The optimal arrangement pays the manager a bonus when "low" cost is observed, and the expected payment to the manager is now $\ddot{I}_H = 11{,}829$. In short, good behavior by the manager means that "low" cost (i.e., $y = 0$) is more likely, and the manager is rewarded when low cost is indeed observed.

Comparing this to the fixed payment of 10,000 when the act is observed leads to the conclusion there is an efficiency loss as a consequence of the nonobservability of the manager's behavior. The expected cost of this is 1,829 (11,829 − 10,000).[26] Also note that the same action supply is motivated as in the earlier perfect market setting. Thus, the increase in the cost

---

[25] This solution is easily verified by using the optimization module in your favorite spreadsheet program.

[26] Again we remind the reader that we assume $q = 1{,}000$ units will be produced using the noted capital and labor quantities. Also notice that the manager's compensation, presuming high action, is a lottery that pays 18,063 and 5,595 with 50–50 odds. What is the manager's certainty equivalent for this lottery?

to the firm is explained only by the changed risk sharing because the manager in the noncooperative setting is accepting a share of the risky outcome. The personal costs are identical in the two settings.

Dwell on this: The manager is offered a pay-for-performance arrangement in which pay is 18,063 if cost turns out to be "low" (i.e., $y = 0$) and 5,595 otherwise, and an instruction to supply a_H. Working through the expected utility calculations, you will see that it is in the manager's best self-interest to accept this offer and then supply a_H.[27] That is, given the offer on the table, the manager's best response is to accept and supply a_H. In turn, how was the offer designed? It is the least costly offer from the firm's perspective, given the manager will apply self-interest calculus to the offer that is placed on the table. In short, this is the solution to a particular noncooperative game. Equilibrium play is for the firm to make the noted offer and for the manager to subsequently accept that offer and then supply a_H.

Actually, we are a bit quick in making this claim. The cost of high action to the firm has gone up relative to the perfect market case. So, we must revisit all of the earlier details. We know high action is best matched with $K = 1,015.14$, $L = 814.12$, and $L' = 402.04$. This gives an overall cost of producing $q = 1,000$ units of

$$C(q; a_H) = p_K K + p_L (L + (1 - \pi_H) L') + E[I \mid a_H] = 214,857$$

Conversely, in the case of low managerial action, we solve the obvious variation on our original program:

$$\ddot{I}_L = \min E[I \mid a_L] = .3I(0) + .7I(1)$$
$$\text{subject to: } E[U \mid I, a_L] = -.3 \exp(-\rho(I(0) - 3,000))$$
$$-.7 \exp(-\rho(I(1) - 3,000))$$
$$\geq -\exp(-\rho \hat{i}) = -\exp(-\rho(5,000)); \text{ and}$$
$$E[U \mid I, a_L] \geq E[U \mid I, a_H] = -.5 \exp(-\rho(I(0) - 5,000))$$
$$-.5 \exp(-\rho(I(1) - 5,000))$$

The solution is $I(0) = I(1) = 8,000$. Offering a flat wage or fixed salary for low action is quite acceptable. The manager is not tempted to supply high action because that would increase his personal cost without any attendant benefit.

From here we recall that the best factor combinations in the low-action case are $K = 1,054.58$, $L = 783.68$, and $L' = 387.00$. The overall cost is just

---

[27] Actually, aside from rounding errors, the manager is indifferent among the various choices, but with indifference there is no reason not to accept the offer and then supply a_H. It is, in fact, instructive to lay out the manager's decision tree, given the noted offer is on the table.

what we had before:

$$C(q; a_L) = p_K K + p_L(L + (1 - \pi_L)L') + E[I \mid a_L] = 218,915$$

Despite the increased cost, then, it does indeed make sense for the firm to continue to use high action.

Parametric Variations

Stepping back, we have a model of trade in which risky (event-contingent) compensation is exchanged for (incentive-compatible) managerial service. The exchange encounter is structured as a noncooperative game in which equilibrium behavior is emphasized. Given the contract and instruction, the manager does as well as possible from a personal perspective. Given the manager will so behave, the firm does as well as possible from its perspective. At issue is motivating the exchange in the face of conflict, the personal cost term, and information asymmetry; the firm knows only signal realization $y \in Y$ while the manager knows the action actually supplied as well as the signal realization. Clearly, $y \in Y$ is the information basis for the exchange. If that information is imperfect, the manager's compensation must be risky by necessity if a_H is to be supplied.

The important forces here are the conflict of interest, the manager's risk aversion, and the "quality" of the information. Consider the conflict. In our simple model, this resides in the personal cost terms, $c_H > c_L$. Other things equal, the firm wants a_H supplied while it is personally desirable for the manager to do otherwise. What happens as we vary the magnitude of this conflict of interest? Using the details (Exhibit 11.3) of our running illustration, we plot in Exhibit 11.5 the expected value of the manager's compensation as we range the cost of low action between $c_L = 2,000$ and $c_L = 5,000$. In effect, this plots the firm's cost of acquiring high action versus the c_L parameter.

EXHIBIT 11.5

$E[I \mid a_H]$ versus c_L

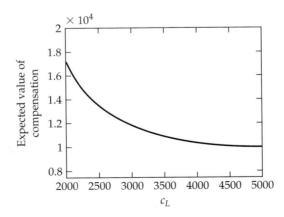

EXHIBIT 11.6
$E[I \mid a_H]$ versus Manager's Risk Aversion, ρ

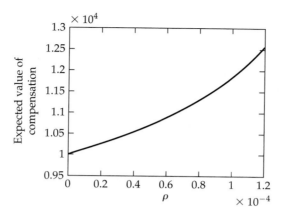

Notice, with $c_H = 5{,}000$, that this ranges the difference between the two cost terms from "large" (i.e., $c_H - c_L = 5{,}000 - 2{,}000 = 3{,}000$) to nonexistent ($c_H - c_L = 5{,}000 - 5{,}000 = 0$). When $c_H = c_L$, we have no conflict of interest, and the efficient exchange is a flat payment of 10,000 for supply of a_H, because at this point the manager is indifferent between low and high action. Then there is no incentive problem, and the cost of implementing high action is exactly 10,000. As the spread increases, however, the steepness of the incentive must be increased to overcome the private cost differential, and, therefore, the expected value of the equilibrium compensation increases.[28] This is consistent with an increase in the incentive problem causing an increase in the cost of implementing the desired solution.

Now consider the second driving force, the manager's risk aversion. If the risk is neutral, the manager is just as capable as the firm's owner of carrying risk, and the efficient solution is to combine risk carrying and action supply. That way the manager-owner will internalize the original conflict of interest. Conversely, increasing the manager's risk aversion increases the firm's cost of high action. The reason is that increasing the risk aversion also increases the incentive problem. This is displayed in Exhibit 11.6 where we plot the expected value of the manager's compensation versus his risk-aversion coefficient, ρ. For ρ near zero, the manager is essentially risk neutral; increasing ρ increases the firm's cost.[29]

Finally, consider the third driving force, the quality of the contracting information. Given the binary nature of the uncertainty, the probability of $y = 0$ (low cost) under the desired high action, π_H, can be used to

[28] The lower bound of $c_L = 2{,}000$ here is not gratuitous. At this point we are getting close to violating the feasibility issue discussed in the Appendix when the cost differential is too great in relation to the "quality" of the information.
[29] Recall that our illustration uses a risk-aversion parameter of $\rho = .0001$. Using $\rho = .00005$, we have less risk aversion and find $I(0) = 16{,}101$, $I(1) = 5{,}331$, and an expected value of compensation of 10,716. Conversely, using $\rho = .00015$, we have more risk aversion and find $I(0) = 23{,}844$, $I(1) = 5{,}811$, and an expected value of compensation of 14,827.

EXHIBIT 11.7

$E[I \mid a_H]$ **versus High- and Low-Action Success Probabilities**

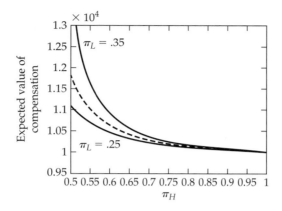

parameterize the quality of the contracting information. In the limit, $\pi_H = 1$ and a high cost ($y = 1$) will materialize only if low action was supplied. In information terms, this is equivalent to having observed low-action supply. In such a case, the information is highly informative, and it is possible to design a forcing contract: That is, offer the reservation wage in combination with a huge penalty whenever high cost (i.e., $y = 1$) is observed. In that case the manager will never select low action because that places the manager in a risky position with a positive probability of getting hit with the penalty. By following instructions and supplying high action, however, the manager will always walk away with the normal wage. Stated differently, the high pay, the "bonus," is guaranteed by good behavior in this case.

Again using our numerical setup in Exhibit 11.3, we illustrate the relationship between the low-cost probability, π_H, and the cost of implementing high action in Exhibit 11.7. The middle curve is our base case in which the low-action probability of low cost is $\pi_L = .3$. Notice how increasing π_H lowers the expected value of the manager's compensation, given we are motivating high action. This reflects the fact that the underlying information signal of low or high cost is becoming more informative about the manager's behavior. Raising the off-equilibrium probability to $\pi_L = .35$ uniformly increases the cost of acquiring high action, just as lowering it to $\pi_L = .25$ uniformly lowers it.

To gain some insight into this information quality theme, examine the pair of (likelihood) ratios:[30]

$$\pi(y = 0 \mid a_L) / \pi(y = 0 \mid a_H) = \pi_L/\pi_H$$
$$\pi(y = 1 \mid a_L) / \pi(y = 1 \mid a_H) = (1 - \pi_L)/(1 - \pi_H)$$

Holding π_L constant, what happens as we increase the π_H? The first ratio becomes smaller, and the second becomes larger; the pair of ratios is

---

[30] Furthermore, $\pi_H > \pi_L$ implies $\pi_L/\pi_H < (1 - \pi_L)/(1 - \pi_H)$.

spread farther apart. This suggests, then, that the information variable is better able to detect choice of a_L versus choice of a_H, and if so, it ought to be cheaper to contract for a_H. Do you see this in the graph? In parallel fashion, what happens as we lower π_L? The first ratio becomes smaller and the second larger; again, we make it easier to detect the choice of action, and so on. Do you see this in the graph?

In this setting it is not the production cost being "low" ($y = 0$) or "high" ($y = 1$) in itself that is the driving force. It is the information content of the random variable, called *production cost*. In fact, any information source that informs about the manager's behavior can serve the role played by the production cost here. That is the reason we motivated the generic story with some abstract information source, $y \in Y$.

Summary

In their legendary monograph, Paton and Littleton (1940, p. 1) observe: "With a condition of detached and scattered investor-interests the service of accounting has necessarily been expanded; the function of reporting information to absentee investors has been added to that of recording and presenting data for owner-operator use." This reporting has a valuation side, which is the subject of Chapters 8, 9, and 10, and a control or evaluation side, as introduced in the present chapter. In the valuation sphere we stressed a simple model of risk-neutral valuation that adequately carries our work of identifying and understanding the use of accounting information in a valuation setting. The same tack is used in the evaluation sphere where we stress a simple model of moral hazard–laden contracting that adequately carries our work of identifying and understanding the use of accounting information in an evaluation setting.

Here, then, cash compensation and personal action cost are the only parameters in the manager's utility function, so only monetary incentives can be used to obtain the desired motivational effect. It is costly to motivate the manager because the residual that accrues to the firm is net of any incentive payment to the manager, and incentive payments, by their very nature, entail less than fully efficient risk sharing.

This is the simplest possible model of a conflict of interest in which there is a demand for motivating the manager to perform and for information that speaks to the question of whether the manager did indeed "perform." On the surface this might appear quite restrictive since benefits and costs of employment come in overwhelming variety. Formally, the results will not change when more parameters are entered into the utility and technology functions. Also, the assumption that only the manager is risk averse is a mere simplification. Adding risk aversion on the part of the firm's owners will not make significant changes. It will introduce a demand for insurance on the part of the owners, which will make the analysis a bit more difficult but without substantial change. Because we do not believe insurance is a first-order effect in our study of accounting in this setting, we have depicted the firm as risk neutral.

Stripping the model down even further, however, is not an interesting option. We want a story in which it is rational to worry about the manager's behavior, that is, to evaluate the manager's performance. Accounting variables are surely widely used in this regard. As Exhibits 11.5, 11.6, and 11.7 suggest, however, removing the personal cost term (Exhibit 11.5), the manager's risk aversion (Exhibit 11.6), or substantive uncertainty (Exhibit 11.7) implies that the trade arrangement would be trivial and there would be no substantive interest in evaluating the manager's performance. This minimal overhead (of personal cost, risk aversion, and uncertainty) is simply essential if we are to study the use of accounting for performance evaluation purposes.

Thus, our model of contracting for managerial services can be viewed as a model of the stewardship role of accounting. One of the long recognized purposes of accounting is to provide information about how management uses the resources entrusted to them. Moral hazard concerns appear to be central to this theme; after all, with no conflict of interest, there is no demand for holding management accountable for the use of resources entrusted to them.

Appendix

Feasibility

Our contracting model in which the firm relies on a pay-for-performance arrangement to acquire a supply of managerial action envisions the firm carefully constructing the arrangement so it is in the firm's best interest, subject to being in the manager's best interest to accept the offer (the individual rationality constraint) and to obey the instructions (the incentive compatibility constraint). As a technical if not an economic or philosophical aside, we should not blithely assume that these constraints can indeed be satisfied.

It turns out that the individual rationality constraint is not an issue. For any payment function that violates this constraint, we can always add a constant amount sufficient to guarantee the constraint is satisfied. Moreover, adding the requisite constant does not affect the incentive compatibility constraint. This is easy to see because constant absolute risk aversion guarantees that if function $I(y)$ satisfies the self-selection constraint, then the perturbed function of an arbitrary constant plus $I(y)$ also satisfies the incentive compatibility constraint.[31] This does presume, however, that the

---

[31] Notice $\exp(-\rho(k + I(y) - c_a)) = \exp(-\rho k) \times \exp(-\rho(I(y) - c_a))$ for any constant k, and the new multiplicative constant, $\exp(-\rho k)$, will factor out of both sides of the incentive compatibility constraint. Try it.

firm faces no limited liability constraint. For example, if times are really bad, will the firm be able to honor its payment arrangement? We presume so. We likewise presume the manager is free of bankruptcy concerns.

The incentive compatibility constraint itself, though, is a more delicate issue. To motivate the supply of high action in the case in which contracting variable $y \in \{0, 1\}$, we require

$$E[U \mid I, a_H] = -\pi_H \exp(-\rho(I(0) - c_H)) - (1 - \pi_H) \exp(-\rho(I(1) - c_H))$$
$$\geq E[U \mid I, a_L] = -\pi_L \exp(-\rho(I(0) - c_L))$$
$$- (1 - \pi_L) \exp(-\rho(I(1) - c_L))$$

Now regroup the terms in the following fashion:

$$-\exp(-\rho I(0))[\exp(\rho c_H)\pi_H - \exp(\rho c_L)\pi_L]$$
$$\geq \exp(-\rho I(1))[\exp(\rho c_H)(1 - \pi_H) - \exp(\rho c_L)(1 - \pi_L)]$$

The left-hand side is negative because $c_H > c_L$ and $\pi_H > \pi_L$ ensure that the term in square brackets is strictly positive, and $-\exp(-\rho I(0))$ is surely negative. On the right-hand side, however, $\exp(-\rho I(1)) > 0$, so we must have the term in square brackets negative, or

$$\exp(\rho c_H)(1 - \pi_H) < \exp(\rho c_L)(1 - \pi_L)$$

Collecting terms again, rewrite the inequality as

$$\frac{1 - \pi_H}{1 - \pi_L} = \frac{\pi(y = 1 \mid a_H)}{\pi(y = 1 \mid a_L)} < \frac{\exp(\rho c_L)}{\exp(\rho c_H)} = \exp(\rho(c_L - c_H))$$

Think of the right-hand side as a "cost differential" in the manager's personal cost sphere. The left-hand side is the likelihood of signal $y = 1$ under high action divided by the likelihood of that signal under low action. If that ratio is sufficiently "low," this contracting variable carries enough information, so to speak, to be able to motivate the more personally noxious action supply.[32]

---

[32] Returning to our numerical illustration, this inequality is $.5/.7 = .714 < \exp(.3 - .5) = .819$. It is also worth noting that we indeed have the payment associated with $y = 0$ strictly greater than that associated with $y = 1$.

Selected References

Stiglitz (1974), Jensen and Meckling (1976), Demski and Feltham (1978), Harris and Raviv (1978), Holmstrom (1979), Shavell (1979), and Grossman and Hart (1983) are primary references for this approach to optimal contracting. Expository treatments are available in Demski (1980; 1994) and Sappington (1991). Lambert (2001), Indjejikian (1999), and Prendergast (1999) provide recent reviews of this literature; Demski and Sappington (1999) stress difficulties in empirical documentation of pay-for-performance arrangement; and Abowd and Kaplan

(1999) and Lazear (2000) provide empirical documentation. Baron and Kreps (1999) provide a substantially broader perspective, and Arrow (1974) provides an exceptionally insightful discussion of frictions that inhibit efficient trade and production.

Key Terms

The manager's **action** is his choice, an act (in the state-act-outcome model of Chapter 5) that determines the possibly random supply of managerial input, factor M in expression (11.2). **Moral hazard** is present when a contractual arrangement, here an arrangement to trade compensation for action, depends on the behavior of at least one of the parties and that behavior is not observable. A **first-best** contractual arrangement is one in which no trade friction, such as that associated with moral hazard, is present. A **second-best** trade arrangement is one in which some trade friction, such as that associated with moral hazard, is present. **Individual rationality** is the requirement, expressed in (11.5), that the contractual arrangement be acceptable to the manager. **Incentive compatibility** is the requirement, expressed in (11.4), that the contractual arrangement render it rational for the manager to supply the desired action.

Exercises

11.1. One of the insights from the contracting setting explored here is the following: If the contracting friction is present and if the contracting information is imperfect, by necessity the manager's compensation must be risky if a_H is to be supplied. Explain.

11.2. Ralph manages a one-product firm. The technology mixes "management," "capital," and "labor" to produce its single product. Capital (K) costs 500 per unit (and cannot exceed an upper bound of 250 units); labor (L) costs 40 per unit. Ralph must produce $q = 700$ units. Technology is given by

$$q \leq M\sqrt{KL}$$

where M denotes managerial services. M can be set at $M = 1$ or at $M = 4$. How much *extra* would Ralph pay to set $M = 4$ instead of $M = 1$? Provide an economic interpretation of factor M.

11.3. This is a continuation of Exercise 11.2. Now suppose factor M is provided by a manager. This manager can supply one of two actions, a_H or a_L. The action determines the stochastic nature of factor M according to the following probabilities:

	$M = 1$	$M = 4$
a_H	.5	.5
a_L	1	0

So action a_H provides 50–50 odds on $M = 1$ or $M = 4$ while action a_L ensures $M = 1$. Moreover, when M is uncertain, Ralph must first select capital (K) and then, after observing M, select labor. Suppose Ralph settles on action a_H.

a. Determine the optimal capital choice and labor choices.

b. What is Ralph's expected expenditure on capital and labor at this point?

c. Contrast Ralph's choice of K with what that choice would be were $M = 2.5$ (i.e., were M guaranteed to equal its expected value).

11.4. Further expanding Exercise 11.3, we now suppose the manager's action is supplied under moral hazard conditions. In particular, the manager's utility measure is given by $U(\$, a) = -\exp(-.0001 \times (\$ - c_a))$ for payment in the amount $\$$ and personal action or "effort" cost in the amount c_a. Act a_H carries a personal "effort" cost of 3,000 while act a_L carries a personal "effort" cost of 0. In addition, this manager has other options, and his next-best employment arrangement promises a certainty equivalent of $CE = 15,000$. Contracting with the manager is confined to the previously noted observation of factor M. Determine the optimal contract that will motivate the manager to supply act a_H. Why does this contract pay more if $M = 4$ than if $M = 1$?

11.5. The contract identified in Exercise 11.4 places the manager at risk despite the fact Ralph is risk neutral.

a. What is the manager's certainty equivalent for this payment lottery?

b. What is Ralph's certainty equivalent for paying this payment lottery? Explain.

11.6. The optimal contract in Exercise 11.4 depends on mutually observed factor M. Ralph's accountant sees this and retorts that she learned in college that since the manager is responsible for producing $q = 700$ units at minimum cost, he should be evaluated based on the cost he incurs. Cost is measured here by the total spent on factors K and L. Carefully evaluate the accountant's suggestion.

11.7. Ralph must produce 900 units of a product. Doing so requires Ralph to mix appropriate amounts of capital (K), labor (L), and managerial services (M). Capital is limited to $K \leq K^{max} = 1,500$. Factor prices on capital and labor are $p_K = p_L = 200$. The managerial service can be set at $M = 1$ or $M = 1.5$. The former costs 30,000 and the latter costs 75,000. The technology is specified by

$$q \leq M\sqrt{KL}$$

Determine Ralph's cost of producing the required 900 units.

11.8. What happens in Exercise 11.7 if the only options for acquiring managerial services are to set $M = 1$, again at a cost of 30,000, or to live with a random M that will be either 1 or 3 with 50–50 odds? The latter costs 75,000. In particular, suppose that the sure ($M = 1$) or the random M can be acquired and that supplemental labor (in the amount L') can be acquired should the actual M turn out to be low.

11.9. Ralph wants to hire an agent. Ralph is risk neutral while the agent is strictly risk averse and incurs a personal cost in supplying labor to Ralph. The agent's utility is given by

$$\sqrt{\$} - \text{cost}$$

where $\$$ denotes compensation and the cost refers to a personal cost incurred by the agent. The agent can supply high input (H) or low input (L). The agent's cost is cost $= 10$ if input H is supplied and cost $= 0$ if input L is supplied. Ralph wants input H, and the agent has an opportunity cost measured in utility units of 40. Thus, if there is no contracting friction, the minimum payment to the agent that will be acceptable is 2,500 because

$$\sqrt{2,500} - 10 = 40$$

a. Assume the two parties can only contract on observable output. This output can be low (q_1) or high (q_2). The probabilities are as follows:

	Output q_1	Output q_2
Input H	.3	.7
Input L	.7	.3

Thus, for example, if input H is supplied, the probability of low output is .3. A consultant has recommended that Ralph motivate the agent with a bonus contract, in effect paying an amount denoted I_j when output q_j is observed. After much study, three possible bonus arrangements have been designed as follows. One of these is optimal. Which one is it, and why?

	Output q_1	Output q_2
Plan 1: Payments	1,049.25	3,311.57
Plan 2: Payments	1,056.25	3,306.25
Plan 3: Payments	765.25	3,106.25

b. Now suppose the agent's utility is given by $-\exp[-.0001(\text{payment less cost of input})]$ where the cost of H is 900 and the cost of L is zero. The agent's next-best alternative guarantees payment less cost of 1,600. Determine an optimal incentive structure that will motivate input H.

11.10. Ralph must produce 900 units of a product. Doing so requires him to mix appropriate amounts of capital (K), labor (L), and managerial services (M). Capital is limited to $K \leq K^{\max} = 1,500$. Factor prices on capital and labor are $p_K = 400$ and $p_L = 200$. Factor M is supplied by a manager. This manager supplies action a, which, in turn, leads to some random supply of factor M. In particular, $M = 1$ or $M = 3$ might materialize. Ralph selects the capital and the manager's action, observes M, and then decides on factor L. The manager is described by a utility function of $U(\iota, a) = -\exp(-.0001(\iota - c_a))$ where ι denotes cash payment and c_a the personal cost of action a. Also, the manager's outside opportunity carries a certainty equivalent of 30,000.

Two possible actions, *high* or *low*, are present. The former carries a personal cost of 5,000 and the latter a personal cost of 0. The *high* action leads to 50–50 odds on M; the *low* action leads to a probability of .9 that $M = 1$.

a. Assume a perfect market for managerial services. Determine Ralph's optimal choices for producing the noted 900 units.

b. Next assume an imperfect market for managerial services in which the only contracting variable is the firm's total cost exclusive of the payment to the manager. Again, determine Ralph's optimal choices for producing the noted 900 units.

11.11. Exhibits 11.5, 11.6, and 11.7, taken together, imply that a control problem is absent in our setting if the manager's personal cost or risk aversion are trivial or if certainty is present. Explain.

11.12. Verify the calculations in Note 29.

11.13. Use the setting of Exercise 11.4 and construct graphs similar to those in Exhibits 11.5 and 11.6.

11.14. Return to Exercise 11.4 where the probability that $M = 4$ under low action is zero. Determine the optimal contract to motivate high action for a series of related cases in which the probability that $M = 4$ under low action (i.e., π_L) increases from 0, to .1, to .2, and so on. What happens? Explain.

Chapter 12

Additional Information in a Managerial Contracting Setting

With the stylized contracting story and the mechanics of identifying an optimal contract in place, it is time to get serious about information questions. We do this by adding a second contracting variable, a second source of information, to the stew. Information content of this second source, naturally conditional on the first source being present, now enters the analysis, but, as we know, information does not just appear at the most convenient time and place. Does the new information arrive early or late in the story? Does it arrive in public format, or is it privately observed and, thus, must be coupled with communication from the informed party to be useful in the contracting venue? These are not gratuitous issues, and we will see in later chapters that being able to identify and deal with them is central to understanding accounting.

We now add additional information to the one-period managerial contracting story introduced in Chapter 11. Timing and possession are critical elements of this extension: When does the additional information arrive and by whom is it observed? Information that arrives "early"—for example, a market research study or a pilot production exercise—can be used to refine the production plan and to evaluate the manager's performance. Information that arrives "late"—for example, a customer satisfaction survey or a set of benchmarking statistics—can be used to evaluate the manager's performance but in our one-period setting arrives too late to affect the production plan itself.[1] Moreover, information that is observed by just one of the two parties creates additional control problems. For example, if late information, such as the customer satisfaction survey, is privately observed by the manager, it must be self-reported if it is to be used in the contracting exercise. Self-reporting, by its very nature, raises veracity concerns.

Initially, we introduce a second source of publicly available information. This information arrives late in the game after decisions have been finalized, and thus is valuable, at most, for evaluating the manager's performance. This allows us to concentrate on the mixing of two information sources absent any direct effect on the production plan itself or concern over self-reporting motives. From there we turn to private information, placing this second source of information first in the hands (metaphorically) of the manager and then in the hands of the firm. This, of course, forces us to confront the veracity issue. Following this, we briefly discuss moving the information forward in time, making it potentially valuable in directing the firm's decisions as well as in evaluating the manager.

Our focus at this point is mixing information sources while varying the timing and possession elements of the story. To keep the setting uncluttered, the new information source is treated in abstract fashion with no explicit connection to accounting measures or concerns. These are addressed in subsequent chapters once the basics are in place.

ADDITIONAL LATE, PUBLIC INFORMATION

Recall that our story in Chapter 11 rests on technology that mixes capital (K), labor (L), and managerial (M) inputs. The managerial input is random with odds that depend on the manager's "effort" action. In turn, the firm was contracting with a manager in a setting in which trade frictions due to an inherent conflict of interest invite opportunism. This led the firm to use cost incurred to evaluate the manager. With the streamlined setup, this cost comes down to whether additional labor is not required ($M = M_H$), coded as $y = 0$, or is required ($M = M_L$), coded as $y = 1$. Important details, drawn from Exhibit 11.3, are summarized in Exhibit 12.1.

With contracting variable y, then, the manager is paid according to the compensation function or contract $I(y)$. The earlier derived optimal pay-for-performance contract is displayed in Exhibit 12.2. For the bulk of this

---

[1] Think of the production plan as the decision point in the story. Then early information is often called *predecision (or decision facilitating) information,* and late information is often called *postdecision (or decision influencing) information.*

EXHIBIT 12.1
Details for
Continuing
Numerical
Illustration

Firm details

Output quantity	$q = 1,000$
Managerial input	$M_H = 1.1$ $(y = 0)$ and $M_L = .9$ $(y = 1)$
Managerial input odds	$\pi_H = .5$ and $\pi_L = .3$

Manager details

Utility measure	$U(\iota, a) = -\exp(-\rho(\iota - c_a))$
Risk-aversion coefficient	$\rho = .0001$
Opportunity certainty equivalent	$\hat{\iota} = 5,000$
Personal costs	$c_H = 5,000$ and $c_L = 3,000$

EXHIBIT 12.2
Base Case Details,
$E[I \mid a_H] = 11,829$

	Signal y	
	$y = 0$	$y = 1$
$\pi(y \mid a_H)$	.50	.50
$\pi(y \mid a_L)$	.30	.70
$I(y)$	18,063	5,595

chapter, we suppress the remaining details of the underlying story.[2] The idea, then, is that the firm seeks unobservable services from the manager, and contracting frictions (here the noted *personal cost term*) lead to using the manager's performance (here the cost incurred to produce $q = 1,000$ units or, equivalently, the realization of the M variable) to infer the supply of unobservable services. So, the manager is paid 5,595 if the observed cost is high (i.e., if $y = 1$) and 18,063 if it is low (i.e., $y = 0$).

We now expand this basic story by adding a second source of information that is also publicly observed and becomes available just as the original contracting variable was observed. To keep things simple, this second source is also binary in nature; its signal will be one of $\{g, b\}$.

You will be relieved to learn that the notation essentials are already in place to deal with this expanded story. Think of the contracting signal now as a pair of signals, $y = (y_1, y_2)$. y_1 is our original signal, so $y_1 \in \{0, 1\}$; y_2 is our new signal, so $y_2 \in \{g, b\}$. The time line is displayed in Exhibit 12.3, which you should contrast with the original story's time line (Exhibit 11.4).

The question now is whether this second source of information is "useful." By design it arrives too late to serve any purpose other than evaluating the manager, and, being public, we need not concern ourselves with veracity issues. The key to answering this question, as we shall see, is the nature of the joint probability, our old friend $\pi(y \mid a)$.

---

[2] These include, given the presumed factor prices, producing $q = 1,000$ units by mixing high action by the manager (a_H) with capital of $K = 1015.14$, initial labor of $L = 814.12$, and supplemental labor (if necessary) of $L' = 402.04$.

EXHIBIT 12.3
Time Line for Contracting Game,
$y_1 \in \{0, 1\}, y_2 \in \{g, b\}$

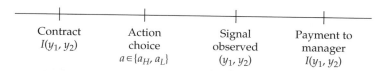

| Contract $I(y_1, y_2)$ | Action choice $a \in \{a_H, a_L\}$ | Signal observed (y_1, y_2) | Payment to manager $I(y_1, y_2)$ |

EXHIBIT 12.4
Case 1 with
$E[I \mid a_H] = 11,063$

	Signal $y = (y_1, y_2)$			
	(0, g)	**(0, b)**	**(1, g)**	**(1, b)**
$\pi(y \mid a_H)$	.30	.20	.30	.20
$\pi(y \mid a_L)$	.15	.15	.35	.35
$I(y)$	15,173	13,665	10,501	3,138

Four Illustrations

To begin, consider the probability specification in Exhibit 12.4. We now have four distinct evaluation combinations because each signal can be one of two possibilities. In addition, this collapses to the original story if we ignore the second signal. In particular, we have $\pi(y_1 = 0 \mid a_H)$ $= \pi(y_1 = (0, g) \mid a_H) + \pi(y_1 = (0, b) \mid a_H) = .30 + .20 = .50$, as well as $\pi(y_1 = 0 \mid a_L) = .15 + .15 = .30$ as in the original story. Consequently, we adopt the interpretation that y_1 is the old signal (managerial input) and y_2 is the new additional signal.

From here we solve for the optimal contract that will motivate the manager to supply action a_H as opposed to a_L. In particular, for some contract defined on both information sources and assuming that high action will be motivated, the firm's expected cost of hiring the manager is

$$E[I \mid a_H] = .30I(0, g) + .20I(0, b) + .30I(1, g) + .20I(1, b)$$

Likewise, with this contract the manager's utility evaluations for high and low action, respectively, are

$$E[U \mid I, a_H]$$
$$= -.30 \exp(-\rho(I(0, g) - 5,000)) - .20 \exp(-\rho(I(0, b) - 5,000))$$
$$- .30 \exp(-\rho(I(1, g) - 5,000)) - .20 \exp(-\rho(I(1, b) - 5,000))$$

$$E[U \mid I, a_L]$$
$$= -.15 \exp(-\rho(I(0, g) - 3,000)) - .15 \exp(-\rho(I(0, b) - 3,000))$$
$$- .35 \exp(-\rho(I(1, g) - 3,000)) - .35 \exp(-\rho(I(1, b) - 3,000))$$

The firm, in turn, designs the contract offer to minimize $E[I \mid a_H]$ subject to the usual individual rationality, $E[U \mid I, a_H] \geq -\exp(-\rho\hat{\imath}) = -\exp(-\rho(5,000))$, and incentive compatibility, $E[U \mid I, a_H] \geq E[U \mid I, a_L]$, constraints. The solution is also reported in Exhibit 12.4 (and can be readily verified with the optimization option in a typical spreadsheet package).[3]

Mechanics aside, what are we to make of this? Notice the second source is more likely to report $y_2 = g$ if a_H is supplied: $\pi(y_2 = g \mid a_H) = .6 > \pi(y_2 = g \mid a_L) = .5$. That is, signal g is more consistent with good behavior by the manager; it is good news, and we see this in the optimal arrangement in which for any realization of the first signal ($y_1 = 0$ or 1), the manager is paid more if $y_2 = g$ than if $y_2 = b$. Likewise, as in our original solution, signal $y_1 = 0$, the case of low cost, is good news, again reflecting the intuition that low cost is more likely under good behavior and is therefore rewarded.[4] Moreover, the optimal solution clearly uses the second signal: For any realization of y_1, the compensation function is not constant across y_2. The firm's (equilibrium) cost is $E[I \mid a_H] = 11,063$, which is lower than our original calculation of 11,829 when the additional information was not present.

Importantly, then, the story is structured so that the first signal has a natural good versus bad news interpretation when viewed in isolation, and the second signal has a natural good versus bad news interpretation when viewed in isolation. Putting the two signals together retains this good versus bad news interpretation. For example, if $y_1 = 1$ is reported, bad news, the manager is penalized; and if $y_2 = b$ is also reported, more bad news, the manager is penalized even more. If $y_2 = g$, however, good news is reported, the good and bad news cut in opposite directions, and the penalty is largely waived.

Focusing on the manager's expected utility calculation, you should verify that the certainty equivalent of the manager's net compensation is precisely $\hat{i} = 5,000$ and that the manager is indifferent between supplying high or low action. Our original solution has the same properties. So, why is the firm's cost less in this case? The answer is noise in the information system or the flip side of noise, the risk imposed on the manager. We have better information now, which means the firm can rely less

---

[3] This is another use of expression (11.6). Using our earlier notation, the optimal contract is the solution to

$$\ddot{I}_H = \min_{I(y)} E[I \mid a_H] = \sum_{y \in Y} I(y) \pi(y \mid a_H)$$

subject to: individual rationality: $E[U \mid I, a_H] \geq -\exp(-\rho \hat{i})$ and
incentive compatibility: $E[U \mid I, a_H] \geq E[U \mid I, a_L]$

[4] This straightforward interpretation depends, as we shall see, on a lack of interaction between the two information sources. Indeed, the signal from the second source here depends on the manager's action but is otherwise independent of the first information source, the cost realization. In fact, we constructed it via $\pi(y_2 = g \mid a_H) = .6 > \pi(y_2 = g \mid a_L) = .5$. With the noted independence, we have $\pi((y_1, y_2) \mid a) = \pi(y_1 \mid a) \pi(y_2 \mid a)$. Try it: $\pi((0, g) \mid a_H) = \pi(y_1 = 0 \mid a_H) \pi(y_2 = g \mid a_H) = .5(.6) = .3$. (Working in the opposite direction, you should examine $\pi(y_2 \mid y_1, a) = \pi((y_1, y_2) \mid a)/\pi(y_1 \mid a)$ and notice that this does not depend on signal y_1 for any of the possible combinations.)

EXHIBIT 12.5
Case 2 with
$E[I \mid a_H] = 10{,}448$

	Signal $y = (y_1, y_2)$			
	(0, g)	**(0, b)**	**(1, g)**	**(1, b)**
$\pi(y \mid a_H)$	.40	.10	.20	.30
$\pi(y \mid a_L)$	.10	.20	.40	.30
$I(y)$	13,302	6,238	6,238	10,854

EXHIBIT 12.6
Case 3 with
$E[I \mid a_H] = 11{,}829$

	Signal $y = (y_1, y_2)$			
	(0, g)	**(0, b)**	**(1, g)**	**(1, b)**
$\pi(y \mid a_H)$	.30	.20	.20	.30
$\pi(y \mid a_L)$	.18	.12	.28	.42
$I(y)$	18,063	18,063	5,595	5,595

on high-powered incentives. This, in turn, means the manager's equilibrium compensation is less risky and the risk premium is therefore reduced.[5] Indeed, it has been reduced from 1,829 to 1,063.

Lest we become euphoric, though, and conclude that mixing information sources is straightforward, we turn to the slightly altered probability structure in Exhibit 12.5. The marginal distributions of the cost realization, $\pi(y_1 \mid a)$, and of the second signal's realization, $\pi(y_2 \mid a)$, remain as before. So, viewed in isolation, each has a good versus bad news interpretation.

However, solving for the optimal contract reveals a different story. If the cost realization is low ($y_1 = 0$), $y_2 = g$ is indeed good news (as $I(0, g) = 13{,}302 > I(0, b) = 6{,}238$), but if it is high ($y_1 = 1$), $y_2 = g$ is bad news (as $I(1, g) < I(1, b)$). Moreover, in the presence of $y_2 = g$, low cost is good news but in the presence of $y_2 = b$, low cost is bad news. Information is difficult to interpret.

The important message is not to think of each information source as an independent source. Interactions are present. With the sources interacting, we cannot interpret one source's report without knowledge of the other's report. As a result, we generally do not have the luxury, or comfort, of being able to label the signals from any specific source as "good" or "bad." The interpretation of one signal depends upon the realization of the other signal.

Exhibit 12.6 presents a third example. $\pi(y_1 \mid a)$ remains as before, although $\pi(y_2 \mid a)$ is altered but in a way that retains the good versus bad news interpretation when viewed in isolation. Now, however, there is no use whatever for the additional information. The optimal contract uses

---

[5] For example, if the manager behaves but high cost is observed, $y_1 = 1$, the second signal offers insurance against such bad luck in the cost domain.

EXHIBIT 12.7
Case 4 with
$E[I \mid a_H] = 10{,}650$

	Signal $y = (y_1, y_2)$			
	(0, g)	(0, b)	(1, g)	(1, b)
$\pi(y \mid a_H)$	.30	.20	.20	.30
$\pi(y \mid a_L)$	.10	.20	.40	.30
$I(y)$	14,040	11,170	4,264	11,170

only the low versus high cost signal, y_1: $I(0, g) = I(0, b)$, and $I(1, g) = I(1, b)$. Also the firm's (equilibrium) cost of high action, $E[I \mid a_H] = 11{,}829$, is identical to what we found when no additional information was present. (See Exhibit 12.2.) The additional information is useless despite the fact that, when viewed in isolation, it is informative about the manager's behavior. Mixing information sources is a delicate matter.

A final example, Exhibit 12.7, adds to the mystery. We again have $\pi(y_1 \mid a)$ as before, but $\pi(y_2 \mid a)$ is now in the category of pure noise because $\pi(y_2 = g \mid a_H) = \pi(y_2 = g \mid a_L) = .5$. Nevertheless, the additional information is found to be useful. Mixing information sources is wonderful (at least sometimes).

Summarizing, the four examples reveal that additional (public) information might improve the contracting with the manager, given we are facing substantive trade frictions. However, this is not always the case. In the first case the new information source was actually independent of the original cost-based information. There we found improvement because the two information sources complemented each other. In the second case we also found improvement due to the additional information. The additional information source had the same characteristics as the independent information source in the first case, although there was correlation between the additional and the original information. Thus, not only the informativeness of the additional information matters but also the interaction with the original information is important. The third example stresses this point even more because there the additional information informs about the manager's behavior, but when combined with the original information, it is utterly useless. Exactly the opposite is found in the final example. There the additional information contains no information on its own about the manager's behavior, but when combined with the original information, it is used in the contracting arrangement.

Information Content

Making sense of this requires us to revisit two earlier notions. First is the notion of *information content*. In Chapter 8, in the risk-neutral valuation setting, we stressed the importance of interaction effects in identifying whether information content is present. With two sources present, with signal $y = (y_1, y_2)$, we said the second source had information content in the presence of the first source only if the valuation varied in nontrivial fashion as a function of y_2 (the second signal) for some y_1 (the first signal).[6] In parallel fashion, then, when two information sources are present in the contracting setting, we say the second source has *information content in the presence of the first source* if the optimal contract, $I(y_1, y_2)$, varies in nontrivial fashion as a function of y_2 for some y_1. Among our four examples, then, Cases 1, 2, and 4 exhibit information content for the second source, but Case 3 does not.

Second is the importance of contrasting equilibrium with off-equilibrium possibilities in the managerial contracting setting. In Chapter 11, when contracting with only the cost or M realization (so $y \in \{0, 1\}$), we saw how, in Exhibit 11.7, spreading out the pair of likelihood ratios,

$$\pi(y = 0 \,|\, a_L)/\pi(y = 0 \,|\, a_H)$$

and

$$\pi(y = 1 \,|\, a_L)/\pi(y = 1 \,|\, a_H)$$

led to improved contracting. Intuitively, we want to distinguish good (supply of a_H) from opportunistic (supply of a_L) behavior, and this is made easier by spreading the noted ratios farther apart. After all, with a larger spread, we make $y = 0$ "more consistent" with supply of a_H.

Combining these two themes requires us to focus on distinguishing good from opportunistic behavior while being careful to look for the second information source's ability to incrementally assist in this "distinguishing exercise." With this in mind, examine the corresponding likelihood ratios in the present case in which two information sources are present. Denoting the ratio $R(y_1, y_2)$, we have the following,

$$R(y_1, y_2) = \frac{\pi((y_1, y_2) \,|\, a_L)}{\pi((y_1, y_2) \,|\, a_H)} = \frac{\pi(y_2 \,|\, y_1, a_L)\,\pi(y_1 \,|\, a_L)}{\pi(y_2 \,|\, y_1, a_H)\,\pi(y_1 \,|\, a_H)} \quad \textbf{(12.1)}$$

where we exploit the rules of conditional probability in the right-hand side of the expression. In our series of examples, then, we have four such ratios: $R(0, g)$, $R(0, b)$, $R(1, g)$, and $R(1, b)$. See Exhibit 12.8 (Case 0 is the base case without additional information present.)

Suppose this ratio does not depend on the second signal, y_2, as in Case 3. The only place y_2 shows up in the likelihood ratio is in the ratio of $\pi(y_2 \,|\, y_1, a_L)$ to $\pi(y_2 \,|\, y_1, a_H)$; the only way signal y_2 can have no influence

---

[6] This means the expected value of future cash flows, conditional on whatever else is known, must vary with what the second source has to say. This, in turn, implies that the conditional probability that describes those future cash flows, conditional on all that is known, is itself a nontrivial function of what the new information source has to say.

EXHIBIT 12.8
Incentive Payments
and Likelihood
Ratios

	Signal $y = (y_1, y_2)$				
	(0, g)	**(0, b)**	**(1, g)**	**(1, b)**	**$E[I \mid a_H]$**
Case 0: $I(y_1)$	18,063	18,063	5,595	5,595	11,829
$\quad R(y_1)$	.60	.60	1.40	1.40	
Case 1: $I(y_1, y_2)$	15,173	13,665	10,501	3,138	11,063
$\quad R(y_1, y_2)$	.50	.75	1.17	1.75	
Case 2: $I(y_1, y_2)$	13,302	6,238	6,238	10,854	10,448
$\quad R(y_1, y_2)$	.25	2.00	2.00	1.00	
Case 3: $I(y_1, y_2)$	18,063	18,063	5,595	5,595	11,829
$\quad R(y_1, y_2)$	.60	.60	1.40	1.40	
Case 4: $I(y_1, y_2)$	14,040	11,170	4,264	11,170	10,650
$\quad R(y_1, y_2)$	.33	1.00	2.00	1.00	

on the overall expression is if $\pi(y_2 \mid y_1, a_L) = \pi(y_2 \mid y_1, a_H)$ for every possible signal from the first source,[7] y_1. This means the second source cannot possibly help us distinguish good from opportunistic behavior, given we are already observing the first source. The second source lacks information content.

Conversely, suppose this ratio does depend on the second signal. This means that for some initial signal y_1, we have unequal likelihood ratios, $R(y_1, y_2') \neq R(y_1, y_2'')$ for two possible signals from the second source. This means, however, that $\pi(y_2 \mid y_1, a_L) \neq \pi(y_2 \mid y_1, a_H)$; in the presence of the first source the second source is capable of helping us further distinguish good from opportunistic behavior.

An important general statement now follows: If the second information source has information content in the presence of the first source in the contracting setting then, by necessity, the likelihood ratio must depend on the second signal. In our running examples, Cases 1, 2, and 4 exhibit information content for the second source because $I(y_1, y_2)$ is a nontrivial function of y_2 in these cases; we see immediately in Exhibit 12.8 that their respective likelihood ratios depend in nontrivial fashion on the second

---

[7] If the ratio does not depend on the second signal, we can write it as depending on only the first, or $R(y_1)$. We then have

$$R(y_1) = \frac{\pi(y_2 \mid y_1, a_L)}{\pi(y_2 \mid y_1, a_H)} \times \frac{\pi(y_1 \mid a_L)}{\pi(y_1 \mid a_H)}$$

and rearranging we have

$$R(y_1) \times \frac{\pi(y_1 \mid a_H)}{\pi(y_1 \mid a_L)} = \frac{\pi(y_2 \mid y_1, a_L)}{\pi(y_2 \mid y_1, a_H)}$$

Importantly, now, the left-hand side does not depend on y_2, so the right-hand side cannot depend on y_2, but this implies that we have $\pi(y_2 \mid y_1, a_L) = \pi(y_2 \mid y_1, a_H)$.

signal.[8] If, then, the second source has information content, it must be capable of revealing something about the manager's behavior, conditional on what is learned from the first source; that is, it must be the case that $\pi(y_2 \mid y_1, a_L) \neq \pi(y_2 \mid y_1, a_H)$ for at least one realization[9] of y_1.

In short, information content in the contracting setting rests on contrasting good with opportunistic—equilibrium with off-equilibrium—behavior by the manager, and with thoroughly conditioning on what is learned from other sources. The latter, of course, is central to information content in a valuation setting as well, but the former is unique to the contracting setting.

Aside

To reinforce the importance of conditioning on other information, recall the oft-heard mantra that a manager should be held responsible for what he or she controls. Stated differently, a particular variable should be used in evaluating a manager if that variable is under the manager's control. In the present setup and focusing on the second source, signal y_2, using that variable to evaluate the manager means that the compensation arrangement

---

[8] In our simple setting in which we have only two possible action supplies, it is possible to make the opposite statement: If the existing arrangement imposes nontrivial risk on the manager and if the likelihood ratio is a nontrivial function of the second signal, then information content is present. This follows from the fact the new source tells us something about high versus low action because those are the only possibilities. In a larger setting we would want to qualify the statement to stress that the additional information must tell us something about a binding part of the larger control problem. This is getting out of hand!

[9] Also notice the connection between the likelihood ratios and the incentive payments in Exhibit 12.8: They vary inversely. Intuitively, the "more likely" the observed signal pair is to have come from the off-equilibrium, low-action supply, the lower the payment. To see this, rewrite the incentive compatibility as $E[U \mid I, a_H] - E[U \mid I, a_H] \geq 0$. Also note that, by construction of the likelihood ratio, $R(y_1, y_2) \times \pi((y_1, y_2) \mid a_H) = \pi((y_1, y_2) \mid a_L)$. Using this along with our usual trick of factoring the manager's utility function, $U(I, a) = -\exp(\rho c_a)\exp(-\rho I)$, we recombine terms in the incentive compatibility constraint as follows:

$$
\begin{aligned}
E[U \mid I, a_H] - E[U \mid I, a_L] &= -\sum \exp(\rho c_H)\exp(-\rho I(y_1, y_2))\,\pi((y_1, y_2) \mid a_H) \\
&\quad + \sum \exp(\rho c_L)\exp(-\rho I(y_1, y_2))\,\pi((y_1, y_2) \mid a_L) \\
&= -\sum \exp(\rho c_H)\exp(-\rho I(y_1, y_2))\,\pi((y_1, y_2) \mid a_H) \\
&\quad + \sum \exp(\rho c_L)\exp(-\rho I(y_1, y_2))\,R(y_1, y_2)\,\pi((y_1, y_2) \mid a_H) \\
&= -\sum \exp(-\rho I(y_1, y_2))[\exp(\rho c_H) \\
&\quad - \exp(\rho c_L)R(y_1, y_2)]\,\pi((y_1, y_2) \mid a_H) \geq 0
\end{aligned}
$$

Concentrate, if possible, on the terms in the square brackets where we see the likelihood ratio. This constraint must be satisfied as cheaply as possible. If the likelihood ratio is "large," we want the multiplier on the term in square brackets to be lower, so we want the payment to be small. The opposite holds for a "small" likelihood ratio. Naturally, the razor's edge case of two identical likelihood ratios leads to identical payments.

depends on that variable. In turn, the manager controls that variable if $\pi(y_2 \mid a)$ depends in nontrivial fashion on the manager's choice of action, a. So the "controllability principle" translates to the imperative that the manager's compensation should depend on the second information source if $\pi(y_2 \mid a)$ depends on the manager's action choice, a.

As we have seen, however, the key to whether it is helpful to use the second information source in this fashion depends on whether $\pi(y_2 \mid y_1, a)$ depends on action a, not on whether $\pi(y_2 \mid a)$ depends on action a. Moreover, there is no necessary connection between $\pi(y_2 \mid y_1, a)$ depending on action a and $\pi(y_2 \mid a)$ depending on action a. For example, in Cases 1 and 2, both $\pi(y_2 \mid y_1, a)$ and $\pi(y_2 \mid a)$ depend on a; in Case 3, $\pi(y_2 \mid a)$ depends on a while $\pi(y_2 \mid y_1, a)$ does not; in Case 4, $\pi(y_2 \mid y_1, a)$ depends on a while $\pi(y_2 \mid a)$ does not.

The important factor in determining whether the second source has information content in the contracting venue is whether it contains new information about the action supply. Think of this as being *conditionally controllable*, conditional in the sense we condition on what we are learning from the other information source.

ADDITIONAL LATE, PRIVATE INFORMATION

Once the notion of additional information is introduced, the question of who has access to that information emerges. The firm, specifically the management team, routinely acquires information about its production process, emerging technologies, factor markets, suppliers, product markets, and competitors, not to mention staying abreast of regulatory mandates and trends. Formal procedures (e.g., time slips, invoices, and periodic customer surveys), specialists (e.g., statistical services and consultants), and informal activities (e.g., casual conversation and trade meetings) are all employed. Competitors' products are analyzed, competitors' employees are hired, and R&D is routinely funded. Management is constantly confronted with new issues relating to its products, its customers, and its production technologies. Indeed, properly designing, managing, and using this array of information sources is a critical activity of the successful management team.

However, parties external to the management team or even to the firm, such as the suppliers of monetary capital, are typically not as well informed as the firm's management team.[10] This means some players know things the other players do not know. Private information is an essential part of the milieu.

---

[10] In parallel fashion, division managers and central management will access different information sources as will be the case of the division managers and their various subordinates. The prospects for drawing this chapter to a close are not very encouraging!

EXHIBIT 12.9 **Time Line for Contracting Game with Late, Private Information**

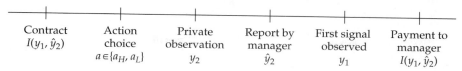

Contract $I(y_1, \hat{y}_2)$	Action choice $a \in \{a_H, a_L\}$	Private observation y_2	Report by manager $\hat{y}_2$	First signal observed y_1	Payment to manager $I(y_1, \hat{y}_2)$

One implication is that management's private information, being private, is not directly available for contracting purposes. Naturally, this information might, if public, be useful for contracting purposes. (In light of the previous section, the information might possess conditional information content.) If so, we have two possibilities for making the private information available for contracting purposes. One is to turn the information source into a public information source. In that case, we are back to the previous section dealing with additional public information.[11] The other possibility is to have the manager self-report the private information. Of course, this means the manager's self-report, not the underlying information, is what becomes available for contracting.

Manager Better Informed

To proceed, we use the same setup as before but with two alterations. First, the second information source, the one that reports $y_2 = g$ or $y_2 = b$, is now observed privately by the manager. Second, this information arrives after the manager supplies action $a = a_H$ or $a = a_L$ but before the first information source, the one that reports $y_1 \in \{0, 1\}$, is observed. This timing convention is summarized in Exhibit 12.9.[12]

The first source, recall, is simply a coded version of the production cost incurred. So, the story is one in which both parties observe the cost, but the manager observes something else, and this observation takes place at the noted time. Given the timing assumption, the only conceivable use of the second information source at the firm level is to aid in evaluating the manager's performance. To do this, however, the manager must reveal what was privately observed.

Naturally, we throw some notation at the story. As hinted in Exhibit 12.9, it is important to distinguish what the manager privately knows, $y_2 \in \{g, b\}$, from what the manager claims to know. To do this, we

---

[11] How to simply "turn the information source into a public information source" is left as an open question.

[12] Recall the larger story that the firm initially acquires capital (K), initial labor (L), and the manager's action. At this point the manager privately observes and then self-reports the second signal. Factor (M) is then observed (the first signal) and supplemental labor is applied as necessary. Reversing the sequence in Exhibit 12.9 so that the public source arrives before the private source is problematic because the public source, as you will see, will now be used to test the veracity of the manager's claim about what was observed.

EXHIBIT 12.10
Late, Private
Information Based
on Case 2
(Exhibit 12.5)

	Signal $y = (y_1, y_2)$, y_1 Public, y_2 Private, Reported as $\hat{y}_2$			
	(0, g)	**(0, b)**	**(1, g)**	**(1, b)**
$\pi((y_1, y_2) \mid a_H)$	.40	.10	.20	.30
$\pi((y_1, y_2) \mid a_L)$	.10	.20	.40	.30
Naive $I(y_1, \hat{y}_2)$	13,302	6,238	6,238	10,854
Defensive $I(y_1, \hat{y}_2)$	18,063	18,063	5,595	5,595
Optimal $I(y_1, \hat{y}_2)$	18,646	12,231	4,965	6,621

begin with the observation that the firm is not naive. The firm knows the manager is observing this private information but just does not know what the manager has observed. So, the firm will ask the manager to reveal what was observed, to reveal whether $y_2 = g$ or $y_2 = b$ was observed. Let $\hat{y}_2 \in \{g, b\}$ denote the manager's claim. The manager knows $y_2 \in \{g, b\}$, and the manager reports $\hat{y}_2 \in \{g, b\}$. Consequently, the manager's compensation now depends on what the public source reported, y_1, and on what the manager claims the private source reported, $\hat{y}_2$. So, we are now dealing with a compensation function denoted $I(y_1, \hat{y}_2)$, not $I(y_1, y_2)$.

To see the significance of this seemingly simple substitution, consider what happens when we use the optimal contract in the Case 2 setting in which both information sources are public. Details are repeated in Exhibit 12.10 where the naive $I(y_1, \hat{y}_2)$ contract is the optimal contract from the original Case 2 setting.

How might the manager respond to such a contract in the private information setting? Presuming it is acceptable to the manager, following an agreement to terms, the manager might respond by supplying high (a_H) or low (a_L) action; following observation of the private signal, the manager might respond by faithfully reporting what was observed or by opportunistically reporting what was observed.

Indeed, for each action supply, the manager has four distinct reporting strategies: Always report what was observed, always report g was observed, always report b was observed, or always report the opposite of what was observed. Opportunism comes in many flavors!

Think of each reporting strategy as mapping what was observed into what is to be reported. Let m denote some such reporting strategy or function. For example, always reporting the opposite is described by $m(y_2 = g) = b$ and $m(y_2 = b) = g$. For later reference also let m^T denote the reporting strategy in which the private observation is always faithfully (i.e., truthfully) reported. In this way, we now characterize the manager's behavior in terms of action supply, a, and reporting strategy, m.

The various combinations are displayed in Exhibit 12.11. Strategy 1, for example, is the desired strategy of high action coupled with factual reporting (i.e., m^T) while strategy 6 is low action coupled with always reporting signal g was observed.

EXHIBIT 12.11   **Strategies for Manager Offered the Naive Contract**

		a, m Pair			Manager's	
		Report of Private Signal			(net) Certainty	
Strategy	Action	$y_2 = g$	$y_2 = b$	$E[U \mid a, m]$	Equivalent	$E[I \mid a, m]$
1	a_H	Report $\hat{y}_2 = g$	Report $\hat{y}_2 = b$	−.6065	5,000	10,448
2	a_H	Report $\hat{y}_2 = g$	Report $\hat{y}_2 = g$	−.6598	4,158	9,770
3	a_H	Report $\hat{y}_2 = b$	Report $\hat{y}_2 = b$	−.7202	3,282	8,546
4	a_H	Report $\hat{y}_2 = b$	Report $\hat{y}_2 = g$	−.7735	2,568	7,867
5	a_L	Report $\hat{y}_2 = g$	Report $\hat{y}_2 = b$	−.6065	5,000	8,329
6	a_L	Report $\hat{y}_2 = g$	Report $\hat{y}_2 = g$	−.6135	4,886	8,357
7	a_L	Report $\hat{y}_2 = b$	Report $\hat{y}_2 = b$	−.5362	6,233	9,469
8	a_L	Report $\hat{y}_2 = b$	Report $\hat{y}_2 = g$	−.5431	6,104	9,497

To decipher Exhibit 12.11, consider the case in which the manager supplies low action, a_L, and reports $\hat{y}_2 = b$ regardless of the underlying information (this is strategy 7). This gives us the following expected utility calculation for the manager:

$$E[U \mid I, a, m] = U(I(0, b), a_L)[\pi((0, g) \mid a_L) + \pi((0, b) \mid a_L)]$$
$$+ U(I(1, b), a_L)[\pi((1, g) \mid a_L) + \pi((1, b) \mid a_L)]$$
$$= -\exp(6.238 - 3)(.1 + .2) - \exp(10.854 - 3)(.4 + .3)$$
$$= -.5362 = U(6,233, 0)$$

Low action results in public signal $y_1 = 0$ with probability .3, and by always reporting that the private signal was b,[13] the manager receives $I(0, b) = 6{,}238$ with probability .3 and $I(1, b) = 10{,}854$ with probability .7. Netting out the action cost (of 3,000) provides the manager with a certainty equivalent of 6,233, well above the reservation or opportunity certainty equivalent of 5,000.

Underneath is a calculated response to the contract that is on the table. Suppose the manager has supplied low action and has privately observed $y_2 = g$. Using the probabilities in Exhibit 12.10, this implies that $y_1 = 0$ will materialize with a probability of $\pi(y_1 = 0 \mid y_2 = g, a_L) = .1/.5. = .2$. So, faithfully reporting that $y_2 = g$ was observed provides a .2 chance at the large payment of $I(0, g) = 13{,}302$, but misreporting provides a .8 chance at the nearly large payment of $I(1, b) = 10{,}854$—case closed. Likewise, if $y_2 = b$ is privately observed, the manager knows $y_1 = 0$ will materialize

---

[13] If the manager always reports that b was observed, the compensation will be $I(0, b)$ if $y_1 = 0$ is subsequently observed and $I(1, b)$ if $y_1 = 1$ is subsequently observed. Now the probability of observing $y_1 = 0$, given the supply of a_L, is the sum of $\pi((0, g) \mid a_L)$ and $\pi((0, b) \mid a_L)$. Additional details are given in the Appendix.

with a probability of $\pi(y_1 = 0 \mid y_2 = b, a_L) = .2/.5 = .4$; it is once again best to report that b was observed. Moreover, the best the manager can do when offered this contract in this circumstance is to supply low action (a_L) and always report $\hat{y}_2 = b$. All of the options are listed in Exhibit 12.11, and strategy 7 beats them all from the manager's perspective.

This is, of course, not a very flattering view of the manager. Naively using the public information contract in this setting, however, invites opportunistic behavior—metaphorically, creative accounting—by the manager. As displayed in Exhibit 12.11, the manager's best response to this contract is to supply low action and always report that b was observed. Equally clear, this is not very attractive from the firm's perspective. By offering the naive contract (designed for the public information case), the firm winds up inadvertently inviting low action and opportunistic reporting. In the process, its expected payment to the manager turns out to be 9,469, well above the payment of 8,000 that would be sufficient to motivate the supply of low action in the first place.

Surely something is amiss; it is the failure to explicitly address the manager's self-reporting incentives. After all, we are now asking the manager to perform two tasks, supply action and self-report, and incentive issues abound in each sphere. One possibility is to offer the manager a defensive contract, one that promises to ignore whatever self-report is delivered. This, of course, returns us to the case in which only the public information source is used in the contracting venue, and it guarantees that the self-reporting incentives are neutral because the parties have mutually agreed to disregard any self-report by the manager. This is the defensive contract in Exhibit 12.10.

Is there room for compromise? Consider the last contract in Exhibit 12.10. Using it, we revisit all of the manager's strategies. Details are given in Exhibit 12.12.

EXHIBIT 12.12 **Strategies for Manager Offered the Optimal Contract**

Strategy	Action	a, m Pair — Report of Private Signal — $y_2 = g$	$y_2 = b$	$E[U \mid a, m]$	Manager's (net) Certainty Equivalent	$E[I \mid a, m]$
1	a_H	Report $\hat{y}_2 = g$	Report $\hat{y}_2 = b$	−.6065	5,000	11,661
2	a_H	Report $\hat{y}_2 = g$	Report $\hat{y}_2 = g$	−.6295	4,628	11,805
3	a_H	Report $\hat{y}_2 = b$	Report $\hat{y}_2 = b$	−.6678	4,038	9,426
4	a_H	Report $\hat{y}_2 = b$	Report $\hat{y}_2 = g$	−.6908	3,699	9,571
5	a_L	Report $\hat{y}_2 = g$	Report $\hat{y}_2 = b$	−.6379	4,496	8,283
6	a_L	Report $\hat{y}_2 = g$	Report $\hat{y}_2 = g$	−.6379	4,496	9,069
7	a_L	Report $\hat{y}_2 = b$	Report $\hat{y}_2 = b$	−.6065	5,000	8,304
8	a_L	Report $\hat{y}_2 = b$	Report $\hat{y}_2 = g$	−.6065	5,000	9,090

The manager now can do no better than supply a_H and faithfully report his private observation. This arrangement and strategy are equivalent to the manager's receiving 5,000, which equals his opportunity certainty equivalent. From the firm's perspective, the expected payment is $E[I \mid a, m] = 11,661$, which is below the expected payment under the defensive contract (of 11,829), but it is also above the expected payment were the information public (10,448). The slippage between the private (11,661) and public (10,448) case is due to the fact that the private information is useful for contracting purposes but must be used less aggressively than in the public case. This less aggressive use is the implicit cost to the firm of maintaining the manager's reporting incentives.

Exhibit 12.12 also hints at how we located this contract. The idea is simple. We want to minimize the firm's cost, its expected payment to the manager, subject to the manager's being willing to accept the terms and being willing to supply a_H and report faithfully. The incentive compatibility issues increase from not only having a_H preferred to a_L (by the manager) but also having a_H and faithful reporting preferred to all other action supply (a) and reporting (m) strategies.

Reprising our earlier notation, the manager's expected utility if contract I is offered, action a is selected, and reporting strategy m is adopted is denoted $E[U \mid I, a, m]$. The faithful truthful reporting strategy is denoted m^T, and the contracting information is denoted $y = (y_1, \hat{y}_2)$. So, the design program is

$$\ddot{I}_H = \min_{I(y)} E[I \mid a_H, m^T] = \sum_{y \in Y} I(y)\pi(y \mid a_H)$$

$$\text{subject to: } E[U \mid I, a_H, m^T] \geq -\exp(-\rho \hat{\imath}) \text{ and}$$

$$E[U \mid I, a_H, m^T] \geq E[U \mid I, a, m] \text{ for all } a \text{ and all } m$$

(12.2)

The first constraint is our old individual rationality condition, requiring that a supply of a_H combined with faithful reporting be as attractive as not accepting the arrangement. The new feature is the family of incentive compatibility constraints. The desired action supply and reporting strategy must, from the manager's perspective, be as desirable as any other option.[14] After all, the firm is unable to observe either the action choice or reporting choice, so proper behavior must be induced via the compensation bundle. In turn, the cost from the firm's perspective is assessed in terms of the underlying probability structure, presuming proper action supply and reliable self-reporting (as guaranteed by the constraints). In other words, the firm designs the arrangement to make best use of the

---

[14] Glance back at Exhibit 12.11 where all possible strategies for the manager are displayed. Strategy 1 is the desired combination of action supply and factual reporting. So, we have seven incentive compatibility constraints: Strategy 1 is preferred to strategy 2, 1 is preferred to 3, and so on. This is explored further in the Appendix.

EXHIBIT 12.13
Late, Private
Information with
Conditional
Independence

	Signal $y = (y_1, y_2)$, y_1 Public, y_2 Private, Reported as $\hat{y}_2$			
	(0, g)	**(0, b)**	**(1, g)**	**(1, b)**
$\pi((y_1, y_2) \mid a_H)$	.30	.20	.30	.20
$\pi((y_1, y_2) \mid a_L)$	.15	.15	.35	.35
Optimal $I(y_1, \hat{y}_2)$	18,063	18,063	5,595	5,595

EXHIBIT 12.14
Late, Private
Information absent
Conditional
Independence

	Signal $y = (y_1, y_2)$, y_1 Public, y_2 Private, Reported as $\hat{y}_2$			
	(0, g)	**(0, b)**	**(1, g)**	**(1, b)**
$\pi((y_1, y_2) \mid a_H)$	.30	.20	.20	.30
$\pi((y_1, y_2) \mid a_L)$	.10	.20	.40	.30
Optimal $I(y_1, \hat{y}_2)$	18,063	18,063	5,595	5,595

private information as long as it remains in the manager's perceived self-interest to be forthcoming with that information.

The intriguing observation here is that the private information is made public through the manager's self-report, but the price paid for that information is that the information is not fully exploited in the performance evaluation. Furthermore, the use of the public report, signal y_1, is noteworthy. The information content of the report by the manager or the possibility for using that report depends critically on the content of the public output. That is the next item on our agenda.

Value of Communication

Our meandering through Exhibits 12.10, 12.11, and 12.12 should convince you that it may be worthwhile for the firm to listen to its manager, but in no case would listening to the manager be more desirable than publicly observing the underlying information.[15] Indeed, there is no guarantee that communication is useful, even though the corresponding public information source has information content. One example of this is when the manager's private information is conditionally independent of the jointly observed public signal. This is illustrated in Exhibit 12.13 where you should notice that the optimal contract ignores the manager's self-report.

A second nihilistic example, one lacking in conditional independence of the private and public information sources, is presented in Exhibit 12.14.

---

[15] Of course, this bold statement rests on having only two players in our game. Suppose there were three. Then private observation and private communication to one of the parties might usefully withhold information from the third party. After all, when the bank manager shares the combination to the vault with the assistant manager, this is not also shared with all employees!

Although we gloss over the details, you should dwell on the fact that both illustrations are slight variations on the original example (Exhibit 12.10), and in both cases, the second information source is useful if it is public. Indeed, Exhibit 12.13 is our original public information Case 1 (Exhibit 12.4), and Exhibit 12.14 is our original Case 4 (Exhibit 12.7).

Summing up, we find communication of private (late) information might, or might not, be useful. It depends on whether the underlying information would be useful were it public and on the other information source. The other source now serves as a veracity check and, consequently, is central to motivating self-revelation. The extreme case, in which the two sources are conditionally independent, is one in which communication is useless because conditional independence implies no connection between the two information sources and thus no ability to use the public source as a veracity check on the self-report of the private source. Even when the two sources are dependent, however, communication is not always useful. The public source serves two purposes in the story: It is used to discipline the action choice of the manager and at the same time it is used to discipline the reporting behavior of the manger.[16] In some cases these two roles conflict, and the best solution is to ignore the communication altogether, in effect removing the use of the information for disciplining the manager's self-reporting.

Firm Better Informed

Private information is not necessarily always in the hands of the manager. The firm, the employer, might be better informed. For example, an important information variable that is useful as an evaluation measure might be privately observed by the employer. After all, the employer and the employee live in the information age. This twists part of the incentive problem upside down. The portion that provides incentives for action choice remains as before; however, the portion that disciplines the reporting now becomes a question of constraining the firm's behavior.

To give some of the flavor, suppose y_2 in our continuing story is privately observed (after the manager acts and before y_1 is publically observed as in Exhibit 12.9) by the firm. The incentive compatibility constraints now become

$$E[U \mid I, a_H, m^T] \geq E[U \mid I, a_L, m^T]$$

and

$$E[I \mid a_H, m^T] \leq E[I \mid a_H, m] \quad \text{for all } m$$

If the firm behaves by faithfully reporting what it observed (policy m^T), the first constraint requires the manager's best response be to supply a_H,

---

[16] For the first purpose, the central point is information about the action and for the second purpose, the public signal has to be correlated with the manager's private information.

EXHIBIT 12.15
Three Information
Regimes for
Additional
Illustration

	Signal $y = (y_1, y_2)$				Expected Payment to Manager
	$(0, g)$	$(0, b)$	$(1, g)$	$(1, b)$	
$\pi((y_1, y_2) \mid a_H)$	.43	.07	.40	.10	
$\pi((y_1, y_2) \mid a_L)$	.10	.20	.10	.60	
$I(y)$, y_2 public	10,526	9,064	10,517	6,975	10,065
$I(y)$, y_2 private to manager	18,063	18,063	5,595	5,595	11,829
$I(y)$, y_2 private to firm	10,314	14,340	10,297	5,969	10,155

as desired. In turn, if the manager behaves by supplying a_H, the second constraint requires that the firm's best response be to faithfully report. Notice this means that its expected payment to the manager is minimized with faithful reporting. Otherwise, the firm has no incentive to self-report what it has observed.

This leads to an important point. In Exhibit 12.15, we provide another variation on the probabilities used in the stream of illustrations. There we summarize the optimal incentive payments for three variations: The second signal is public, the second signal is privately observed by the manager, and the second signal is privately observed by the firm. Notice that the information is useful if it is public, somewhat less so if it is private but in the hands of the firm, and useless if it is private and in the hands of the manager. Moreover, when in the hands of the firm, the forthcoming public signal (y_1) is again used to discipline the reporting behavior of the informed party.[17]

The larger point should not be missed. It is one thing to say an information source is potentially useful, but it is quite another to say it can be used, or is used best, in a particular way. Part of the information story is providing the necessary incentives for that information to be produced and conveyed in the first place, and doing so has a great deal to say about how the information will be used.

OTHER TIMING POSSIBILITIES

The story to this point, information arriving late in the production process, reflects an extreme timing assumption. Realistically, the firm and its agents acquire information nearly continuously. In our stylized setting,

---

[17] Although details are wearing thin, the pattern in the incentive payments is revealing. If the second source (y_2) is public, a report of $y_2 = g$ is good news for the manager, regardless of what the first source reports. When we must also provide the firm with self-reporting incentives, however, this good news pattern is reversed when $y_1 = 0$ is reported. This is done to keep the firm's self-reporting incentives in line.

the information might arrive anywhere on the time line, perhaps before or just after capital is chosen.

To lay out some of the issues in a richer information environment, suppose that in a setting similar to that of the numerical examples, public information arrives after capital has been acquired and after the contract with the manager has been determined but before the manager's action has been selected. Two additional issues now surface: How the manager's action should vary with the information and how the manager should be motivated to follow the desired policy. For example, it might turn out that for one signal (say $y_2 = g$), action a_H is desired while for the other ($y_2 = b$), action a_L is desired. The incentive structure, again based on what is eventually reported by the two information sources, must now be designed so the manager finds it incentive compatible to supply a_H when signal g is observed but also finds it incentive compatible to supply a_L when b is observed. Of course, the strains on incentive compatibility would be even greater if this additional information were privately observed by the manager. We will return to this in the next chapter.

Summary

Our streamlined contracting model emphasizes unobservable action supply by the manager coupled with an inherent conflict of interest. This leads to pay-for-performance arrangements in which performance is used, literally, as an information source to infer the unobservable action. Equilibrium behavior is stressed, meaning the pay-for-performance arrangement is designed so the manager's best response is to supply the contracted for, although unobservable, service.

Performance, then, is an information source. It is the basis on which the manager is evaluated. Moreover, reflecting the importance of equilibrium behavior, this information source's importance depends on the contrast between what it might report if the manager supplies the desired service as opposed to engaging in opportunistic behavior.

It is, of course, natural to add additional information to this story, although doing so raises issues of timing, precisely when the additional information is available, and possession, precisely who is observing the additional information. We concentrated on "late" arrival, simultaneous to or just before the observance of the original performance variable. This stresses evaluation of the manager because, by definition, the information arrives too late in the story to be used for any other purpose. So, information content is present if the optimal contract uses the additional information. In turn, if this is the case, then the additional information must be informative about the manager's behavior. Conditional on what is learned from the original source, then, what this new source might report must depend on what the manager does. Otherwise, it offers no additional insight into what the manager actually did.

In our highly stylized setting, this ability to bring new information to the table can be identified by likelihood ratios that vary with the new source's report or, equivalently, by the conditional probability associated with those signals. Importantly, though, this ability to bring new information to the table cannot be discerned without first controlling for or conditioning on what is learned from the original information source. This is the notion of *conditional controllability*. We have repeatedly flagged the importance of identifying other information sources when studying accounting information, and this is no exception.

Of course, this additional information might be privately observed. The manager might, for example, privately observe product or factor market conditions (e.g., the fair value of inventory). Similarly, the firm might privately observe, say, benchmark statistics that it has compiled. Either way, we then expand the web of incentives to provide requisite motivation, or absence of temptations, so self-reporting that private information is a reliable exercise. Then the public information serves two purposes: one is to feed directly the evaluation of the manager, and the other is to discipline the reporting incentives of the privately informed party.

From here, we readily envision more involved timing and possession stories. The information might, for example, be a consultant's report that is delivered early in the story, even before capital is invested. Presumably, then, the firm's overall plan, including capital, labor, and managerial choices, will be influenced by the new information. Alternatively, the manager's initial task might be to study and devise a strategy for the firm, in effect turning the consultant's report into private information generated and held by the manager.

The overall message of the chapter is straightforward. Incentives heavily influence the use and dispersion of information in an organization. Using and controlling the organization's information system is a delicate matter that requires close attention to reporting incentives. Additional information might improve contracting with the manager, but not always. Additional and old information interact. It is not the information content of the information source in question that matters. It is the information content of the information source, conditional on the presence of the other source or sources. This is the essential feature of focusing on conditional controllability to determine whether a late reporting public source has information content in the contracting domain. Of course, the issue becomes more complex when the reporting incentives of the manager are considered because private information might be present. Then we expand beyond the notion of conditional controllability because dealing with the reporting incentives also enters the fray at this point. The public information source then serves two purposes, disciplining the action choice and disciplining the reporting behavior. These roles might well conflict.

Appendix

Contract Design under Late, Private Information

As sketched in (12.2), the key to contract design when the (late) information is private is to maintain incentive compatibility across all combinations of action supply and self-reporting possibilities. To develop this more fully, return to the setting of Exhibit 12.10 where there are two possible actions and two possible signals from the private information source. We have, then, eight possible modes of behavior, or strategies, available to the manager. (Recall Exhibit 12.11.) These behavior modes, or a, m pairs, are repeated in Exhibit 12.16 along with their respective induced compensation probabilities.

With private signal self-report $\hat{y}_2 \in \{g, b\}$ and public signal $y_1 \in \{0, 1\}$, there are four possible payments to the manager: $I(0, g)$, $I(0, b)$, $I(1, g)$, and $I(1, b)$. The first variable, $y_1 \in \{0, 1\}$, is public while the second, $\hat{y}_2 \in \{g, b\}$, is what the manager claims to have privately observed. So, the probability of receiving payment $I(y)$ depends on the manager's action (a) and on his reporting strategy (m). For example, if he supplies action a_H and always reports that signal g was observed (strategy 2 in Exhibit 12.16), $y = (0, g)$ will be observed with probability .50, as will $y = (1, g)$.

Continuing, if a_H and m^T are motivated with contract $I(y)$, the firm's expected compensation cost is given by

$$E[I \mid a_H, m^T] = \sum_{y \in Y} \pi(y \mid a_H) I(y)$$
$$= .40 I(0, g) + .10 I(0, b) + .20 I(1, g) + .30 I(1, b)$$

(12.3)

EXHIBIT 12.16   Induced Payment Probabilities

Strategy	Action	Report of Private Signal $y_2 = g$	Report of Private Signal $y_2 = b$	(0, g)	(0, b)	(1, g)	(1, b)
1	a_H	Report $\hat{y}_2 = g$	Report $\hat{y}_2 = b$	.40	.10	.20	.30
2	a_H	Report $\hat{y}_2 = g$	Report $\hat{y}_2 = g$	.50	0	.50	0
3	a_H	Report $\hat{y}_2 = b$	Report $\hat{y}_2 = b$	0	.50	0	.50
4	a_H	Report $\hat{y}_2 = b$	Report $\hat{y}_2 = g$	.10	.40	.30	.20
5	a_L	Report $\hat{y}_2 = g$	Report $\hat{y}_2 = b$	.10	.20	.40	.30
6	a_L	Report $\hat{y}_2 = g$	Report $\hat{y}_2 = g$	.30	0	.70	0
7	a_L	Report $\hat{y}_2 = b$	Report $\hat{y}_2 = b$	0	.30	0	.70
8	a_L	Report $\hat{y}_2 = b$	Report $\hat{y}_2 = g$	.20	.10	.30	.40

The table header spans: "a, m Pair" over "Report of Private Signal" ($y_2 = g$, $y_2 = b$), and "Signal $y = (y_1, y_2)$, y_1 Public, y_2 Private, Reported as $\hat{y}_2$" over ((0, g), (0, b), (1, g), (1, b)).

Conversely, if the manager supplies a_H and reports truthfully, his expected utility is given by

$$E[U \mid I, a_H, m^T] = .40U(I(0, g), a_H) + .10U(I(0, b), a_H)$$
$$+ .20U(I(1, g), a_H) + .30U(I(1, b), a_H)$$

where, of course, $U(I, a_H) = -\exp(-.0001(I - 5,000))$.

Incentive compatibility deals with every other combination of action and reporting strategy the manager might choose. The manager's utility score for supplying a_H but always reporting that g was observed is

$$E[U \mid I, a_H, g \text{ always}] = .50U(I(0, g), a_H) + 0U(I(0, b), a_H)$$
$$+ .50U(I(1, g), a_H) + 0U(I(1, b), a_H)$$

The remaining utility calculations are

$$E[U \mid I, a_H, b \text{ always}] = 0U(I(0, g), a_H) + .50U(I(0, b), a_H)$$
$$+ 0U(I(1, g), a_H) + .50U(I(1, b), a_H)$$

$$E[U \mid I, a_H, \text{report opposite}] = .10U(I(0, g), a_H) + .40U(I(0, b), a_H)$$
$$+ .30U(I(1, g), a_H) + .20U(I(1, b), a_H)$$

$$E[U \mid I, a_L, m^T] = .10U(I(0, g), a_L) + .20U(I(0, b), a_L)$$
$$+ .40U(I(1, g), a_L) + .30U(I(1, b), a_L)$$

$$E[U \mid I, a_L, g \text{ always}] = .30U(I(0, g), a_L) + 0U(I(0, b), a_L)$$
$$+ .70U(I(1, g), a_L) + 0U(I(1, b), a_L)$$

$$E[U \mid I, a_L, b \text{ always}] = 0U(I(0, g), a_L) + .30U(I(0, b), a_L)$$
$$+ 0U(I(1, g), a_L) + .70U(I(1, b), a_L)$$

and

$$E[U \mid I, a_L, \text{report opposite}] = .20U(I(0, g), a_L) + .10U(I(0, b), a_L)$$
$$+ .30U(I(1, g), a_L) + .40U(I(1, b), a_L)$$

From here the optimal contract is located by finding the four contractual payments, that is, $I(0, g)$, $I(0, b)$, $I(1, g)$, and $I(1, b)$ that minimize $E[I \mid a_H, m^T]$ (i.e. (12.3)) subject to the usual individual rationality constraint,

$$E[U \mid I, a_H, m^T] \geq -\exp(-.0001\,\hat{\imath}) = -\exp(-.5)$$

and subject to the following family of incentive compatibility constraints (where we engage in a slight amount of redundancy in the interest of exposition):

$$E[U \mid I, a_H, m^T] \geq E[U \mid I, a_H, g \text{ always}]$$

$$E[U \mid I, a_H, m^T] \geq E[U \mid I, a_H, b \text{ always}]$$

$$E[U \mid I, a_H, m^T] \geq E[U \mid I, a_H, \text{ report opposite}]$$

$$E[U \mid I, a_H, m^T] \geq E[U \mid I, a_L, m^T]$$

$$E[U \mid I, a_H, m^T] \geq E[U \mid I, a_L, g \text{ always}]$$

$$E[U \mid I, a_H, m^T] \geq E[U \mid I, a_L, b \text{ always}]$$

and

$$E[U \mid I, a_H, m^T] \geq E[U \mid I, a_L, \text{ report opposite}]$$

Notice that, using the numbering scheme in Exhibit 12.16, the incentive compatibility conditions require, from the manager's perspective, strategy 1 is preferred to 2, 1 is preferred to 3, 1 is preferred to 4, and so on.[18]

[18] Notice this is equivalent to the manager choosing a compensation function based upon private information. The firm specifies the menu from which the manager must choose. That choice reflects the manager's private observation. Each signal from the private information system will lead to one particular item on the menu being selected. In the reverse, each selected item of the menu will have its origin in the manager's having observed the signal that leads to that selection. The only way information is lost in this reporting scheme is if the manager chooses the same report for different signals.

The consequence of this argument is that the contract we found with the noted optimization is indeed overall optimal. Relaxing the assumption that only truth-inducing contracts were considered would not change the solution. However, an important part of this argument leading to only considering truth-telling contracts is the ability to commit. The firm commits to following the incentive scheme that was specified in the contract. As suggested by the example, this also means the firm does not fully exploit the information that is passed from the manager. Additionally, this focus on full revelation rests on optimal contracts and no aggregation in the communication process. This subtlety will resurface when we subsequently visit intertemporal accruals and "earnings management."

Selected References	The remarkable conclusion linking information content to the likelihood ratio (or, equivalently, the appropriate conditional probability) was developed by Holmstrom (1979) and Shavell (1979). Application to the so-called controllability principle is developed in Antle and Demski (1988); also see Demski (1994). Communication incentives and usefulness, with an emphasis on an informed agent or manager, are explored in, for example, Christensen (1981; 1982), Melumad and Reichelstein (1989), Christensen and Feltham (1993; 1997), and Penno (1990). Demski and Sappington (1993) stress an informed principal. Also, our work on communication presumes that it makes sense to invite full, honest communication. This is without loss of generality, and the argument goes by the name the *revelation principle*. If in some trading game the players face no explicit

costs to conveying and processing information and if they can commit up front to precisely how that information will be used, then any equilibrium in the trading game can be replicated by one in which full disclosure is motivated and engaged. We will see this used later in our study. A basic reference is provided by Myerson (1979; 1991).

Key Terms

Paralleling our earlier definitions of information content in a single-person decision-making setting or in a risk-neutral valuation setting, a single, stand-alone information source has **information content** in the managerial contracting setting if the optimal contract uses that information, if the optimal contract is a nontrivial function of what the information source might report. Turning to additional information when two information sources are present in the contracting setting, a second source has **information content in the presence of the first source** if the optimal contract, $I(y_1, y_2)$, varies in nontrivial fashion as a function of y_2 for some y_1. Closely related, we say the second source is **conditionally controllable** by the manager if the odds on what the second source reports, conditional on the first source's report, depend on the manager's action. In the basic case in which the additional information is both late and public, information content implies conditional controllability. This reflects the basic idea of contrasting good (high-action) with opportunistic (low-action) behavior conditional on what is being learned from the other source or sources.

Exercises

12.1. Explain the difference between information content in the (risk-neutral) valuation setting and in the managerial contracting setting.

12.2. Suppose we are considering the use of a second performance variable for contracting purposes in a contracting game as used throughout the present chapter. This second variable will be observed at the end of the contracting game. However, the likelihood ratio, as in (12.1), does not depend on the second source's signal. Carefully explain why this implies that the second performance variable has no information content.

12.3. Consider a setting in which two late, public information sources are present with respective signals denoted y_1 and y_2. We say the second variable is controllable by the manager if $\pi(y_2 \mid a)$ depends nontrivially on the manager's action, a. Using a setup similar to that in Exhibits 12.4 through 12.7 give four different probability matrices (i.e., $\pi((y_1, y_2) \mid a)$) such that (a) the second source is controllable and has information content; (b) the second source is controllable and lacks information content; (c) the second source is not controllable but has information content; and (d) the second source is not controllable and lacks information content. What does this tell you about relying on controllability to gauge information content?

12.4. A key notion in maintaining the manager's incentives to self-report private information is to "underutilize" that information relative to how it would be used were it public in the first place.

    a. Does this underutilization theme appear in Exhibit 12.10? Explain.

    b. Is it apparent in the use of a so-called state's witness in a criminal prosecution? Again, explain.

12.5. Return to Exhibit 12.11. Verify the expected utility calculations and associated certainty equivalents for each of the (a, m) combinations. Then draw the manager's decision tree and "roll it back" to identify the manager's optimal behavior. Explain the connection between the verified calculations and your analysis of the manager's decision tree.

12.6. This is a continuation of Exercise 11.10. Everything remains as before except that we introduce a second contracting variable. The original variable is the firm's cost exclusive of the manager's compensation. (That cost can be "high" or "low," which corresponds to $M = 1$ or $M = 3$.) The *high* action leads to a probability of α that $M = 3$; the *low* action leads to a probability of .1 that $M = 3$. (So, $\alpha = .50$ is the original story.) The new information is a monitor that will report $y_2 = good$ or *bad*. The monitor reports *good* with probability .8 if *high* is supplied; it reports *bad* with probability .8 if *low* is supplied. The monitor is otherwise independent of M. (Technically, $\pi(y_2 \mid M, a) = \pi(y_2 \mid a)$.) So, with cost and the monitor, we have four possible combinations of performance events: "high" and *good,* "high" and *bad,* "low" and *good,* and "low" and *bad.* Determine Ralph's optimal contract offer for $\alpha \in \{.5, .6, .7, .8, .9, .95, 1\}$. Explain your findings.

12.7. This is a continuation of Exercise 12.6. Everything remains as before in the imperfect market setting in which we must rely on pay-for-performance with the manager except that we now have a different information source. Joint probabilities are given in the following table where the first variable is, again, the firm's cost exclusive of the manager's compensation. (That cost can be "high" or "low," which corresponds to $M = 1$ or $M = 3$.)

	Signal $y = (y_1, y_2)$			
	(3, *g*)	**(3, *b*)**	**(1, *g*)**	**(1, *b*)**
$\pi(y \mid a_H)$	.25	.25	.45	.05
$\pi(y \mid a_L)$	.09	.01	.01	.89

    a. Find the optimal contract when only the first signal is available for contracting.

b. Find the optimal contract when only the second signal is available for contracting.

c. Find the optimal contract when both signals are available for contracting.

d. Contrast your contracts.

12.8. Suppose that in Exercise 12.7, the second signal is privately observed by the manager after acting and will be self-reported before the cost variable is observed. Is the originally determined contract feasible? Explain. Determine and interpret an optimal contract.

12.9. Repeat Exercise 12.8 for the case in which the firm rather than the manager privately observes the second variable.

12.10. Repeat Exercise 12.8, but now assume that the private information arrives after the cost variable is observed. Explain your findings.

12.11. Repeat Exercises 12.8 and 12.9, but assuming the following joint probabilities

| | Signal $y = (y_1, y_2)$ | | | |
	(3, g)	(3, b)	(1, g)	(1, b)
$\pi(y \mid a_H)$	.20	.30	.45	.05
$\pi(y \mid a_L)$	.05	.05	.45	.45

12.12. Consider a setting as described in Exhibit 12.1 where two information sources are present and where the second signal, $y_2 = g$ or $y_2 = b$, is public but is observed after capital (K) is chosen but before the manager's action and subsequent labor supply are chosen. Probabilities and some suggestive polices follow.

| | Signal $y = (y_1, y_2)$ | | | |
	(0, g)	(0, b)	(1, g)	(1, b)
$\pi((y_1, y_2) \mid a_H)$	.30	.20	.20	.30
$\pi((y_1, y_2) \mid a_L)$	.25	.05	.25	.45
$I(y)$, a_H always	31,682	15,848	1,548	7,413
$I(y)$, a_H only under $y_2 = b$	8,000	15,848	8,000	7,413

a. One possibility is to motivate the manager to supply a_H regardless of what information is received. Verify that the contract denoted "a_H always" makes it in the manager's best interest both to accept that contract and to supply a_H for each possible signal from the second source.

b. Another possibility is to motivate the manager to supply a_L when $y_2 = g$ is observed and a_H when $y_2 = b$ is observed. Verify that the contract denoted "a_H only under $y_2 = b$" makes it in the manager's best interest both to accept that contract and to follow the desired action supply policy. The cost to the firm of this second policy is $E[I \,|\, a_H$ only under $y_2 = b] = 9{,}394$, which is substantially less than the cost of the high-action always policy, $E[I \,|\, a_H$ always$] = 15{,}208$. What explains this dramatic reduction in contracting cost?

c. Finally, to fully contrast the two managerial action policies, we must track through the corresponding labor and capital choices. Determine the firm's total cost of producing the noted 1,000 units using the (1) a_H always and (2) a_H only under $y_2 = b$ policies. (*Hint:* $K = 1{,}015.14$ under the first policy and $K = 1{,}025.14$ under the second, although you should derive these conclusions on your own.)

Chapter 13

Conflict among Uses

We now combine the valuation and contracting themes. This is an important, essential step because information content in the valuation setting does not imply information content in the contracting setting and vice versa. To develop this insight, we continue with the contracting story of Chapter 12 but switch from late to early information and concentrate on public information. From here we apply our information content lens in both the valuation and contracting spheres. As you will see, there is no guarantee that information content in one domain is associated with information content in the other. Moreover, it is possible to have information content in both domains yet have the firm worse off, have value destroyed, so to speak, by virtue of producing the information. This is the reason we identify valuation and contracting uses and the reason we continue to stress the folly of simple answers in the world of accounting theory.

Having completed our (admittedly long but nonetheless abbreviated) examination of information in valuation and managerial contracting settings, we turn to the important topic of *conflict*. Casual conversation and even formal rhetoric often suggest that information content in one domain implies information content in another. For example, we often hear of the importance of stressing "value added" in evaluating and compensating upper management, thereby implicitly suggesting that a valuation-based approach is the appropriate approach to evaluating the management. We are equally familiar with the FASB's focus on valuation essentials,[1] for example.

---

[1] The IASC, now the IASB, has a similar focus: "The providers of risk capital and their advisers are concerned with the risk inherent in, and returns provided by, their investments. They need information to help them determine whether they should buy, hold, or sell. Shareholders are also interested in information which enables them to assess the ability of the enterprise to pay dividends." (IASC, 1989, Section 9(a)).

FASB (1978), *Concepts Statement No. 1*, paragraph 34, states

> Financial reporting should provide information that is useful to present and potential investors and creditors and other users in making rational investment, credit, and similar decisions.

The following is from FASB (1980a), *Concepts Statement No. 4*, paragraph 35:

> Financial reporting by nonbusiness organizations should provide information that is useful to present and potential resource providers and other users in making rational decisions about the allocation of resources to those organizations.

It turns out, however, there is no necessary connection between information that is useful, has information content, in a valuation setting and information that is useful in a labor-contracting setting. The underlying reason is straightforward: Information can reduce or increase trade frictions, and its effect can vary highly from setting to setting. Early disclosure might be welcomed by the financial market, other things equal, but such disclosure might tip the firm's hand and diminish its competitive advantage. Detailed monitoring by, for example, the board of directors' compensation committee might be essential but of no explicit relevance in the valuation market as long as it is well known that the monitoring is indeed taking place (and if the monitoring result is highly predictable when the management team is well functioning). Aggressive release of information may indeed weaken the usefulness of that information in the control arena. For example, it would be foolish for a bank to publicly reveal that its surveillance cameras were not working! All in all, this suggests a far more delicate approach to modeling and managing the firm's information practices.

We rely again on our prototypical reporting firm to document the possibilities: information that is useful in both settings, information that is useful in only one of the settings, and information that is useful in one setting but harmful in the other. From there we turn to broader issues of disclosure.

EXPANDED SETTING WITH PUBLIC, "EARLY" INFORMATION

As in Chapter 12, we focus on a setting in which the firm is committed to supplying a customer a stated number of units ($q = 1,000$). As usual, capital (K), labor (L), and managerial (M) inputs are mixed in light of prices and trading frictions, and input M is a random variable under the influence of the manager.

In the simplest case this managerial input can be low (M_L) or high (M_H), and low input is dealt with by hiring additional labor. The productive

EXHIBIT 13.1

Time Line with $y_2 \in \{g, b\}$ **Preceding Manager's Action Choice**

Contract $I(y_1, y_2)$	Public observation $y_2 \in \{g, b\}$	Action choice $a \in \{a_L, a_H\}$	Public observation $y_1 \in \{0, 1\}$	Payment to agent $I(y_1, y_2)$

EXHIBIT 13.2

Details for Series of Illustrations

Firm details

Output quantity	$q = 1,000$
Managerial input	$M_H = 1.1$ and $M_L = .9$
Managerial input odds	$\pi(M = M_H \mid a_H) = .75$ and $\pi(M = M_H \mid a_L) = .2$
Capacity constraint	$K^{max} = 1,500$

Manager details

Risk-aversion coefficient	$\rho = .0001$
Opportunity certainty equivalent	$\hat{\imath} = 5,000$
Personal costs	$c_H = 5,000$ and $c_L = 3,000$

Market prices

Capital	$p_K = 100$
Labor	$p_L = 100$

managerial input, M_H, is more likely when the manager supplies high (a_H) as opposed to low action (a_L). Thus, the evaluation issue is whether additional labor is (i.e., $M = M_L$) or is not (i.e., $M = M_H$) required. To highlight the underlying information theme, this cost event is again coded as $y_1 = 1$ (high cost via $M = M_L$) or $y_1 = 0$ (low cost via $M = M_H$).

We now impose a public information source that will once again report $y_2 = g$ or $y_2 = b$. Importantly, though, this second source is now observed at an earlier point on the time line: after capital (K) is acquired but before the manager's action (a) is supplied. So, the timing is as follows: Capital is acquired and signal $y_2 \in \{g, b\}$ is then observed; managerial action $a \in \{a_H, a_L\}$ and initial labor L are next supplied; finally, $M \in \{M_H, M_L\}$ is observed and supplemental labor, if necessary, is supplied.[2] The timing details, as they pertain to contracting with the manager, are summarized in Exhibit 13.1, and remaining details are summarized in Exhibit 13.2.

Before proceeding, though, it is important to identify the expanded contracting problem that is associated with these timing details. The manager's compensation depends on signals y_1 and y_2, yet the manager already has observed signal y_2 when it is time to make the action choice.

---

[2] Recall that capital K and labor L are chosen so

$$\text{output } q = 1,000 = M_H \sqrt{KL}$$

If $M_L < M_H$ is observed, however, supplemental labor is chosen to satisfy

$$q = M_L \sqrt{K(L + L')}$$

EXHIBIT 13.3
Probability
Specification for
Illustrative Case

	Signal $y = (y_1, y_2)$			
	$(0, g)$	$(0, b)$	$(1, g)$	$(1, b)$
$\pi(y \mid a_H)$	.45	.30	.05	.20
$\pi(y \mid a_L)$	.20	0	.30	.50
$\pi(y \mid y_2 = g, a_H)$	.90	0	.10	0
$\pi(y \mid y_2 = g, a_L)$	.40	0	.60	0
$\pi(y \mid y_2 = b, a_H)$	0	.60	0	.40
$\pi(y \mid y_2 = b, a_L)$	0	0	0	1
$I(y_1, y_2)$	10,453	11,597	6,646	8,000

This expands the incentive compatibility issues because we have to worry about what the manager knows at the time of action choice.

To see this, consider the probability specification, $\pi((y_1, y_2) \mid a)$ in Exhibit 13.3, and assume that we want the manager to supply high action regardless of what the early reporting information source has to say. Furthermore, suppose the early reporting source reports $y_2 = g$. At the time of action choice, then, the manager already knows $y_2 = g$, so the remaining uncertainty is characterized by the revised probability assessment, $\pi(y \mid y_2 = g, a)$, displayed in Exhibit 13.3.

At this point and facing compensation schedule $I(y_1, y_2)$, the manager evaluates the high and low action options as follows:

$$E[U \mid I, y_2 = g, a_H] = -.90 \exp(-\rho(I(0, g) - 5,000))$$
$$-.10 \exp(-\rho(I(1, g) - 5,000))$$

and

$$E[U \mid I, y_2 = g, a_L] = -.40 \exp(-\rho(I(0, g) - 3,000))$$
$$-.60 \exp(-\rho(I(1, g) - 3,000))$$

Likewise, had $y_2 = b$ been observed, the evaluations would be

$$E[U \mid I, y_2 = b, a_H] = -.60 \exp(-\rho(I(0, b) - 5,000))$$
$$-.40 \exp(-\rho(I(1, b) - 5,000))$$

and

$$E[U \mid I, y_2 = b, a_L] = -\exp(-\rho(I(1, b) - 3,000))$$

Now, by assumption, we want the manager to select a_H in each instance. This implies the incentive function, $I(y_1, y_2)$, must simultaneously satisfy $E[U \mid I, y_2 = g, a_H] \geq E[U \mid I, y_2 = g, a_L]$ and $E[U \mid I, y_2 = b, a_H] \geq E[U \mid I, y_2 = b, a_L]$. That is, we have a separate incentive compatibility concern for each signal the manager might observe.

In turn, if the manager so behaves, the contractual arrangement viewed at the start before the first information arrives is

$$E[U \mid I, a_H \text{ always}]$$
$$= -.45 \exp(-\rho(I(0, g) - 5,000)) - .30 \exp(-\rho(I(0, b) - 5,000))$$
$$- .05 \exp(-\rho(I(1, g) - 5,000)) - .20 \exp(-\rho(I(1, b) - 5,000))$$

If this is going to be attractive for the manager, it must satisfy the usual individual rationality condition, here expressed as $E[U \mid I, a_H \text{ always}] \geq -\exp(-\rho \hat{\imath})$.

Using the remaining details in Exhibit 13.2, the optimal contract is the solution to[3]

$$\min_{I(y)} E[I \mid a_H \text{ always}] = .45I(0, g) + .30I(0, b) + .05I(1, g) + .20I(1, b)$$

subject to: $E[U \mid I, a_H \text{ always}] \geq -\exp(-\rho \hat{\imath}) = -\exp(-.5)$

$$E[U \mid I, y_2 = g, a_H] \geq E[U \mid I, y_2 = g, a_L]$$

$$E[U \mid I, y_2 = b, a_H] \geq E[U \mid I, y_2 = b, a_L]$$

The solution is also displayed in Exhibit 13.3, and the firm's cost of contracting for "a_H always" in this environment is $E[I \mid a_H \text{ always}] = 10,115$.

In the following section we examine a number of closely related cases, all geared to the joint probability $\pi((y_1, y_2) \mid a)$. With the additional information arriving just before the manager's action choice is finalized, it is possible that the information will be useful in directing that choice. The cases are designed, however, so the firm always finds it efficient to acquire high action from the manager regardless of signal $y_2 \in \{g, b\}$. This ensures we are dealing with the same underlying managerial activity as we work through the cases.

SIMULTANEOUS INFORMATION CONTENT

The overriding question is whether introducing public signal $y_2 \in \{g, b\}$ at the noted time is a good idea. This is addressed in two venues. First, does the second signal improve the firm's contracting with the manager? Does it lower the expected value of the manager's compensation, given we continue to motivate supply of high action by the manager? Stated differently, does the new information lower the firm's cost of acquiring the managerial factor? This is a contracting setting.

Second, does the second signal improve the predictability of the firm's overall results? Here, with the firm committed to supplying $q = 1,000$ units, we concentrate on what can be learned about its expenditures on capital and labor: $p_K K + p_L L$ if no supplemental labor is required (if managerial input $M = M_H(y_1 = 0)$ occurs) or $p_K K + p_L(L + L')$ if supplemental labor is required (if $M = M_L(y_1 = 1)$ occurs). Stated differently, does the new information inform about whether the firm will subsequently

---

[3] Thus, the optimal incentive arrangement is located in the usual fashion; the only novelty is that incentive compatibility must now address the manager's behavior when $y_2 = g$ is observed and when $y_2 = b$ is observed:

$$\hat{\imath} = \min_{I(y)} E[I \mid a_H \text{ always}] = \sum_{y \in Y} I(y)\pi(y \mid a_H)$$

subject to: $E[U \mid I, a_H \text{ always}] \geq -\exp(-\rho \hat{\imath})$

$$E[U \mid I, a_H, y_2 = g] \geq E[U \mid I, a_L, y_2 = g], \text{ and}$$

$$E[U \mid I, a_H, y_2 = b] \geq E[U \mid I, a_L, y_2 = b]$$

incur supplemental labor cost? This is a valuation setting in which we have purposely focused on the totality of the firm's activities exclusive of the contracting for managerial factor M.

Combining these themes leads to a focus on simultaneous information content, i.e., information content in both the valuation and contracting venues. Two features of the exploration should be kept in mind. First, since the new information arrives before the manager acts, it provides the manager additional possibilities including opportunism temptations. The manager can be more selective here, thanks to the new information arriving early in the game. This might lead to improved decision making because the action can be fine tuned to the environment, but it might also lead to an increased control problem because the manager knows more about the controls he is facing. We thus have a tension between expanding opportunities, including temptations, and an expanding evaluation base. As we shall see, the implied horse race can be positive or negative.

Second, our focus on the valuation side is whether the new information alters the expected value of the firm's cash flow (in the single-period setting). This focus on the expected value is convenient but problematic. After all, with risk-neutral valuation in a well-functioning valuation market, two instruments with the same initial cash flow distributions would be priced identically, even if one had more intermediate information releases than the other.[4]

Two-Sided Information Content

Our initial case illustrates the intuitive possibility that the new information is useful simultaneously in contracting and in forecasting the firm's results. The probability specification is none other than the earlier illustration in Exhibit 13.3.

We already know the optimal contract provided the information is present and provided it is optimal to motivate "a_H always," but the wisdom of motivating "a_H always" is not obvious. If the manager supplies a_H always, $M = M_L$, the event when supplemental labor is required, will occur

---

[4] Notice we are asking whether the second source has information content. This is straightforward on the valuation side. The new information arrives before the original source reports; so, we merely ask whether the new source has information content at the time it reports. This boils down to asking whether the expected value of the firm's expenditures on capital and labor vary nontrivially with signal $y_2 \in \{g, b\}$. Simply stated, the second source has information content in the valuation domain if it will affect the time path of valuation. Information content in the contracting side, though, is a somewhat different issue. The manager's compensation depends on all information accumulated through the encounter; so, here we focus on information content of the second source, given the first source is also reporting. As you will see, though, our focus is on whether the new information allows the firm to lower its cost of acquiring the (high-action) services of the manager. This is more subtle than simply documenting whether the new information is used in nontrivial fashion in the efficient contracting arrangement. The difficulty is that the manager's choice between low and high action is now informed by the new information, so the control problem expands to each information event the manager might encounter, and it is possible for contracting cost to increase even though the efficient contract uses the new information.

with probability .25. (Reading from Exhibit 13.3, we see $\pi(y_1 = 1 \mid a_H$ always$) = .05 + .20 = .25$). The best capital (K) and labor (L) to mix with a_H always is now located in the following, hopefully familiar, fashion:

$$C(q; a_H \text{ always}) \equiv \underset{K,L,L' \geq 0}{\text{minimum}} \; p_K K + p_L(L + \pi(y_1 = 1 \mid a_H \text{ always})L')$$

$$+ E[I \mid a_H \text{ always}]$$

$$\text{subject to}: q \leq M_H \sqrt{KL};$$

$$q \leq M_L \sqrt{K(L + L')}; \text{ and}$$

$$K \leq K^{\max}$$

Solving this in our particular case provides $K = 963.57$, $L = 857.69$, and $L' = 423.55$, implying $C(q; a_H \text{ always}) = 192{,}715 + 10{,}115 = 202{,}830$. Moreover, the firm's expenditures on capital and labor will total 182,126 if no supplemental labor is required and 224,481 otherwise.

From here we must test the other policies: contract for "a_L always," for "a_H only under $y_2 = g$," and for "a_H only under $y_2 = b$." Matching each combination with the best associated choices of K and L, we determine that "a_H always" is indeed the efficient arrangement. In the hope of fostering a productive working relationship between authors and readers, though, we spare you the details.

With these ancillary details in place, we redisplay the presumed probability structure and optimal contract in Exhibit 13.4. Notice that the optimal arrangement does indeed use the $y_2 \in \{g, b\}$ observation, increasing the steepness of the incentives when $y_2 = g$ is observed. We also display in Exhibit 13.4 the benchmark solution for motivating high action when the second source of information is not present. This is contract $\bar{I}(y_1)$ in Exhibit 13.4. Also notice that it is less costly (in expectation) to the firm to acquire the manager's services when the information is present, but this is only part of the story.[5]

Given "a_H always" is the optimal policy, will public observation of signal $y_2 \in \{g, b\}$ be useful in the valuation arena? The primary issue here is whether the firm's costs will eventually turn out to be high or low. Low cost

---

[5] This is the horse race mentioned earlier. Here the additional information allows for fine tuning the incentives and to such an extent that we overcome the additional friction of having to satisfy incentive compatibility conditions for each signal rather than for an uninformed manager. Also, the benchmark case in which the additional information is absent is identified in the usual case. We contract on only the first signal, using the probability structure implied by Exhibit 13.4:

	Signal y_1	
	$y_1 = 0$	$y_1 = 1$
$\pi(y \mid a_H)$	.75	.25
$\pi(y \mid a_L)$	.20	.80
$\bar{I}(y_1)$	11,061	7,362

The optimal contract, denoted $\bar{I}(y_1)$, has an expected value of $E[\bar{I} \mid a_H] = 10{,}136$.

EXHIBIT 13.4
Case 1 with
$E[I \mid a_H \text{ always}] =$
10,115 (vs. $E[\bar{I} \mid a_H] =$
10,136 absent y_2)

	Signal $y = (y_1, y_2)$			
	(0, g)	**(0, b)**	**(1, g)**	**(1, b)**
$\pi(y \mid a_H)$	.45	.30	.05	.20
$\pi(y \mid a_L)$	.20	0	.30	.50
$I(y_1, y_2)$	10,453	11,597	6,646	8,000
$\bar{I}(y_1)$	11,061	11,061	7,362	7,362

EXHIBIT 13.5
Case 2 with
$E[I \mid a_H \text{ always}] =$
10,225 (vs. $E[\bar{I} \mid a_H] =$
10,188 absent y_2)

	Signal $y = (y_1, y_2)$			
	(0, g)	**(0, b)**	**(1, g)**	**(1, b)**
$\pi(y \mid a_H)$	.40	.30	.10	.20
$\pi(y \mid a_L)$	.10	.10	.40	.40
$I(y_1, y_2)$	10,767	12,503	7,413	7,132
$\bar{I}(y_1)$	11,425	11,425	7,300	7,300

is associated with factor $M = M_H$ or $y_1 = 0$. Glance back at Exhibit 13.4. Absent any information, the probability of low cost is $\pi(y_1 = 0 \mid a_H) = .45 + .30 = .75$. Having observed signal y_2, however, this probability increases under $y_2 = g$ but decreases under $y_2 = b$:

$$\pi(M = M_H \mid a_H, y_2 = g) = \pi(y_1 = 0 \mid a_H, y_2 = g) = .45/(.45 + .05) = .90$$

and

$$\pi(M = M_H \mid a_H, y_2 = b) = \pi(y_1 = 0 \mid a_H, y_2 = b) = .30/(.30 + .20) = .60$$

Thus, we see that the second information source in this setting provides information used both for valuing the firm's prospects and for contracting with its manager. Information content is present in both arenas.

Perverse Information Content

This happy state of affairs, though, is not guaranteed. In our streamlined setting, the new information will or will not be useful in predicting whether the firm's costs will be high or low. The worst case simply tells us nothing about the firm's prospects and is therefore of no use in the valuation arena. So, from a valuation perspective, the information in this setting is either useful or neutral.[6] The contracting side, however, is another story.

Case 2 in Exhibit 13.5 is illustrative. If the new information is not available, the firm's best choice is to motivate the supply of high action, and the firm's contracting cost is $E[\bar{I} \mid a_H] = 10,188$. (This is contract $\bar{I}(y_1)$ in Exhibit 13.5.) If the new information is introduced, however, the added

---

[6] In other words, the new, early information source either tells us something about the forthcoming cash flows or it does not. In the risk-neutral case, this boils down to asking whether it tells us something about the expected value of the cash flows. More broadly, suppose the market priced the risk as well. Then the question would be whether the information tells us something about either the expected value or about the risk that is being priced.

friction of expanding the control system to motivate high action from an informed manager results in a higher contracting cost, $E[I \mid a_H \text{ always}] = 10{,}225 > 10{,}188$.

Working through the remaining details, it remains optimal to motivate "a_H always" in this setting. Moreover, the public information is again used in the valuation setting:

$$\pi(M = M_H \mid a_H, y_2 = g) = \pi(y_1 = 0 \mid a_H, y_2 = g) = .40/(.40 + .10) = .80$$

and

$$\pi(M = M_H \mid a_H, y_2 = b) = \pi(y_1 = 0 \mid a_H, y_2 = b) = .30/(.30 + .20) = .60$$

We thus have a setting in which the firm's total cost actually increases if the information is produced, even though that information is used in the valuation setting.[7] Information content can be a mixed blessing!

An additional observation here is the fact that the optimal contract actually uses the new information when it is available. On the surface, then, the information is used in the contracting domain; it appears to be useful. The firm, however, is not in the position of denying the existence of the information, given it is available. Here the best way to deal with the fact that the information is public is to explicitly incorporate it into the contracting arrangement, but the firm would be strictly better off if the information were simply not available.[8]

---

[7] We find $K = 974.11$, $L = 848.42$, and $L' = 418.97$, implying $C(q; a_H \text{ always}) = 194{,}821 + 10{,}225 = 205{,}046$; and the firm's expenditures on capital and labor will total 182,252 if no supplemental labor is required and 224,149 otherwise. Added to this is the firm's cost of acquiring factor M, which is $E[I \mid a_H \text{ always}] = 10{,}225$ if the information is produced but $E[\bar{I} \mid a_H] = 10{,}188$ if it is not produced.

[8] For that matter, it is possible to have no information content in the valuation domain coupled with the firm's being harmed by the presence of the information. The following is illustrative:

	Signal $y = (y_1, y_2)$			
	(0, g)	**(0, b)**	**(1, g)**	**(1, b)**
$\pi(y \mid a_H)$	.25	.25	.25	.25
$\pi(y \mid a_L)$	.10	.15	.40	.35
$I(y_1, y_2)$	14,605	18,063	6,859	5,595
$\bar{I}(y_1)$	15,848	15,848	6,334	6,334

Working through the details, you will discover that it is optimal to motivate high action in all cases; given this, the first signal carries no information whatever about whether the firm's labor cost will eventually be high or low. In addition, $E[I \mid a_H \text{ always}] = 11{,}280 > E[\bar{I} \mid a_H] = 11{,}091$.

The lack of use in the valuation domain depends on $\pi(y_1 = 0 \mid a_H, y_2) = \pi(y_1 = 0 \mid a_H)$. A modest change in $\pi(y \mid a_H)$ will, of course, lead to signal y_2 being informative here. So, the illustration is a razor's edge case, but the noted modest change will also ensure that the change in the expected value of the firm's expenditures on capital and labor is itself modest. So, an alternative interpretation is that the second source of information is of first-order importance in the contracting domain but of second-order importance in the valuation domain.

One-Sided Information Content

It is also possible that we may have information content in one domain but its complete absence in the other. This stems from the fact that the valuation exercise focuses on the firm's equilibrium cash flow prospects while the contracting exercise supports that equilibrium via its threat, so to speak, of what might be reported should the manager behave opportunistically. In our series of cases in which "a_H always" is the equilibrium, information content in the valuation setting rests on $\pi(y_1 \mid a_H)$ while in the contracting setting it rests on $\pi(y \mid a_H)$ versus $\pi(y \mid a_L)$.

Illustrating the one-sided possibility requires slightly more degrees of freedom in our running setup. So, for the next few paragraphs, suppose the managerial input can be $M = 1.1$, $M = 1.0$, or $M = .9$. Code these respectively as $y_1 = 0, 1,$ or 2. Supplemental labor then will be nil, modest, or large. The assumed probability structure is given in Exhibit 13.6.

The setting is again designed so "a_H always" is the optimal policy. The firm's cost, however, can now be low, medium, or high. Notice that low cost ($y_1 = 0$) is more likely and medium cost ($y_1 = 1$) is less likely when $y_2 = g$ is observed while the opposite is true when $y_2 = b$ is observed. The second information source clearly exhibits information content in the valuation domain.

The contracting side, though, is another story. The high-cost odds do not vary with what the second source might report, and the optimal incentive arrangement does not distinguish low from medium cost. (This should be clear from the likelihood ratios.) So, we wind up with a setting in which the additional information is not useful in the contracting domain if it is present but does not pollute the underlying control problem. All the action, so to speak, is on the valuation side.

The opposite is also readily illustrated. Consider Case 4 in Exhibit 13.7. We begin with a specification in which the new information, $y_2 \in \{g, b\}$, tells us nothing about what the firm's cost might be (given policy "a_H always," which continues to be optimal). The off-equilibrium story, though, is quite different. If $y_2 = g$, $y_1 = 1$ is bad news, but if $y_2 = b$, $y_1 = 2$ is bad news. (Again, this should be clear from the likelihood ratios.) Importantly, the new information allows the incentive structure to be fine tuned to the environment, and this fine tuning outweighs any pollution caused by the manager's being better informed before acting.

	Signal $y = (y_1, y_2)$					
	(0, g)	**(0, b)**	**(1, g)**	**(1, b)**	**(2, g)**	**(2, b)**
$\pi(y \mid a_H)$	.35	.25	.05	.15	.10	.10
$\pi(y \mid a_L)$	0	0	0	0	.50	.50
$I(y_1, y_2)$	10,569	10,569	10,569	10,569	8,000	8,000
$\bar{I}(y_1)$	10,569	10,569	10,569	10,569	8,000	8,000

EXHIBIT 13.6
Case 3 with $E[I \mid a_H] = 10{,}056$ (vs. $E[\bar{I} \mid a_H] = 10{,}056$ absent y_2)

EXHIBIT 13.7
Case 4 with
$E[I \mid a_H] = 10,024$
(vs. $E[\bar{I} \mid a_H] =$
10,055 absent y_2)

	Signal $y = (y_1, y_2)$					
	(0, g)	(0, b)	(1, g)	(1, b)	(2, g)	(2, b)
$\pi(y \mid a_H)$	.40	.40	.05	.05	.05	.05
$\pi(y \mid a_L)$	0	0	.50	0	0	.50
$I(y_1, y_2)$	10,249	10,249	8,000	10,249	10,249	8,000
$\bar{I}(y_1)$	10,569	10,569	8,000	8,000	8,000	8,000

We thus have a setting in which the second information source provides information content in the contracting domain but not in the valuation domain.[9]

Clearly, now, the valuation and contracting domains are not coextensive. We cannot focus, for example, on a valuation perspective and hope to capture the full flavor of the reporting firm's information stew. The two do not move in tandem because they concentrate on different aspects of the reporting environment.

Our particular exploration highlighted a single-period setting in which the additional information arrived after contracting and capital acquisition arrangements had been made but before the manager's action supply was in place. The new information, then, might inform (or not inform) about the firm's prospects. It also might be of help in the contracting arena, be neutral, or be negative. The latter is possible because additional information that arrives before the manager acts is a "two-edged sword." It might allow for fine tuning the action decision to the underlying environment, but it also might increase the opportunism opportunities.[10]

Yet Another Story

What happens, then, if we alter the time at which the new information arrives? To glimpse the possibilities, suppose the new public information arrives late in the game after the manager acts but before the firm's labor expenditures are known (i.e., before $y_1 \in \{0, 1\}$ is observed).[11] This means the information cannot increase the opportunism opportunities because it arrives too late in the game. It can be useful, however, in evaluating the manager, as well as in predicting the firm's prospects.

[9] Naturally, strictly useless in the valuation domain is a razor's edge case, but as noted before, a slight modification will render the valuation effect positive but of clearly second-order importance.
[10] Although we spare you the details, an utterly random second signal would provide a setting in which information content was lacking in both the valuation and contracting domains.
[11] An alternative is to move the new information even earlier in time so the firm's capital choice can also be influenced by the information.

Consider the probability structure in Exhibit 13.8. This is a modest variation of the original story in Exhibits 13.3 and 13.4; all other details remain as before except that the new information, $y_2 \in \{g, b\}$, arrives after the manager acts. (So, acquiring $a = a_H$ remains optimal although we skip the details, thankfully.)

The trick here is that the new information is a perfect monitor: It will report $y_2 = g$ only if action $a = a_H$ is supplied (and $y_2 = b$ only if action $a = a_L$ is supplied). With a perfect monitor, the well-behaved manager is guaranteed a payment of 10,000 just as the opportunistic manager is guaranteed a payment of zero! In equilibrium, action $a = a_H$ is surely supplied, signal $y_2 = g$ is surely observed, and we learn at that time nothing whatever about the firm's prospects. The information is clearly important in the contracting domain ($E[I \mid a_H] = 10{,}000$ vs. $E[\bar{I} \mid a_H] = 10{,}136$ absent y_2) and utterly useless in the valuation domain.

Just the opposite surfaces in Exhibit 13.9. There the information is clearly useful in the valuation domain because either signal has positive probability when the manager behaves, and each carries different implications for whether the firm will require supplemental labor:

$$\pi(M = M_H \mid a_H, y_2 = g) = \pi(y_1 = 0 \mid a_H, y_2 = g) = .50/(.50 + .10) = 5/6$$

and

$$\pi(M = M_H \mid a_H, y_2 = b) = \pi(y_1 = 0 \mid a_H, y_2 = b) = .25/(.25 + .15) = 5/8$$

Equally clear is the fact that the information is useless in the contracting domain. Indeed, we designed the setting so the likelihood ratios do not depend on the new information.

The conflict, then, does not depend on our timing assumptions. Information content may be present in both or in only one of the settings, given

EXHIBIT 13.8
Case 1A with
$E[I \mid a_H] = 10{,}000$
(vs. $E[\bar{I} \mid a_H] =$
$10{,}136$ absent y_2)

	Signal $y = (y_1, y_2)$			
	(0, g)	**(0, b)**	**(1, g)**	**(1, b)**
$\pi(y \mid a_H)$	.75	0	.25	0
$\pi(y \mid a_L)$	0	.20	0	.80
$I(y_1, y_2)$	10,000	0	10,000	0
$\bar{I}(y_1)$	11,061	11,061	7,362	7,362

EXHIBIT 13.9
Case 1B with
$E[I \mid a_H] = 10{,}136$
(vs. $E[\bar{I} \mid a_H] =$
$10{,}136$ absent y_2)

	Signal $y = (y_1, y_2)$			
	(0, g)	**(0, b)**	**(1, g)**	**(1, b)**
$\pi(y \mid a_H)$	.50	.25	.10	.15
$\pi(y \mid a_L)$	2/15	1/15	.32	.48
$I(y_1, y_2)$	11,061	11,061	7,362	7,362
$\bar{I}(y_1)$	11,061	11,061	7,362	7,362

that it arrives "late" in the game. Information content comes in a variety of settings and flavors.

FULL AND FAIR DISCLOSURE

In a larger sense, two themes are being mixed in this chapter. One is the importance of understanding potential use beyond that of the traditional valuation emphasis. The control side is ever present. We have used managerial contracting as a prototypical setting laden with contracting frictions, but the underlying theme of dealing with frictions extends to most settings in which we encounter strategic behavior, and information clearly has an impact on such behavior. The insight here is the fact that information content in one domain does not imply information content in the other. Second is the sheer delicacy of information. By no means does it follow that "more" information is better than "less" information even if it is not costly to produce and use that information. Information content can be present even though it is inefficient to produce that information in the first place.

Of course, in a strictly single-person setting—the proverbial Robinson Crusoe setting—"more" information is better than "less" information, and there is no possibility for *perverse* information content. It is, however, naive to extend this observation to interactive settings as it is to presume that content in one domain implies content (or at least no harm) in another setting.

This leads to the broader issue of disclosure in general. What information about the reporting firm should be produced and distributed both within and across its boundaries? The straightforward, if exasperating, answer is that "it all depends." There is simply no general rule or guideline.[12]

Our modest exploration here illustrates the fact that additional information in the hands of the manager can increase the control problem, the trade frictions encountered, but this only scratches the surface. A larger perspective would focus on strategically creating, reducing, and maintaining the trade frictions. For example, the firm may or may not want its competitors to know what it knows. A well-timed new product announcement may keep the customer base from jumping to a competitor just as it might deter entry by a rival. On the other hand, the firm might be foolish to announce a setback in its new product development efforts. Similarly, the firm expects its auditor, its consultant, and its investment banker not to share its proprietary information.

---

[12] An added dimension is the question of to whom this information should be distributed. The SEC has, for example, stringent disclosure regulations that are aimed at preventing some classes of investors from being advantaged over other classes simply because of more timely access to management's disclosures.

We also know that longer-term relationships—arrangements with suppliers, labor sources, and customer groups, for example—are often renegotiated. Renegotiation, though, can be dramatically affected by information, again suggesting that the story is much deeper than ensuring that the firm report all it knows or might know.

Multiple producers of information are also commonplace. This suggests that reactive response to disclosures is an important institutional detail. To illustrate, suppose a new financial reporting regulation calls for some additional disclosure. Will management then alter what it reports in advance of the forthcoming financial report? Will institutional actors seek more or less information knowing that these additional disclosures are forthcoming? Indeed, we would expect far from passive behavior by the parties in such a setting.

Summary

We have a tendency in our study of accounting to focus on specific settings, for example, financial reporting, and what should be disclosed to the financial market or managerial reporting and what financial (and nonfinancial) measures are most useful inside the organization. We also know, however, that accounting is multipurpose and that reports aimed at the financial sector inform us about management's stewardship. This raises the question of conflict between or among the various purposes.

The folklore here is comforting: A focus on the financial sector will sort this all out; what is best for the financial sector is best for contracting. After all, we should, in one of today's colloquialisms, emphasize value creation, and what better way to do that than to use "the market"? Accounting in all its spheres should prove a value-added service, so the argument goes, and this implies an unwavering focus on the valuation market.

The difficulty is that markets are not complete and perfect, and so we cannot rely on them for unambiguous guides to resource allocation. This simple fact is what produces the conflict examined in the current chapter. Information content in a contracting setting does not imply information content in a valuation setting, and information content in a valuation setting does not imply information content in a contracting setting. Information content is not a straightforward proposition. The valuation setting emphasizes the firm's prospects, given equilibrium play, given the management team is well behaved, so to speak. The contracting setting emphasizes good behavior by the management team, essentially contrasting what might be reported if the management team behaves with what might be reported if it misbehaves. The focus, so to speak, is on contrasting equilibrium with off-equilibrium play. There is an interest in this contrast simply because of frictions in the managerial labor market.

The valuation and contracting settings, then, are not coextensive. Now you know why our analysis of the use of accounting information moved well beyond the usual setting of trade-based (market) valuation.

Selected References

The conflict between valuation and contracting settings emphasized here was originally reported by Gjesdal (1981). Subsequent articles include Feltham and Xie (1994), Kim (1995), and Arya, Glover, and Sivaramakrishnan (1997). Timing issues are explored in, for example, Demski and Sappington (1986) and Christensen and Feltham (1997). More broadly illustrative work on disclosure issues can be found in Demski and Frimor (1999), Dye (2001), and Verrecchia (2001). Baiman and Verrecchia (1995) and Farlee, Fellingham, and Young (1996) emphasize simultaneous valuation and evaluation issues.

Key Terms

Simultaneous information content is present when the information source displays information content in the valuation and in the contracting settings. This applies regardless of whether other information is present, and we therefore appropriately condition on the presence of that other information. Likewise, information can be **perverse** if the firm is better off were that information unavailable in the first place.

Exercises

13.1. Explain why it is possible to have information content in the (risk-neutral) valuation setting but not in the managerial contracting setting.

13.2. Explain why it is possible to have information content in the managerial contracting setting but not in the (risk-neutral) valuation setting.

13.3. Explain why it is possible that an optimal contract would use public, early information while the firm would be better off if the information were not available.

13.4. An often-heard assertion is that managers should be paid for the value they create, implying that the ideal performance measure for contracting with the manager is value created. Carefully explain the flaw in this assertion.

13.5. Verify that the contracts in Exhibits 13.3 and 13.4 motivate the manager to supply $a = a_H$ regardless of what the public source reports.

13.6. Return to the setting of Exhibit 13.4. Determine the manager's risk premium for the case in which the second information source is present, and contrast that risk premium with its counterpart for the case in which the second information source is absent. Explain your findings.

13.7. Return again to the setting of Exhibit 13.4. Verify that the firm's optimal policy is to instruct the manager to supply $a = a_H$ regardless of what the public source reports.

13.8. Return again to the setting of Exhibit 13.4. Determine the firm's expected cost exclusive of payments to the manager if signal $y_2 = g$ is reported and if signal $y_2 = b$ is reported.

13.9. Consider the following variation on the setting of Exhibit 13.4.

	Signal $y = (y_1, y_2)$			
	(0, g)	**(0, b)**	**(1, g)**	**(1, b)**
$\pi(y \mid a_H)$	.60	.15	.10	.15
$\pi(y \mid a_L)$	.05	.15	.65	.15

Determine the firm's optimal combination of factors including instruction to the manager. Contrast your analysis with that in the Exhibit 13.4 setting.

13.10. In the setting of Exhibit 13.5, suppose the second information source is late reporting (i.e., it reports when the first information source reports). Determine an optimal contract, and explain the difference with that detailed in Exhibit 13.5.

13.11. Assume a setting as detailed in Exhibits 13.1 and 13.2 except that the market price of capital is $p_K = 500$ and the probability structure is as follows:

	Signal $y = (y_1, y_2)$			
	(0, g)	**(0, b)**	**(1, g)**	**(1, b)**
$\pi(y \mid a_H)$	.45	.35	.05	.15
$\pi(y \mid a_L)$	.05	.15	.45	.35

Determine the firm's optimal factor mix and contract with the manager.

13.12. Ralph is studying principal-agent problems in which the principal's claim to the net cash flow (net after payment to the agent) is valued in a risk neutral valuation market. For convenience, there is no discounting. The agent is risk averse and incurs a personal cost. The agent can supply input L or input H. The agent's preferences are given by

$$\sqrt{Payment} - (Cost\ of\ input)$$

where the agent's input cost is 25 if input H is supplied and 5 if input L is supplied. In addition, the agent must face an expected utility of at least 75 "units" if this is to be an attractive option. Input H is desired in all that follows. As usual, the agent will not supply H unless explicitly motivated. The output prior to paying the agent will be $x_1 = 20,000$ or $x_2 = 80,000$. In addition, the agent does not buy or short any fraction of the mentioned security.

The catch now is that a monitor is also available; it will report $y = g$ or $y = b$. So, the agent's contract can depend on both monitor report y and output x. The timing should be familiar. After the labor contract is signed, the financial market meets and values the enterprise. Then the agent acts, and the monitor is publically observed. At this point the market revises its value of the enterprise. Finally, output is observed, payments are made, and the game ends.

Consider the following probability structure.

	(g, x_1)	(b, x_1)	(g, x_2)	(b, x_2)
Input H	.20	0	.80	0
Input L	0	.50	0	.50

a. Is the monitor useful in the labor market? Is it useful in the financial market?

b. Now consider the following probability structure.

	(g, x_1)	(b, x_1)	(g, x_2)	(b, x_2)
Input H	.02	.18	.64	.16
Input L	.05	.45	.40	.10

Is this monitor useful in the labor market? Is it useful in the financial market?

c. Write a brief paragraph interpreting what you have observed here.

Comparative Advantage

Chapter

14

Recognition

Having deepened our understanding of information use in the valuation and managerial contracting domains, we now return to accounting as an explicit supplier of information. The initial step is the topic of recognition. As we know, information is conceptually viewed as a partition of some underlying set. Accounting information is no different. The recognition policy or rule defines the partition by specifying the linkage between what the firm knows and what and when it reports. In subsequent chapters we will link the choice of recognition rule to the accounting system's comparative advantage of one among many suppliers of information.

We now turn our attention to the contents of and the information to be conveyed by the accounting system. We do this in stages. Initially in this chapter, we explore recognition, stressing the theme of temporal aggregation. In Chapter 15 we focus the recognition issue on the importance of an audit trail, the notion that whatever is recognized by the accounting system can be audited. After that, we introduce a refined version of recognition that allows the recognition decision to be based on other information. This last step allows us to view the accounting system as a source of information and, simultaneously, to stress its comparative advantage among competing and complementary sources of information.

The recurring theme is that of recognition: When are particular phenomena recognized and recorded in the accounting system's rendering of the entity's financial history?[1] Recognition is the workhorse of accounting system design. The firm's recognition policy prescribes the boundaries of the recording process. It governs exclusion and inclusion. It defines the measurement that takes place. In short, it defines the information system.

[1] The substantive issue, of course, is the partition or the information, not the scale with which that partition is described or recorded.

An emphasis on historical cost, for example, excludes various price changes from the accounting system just as an emphasis on "fair value" calls for aggressive searching out of price changes. Encumbrance accounting is quick to acknowledge purchases, just as the supplier's associated revenue recognition policy will likely be less aggressive in acknowledging the same purchase.[2] Extensive aggregation over various products mutes product-specific details. Cash and accrual measures are simply two sets of accounting measures that use different recognition rules. You get the picture.

We begin with a review of the rhetoric of recognition. This is followed by a brief look at matching. We then step behind the rhetoric and invoke the information content theme. This is done by interpreting recognition issues in terms of temporal aggregation. Following this, we look more closely at information content issues.

RHETORIC OF RECOGNITION

Recognition issues stand out when we worry about "properly" identifying and measuring a reporting entity's accounting assets, liabilities, expenses, revenues, and so on. In an ideal world of perfect markets, Chapter 3, we would know the economic value of assets, liabilities, and so forth. Economic stocks and flows would be known, and accounting stocks and flows could mirror their economic counterparts. Recognition issues would then be trivial: All recognition would be market based. After all, market values would be readily available at all points in time. Of course, we do have the problem that accounting is so easy in such a setting precisely because it has nothing to offer. No one would pay for such an accounting system in an ideal environment, because it merely reflects what everyone is presumed to know in the first place.

Reality, as we know, intrudes on the ideal of well-known economic stocks and flows. Accounting thought and practice retain the notions of economic stocks and flows but give them an accounting stamp. The accounting stocks and flows are defined and inferred as opposed to being directly observed in current market prices. This is the role of accounting recognition. We begin with notions of assets, liabilities, expenses, revenues, and so on. We then impose a recognition test to decide, for example, when an asset or a particular revenue item is to be recognized and recorded in the accounting system. Broadly interpreted, this recognition

---

[2] For example, a municipality will use encumbrance accounting, a system that focuses on commitment and not exceeding authorized spending limits. When supplies are ordered, the accounting system recognizes this commitment at the time the order is placed, in effect expensing the supplies when the purchase order is placed. In sharp contrast, the supplier's accounting system would not recognize the receipt of the purchase order per se but would defer recognition until the ordered supplies were shipped or delivered.

test governs the inclusion and exclusion of events in the accounting system and specifies how they are recorded.

Analyses of this sort were prevalent in academic writings earlier in the prior century and in various pronouncements of financial reporting regulatory agencies such as the FASB and IASB.[3] For example, the FASB (1985, paragraph 143), defines recognition as "the process of formally recording or incorporating an item in the financial statements of an entity." We also know that for publically traded entities in the United States, a major focus of the FASB, the ratio of market value of the entity's equity claims to book value of those claims is typically well below unity. (Recall our survey in Chapter 10.) Economic value evidenced by trading behavior in organized markets is typically well above accounting value. If the calculus of accounting valuation is not far removed from the valuation calculus in the trading market, the trading market appears to be "recognizing" much more than its accounting counterpart.

What, then, governs or explains the accounting side of this seeming mismatch? The FASB offers four essentials for inclusion in the financial calculations of those entities it regulates: definitional appropriateness, measurability, relevance, and reliability. Paraphrasing, recognition of some item or phenomenon is called for when and if that item (1) meets the definition of an element of financial statements (asset, liability, etc.), (2) possesses an attribute that is relevant and measurable with sufficient reliability, (3) is capable of making a difference to users of the financial statements, and (4) can be portrayed in a representationally faithful, verifiable, and neutral manner (FASB, 1984). These essentials, in turn, are muted by materiality and cost-benefit considerations.

Revenue recognition is illustrative. It is common to recognize revenue as soon as the major revenue-producing activity has been completed and an asset that can be "reliably valued" has been received. This leads, in varying circumstances, to recognition at the time of production (e.g., long-term construction), delivery (e.g., fast food), cash collection (e.g., problematic real estate sales), or perhaps after a right of return has expired (e.g., software sales with trial periods or book publishing). In turn, pragmatic considerations diminish the purity of the recipe. For example, we usually do not line up all sales-related expenses with the revenue recognition event; rather, order-getting and collection costs are usually expensed as incurred.[4]

---

[3] The International Accounting Standards Committee (IASC) was recently restructured and renamed The International Accounting Standards Board (IASB).
[4] Moreover, the transactions themselves can be disconcertingly complex. For example, the product might be shipped on a consignment basis with title not passing until the delivered product is actually put in use. Alternatively, elaborate price adjustment clauses may be present with the adjustment depending on observed prices as well as the buyer's cost experience.

The IASC (1989) offers a similar approach. It stresses that an element of financial statements that is likely to lead to economic flows and can be measured reliably should be recognized. Some type of threshold in terms of likelihood and reliability triggers the recognition.

Auditors also worry about these issues but often invoke their own rhetoric of satisfying "audit objectives." Are recorded transactions legitimate (existence)? Are all appropriate transactions recorded (completeness)? Are they recorded in the appropriate periods (timing)? Are appropriate valuations employed (accuracy)?

Economic Indicators

A little reflection now should convince you that these types of issues are not unique to economic activity within, for example, the purview of present-day financial reporting (as exemplified by FASB or IASB activities). Managerial reporting provides a ready example. Here we are familiar with the theme of responsibility accounting or which financial measures are best used in evaluating a manager's performance. Frequently encountered issues include: Should the price variance for labor and materials be removed from the manager's evaluation?[5] Should various overhead items be allocated? Should an explicit capital charge as in residual income or so-called economic value-added calculations be included?

We also know that tax recognition can differ in important ways from financial reporting recognition, just as recognition rules for internal purposes are not bound by regulatory reporting requirements. Likewise, recognition policy is not constant across for-profit, not-for-profit, and governmental entities. As noted earlier, for example, encumbrance accounting is commonplace in municipal accounting.

Even this range of anecdotes does not exhaust the possibilities. Consider economywide reporting. Gross domestic product (GDP) is a well-known and well-publicized measure of aggregate activity at the economy level. It can be calculated using the so-called product approach, expenditure approach, or income approach. All three give the same total but emphasize different categorizations or approaches.

The product approach tallies the economic value of goods and services produced within an economy during a period of time. One can imagine the market value of, for example, food services and automobiles produced during a year. Government services, though, are problematic because market prices are missing. In their absence, we "value" things such as public education, defense, the judiciary, and highways at their cost.

The expenditure approach tallies GDP as the sum of consumption, investment, government purchases, and net exports of goods and services. The income approach tallies compensation of employees, proprietors'

---

[5] Invoking a recently observed torturing of the English language, this would be referred to in some circles as *derecognition*.

income, rental income of individuals, corporate profits, and net interest, all adjusted for indirect business taxes, depreciation, and net factor payments.

Are you spotting recognition issues? How are corporate profits calculated? What valuation concept is used in valuing government services? How do we handle depletion of natural resources or environmental degradation (or restoration)? What about human capital?

As a final illustration, consider the consumer price index (CPI) as compiled by the U.S. Labor Department's Bureau of Labor Statistics. This is a so-called Laspeyres index because it measures the current cost, relative to the past cost, of a particular fixed bundle of goods and services. It is well known that such an index overstates inflation because it does not acknowledge the ability to substitute, for example, away from goods and services whose prices are increasing relatively quickly. The CPI is also slow to introduce new products (such as cellular phones), has difficulty treating quality improvements, incorporates the full price of consumer durables, and does not utilize sale prices for weekend sales.

An arguably better measure of inflation is available when we combine this type of index with a Paasche index that measures the current cost relative to the past cost of the currently consumed bundle of goods and services. The difficulty is that the Paasche index requires knowledge of current consumption. In short, it relies on more aggressive recognition of consumer behavior.[6]

The common theme in these stories is selectivity. Particular phenomena are included and others are excluded. This is not unique to financial accounting, nor is it unique to accounting more broadly interpreted. Any information source is selective. Consider the editorial policies of your favorite news source. This is the reason that we call recognition the workhorse of accounting system design. Recognition is the key to what phenomena are reflected in the accounting stocks and flows, and designing an appropriate recognition policy is the key to identifying and exploiting the accounting system's comparative advantage among information sources.

Matching

We stress a broad view of recognition that governs the contents of the accounting system. (We will offer a formal definition based on our information content theme shortly.) Matching is a derivative concept. When used in a narrow sense, it refers to recognizing factor costs as expenses associated with revenue that is being recognized: The expenses are

---

[6] A Tornqvist index is a weighted average of price increases in which the weights are the average of those in the Laspeyres and Paasche indices. Also notice that contrary to the world of the FASB, it is routine to adjust macro statistics for inflation; acknowledging the noted difficulties with the CPI, it is not the index used, for example, for converting the GDP series to its real counterpart.

matched, so to speak, with the revenue.[7] Inventory accounting for a merchandising firm is illustrative. More broadly, *matching* refers to recognizing the expenses, losses, and gains of a period. In the limit, it is a synonym for recognition.

Consider the accounting treatment of a capital asset. A cash basis recognition rule would expense the purchase price when the supplier is paid. Recording the purchase of a small consumer durable in the household checkbook provides a ready illustration. The cash basis system aggressively expenses assets. No degrees of freedom are left for the matching process. The result is that no assets other than cash, are recorded in the accounting system, literally. An economic value orientation would track the period-by-period economic value of the asset, thereby recognizing discernible value changes. The typical historical cost orientation would spread the asset's original cost over some "appropriate" time frame in some "appropriate" fashion. How this is done is specified by the matching rules.

Paton and Littleton (1940), in their classic monograph, stress the idea that costs measure "effort" while revenues measure "accomplishment." This leads to a "proper" matching of effort and accomplishment in the historical cost model (p. 14):

> The realization of revenue from sales therefore marks the time and measures the amount of (1) recapture of costs previously advanced in productive efforts, and (2) capture of additional assets (income) representing amount of compensation for capital service rendered, responsibility taken, and risk assumed in the process of production. Inventories and plant are not "values," but cost accumulations in suspense, as it were, awaiting their destiny. In order to learn what costs have already met the test (recapture) and what costs still await the test, accounting assumes that acquisition costs are mobile and may be apportioned or regrouped, and that costs reassembled have a natural affinity for each other which identifies them with the group.

We also know from our earlier study of accounting that accounting stocks and flows often reflect a conservative orientation. This can be visualized in terms of a bias in the matching process. Specifically, suppose that we design the recognition policy to delay revenue recognition until virtually all details have been resolved and combine this policy with a more aggressive recognition on the expense (and loss) side of the equation. This quickly degenerates to the dictum of delay all revenues and anticipate all expenses!

---

[7] For example, in *Statement of Financial Accounting Concepts No. 6* (FASB, 1985), the FASB states "recognition of revenues, expenses, gains, and losses and the related increments or decrements in assets and liabilities—including matching of costs and revenues, allocation, and amortization—is the essence of using accrual accounting to measure performance of entities" (paragraph 145). Continuing (paragraph 146), we find that matching "is simultaneous or combined recognition of the revenues and expenses that result directly and jointly from the same transactions or other events."

The point, though, is that the recognition policy (including the matching policy) governs the behavior of the accounting system. It is, as we said earlier, the workhorse of accounting system design. Our task now is to put some structure on this elusive, if not evasive, notion.

TEMPORAL AGGREGATION

The key, of course, is to explicitly view the accounting system as a source of information, a mapping, so to speak, from states into signals (or, equivalently, a partition of the set of states). Naturally, this goes on each and every period, and we hardly expect the firm to reveal all that it knows at each and every instance. So, the central theme is temporal aggregation.

Earlier Illustration

One illustration of this connection is provided by our earlier work in Chapter 7. There we dealt with a firm whose uncertain cash flows, over a three-year horizon, were as given in Exhibit 14.1. Notice the initial investment of 25,000 is followed by uncertain cash inflows over the next three periods.

We then calculated the firm's periodic income, $\hat{I}_t$, by treating the cash inflow as "net revenue" and depreciating the original asset.[8] This led to the income numbers in Exhibit 14.2 where the depreciation in period 1 is d_1 and so on.

For the moment, ignore the additional expense in amount d at time $t = 1$ in state s_1. The income series then induces the following partitions of the states:

$t = 0$: null.

$t = 1$: $\{\{s_1, s_2\}, \{s_3, s_4\}\}$.

$t = 2$: $\{\{s_1, s_2\}, \{s_3, s_4\}\}$.

$t = 3$: $\{\{s_1\}, \{s_2\}, \{s_3\}, \{s_4\}\}$.

Equally clear is the fact that identical partitions are induced by the cash flows themselves. From an information perspective, the firm has chosen to recognize nothing beyond the structure of the cash flows themselves. It is reporting "net revenue" on a cash basis, and the (accrual) depreciation series is simply a scaling.

Contrast this with the case in which the additional expense, the restructuring charge of d in the first period under state s_1, is nontrivial. There the firm elects to communicate at time $t = 1$ what it has learned about future "net revenues." It thus employs a more aggressive recognition rule

---

[8] We actually identified cash inflows from customers and outflows for labor and capital, but the summarization in terms of "net revenue" is adequate for the immediate purpose.

EXHIBIT 14.1
Cash Flow Vector as a Function of State

$CF_t(s)$	s_1	s_2	s_3	s_4
$CF_0(s)$	−25,000	−25,000	−25,000	−25,000
$CF_1(s)$	5,700	5,700	4,200	4,200
$CF_2(s)$	9,680	9,680	9,680	9,680
$CF_3(s)$	15,387.50	17,887.50	15,387.50	17,887.50
$\sum_t CF_t(s)$	5,767.50	8,267.50	4,267.50	6,767.50

EXHIBIT 14.2 **Accounting Income Calculations**

$\hat{I}_t$	s_1	s_2	s_3	s_4
$\hat{I}_1$	$5,700 - d_1 - d$	$5,700 - d_1$	$4,200 - d_1$	$4,200 - d_1$
$\hat{I}_2$	$9,680 - d_2$	$9,680 - d_2$	$9,680 - d_2$	$9,680 - d_2$
$\hat{I}_3$	$d_1 + d_2 + d - 9,612.50$	$d_1 + d_2 - 7,112.50$	$d_1 + d_2 - 9,612.50$	$d_1 + d_2 - 7,112.50$
$\sum \hat{I}_t$	5,767.50	8,267.50	4,267.50	6,767.50

that admits more into the accounting records and results in the following sequence of partitions.

$t = 0$: null.

$t = 1$: $\{\{s_1\}, \{s_2\}, \{s_3, s_4\}\}$.

$t = 2$: $\{\{s_1\}, \{s_2\}, \{s_3, s_4\}\}$.

$t = 3$: $\{\{s_1\}, \{s_2\}, \{s_3\}, \{s_4\}\}$.

Extended Example

More structure will be helpful as we dig more deeply into the recognition theme. For this purpose we consider a single-product version of our reporting firm whose success depends on selling its single product to a customer and eventually collecting from that customer. Production cost is C, and the selling price is $P > C$. Should a sale not take place or the item be repossessed due to nonpayment, the item will be liquidated for amount C, thereby covering the firm's initial cost. This stylization minimizes details—always an advantage—and stresses the familiar issue of when to recognize revenue.[9]

The revenue side of the story is a sequence of four events suggestive of an earnings cycle: (1) locating a potential customer, (2) selling to that

---

[9] The underlying details are tangential except it is important to understand that all of this is a nonissue without some type of market imperfection. For the record, we return to the ongoing setting first introduced in Chapter 2 where the firm uses capital (K) and labor (L) to produce its single product. The physical capacity limit of K^{max} limits its scale. The catch is that it must manufacture the output and then hope it can locate a customer who will eventually pay. The expected value of the customer's payment is, say, 400. Capital and labor each cost 100, and $K^{max} = 0.50$. If you work through the details, you will see that it pays the firm to produce and try to sell one unit while incurring factor expenditures of 250.

customer, (3) dealing with any postsale return from that customer, and (4) collecting from that customer. A zero interest rate is also assumed. This is admittedly simplified to the point of naivete, but it serves our purpose.

If the firm has unbounded success, it will have located the customer, consummated a sale with that customer, not experienced any return from the customer, and collected the sales price. Naturally, there are pitfalls along the way. If the customer cannot be located, no sale takes place. If a sale takes place but the good is returned, there will be no second customer, and we are back to the no-sale story. Either way, the good is then sold in the liquidation market for an amount that just covers its production cost. If the customer turns out to be a deadbeat, we have an even more awkward situation. For simplicity, we assume that a deadbeat eventually pays amount C, again just covering the initial production cost. In all events, the cash inflow, be it C or P in amount, occurs at time $t = 4$.

Recall our device for modeling uncertainty in which an uncertain outcome is modeled as depending on some underlying (and uncertain) state. State s_1 is the case in which no potential customer exists; s_2 is the case in which a potential customer exists but no sale can be consummated; s_3 covers the case of a consummated sale followed by a return; and so on. Details are displayed in Exhibit 14.3 with the net cash flow to the firm.

Ponder the sequence of events. Initially, at time $t = 0$, the firm expends amount C in hopes of subsequently locating a paying customer. At time $t = 1$, it knows whether a potential customer exists. It has either succeeded or failed in locating a potential customer. At time $t = 2$ it knows whether a potential customer exists and, if so, whether a sale was consummated. Continuing, the firm observes the following temporal partitions:

$t = 0$: null.

$t = 1$: $\{\{s_1\}, \{s_2, s_3, s_4, s_5\}\}$.

$t = 2$: $\{\{s_1\}, \{s_2\}, \{s_3, s_4, s_5\}\}$.

$t = 3$: $\{\{s_1\}, \{s_2\}, \{s_3\}, \{s_4, s_5\}\}$.

$t = 4$: $\{\{s_1\}, \{s_2\}, \{s_3\}, \{s_4\}, \{s_5\}\}$.

The firm learns more and more about its fate with the passage of time. If state s_1 is present, it learns this fact at time $t = 1$. If state s_2 is present, it

	State				
	s_1	s_2	s_3	s_4	s_5
Description					
Locate ($t = 1$)	No	Yes	Yes	Yes	Yes
Sale ($t = 2$)		No	Yes	Yes	Yes
Return ($t = 3$)			Yes	No	No
Collect ($t = 4$)				No	Yes
Cash inflow ($t = 4$)	C	C	C	C	P
Cash outflow ($t = 0$)	$\underline{C}$	$\underline{C}$	$\underline{C}$	$\underline{C}$	$\underline{C}$
Net cash flow	0	0	0	0	$P - C$

EXHIBIT 14.3
State and Cash Flow Description for Recognition Story

learns this fact at time $t = 2$, and so on. Its information is refined with the passage of time. This is the information we assume is available to the firm.

Now impose an accounting system that will record revenue at some appropriate time and match the production cost appropriately. Cash basis recognition is the easiest to envision. Under such a policy, a cash expenditure of C would be immediately recognized. Subsequently, a cash collection of P at time $t = 4$ would be recognized if and only if the customer actually paid at that time. Otherwise, a cash inflow of C would be reported at that time. Of course, cash inflow of C might mean that no customer was located, the potential customer refused to purchase, the customer actually purchased and returned the good, or, in the limit, the customer turned out to be a deadbeat. So, under cash basis recognition, the story is told as follows:

$t = 0$: Cash expenditure of C recognized.

$t = 1$: Nothing recognized.

$t = 2$: Nothing recognized.

$t = 3$: Nothing recognized.

$t = 4$: Cash inflow of P recognized if collection takes place; otherwise cash inflow C recognized.

This is informationally equivalent to the following sequence of partitions:

$t = 0$: null.

$t = 1$: $\{\{s_1, s_2, s_3, s_4, s_5\}\}$.

$t = 2$: $\{\{s_1, s_2, s_3, s_4, s_5\}\}$.

$t = 3$: $\{\{s_1, s_2, s_3, s_4, s_5\}\}$.

$t = 4$: $\{\{s_1, s_2, s_3, s_4\}, \{s_5\}\}$.

The original expenditure is immediately recognized, and nothing else enters the records until cash inflow takes place at time $t = 4$. Thus, cash basis recognition distinguishes state s_5 from the other states and does so at time $t = 4$. Otherwise, it has nothing to tell us. It routinely reveals less than the firm knows.

Contrast this with recognition at the time of sale. Under this policy, the initial expenditure of C is recorded as an inventory accrual. At time $t = 1$ the firm knows whether a customer has been located. If a customer has been located, it is premature to recognize revenue, so no accrual would be recorded. Conversely, if no customer is located, the firm knows the inventory will eventually be liquidated for amount C, so a lower-of-cost-or-market write-down is not called for; again, no accrual would be recorded.

If a sale is consummated at time $t = 2$, the sale is recognized. This calls for accruing a receivable in the amount P and expensing the inventory, C. Dealing with the return and uncollectibility states is a little messy. For now, assume that the necessary adjustments are made as indicated in Exhibit 14.4 (essentially at times $t = 3$ or 4, as appropriate). Under

EXHIBIT 14.4
Income Measures
Given Recognition
at Time of Sale

	State				
	s_1	s_2	s_3	s_4	s_5
$t = 1$ income	0	0	0	0	0
$t = 2$ income	0	0	$(P - C)$	$(P - C)$	$(P - C)$
$t = 3$ income	0	0	$-(P - C)$	0	0
$t = 4$ income	0	0	0	$-(P - C)$	0
Total income	0	0	0	0	$P - C$

recognition at time of sale, then, the firm's story would be told as follows:

$t = 0$: Inventory in amount C is accrued.

$t = 1$: Nothing recognized.

$t = 2$: Report of accrued revenue $= P$ if sale takes place, along with expense accrual; no entry otherwise.

$t = 3$: Report of revenue adjustment $= C - P$ if good returned at time $t = 3$.

$t = 4$: Report of revenue adjustment $= C - P$ if account deemed uncollectible at time $t = 4$.

This recording is most evident when we examine the implied sequence of income measures. This is laid out in Exhibit 14.4.

Notice that, following a revenue accrual of P and associated (i.e., matched) expense of C at time $t = 2$, the adjustment at time $t = 3$ reveals the return, and the adjustment at time $t = 4$ reveals that the deadbeat state is present just as no adjustment at that time reveals that collection occurred.[10] This recognition policy is informationally equivalent to the following sequence of state partitions:

$t = 0$: null.

$t = 1$: $\{\{s_1, s_2, s_3, s_4, s_5\}\}$.

$t = 2$: $\{\{s_1, s_2\}, \{s_3, s_4, s_5\}\}$.

$t = 3$: $\{\{s_1, s_2\}, \{s_3\}, \{s_4, s_5\}\}$.

$t = 4$: $\{\{s_1, s_2\}, \{s_3\}, \{s_4\}, \{s_5\}\}$.

Continuing, we can also amuse ourselves by examining a policy of recognizing only after the return possibility has been observed. We call this *late recognition*. We also might examine a hybrid in which the location and

---

[10] You may be wondering about recording a potential bad debt expense at the time the sale is recognized. If you work through the details, though, you will see that such a procedure is informationally equivalent to the one we have described. The reason is, conveniently, whether the firm suffers a return or a deadbeat, it must reverse a net of $P - C$ less whatever allowance for an uncollectible was originally accrued. No inventory accounting is called for. Moreover, we might embellish the story by having the firm acquire and systematically refine its information concerning the customer's creditworthiness.

EXHIBIT 14.5   Partitions Induced by Various Recognition Rules

Recognition Rule	Partition at Time t			
	$t = 1$	$t = 2$	$t = 3$	$t = 4$
Cash	$\{\{s_1, s_2, s_3, s_4, s_5\}\}$	$\{\{s_1, s_2, s_3, s_4, s_5\}\}$	$\{\{s_1, s_2, s_3, s_4, s_5\}\}$	$\{\{s_1, s_2, s_3, s_4\}, \{s_5\}\}$
Early	$\{\{s_1\}, \{s_2, s_3, s_4, s_5\}\}$	$\{\{s_1\}, \{s_2, s_3, s_4, s_5\}\}$	$\{\{s_1\}, \{s_2, s_3, s_4, s_5\}\}$	$\{\{s_1\}, \{s_2, s_3, s_4\}, \{s_5\}\}$
Sale	$\{\{s_1, s_2, s_3, s_4, s_5\}\}$	$\{\{s_1, s_2\}, \{s_3, s_4, s_5\}\}$	$\{\{s_1, s_2\}, \{s_3\}, \{s_4, s_5\}\}$	$\{\{s_1, s_2\}, \{s_3\}, \{s_4\}, \{s_5\}\}$
Late	$\{\{s_1, s_2, s_3, s_4, s_5\}\}$	$\{\{s_1, s_2, s_3, s_4, s_5\}\}$	$\{\{s_1, s_2, s_3\}, \{s_4, s_5\}\}$	$\{\{s_1, s_2, s_3\}, \{s_4\}, \{s_5\}\}$
Hybrid	$\{\{s_1\}, \{s_2, s_3, s_4, s_5\}\}$	$\{\{s_1\}, \{s_2\}, \{s_3, s_4, s_5\}\}$	$\{\{s_1\}, \{s_2\}, \{s_3, s_4, s_5\}\}$	$\{\{s_1\}, \{s_2\}, \{s_3\}, \{s_4\}, \{s_5\}\}$
Full	$\{\{s_1\}, \{s_2, s_3, s_4, s_5\}\}$	$\{\{s_1\}, \{s_2\}, \{s_3, s_4, s_5\}\}$	$\{\{s_1\}, \{s_2\}, \{s_3\}, \{s_4, s_5\}\}$	$\{\{s_1\}, \{s_2\}, \{s_3\}, \{s_4\}, \{s_5\}\}$

sale states are distinguished. This would call for a reversal of any time $t = 1$ accrual if the sale did not take place at time $t = 2$. Can you think of other possibilities?

The partitions induced by various recognition policies are summarized in Exhibit 14.5. *Full recognition* refers to the limiting case in which everything the firm learns is recognized as soon as it is learned. The other policies are fairly transparent, and we leave designing the underlying accruals to the reader. Just remember, anything the recognition rule reports over and above what is discernible from cash basis recognition must be done with accruals.

This display illustrates the reason we refer to *recognition* as the workhorse of accounting system design. Full recognition amounts to recording and reporting all events of which the firm becomes aware at the time this awareness takes place. We surely do not observe full, instantaneous disclosure of all the firm knows. This would be overwhelming, not to mention ridiculously costly. A more modest approach is taken instead.

Continuing with the visualization in Exhibit 14.5, any such "more modest" approach boils down to choosing a sequence of partitions that is less refined than the partition induced by the full recognition policy. Events are combined in the recognition process.

Think of this as aggregating states for accounting purposes. This aggregation takes place across states at any instant in time but also takes place as we march through time. Something ostensibly known at time t need not be reported, even in aggregate fashion, until a later date. As our story stresses, revenue recognition is a ready illustration. We wait until some threshold event has taken place; only then do we record something. Likewise, how do we typically handle difficult-to-estimate low-probability liabilities? What about the market value of a coupon bond that we hold or that we issued?[11]

---

[11] Likewise, the going concern concept reflects the idea that accounting accruals are executed on the assumption that the firm is not seriously troubled barring important evidence to the contrary.

EXHIBIT 14.6
**Fineness
(Subpartition)
Relationships
among Recognition
Rules**

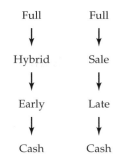

Viewed in this manner, a recognition policy specifies the temporal aggregation in the accounting system. We do not record and report every single item at each instant in time. Rather, we pick and choose; we aggregate. We engineer the degree of temporal aggregation.

Continuing, some recognition policies provide "more or less" information than others; that is, these policies can be ranked by the subpartition or fineness relationship among the state partitions they induce; others, however, are noncomparable. A little thought should convince you that our simple story exhibits the fineness relationships displayed in Exhibit 14.6.

Cash reporting, of course, is the least informative of the policies, just as full reporting is the most informative. In turn, we can move from the full to the hybrid to the early and on to the cash partitions (Full → Hybrid → Early → Cash) as they are readily ranked in terms of fineness. (Study the partitions in Exhibit 14.5, making certain you work period by period to verify each fineness or subpartition relationship.) Full-to-sale-to-late-to-cash is another string. Hybrid and late are noncomparable, however, as are hybrid and sale, sale and early, and so on. For example, contrast the late and hybrid partitions at time $t = 3$. We simply cannot convert partition $\{\{s_1, s_2, s_3\}, \{s_4, s_5\}\}$ to partition $\{\{s_1\}, \{s_2\}, \{s_3, s_4, s_5\}\}$ or vice versa.

Definition

Now recall that the typical accounting system reports cash- and accrual-based measures. This amounts to the use, in parallel, of two recognition rules. It also implies, as we have repeatedly stressed, that the information content of the accrual process is incremental to that provided by the cash basis recognition rule. This important fact is evident in Exhibit 14.5. If we combine one of the accrual rules with cash basis reporting, we see that any information conveyed before $t = 4$ is conveyed by the accrual rule. It is the accruals that carry the additional information. Indeed, in our simple story, cash basis recognition is a redundant information source when combined with any of the other rules simply because we have a one-product firm and track it to the end of its economic life.

In information content terms, then, a *recognition policy* is a specification of the information that will be conveyed in each period by the accounting system. In our simple setting it amounts to a specification of the sequence of partitions of the noted state space.[12]

To be formal and to take us back to the earlier formalization of accounting as an information source (Chapter 7), suppose the firm is observing the following sequence of information sources (from its cash flow series coupled with all other available sources of information):

$$\hat{\eta}(s) = [\hat{\eta}_0(s), \hat{\eta}_1(s), \ldots, \hat{\eta}_T(s)] \qquad \textbf{(14.1)}$$

where S is a set of states and each $\hat{\eta}_t(s)$ defines a partition of S. In a larger sense, we should treat $\hat{\eta}(s)$ as endogenous or as actually chosen by the firm, but we simply take it as given.[13]

Now, suppose the firm wants to convey via its accounting system the information—the partitions—defined by the following:

$$\eta(s) = [\eta_0(s), \eta_1(s), \ldots, \eta_T(s)] \qquad \textbf{(14.2)}$$

where, for each time t, what the firm knows—its combined partitions of $\hat{\eta}_0(s), \ldots, \hat{\eta}_t(s)$—is a subpartition of what has been "recorded" in the accounting system, that is, the combined partitions of $\eta_1(s), \ldots, \eta_t(s)$. A recognition rule now is simply a rule or a mapping that specifies the $\eta(s)$ that is associated with $\hat{\eta}(s)$.[14]

As implied by the description in Exhibit 14.3, the firm's information is refined from $\{\{s_1\}, \{s_2, s_3, s_4, s_5\}\}$ at time $t = 1$ to $\{\{s_1\}, \{s_2\}, \{s_3\}, \{s_4\}, \{s_5\}\}$ at time $t = 4$. A recognition rule specifies how much of what the firm knows is revealed by the accounting measures at each point in time. The recognition rule defines a sequence of partitions or an information plan, so to speak.

Recognition then defines the partition, that is, the information to be carried. The scale with which this is to be accomplished must also be

---

[12] Pandering to the notation connoisseur, think of the firm as managing a production function described by $f(s, a)$ where $s \in S$ is an uncertain state and $a \in A$ is some act or activity. In broadest terms, then, a recognition rule would identify some partition of $S \times A$; it would reveal something about the uncertainty and behavior of the firm. In the managerial contracting case, for example, a perfect monitor would report a distinct message for each act choice by the manager regardless of the state.

[13] Of course, a reporting regulation might require the firm to acquire some underlying information just as the firm might decide to acquire some underlying information because it wants to disclose that information, perhaps even via its formal accounting reports.

[14] Some call what the firm knows at time t, the combined partitions of $\hat{\eta}_0(s), \ldots, \hat{\eta}_t(s)$, its *information set* at time t. In this terminology, then, a recognition rule is simply a mapping from the firm's information set in each and every period into its accounting system. Notice that, being true to the information content theme, the definition emphasizes partitions, not the particular scale with which those partitions are to be conveyed.

specified. Think back to our earlier work on scaling and the importance of being able to decode or invert the accounting measure to identify the underlying phenomena (Chapter 7). The valuation function is constrained by the usual endpoints, in our case a beginning asset balance of $A_0 = C$ (presuming C was invested to fund the enterprise) and an ending asset balance of $A_5 = 0$ (presuming the accumulated cash of C or $P - C$ is paid out as a dividend). Other than specifying the endpoints, the valuation function per se is unconstrained.[15] From here we also want the valuation measures to be consistent with whatever underlying information they are to reflect. Degrees of freedom remain, however; the resulting scale is hardly unique. For example, the use of straight-line or accelerated depreciation as the standard vehicle for dealing with depreciable assets is merely a scaling issue, but our focus at this juncture is the information content (the partition), not the scale.[16]

SELECTION AMONG RECOGNITION RULES

Thus, the firm's recognition rule defines its accounting information structure. Different recognition rules provide different accounting information structures and vice versa. This theme was initially developed in Chapter 7 where we analyzed the accounting system as an information channel. There we also stressed the temporal development of the accounting system and the importance of invertibility, the ability to decipher the accounting report. There too, the definition of the accounting system, the recognition rule, was given. Here it is a matter of choice.

Selecting among the recognition rules requires us to say something about the use to which this information might be put. This leads, as we shall see, to a more subtle view of the recognition issue.

One possible avenue is to think of this as a story whose firm will distribute a liquidating dividend at time $t = 4$. This dividend will total $P - C$ or zero, depending on which state is present. From here, notice that the various recognition rules reveal "more or less" about this dividend prospect at various points in time. For example, cash and late recognition tell us nothing through time $t = 2$, while the early, sale, and hybrid rules are informative in the early part of the story.

To what end is this useful? Suppose we think of this dividend claim as being valued in a risk-neutral manner. Then different recognition rules

---

[15] Likewise, under articulation, accounting income will total $C - C = 0$ or $P - C$, but the period-by-period amounts are otherwise unconstrained.

[16] Think back to the rhetoric we often encounter here, for example, the concern for definitional appropriateness, measurability, relevance, and reliability. Do you see the implied concern for what is and what is not to be recognized?

lead to different valuation paths, but all begin and end at the same point, and risk-neutral valuation implies indifference among these various paths.[17] There is no explicit demand for early resolution of uncertainty in such a setting. Taken literally, the setting implies an indifference among the various recognition rules.

At the other extreme, we might assume that this information is used by a dividend claimant who is faced with the task of planning consumption over the four periods. Learning about the $t = 4$ dividend sooner is important here because it allows for improved consumption planning. Glancing back at Exhibit 14.5, we find that if the full policy is unavailable and by ignoring any cost considerations, the interesting choice is between the hybrid and sale policies. The late, early, and cash policies are dominated. From here we cannot say anything definitive without additional details on the plight of the dividend claimant. The hybrid policy reveals a lot early on but is silent at $t = 3$ while the sale policy is rather candid at $t = 3$. Pick your poison, so to speak.[18]

A second avenue is a managerial contracting story in which the firm seeks the input of a manager. As usual, we posit a conflict of interest between the manager and the firm. Without belaboring the details, think of this as our familiar high (a_H) versus low (a_L) action story. Low action is unusually unproductive and leads to zero customer identification in the first place as well as an inability to dispose of the unsold product.[19] So, under low output we always see a net cash flow of $-C$. Further change the story so that in state s_4 where the customer is a deadbeat, no collection whatever takes place; this, too, implies a net cash flow of $-C$. Thus, when a negative net cash flow is observed, it is consistent with good behavior by the manager coupled with bad luck or with opportunistic behavior by the manager. Exhibit 14.7 summarizes the revised and expanded setting.[20]

For the moment, concentrate on cash basis recognition. Presuming the manager behaves, at time $t = 4$ cash basis recognition provides a partition of $\{\{s_1, s_2, s_3\}, \{s_4\}, \{s_5\}\}$. After all, zero net cash flow arises in the first three

---

[17] This indifference is driven by risk neutrality and the martingale structure of revised expectations.

[18] In between, we might return to the auction theme in Chapter 8. Arguing by analogy, suppose we are at time $t = 0$ and the present owner of this dividend claim wants to sell that claim at auction. The auction will take place at time $t = 2$. Furthermore, suppose the seller privately observes the full partition. Moreover, it is possible to arrange now, at time $t = 0$, to issue an accounting report at $t = 2$ just prior to the auction. Is the seller indifferent among the various recognition rules at this point?

[19] The technology specification at this point can be interpreted as

$$q \leq M\sqrt{KL}$$

for capital (K), labor (L), and managerial input (M). Our unusual although convenient story at this point is $M = 1$ under high effort but $M = 0$ under low effort.

[20] Moreover, if we fill in the details, we will discover the optimal pay-for-performance arrangement has "high" pay if $-C$ is not observed and "low" pay if it is observed.

EXHIBIT 14.7
State and Cash Flow Description for Revised Recognition Story

	State				
Manager's Effort	s_1	s_2	s_3	s_4	s_5
a_H	0	0	0	$-C$	$P - C$
a_L	$-C$	$-C$	$-C$	$-C$	$-C$

states, a loss of C in the fourth, and a gain of $P - C$ in the fifth. If the manager behaves opportunistically, however, cash basis recognition provides a partition of $\{\{s_1, s_2, s_3, s_4, s_5\}\}$.

Now introduce an accrual reporting system, for example, revenue recognition at the point of sale ($t = 2$). Presuming the manager behaves, we have an accrual for the initial expenditure of C followed by recognition of the sale (and attendant expense) if the sale is consummated. The only difference from what we saw in the earlier story is that if the customer turns out to be a deadbeat, the eventual revenue adjustment is in the amount P rather than in the amount $P - C$. At time $t = 4$, this induces a partition of $\{\{s_1, s_2\}, \{s_3\}, \{s_4\}, \{s_5\}\}$. This is surely finer than or a subpartition of what we have with cash basis recognition, but notice that it distinguishes the events that appear not to be useful for contracting purposes. In particular, if we see a net cash flow other than $-C$, regardless of the state, we know the manager behaved.

Not so fast: What will revenue recognition at time of sale report if the manager behaves opportunistically? On the surface, no sale takes place, so no revenue will be recognized. Remember, however, that the accrual system begins by setting up an accrual for inventory. Suppose this is done and we also apply a lower-of-cost-or-market rule to that inventory. Appropriate inventory valuation might reveal opportunistic behavior by the manager.

This begs a number of questions. Does the manager self-report when the inventory is useless? Is the initial inventory accrual audited, and is the auditor of sufficient quality to invoke a lower-of-cost-or-market rule at this point? We will take these matters up in Chapter 15.

The important point for now is to identify the subtle side of the recognition rule. In the valuation setting we are concerned with the induced state partition and which recognition rule best supports some valuation purpose. In the labor market setting we are concerned with evaluating the manager, which boils down to a concern for what the information source will report if the manager behaves versus what that information source will report if the manager does not behave. The significance of a recognition rule is not only what information it conveys but also what information it might convey if alternate behavior (the off-equilibrium behavior) were engaged. The threat of what might be reported is important. Indeed, it is possible that the recognition rule leads to the appearance of negligible information content simply because its power is in the threat of what it would report under alternate circumstances. For example, if its primary purpose is to discipline earlier self-reporting by the management team and if all is working according to plan, we should see almost nothing in the accrual-based accounting system that we had not learned earlier.

Now, to be sure, we have considered only the most rudimentary of managerial market settings in the Exhibit 14.7 story. By expanding the story, we can easily envision settings that lead to each of the proposed recognition rules being the most appropriate. For example, if the main control problem is located in the sale to the customer, the recognition rules that zoom in on this event will be preferred. Consequently, even from a contracting point of view, the choice of recognition rule is highly contextual. Adding the valuation setting to the stew leads us back to Chapter 13 because we might have a conflict between the control and valuation uses. Different uses impose different rankings of information sources. Choice of a recognition rule requires balancing a variety of uses of the accounting system.

The final complicating feature of this choice problem that is carried forward is a feasibility issue. Recall that the recognition rule was defined as a mapping from what the firm knows to what is entered into the accounting system. What the firm knows might be largely private, and reporting incentives then enter the choice problem as well. The feasibility of a given recognition rule depends on the use of the information that is conveyed. Alternatively, we might be concerned with the possibility of doing a veracity check on a report issued by management, and, at this point, demand for auditing services surfaces as part of the larger choice problem that deals with recognition.[21] This calls for the next chapter.

Summary

Recognition defines which phenomena are entered into the accounting records as well as the time at which this recording takes place. A so-called fair value approach, for example, demands close attention to current prices, just as the historical cost approach emphasizes prices at the time the original transactions were recorded. As such, the firm's recognition rules govern the inclusion and, therefore, the exclusion rules for its accounting system.

Elaborate rules are often associated with recognition policies. Cost allocation in the product-costing arena, present-day reporting on financial instruments, and revenue recognition in general are illustrative. Abstracting from the rhetoric, however, the idea is both straightforward and essential.

In information content terms, the firm's accounting system is an information source, here modeled as a partition of some underlying set of

---

[21] This feasibility concern is embedded in the rhetoric of recognition where we see concerns for audit objectives and verifiability included in the auditing and reporting standards.

states and actions. Of course, this begs the question of just what partition we have in mind. This is where recognition enters. The recognition rules that the firm adopts serve to specify the partition. Indeed, without some such specification, we would have an undefined information source, that is, an accounting system committed to anarchy. As we said, the idea is both straightforward and essential.

It is one thing to conceptually identify the substance of the accounting system with its recognition rules, but it is quite another to specify those rules. This is our next step.

Selected References

We highlight the FASB's literature here because of its prominence in present-day regulatory activities. The FASB's conceptual writings, as well as those of the IASB (formerly IASC), though, follow a long line of earlier writings. Vatter (1947) is one of our particular favorites. He stresses the central role of assets as "embodiments of future want satisfaction in the form of service potentials" (p. 17). In turn, "a fund is a collection of service potentials that have been brought together for some functional purpose" (p. 18); and equities are "restrictions that apply to assets in the fund" (p. 19). This leads, for example, to viewing an expense as "a release of service to the designated objectives of the fund" (p. 23) and viewing revenue as an asset-increasing transaction in which "the new assets are completely free of equity restrictions other than the residual equity of the fund itself" (p. 25). Also see Paton (1922) and Canning (1929). Sorter (1969) is particularly eloquent on the theme of recording "events." Antle and Demski (1989) and Liang (2000, 2001) explicitly link the recognition and information content themes.

Key Terms

The firm's **recognition rule** is a specification of the information, the partition, that will be conveyed in each period by the accounting system. It is the relationship between expressions (14.1) and (14.2). **Matching** is a derivative concept. When revenue is recognized, the associated factor costs are recognized as expenses simultaneously. In this way the revenue recognition rule and the matching principle jointly specify how the firm's information is aggregated into the accounting information system.

Exercises

14.1. We have repeatedly stressed that accrual basis and cash basis accounting use different recognition rules. Explain.

14.2. Recognition is the "workhorse of accounting." Explain.

14.3. Suppose a firm faces a problematic potential liability, for example, one associated with a possible legal action. Discuss current applicable financial reporting regulations for dealing with this potential liability, and interpret them in terms of recognition.

14.4. Provide recording entries for each of the recognition rules summarized in Exhibit 14.3. Describe the revenue recognition and expense matching associated with each set of entries.

14.5. Suppose a firm purchases for 1,000 a long-lived asset with an estimated life of five years. It is considering straight-line or sum-of-the-years'-digits depreciation. Discuss this choice in terms of recognition. Contrast either choice with immediate expensing of the acquisition.

14.6. Suppose the states in Exhibit 14.3 are equally likely, $P = 1,000$ and $C = 200$. Further assume risk-neutral valuation and, conveniently, a zero interest rate. Determine the value of the claim to the eventual cash flow (at time $t = 4$) at times $t = 0, 1, 2,$ and 3 for each of the recognition rules in Exhibit 14.5. Interpret your findings.

14.7. Verify the claim in Note 10 that appending a perfunctory bad debt anticipation to the revenue recognition approach in the Exhibit 14.1 story is merely a scaling issue.

14.8. Using the manager's risk aversion and personal cost specification in Chapter 13, verify the claim in Note 19. Assume the states are equally likely.

14.9. This is a slight modification of the story in Exercise 7.8. The cash flow when Ralph is dealing with a two-period setting in which there are six equally likely states follows. (Notice the expected cash flow in the first period is 110, and its counterpart in the second period is 121.) Naturally, the interest rate is 10 percent. The information, signal y, is privately observed by Ralph as is the first-period cash flow. Construct an accounting system so that by reporting cash flow and accounting income (and accounting value), Ralph will de facto reveal the private information at time $t = 1$. Discuss your system in terms of the concept of recognition.

	s_1	s_2	s_3	s_4	s_5	s_6
CF_0	-200	-200	-200	-200	-200	-200
CF_1	110	110	110	110	110	110
CF_2	101	101	141	141	141	101
Signal y	y_1	y_2	y_2	y_3	y_2	y_2

14.10. We now find Ralph worrying about consumption. Ralph has a $T = 3$ period horizon and will consume some commodity (let's call it cash) in each of the three periods. Denote consumption in period t by c_t. Ralph's utility for consumption of $c_1, c_2,$ and c_3 is given by the following expression:

$$U(c_1, c_2, c_3) = \sqrt{c_1} + \sqrt{c_2} + \sqrt{c_3}$$

Notice that negative consumption is not feasible. For convenience, the interest rate is zero. Ralph has an endowment of $w = 1,000$, so consuming $1,000/3$ each period is feasible, but he also owns a factory. This factory is attempting to make a sale to a customer. If it is successful, it will have available additional cash of 1,000 for consumption in the final period. So, for example, if Ralph knew this sale were certain, respective consumption amounts of $c_1 = c_2 = 500$ and $c_3 = 1,000$ would be feasible. The trouble is that this sale is uncertain. If it falls through, there is no gain or loss, nor can Ralph go to the bank. An earlier bankruptcy has ruined his credit rating.

The would-be sale works as follows: It must go through three successive, independent stages to be successful. Each stage has a .8 probability of being successful. Failure at any one stage means no sale takes place. So, the probability of a sale is $(.8)(.8)(.8) = .512$. Initially suppose Ralph has no information.

a. Determine Ralph's optimal consumption. To do this, you should maximize the following expression

$$\sqrt{c_1} + \sqrt{c_2} + .488\sqrt{w - c_1 - c_2} + .512\sqrt{w + 1,000 - c_1 - c_2}$$

subject to $c_1 \geq 0$, $c_2 \geq 0$ and $w - c_1 - c_2 \geq 0$. Interpret your solution.

b. Now assume Ralph decides to put in a fancy accounting system. One version can observe success or failure in the first period and will make its report just before Ralph decides on c_1. A second version can observe success or failure through the first two stages and then make a report before Ralph decides on c_2 but after he has decided on c_1. Notice that the first version reports sooner but is less accurate. Determine which of these two reporting systems Ralph prefers. (Adapted from Antle and Demski, 1989.)

14.11. Interpret your analysis in Exercise 14.10 as a choice between recognition rules.

14.12. Return again to Exercise 14.10. Notice that Ralph can neither borrow nor contract with other individuals to share the consumption risk. This is a story of market frictions and an unbalanced portfolio. Discuss the differences between this type of setting and our usual approach to valuation.

14.13. Ralph is now trying to understand some subtle features of how a revenue recognition rule works. For this purpose, think of a process in which three binary gates must be successfully traversed for revenue to be actually collected. Each gate will be good news (g) or bad news (b). A customer is successfully identified only if each gate reports good news. The probability of good news in gate i is denoted π_i and the three gates operate in independent fashion, so the probability of success is $\pi_1\pi_2\pi_3$. Success leads to cash flow of P; failure leads to cash flow of zero.

Now overlay an accounting story. At the end, after gate 3 is traversed, the accounting system will record the actual revenue. The accounting system also may issue one intermediate report after gate 1 has been traversed (aggressive reporting) or after gates 1 and 2 have been traversed (conservative reporting). Think of this as revenue recognition. The aggressive system will report revenue of P if gate 1 is successfully traversed and revenue of 0 otherwise. The report is issued at the end of period 1; no period 2 report is issued. If failure occurs somewhere between gates 2 and 3, the final report will contain a "correction." The conservative system will issue no report at period 1; it will report revenue of P at the end of period 2 if gates 1 and 2 are successfully traversed and revenue of 0 otherwise. If revenue of P is recognized in period 2 but failure occurs in period 3, a correction will be issued in period 3.

Which revenue recognition rule is more "timely?" Which revenue recognition rule is more "accurate?" Which do you think is easier to audit? Which do you think is easier to manipulate?

Chapter 15

Information Content of Audited Accruals

The substantive information conveyed by the accounting system is conveyed by the accruals. After all, the accrual-free approach of cash basis recognition is both perfunctory and reported, so it behooves us to concentrate on the accruals. This we do here with the added notion that the accruals are audited, or vetted, by an independent third party. In particular, we now endow the manager with private information about an inventory level, for example, and then introduce another information source that is both public and a garbling of what the manager knows. This new source, interpreted as an audit of what the manager claims, has information content because it speaks to the veracity of the manager's claim.

We now introduce *audited accruals*, the backbone of the accounting system. We know from our work to date that any substantive information carried by the accounting system is carried by the accruals. We also know, institutionally, that accounting reports are often audited. Annual financial reports, a lender's requirement that a financial statement accompany the loan application, and the very existence of an internal audit group are illustrative. These themes are now combined: Important information will be carried by the accruals, and an auditor will play a central role in the process.

Initially, we revisit the earlier contracting setting. An additional contracting variable is introduced, but it is one that is private to the manager and thus must be self-reported. From here we introduce a third variable that provides a check on the veracity of the manager's self-report of the second variable.

We then develop the underlying structure of the setting and interpret the private information as an inventory variable: The firm may have work-in-process inventory, but the manager privately knows the level of inventory. Naturally, if inventory is present, it should be recognized by the accounting system, as an accrual to be sure. As it turns out, veracity issues arise when the manager is asked to self-report the inventory level, thereby creating difficulties with our desire to recognize the inventory. (It is no accident that audit regulations require inventory verification.) From here we interpret the third variable as an auditor who, with error, can verify, can attest to the claimed inventory level.

Of course, we often think of accounting and auditing as closely related, yet this is the first time we introduce an auditor. It is no accident that this occurs in a setting in which trade frictions are present. Absent some such friction, the parties could simply ask the informed parties to put the desired information "on the table," and that would be the end of the matter. Here that trading friction takes the form of wanting to use various measures to gauge the manager's performance, and using the measures in this fashion plays havoc with the manager's willingness to provide the desired information. So, we turn to the (independent) auditor to provide a countervailing incentive.

The resulting picture carries two important themes. First, the audited inventory record, the audited accrual, is useful in disciplining the manager's self-report, and its information content therefore becomes rather subtle. Second, there would be no interest whatever in auditing were the manager not present. Indeed, the accounting system is designed to accommodate this attestation because the accruals are constructed in a way that facilitates auditing.

SETTING

We begin with a streamlined illustration in which the firm is once again contracting with a manager. Two action choices are possible, $a \in \{a_H, a_L\}$. The manager is specified in familiar fashion, complete with preference measure $U(\iota, a) = -\exp(-\rho(\iota - c_a))$ for compensation ι and action a. We also set the personal cost terms at $c_H = 5{,}000$ and $c_L = 3{,}000$, the risk-aversion measure at $\rho = .0001$, and the manager's opportunity certainty equivalent at $\hat{\iota} = 5{,}000$. (These details, in fact, are a carryover from the illustrations in Chapters 11 and 12.)

The firm seeks supply of action a_H. The possible contracting variables for now are the pair of signals, $y_1 \in \{0, 1\}$ and $y_2 \in \{g, b\}$. Both are late sources arriving after the manager acts. Probabilities are given in Exhibit 15.1. Notice that $\pi(y_1 = 0 \mid a_H) = .50$ while $\pi(y_1 = 0 \mid a_L) = .30$.

EXHIBIT 15.1
Probabilities for
Base Case
Illustration

	Signal $y = (y_1, y_2)$			
	(0, g)	(0, b)	(1, g)	(1, b)
$\pi((y_1, y_2) \mid a_H)$	.44	.06	.36	.14
$\pi((y_1, y_2) \mid a_L)$	0	.30	0	.70

From here we solve for optimal contracts in three cases displayed in Exhibit 15.2. The first case confines the contracting to the first information source, $y_1 \in \{0, 1\}$. It should have a familiar look!

The second case occurs when both sources are available. Notice that the second source not only has information content in the presence of the first but also is unusually informative. It completely overshadows the first source. Indeed, the first source has no information content in the presence of the second source.

Self-Reporting

The third case occurs when this powerful second source, y_2, is privately observed by the manager. Here we ask the manager to self-report his private observation. We further assume that the second source is privately observed and self-reported before the first source reports. Otherwise, we have no forthcoming observation that can be used to check the veracity of the manager's self-report. Notice that the incentives are turned off if the manager claims $y_2 = b$, but if he claims $y_2 = g$, a large bonus accompanies $y_1 = 0$ and a serious penalty accompanies $y_1 = 1$.[1]

---

[1] Recall that we want the manager to supply action a_H and to tell the truth. Pedantically, other than telling the truth, the manager could follow a strategy of claiming $y_2 = g$ no matter what, $y_2 = b$ no matter what, or always reporting the opposite of what is known. We tabulate the various options as follows:

Action and Report Strategy	(0, g)	(0, b)	(1, g)	(1, b)
a_H, truth	.44	.06	.36	.14
a_H, $y_2 = g$ always	.50	0	.50	0
a_H, $y_2 = b$ always	0	.50	0	.50
a_H, always opposite	.06	.44	.14	.36
a_L, truth	0	.30	0	.70
a_L, $y_2 = g$ always	.30	0	.70	0
a_L, $y_2 = b$ always	0	.30	0	.70
a_L, always opposite	.30	0	.70	0

For example, if the manager supplies action a_H and always claims that $y_2 = g$ was observed (reprising our earlier notation, the manager always reports $\hat{y} = g$), the (0, g) pair will show up with probability .50. So, we design the contract to minimize the expected payment subject to the constraints that high action and truth satisfy the manager's opportunity cost and beat, from the manager's perspective, every other combination (i.e., every other row) in the preceding table.

EXHIBIT 15.2 **Optimal Pay-for-Performance for Various Information Structures**

Contracting Information	Signal $y = (y_1, y_2)$				
	$(0, g)$	$(0, b)$	$(1, g)$	$(1, b)$	$E[I \mid a_H]$
$y = y_1$	18,063	18,063	5,595	5,595	11,829
$y = (y_1, y_2)$	10,569	8,000	10,569	8,000	10,056
$y = (y_1, y_2)$, y_2 self-reported	18,063	8,000	5,595	8,000	11,562

We are now in a position in which contracting on both variables, given they are public, uses only the second variable, but contracting on a self-report of the second variable followed by public observation of the first uses both variables in the optimal contract. Why is it useful to use the first variable in the self-report case?

In the self-report case the manager is asked to do two things: supply a_H and candidly report what was privately observed. The y_2 realization, were it public, carries information about the manager's action. Although useless in the presence of a public second source, the first variable carries information about the manager's veracity. If the manager claims $y_2 = g$ is indeed present, we use the forthcoming y_1 realization as a back door check on that claim. If the claim is factual, the probability of subsequently observing $y_1 = 0$ is $.44/(.44 + .36) = .55 > .50$; but if it is false, the probability is $.06/(.14 + .06) = .30$. In effect, when the manager claims $y_2 = g$ was observed, that claim is backed up by accepting a bet on whether $y_1 = 0$ will be subsequently observed. By design, the bet is favorable only when a_H is chosen and g is observed. In equilibrium, that is, the manager accepts the bet, so to speak, under the intended circumstance.

The usefulness of the first source in disciplining the manager's veracity stems from two facts. First, the manager does not yet know what that source will report when he is called upon to self-report his private observation. Second, the odds on what that forthcoming report will convey depend on what the manager has actually observed. If the manager already knows the y_1 realization, that realization cannot be used to check his veracity. Likewise, if the odds on what the y_1 report will be do not vary with the y_2 realization, y_1 cannot possibly be used to check the self-report.

In Chapter 12 we stressed conditional information content in understanding when an additional measure might be useful for contracting purposes. There we were examining public information, and the concern was the manager's possible opportunistic supply of effort or action. A parallel test surfaces here to deal with the manager's possible opportunistic self-reporting. Think of the second variable, y_2, as now being self-reported. If it is true that the first variable is useful in the presence of a self-reported second variable, then either (1) the first tells us something new about the manager's action choice (i.e., has conditional information content as defined earlier) or (2) tells us something about the manager's self-report. The first condition can be expressed as $\pi(y_1 \mid y_2, a)$, must depend nontrivially on action a for some y_2; the second, can be expressed as $\pi(y_1 \mid y_2, a)$, must depend nontrivially on y_2 for some action a.

An important similarity should be coming into focus. If there is any hope the additional information might be useful for evaluating and therefore contracting with the manager, it must tell us something we do not know, so we condition on the in place second observation, y_2. It must also tell us something that is useful to know, something about the underlying opportunism concerns. In our stylized model, this boils down to telling us something about the action choice or something about the self-report.

Third Contracting Variable

Sensing victory, we now forge ahead and introduce a third contracting variable. This third variable is publicly observed after the manager has privately observed and self-reported the second source's signal.[2] It is also a garbling of the second variable. In particular, it will report $y_3 = b$ whenever (the second source reports) $y_2 = b$. If the second source reports $y_2 = g$, however, it will report $y_3 = g$ with probability $\alpha > .5$ and $y_3 = b$ with probability $1 - \alpha$. It is simply an inferior but public version of what the manager is privately observing.

This leads to the signal combinations and probabilities in Exhibit 15.3. Of course, $\alpha = 1$ is the case in which the third source perfectly mimics the second and de facto converts it to public information. On the other hand, $\alpha = 0$ is the case in which the third source is useless and reports the same thing regardless of underlying events. Also notice that we have only six combinations of the three signals since $y_2 = b$ is always accompanied by $y_3 = b$.

Now let $\alpha = .90$. Various pay-for-performance arrangements are displayed in Exhibit 15.4. Case 1 is our earlier setting in which the manager self-reports his private observation of the second source, and the first source is subsequently observed. This amounts to ignoring the third source.

To understand the third source's role here, a self-report by the manager that $y_2 = g$ is also a claim that the third source is likely to report $y_3 = g$. After all, the third source has a probability of $\alpha = .90$ of confirming such a claim if it is factual.[3] This suggests that we look to the third source as the primary backup to the self-report.

This is what we see in Case 2 in which both public signals as well as the manager's self-report are used. As before, the incentives are turned off

---

[2] So the timing is as follows: After contracting, the manager acts, privately observes the signal from the second source, and then issues a self-report. The first and third sources then publicly report, and compensation is delivered according to the contract.

[3] In parallel fashion, the manager has no interest whatever in claiming that $y_2 = b$ was observed when, in fact, $y_2 = g$ was observed.

EXHIBIT 15.3
Probabilities for
Expanded
Illustration

	Signal $y = (y_1, y_2, y_3)$					
	(0, g, g)	(0, g, b)	(0, b, b)	(1, g, g)	(1, g, b)	(1, b, b)
a_H	.44α	.44(1 − α)	.06	.36α	.36(1 − α)	.14
a_L	0	0	.30	0	0	.70

EXHIBIT 15.4   **Optimal Pay-for-Performance for Various Information Structures**
with Third Signal

Contracting Information	Signal $y = (y_1, y_2, y_3)$						
	(0, g, g)	(0, g, b)	(0, b, b)	(1, g, g)	(1, g, b)	(1, b, b)	$E[I \mid a_H]$
Case 1: $y = (y_1, y_2)$, y_2 self-reported	18,063	18,063	8,000	5,595	5,595	8,000	11,562
Case 2: $y = (y_1, y_2, y_3)$, y_2 self-reported	10,816	9,730	8,000	10,816	7,341	8,000	10,080
Case 3: $y = (y_1, y_3)$	10,865	8,687	8,687	10,865	7,720	7,720	10,085
Case 4: $y = (y_1, y_2)$, y_2 public	10,569	10,569	8,000	10,569	10,569	8,000	10,056
Case 5: $y = (y_1, y_2, y_3)$, y_2 public	10,569	10,569	8,000	10,569	10,569	8,000	10,056

when the manager self-reports that $y_2 = b$ was observed, but a claim that $y_2 = g$ was observed is handsomely rewarded if it is confirmed by the third source. Conversely, if that claim is not confirmed by the third source and is also followed by $y_1 = 1$ (the original bad news signal), we have a double dose of bad news, and that is when the penalty side of the arrangement is administered. All in all, the information base on which to evaluate the manager has improved.

A less efficient arrangement is to totally ignore the manager's self-report. This is Case 3 in which we rely on only the public sources, the first and third sources. The point here is that the manager knows whether the third source is in error relative to what has been privately observed; it is possible to use the manager's private information to improve the contracting information base. Of course, the manager's report must precede the public reports. Otherwise, the manager is too informed!

Finally, we also display Case 5 in which all three signals are publicly observed. Here we see that the third source has no information content in the presence of the first two sources. It is, after all, a garbling of the second source. Indeed, this is transparent when we contrast Case 5 with Case 4 in which the first two sources are presumed to be public.[4]

---

[4] We also see once more the fact that the first source has no information content in the presence of the second source provided the second source is public.

RICHER STORY

We now divulge the underlying details of this particular story. Return—where else?—to our prototypical firm that uses capital (K), labor (L), and managerial (M) inputs to produce output q, with technology specified by

$$q \leq M\sqrt{KL}$$

Now, however, the firm produces two products over two periods. It must supply $q_1 = 300$ of the first product in the first period followed by $q_2 = 1,000$ of the second product in the second period. Capital is acquired, as usual, at the start and is common to the two products.

Technology in the first period is simply

$$q_1 \leq \sqrt{KL_1}$$

where L_1 denotes labor in the first period. The second period labor requirements, however, depend on the managerial input, $M \in \{M_H, M_L\}$. We thus have the usual pair of requirements:

$$q_2 \leq M_H\sqrt{KL_2}$$

and

$$q_2 \leq M_L\sqrt{K(L_2 + L_2')}$$

where L_2 denotes labor in the second period, presuming that M_H materializes, and L_2' denotes the supplemental second period labor should M_L materialize.

The odds on the managerial input, M, depend on the manager's action, $a \in \{a_H, a_L\}$. For simplicity, the manager acts only once, at the beginning. A somewhat condensed time line is displayed in Exhibit 15.5.

Add to this the fact that the manager is specified precisely as in the earlier illustration. Important additional details including prices, probabilities, and the manager's specifics are given in Exhibit 15.6. To avoid clutter, a zero interest rate is assumed.

You should be able to verify that if action a_H is supplied, which implies 50–50 odds on the M variable, the firm's optimal choices are $K = 1,058.54$, $L_1 = 85.02$, $L_2 = 780.74$, and $L_2' = 385.55$.[5] Notice that at this point the single indicator of managerial input is whether second period labor must be supplemented. In particular, if the manager is productive, we will see a labor usage in the second period of $L_2 = 780.74$; but if the manager is not productive, the usage will be increased to $L_2 + L_2' = 1,166.29$.

From here notice that the labor cost (or usage) variable is the first information source in our earlier illustration: $y_1 = 0$ corresponds to no supplemental labor ($M = M_H$) and so on.

---

[5] We minimize the expected value (of the present value) of expenditures on capital and labor, or $100K + 100L_1 + 100L_2 + .5(100)L_2'$, subject to the three technology constraints (along with $q_1 = 300$ and $q_2 = 1,000$). For the record, the choices if action level a_L is supplied by the manager are $K = 1,096.42$, $L_1 = 82.09$, $L_2 = 753.77$, and $L_2' = 372.23$. Also, the firm's best choice of managerial action is a_H in all that follows.

EXHIBIT 15.5
Time Line for
Two-Period Setting

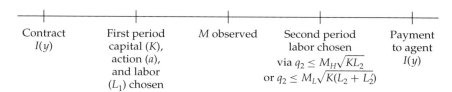

| Contract $I(y)$ | First period capital (K), action (a), and labor (L_1) chosen | M observed | Second period labor chosen via $q_2 \leq M_H\sqrt{KL_2}$ or $q_2 \leq M_L\sqrt{K(L_2 + L_2')}$ | Payment to agent $I(y)$ |

EXHIBIT 15.6
Details for
Two-Period Setting

> **Firm details**
>
> | | |
> |---|---|
> | Output quantities | $q_1 = 300$ and $q_2 = 1{,}000$ |
> | Managerial input | $M_H = 1.1$ and $M_L = .9$ |
> | Managerial input odds | $\pi(M_H \mid a_H) = .5$; $\pi(M_H \mid a_L) = .3$ |
> | Maximum capital | $K^{max} = 1{,}500$ |
>
> **Manager details**
>
> | | |
> |---|---|
> | Risk-aversion coefficient | $\rho = .0001$ |
> | Opportunity certainty equivalent | $\hat{\imath} = 5{,}000$ |
> | Personal costs | $c_H = 5{,}000$ and $c_L = 3{,}000$ |
>
> **(Spot) Market prices**
>
> | | |
> |---|---|
> | Capital | $p_K = 100$ |
> | Labor | $p_{L1} = 100$ and $p_{L2} = 100$ |

Inventory

This is just our starting point, however. By design, the manager's action affects the productivity of capital and labor in the second period. We now put some structure on this, albeit in a stylized fashion. If the manager exerts high action, it may be possible to begin work early on the second product. Think of this as prefabrication that, if successful, leads to work in process at the end of the first period. The ability to do this is not guaranteed, but if it can be done, it reduces the odds of requiring extra labor in the second period. So, we have a story in which M can take on one of two values and inventory can take on one of two values (present or absent).

This inventory variable is, in fact, the second information source in the earlier illustration. Glance back at Exhibit 15.1 and think of signal $y_2 = g$ as inventory being present and of signal $y_2 = b$ as no inventory being present. If the manager supplies action a_L, inventory never materializes, but if the manager supplies action a_H, inventory materializes with probability $.8 = \pi(y_2 = g \mid a_H)$. Moreover, the odds of requiring supplemental labor decline when the inventory is present: The probability of M_L if inventory is true and the manager has supplied a_H is $.36/(.44 + .36) = .45 < .50$.

The idea, then, is that good behavior by the manager (i.e., supply of a_H) creates the possibility that second period production can begin early (i.e., inventory is present). In turn, if this is the case, the odds of requiring extra labor go down.

Naturally, we want the accounting system to recognize inventory when it is present. If we are able to accomplish this, the inventory report amounts to conveying the second signal, and if this is publicly observed, we are back to Case 4 (or, for that matter, Case 5) in Exhibit 15.4. All is well.

What happens, however, if the inventory is privately observed by the manager?

Self-Reporting

We might simply ask the manager to self-report the presence (or absence) of inventory. Ideally, we could do this while relying on the Case 4 contract exhibited in Exhibit 15.4, the one in which the inventory observation is presumed public and therefore used aggressively by the contract. As we know, this places the manager in an awkward position: The only way to make bonus is to claim the inventory is present. It does not seem wise to encourage inventory fraud.

Expanding the incentives to motivate faithful reporting of the inventory, then, reduces us to Case 1 in Exhibit 15.4 in which the first variable is public but the second, the inventory observation, is private and self-reported. In effect, the inventory will be reliably reported here but at the implicit cost of not being able to make full use of that report in the contracting arrangement.[6]

Audited Accruals

At this point we introduce an auditor. The *auditor*, of course, provides an attestation service, or a report, if you will, on someone else's report. (Indeed, the auditor must make certain that inventory has been verified.)

Importantly, the auditor will begin with management's claim and proceed from there. If the manager claims that inventory is present, the auditor will attempt to verify that claim. Think of this as follows: The accounting records tentatively show work-in-process inventory, an accrual, and the auditor then attempts to verify the propriety of this accrual by attempting to verify the presence of the inventory.

To capture the idea of attestation, suppose the auditor correctly verifies inventory that is present with probability α and fails to verify such inventory with probability $1 - \alpha$. Conversely, if no inventory is present, the auditor never erroneously claims otherwise. Thus, attestation is perfect if $\alpha = 1$ but possibly in error otherwise. Moreover, in a technical sense, this

---

[6] A subtle issue also arises here. A key assumption in Case 1 in Exhibit 15.4 is that the firm is able to commit to how it will use the manager's self-report. Suppose, however, that the manager also has an equity position in the firm and that the self-report affects the market value of that equity position. The market, then, is also using that self-report and in a way the firm cannot possibly control. Absent some mythical way to perfectly foresee the valuation implications of the self-report, then, we have lost the ability to fully commit to how the manager's self-report will be used.

EXHIBIT 15.7 **Time Line for Information Events Including Audit Report**

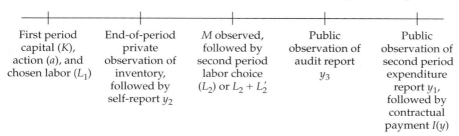

| First period capital (K), action (a), and chosen labor (L_1) | End-of-period private observation of inventory, followed by self-report y_2 | M observed, followed by second period labor choice (L_2) or $L_2 + L_2'$ | Public observation of audit report y_3 | Public observation of second period expenditure report y_1, followed by contractual payment $I(y)$ |

attestation is simply a garbling of the underlying, although privately known, information.

In effect, the auditor is able, although with error, to confirm or to attest to the manager's recorded claim or self-report. Moreover, this auditor is none other than the third contracting variable in Exhibit 15.4 in which confirmed inventory is reported as $y_3 = g$ and so on.[7] Essential timing details are displayed in Exhibit 15.7.

Do not, however, pass this off as another pithy comment. There is no reason here whatever to have an audit function if the manager is not present. The sole function of the auditor is to confirm the manager's self-report. If the manager does not have something worth self-reporting or does not have an incentive to manipulate this self-report in some fashion, we have no reason to introduce an auditor. This is evident in Exhibit 15.4. If the second source were public or supplied by a mechanical as opposed to a self-interested manager, the third information source would have no information content, be it in a contracting exercise or in a valuation exercise.[8]

Likewise, we see in Exhibit 15.4 that with a self-interested manager, the auditor's work is strictly valuable, even though it amounts to a garbling of what is already known by the manager. The garbled information is useful simply because we do not have costless access to what the manager privately knows. The only way to gain access to what the manager knows is through an evaluation arrangement that purposely underutilizes the forthcoming self-report. Otherwise, too much stress is placed on that self-report.

[7] The timing details are important. Initially, the manager privately observes whether prefabrication took place, that is, whether inventory is present. Any self-report takes place at this time. The auditor then seeks to verify a claim that inventory is present. Finally, second period expenditures, revealing whether M was M_H or M_L, are observed. First period expenditures are also observed, but they are, recall, completely determined by the initial K and L_1 expenditures and thus carry no information whatever.

[8] Of course, a larger story would allow the auditor the possibility of producing information that is complimentary or even superior to that of the manager, but the primary issue is verification of the manager's claim, and that is the reason we treat the third signal, the auditor's report, as a garbling of what the manager knows. After all, the auditor is performing an attestation service.

Here, then, we see in a microcosm the comparative advantage of the accounting system. The manager possesses important private information but lacks incentives to bring that information forward. The implicit price for bringing it forward is to underutilize that information relative to the way it would be used were it publicly observed. Some of what the manager privately knows, though, can be attested to (with error) by an auditor.

We thus see the power of the accrual recording. The information over and above the cash observation (equivalent to the M observation here) that is conveyed by the accounting system is carried by the accruals. Here the only substantive accrual is one that recognizes work-in-process inventory. In turn, the comparative advantage is that this accrual must pass the auditor's inspection. The accruals, that is, are carefully crafted to lend themselves to auditing.

The contracting arrangement in which cost, self-report, and the audited accrual are all used should now fall into place. Think of this as a financial reporting system that reports cash flow and the audited accrual.[9] Other information, here the manager's self-report, is also added to the stew. We thus arrive at a subtle mixing of information sources including the significant role played by the audited accruals.[10]

Parametric Variations

This view of mixing information sources is reinforced when we vary the quality of the auditor. In Exhibit 15.8, we plot the expected value of the manager's compensation for various information combinations as we vary the auditor's quality, the α, from $\alpha = 0$ when the auditor has a zero chance of doing anything useful, to $\alpha = 1$ when the auditor is a mythical error-free machine.

As a reference point, contracting on only the cost observation (see Exhibit 15.4) entails a compensation cost to the firm of $E[I \mid a_H] = 11{,}829$. This, of course, is the same as contracting on the cost and audit reports when the audit quality is nil, or $\alpha = 0$. Conversely, contracting on the manager's self-report and the cost observation entails a compensation cost of $E[I \mid a_H] = 11{,}562$. One thing to notice in the exhibit is that if the auditor is of sufficiently low quality, if α is near zero, the firm is better off contracting on the self-report and cost than it is contracting on the audit report and cost. The second thing to notice in the exhibit is that contracting on the cost, self-report, and audit strictly dominates contracting on the

---

[9] In turn, we could be more explicit about the channel through which the manager's self-report is conveyed. This might be an unaudited accrual, or it might be outside the accounting system altogether.

[10] Institutionally, the story can be interpreted as follows: The financial reporting system reports cash flow and audited accrual measures, and the management team also self-reports to the board of directors.

EXHIBIT 15.8
E[I | a$_H$] versus α for **Various Information Structures**

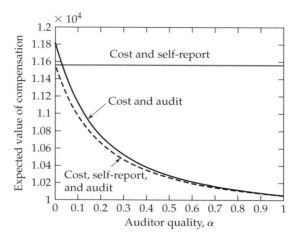

cost and audit report as long as the auditor is not error free, as long as α ≠ 1.

Back to Recognition

It is also important for us to link this audited accrual to the theme of recognition. Recall from Chapter 14 that the firm's recognition policy specifies the information that is to be collected and admitted into the accounting system. In our extended example, the firm's accounting system will record the cash flows as well as any inventory whose presence is confirmed by the auditor.[11] This is the accounting system's recognition policy. The accounting system does not simply enter the manager's claim about inventory but relies instead on the audit of that claim.

As in Chapter 14, it is convenient to represent the information as a partition of some set of states. We reformat the details in terms of an underlying state specification, and associated probabilities which reflect the audit specification of α = .9 in Exhibit 15.9. Be certain you see the connection between this display and our earlier exhibits.

Notice that the temporal partitions provided by any of the information sources, as displayed in Exhibit 15.10, depend on the manager's behavior. For example, if a$_H$ is supplied, the cost variable provides one partition of the eight states while the supply of a$_L$ provides a different partition of those states. This is inevitable because the manager's behavior specifies the connection between what is observed and the underlying states. This connection also dramatizes the important fact that a change in that behavior or a mere unanticipated behavior can lead us to unwittingly think we

---

[11] This recording is particularly simple because inventory in this case is a binary variable. Any nonzero valuation will convey the fact that the manager was successful in getting a leg up on the second period production.

EXHIBIT 15.9   **Recast of Exhibit 15.3 into States and Signals Format**

	s_1	s_2	s_3	s_4	s_5	s_6	s_7	s_8
$\pi(s_j)$	.044	.156	.240	.060	.036	.164	.160	.140
Cost, if a_H	$y_1 = 0$	$y_1 = 0$	$y_1 = 0$	$y_1 = 0$	$y_1 = 1$	$y_1 = 1$	$y_1 = 1$	$y_1 = 1$
Inventory, if a_H	$y_2 = g$	$y_2 = g$	$y_2 = g$	$y_2 = b$	$y_2 = g$	$y_2 = g$	$y_2 = g$	$y_2 = b$
Audit, if a_H	$y_3 = b$	$y_3 = g$	$y_3 = g$	$y_3 = b$	$y_3 = b$	$y_3 = g$	$y_3 = g$	$y_3 = b$
Cost, if a_L	$y_1 = 1$	$y_1 = 1$	$y_1 = 0$	$y_1 = 0$	$y_1 = 1$	$y_1 = 1$	$y_1 = 1$	$y_1 = 1$
Inventory, if a_L	$y_2 = b$	$y_2 = b$	$y_2 = b$	$y_2 = b$	$y_2 = b$	$y_2 = b$	$y_2 = b$	$y_2 = b$
Audit, if a_L	$y_3 = b$	$y_3 = b$	$y_3 = b$	$y_3 = b$	$y_3 = b$	$y_3 = b$	$y_3 = b$	$y_3 = b$

EXHIBIT 15.10   **Temporal Partitions Induced by Information Sources in Exhibit 15.9**

Information	$t = 1$ Partition	$t = 2$ Partition
Cost, if a_H (y_1)	$\{s_1, s_2, s_3, s_4, s_5, s_6, s_7, s_8\}$	$\{\{s_1, s_2, s_3, s_4\}, \{s_5, s_6, s_7, s_8\}\}$
Inventory, if a_H (y_2)	$\{\{s_1, s_2, s_3, s_5, s_6, s_7\}, \{s_4, s_8\}\}$	$\{\{s_1, s_2, s_3, s_5, s_6, s_7\}, \{s_4, s_8\}\}$
Audit, if a_H (y_3)	$\{\{s_1, s_4, s_5, s_8\}, \{s_2, s_3, s_6, s_7\}\}$	$\{\{s_1, s_4, s_5, s_8\}, \{s_2, s_3, s_6, s_7\}\}$
Cost, if a_L (y_1)	$\{s_1, s_2, s_3, s_4, s_5, s_6, s_7, s_8\}$	$\{\{s_3, s_4\}, \{s_1, s_2, s_5, s_6, s_7, s_8\}\}$
Inventory, if a_L (y_2)	$\{s_1, s_2, s_3, s_4, s_5, s_6, s_7, s_8\}$	$\{s_1, s_2, s_3, s_4, s_5, s_6, s_7, s_8\}$
Audit, if a_L (y_3)	$\{s_1, s_2, s_3, s_4, s_5, s_6, s_7, s_8\}$	$\{s_1, s_2, s_3, s_4, s_5, s_6, s_7, s_8\}$

EXHIBIT 15.11   **Equilibrium Temporal Partitions**

Information	$t = 1$ Partition	$t = 2$ Partition
All available (y_1, y_2, y_3)	$\{\{s_1, s_5\}, \{s_2, s_3, s_6, s_7\}, \{s_4, s_8\}\}$	$\{\{s_1\}, \{s_5\}, \{s_2, s_3\}, \{s_6, s_7\}, \{s_4\}, \{s_8\}\}$
Accounting (y_1, y_3)	$\{\{s_1, s_4, s_5, s_8\}, \{s_2, s_3, s_6, s_7\}\}$	$\{\{s_1, s_4\}, \{s_2, s_3\}, \{s_5, s_8\}, \{s_6, s_7\}\}$

are observing signals from one system when in fact they are being produced by another system. We expect that the parties' behavior will lead to a specific set of temporal partitions, the equilibrium temporal partitions highlighted in Exhibit 15.11.

Exhibit 15.10, of course, displays the possible partitions, but we must also remember that the manager is being motivated to supply action a_H. In equilibrium, then, when the manager rationally responds to the well-designed incentive arrangement, we expect action a_H will be supplied. This means that we expect the observed partitions will be those displayed in Exhibit 15.11.

In particular, if the manager is well behaved, the accounting system will report any audited inventory accrual at time $t = 1$, and, of course, will report the receipts and expenditures at times $t = 1$ and $t = 2$. In these latter categories, however, the only uncertainty is the labor expenditure in the second period. In short, the accounting system will be reporting the pair of signals, (y_1, y_3), and the underlying stochastic structure will be governed by the manager's equilibrium behavior. The accounting partitions will be those associated with the recognition rules (capture the cash and the audited accruals) and the manager's behavior.

Moreover, the accounting partition will be but a subset of what is known at each point. All available information, which reflects the manager's self-report as well, is the other display in Exhibit 15.11. Now you see the reason we refer to recognition as defining the partitions and to those partitions as being temporal aggregations of all available information.

We should not lose sight of the adjective in the title of Exhibit 15.11. These are the *temporal partitions* that will be observed in equilibrium, meaning when the parties are well behaved. It is the threat of what partitions would be observed were the parties not well behaved that is the strength of the control system. Recognition requires us to specify the equilibrium and the off-equilibrium partitions.[12]

Summary

In purely mechanical terms, the story in this chapter is friction-laden contracting with a manager. An important, even powerful information source is present, but it is privately observed by the manager. A garbling of that private information is publicly available and can be used to discipline the manager's self-reporting.

It is the tie to institutional details that captures our interest. The information content perspective is uncompromising. Accounting must, in this view, carry information. A closer look brings us to the position that the substantive information carried by the accounting system is carried by the accruals because cash flow (another source of information) is a vastly easier approach to accounting, and cash flow is routinely reported in conjunction with the usual accrual reports. In addition, we know that there are many sources of information. We thus arrive at the view that accounting is a source of information but is also a source that coexists with other sources.

Coexistence implies that the accounting system has a comparative advantage: It is designed to be difficult to manipulate. This implies that it is slow to report because the auditor requires time to perform the necessary audit functions; the system is also careful about what information is allowed into its structure, into the accruals. Otherwise, we would be asking the auditor to audit, to attest to, to verify the essentially unverifiable!

This view is the centerpiece of our work in this chapter. The cash flow boils down to the level of second period labor expenditures, which is equivalent to observing the M variable. Other information is conveyed by the manager's self-report on the success or failure of prefabrication, that

---

[12] To reinforce this point, we often think of an auditor as sampling from a population, but this population is endogenous; it is affected by the manager's behavior. It is the threat of what the auditor's sampling rule might uncover were the manager to engineer a different population that is the key idea in the control system design.

is, on the presence or absence of work-in-process inventory in the first period. This self-report is not acted upon or conveyed by the formal accounting structure. Rather, the accounting structure rests on the auditor's report. If the auditor reports that work-in-process inventory is present, that fact is reflected in an appropriate accrual.

In a sense, then, this is all about recognition. Two features add some spice and subtlety to the stew. First, if we are to have an interest in the information, there must be some explicit use of that information to be made. Since we are dealing with a service, the auditing of accruals, that would be difficult to rationalize without some sort of contracting friction, we place the story squarely in the context of a contracting exercise. Second, once this is done, we see that the recognition rules must be viewed from the perspective of what might be reported if the manager is well behaved and what might be reported if the manager is not so well behaved. Proper design requires attention to both "paths."

Selected References

The additional nuance in this chapter is a veracity check of a self-report, a check that in and of itself would be superfluous if the self-report were utterly reliable. We interpret this veracity check as an auditor, an attestation, although we sidestep the important issue of how the audit service itself is well controlled. Favorite expositions of this attestation theme are Ijiri (1975), who stresses "hardness"; Sundem, Dukes, and Elliott (1996), who stress veracity; and Kinney (2000), who stresses "quality" and its perception. Extension into explicit strategic aspects is well illustrated by Fellingham and Newman (1985); controlling the auditor is illustrated by Datar, Feltham, and Hughes (1991) and Arya and Glover (1996). Connections to voluntary disclosures in a valuation market are illustrated by Gigler (1994).

Key Terms

A **temporal partition** is simply a sequence of partitions through time. An **equilibrium temporal partition** is a temporal partition that, given equilibrium play by the parties—the firm and the manager—in the contracting game, is the partition whose element will be observed by an outside party, the temporal partition, so to speak, that will be played in the game. An **auditor** is able to confirm or attest to a report filed by the manager (or management). This confirmation or attestation is hardly flawless because errors are associated with the auditor's report. That report takes the form of **audited accruals**.

Exercises

15.1. Explain why, from a contracting perspective, the first information source in Exhibit 15.1 has no information content in the presence of the second source, yet the second source has information content in the presence of the first source. (Assume that both sources are public.)

15.2. Verify that the contract for the self-reporting case in Exhibit 15.2 does motivate the manager to both supply action a_H and candidly report what is privately observed. Explain the connection between your verification and the table in Note 1.

15.3. Change the probabilities in Exhibit 15.1 so the first source has no information content if the second source is public, but the second source has no information content if that source is privately observed by the manager (before the first signal is observed, of course). Explain the intuition behind your alteration of the probabilities.

15.4. Chapter 15 relies on the idea that accruals carry information and on the claim that a formal recording of an inventory balance is in fact an accrual. Is it? Explain.

15.5. Return to Exhibits 15.5 and 15.6 and assume that payment for capital is made at time $t = 0$, payment for labor is made at the end of the respective periods, and the manager is paid at the end of the second period. Furthermore, suppose that, to save needless details, the manager is actually paid a flat wage of 10,000 and supplies a_H (so some type of highly useful monitor is in place). Also suppose that the customers pay upon delivery, say, P per unit. Determine the cash flow at each point in time.

15.6. Using your cash flow calculations in Exercise 15.5, determine whether, from a valuation perspective, the second information source reporting at time $t = 1$ has information content. Repeat for the third source, first when the second source is not available and second when the second source is also available. What does this tell you about the usefulness of the audit function, given no contracting friction, in this case?

15.7. This is another extension of Exercise 15.5. Suppose that the recognition rule described in Exhibits 15.9 and 15.10 is in place and that at time $t = 1$, the manager's self-report is observed by the market, and, following that self-report, the audited financial statement for the first period is reported. Determine the value of the overall cash flow series at $t = 0$ just after the self-report is observed, and, finally, just after the audited financial statement is observed. Relate your findings to the Ball and Brown experiment, Exhibit 10.8. (Remember that we assume a zero interest rate here.)

15.8. Once again, Ralph seeks labor input from a manager. The output is one of two quantities: $x_1 < x_2$, and the manager's input can be one of two quantities, $L < H$. If the manager supplies input a and is paid compensation ι, his utility measure is $-\exp(-\rho(\iota - c_a))$, with $\rho = .0001$; also, the manager's opportunity certainty equivalent is $\hat{\iota} = 10,000$; $c_H = 4,000$ and $c_L = 0$. Ralph is risk neutral and seeks input H.

For most of the exercise, a monitor is also available for contracting purposes. The monitor will report g or b. Probabilities follow.

	(g, x_1)	(b, x_1)	(g, x_2)	(b, x_2)
Input H	.2	.1	.6	.1
Input L	0	.8	0	.2

a. Initially suppose that the monitor is not available, so the contract can depend on only the output. Determine an optimal contract.
b. Now suppose that both the monitor and the output are available. Determine an optimal contract. Provide an intuitive explanation for your finding.
c. Next suppose that the manager privately observes the monitor (after acting, of course, but before the output is observed). Determine an optimal contract that will motivate the manager to supply $a = H$ and to candidly reveal his private information.
d. Finally, suppose that a veracity check is also possible. This will report b if the manager's private information is signal b, but if the manager's private information is signal g, this veracity check will report g with probability .95 and b with probability .05. Determine an optimal contract. Provide an intuitive explanation for your contract.

15.9. This is a continuation of Exercise 15.8. Now suppose that the veracity check works in the opposite manner. If the manager's private signal is g, the veracity check always reports g; but if the private signal is b, the veracity check calls it correct with probability .95. Determine an optimal contract, and explain the difference between what you found here and what you found in Exercise 15.8.

15.10. Repeat Exercises 15.8 and 15.9 for the case in which the probabilities are given by the following:

	(g, x_1)	(b, x_1)	(g, x_2)	(b, x_2)
Input H	.2	.1	.1	.6
Input L	.4	.4	.1	.1

15.11. Is it possible that an audited accrual could have information content, conditional on all other information, for contracting purposes but not for valuation purposes? Explain.

16

Conditional Recognition

The firm's recognition rule governs what it reports via its accounting system, and the focus is, naturally, on the accruals. We also know that the integrity of what is so reported is well defended, a feature we highlighted in Chapter 15 by interpreting the accounting report as a public although garbled version of what the firm wished to self-report. A final institutional detail is now added to the story: What is entered into the accounting system is often conditional on what is learned from other sources. Lower of cost or market, for example, requires market price be reported only if it is below cost. We call this *conditional recognition*. As you will see, this feature brings efficiency to the task of attesting to the accounting report and ties to the *conservatism* we associate with the accounting channel.

We now deepen our view of recognition to acknowledge the important institutional detail that recognition is often conditional in nature. Whether to recognize some activity or event often depends on what has been learned from other information sources. For example, a potential loss arising from a lawsuit will be recognized under U.S. GAAP if the loss is probable and if it can be reasonably well estimated. If the available information indicates that the loss is probable, the reporting firm then searches for information on which to base an estimate of the loss; if the resulting loss can be sufficiently well estimated, it will be recognized. The loss recognition, so to speak, is conditional on other information indicating the likelihood of the contingency occurring, and once this likelihood passes a threshold of being probable, additional information is brought to bear on the estimation issue.

In similar fashion, suppose the firm's debt is troubled and the firm exchanges some of its assets for the outstanding debt. At this point we typically require the fair value of the assets so exchanged to be estimated and any gain or loss associated with the exchange to be recognized. Here, too, we see conditional recognition. The exchange of assets for the liability calls for an estimate of the then fair value of the assets exchanged; otherwise, absent the exchange, no fair value estimate would be recognized.

The audit process itself exhibits the same pattern. The auditor, for example, searches transactions and events after the statements' closing date to check whether important items have escaped recognition or disclosure. In a deeper sense, the entire audit is an exercise in contingent recognition because all of the information that the audit team has is brought to bear on the questions of what evidence to gather, how to interpret the gathered evidence, and, in the limit, whether the accumulated evidence is sufficient to sustain the auditor's opinion.

Our task here is to expand the comparative advantage theme of audited accruals to highlight this detail of conditional recognition. As we know, the substantive information carried by the accounting system is carried by the accruals. Conditional recognition expands this idea to allow the choice of what information to convey to depend on what other information sources have to say.[1] Moreover, combining the comparative advantage and conditional recognition themes points toward an endogenous and asymmetric tendency to challenge "good news" but accept "bad news" without question.

We begin by revisiting the work-in-process illustration used in Chapter 15. From there, we modify the story by introducing a new public information source and formalize the conditional recognition theme. Then we add an intermediate layer of self-reporting by the manager. When the smoke clears, we will have a setting in which so-called conservative reporting is efficient.

PRIOR ACQUAINTANCE

As it turns out (thanks to your authors), the work-in-process illustration from Chapter 15 well illustrates the theme of conditional recognition. The story there, recall, was a two-period setting in which the manager's input in the second period could turn out to be highly ($M = M_H$) or not so highly ($M = M_L$) productive; the setting was crafted so the contract with the

---

[1] In this sense, conditional recognition is a form of "management by exception": If circumstances warrant, additional information is produced and admitted into the accounting system. Recall the more abstract definition of recognition in Chapter 14, especially (14.1) and (14.2), as a mapping from the information to which the firm has access to what is formally included in the accounting system. Conditional recognition now simply means we are working with a more subtle mapping or rule.

EXHIBIT 16.1
Details for Earlier
Numerical
Illustration

Firm details	
Output quantities	$q_1 = 300$ and $q_2 = 1{,}000$
Managerial input	$M_H = 1.1$ and $M_L = .9$
Managerial input odds	$\pi(M_H \mid a_H) = .5$; $\pi(M_H \mid a_L) = .3$
Maximum capital	$K^{max} = 1{,}500$
Manager details	
Risk-aversion coefficient	$\rho = .0001$
Opportunity certainty equivalent	$\hat{\imath} = 5{,}000$
Personal costs	$c_H = 5{,}000$ and $c_L = 3{,}000$

manager relied on a pay-for-performance structure. Details are summarized in Exhibit 16.1.

The manager also might be able to begin work on the second period product in the first period, resulting in work-in-process inventory. Importantly, the presence of such inventory is an informative indicator of the manager's behavior. This led to a setting in which the manager could claim, at the end of the first period, that work-in-process inventory was or was not present. Such self-reporting invites opportunistic behavior, and we then added to the stew an auditor who could, with error, verify the presence of inventory. The story illustrates the common theme that inventory misreporting can be an overwhelming temptation, and, as a result, verification of inventory is an essential step for the auditor.

Notice the chain of events. If the manager claims that inventory is present, the auditor has reason to verify that claim. In turn, if the claim is indeed verified, the inventory will be acknowledged and will be recognized by the accounting system. The recognition of work in process depends on the claim that such inventory is present backed by the verification of that claim. Recognition is conditional on the claim and its verification.

EXPANDED MOSAIC

We now embellish the setting to better explore the conditional recognition theme. We make two changes. First, to keep the number of information variables at a reasonable level, we now assume only one period and consequently no intermediate inventory. Thus, without additional information, the parties will contract on the cost incurred or, equivalently, whether the managerial input was M_H or M_L. As usual, this is the first information source, with $y_1 = 0$ corresponding to low cost incurred and so on.

Second, we also suppose that an additional information source, a second source, is available. It will report good ($y_2 = g$) or bad ($y_2 = b$) news. This second source is a late-reporting source, or a monitor, because it reports after the manager has acted. Although it strains credulity in a single-period model, it is intuitively helpful to think of this new source as an estimate of the "fair value" of an end-of-period inventory or some other accrual. Regardless, the probability of a good or bad news report depends only on the manager's input: $\pi(y_2 \mid y_1, a) = \pi(y_2 \mid a)$. It is also symmetric in that

$$\pi(y_2 = g \mid a_H) = \pi(y_2 = b \mid a_L) = \beta \geq .50 \qquad \textbf{(16.1)}$$

A well-behaved manager has probability $\beta \geq .50$ of receiving a good news report from the monitor, just as an opportunistic manager has probability $\beta \geq .50$ of receiving a bad news report from the monitor.

The event structure implied in Exhibit 16.1 now expands as displayed in Exhibit 16.2. If $\beta = .50$, the source is complete noise, a coin flip. Otherwise, a good news report is more likely under a_H, just as a bad news report is more likely under a_L. This is further evidenced by the likelihood ratios displayed in Exhibit 16.2, and this is what justifies the labels of good and bad news.

Optimal pay-for-performance arrangements for several variations on this theme are displayed in Exhibit 16.3. The first row, the $\beta = .50$ case, is the noted benchmark in which the monitor is useless. Here the only useful contracting variable is the first source, the cost realization: We pay 18,063 for $y_1 = 0$ and 5,595 for $y_1 = 1$. This is the same benchmark as in Chapter 15.

Next we endow the second source with serious information content, setting $\beta = .80$. Here you should notice that less risk is imposed on the manager; for any cost (or y_1) realization, pay is higher if the monitor reports good news (g) rather than bad news (b), and the two sources of information complement each other. The highest pay is when both sources report "good news," just as the lowest pay is when both report "bad news."

EXHIBIT 16.2
Probabilities for Base Case Illustrations

	Signal $y = (y_1, y_2)$			
	(0, g)	**(0, b)**	**(1, g)**	**(1, b)**
$\pi((y_1, y_2) \mid a_H)$	$.50\beta$	$.50(1 - \beta)$	$.50\beta$	$.50(1 - \beta)$
$\pi((y_1, y_2) \mid a_L)$	$.30(1 - \beta)$	$.30\beta$	$.70(1 - \beta)$	$.70\beta$
Likelihood ratio	$.6(1 - \beta)/\beta$	$.6\beta/(1 - \beta)$	$1.4(1 - \beta)/\beta$	$1.4\beta/(1 - \beta)$

EXHIBIT 16.3   **Optimal Pay-for-Performance for Various Information Structures**

	Signal $y = (y_1, y_2)$				
Contracting Information	**(0, g)**	**(0, b)**	**(1, g)**	**(1, b)**	$E[I \mid a_H]$
$y = (y_1, y_2),\ \beta = .5$	18,063	18,063	5,595	5,595	11,829
$y = (y_1, y_2),\ \beta = .8$	10,653	9,229	10,534	6,774	10,075
$y = (y_1, y_2),\ y_2$ only if $y_1 = 0,\ \beta = .8$	13,364	4,203	9,310	9,310	10,421
$y = (y_1, y_2),\ y_2$ only if $y_1 = 1,\ \beta = .8$	10,419	10,419	10,583	6,413	10,084

EXHIBIT 16.4
**Time Line for
Conditional
Production of
Second Source**

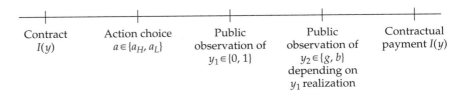

Conditional Monitoring

The latter two rows of Exhibit 16.3 illustrate conditional monitoring. Here we wait until the first information source, the cost realization, is observed; depending on what that realization is, we decide whether to invoke the second source, which is the monitor. The time line is displayed in Exhibit 16.4.[2]

Although unmodeled, the idea is simple. Think of the second source as costly. To save on information cost, then, we defer the decision on whether to acquire the second source until after we have observed the first source's report. Naturally, if we do not acquire the second source all the time, we have reduced the information available for evaluating the manager—but to what effect?

In our setting there are two ways to proceed. One is to order the second source when the first source reports $y_1 = 0$ (low cost is observed). The other is to order it when the first source reports $y_1 = 1$ (high cost is observed). These are the latter two rows of Exhibit 16.3.

Consider the "only if $y_1 = 0$" case in which we order the new monitor only if $y_1 = 0$ is observed. Restricting the second source to be present only when $y_1 = 0$ is present amounts to forcing the manager's payment to be the same for the $y = (1, g)$ and $y = (1, b)$ events because the second source is now not available when $y_1 = 1$ is observed. Parallel comments apply to the "only if $y_1 = 1$" case.

The important point to notice now is the difference in the firm's cost of acquiring action a_H from the manager. If we are going to condition acquisition of the second monitor on what the first source reports, it is better to acquire the second monitor when the first source reports $y_1 = 1$ rather than when it reports $y_1 = 0$ ($E[I \mid a_H] = 10,084$ versus $10,421$). Stated differently, the first source reports either good ($y_1 = 0$) or bad ($y_1 = 1$) news, and it is better to supplement that report, to look further into the matter, when bad news is reported than when good news is reported. Chase bad news!

Why the difference—why does it pay to chase the bad news? We carefully set the exercise so we have 50–50 odds on $y_1 = 0$ versus $y_1 = 1$. So, regardless of which realization we condition on, we are producing the

---

[2] The time line is heavily condensed in order to display the information timing assumptions. Just underneath we have the usual capital (K) and labor (L) stories.

additional information with probability .50. The new information is also conditionally independent of the y_1 realization.[3] This means that the odds on what the new information source will report depend on the manager's behavior but not additionally on what the first source has reported. In short, the setting is neutralized, so the monitor's information content is unaffected by whether its acquisition is conditioned on a good or bad news report.

With this in mind, now think of the monitor as offering insurance to a well-behaved manager. If the earlier source reports good news, there is little to insure, but if it reports bad news, it is efficient to have insurance. Presuming the manager has behaved but had the misfortune of a bad news initial evaluation, providing a second evaluation at that point offers attractive odds of countering the initial bad news. This second evaluation is, of course, the noted monitor. We thus chase the bad news.

Likewise, if the manager behaves opportunistically, bad news from the first source is more likely. Chasing the bad news now increases the odds of producing the additional information; if that information is produced, it is likely to double the supply of bad news facing the (opportunistic) manager.[4] (Remember that we identify information content in a contracting environment by contrasting what might be reported if the manager behaves with what might be reported if the manager misbehaves.)

In fact, as is evident in Exhibit 16.5, this overall pattern remains as we vary the quality of the second source, the monitor. There we plot the expected compensation to the manager versus the second source's quality, β, for the three information structures exhibited previously: acquire the second source only if the first source reports $y_1 = 0$, only if the first source reports $y_1 = 1$, or regardless of what the first source reports.[5] If $\beta = .50$, the monitor is useless, and all three structures are equally ineffective. After all, the second source is pure noise in the $\beta = .50$ case, so producing it all the time or conditional on the first source's report is of no import. Noise is noise.

---

[3] Return to Exhibit 16.2 and look at the likelihood ratios. They are, under $\beta = .8$, respectively, .15, 2.4, .35, and 5.6. If $y_1 = 0$ is observed, its likelihood ratio is spread from .6 to .15 and 2.4 by appending the monitor; similarly, if $y_1 = 1$ is observed, its likelihood ratio is spread from 1.4 to .35 and 5.6. The two "spreads" are in the same proportions because the "amount" of new information conveyed by the second source is conditionally independent of the y_1 realization.

[4] The insurance explanation, then, rests on the manager's risk aversion. It is also important to note the manager is modeled with constant risk aversion; the degree of risk aversion, presuming it remains nontrivial, does not affect the pattern in Exhibit 16.3.

[5] Here and in the following related exhibits, we plot the expected value of the manager's compensation against the quality of the information. Each such plot is based on the optimal pay-for-performance arrangement; it is optimal given the information quality identified on the horizontal axis.

EXHIBIT 16.5
$E[I \mid a_H]$ versus
**Second Source
Quality β for
Various Information
Structures**

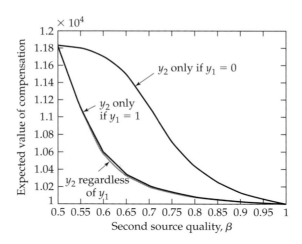

Likewise, if $\beta = 1$, the three information structures are equally effective and rather powerful. Suppose the manager supplies low action. With $\beta = 1$, any report by the second source will unequivocally identify this opportunistic behavior. The new information is now so powerful it makes no difference whether it is produced all the time or simply with positive probability. Any report of opportunistic behavior coupled with a severe penalty attached thereto is all we require.

In between ($.5 < \beta < 1$), chasing the bad news strictly dominates chasing the good news. Moreover, the slippage between chasing the bad news and acquiring the second source unconditionally is nearly trivial.[6]

Self-Reporting

An important extension now is the case in which the manager privately observes the second source. This private observation story again fits nicely with our running (somewhat tongue-in-cheek) interpretation that the second source reports the end-of-period inventory's fair value. Naturally, to make this interesting, we must reverse the sequence in which the two information sources report and now assume that the second source, or inventory valuation, is (privately) observed before the first source, or total cost incurred, is observed. Might we then ask the manager to self-report the private observation?

In principle, this has considerable appeal. We ask the manager to self-report before the first source, the cost observation, is observed. That way

---

[6] To be sure, this pattern is not universal. Altering the story in significant ways would allow us to demonstrate a setting in which chasing good news dominates chasing bad news. Also notice that we endow the firm with important commitment power here. It can presumably commit to following some such conditional information acquisition policy.

the first source can be used not only to evaluate the manager's action choice or effort supply but also to discipline the self-report.

Unfortunately, it is useless to explore this avenue. Recall that what the second source reports depends on the manager's action but not on the first source's realization. This means the first source cannot be used to check the veracity of the manager's report. If you track down the optimal contract in this case, you will discover that it does not use the manager's self-report. We have designed the setting so that self-reporting is useless.[7]

EXPANDED STORY

Our next step is to introduce yet additional information. (Surprise!) This new source is the third in the story, so its signal is denoted y_3. This source is a noisy indicator or a garbling of the second source and is conditionally independent of the first source or of the manager's action. Think of it as an audit of the end-of-period inventory valuation, and therefore accrual.

Again we use the good (g) and bad (b) nomenclature, and symmetry is imposed: $\pi(y_3 \mid y_2, y_1, a) = \pi(y_3 \mid y_2)$ along with

$$\pi(y_3 = g \mid y_2 = g) = \pi(y_3 = b \mid y_2 = b) = \gamma \geq .50 \qquad \textbf{(16.2)}$$

This new source, then, is simply a symmetric garbling of the second source. With probability γ, it reports what the second source reported, and with probability $1 - \gamma$, it reports the opposite. Naturally, if the second source is publicly observed, this garbling is utterly useless; it is a rare combination of redundancy and error.[8]

We also know, however, that if the second source is self-reported, this redundant, error-prone backup can be used to discipline that self-reporting. Let the second source be 80 percent accurate, $\beta = .80$. Also let the third source mimic the second source 70 percent of the time, $\gamma = .70$. Furthermore, suppose the manager privately observes and self-reports what the second source revealed, and following that report, the third and

[7] You might enjoy verifying our self-report that self-reporting here is useless. The manager's possible strategies and associated event probabilities follow.

Action and Report Strategy	(0, g)	(0, b)	(1, g)	(1, b)
a_H, truth	.5β	.5(1 − β)	.5β	.5(1 − β)
a_H, g always	.50	0	.50	0
a_H, b always	0	.50	0	.50
a_H, always opposite	.5(1 − β)	.5β	.5(1 − β)	.5β
a_L, truth	.3(1 − β)	.3β	.7(1 − β)	.7β
a_L, g always	.30	0	.70	0
a_L, b always	0	.30	0	.70
a_L, always opposite	.3β	.3(1 − β)	.7β	.7(1 − β)

[8] Of course, what we mean by *rare* depends on the baseline. Consider speeches at public meetings or political promises.

EXHIBIT 16.6
Time Line for
Expanded, Private
Information Setting

Contract $I(y)$	Action choice $a \in \{a_H, a_L\}$	Private observation and self-report of $y_2 \in \{g, b\}$	Public observation of $y_3 \in \{g, b\}$ (possibly depending on self-report of y_2)	Public observation of $y_1 \in \{0, 1\}$, followed by contractual payment $I(y)$

EXHIBIT 16.7 **Optimal Pay-for-Performance Using Self-report of y_2**

				$y = (y_1, y_2, y_3)$					
$(0, g, g)$	$(0, g, b)$	$(0, b, g)$	$(0, b, b)$	$(1, g, g)$	$(1, g, b)$	$(1, b, g)$	$(1, b, b)$	$E[I \mid a_H]$
12,739	10,584	11,183	11,183	11,591	4,767	6,373	6,373	10,410

first sources are publicly observed. This gives us eight distinct events in the contracting exercise and the time line displayed in Exhibit 16.6.[9] (Clearly, this is getting out of hand.)

The optimal pay-for-performance arrangement is displayed in Exhibit 16.7. Notice the pattern. If the manager self-reports good news (claims $y_2 = g$ is true), subsequent confirmation (by observing $y_3 = g$) is rewarded, just as subsequent lack of confirmation (by observing $y_3 = b$) is penalized. Self-reporting $y_2 = g$ is accompanied by a bet, so to speak, on what the new source will report. In addition, the penalty when the second and third sources disagree in this fashion is most severe when $y_1 = 1$, high cost, is also observed.

Conversely, if the manager self-reports bad news (claims $y_2 = b$ is true), this claim is not subjected to a veracity check (via the third source, the information from (16.2)). Instead, following such a claim, the manager is paid 11,183 if $y_1 = 0$ is observed and 6,373 if $y_1 = 1$ is observed. Intuitively, the arrangement uses the third source only when the manager self-reports good news from the first source because self-reporting good news is a pressure point in the control system.

The overall cost to the firm, $E[I \mid a_H] = 10,410$, is strictly below its counterpart of 11,829 if the firm contracted on only the manager's self-report and the first source. (Glance back at Exhibit 16.3 to confirm the 11,829 amount.) Naturally, we incur some slippage because, even with the veracity check, it is not possible to aggressively use the manager's self-report as we would were the initial source's revelation public.

Now consider our earlier theme of producing the additional information conditional on what the earlier source reports. Of course, this implies

[9] Recall that we modified the initial story so observation of work-in-process inventory has no information content. Had we not done that, we would have not 8 but 16 distinct events in the pay-for-performance arrangement.

EXHIBIT 16.8

E[I | a_H] versus
**Third Source
Quality γ for
Various Information
Structures ($\beta = .8$)**

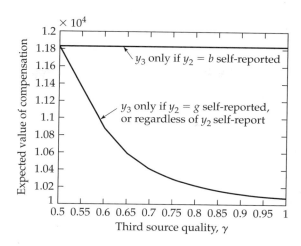

that we now condition the acquisition of the third source on what the manager claims the second source reported. The two ways to proceed are to produce the additional information or invoke (16.2) only if the manager self-reports good news or only if the manager self-reports bad news. Chasing the good news report is, of course, equivalent to what we have in Exhibit 16.7. The reason is that a self-report of bad news is not subsequently tested. Likewise, chasing only the bad news report whose veracity is hardly in question returns us to the case in which the third source is never available simply because in this case the source is invoked precisely when it is useless—not a good idea.

This pattern is also evident in more general fashion in Exhibit 16.8. There we plot the firm's cost of acquiring action a_H, $E[I | a_H]$ versus the quality of the third source, which is the garbling parameter γ, all presuming that the second source—the privately observed source—has a quality level of $\beta = .8$. Chasing the bad news has no effect regardless of γ. Chasing the good news is uniformly productive, and in this case is equivalent to producing the third source regardless of the manager's self-report.

The take away here is that we are concerned about the veracity of the manager's self-report and that we have access to a garbled version of what the manager actually observed in private. The best way to use this additional source is to chase a good news report, presuming we want to condition its acquisition on the earlier information. The reason is that claiming good news is the point at which the manager faces the greatest temptation; it is the point where the self-reporting friction is present. Moreover, chasing good news is just the opposite of what we saw earlier when self-reporting was not at issue. This phenomenon is most evident in Exhibits 16.5 and 16.8. In Exhibit 16.5 it is best to chase the bad news event, $y_1 = 1$. In Exhibit 16.8, it is best to chase the good news event, which is a self-report of good news by the manager. The additional information in

Exhibit 16.5 is used to help discipline the manager's action choice, but in Exhibit 16.8, it is used to help discipline the manager's self-reporting of information that can, in turn, be used to help discipline the underlying action choice.

Aside

It is also important to acknowledge that the comparison here is based on different conditioning events using the first source, or cost realization, in the first case and the manager's self-report of the second source in the second case. What if instead we condition on the first source, on y_1, as we did in the earlier foray? Exhibit 16.9 provides the answer.

In Exhibit 16.9 we replicate the Exhibit 16.8 story in which the manager privately observes and self-reports the second source but now base the invocation of the third source on what the first source reports instead of on the manager's self-report.

Not surprisingly, we now revert to the earlier pattern of chasing the bad news, $y_1 = 1$. The intuition is straightforward. If $y_1 = 1$ is observed, a well-behaved manager has had bad luck, and the third source now plays an insurance role for the manager, although somewhat indirectly. This effect dominates the veracity check because that check can no longer be directed precisely at the problematic claim of good news.

Although this discourse is surely wearing thin, we provide a summary comparison in Exhibit 16.10. Several patterns are illustrated. The firm can do no better than contract on the first two sources provided they can be publicly observed. In a related manner, conditioning the acquisition of the second source on a bad news observation from the first source is remarkably efficient. If the manager privately observes the second source, however, self-reporting is useful provided it is backed up by the garbled although

EXHIBIT 16.9

$E[I \mid a_H]$ versus Third Source Quality γ for Various Information Structures ($\beta = .8$)

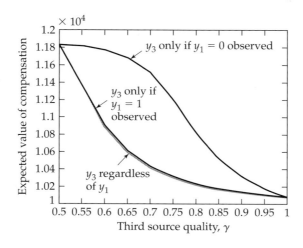

EXHIBIT 16.10
Summary
Comparison of
Various Information
Structures (using
$\beta = .8$ and $\gamma = .7$)

Information Structure	$E[I \mid a_H]$
Public y_1, public y_2	10,075
Public y_1, public y_2 only if $y_1 = 0$	10,421
Public y_1, public y_2 only if $y_1 = 1$	10,084
Public y_1, y_2 self-report, public y_3	10,410
Public y_1, y_2 self-report, public y_3 only if $y_2 = g$ self-reported	10,410
Public y_1, y_2 self-report, public y_3 only if $y_2 = b$ self-reported	11,829
Public y_1, y_2 self-report, public y_3 only if $y_1 = 0$ observed	11,517
Public y_1, y_2 self-report, public y_3 only if $y_1 = 1$ observed	10,433

public third source. Conditioning the acquisition of that third source on what the manager had to say is efficient and is slightly better than conditioning on the first source.[10]

More important, we now have a story in which the manager self-reports and the firm responds by selectively producing additional information depending on the self-report the manager puts forward.

Back to Recognition

In Chapter 14 we were careful to recast the uncertainty into a "states-of-the-world" format and specified two sequences of partitions, one ($\hat{\eta}(s)$) reflecting the information to which the firm had access and the second ($\eta(s)$) the information the firm wanted reflected in its accounting system, that is, in its formal financial history, so to speak. A recognition rule was then defined as a rule that specifies the $\eta(s)$ that is associated with $\hat{\eta}(s)$.

Here we emphasize sophisticated or conditional forms of such a rule. As suggested, think of the third source in our running illustrations as an audited accrual. In Exhibit 16.8 we have a case in which it makes sense to produce this audited accrual when the manager self-reports good news but not when the manager self-reports bad news. So the information, or partition, that is chosen at this juncture depends on what other information sources, here the self-report, tell the firm. In short, the recognition rule continues to specify "the $\eta(s)$ that is associated with $\hat{\eta}(s)$"; the added feature is the conditional switching, which is conditional on what becomes known or observed.

ENDOGENOUS CONSERVATISM

This odyssey also links to accounting in a less abstract manner. We are well aware that the typical accounting system is conservative in nature. It displays a tendency toward early, aggressive recognition of unfavorable

---

[10] We admit to the temptation to go on and condition on various combinations of what the manager had to say and what cost level was observed.

events resulting in minimization of net assets and accounting income. Inventory is generally valued at the lower of cost or market, goodwill and human capital are problematic, revenue is not recognized until late in the earnings cycle, research and development costs are aggressively expensed, and so on. The market-to-book ratio is typically well above unity. Prudence is everywhere, and in the limit, we have the cynical expression to anticipate all losses but no gains.

When pressed for an explanation of such conservative behavior, we often encounter personality disorders (i.e., those who submit to professional training in accounting are inherently conservative to begin with) and legal liability. The reporting firm and its auditor are exposed to legal liability if their financial statements are overly optimistic, so a natural, indeed inevitable, response is to make certain that no optimism ever surfaces in the financial records. The presence of these forces is undeniable, but we are left with the question of where the liability rules came from in the first place.[11]

Conditional recognition and scaling are also at work. Glance back at Exhibit 16.8 again. If the manager is called upon to self-report progress and if it is possible to produce (at some cost) a noisy, garbled version of what the manager knows, it is better to produce this additional information when the manager reports good rather than bad news. Accept the bad news without question, but challenge the good news with a veracity check. This suggests a bias against good news.

Now think of this third information source as the accounting system that must be audited and is costly, and verifying all that the manager knows will be difficult.[12] (This is the reason we modeled it, in (16.2), as a garbling of what the manager knows.) Bad news is readily accepted, but good news is challenged and allowed to stand in the formal records only if it survives the auditor's (noisy) challenge.

With a solid dose of fantasy, we can illustrate this with the themes in our running illustration. Recall that inventory is present, so we will focus on its valuation. To put some numbers down, suppose the inventory will eventually sell for a net of 50 or 100 (selling price less additional cost to be incurred in the second period) with 50–50 odds; the accounting cost at the end of the first period is 70. (Any additional labor, recall, occurs in the second period, so the inventory valuation does not in any way depend on the overall cost, or y_1.) Again, this is all thrown in just to give us some convenient numbers on which to focus.

---

[11] Legal liability is a complex issue covering management (including the chief financial officer, of course) and the auditor. Securities law is omnipresent (e.g., U.S. Rule 10b-5), as is common law (e.g., contributory negligence).

[12] Not all information lends itself to a veracity check. Consequently, some of what the manager privately knows will not be included in the accounting system, even if it would otherwise be desirable to have that private information public.

EXHIBIT 16.11
Probabilities for
Inventory
Illustration

	$y = (y_2, y_3)$			
Net Selling Price	(g, g)	(g, b)	(b, g)	(b, b)
100	.28	.12	.03	.07
50	.07	.03	.12	.28

EXHIBIT 16.12
Valuations
Conditional on
Various Information
Sources

	$y = (y_2, y_3)$				
Valuation Method	(g, g)	(g, b)	(b, g)	(b, b)	E[net]
Historical cost	70	70	70	70	70
Market, given all information	90	90	60	60	75
"Market," given second source (y_3)	81	69	81	69	75
LCM, given all information	70	70	60	60	65
LCM, given conditional second source	70	69	60	60	64.85
NRV, given conditional second source	81	69	60	60	68.7

Now we overlay the second and third sources with the third a garbling of the second, but we also link this information to the inventory valuation task. Probabilities are given in Exhibit 16.11. Of the two sources displayed, y_2 is meant to suggest (16.1) and y_3 is meant to suggest (16.2). The original, y_1, source is not displayed because it arrives at the end of the second period and thus has nothing to say about the inventory valuation at the end of the first period.

Prior to any information arriving, the expected value of the net is $E[net] = 75$. Furthermore, notice that if $y_2 = g$, the expected value is revised upward to $E[net \mid y_2 = g] = 90$ but is revised downward to $E[net \mid y_2 = b] = 60$ in the event of bad news. Moreover, because y_3 is a garbling of y_2, appending the y_3 to the y_2 report does not revise these conditional assessments. Also, if we use only the garbled source, we have respective revised expected values of $E[net \mid y_3 = g] = 81$ and $E[net \mid y_3 = b] = 69$.[13]

Now apply some accounting skills. Several valuation methods are displayed in Exhibit 16.12. The first method is brute force historical cost; regardless of what we know or might know, maintain the accounting value at accounting cost of 70.

The second method is a market-based net realizable value approach, given all of the information available when we value the inventory at its expected (net) value. The third method focuses on market value as well but uses the inferior y_3 information source.

[13] To illustrate, we have $E[net] = 100(.28 + .12 + .03 + .07) + 50(.07 + .03 + .12 + .28) = 100(.50) + 50(.50) = 75$. Similarly, we have $E[net \mid y_3 = b] = 100(.12 + .07)/.50 + 50(.03 + .28)/.5 = 69$.

Next is a lower-of-cost-or-market (LCM) method when *market* is defined by the second method that used all available information. In parallel fashion, we also present a modified LCM approach that relies on conditional recognition. If the y_2 source reveals bad news, implying a market value of 60, this estimate is accepted, and the inventory is written down to a value of 60. If the source reveals good news, however, that claim is challenged by the accounting system. In particular, the presumed value of 80 is not accepted; rather, the accounting source now accesses the y_3 source and uses its report to estimate value. If $y_3 = g$ is observed, if the second source confirms the first, a value of $E[\text{net} \mid y_3 = g] = 81$ is implied (using only the second source to revise the value estimate). If it is not confirmed, however, a value of $E[\text{net} \mid y_3 = b] = 69$ (below cost of 70) is implied; so the inventory is written down. Notice the resulting pattern of conservative valuation driven by the conditional challenging of the earlier source's report coupled with strict reliance on the audited source.

Finally, we throw in a hybrid net realizable value (NRV) method that accepts the y_2 source's report of bad news but challenges a good news claim. When the claim is challenged, only the y_3 information is allowed to influence the accounting valuation. Again, we see the power of conditional recognition in developing a pattern of conservative accounting valuation.

Notice the ability of the LCM filter to provide an "on-average" valuation (the $E[\text{net}]$ column in Exhibit 16.12) that is downward biased. It is also apparent that the variability of the valuation is affected.

Of course, we must not forget the information content theme. Each of the valuation methods in Exhibit 16.12 provides some type of event partition. Mixing in management's behavior then leads us to a precise specification of information content. As we have repeatedly stressed, information from other sources is critical to identifying information content. The accounting system's recognition rule is a carefully crafted response to the firm's information environment. The end result is a mix of the three types of information sources we have analyzed in this chapter: Hard evidence (cash flows), management reports, and audited accruals. For now, though, it is important to understand that the auditor's perspective invites conditional recognition, and conditional recognition naturally leads to the appearance of conservatism, but the information content theme remains paramount.

Summary

This completes our three-part development of the concept of recognition. Initially, in Chapter 14, we viewed recognition as a choice to place some specific subset of all the firm knows or might know into its accounting records. The firm knows it has just sold a unit to a customer who immediately paid in cash. This is immediately recorded in the accounting records.

Reporting regulations require selected instruments be reported at fair value. If the firm does not yet know the fair value of these instruments it must discover them and record same in its accounting records. The firm receives an important order from a major customer. Because no payment has been received, the firm does not record this order in its accounting records. The firm's chief designer presents an exciting new product proposal to the executive committee. The committee decides to proceed immediately into pilot production and market testing. As important and exciting as this new development is, the firm at present makes no recording in its accounting records.

The second step was to bring in the comparative advantage of the accounting channel. Accounting uses the language and algebra of valuation to convey information that is well defended, and it is difficult to manipulate. Thus, in Chapter 15, we stressed the idea that the substantive information in the accounting channel is carried by the accruals, and these accruals are, in general, audited. They must pass muster with the auditor.[14] This implies that the mapping from what the firm knows to what is recorded in the accounting system is not unconstrained. Indeed, some of what the firm knows is kept out simply because the auditor would be at serious disadvantage in attesting to these items.

The third step, Chapter 16, exposes some of the subtlety of recognition policies. The firm does not design a policy that records various observations regardless of surrounding circumstances. A problematic liability is recorded only if it passes a threshold test, and even then only if additional information can provide a reasonably defensible estimate. A lower-of-cost-or-market rule brings the market price to bear only if it is below cost. Hence, we stressed here the idea of conditional recognition when we seek additional information depending on the surrounding circumstances and on what is learned from other sources.

Even so, the choice of recognition policy itself is far from straightforward. We already know that information content viewed from a valuation perspective is not the same as information content viewed from a contracting perspective.

Closely related is the idea of deliberately providing for some slack, that is, some discretion, in the recognition policy. This provision, it turns out, is yet another way in which the overall integrity of the accounting channel is protected. It is the subject of Chapters 17 and 18.

---

[14] Naturally, this association with the auditor might be indirect. For example, the firm might use different recognition rules for internal purposes but will nonetheless contrast what these rules report with what is contained in the audited financial statements. Likewise, the auditor's veracity check of a particular item might itself be indirect. Outside a theory text, multiple items are present, double entry recording is in evidence, and its built in correlations are well exploited by the auditor.

Selected References

The central theme in this chapter is looking for additional information depending on what the in-place information source has reported. This is an old idea that is often associated with the phrase "management by exception" when we focus on the exceptional or the extraordinary. Baiman and Demski (1980) and Lambert (1985) illustrate this conditional approach in a contracting setting. The important point, relative to the more familiar sampling literature, is to regard the population from which the additional information is drawn as endogenous. That is, anticipation of the "sampling procedure" affects the population. (This is another example of the importance of thinking in equilibrium terms.) Christensen and Demski (2001) connect this to the veracity check theme explored here and to the familiar statistical pattern of conservative valuation.

Key Terms

The accounting system's comparative advantage, its unique feature, in the vast array of information sources is that the system is well defended against unintentional error and opportunism. This means that the system is typically audited and shies away from underlying data or claims that are difficult to verify. This leads to **conditional recognition,** or the idea that what is entered into the accounting channel depends in important ways on what other information sources are reporting. This often results in an accounting system that exhibits **conservatism:** a bias toward early (aggressive) recognition of unfavorable events—bad news—and late recognition of favorable events—good news. Note well: This conservatism does not simply happen, but it is the product of careful design of the accounting system; it is endogenous.

Exercises

16.1. Throughout the chapter we refer to signals as being "good" or "bad." What allows us to assign these labels or interpretations with such confidence? (*Hint:* Examine the presumed probability structures.)

16.2. This chapter presents a running illustration in which the choice of whether to acquire one of the information sources depends on what an earlier information source has reported. In the first such case, the optimal policy is to "chase the bad news" (Exhibit 16.5), but in the second, it is to "chase the good news" (Exhibit 16.8). What is the explanation for these stark policy differences?

16.3. In the setting of Exhibit 16.5, solve for the optimal contracts for each of the three information policies, assuming $\beta = .55$ and $\beta = .85$. Explain the difference among your contracts. Also verify that they are consistent with the plots in Exhibit 16.5.

16.4. Prepare a short essay explaining the connection between conditional recognition and the Ball and Brown diagram (Exhibit 10.8).

16.5. Using the same setup as in the chapter, especially Exhibit 16.1, consider the following probability structure. (Both are public sources.) Determine an optimal contract for three cases: only the first source is available, only the second source is available, and both sources are available. Explain your findings.

	Signal $y = (y_1, y_2)$			
	(0, g)	**(0, b)**	**(1, g)**	**(1, b)**
$\pi((y_1, y_2)\,\|\,a_H)$	.5	0	.5	0
$\pi((y_1, y_2)\,\|\,a_L)$	0	.3	.7	0

16.6. This is a continuation of Exercise 16.5. Now suppose production of the second source can be conditioned on what the first source reports. Is it better to condition on good news or on bad news from the first source? Explain. Now read Note 6.

16.7. This is a continuation of Exercise 12.6. Suppose the manager privately observes the second information source, the monitor, and is asked to self-report.

a. Determine an optimal contract, again for $\alpha \in \{.5, .6, .7, .8, .9, .95, 1\}$. Explain your findings.

b. Suppose a third information source, the veracity check in (16.2), can also be used for contracting purposes. Let $\gamma = .9$, and again determine an optimal contract for each $\alpha \in \{.5, .6, .7, .8, .9, .95, 1\}$. Explain your findings.

16.8. Retain all of the details in Exhibit 16.1 except that the personal cost of a_L is now $c_L = 0$. Continue to assume that the firm seeks a supply of a_H. The probability structure for the first two information sources (paralleling Exhibit 16.3), is

	Signal $y = (y_1, y_2)$			
	(0, g)	**(0, b)**	**(1, g)**	**(1, b)**
$\pi((y_1, y_2)\,\|\,a_H)$	.60	.10	.20	.10
$\pi((y_1, y_2)\,\|\,a_L)$	.10	.10	.40	.40

a. Determine optimal contracts for the case in which the parties contract on the first source, on the second source, and on both sources. Explain your findings.

b. Is it still evident that we are free to label the signals "good" and "bad"? Explain.

16.9. This is a continuation of Exercise 16.8. Now suppose the second source is privately observed and self-reported. Determine an optimal contract.

16.10. This is a continuation of Exercise 16.9. Now introduce a third source, the garbling in (16.2).

 a. Determine optimal contracts for $\gamma \in \{.55, .6, .7, .8, .9, 1\}$; do this for the three recognition rules in Exhibit 16.5.

 b. Construct a plot similar to Exhibit 16.8. Comment on your plot.

16.11. This is a continuation of Exercise 16.9. Repeat the exercise but now for the case in which the conditioning is based on the y_1 report. Construct a plot similar to Exhibit 16.9. Comment on your plot.

16.12. Calculate the variance of the recorded inventory value for each of the recognition rules in Exhibit 16.12. Why is the variance lower when the third rather than the second method is used to estimate value?

Chapter 17

Intertemporal Accruals

As we know, accounting is most interesting in a multiproduct or a multiperiod setting. After all, accruals carry the substantive information, but accruals are moot if the firm has only one product and lives for only one period. Here we emphasize multiple periods and the associated timing issues. Should revenue be recognized in aggressive fashion and, therefore, in the current period or in conservative fashion and, therefore, in the following period? On the surface, this timing issue is only a specific application of the recognition apparatus developed in earlier chapters. There is more to the story, however: Might management be opportunistic or aggressive here when suiting its purpose but conservative otherwise? To properly explore this issue, we require at least two periods, a nontrivial contracting friction, and private information in the hands of management. As you will see, however, the exploration is revealing: So-called earnings management arises endogenously and may (or may not) be both rational and efficiency enhancing. The reason is that earnings management alters the sequence of information releases, and there is no reason in a world of contracting frictions (let along product market frictions) for the firm to routinely and inexorably disclose all that it knows.

We now turn to the ubiquitous question of timing. Our work to date on recognition policy stresses one side of the issue: If the evidence is accumulating, at what point do we formally recognize that evidence? For example, at what point in the earnings cycle do we recognize revenue, or at what point do we recognize a problematic liability? As usual, other sources of information are important in the calculus, and we must keep an eye on the accounting system's comparative advantage in the information supply chain.

Here we explore a second side of the issue: Should we allow the privately informed manager to engineer or to decide when an important event enters the accounting system? Should discretion or slack possibilities be part of the overall policy? Cash basis accounting adopts an extreme answer: Only cash transactions (as consummated) enter the records, so the privately informed manager must trigger a cash-based transaction to trigger an entry in the accounting records. An accrual system offers considerable leeway. Suppose the management team contemplates a major reorganization. Is an immediate restructuring charge, an accrual appropriate? If so, how large? Similarly, if demand has waned and inventory has accumulated, is an inventory write-down appropriate? Notice in both cases we are concerned about the time at which something is recognized, but we also sense a potential for opportunism.

Earnings management is the popular euphemism here. If we are having a banner year, it might be a good idea to hold back some of the good news, that is, to create a reserve for the inevitable downturn. Likewise, when that downturn arrives, this might be a good time to harvest some of that reserve. In the limit, do we aggressively work to avoid showing a decline, let alone a loss, in reported earnings? Do we aggressively search for additional income to "meet our numbers"? Similarly, do we aggressively book income just before taking the firm public? Do we aggressively hide income just before entering a contentious labor negotiation?

There are two keys to understanding the opportunism side of the issue. One is to remember that we use accruals to convey information. Altering the dimensions or the timing of accruals alters the information that is being conveyed. So, we are concerned fundamentally about information conveyance, be it via the accounting system or some alternative disclosure mechanism. The second key is to realize that there are limits to full, unfettered information conveyance. If these limits are present, the firm's information practices will not necessarily come down to full, timely disclosure in all circumstances. To put it emphatically, the idea that discretion should be absent, that is, that earnings management is an unequivocally negative activity, is simply false. This adds a serious element of subtlety to the opportunism theme.

Even with modern era technology, information transmission, receipt, and processing are not costless exercises, so on this basis alone we should not expect complete disclosure of all the firm knows. Equally clear is the fact that the firm may be seriously disadvantaged by some disclosures. Revelation of a new product design may reduce the firm's first mover advantage in that product market; likewise, a competitor's discovery that it is about to be seriously threatened by the firm may invite the competitor to seek relief in the political arena. Antidumping proceedings are an example.

On a more elusive side, contracts can always be renegotiated. At a future date when renegotiation is possible, for example, between the owners and the manager or between the firm and a critical supplier, information in the hands of one or the other party can have a profound effect on the renegotiation.[1] For example, would you rather bargain over an heirloom with someone who is fully informed or with someone who is not so fully informed? Or would you like to be well informed and bargain with someone who is not so informed? With renegotiation always on the horizon, the parties have a keen interest in managing the flow of information. Full disclosure at each and every step along the way is the exception.[2] Instead, a delicate game of managed information flow is the norm. Viewed from this perspective, earnings management, a garbling of the underlying information, is part and parcel of the game of managed information flows.

Our exploration begins with a return to our ever-present model firm to construct a setting in which the time when accruals can be recorded is open. This gives us something on which to hang the accrual reckoning. We then expand the setting to include private information in the hands of the manager, and this creates the possibility of opportunistic accrual timing. From there we explore two illustrations, one in which it is best to motivate rejection of any such opportunity and the other in which it is best to exploit any such opportunity. The overall message is that these timing games are natural and have a natural, indeed inevitable, interpretation of managing the firm's release of information.

TWO-PERIOD SETTING

As usual, the beginning point is to exhibit the issue, here a natural accrual timing issue, in our prototypical firm. An intuitive way to do this is to spread output over two periods and further structure the setting so output itself is uncertain. As we shall see, this creates a setting in which proper identification of output in each period is an issue.

The firm continues to use capital (K), labor (L), and managerial (M) inputs to produce output q, with technology specified by

$$q \leq M\sqrt{KL}$$

The underlying details, though, are more elaborate than usual. Production and sale take place over two periods. Capital (K) is acquired at the start

---

[1] For that matter, anticipation of the arrival of information following the renegotiation can also affect the parties' behavior.

[2] More broadly, recall, from Chapter 12 we have what is called the *revelation principle*. If in some trading arrangement the parties have the capacity for full, complete communication (meaning there are no explicit costs to conveying and processing information) and if the parties can commit up front to precisely how that information will be used, then any equilibrium in the trading game can be replicated by one in which full disclosure is motivated and engaged. Take away the capacity to tell all, for example by using statistical summaries, or to commit without equivocation, for example by admitting that we might turn around and renegotiate the arrangement, however, and all bets are off.

EXHIBIT 17.1 Action Induced Managerial Input Probabilities for $t = 1, 2$

Period t Action	$M_t = 10$	$M_t = 11$	$M_t = 12$
$\pi(M_t \mid a_t = a_H)$	.04	.32	.64
$\pi(M_t \mid a_t = a_L)$	.64	.32	.04

EXHIBIT 17.2 Time Line for Two-Period Setting with Uncertain Output

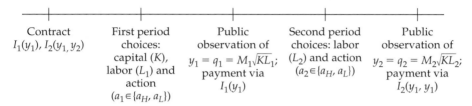

| Contract $I_1(y_1), I_2(y_1, y_2)$ | First period choices: capital (K), labor (L_1) and action $(a_1 \in \{a_H, a_L\})$ | Public observation of $y_1 = q_1 = M_1\sqrt{KL_1}$; payment via $I_1(y_1)$ | Second period choices: labor (L_2) and action $(a_2 \in \{a_H, a_L\})$ | Public observation of $y_2 = q_2 = M_2\sqrt{KL_2}$; payment via $I_2(y_1, y_1)$ |

and then first period labor (L_1) and managerial input (M_1) are supplied, and first period output of

$$q_1 = M_1\sqrt{KL_1}$$

is realized. The labor and managerial inputs are supplied simultaneously, so labor cannot be determined once the M realization is known. Next, second period labor (L_2) and managerial input (M_2) are supplied, and second period output of

$$q_2 = M_2\sqrt{KL_2}$$

is realized.

Each period's managerial input is random. It will be either "high" $(M_t = 12)$, "medium" $(M_t = 11)$, or "low" $(M_t = 10)$. The two inputs are independent, so knowledge of the first tells us nothing about the second, although the odds again depend on the manager's action or effort supply in each period. In particular, if the manager supplies high action, $a_t = a_H$, at the start of period t, that period's managerial input is likely to be high. If the manager supplies low action, $a_t = a_L$, however, that period's managerial input is likely to be low. The presumed probability structure is given in Exhibit 17.1.[3]

The timing details laid out in Exhibit 17.2 are important. Once capital is chosen, the manager simultaneously selects first period labor and action supply. The M_1 realization determines first period output, and the manager is then paid for first period services, $I_1(y_1)$. The manager next selects

---

[3] The action in period t affects the managerial input odds only in period t:
$\pi(M_1, M_2 \mid a_1, a_2) = \pi(M_1 \mid a_1)\pi(M_2 \mid a_2)$.

second period labor and effort supply. The M_2 realization determines the second period output, and second period compensation is then delivered, $I_2(y_1, y_2)$. Thus, the manager now makes a sequence of action choices, and the second period choices are made after first period results are known to the manager. Also, as we shall see, the contracting information, y, is the output produced in each of the two periods.

As usual, the manager prefers to supply a_L each period while the firm will turn out to prefer a supply of a_H each period, but we also have to deal with two periods. We do this with a convenient extension of our earlier work. Suppose in period t the manager has supplied action a_t, which carries a personal cost of $c(a_t) = c_H$ if $a_t = a_H$ and $c(a_t) = c_L$ if $a_t = a_L$, and has received compensation of I_t, for periods $t = 1, 2$. Overall, the manager's utility measure is given by

$$U(\cdot) = -\exp(-\rho(I_1 - c(a_1))) \times \exp(-\rho(I_2 - c(a_2)))$$
$$= -\exp(-\rho(I_1 + I_2 - c(a_1) - c(a_2))) \qquad \textbf{(17.1)}$$

where, again, $\rho > 0$ is the risk-aversion measure. Although alarming in appearance, the idea is simple. The manager cares about total compensation and total personal cost and exhibits nontrivial although constant risk aversion. So, the manager's attitude toward risk in the second period is precisely what it was in the first period regardless of what happened in the first period. Stated differently, the manager cares only about total net compensation, $I_1 + I_2 - c(a_1) - c(a_2)$ and displays constant risk aversion.

The manager's opportunity certainty equivalent is $\hat{\imath} = 10,000$ for the two periods combined. The personal cost terms are $c_H = 5,000$ and $c_L = 0$; the manager's risk aversion parameter is $\rho = .0001$. If, then, the firm wanted a_H supplied each period and if perfect market conditions prevailed, the firm would offer the manager $2c_H + \hat{\imath} = 20,000$. (We hope this is sounding familiar.)

For convenience, we use a zero interest rate throughout. As usual, capital and labor are acquired in well-organized markets. The price of capital is $p_K = 1,000$ per unit of capital, and the labor prices are $p_{L1} = p_{L2} = 29,000$ per unit of labor.[4] The firm's capital constraint is $K^{\max} = 1$ unit. Each unit of output sells for 5,000 in either period. Finally, all payments for labor and capital as well as those from customers occur at the end of the second period and are observed only in aggregate. This timing assumption guarantees that cash flow in the first period is nil and that accruals therefore must carry whatever information is to be provided. These various details are summarized in Exhibit 17.3.

For the moment, suppose the firm will use high action each period and acquire the maximum capital of $K = 1$. High action implies an

---

[4] Here we work with a composite of labor requirements. If $M = 10$ and $K = 1$, we require $L = 1$ to produce 10 units; and the necessary labor for "$L = 1$" costs the firm 29,000.

EXHIBIT 17.3
Details for Two-
Period Setting

Firm details	
Labor input	L_1, L_2
Maximum capital	$K^{max} = 1$
Managerial input	$M_t = 10, 11,$ or 12 (Exhibit 17.1)
Manager details	
Risk-aversion coefficient	$\rho = .0001$
Opportunity certainty equivalent	$\hat{\imath} = 10,000$
Personal costs	$c_H = 5,000$ and $c_L = 0$
Market prices	
Capital	$p_K = 1,000$
Labor	$p_{L1} = 29,000$ and $p_{L2} = 29,000$
Product	$5,000$

expected managerial input each period of $E[M \,|\, a_H] = .04(10) + .32(11) + .64(12) = 11.6$. This implies that the expected output in period t, the expected value of

$$E[q_t] = E[M_t]\sqrt{KL}$$

is simply

$$E[q_t] = 11.6\sqrt{L_t}$$

Seeking to maximize the expected value of its total profit (since the interest rate is zero and it behaves in risk-neutral fashion), the firm will now select output and labor quantities to maximize

$$5,000E[q_1] - 29,000L_1 + 5,000E[q_2] - 29,000L_2 - 1,000$$
$$-E[I_1 + I_2 \,|\, a_t = a_H]$$

Notice that we have revenue less labor expenditure for each product less the capital expenditure of 1,000 (as $K = 1$) less the expected payment to the manager.

Now substitute

$$E[q_t] = 11.6\sqrt{L_t}$$

and differentiate with respect to L_t (or use your favorite spreadsheet program). The firm's optimal choice is $L_1 = L_2 = 1$. Its expected output in either period is then $E[q_t] = 11.6$. Its expected profit is[5]

$$2(11.6)5,000 - 2(29,000) - 1,000 - E[I_1 + I_2 \,|\, a_t = a_H]$$
$$= 57,000 - E[I_1 + I_2 \,|\, a_t = a_H]$$

---

[5] For the record, suppose the firm uses low action in each period. This implies an expected managerial input of $E[M_t \,|\, a_L] = 10.4$. Proceeding as before, you will find the labor choices would be $L_1 = L_2 = .8038$, which implies an expected output each period (given a_L) of 9.3241. The expected profit would be $45,620 - E[I_1 + I_2 \,|\, a_t = a_L]$. (Likewise, $K < 1$ is not very interesting.)

With $K = L_t = 1$, output in either period is

$$q_t = M_t \sqrt{KL_t} = M_t$$

Output, then, will be 10, 11, or 12 units in each period.[6]

The remaining question is the manager's compensation, presuming we stick with the preceding noted plan of high action and $L_1 = L_2 = K = 1$. Here we assume the contractible information is the output produced each period and the aggregate cash flow (which occurs only at the end of the second period). Knowing output and the cash flow, it will be clear at the end if the labor or capital choices were inappropriate.[7] So, the only substantive incentive issue is whether the manager behaved opportunistically in either period (by supplying a_L instead of a_H). For this purpose, all information is contained in the output itself. Conveniently, then, the manager's compensation will depend on output, but only on output, in each of the two periods.[8]

At this point the story gets messy, but it is important to understand the details. The manager's first period compensation depends on first period output, so we write it as $I_1(q_1)$, as in Exhibit 17.2. Likewise, the second period compensation can, in principle, depend on output in both periods, so we write it as $I_2(q_1, q_2)$.[9]

In turn, the odds on what output is produced depend on the manager's action. In the first period the manager is confronted with a choice between a_H and a_L. In the second period, this choice is confronted again, but the manager then knows the actual first period output. (See Exhibit 17.2.) So, we have to worry about the manager's second choice if $q_1 = 10$ was observed, if $q_1 = 11$ was observed, or if $q_1 = 12$ was observed. For example, if the manager was lucky in the first period ($q_1 = 12$) might slacking off in the second period be tempting? To handle these possibilities, let $a_2 = \delta(q_1)$ denote some specification of the second period action choice depending on first period output, such as a_H always or a_H unless $q_1 = 12$. There are eight such policies or functions with δ^H denoting the one that

---

[6] We purposely set the technology and prices so that, given optimal behavior, the firm's output in each period will be an integer (10, 11, or 12 units, in particular). This supports the intuitive idea of worrying about how many units of total output were produced in each of the two periods. Also notice in the derivation of the optimal behavior that, in principle, the second period output could depend on first period output, but given the technology and prices, there is no interest in such a refined policy.

[7] We also assume that sufficient penalties are available to guarantee that it is in the best interest of the manager to adopt the preferred capital and labor amounts.

[8] Notice the firm is committed to spending $1,000K + 29,000(L_1 + L_2) = 59,000$, but output each period is a random variable. Output carries the essential contracting information. In turn, with all cash flow at the end, output will lead to an accounting accrual, and in this fashion we have the accruals carrying the essential contracting information.

[9] However, the manager's utility measure depends on total compensation, $I_1 + I_2$. So, in this case we can concentrate on total compensation that depends on output in both periods. This will become apparent as we proceed.

selects a_H regardless of first period output.[10] If we are to motivate high effort throughout, δ^H is the policy we must motivate.

Now suppose we have specified a pair of compensation functions. (Continuing the notational assault, this would be $I_1(q_1)$ and $I_2(q_1, q_2)$ introduced earlier.) If the manager now decides to supply action a_1 in the first period and then use policy δ to specify the second period action choice, we readily identify the expected utility calculation, denoted $E[U \mid a_1, \delta]$. (Details are presented in the Appendix.) If the manager is to be relied upon to supply a_H each period regardless of first period output, we must satisfy an entire family of incentive compatibility constraints:

$$E[U \mid a_H, \delta^H] \geq E[U \mid a_1, \delta] \text{ for all } a_1 \text{ and for all } \delta \qquad \textbf{(17.2)}$$

Likewise, if this arrangement is to be attractive to the manager in the first place, we must also satisfy[11]

$$E[U \mid a_H, \delta^H] \geq U(\hat{\imath}) \qquad \textbf{(17.3)}$$

From here, the firm selects the minimal cost compensation arrangement subject to acceptance (17.3) and obedience (17.2) by the manager:

$$\underset{I_1(q_1), I_2(q_1, q_2)}{\text{minimize }} E[I_1 + I_2 \mid a_H, \delta^H]$$
$$\text{subject to: (17.2), (17.3)} \qquad \textbf{(17.4)}$$

The solution is displayed in Exhibit 17.4; the firm's cost is $E[I_1 + I_2 \mid a_H \delta^H] = 20{,}277$. Moreover, it is routine (although tedious) at this point to verify that the firm's best overall choice is to acquire $K = L_t = 1$ and to motivate initial choice of a_H followed by δ^H (a_H always).

Notice that the optimal arrangement treats the periods as being independent. The manager is offered a contract that pays 2,929 for

---

[10] We enumerate the policies as follows. Notice the first one enumerated is δ^H.

$q_1 = 10$	$q_1 = 11$	$q_1 = 12$
a_H	a_H	a_H
a_H	a_H	a_L
a_H	a_L	a_H
a_H	a_L	a_L
a_L	a_H	a_H
a_L	a_H	a_L
a_L	a_L	a_H
a_L	a_L	a_L

[11] From this point forward we suppress the dependence of the expected utility calculation on the incentive functions. Also, it is instructive to sketch the manager's decision tree. The initial choice is either to reject the contract, to accept it and supply a_H, or to accept it and supply a_L. Presuming acceptance, $q_1 = 10$, 11, or 12 is then observed. At this point, the manager must select a_H or a_L for the second period. Following this, second period output of $q_2 = 10$, 11, or 12 is observed. The family of constraints in (17.2) guarantees that, if the contract is accepted, the initial supply of a_H followed by supply of a_H in the second period regardless of q_1 beats every other path through the tree. Similarly, (17.3) guarantees that the contract offer will be accepted.

EXHIBIT 17.4   Optimal Compensation Arrangement to Motivate Policy a_H, δ^H

Period t Compensation	$q_t = 10$	$q_t = 11$	$q_t = 12$
$l_1(q_1)$	2,929	10,227	10,545
$l_2(q_1, q_2) = l_2(q_2)$	2,929	10,227	10,545

$q_t = 10$, 10,227 for $q_t = 11$, and 10,545 for $q_t = 12$. Second period compensation depends only on second period output. Intuitively, the two periods themselves are independent; there is no information spillover between periods. The manager has constant risk aversion and cares only about total net compensation. In addition, the probability structure itself is the same for each period. This is the reason we see the stationary compensation arrangement. Indeed, you could locate this arrangement by modeling a one-period problem but reducing the manager's opportunity certainty equivalent to half of that assumed.[12]

As we collect the various threads, remember that all cash payments occur at the end. Through appropriate accruals, the accounting system reports output in each of the periods (e.g., by recognizing an appropriate revenue accrual). We thus have a setting in which it is rational for the firm to produce in each period, to compensate the manager based on the accruals, the output, in each period, and to deliver this compensation with a stationary pay-for-performance arrangement.

INADVERTENT INVITATION

Review the payment arrangement in Exhibit 17.4. A large increment is delivered if output is 11 instead of 10 units, and a small additional increment is delivered if output is 12 instead of 11 units. Larger output is good news, but the arrangement also displays decreasing returns to good news. Importantly, varying increments of this nature invite arbitrage.

Ubiquitous Reserve

One way to see this arbitrage temptation is to suppose that first period output is $q_1 = 12$, but the manager is somehow able to surreptitiously hide one unit in reserve, so only $q_1 = 11$ units are observed. In the next, and final, period, this reserve is "harvested": $q_2 = 10$ is reported as $10 + 1 = 11$, $q_2 = 11$ is reported as $11 + 1 = 12$, and $q_2 = 12$ is reported as, well, 12. In the latter case we assume that the extra output is simply

---

[12] Given this, you are probably wondering why we have woven this elaborate web of cascading details. Read on.

EXHIBIT 17.5 Arbitrage Possibilities with Original Compensation Arrangement Given $q_1 = 12$, $a_2 = a_H$, and Reserving

	Second Period Output, q_t			CE of
	$q_t = 10$	$q_t = 11$	$q_t = 12$	Compensation
$\pi(q_2 \mid a_2 = a_H)$	.04	.32	.64	Lottery
Reported $q = (q_1, q_2)$, given truth	(12,10)	(12,11)	(12,12)	
Total compensation, given reported q	$10{,}545 + 2{,}929$ $= 13{,}474$	$10{,}545 + 10{,}227$ $= 20{,}772$	$10{,}545 + 10{,}545$ $= 21{,}090$	20,545
Reported $q = (q_1, q_2)$, given reserve 1 unit	(11,11)	(11,12)	(11,12)	
Total compensation, given reported q	$10{,}227 + 10{,}227$ $= 20{,}454$	$10{,}227 + 10{,}545$ $= 20{,}772$	$10{,}227 + 10{,}545$ $= 20{,}772$	20,759

destroyed because revealing it at that point would de facto reveal that opportunistic reserving had taken place.[13]

Unfortunately, this invitation is now more than a little tempting when the manager faces the compensation arrangement in Exhibit 17.4. Details are summarized in Exhibit 17.5.

If the reserve is not created, the manager receives total compensation of $I(12) + I(q_2)$, where $I(q_2) = I(10)$ with probability .04, $I(11)$ with probability .32, and $I(12)$ with probability .64, presuming $a_2 = a_H$. This has a certainty equivalent (*CE*) of 20,545.[14] If the manager does create the reserve, 11 units will be reported in the first period, and total compensation will be $I(11) + I(q_2)$, where $I(q_2) = I(10)$ with probability 0, $I(11)$ with probability .04, and $I(12)$ with probability $.32 + .64 = .96$. The certainty equivalent of this compensation lottery is $20{,}759 > 20{,}545$.

Contrast the two possibilities. If second period output turns out to be 10 units, the reserving scheme delivers additional compensation of $2I(11) - I(10) - I(12) = 6{,}980$, but if it turns out to be 12 units, the difference is $I(11) + I(12) - 2I(12) = -318$. A small amount of compensation in the $q_2 = 12$ case is sacrificed to avoid the low compensation associated with $q_2 = 10$. Even weighting these outcomes with the appropriate probabilities will not tilt this imbalance. Of course, the firm is none too pleased

[13] If reserving of this nature is to be effective, it must be subtle. Claiming way, way too much good news when the reserve is harvested is an invitation to discovery. So, we simply assume second period output must be one of 10, 11, or 12 units. Any other output is a sure sign something is amiss.

[14] At this point, both actions have been supplied, and their personal costs are sunk, so we focus on the compensation per se. This gives us, for the truth case, $20{,}545 = (-1/.0001)\ln(.04\exp(-1.3474) + .32\exp(-2.0772) + .64\exp(-2.1090))$.

EXHIBIT 17.6
Arbitrage
Possibilities
with Original
Compensation
Arrangement and
Foreknowledge of
Second Period
Output

	q_1	q_2	$q_1 + q_2$	$I(q_1) + I(q_2)$	Probability
Case A	12	10	22	$10{,}545 + 2{,}929 = 13{,}474$	$1 - \alpha$
	12	11	23	$10{,}545 + 10{,}227 = 20{,}772$	α
Case B	11	11	22	$10{,}227 + 10{,}227 = 20{,}454$	$1 - \alpha$
	11	12	23	$10{,}227 + 10{,}545 = 20{,}772$	α
Case C	10	11	21	$2{,}929 + 10{,}227 = 13{,}156$	$1 - \alpha$
	10	12	22	$2{,}929 + 10{,}545 = 13{,}474$	α
Case D	11	10	21	$10{,}227 + 2{,}929 = 13{,}156$	$1 - \alpha$
	11	11	22	$10{,}227 + 10{,}227 = 20{,}454$	α

if this happens because its compensation cost has increased and output has a positive chance of actually being destroyed![15]

More Subtle Timing Temptation

A second way to illustrate arbitrage temptations is to focus on the fact that the management team generally knows some things about the coming period as it finalizes its accounting treatment for the current period.

Once again, suppose that first period output is $q_1 = 12$ but the manager has also learned second period output will be $q_2 = 10$ (with probability $1 - \alpha$) or $q_2 = 11$ (with probability α) but will definitely not be $q_2 = 12$. Think of this as middling prospects for the second period. Overall, then, total output will be $12 + 10 = 22$ with probability $1 - \alpha$ or $12 + 11 = 23$ with probability α. This is Case A in Exhibit 17.6.

Now translate this into the manager's perspective using the payment arrangement in Exhibit 17.4. At this point the manager faces total compensation of $10{,}545 + 2{,}229 = 13{,}474$ with probability $1 - \alpha$ and $10{,}595 + 10{,}227 = 20{,}772$ with probability α.

Conversely, suppose instead that the manager knows first period output is $q_1 = 11$ and has learned that second period output will be $q_2 = 11$ (with probability $1 - \alpha$) or $q_2 = 12$ (with probability α) but will not be $q_2 = 10$. Think of this as excellent prospects for the second period. Total output will be $11 + 11 = 22$ with probability $1 - \alpha$ and $11 + 12 = 23$ with probability α, just as before. This is Case B in Exhibit 17.6.

Again translate this into the manager's perspective. The manager now faces total compensation of $10{,}227 + 10{,}227 = 20{,}454$ with probability $1 - \alpha$ and $10{,}227 + 10{,}595 = 20{,}772$ with probability α.

[15] This is, to be sure, a bit apocryphal, but it well illustrates the larger point that inadvertent temptations can have real effects on behavior. For example, consider the case in which the firm fraudulently hides poor sales in the hope of a convenient recovery in the not-too-distant future or inefficiently delays maintenance in the hope of boosting current period income. More broadly, think about the case in which the firm goes out of its way to design a transaction to keep that transaction off its balance sheet.

EXHIBIT 17.7
Induced
Compensation
Lotteries

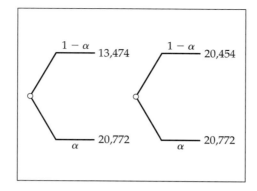

The thing to notice is that the total output lotteries are the same in Cases A and B, but the manager strictly prefers the Case B to the Case A story. This strict preference is illustrated in Exhibit 17.7 where we sketch the two compensation lotteries. In both cases the manager will receive 20,772 with probability α, but the other branch of the tree delivers strictly more compensation in the Case B story. So, we have a simple case of dominance! Cases C and D in Exhibit 17.6 provide a parallel possibility.

The intriguing question now is whether a manager who finds himself in the middle of the exercise has the opportunity, for example, to make Case A look to an outsider like Case B? This requires only an ability to take one unit of output in the first period and shift it to the second period. Cases C and D work in the opposite direction; in Case C the temptation would be to take one unit of output in the second period and claim it was produced in the first period.

PRIVATE INFORMATION

Of course, being able to make vinegar look like cognac requires some sleight of hand, and in our world sleight of hand calls for private information. So, we now change the story in an important detail: Let the manager—but only the manager—see output in each period. The manager will be asked to self-report each period's output.

The self-report, which leads to accrued revenue (as customers pay at the end of the second period), will be audited. To avoid unnecessary complications, we assume the auditor is able to ensure that the self-reports are accurate in total. Thus, total reported output equals total output (otherwise the manager is severely penalized), but the auditor cannot detect the subtle shifting of output between periods. This rules out the first temptation sketched above, reserving and destroying some output if necessary, but leaves the more subtle version in play.

Some additional details will now tie this together. Output either period will be 10, 11, or 12 units. Think of this as a customer (or output) base of 10

EXHIBIT 17.8   **Time Line with Private Information**

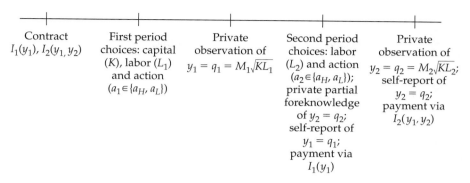

Contract
$I_1(y_1), I_2(y_1, y_2)$

First period
choices: capital
(K), labor (L_1)
and action
$(a_1 \in \{a_H, a_L\})$

Private
observation of
$y_1 = q_1 = M_1 \sqrt{KL_1}$

Second period
choices: labor
(L_2) and action
$(a_2 \in \{a_H, a_L\})$;
private partial
foreknowledge
of $y_2 = q_2$;
self-report of
$y_1 = q_1$;
payment via
$I_1(y_1)$

Private
observation of
$y_2 = q_2 = M_2 \sqrt{KL_2}$;
self-report of
$y_2 = q_2$;
payment via
$I_2(y_1, y_2)$

with prospects for one or two additional sales (or units of output). The extra customers arrive in independent fashion with probability .8. So, the probability of two extra customers (or two extra units of output) is .8(.8) = .64, the probability of no extra customer is .2(.2) = .04, and the probability of one extra customer is .8(.2) + .2(.8) = .32.

This, of course, presumes the manager supplies action a_H. Supply of a_L leads to the same structure but with a "success" probability of .2. The resulting probabilities are what we displayed in Exhibit 17.1.[16] Notice that action a_H gives us $\alpha = .8$ in Exhibit 17.7.

We assume furthermore that the manager has limited foreknowledge about the second period when it is time to make the first period output report. In particular, at the time of the report, the manager knows not only first period output (of $q_1 = 10$, 11, or 12) but also whether the first additional customer (or additional unit of output) in the second period has materialized. Think of this as the usual reporting delay and knowledge of first quarter results at the time the year-end financials are finalized.[17] The revised time line is displayed in Exhibit 17.8.

The resulting possibilities are listed in Exhibit 17.9. Since we know that output will be either 10, 11, or 12 units, the auditor insists on a report that claims 10, 11, or 12 units; otherwise, the report would be patently false. Suppose the manager winds up in Case 1 with $q_1 = 10$ and knows the first additional unit in the second period was a success. So, faithfully reporting first period output of 10 units implies second period output will be 11 or 12 units. The manager can also "borrow" a unit from the second period and claim first period output was 11 units, thus implying that second

---

[16] In other words, the number of extra customers is a Bernoulli random variable with success probability .8, presuming action a_H is supplied; otherwise, under a_L, the success probability is .2. You now know how Exhibit 17.1 was constructed.

[17] Alternatively, think of it as a single year with the manager having advance insight into the second half when it is time to report first-half results.

EXHIBIT 17.9 Smoothing Options for Privately Informed Manager

Manager's Private Knowledge at Time of Report	Implied Second Period Output	Feasible First Period Report and Implied Second Period Report
Case 1: $q_1 = 10$ and first additional unit success	$q_2 = 11$ or 12	$q_1 = 10$ and $q_2 = 11$ or 12; or $q_1 = 11$ and $q_2 = 10$ or 11
Case 2: $q_1 = 10$ and first additional unit failure	$q_2 = 10$ or 11	$q_1 = 10$ and $q_2 = 10$ or 11
Case 3: $q_1 = 11$ and first additional unit success	$q_2 = 11$ or 12	$q_1 = 11$ and $q_2 = 11$ or 12
Case 4: $q_1 = 11$ and first additional unit failure	$q_2 = 10$ or 11	$q_1 = 11$ and $q_2 = 10$ or 11
Case 5: $q_1 = 12$ and first additional unit success	$q_2 = 11$ or 12	$q_1 = 12$ and $q_2 = 11$ or 12
Case 6: $q_1 = 12$ and first additional unit failure	$q_2 = 10$ or 11	$q_1 = 11$ and $q_2 = 11$ or 12; or $q_1 = 12$ and $q_2 = 10$ or 11

period output will be reported as $11 - 1 = 10$ or $12 - 1 = 11$ units. We assume that the auditor cannot detect this subtle movement of output that should be recognized in the second period but is actually being booked in the first period. Returning to Exhibit 17.6, the manager in this instance can make Case C appear as Case D.

In other words, the manager has viable "smoothing" options because revenue might be recognized early when current period sales are low or late when current period sales are high. Of course, such misreporting is a form of earnings management. In this particular case it has the effect of smoothing the earnings series, so we proceed with the explicit, intuitive interpretation of smoothing.

Case 2, in which $q_1 = 10$ but the first additional unit in the second period is a failure, offers no such opportunity. If output is "borrowed" from the second period, there is a possibility that total output will be $10 + 10 = 20$, but with 11 claimed in the first period, this is clearly impossible unless the self-reporting has been nefarious. This is a case in which the auditor is able to deter any inappropriate early (or late) recognition. Case 5 is a parallel story, and Case 6 is a story in which the manager can "loan" or reserve a unit of first period output to the second period, effectively delaying recognition, in a manner that the auditor cannot detect.

The intermediate cases in which first period output is $q_1 = 11$ units also in principle invite use of the borrow (Case 3) or loan (Case 4) options, but we rule this out, just to cut down on the details. Think of this as a setting in which the auditor can be fooled only in the extreme cases. (Regardless, this does not affect the substance of what follows.)

Where does this leave us? The enlarged, revised, and well-tortured story has the manager possibly confronting subtle earnings management possibilities. Returning to Exhibit 17.6, we recognize the important detail is that the manager can now make Case A look like Case B and Case C look like Case D.

To proceed, we have to pick our poison. We know that using the original contract (Exhibit 17.4), designed for the setting in which no such option arises, is naive. It not only invites smoothing (the substance of Exhibits 17.6 and 17.7) but also turns out not even to motivate the supply of high action in all cases.[18]

One avenue is to design the incentives so the manager will always supply high action and will shy away from any earnings management option that presents itself. Paraphrasing our earlier work, we identify the efficient incentive structure with the following exercise (where, recall, δ^H is the action choice policy that selects a_H at each opportunity):

$$\underset{I_1(q_1), I_2(q_1,q_2)}{\text{minimize }} E[I_1 + I_2 \mid a_H, \delta^H, \text{truth}]$$

subject to: $E[U \mid a_H, \delta^H, \text{truth}] \geq U(\hat{\imath})$;

$$E[U \mid a_H, \delta^H, \text{truth}] \geq E[U \mid a_1, \delta, \text{truth}]$$
for all a_1 and for all δ; and

$$E[U \mid a_H, \delta^H, \text{truth}] \geq E[U \mid a_1, \delta, \text{smooth}]$$
for all a_1 and for all δ **(17.5)**

The first two constraints are expressions (17.2) and (17.3) in the original formulation where output was publicly observed. The third constraint ensures no combination of action, and explicit earnings management is tempting to the manager.

The optimal incentive structure is displayed in Exhibit 17.10 (the Motivate Truth column). Notice how, relative to the original case, the payments are distorted to remove the smoothing temptation. For example, the payment when 11 units are claimed in each period, the attractive smoothing prize so to speak, is now lowered. Naturally, contracting with the additional friction of removing the otherwise natural earnings management incentives means we must be less aggressive in using the contracting information. Consequently, the firm's cost of acquiring high effort increases (from 20,277 to 20,518).

A second avenue is to invite, indeed, to motivate smoothing. To identify the optimal arrangement in this case, we proceed exactly as before except that we design the incentives so the manager will always smooth when possible but will again provide high action throughout. Details are also provided in Exhibit 17.10, in the Motivate Smoothing column. Here you

---

[18] This is readily verified by working through the manager's decision tree. One difficulty arises when $q_1 = 12$, where the prospect of being able to smooth now invites supply of a_L in the second period at that point.

EXHIBIT 17.10
Efficient
Compensation
Arrangements

Reported Output		Original Case	Motivate Truth	Motivate Smoothing	Revised Story
q_1	q_2				
10	10	5,858	6,833	6,760	20,000
10	11	13,156	12,300	12,289	20,000
10	12	13,474	14,883	penalty	penalty
11	10	13,156	11,674	12,122	12,929
11	11	20,454	15,094	14,815	20,227
11	12	20,772	20,344	21,057	20,545
12	10	13,474	14,883	penalty	penalty
12	11	20,772	21,904	21,469	20,000
12	12	21,090	22,559	22,621	20,000
$E[I_1 + I_2 | \cdots]$		20,277	20,518	20,530	20,067

should notice that "unsmoothed" reports of 10 and 12 or 12 and 10 units, respectively, should not appear if the manager follows instructions; hence the penalty in these cells. The overall approach is inferior to motivating the manager not to acquiesce to earnings management temptations in the first place.

The underlying tension is important. The natural incentives invite the manager to smooth in this setting. One way to proceed is to dampen the incentives, to remove the smoothing incentives. This amounts to staying with the same underlying information base but using that information less aggressively in the contracting arrangement. A second way to proceed is to live with the smoothing. Of course, relying on a smoothed report amounts to relying on a garbling of what the manager privately knows. So, we now use lower-quality information but are able to use it more aggressively. Which horse wins the race? The former does in this case.

Damping the incentives to remove smoothing temptations is not the universal answer, however. For example, if the manager is able to obtain the critical foreknowledge here with only 50–50 odds, we would find it is best to tolerate the smoothing. (With 50–50 odds, the garbling is actually less, and this implies less of a reduction in the information content of the smoothed accrual series; yet the incentive restrictions not to exploit the garbling remain as before, and the trade-off now flips to favor the smoothing approach.)

More interesting is another variation on our never-ending story. Suppose that a by-product of supplying high action is unusual insight into the production and sales process and that the only way to acquire the foreknowledge that allows smoothing to be both executed and hidden from the auditor is to supply action a_H in both periods. This is the last column in Exhibit 17.10 where we see that the firm is better off (paying 20,067 versus the original 20,277 for the manager's services). Here the trick is to motivate smoothing—again, a garbling of the underlying information—but the manager can do this only if high action is supplied throughout. So, smoothing, so to speak, now becomes a signal of good behavior!

LARGER PICTURE

It is time to step back and put these observations in perspective. We began with a setting in which the pay-for-performance arrangement that the firm would like to employ inadvertently creates an incentive to manage earnings (explicitly, to smooth performance) over the two periods. Moreover, this smoothing takes place in the accruals by manipulating the time at which selective accruals are recorded. In this sense we are dealing with the management of intertemporal accruals. Likewise, in the following chapter we will confront the companion issue of managing intratemporal accruals.

Now, the firm might be better or worse off when its manager is put in a position in which earnings management is possible. If such opportunism possibilities are tempting and gratuitous, they destroy valuable contracting information. The firm then must decide whether it is better to tolerate this secondary incentive effect or to dampen its use of the underlying information to remove the temptation to smooth the performance series. It is easy to arrive at cases in which either approach is superior to the other. Indeed, if the possibilities are tempting and signal unusual but desirable attention to detail, they provide a superior contracting venue. So, there is no universal answer in this sphere.

We also must acknowledge the firm's incentive to dampen the information content of the reporting and the stability of the contracting itself. The market for managerial services might well see the manager's reported performance, thus reducing, via the market's assessment of the manager's talent, the firm's ability to craft the most desirable connection between pay and performance. Similarly, the firm and manager are always free to renegotiate their contractual arrangement. This freedom also raises issues of how much that is known should actually be made public, that is, made available for contracting purposes at any point in time, just as it raises issues of how much information the parties should seek to acquire at any point in time.

Valuation issues may also be part of the stew. Of course, our continued reliance on risk-neutral valuation renders any such concern moot because there is no demand for early resolution of uncertainty in such a setting and because rational expectations are in place to ensure that the valuation market is aware of whatever earnings management activities are being motivated. Introducing frictions in the valuation market in one form or another will spread the information timing concerns from the contracting to the contracting and to the valuation spheres.

Most important, incentives to smooth or, more expansively, to manage *intertemporal accruals* are endogenous. Dealing with these issues is part of the firm's overall contracting exercise, not to mention being far from routine and straightforward.[19] In a larger sense, the firm seeks to inter-temporally manage the information flow among various parties. Information is costly, and information can have a deleterious effect on some encounters. So, we do not expect full and timely disclosure of all that the parties know; managing intertemporal accruals is simply one manifestation of that fact.

Summary

Stories of presumptively opportunistic earnings management are well known as are regulatory interventions and enforcement proceedings, yet reporting discretion remains. The key to understanding why this is not a cynic's feast is to view the exercise of reporting discretion as managing the release of information. Viewed in this fashion, earnings management is a garbling of what the management team knows, just as government secrecy is a garbling of what the government knows. From here it is a short step to remember that incentives are endogenous and that we are dealing with audited accruals. This means that the exercise of the reporting discretion is itself endogenous and must survive the auditor's scrutiny.

This is precisely what comes into view when we extend our prototypical firm to include output in each of two periods. The manager acts in each period, so incentive issues are also present in each period. Add to this the ability of the manager to "time" when some of the output, that is, some of the accounting income, is recognized, and we immediately see the delicate interplay between maintaining action incentives and managing the flow of information, the accruals, across the periods.

One possibility then is that the manager's timing (i.e., reporting) discretion is inevitable and the auditor is not superhuman. So, we cannot rely on the auditor to catch all forms of opportunistic reporting. The remaining question is whether to aggressively use the reported information knowing that some opportunism will thus be motivated or whether to less aggressively use the reported information and thereby remove or lessen the temptations.

Another possibility is that this discretion is not inevitable but follows from otherwise productive behavior by the manager. In this instance, the

---

[19] Placing considerable pressure on some set of performance measures naturally invites attention to be directed at manipulating those measures. Here, then, we struggle with the choice of tolerating the manipulation or removing the strong pressure on the measures. Tolerating, of course, is a form of incomplete communication; the manager purposely reveals less than is privately known. A subtle point now arises: Why have we not pursued a revelation argument at this point? The reason is that communication is limited. The manager reports output but not whether the output report is or could have been manipulated. Think about it.

well-managed performance series is indicative of good behavior and should be both encouraged and rewarded.

More broadly, we arrive at a recurring theme in our study. Universal answers are in the realm of fiction. Information matters as does the time at which information is released, and accounting is a source of information.

Appendix

Two-Period Optimal Contracts

Solving for an optimal contract in this two-period setting in which the manager acts twice follows the pattern of our earlier work, but the amount of detail expands. To begin, although it is natural to think of the manager as being paid $I_1(q_1)$ in the first period followed by $I_2(q_1, q_2)$ in the second period, what matters to both the manager and the firm is the total payment. So, we may as well collapse the payment into the total that is delivered at the end of the second period, $I_1(q_1) + I_2(q_1, q_2) = \bar{I}_2(q_1, q_2)$. (This follows from our definition of the manager's preference measure in (17.1).)

OUTPUT PUBLICLY OBSERVED

We begin with the case in Exhibit 17.2 in which each period's output is publicly observed. Recall that the manager faces an initial choice of $a_1 \in \{a_H, a_L\}$, and then, following the observation of $q_1 \in \{10, 11, 12\}$, a second choice of $a_2 \in \{a_H, a_L\}$. This second choice is described by the function $a_2 = \delta(q_1)$. There are eight such possible patterns or functions. Overall, then, we must worry about all possible combinations of two initial choices coupled with one of eight such functions, or 16 possible combinations in all.

Brute force is the easiest way to sort through this morass. Any combination of a_1 and $a_2 = \delta(q_1)$ induces a probability distribution over the $q = (q_1, q_2)$ possibilities, denoted $\pi(q_1, q_2 \,|\, a_1, \delta)$. These are displayed in Exhibit 17.11 for all the world to see.[20]

---

[20] To verify these probabilities, further recall that the firm's capital and labor choices result in $q_t = M_t$, and that $\pi(M_t \,|\, a_t)$ is given in Exhibit 17.1. Now suppose that the manager initially supplies a_H and continues to supply a_H in the second period unless $q_1 = 12$. This is the second policy listed in Exhibit 17.11. From here, the probability of observing, for example, 12 units in each period is $.64(.04) = .0256$ because from Exhibit 17.1, we have $\pi(M_1 = 12 \,|\, a_1 = a_H) = .64$ and $\pi(M_2 = 12 \,|\, a_2 = a_L) = .04$. Furthermore, notice that the first policy listed is the desired one of high action followed by high action regardless, or (a_H, δ^H).

EXHIBIT 17.11   Output Probabilities for Manager's Two-Period Strategies

$a_2 = \delta(q_1)$			$\pi(q_1, q_2 \mid a_1, \delta)$								
$q_1 =$			(q_1, q_2)								
a_1	10	11	12	(10,10)	(10,11)	(10,12)	(11,10)	(11,11)	(11,12)	(12,10)	(12,11)	(12,12)
a_H	a_H	a_H	a_H	0.0016	0.0128	0.0256	0.0128	0.1024	0.2048	0.0256	0.2048	0.4096
a_H	a_H	a_H	a_L	0.0016	0.0128	0.0256	0.0128	0.1024	0.2048	0.4096	0.2048	0.0256
a_H	a_H	a_L	a_H	0.0016	0.0128	0.0256	0.2048	0.1024	0.0128	0.0256	0.2048	0.4096
a_H	a_H	a_L	a_L	0.0016	0.0128	0.0256	0.2048	0.1024	0.0128	0.4096	0.2048	0.0256
a_H	a_L	a_H	a_H	0.0256	0.0128	0.0016	0.0128	0.1024	0.2048	0.0256	0.2048	0.4096
a_H	a_L	a_H	a_L	0.0256	0.0128	0.0016	0.0128	0.1024	0.2048	0.4096	0.2048	0.0256
a_H	a_L	a_L	a_H	0.0256	0.0128	0.0016	0.2048	0.1024	0.0128	0.0256	0.2048	0.4096
a_H	a_L	a_L	a_L	0.0256	0.0128	0.0016	0.2048	0.1024	0.0128	0.4096	0.2048	0.0256
a_L	a_H	a_H	a_H	0.0256	0.2048	0.4096	0.0128	0.1024	0.2048	0.0016	0.0128	0.0256
a_L	a_H	a_H	a_L	0.0256	0.2048	0.4096	0.0128	0.1024	0.2048	0.0256	0.0128	0.0016
a_L	a_H	a_L	a_H	0.0256	0.2048	0.4096	0.2048	0.1024	0.0128	0.0016	0.0128	0.0256
a_L	a_H	a_L	a_L	0.0256	0.2048	0.4096	0.2048	0.1024	0.0128	0.0256	0.0128	0.0016
a_L	a_L	a_H	a_H	0.4096	0.2048	0.0256	0.0128	0.1024	0.2048	0.0016	0.0128	0.0256
a_L	a_L	a_H	a_L	0.4096	0.2048	0.0256	0.0128	0.1024	0.2048	0.0256	0.0128	0.0016
a_L	a_L	a_L	a_H	0.4096	0.2048	0.0256	0.2048	0.1024	0.0128	0.0016	0.0128	0.0256
a_L	a_L	a_L	a_L	0.4096	0.2048	0.0256	0.2048	0.1024	0.0128	0.0256	0.0128	0.0016
$\bar{I}(q_1, q_2)$				5,858	13,156	13,474	13,156	20,454	20,772	13,474	20,772	21,090

From here we calculate the manager's expected utility score for each of these two-period strategies. The only added complexity is to remember that the second period choice occurs after first period output is observed, $a_2 = \delta(q_1)$, so we must track second period action cost via $c(a_2) = c(\delta(q_1))$. This leads to the following calculation, given total payment function $\bar{I}(q_1, q_2)$:

$$E[U \mid a_1, \delta] = \sum_{q_1} \sum_{q_2} -\exp(-\rho(\bar{I}(q_1, q_2) - c(a_1) - c(\delta(q_1))))$$
$$\times \pi(q_1, q_2 \mid a_1, \delta) \qquad \textbf{(17.6)}$$

From here we have the design program identified in the chapter:

$$\underset{\bar{I}(q_1, q_2)}{\text{minimize }} E[I_1 + I_2 = \bar{I} \mid a_H \delta^H]$$
$$\text{subject to: } E[U \mid a_H, \delta^H] \geq U(\hat{\imath}) \text{ and}$$
$$E[U \mid a_H, \delta^H] \geq E[U \mid a_1, \delta]$$
$$\text{for all } a_1 \text{ and for all } \delta \qquad \textbf{(17.7)}$$

Solving provides the total payment function displayed in the last row of Exhibit 17.11.

Now glance back at the stationary payment function in Exhibit 17.4. We have, as you can readily verify, $\bar{I}(q_1, q_2) = I(q_1) + I(q_2)$. This convenience is driven by the manager's constant risk aversion, the identical but independent probability structure across the two periods, and the public observability of output.

It is possible, not to mention desirable, however, to streamline the analysis, thanks to these assumptions. Suppose the manager initially chose $a_1 = a_H$, then observed first period output of q_1, and is contemplating choice of $a_2 \in \{a_H, a_L\}$. The expected utility calculation at this point is

$$E[U \mid a_H, q_1, a_2] = \sum_{q_2} -\exp(-\rho(\bar{I}(q_1, q_2) - c(a_H) - c(a_2)))$$
$$\times \pi(q_2 \mid a_2)$$
$$= -\exp(-\rho(CE(q_1, a_2) - c(a_H) - c(a_2)))$$

(17.8)

when $CE(q_1, a_2)$ is the certainty equivalent of the payment lottery, given q_1 was observed and action a_2 is chosen.[21]

This allows us to rewrite the design program in (17.7) as

$$\underset{\bar{I}(q_1, q_2)}{\text{minimize}} \; E[I_1 + I_2 = \bar{I} \mid a_H, \delta^H]$$

subject to: $E[U \mid a_H, \delta^H] \geq U(\hat{\imath})$;

$$CE(q_1, a_H) - c(a_H) \geq CE(q_1, a_L) - c(a_L) \text{ for all } q_1; \text{ and}$$

$$\sum_{q_1} -\exp\big(-\rho(CE(q_1, a_H) - c(a_H))\big)\pi(q_1 \mid a_H)$$

$$\geq \sum_{q_1} -\exp\big(-\rho(CE(q_1, a_H) - c(a_L))\big)\pi(q_1 \mid a_L)$$

(17.9)

Intuitively, the personal cost of the first period action is sunk at the start of the second period, and the manager's risk aversion is unaffected by the payment implications of whatever first period output materialized. This means motivating high action following q_1, presuming initial high action, also motivates high action following initial low action. That being the case, we must motivate high action only in the first period, knowing the other constraints ensure high or low action in the first period will be coupled with high action in the second period.

OUTPUT PRIVATELY OBSERVED

Now assume output is privately observed and self-reported by the manager. We concentrate on the subtle case in which the manager does not destroy output but relies on shifting a unit from one to the other period only when such shifting is completely invisible as in Exhibits 17.9 and 17.10. The constraints in (17.7) ensure that the manager will supply high action

---

[21] Since the two periods are independent, output q_1 has no effect on the output distribution in the second period, so the certainty equivalent depends only on how q_1 affects the eventual payment and on how action a_2 affects the probability of that payment.

in both periods, provided no earnings management or smoothing takes place. To this list of constraints we must now add constraints to ensure the manager is not tempted to shift output between periods. These are Cases 1 and 6 in Exhibit 17.9.

The underlying story is that a customer base of 10 is present with two additional potential customers. The latter two arrive in sequence with independent success probabilities of .8 under action a_H. So, we have four possibilities in either period, given the supply of $a_t = a_H$:

1. $q_t = 10 + 1 + 1$ with probability $(.8)(.8) = .64$.

2. $q_t = 10 + 1 + 0$ with probability $(.8)(.2) = .16$.

3. $q_t = 10 + 0 + 1$ with probability $(.2)(.8) = .16$.

4. $q_t = 10 + 0 + 0$ with probability $(.2)(.2) = .04$.

Now suppose the manager has observed $q_1 = 12$, supplied $a_2 = a_H$, but gives in to the temptation to smooth the output series. So item 3 would now be self-reported as $q = (11, 12)$ instead of $(12, 11)$, and item 4 would be self-reported as $q = (11, 11)$ instead of $(12, 10)$. (This is Case 6 in Exhibit 17.9.) So, having observed $q_2 = 12$, supplied $a_2 = a_H$, and given in to temptation, the manager has expected utility at this point (ignoring the sunk cost of whatever a_1 was chosen) as follows:

$$E[U \mid q_1 = 12, a_H, \text{smooth}]$$
$$= -.64 \exp(-\rho(\bar{I}(12, 12) - c_H)) - .16 \exp(-\rho(\bar{I}(12, 11) - c_H))$$
$$-.16 \exp(-\rho(\bar{I}(11, 12) - c_H)) - .04 \exp(-\rho(\bar{I}(11, 11) - c_H))$$

(17.10)

If the manager does not smooth, however, the parallel calculation is

$$E[U \mid q_1 = 12, a_H, \text{truth}]$$
$$= -.64 \exp(-\rho(\bar{I}(12, 12) - c_H)) - .32 \exp(-\rho(\bar{I}(12, 11) - c_H))$$
$$-.04 \exp(-\rho(\bar{I}(12, 10) - c_H))$$ **(17.11)**

Of course, the manager might also smooth, following observation of $q_1 = 12$ and supply of $a_2 = a_L$. Since low action has a success probability of .2, we readily calculate the expected utility measure for this possibility as

$$E[U \mid q_1 = 12, a_L, \text{smooth}]$$
$$= -.04 \exp(-\rho(\bar{I}(12, 12) - c_L)) - .16 \exp(-\rho(\bar{I}(12, 11) - c_L))$$
$$-.16 \exp(-\rho(\bar{I}(11, 12) - c_L)) - .64 \exp(-\rho(\bar{I}(11, 11) - c_L))$$

(17.12)

Parallel calculations surface for the $q_1 = 10$ possibility. There, however, it is the first two rather than the last two possibilities that are misreported.

(This is Case 1 in Exhibit 17.9). We have

$$E[U \mid q_1 = 10, a_H, \text{smooth}]$$
$$= -.64 \exp(-\rho(\bar{I}(11, 11) - c_H)) - .16 \exp(-\rho(\bar{I}(11, 10) - c_H))$$
$$-.16 \exp(-\rho(\bar{I}(10, 11) - c_H)) - .04 \exp(-\rho(\bar{I}(10, 10) - c_H))$$

(17.13)

$$E[U \mid q_1 = 10, a_H, \text{truth}]$$
$$= -.64 \exp(-\rho(\bar{I}(10, 12) - c_H)) - .32 \exp(-\rho(\bar{I}(10, 11) - c_H))$$
$$-.04 \exp(-\rho(\bar{I}(10, 10) - c_H))$$

(17.14)

and

$$E[U \mid q_1 = 10, a_L, \text{smooth}]$$
$$= -.04 \exp(-\rho(\bar{I}(11, 11) - c_L)) - .16 \exp(-\rho(\bar{I}(11, 10) - c_L))$$
$$-.16 \exp(-\rho(\bar{I}(10, 11) - c_L)) - .64 \exp(-\rho(\bar{I}(10, 10) - c_L))$$

(17.15)

The design program to motivate supply of high action in all eventualities and to motivate truthful self-reporting now follows the earlier program (17.9) except that we also append constraints to ensure that no earnings management temptations remain:

$$\underset{\bar{I}(q_1, q_2)}{\text{minimize}} \; E[I_1 + I_2 = \bar{I} \mid a_H, \delta^H, \text{ truth}]$$

$$\text{subject to: } E[U \mid a_H, \delta^H] \geq U(\hat{\imath});$$

$$CE(q_1, a_H) - c(a_H) \geq CE(q_1, a_L) - c(a_L) \text{ for all } q_1;$$

$$\sum_{q_1} -\exp\big(- \rho(CE(q_1, a_H) - c(a_H))\big)\pi(q_1 \mid a_H)$$

$$\geq \sum_{q_1} -\exp\big(- \rho(CE(q_1, a_H) - c(a_L))\big)\pi(q_1 \mid a_L)$$

$$E[U \mid q_1 = 12, a_H, \text{truth}] \geq E[U \mid q_1 = 12, a_H, \text{smooth}];$$

$$E[U \mid q_1 = 12, a_H, \text{truth}] \geq E[U \mid q_1 = 12, a_L, \text{smooth}];$$

$$E[U \mid q_1 = 10, a_H, \text{truth}] \geq E[U \mid q_1 = 10, a_H, \text{smooth}]; \text{ and}$$

$$E[U \mid q_1 = 10, a_H, \text{truth}] \geq E[U \mid q_1 = 10, a_L, \text{smooth}]$$

(17.16)

The solution is displayed in Exhibit 17.10; the firm's cost is $E[I_1 + I_2 \mid a_H, \delta^H, \text{truth}] = 20{,}518$.

The companion cases in Exhibit 17.10 follow in parallel fashion. In each instance the presumed behavior must be motivated, and the probabilities must reflect the presumed and motivated behavior.

Selected References

The topic of earnings management appears with regularity in the business press and is the subject of regular enforcement action by, for example, the SEC. Empirical documentation has been approached from a variety of angles, including Burgstahler and Dichev (1997); recall Chapter 10; Thomas (1989), Niskanen and Keloharju (2000); and Barton (2001). Many approach documentation by focusing on how reported accruals differ from their statistical norm during some unusual event, such as an auditor change or major acquisition. (The "unusual" accruals are called *discretionary accruals*.) Collins and Hribar (2001) provide an excellent review. Also see Schipper (1989) and Dechow and Skinner (2000). From a theoretical perspective, earnings management is a garbling of the underlying information, and this implies we have violated at least one of the assumptions in the revelation principle. Via these assumptions, Arya, Glover, and Sunder (1998) review and catalog the various approaches to modeling such garbling. The particular approach emphasized here is based on Demski (1998); Demski and Frimor (1999) add renegotiation to that setting. Dye (1988) connects frictions in the managerial and the valuation markets to the earnings management theme. Fellingham, Newman, and Suh (1985) is the source for the initial, stationary contract in the two-period setting; also see Holmstrom and Milgrom (1987). Aghion and Tirole (1997) deal with the broader issue of who should make which decisions in an organization, stressing the tension between initiative and loss of control. Discretion in reporting is clearly one such phenomenon.

Key Terms

Accruals can be associated with various time periods, **intertemporal accruals** (e.g., depreciation), and they can be associated with a single time period, **intratemporal accruals** (e.g., assignment of a given period's depreciation to various products). **Earnings management** arises when the underlying information is garbled so as to provide a sequence of accounting measures that differs from what would be reported were the garbling not invoked.

Exercises

17.1. Might earnings management be called balance sheet management? Explain.

17.2. Earnings management is a garbling of the firm's information. Explain.

17.3. Using the contract in Exhibit 17.4, verify that regardless of first period output, the manager can do no better than supply high action in the second period. Then, knowing that high action will be supplied in the second period, verify that the manager can do no better than accept the contract offer and supply high action in the first period as well.

17.4. For the setting in Exhibits 17.1, 17.2, and 17.3 (or in Exhibit 17.10 where factual reporting is motivated), determine the firm's accounting income for the first period and its end of first period balance sheet.

17.5. Consider a contracting setting in which a manager will supply one of two possible actions, $a \in \{a_H, a_L\}$, and the contracting information, y, can take on one of three possible values, $y \in \{10, 11, 12\}$. Probabilities follow; action a_H is desired.

	$y = 10$	$y = 11$	$y = 12$
$\pi(y \mid a_H)$	.04	.32	.64
$\pi(y \mid a_L)$	.64	.32	.04

The manager's utility measure is $U(\$, a) = -\exp(-.0001(\$ - c_a))$ for payment in the amount $\$$ and personal cost amount c_a. Action a_H carries a personal cost of 5,000 while action a_L carries a personal cost of zero. In addition, the manager's next best employment arrangement promises a certainty equivalent of $\hat{\imath} = 5,000$.

a. Determine the optimal contract that will motivate the manager to supply action a_H.

b. Suppose the manager has payment w from some other source. If $w = -2,071$, will the contract you determined continue to motivate supply of action a_H? What if $w = 5,227$? What if $w = 5,545$? What is the connection to the story in Exhibit 17.4?

17.6. Return to the setting in Exhibits 17.9 and 17.10 in which the manager is able to smooth in the indicated manner. Suppose the firm naively ignores this possibility and offers the manager the contract in Exhibit 17.4.

a. What will the manager do?

b. What is the manager's certainty equivalent, given optimal response to being offered this contract?

c. What is the firm's expected payment to the manager? (*Hint:* Draw the manager's decision tree.)

17.7. Repeat Exercise 17.6 for the case in which the firm anticipates the manager's smoothing options, instructs the manager to report factually, and offers the contract in the Motivate Truth column in Exhibit 17.10.

17.8. Repeat Exercise 17.6 for the case in which the firm again anticipates the manager's smoothing options but now instructs the manager to smooth whenever possible and offers the contract in the Motivate Smoothing column of Exhibit 17.10.

17.9. Repeat Exercise 17.6—yes, again!—for the case in which the manager will encounter the smoothing option only when $a_1 = a_2 = a_H$, and assume the firm offers the contract in the last column of Exhibit 17.10.

a. Why is this "arrangement" more efficient than the others in Exhibit 17.10?

    b. Why is garbled information a superior contracting venue in this case?

    c. What does this tell you about earnings management in general?

17.10. What role is played by the presumed form of the manager's preferences in developing the streamlined design program in (17.9)?

17.11. Verify that the contract in Exhibit 17.4 satisfies the constraints in (17.9).

17.12. Consider a setting in which the manager is as described in the chapter and the firm wants a supply of high action in each and every circumstance. The only difference is that the output probabilities are as follows:

Period t Action	$M_t = 10$	$M_t = 11$	$M_t = 12$
$\pi(M_t \mid a_t = a_H)$	.01	.18	.81
$\pi(M_t \mid a_t = a_L)$	1	0	0

Determine an optimal contract, presuming output is publicly observed each period.

17.13. Return to Exercise 17.12, but now assume that the manager also privately observes output in the fashion assumed in Exhibit 17.10. The "success" probability under high action is now .9. So, .9(.9) = .81, and so on. Determine optimal contracts corresponding to each of the columns in Exhibit 17.10. What qualitative differences do you notice?

17.14. Return to the setting of Exhibit 17.10, but now suppose that, instead of privately knowing first period output and something about second period output at the time of the initial self-report, the manager knows only the first period output. Furthermore, suppose that the manager can create a reserve of one unit and hide this fact in the second period if it turns out that $q_2 = 12$, simply by canceling the embarrassing customer's order. Will the following pay-for-performance arrangement motivate a supply of high action in all circumstances as well as no such secret reserving?

(10,10)	(10,11)	(10,12)	(11,10)	(11,11)	(11,12)	(12,10)	(12,11)	(12,12)
7,017	11,716	15,281	11,450	15,595	19,881	14,865	22,162	22,481

Chapter 18

Intratemporal Accruals

Accrual issues also arise within the confines of a single period, provided, of course, the firm produces multiple products or operates with a nontrivial organization arrangement. What is the best estimate of this particular product's marginal cost? How much of this period's income is attributable to this set of customers or to this division? To be sure, these intratemporal issues arise in the valuation (e.g., line-of-business reporting) and contracting (e.g., effort allocation across various products) domains studied to date, but they are most often associated with intraorganization activities (e.g., two managers sharing a common resource). For that reason, we emphasize the intraorganization setting. This is accomplished by focusing on two products and two managers in a single-period version of our prototypical firm. This focus on intraorganization activities also serves to remind us that accounting plays important roles within and across organization boundaries and that accounting theory is equally adept in either arena. The focus also serves to remind us again that nonseparability concerns are ever present.

Information, including accounting information, is used in a variety of settings. Having explored the use of information in valuation and labor-contracting settings, essentially interorganization settings, we now explore the use of information inside an organization. In broadest terms, this organization might be a manufacturing or service firm, a municipality, a government bureau, a legal entity and its suppliers, or an entire economy.[1]

[1] It is important not to confuse an organization's boundaries with its legal boundaries. Accounting stresses the notion of the reporting *entity*. Consolidation policy and the question of when to include a partially owned subsidiary well illustrate the notion in terms of formal accounting reports. Contrast this with a firm and a separately owned although captive supplier. Economic and legally specified organization boundaries are not coextensive.

For concreteness, though, we stress our familiar firm, now in a two-product, single-period interpretation. Information questions now arise in terms of measuring the performance of the management team (e.g., has a manager been sufficiently productive) and in terms of managing the products (e.g., is one sufficiently profitable or should a special order be pursued). Notice the first has an evaluation flavor while the second has a valuation flavor. The added nuance at this point is that these activities take place within the firm and cover multiple products and managers.

An important point to keep in mind as we proceed is the presumed lack of separability. One product's valuation is not generally separable from that of other products, just as one manager's evaluation is not generally separable from that of other managers. The organization has chosen to combine these products and labor sources for some reason. This creates the presumption that economic forces are favorable to such combination, and, if that is the case, the activities are prima facie not separable: The "whole" is more productive than the "sum of the parts." In other words, the firm faces economics of scope.

On the other hand, accounting procedures offer the appearance of separability. We speak routinely of the cost of producing one of the products, of the profitability of one of the products, of the manager's financial responsibility and financial contribution to the organization, and so on. The accounting procedures are designed in this manner—but this is getting ahead of the story.[2]

We begin by filling in the details for the two-product story and then turn to the case in which a single manager deals with both products. This case allows us to stress the evaluation theme and to draw a close connection to our just concluded study of intertemporal accruals. From here we turn to the case in which a separate manager is assigned to each product, a setting suggestive of separate division managers. Eventually, coordinated behavior arises when one division supplies the other and the proper recording of this transfer becomes an issue in the managers' evaluations. We then switch to a valuation theme by returning to the product cost and profitability concerns originally broached in Chapter 2. Finally, some reflective comments on less than arm's-length relationships between organizations rounds out the exploration.

As usual, in all these variations we are asking the accounting system to convey information, meaning that it must tell us something over and above what is discernible from the cash flows themselves. This explains the continued emphasis on accruals.

---

[2] Were markets perfect and complete, we would have all transactions taking place in markets, and separability would be present. A firm, a nonmarket organization, arises simply because such market richness exists only in textbooks.

TWO-PRODUCT SETTING

As usual, our firm uses capital (K), labor (L), and managerial (M) inputs to produce output q, with technology specified by

$$q \leq M\sqrt{KL}$$

The added feature is that the firm now produces two products but in one period. Common capital (K) is used for production of both products. Labor and managerial inputs, however, are specific to each of the products. For the first product,

$$q_1 = M_1\sqrt{KL_1}$$

units are produced when labor input L_1 and managerial input M_1 are combined with capital K. Likewise, $q_2 = M_2\sqrt{KL_2}$ units of the second product are produced when labor input L_2 and managerial input M_2 are combined with capital K. The labor and managerial inputs are supplied simultaneously, so labor is not determined once the M realization is known. Uncertainty is placed in the output itself as in Chapter 17.

Each product's managerial input is random. It will be either "high" ($M_i = 12$), "medium" ($M_i = 11$), or "low" ($M_i = 10$). The two inputs are independent, so knowledge of the first tells us nothing about the second. The odds, though, again depend on the manager's action or effort supply, which can be "high" or "low" for each product, $a_i \in \{a_H, a_L\}$. Details are given in Exhibit 18.1 where you should notice a strong similarity with Exhibit 17.1.

The timing is also important. Once capital is chosen, the manager selects labor and action supply for the two products simultaneously. The M_1 realization then determines the first product's output, the M_2 realization determines the second product's output, and an accounting system (conveniently) reports both outputs. The manager's compensation is based on the noted output report. (See Exhibit 18.2.) With a single-period setting, we further assume that the cash flows are close to being timeless and occur at the end of the period. No discounting is present, and the firm operates in risk-neutral fashion.

As usual, the manager prefers to supply a_L, now to each product, while the firm will turn out to prefer a supply of a_H for each. The manager's

EXHIBIT 18.1 **Action-Induced Managerial Input Probabilities for $i = 1, 2$**

Product i Action	$M_i = 10$	$M_i = 11$	$M_i = 12$
$\pi(M_i \mid a_i = a_H)$	.04	.32	.64
$\pi(M_i \mid a_i = a_L)$	.64	.32	.04

EXHIBIT 18.2
Time Line for
Two-Product
Setting with
Uncertain Output

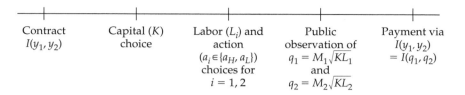

| Contract $I(y_1, y_2)$ | Capital (K) choice | Labor (L_i) and action ($a_i \in \{a_H, a_L\}$) choices for $i = 1, 2$ | Public observation of $q_1 = M_1\sqrt{KL_1}$ and $q_2 = M_2\sqrt{KL_2}$ | Payment via $I(y_1, y_2)$ $= I(q_1, q_2)$ |

EXHIBIT 18.3
Details for
Two-Product
Setting

Firm details

Labor input	L_1, L_2
Maximum capital	$K^{max} = 1$
Managerial input	$M_i = 10, 11, \text{ or } 12$ (Exhibit 18.1)

Manager details

Risk-aversion coefficient	$\rho = .0001$
Opportunity certainty equivalent	$\hat{\iota} = 10,000$
Personal costs (each product)	$c(a_H) = 5,000$ and $c(a_L) = 0$

Market prices

Capital	$p_K = 1,000$
Labor	$p_{L1} = 29,000$ and $p_{L2} = 29,000$
Product	$5,000$

utility measure is also familiar, we trust. Suppose the manager has supplied action a_i to product i, which carries a personal cost of $c(a_i)$, and received a total compensation of ι. Overall, then, the manager's utility measure is given by

$$U(\cdot) = -\exp(-\rho(\iota - c(a_1) - c(a_2)))$$

where, again, $\rho > 0$ is the risk-aversion measure. Importantly, total compensation less the total of the personal costs is what matters to the manager.

The manager's opportunity certainty equivalent is $\hat{\iota} = 10,000$. The personal cost terms are $c(a_H) = 5,000$ and $c(a_L) = 0$ for each product; the manager's risk-aversion parameter is $\rho = .0001$. If the firm then wanted a_H supplied for each product and if perfect market conditions prevailed, the firm would offer the manager $2c(a_H) + \hat{\iota} = 20,000$.

As usual, capital and labor are acquired in well-organized markets. The price of capital is $p_K = 1,000$ per unit, and the labor prices are $p_{L1} = p_{L2} = 29,000$ per unit. The firm's capital constraint is $K^{max} = 1$ unit. Each unit of either output sells for 5,000. The various details are summarized in Exhibit 18.3. The setting is by design a close cousin to the intertemporal timing story in Chapter 17. It is straightforward to verify that the firm will set $K = L_i = 1$ (implying $q_i \in \{10, 11, 12\}$) and will seek high action applied to each of the products.[3]

The important question for us is the manager's compensation. As noted, the contractible information is the output produced and the cash flow. Knowing output and the cash flow, it will be clear at the end whether the labor or capital choices were inappropriate. So the only substantive incentive issue is whether the manager behaved opportunistically in relation to either of the two products (by supplying a_L instead of a_H). For this purpose, all the information is contained in the output itself. Conveniently, then, the manager's compensation will depend on the output for each of the two products.[4]

Of course, the odds on what output is produced depend on the manager's supply of action. For each product the manager is confronted with a choice between a_H and a_L, and the two choices are made at the same time. Overall, then, four combinations are possible: (a_H, a_H), (a_H, a_L), (a_L, a_H), and (a_L, a_L). If the manager is to be relied upon to supply a_H for each product, we must satisfy an entire family of incentive compatibility constraints:

$$E[U \mid (a_H, a_H)] \geq E[U \mid (a_i, a_j)] \text{ for all } a_i, a_j \in \{a_H, a_L\} \quad \textbf{(18.1)}$$

Likewise, if this arrangement is to be attractive to the manager in the first place, we must also satisfy

$$E[U \mid (a_H, a_H)] \geq U(\hat{\imath}) \quad \textbf{(18.2)}$$

---

[3] Indeed, we merely revisit the analysis in Chapter 17. Suppose the firm will use high action for each product and acquire the maximum capital of $K = 1$. High action implies an expected managerial input for each product of $E[M \mid a_H] = .04(10) + .32(11) + .64(12) = 11.6$. This implies that the expected output of product i is simply

$$E[q_i \mid a_H] = E[M \mid a_H]\sqrt{KL_i} = 11.6\sqrt{L_i}$$

Now seeking to maximize the expected value of its total profit and again assuming that high action is supplied to each product along with $K = 1$, the firm will maximize:

$$5,000(11.6\sqrt{L_1}) - 29,000L_1 + 5,000(11.6\sqrt{L_2}) - 29,000L_2 - 1,000 - E[\imath \mid (a_H, a_H)]$$

The optimal choice is $L_1 = L_2 = 1$. So, the expected output of either product is $E[q_i \mid a_H] = 11.6$. The expected profit is simply

$$2(11.6)5,000 - 2(29,000) - 1,000 - E[\imath \mid a_i = a_H] = 57,000 - E[\imath \mid (a_H, a_H)]$$

And, with $K = L_i = 1$, output of either product is

$$q_i = M_i\sqrt{KL_i} = M_i$$

From here we fold in the forthcoming compensation cost for the manager and then verify that high action does indeed beat low action for each product. (Likewise, $K < 1$ is not very attrative.)

[4] Notice the firm is committed to spending $1,000K + 29,000(L_1 + L_2) = 59,000$, but output is a random variable. Output carries the essential contracting information.

EXHIBIT 18.4   Optimal $I(q_1, q_2)$ to Motivate Policy (a_H, a_H)

Regime $(E[I \mid (a_H, a_H)])$	Output Pair (q_1, q_2)								
	10, 10	10, 11	10, 12	11, 10	11, 11	11, 12	12, 10	12, 11	12, 12
Benchmark (20,264)	−3,051	14,383	14,890	14,383	20,399	20,678	14,890	20,678	20,948
Switch (12, 10) (20,302)	−7,196	15,882	16,430	11,918	19,249	20,765	19,249	20,639	20,983
Only if (a_H, a_H) 20,000	20,000	20,000	20,000	20,000	20,000	20,000	penalty	20,000	20,000
Aggregate (20,316)	−8,646	14,018	18,819	14,018	18,819	20,709	18,819	20,709	20,991

From here, the firm selects the minimal cost compensation arrangement subject to acceptance, individual rationality constraint (18.2), and obedience, incentive compatibility constraints (18.1), by the manager:

$$\underset{I(q_1, q_2)}{\text{minimize}} \; E[I \mid (a_H, a_H)]$$

$$\text{subject to: (18.1), (18.2)} \qquad \textbf{(18.3)}$$

The solution is displayed in Exhibit 18.4 for the case labeled Benchmark. The firm's compensation cost is $E[I \mid (a_H, a_H)] = 20{,}264.$[5]

As we collect the various threads, remember that this benchmark case presumes the accounting system reports output for each of the products and that all cash payments occur at the end of the period. We thus have a setting in which it is rational for the firm to produce each of the products and to compensate the manager based on the output of each of the products.

---

[5] To verify this $I(q_1, q_2)$ solution, we proceed in the usual fashion. As noted, the manager faces four possible combined action possibilities. Using the probabilities in Exhibit 18.1 and remembering we have $\pi(q_1, q_2 \mid a_1, a_2) = \pi(q_1 \mid a_1)\pi(q_2 \mid a_2)$, we have the following:

Action (a_1, a_2)	$\pi(q_1, q_2 \mid a_1, a_2)$								
	10, 10	10, 11	10, 12	11, 10	11, 11	11, 12	12, 10	12, 11	12, 12
(a_H, a_H)	.0016	.0128	.0256	.0128	.1024	.2048	.0256	.2048	.4096
(a_H, a_L)	.0256	.0128	.0016	.2048	.1024	.0128	.4096	.2048	.0256
(a_L, a_H)	.0256	.2048	.4096	.0128	.1024	.2048	.0016	.0128	.0256
(a_L, a_L)	.4096	.2048	.0256	.2048	.1024	.0128	.0256	.0128	.0016

This gives us a setting in which we want to motive one of four choices (the first) with respective personal costs of 10,000, 5,000, 5,000, and 0. It turns out that supplying low action to each product is not a concern because the action choices for the two products are made simultaneously.

Accounting Discretion

Now suppose the manager also has some reporting discretion. In Chapter 17 this freedom had an intertemporal nature because the manager was able to "smooth" reported income across periods. Now, in this intratemporal setting, what happens if the manager is able to shift some of the accounting income between the two products, if the manager has accounting discretion when it comes to reporting income for each of the products?

To keep the story within bounds, suppose the manager has the ability to surreptitiously report $q_1 = 12$ and $q_2 = 10$ as $q_1 = q_2 = 11$ but must otherwise factually report output.[6] For example, the two products might be essentially the same product produced on two separate lines, or they might be intended for two customer groups. What we have in mind is that the manager is able to effectuate some type of accrual or misclassification that results in some output or income from one line being reported as having originated in the other.

Glance back at Exhibit 18.4. Regardless of the finer details, this ability to selectively misclassify creates an awkward temptation for the manager. Misreporting in this fashion would increase the compensation from $I(12, 10) = 14,890$ to $I(11, 11) = 20,399$.

Stated differently, the incentive package designed on the assumption that the accounting system perfectly reports the output of each product is vulnerable to misclassification. If this possibility is present, we must perturb the incentive system. This is the case labeled Switch $(12, 10)$ in Exhibit 18.4. The key is to extend the incentive compatibility to not misclassifying output as well as to supplying a_H for each product. Notice that this accounting discretion results in equal pay for the $q = (12, 10)$ and $q = (11, 11)$ cases. It also results in an increase in expected compensation from 20,264 to 20,302. Are you surprised? After all, the incentive scheme was designed on the presumption that any such temptation could not be acted upon.[7]

A different view emerges if we assume that this ability to misclassify is present only when the manager provides high action for each product. This means $q_1 = 12$ and $q_2 = 10$ can be guaranteed never to occur if (and only if) the manager supplies the desired actions and appropriately exercises the reporting discretion. So, now opportunistic reporting or misclassifying $(12, 10)$ as $(11, 11)$ is a signal that in more important things the manager did not behave opportunistically. This is the case labeled Only if (a_H, a_H) in Exhibit 18.4. Notice the compensation is 20,000 unless $(12, 10)$ is

---

[6] That is, except in the case of $q_1 = 12$ and $q_2 = 10$, output is publicly observed, but in the case of $q_1 = 12$ and $q_2 = 10$, the manager is able to have this output reported as $(12, 10)$ or as $(11, 11)$.

[7] To verify the pay-for-performance arrangement, we proceed as in the benchmark case but append the additional constraint that rules out any temptation to report $(12, 10)$ as $(11, 11)$: $I(11, 11) \leq I(12, 10)$.

observed, and (12, 10) can be avoided for certain if the manager behaves. Literally, then, the opportunistic accrual carries information about the manager's action, and it is in the interest of the manager to reveal this type of information. Consequently, the contracting can rely on this information, and the contract is improved.

As in the earlier intertemporal case, the subtlety of contracting is once more on display. The manager has the possibility of influencing the accounting report by (literally) changing the accounting method by exercising reporting discretion. In one case the firm loses by this and in another case it gains. Inter- and intratemporal "smoothing" concerns are, indeed, close cousins.

Aggregation

The limit point of this theme occurs when the manager has complete discretion when it comes to allocating output or income between the two products. Only the total must be correct. Here the manager privately observes each product's output and is free to self-report any allocation of the total. (So, the auditor can guarantee that the total is correct but nothing else.) The consequence of this freedom to misclassify is the case labeled Aggregate in Exhibit 18.4.

Suppose the manager privately observes $q_1 = 10$ and $q_2 = 12$. With complete freedom, this could be reported as (10, 12), (11, 11), or (12, 10).[8] As we work through the other cases as well, it quickly becomes apparent that the compensation arrangement can distinguish only among output totals, not their allocation between the products. This follows from the fact that the manager reports after privately observing the output of each product and can, by assumption, misclassify with impunity. For all options having a total production of 22 units, for example, the manager will report the most advantageous combination, and that report will be issued every time 22 pops up. Thus, the incentive scheme might as well pay a constant amount for all combinations leading to 22. This is the aggregate scheme in Exhibit 18.4. De facto, we rely on complete aggregation. Anything else invites opportunistic reporting without advantage.

Naturally, this comes at some loss in performance as the expected compensation increases to 20,316. Knowing both outputs is simply more informative about the action taken by the manager. This is the nature of

[8] Presumably, the manager would not claim an output for either product that was different from 10, 11, or 12 units. Such a claim would be preposterous and thereby confirm opportunistic reporting. Moreover, this discretion leads to contracting on the total, not its allocation. For example, if (12, 10) is observed, we require $I(12, 10) \geq I(11, 11)$ to prevent misclassifying (12, 10) as (11, 11). Conversely, if (11, 11) is observed, we require $I(11, 11) \geq I(12, 10)$ to prevent misclassifying (11, 11) as (12, 10). Combining, this requires $I(11, 11) = I(12, 10)$. Working through the other possibilities confirms the fact that we end up contracting on the total, period.

aggregation. Only in rare cases can we expect aggregation to perform as well as reliance on the underlying, disaggregated data.[9]

TWO MANAGERS

We next expand the setting to include two managers, one for each product. This provides a setting in which decision rights (who designs the product), coordinated behavior (engineering and design personnel ought to communicate), evaluation tournaments (the sales force faces a contest to identify the best salesperson), and so on arise. Naturally, related accounting issues, such as the perennial themes of responsibility accounting and transfer pricing, come into focus.

Independent Evaluations

To begin, suppose the firm is exactly as before (Exhibits 18.1 through 18.3) except that a separate manager supplies managerial input for each product. Each manager is as described before except that the reservation wage or opportunity certainty equivalent is half of what it was in the original story (i.e., we now use $\hat{\imath} = 5,000$). This allows us to maintain some comparability, as you will see.

Now, since the two managers are identical and the two production settings are identical although independent, it readily follows that each manager is evaluated solely on the basis of the output of the product to which he is assigned. The optimal arrangement is given in Exhibit 18.5. With two such managers, then, the firm faces a total expected compensation of $2(10,139) = 20,278$ to the managers.

This total is slightly above the benchmark case in Exhibit 18.4 where a single manager supplied both inputs. The reason is that the benchmark case exploits the fact that the single manager must simultaneously supply the two inputs, and this leads to a modest efficiency gain because it eases the contracting difficulties in our particular setting.

It is also important to understand that this strict separation of the evaluations, when each manager's evaluation depends exclusively on his product's output, is driven by the lack of coordination and independence in the two environments. Often, though, managers interact, explicitly or

---

[9] A pithy caveat is in order. It is also possible to aggregate the underlying data in precisely the way they are treated in the optimal incentive structure. In that case, the optimal contract can be written as depending on the optimally aggregated performance measure—as we said, pithy! The statistical parallel to this is the idea of a *sufficient statistic*. In estimation of the mean of a normal distribution, for example, the arithmetic mean of a random sample is a sufficient statistic for the original data. In that case, the sample mean contains all relevant information of the data set, which is used for estimating the mean of the distribution.

EXHIBIT 18.5
Optimal $I(q_i)$ for
Manager i

$E[I \mid a_H]$	Output (q_i)		
	10	**11**	**12**
10,139	2,929	10,227	10,545

implicitly. Then it is likely that the evaluation measure for one manager will contain information useful in the evaluation of the other. For example, suppose the two M_i's are positively correlated when each manager supplies a_H. We would then find that the optimal contract for one manager depends on that manager's output as well as the other's output simply because the correlated variable helps understand the "noise" under which the manager works.

Separation of Duties

A closely related issue is *decision rights*, or which manager is assigned which set of tasks. For example, does the manager who proposes new investments also evaluate those proposals, or are they passed to a second group for evaluation? Does the design team carry the new product through manufacturing?

Our simple story already illustrates this theme; we noted that having two separate managers is less efficient than the benchmark case of having a single manager, given simultaneous action choice coupled with full observability of both outputs. This only scratches the surface, however. We know, for example, that the typical organization pays close attention to separating the production and use of various types of information. For example, it is common practice to separate "doing the books" and "working the cash." Putting control of both in one person's hands is simply too tempting, and auditors are well trained to document appropriate separation of duties. Likewise, we think of accounting as providing "hard" data that are used to control the use of resources and to keep track of the organization's performance. Lack of "hard" evidence of this sort makes it difficult, if not hopeless, to construct and maintain an efficient web of incentives.

The general idea in the *separation of duties* theme is that it is more difficult for a group of persons to agree on exploiting the informational advantage they share than for a single individual who has the same opportunity. It is easy for a single individual to underperform if he controls both the action selection and the information production. Then bad news would be an event that occurred only in rare circumstances.

This separation theme, too, can be illustrated with our running example. Suppose only total output is observed. Using a single manager, we revert to the aggregate reporting case in Exhibit 18.4 simply because maintaining the manager's incentives to accurately report the output of each product requires that the incentive scheme not make distinctions between how much of a given total is associated with either product.

Now suppose we separate the duties, so to speak, and use a pair of managers. Let's also use the incentive scheme in Exhibit 18.5 and ask each manager not only to supply high action but also to self-report the output produced. This self-report takes place before the total output is publicly observed. If the sum of the two self-reports does not equal the observed total, a serious penalty is administered (for example, both managers are dismissed). It is easy now to verify that equilibrium behavior is to honestly self-report.[10] So, separation of duties now leads to a more efficient arrangement simply because it removes the sole manager's reporting discretion.

Of course, there is a darker side. Fraud is not unheard of in reporting circles, and separation of duties does carry a degree of temptation for unanticipated and unwanted coordination. Suppose, for example, that one manager's output is 10 and the other's is 12. If they both report 11, their malfeasance will not be flagged and their combined compensation will be larger, although a side payment will be necessary if both are to strictly gain from so gaming the system. From here we enter the world of whistle-blowers, coalition stability, and similar arrangements. For example, would the manager whose output claim was padded by the other actually deliver the anticipated side payment at the end of the exercise?

The important point is that the incentives of the managers are not aligned throughout the process; because the intermanager arrangement is hardly enforceable, there is some residual concern over deviation from the coordinated strategy to sabotage the firm's control system. This argument is the central idea of separation on duties, not to mention all internal control mechanisms.

Interdivisional Transfer

Of course, it is also possible that we want to motivate the two managers to coordinate their activities. The classic example is the so-called transfer pricing setting in which one division supplies another division or, stated differently, in which the divisions engage in trade. This is, in turn, of little interest unless there is some reason to place the decision to trade in the hands of the managers themselves. Naturally, we adopt a private information perspective: The managers themselves privately know whether trading opportunities are present, and the firm for some unmodeled reason finds it convenient to let the divisions' managers sort this out on their own.

A slight variation in our running story provides a ready illustration. Think of each manager as managing separate, autonomous divisions. Furthermore, suppose that if, but only if, both managers supply action a_H, which is desired, there is a .25 probability that a "profitable trade" or

---

[10] In particular, if one manager is truthfully reporting output and given that total output is publicly observed, the only way the other manager can escape observable malfeasance is to report truthfully.

EXHIBIT 18.6
Action Induced
Managerial Input
Probabilities

Division 1 Action, $i = 1$	$q_1 = 10$	$q_1 = 11$	$q_1 = 12$
a_H and no transfer	.16	.48	.36
a_H and transfer	.40	.60	.00
a_L	.36	.48	.16
a_H aggregated	.22	.51	.27
Division 2 Action, $i = 2$	$q_2 = 10$	$q_2 = 11$	$q_2 = 12$
a_H and no transfer	.16	.48	.36
a_H and transfer	0	0	1.00
a_L	.36	.48	.16
a_H aggregated	.12	.36	.52

coordination opportunity arises. If so, it arises after both managers have acted but before any output is observed. The nature of this opportunity is laid out in Exhibit 18.6.

If no coordination opportunity arises, high action by either manager results in $M_i = 10$, 11, or 12, with respective probabilities of .16, .48, and .36. Alternatively, low action "reverses" these probabilities to .36, .48, and .16, but if a coordination possibility arises—and this is possible only if both managers supply high action—the first manager's output odds drop to .4, .6, and 0 while the second manager's odds increase to 0, 0, and 1. This idea is simple: The transfer improves the second manager's performance, guaranteeing $q_2 = 12$, but comes at a cost of decreasing the first manager's performance.[11] After all, the transfer shifts useful resources from the one to the other manager, which, other things equal, lowers the performance of the first manager and increases the performance of the second.

Again, this transfer or coordination opportunity is available only if both managers supply high action and even then only with probability .25. So the "a_H aggregated" probabilities in Exhibit 18.6 are simply .25 of the transfer probabilities plus .75 of the no transfer probabilities.

Otherwise, with the exception that we now use a low-action cost of $c(a_L) = 3{,}000$, everything remains as originally specified in Exhibit 18.3. The firm wants high action, K and L_i choices are unity, implying $M_i = q_i$, and so on. In addition, it is easy to verify that the firm wants any such transfer opportunity acted upon. So, we have a setting in which divisions are encouraged to trade based upon their private information.

With this (elaborate) setup, let's begin with the simple case in which the transfer or coordination opportunity is absent. In this case, with

[11] For the numerically curious, think of q_i as equal to 10 plus the sum of two (0 or 1) Bernoulli random variables. The success probability is .6 under high action but .4 under low action. So, the probability of two successes (and thus $q_i = 12$) is .6(.6) = .36, and so on. Conversely, if a transfer takes place, the second division is guaranteed full success while the first is reduced to only one of the original two Bernoulli random variables, implying the noted .4 and .6 probabilities.

EXHIBIT 18.7
Optimal $I(q_i)$ for
Manager i

	Output (q_i)		
$E[I \mid a_H]$	10	11	12
10,541	3,851	10,943	12,978

independence between the two division's activities, the optimal incentive structure rests each evaluation on the output of the respective division, just as we saw in the earlier case of two managers. With the settings and managers being identical, the incentive packages are also identical. See Exhibit 18.7.[12]

Now suppose the noted transfer opportunity is indeed present (with probability .25). Can we depend on these contracts? Hardly. If the opportunity is present and the first manager agrees to coordinated activity, his utility score (where we ignore the personal cost because it is sunk at this point) is

$$E[U \mid a_H, \text{transfer}] = .4U(3,851) + .6U(10,943) = U(7,486)$$

Conversely, refusing the transfer carries a utility score of

$$E[U \mid a_H, \text{no transfer}] = .16U(3,851) + .48U(10,943) + .36U(12,978)$$
$$= U(10,000)$$

Our poor manager faces a certainty equivalent of 7,486 if instructions are followed but 10,000 if they are abandoned. We are placing too much stress on the initial contract. This is all rather obvious because the benchmark setting calls for evaluation based on output, and agreeing to a transfer results in less output being reported for this division.

The firm has several options at this point. One is to continue to myopically evaluate each manager on his own division's output but to have the managers arrange an internal market. In that case the managers adjust their respective accounting reports to reflect the trade. De facto they transform their respective reports, in effect introducing an accrual, in a manner that reflects the coordinated behavior. Another option is to use this internal market approach but to use both division outcomes in the evaluation of each manager. A third option is to have the managers report the presence of any such coordination possibility and explicitly use this self-report in the evaluations along with the observed division outputs. These options are explored in turn.

The first option rests on an adjustment to the accounting records to recognize any trade that takes place. Basically, this is an accounting transfer

---

[12] Parenthetically, the incentive scheme is more powerful than in the Exhibit 18.5 benchmark because the change in probabilities, despite the lessening of the difference in the manager's personal cost, leads to a more difficult control problem.

EXHIBIT 18.8
Optimal Division
Output-Based
Compensation

$I(q)$	$q_i = 10$	$q_i = 11$	$q_i = 12$
$I_1(q_1)$	4,437	10,418	11,837
$I_2(q_2)$	4,085	11,035	11,466

in which one division pays the other in "accounting currency." In our simple setting, let's assume this price is one unit of output. So, recalling the setup in Exhibit 18.6, if a transfer takes place, the second division's output will be reported as $12 - 1 = 11$ units, and the first division's will be reported as $10 + 1 = 11$ units (with probability .4) or $11 + 1 = 12$ units (with probability .6). Do not lose sight of the fact we are once again rearranging the output reports![13]

Continuing, suppose we evaluate each manager on his division's (thus altered) reported output. Designing the incentive contract also requires that the managers indeed be willing to go forward with any transfer opportunity. This entails adding a constraint of the form

$$E[U \mid a_H, \text{transfer}] \geq E[U \mid a_H, \text{no transfer}] \quad \textbf{(18.4)}$$

to the usual individual rationality and incentive compatibility constraints for each manager.

Proceeding in the usual fashion leads then to the optimal contracts displayed in Exhibit 18.8. Respective expected payments are $E[I_1 \mid a_H,$ transfer when available$] = 10,296$ and $E[I_2 \mid a_H,$ transfer when available$] = 10,318$, for a total of 20,614. Notice that each contract explicitly motivates each manager to jump on the transfer opportunity should it materialize; you should verify this claim. This is driven, of course, in the supplying manager's case by reducing the bonus associated with reporting output of 12 as opposed to 11 units.

If you are on your toes, you are wondering why this arrangement confines each manager's evaluation to the results reported, given the transfer arrangement. After all, coordinated behavior induces a degree of

---

[13] For the record, this reclassification of the output report or transfer pricing device results in the following probability specifications for the two managers.

Division 1 Action	$q_1 = 10$	$q_1 = 11$	$q_1 = 12$
a_H and transfer	.00	.40	.60
a_H and no transfer	.16	.48	.36
a_H aggregated	.12	.46	.42
a_L	.36	.48	.16
Division 2 Action	$q_2 = 10$	$q_2 = 11$	$q_2 = 12$
a_H and transfer	.00	1.00	.00
a_H and no transfer	.16	.48	.36
a_H aggregated	.12	.61	.27
a_L	.36	.48	.16

EXHIBIT 18.9 Optimal Division and Firmwide Compensation
Arrangement to Motivate Policy (a_H, a_H)

					Output Pair (q_1, q_2)				
$I(q)$	**10, 10**	**10, 11**	**10, 12**	**11, 10**	**11, 11**	**11, 12**	**12, 10**	**12, 11**	**12, 12**
$I_1(q_1)$	4,595	4,595	4,595	9,734	10,847	9,734	11,378	12,007	11,378
$I_2(q_2)$	4,202	9,721	11,446	4,202	10,891	11,446	4,202	11,392	11,446

EXHIBIT 18.10 Optimal Division and Firmwide Compensation
Arrangement to Motivate Policy (a_H, a_H) When No Adjustment Is Made

					Output Pair (q_1, q_2)				
$I(q)$	**10, 10**	**10, 11**	**10, 12**	**11, 10**	**11, 11**	**11, 12**	**12, 10**	**12, 11**	**12, 12**
$I_1(q_1)$	2,151	2,151	10,923	9,652	9,652	11,693	11,758	11,758	11,758
$I_2(q_2)$	4,986	9,749	12,080	4,986	9,749	11,905	4,986	9,749	11,305

dependency between the managers' reported outputs, so at the margin, one manager's output is now informative about the other. For example, if the second manager reports 11 units, it is likely that a transfer actually took place. (Moreover, common practice is to use both division and firmwide results in evaluating division managers.) Anyway, solving for yet another round of contracts gives us the details in Exhibit 18.9. Here, the respective expected payments are $E[I_1 \mid a_H$, transfer when available$] = 10,287$ and $E[I_2 \mid a_H$, transfer when available$] = 10,311$, for a total of 20,599.

Alternatively, we might use both outputs in both evaluations but not make any adjustment for the transfer. This results in the incentive packages in Exhibit 18.10, along with $E[I_1 \mid a_H$, transfer when available$] = 10,397$ and $E[I_2 \mid a_H$, transfer when available$] = 10,265$, for a total of 20,662.

The third option in our trilogy is to have the managers self-report when a transfer takes place. This way we are not relying on the accounting to aggregate the information. The communication constraint is particularly simple in this case because an output of 12 is guaranteed in the second division should a transfer take place. So, incentive compatibility (with respect to capturing any trading opportunity and faithfully reporting same) is readily provided by a payment of 12,365 when a transfer is reported. Absent a transfer, we evaluate the managers in independent fashion, again because of the underlying independence in the two technologies. For the record, the optimal contracts are reported in Exhibit 18.11. The total expected compensation is now 2(10,259) = 20,518. Naturally, with full use of all information, we have reached a minimum compensation cost.

EXHIBIT 18.11 Optimal Division Output-Based Compensation When Transfer Is Self-Reported

$I(q)$	Transfer	$q_i = 10$	$q_i = 11$	$q_i = 12$
$I_1(q_1)$	12,365	5,082	9,752	11,287
$I_2(q_2)$	12,365	5,082	9,752	11,287

Summarizing, the managers directly communicate between themselves, and we seek some way to reflect their "trading behavior" in their evaluations. To this end, we see that explicitly self-reporting the transfer beats the other approaches, which rely on encoding the fact of a transfer in the accounting reports themselves. The coding, however, is not perfect, and this results in the slippage between the third and the first two approaches. The second best option is the transfer payment arrangement. In that case the only communication of a trade is its recognition in the accounting records. The noteworthy fact is this arrangement beats an evaluation scheme that uses the unadjusted joint outcomes of the two divisions. In other words, recording the transfer in the accounting records serves to indirectly acknowledge, although with some ambiguity, the presence of the transfer from the first to the second division. Once more we see the accruals carrying information!

PRODUCT LINE REPORTING

We now turn to the issue of product line reporting, one of the all-time favorite sinkholes in accounting. On the surface the theme here is reporting or estimating the profitability of some product line, customer group, or special order. Costing art surfaces in the form of cost allocation, activity-based costing, and so on.[14]

From an information content perspective, two issues now merge. One is using the accounting calculations to carry information. The other is scaling the information-laden measure so it directly reports the information in a "user friendly" fashion.

We illustrate this merging of issues with a slight variation on the two-product setup used earlier in the chapter. One difference is that we now remove the agency problem in dealing with the manager, for example, because the personal cost is irrelevant via $c(a_H) = c(a_L)$. This is done to reduce clutter in what follows. The second difference is that we assume the managerial input for each product, M_i, is observed before capital (K)

---

[14] Naturally, costing art is present in the transfer pricing arena where the managers must decide whether trade is profitable and the accounting system is used to distribute the profit from any such trade between the divisions.

and labor (L_i) choices are made. This, too, eases our work a bit and well illustrates an important insight.

Product Profitability

Initially, we focus on a setting in which the primary concern is the profitability of the separate products. To give this context, we simply focus on measuring the marginal cost of each product at some point. We might worry more broadly about adding or dropping products, large variations in a customer base, and so on, but the straightforward story is adequate for our purpose.

Suppose then that having observed M_1 and M_2, the firm seeks to produce q_1 and q_2 units. As usual, the firm faces prices of p_K in the capital market and p_{Li} in the respective labor markets. So, its cost is determined in the usual fashion via

$$C(q_1, q_2; M_1, M_2) \equiv \underset{K, L_1, L_2 \geq 0}{\text{minimum}} \ p_K K + p_{L1} L_1 + p_{L2} L_2$$

$$\text{subject to: } q_1 \leq M_1 \sqrt{KL_1};$$

$$q_2 \leq M_2 \sqrt{KL_2}; \quad \text{and}$$

$$K \leq K^{\max} \qquad \qquad \textbf{(18.5)}$$

Again, nothing unusual is present here; the firm simply observes the important M_i terms before selecting the efficient combination of capital and labor, so we condition the cost expression on both the product quantities and the M_i terms. (Also, for simplicity, we do not explicitly show the manager's compensation or deal with selecting the most desirable input from the manager.)

To illustrate, let capital be priced at $p_K = 200$ and labor at $p_{L1} = p_{L2} = 100$, along with $K^{\max} = 150$. Also let $M_i = 8$ or 12, with equal odds; furthermore, assume that the two M_i realizations are independent. Factor choices for output of $q_1 = q_2 = 1{,}000$ units are displayed in Exhibit 18.12. Notice how the larger M_i increases the productivity of the other factors, which results in lower total cost. We are also working in a region where the $K^{\max}$ constraint is not binding. In addition, we display the respective

EXHIBIT 18.12 Factor Choices and Marginal Costs for $q_1 = q_2 = 1{,}000$ ($K^{\max}$ not binding)

M_1	M_2	K	L_1	L_2	MC_1	MC_2	$C(\cdot; M_1, M_2)$
8	8	125	125	125	25	25	50,000
8	12	106.230	147.087	65.372	29.42	13.07	42,492
12	8	106.230	65.372	147.087	13.07	29.42	42,492
12	12	83.333	83.333	83.333	16.67	16.67	33,333

marginal cost calculations (denoted MC_1 and MC_2, respectively) in the exhibit.[15]

Now suppose the accounting system aggregates the various factor expenditures, so all we observe is the total cost incurred. A low total cost (33,333) reveals that both M_i are large, just as a high total cost (50,000) reveals that both are small. The intermediate total (42,492) leads to ambiguity. Here one M_i is large and the other small, but which is which?

Let's sharpen our product-costing skills. In the story, the unknown is the productivity of the managerial input for each product; it can be low for each, high for each, or split. Notice in Exhibit 18.12 that reporting the pair of marginal costs tells us exactly what is going on. A product's marginal cost is high only when its M_i is low. This is another example of scaling.

Moreover, the scheme is tidy in the sense that the thus calculated product costs fully assign the total cost pool to the products. For every combination, total cost equals $q_1 \times MC_1 + q_2 \times MC_2$. (For example, in the second row in Exhibit 18.12, we have $1,000(29.42) + 1,000(13.07) = 42,492$, subject to rounding.) In fact, this property holds in general here so long as the K^{max} constraint is not binding. Best of all, this scaling is accomplished in a user friendly fashion. We have the best of all worlds: The scheme fully reveals the productivity realizations, it obeys the accounting convention of adding up to the total, and it carries the information by summarizing the information in a highly useful calculation, each product's marginal cost. It just does not get any better in an accounting theory text!

From an information content perspective, this is the central idea in product costing. We want the calculated costs to reveal what is to be revealed; and we want it to be "predigested" or "prefabricated" so it arrives in useful format. This is the reason we resorted to marginal cost

---

[15] For the curious, notice the technology constraint,

$$q_i \leq M_i \sqrt{KL_1}$$

can be written as $(1/K)(q_i/M_i)^2 \leq L_1$. Surely labor would not be acquired to excess, so we have $(1/K)(q_i/M_i)^2 = L_i$ for $K > 0$. Substitute these labor choices into the factor expenditure tally, and we have an expression that depends only on the capital choice, K:

$$\min p_K K + p_{L1}(1/K)(q_1/M_1)^2 + p_{L2}(1/K)(q_2/M_2)^2$$

Differentiating and setting the expression to zero identifies the optimal K (so long as it is not so large K^{max} becomes an issue):

$$p_K - (p_{L1}(q_1/M_1)^2 + p_{L2}(q_2/M_2)^2)/K^2 = 0$$

Now use the thus identified K choice to back out the respective L_i choices. Collecting terms and a little algebra then gives us the following cost expression, as long as the quantities are not so large that the desired K exceeds K^{max}:

$$C(q_1, q_2; M_1, M_2) = 2\sqrt{p_K(p_{L1}q_1^2/M_1^2 + p_{L2}q_2^2/M_2^2)}$$

From here differentiation gives us the expression for product i's marginal cost (again presuming K^{max} is not binding):

$$\partial C(q_1, q_2; M_1, M_2)/\partial q_i = MC_i = 2(p_{Li}q_i/M_i^2)\sqrt{(p_K)/(p_{L1}q_1^2/M_1^2 + p_{L2}q_2^2/M_2^2)}$$

EXHIBIT 18.13   **Factor Choices and Marginal Costs, for $q_1 = q_2 = 1,000$**
($K^{\max} = 100$)

M_1	M_2	K	L_1	L_2	MC_1	MC_2	$C(\cdot; M_1, M_2)$
8	8	100	156.250	156.250	31.25	31.25	51,250
8	12	100	156.250	69.444	31.25	13.89	42,569
12	8	100	69.444	156.250	13.89	31.25	42,569
12	12	83.333	83.333	83.333	16.67	16.67	33,333

calculations here. Imagine, for example, the firm wondering how to respond to an extra customer. Its response depends on the uncertain marginal cost, and the accounting system resolves fully the uncertainty and delivers a correctly calculated marginal cost measure.

Continuing, now suppose the $K^{\max}$ constraint is not so friendly. In Exhibit 18.13 we repeat the story but now assume $K^{\max} = 100$. This has the effect of forcing the firm to use inefficient mixes of labor and capital except in the most productive state. Also notice that our allegiance to reporting marginal cost remains rewarded. The pair of marginal cost measures fully reveals all there is to know in the story.

All is not well, however. If we tally the assigned cost, $q_1 \times MC_1 + q_2 \times MC_2$, for each combination, we find totals of 62,500 > 51,250 for the low productivity event, 45,139 > 42,569 for the mixed case, and 33,333 for the high productivity event. If the firm is forced to use an inefficient combination of factors, perhaps because $K^{\max}$ is binding or the firm finds itself in a particularly onerous short-run position, it is in a region of diseconomies of scale. In such a region, the marginal costs are high due to inefficient factor combinations. The net effect is that we cannot simultaneously reveal all that is to be known, do this with well-calculated marginal cost measures, and have the thus assigned costs tally to the total cost in question.

The implication should not be missed. From an information content perspective, we want the product cost calculations to convey information. Otherwise, they are not telling us anything we do not already know. In addition, we want the cost calculations, that is, the accruals, to arrive in friendly format, presumably something akin to marginal cost.[16] We cannot in general accomplish both purposes and still have everything add up, however, and we definitely want the system to be tidy. As a result, we generally think of a product-costing system as "favoring" some products in the sense that they provide reliable estimates of marginal costs but at the expense, so to speak, of having to rely on less insightful formatting for the others. Such is the nature of intratemporal accruals in the product costing arena from an information content perspective.

[16] Recall that average cost is meaningless in the multiproduct setting, absent extreme separability assumptions, conditions that are clearly violated here.

Control

Although suppressed in our simple story, control issues are also present in the product line reporting arena. This, in fact, is well illustrated by our earlier look at transfer pricing and the importance of useful contracting information and maintaining self-reporting incentives. From here it is easy to visualize another round of coordination issues, such as each product's manager having significant private information that affects the capital choice and designing a product profitability measure that responds well to this private information.

Regardless, it is important to remind ourselves of the two perspectives at work here. The control side emphasizes information content with respect to the manager's behavior. The product profitability side emphasizes information content with respect to the product. The latter is, essentially, a valuation perspective while the former, of course, is a control or contracting perspective. We rely on the accounting system to serve both masters, so to speak.

ODDS AND ENDS

The issues stressed here concern the use of accounting information within an organization, yet organization boundaries are hardly well defined or rigid. Alliances, joint ventures, and supply chains are illustrative. Acknowledging this important fact brings us to the use of accounting information, including intratemporal accrual issues, in interorganization settings. The common theme here is that an organized market is put aside and replaced by an elaborate set of complex (explicit and implicit) contracts and an organization setup that distributes decision rights among the participants, specifies the set of rules to be followed, and defines how the proceeds are split. The organization setup is the governance device that deals with unforeseen circumstances and specific situations as they occur.

The use of accounting as part of the governance structure in such arrangements increases the concern for incentive issues—in terms of reporting—and the use of resources within each of the more or less independent units of the network. We sketch this briefly with an emphasis on government procurement and supply chains that connect otherwise independent firms. Both are important institutional settings in their own right, and they serve to illustrate important features and concerns in these types of arrangements.

Government Procurement

Government procurement is unusual in terms of the sheer size of a single buyer (e.g., for infrastructure, education, or health research) and for the complexity of some of the products and services (e.g., for air-traffic control systems or national defense).

The defense story itself is distinguished on a number of dimensions, including the product, the small number of suppliers, and regulation. We are talking about unusual products and products that are not to be sold on a free market. Only the customer and perhaps other designated customers (i.e., nations) are able (or allowed) to buy the products. Furthermore, the products are often highly specialized, implying significant research and development cost, and are developed specifically for a single costumer. Product development is often highly risky. Product specifications are often unknown at the time of initial contracting, and development and production costs are highly uncertain. Add to this the customer's keen interest in maintaining development and production capacity, an obvious option.

The nature of the production technology means that only a few firms are able to participate in the development of a new product. This limits competition; information, it seems, plays a heavy role in the supplier-customer relationship. The government, for example, likely knows more about what it is willing to accept as the product evolves, and the supplying firm is likely to have an edge in estimating costs. In some cases even the technology is classified, and this points toward even more uncertainty in the cost estimates. In addition, the technology often leads to a multi-product firm for which defense accounts for only some of the products (e.g., military and commercial aircraft).[17]

Given these various details, it should come as no surprise that incentive contracts are commonplace here. A common form is a "cost-plus incentive fee" arrangement designed to share risk between the supplier and the customer but to maintain pressure to control costs. Remembering that the supplier is a multiproduct firm, this arrangement in turn places noticeable pressure on the accounting system. There is a temptation to mold the system to assign costs to the products under cost-based pricing, and this leads us back to the accounting discretion issue with which we opened this chapter. (Surprise!) Naturally, the accounting systems themselves are regulated via an elaborate administrative apparatus, a formal regulatory group (the Cost Accounting Standards Board), and stringent audit requirements.[18]

---

[17] Given this, one might wonder why this industry exists in the private as opposed to the public sector. Presumably, the answer is that the present arrangement has advantages in terms of efficiency and adaptability. Furthermore, there are economies of scale in the development area. The research done for government products might be useful for products aimed at civilian purposes. Also, for a given task, the government might have several potential suppliers. In addition, the private firm offers important governance stability in its own right.

[18] The finer details of these arrangements are also important. For example, costing is approached in terms of direct and indirect costs with prices attached to each. In simple terms, we might have direct costs reimbursed at 100 percent and indirect costs at some other rate. The rate on an indirect pool might be close to or far removed from marginal effects. So, suppose the firm has the option of producing a part or buying it from a supplier. It might be efficient to buy from the supplier but, depending on the contractual rate for indirect cost recovery, it might nonetheless be profitable for the firm to produce internally. The result is an inefficient production decision on this specific part.

Taken together, we have an unusual ongoing relationship between the customer and the suppliers in this arena. This places considerable stress on the information environment and the accounting system itself.

Supply Chain Management

Interorganization dependencies are hardly limited to government procurement. A parallel pattern emerges in the web of interrelationships among a firm and its various suppliers. Close coordination between supplier and buyer has become commonplace. This coordination embraces all facets of the production process. In the first level, the concern is just coordination of production schedules and delivery times. This way unnecessary inventories are avoided and quality is more readily monitored. In the next level, joint work on the design might further ease the production process, and, finally, research might also be part of the common work. Just below the surface we find investment in common software, transportation links, interpersonal relationships, and so on.

Now go one step further and suppose the supplying firm enjoys a scope advantage, so it is economical to supply a number of customers. Uncertainty with respect to product development, production technology, consumer tastes, competitor reaction, and so on quickly leads to a setting in which the relationship is far from stable and requires constant care and management.

As we saw in the government procurement case, the resulting incentive issues caused by this close cooperation are many and complex. The detailed planning of the operation requires information flows among the parties. This includes the accounting and physical planning systems. Product costing becomes a special issue because the relationship is extended to more than just one batch of a specific product and learning takes place. In turn, development activities and the aforementioned investment issues become part of the milieu. For example, are supplier personnel trained at the buyer's plant or design center, an activity with little apparent purpose outside the supply chain? The glue that holds this together is the stable arrangement between the supplier and buyer. This, of course, is the governance issue mentioned earlier.

Summary

Accruals are the information carriers in an accounting system. This simple fact is evident when we examine the "time series" pattern of accruals, the intertemporal setting stressed in Chapter 17, or the "cross-sectional" pattern of accruals, the intratemporal setting stressed in the present chapter. Moreover, discretion in recording these accruals is an important component of the story. We saw this in the intertemporal setting where the stylized smoothing story reflected the fundamental nature of earnings management as a garbling of the underlying information base, a garbling that is central to the larger issue of managing the flow of information. We also see the discretion issue in the intratemporal setting where product line profitability, division-specific performance measures, and product costs themselves reflect accruals, accruals that are passed through the reporting discretion filter. Managing the flow of information implies that the firm manages the information released at any point in time, both within and external to its boundaries. So, it is natural and inevitable that we view the accruals at any instant in time as reflecting a specific approach to accounting measurement that is designed to convey the desired "amount" of information. The accounting system, after all, is not a mundane repository of what the firm knows. It operates with carefully designed and maintained recognition rules.

Reporting discretion surfaces here when the firm produces multiple products and the manager enjoys some accounting discretion over ascribing which portion of total income belongs to or was earned with each of the products. This is, of course, a timeless version of the earnings management setting of Chapter 17 and leads to the same conclusions: Reporting discretion may or may not be desirable, but ignoring it does not appear to be well advised.

From here we turn to multiple managers and, eventually, to a more subtle version of the story in which the managers may be able to trade and, absent full communication of these trading arrangements, we rely on the managers to exercise reporting discretion to embed the details of such trading in the accruals themselves. This leads to a transfer pricing story. Finally, we revisit the important themes of lack of separability and scaling in the product costing arena. In an ideal world, product costs would be well-designed estimates of marginal costs, but lack of separability implies that these estimates will in general depend on a variety of the firm's activities, not just on those associated with the product in question. This returns us to our earlier scaling theme where we see that it is possible to design the costing system so some of the products have well-engineered marginal cost estimates but the others do not simply because we insist that the total of the product costs sum to the total of the accounting costs recognized.

Selected References

Of course, the broad topic of intratemporal accruals is closely associated with such issues as product profitability, responsibility accounting, and divisional performance measurement, issues of concern in management accounting. See, for example, Demski (1994), Horngren, Foster, and Datar (1999), and Zimmerman (1999). Also see Brickley, Smith, and Zimmerman (2000). The hardness metaphor is due to Ijiri (1975). Transfer pricing has been studied in a variety of contexts; Harris, Kriebel, and Raviv (1982) and Christensen and Demski (1998) stress an information content perspective. Costing issues are closely linked to cost allocation (Demski, 1994, and Zimmerman, 1979), and the inability to simultaneously convey the full list of marginal costs is developed in Christensen and Demski (1997). Rogerson (1992; 1994) is particularly insightful on the subject of perverse incentives in a cost-based contracting regime so prevalent in defense contracting; also see Cavalluzzo, Ittner, and Larcker (1998). Gietzmann and Larsen (1998) provide an extensive discussion of firm-supplier relations and draw a parallel with promotion ladders.

Key Terms

The typical firm produces a variety of products and employs an elaborate organization arrangement. This leads to a system of **decision rights** that specify which individual or group of individuals has the authority to make specific decisions. For example, **separation of duties** simply parcels out decision rights in a manner that makes malfeasance and error less likely. In turn, the firm's accounting system is also designed to reflect these multiple products and arrangements. This leads to increased **accounting discretion** in that a manager is potentially able to shift income among products or otherwise misclassify costs. **Transfer prices** are designed to shift or reclassify cost and income in response to trade among an organization's subunits.

Exercises

18.1. Intra- and intertemporal accrual issues are closely related. Explain.

18.2. Consider Exhibits 18.8, 18.9, and 18.11.

    a. What accruals are associated with the evaluation and compensation arrangement in Exhibits 18.8 and 18.9?

    b. Contrast this with the arrangement in Exhibit 18.11. Explain.

    c. Is it important the accruals you have identified be audited? Explain.

18.3. We have stressed, for example in Chapter 2, the importance of nonseparability in understanding a firm's activities and prospects. How does this nonseparability theme arise in Exhibits 18.12 and 18.13?

18.4. The pay-for-performance solutions in Exhibit 18.4 presume that, in conjunction with any of these arrangements, the firm's best policy is to set capital and each labor factor to unity. Verify that this is indeed the case.

18.5. In the setting of Exhibit 18.4, suppose that the manager is able to self-report $q = (12, 10)$ as $q = (11, 11)$ and that the firm naively offers the manager the noted benchmark contract.

    a. What will the manager do?

    b. Given this, what is the certainty equivalent of the resulting compensation lottery?

18.6. Return to Exhibit 18.4 and the Only if (a_H, a_H) case.

    a. Draw the manager's decision tree and identify the optimal path through that tree.

    b. What do you notice, relative to the manager's decision tree in the benchmark case?

18.7. The setting in Exhibit 18.5 presumes each manager's output is independent of the other. Suppose everything remains as in the setting except that the two outputs are perfectly (positively) correlated when the two managers supply the same action but are independent if they do not supply the same action. Determine an optimal contract. Comment on the nature of the contract and any additional temptations you notice.

18.8. Return to the benchmark setting of Exhibit 18.4 (where output is publicly observed), but now assume the manager supplies action to the second product after observing the first product's output. Determine an optimal contract, and contrast your contract with that in Exhibit 18.5.

18.9. Verify that the pay-for-performance arrangements in Exhibit 18.8, given the transfer pricing arrangement will motivate each manager to supply high action and to capitalize on the trading opportunity, should it materialize.

18.10. Repeat the verification in Exercise 18.9 for the arrangements in Exhibit 18.9. What qualitative difference do you observe in the two pairs of arrangements?

18.11. Return to the transfer pricing illustration, Exhibits 18.6 through 18.11, but now assume that the probability a trading opportunity arises is .50 (as opposed to .25), presuming high actions. Explain what effect you think this will have on the pay-for-performance arrangements in Exhibits 18.8, 18.9, and 18.11.

18.12. This is a continuation of Exercise 18.11. Now solve for the optimal contracts in each of the regimes corresponding to Exhibits 18.8, 18.9, and 18.11. Then rewrite your noted explanation.

18.13. Consider a setting identical to that of Exhibits 18.12 and 18.13 except that the price of capital is $p_K = 300$. Repeat the factor choice, marginal cost, and total cost calculations in both Exhibits 18.12 and 18.13.

18.14. Ralph is trying to hire an agent to supply managerial input. The agent's choices are H or L; Ralph prefers H, and the agent prefers L. Ralph is risk neutral, and the agent is strictly risk averse. Output is uncertain and will depend on the agent's input as well as which of 10 equally likely states is present. The possibilities are detailed in the following table where x is some positive number and the states are denoted $s_1, \ldots s_{10}$. For example, if input H is supplied and the state turns out to be s_5, output will be $2x$.

	s_1	s_2	s_3	s_4	s_5	s_6	s_7	s_8	s_9	s_{10}
Input H	x	x	x	x	$2x$	$2x$	$2x$	$3x$	$3x$	$4x$
Input L	x	x	x	x	x	x	x	x	x	x

a. In qualitative terms, describe all details of the contractual arrangement between Ralph and the agent, presuming output is the only contracting variable.
b. Now suppose that a derivative instrument is available. It will pay x if the true state is one of the first five states and will require a payment of x if the true state is one of the last five. Assume that this instrument is priced at its expected value. (So the price is zero.) Now suppose Ralph buys such an instrument and the parties contract on the total of (1) the noted output of x, $2x$, and so on and (2) the net cash transaction associated with the financial instrument. Describe all details of the contractual arrangement between Ralph and the agent. Do you see any new moral hazard concerns at this point?
c. Repeat parts a and b for the following technology.

	S_2	S_1	S_3	S_4	S_5	S_6	S_7	S_8	S_9	S_{10}
Input H	x	x	x	x	$2x$	$2x$	$2x$	$3x$	$3x$	$4x$
Input L	0	0	0	0	0	$2x$	$2x$	$2x$	$2x$	$2x$

d. Carefully comment on what you have discovered. Do you see any connection to the interest in disclosing a firm's use of derivative instruments?

Part 4

End Game

Chapter 19

Institutional Considerations

Our information content focus necessitates close attention to the organization unit, the firm in our story, and how information might be used by whom. The final step in the odyssey is to admit to multiple firms and to dynamics. The admission of multiple firms creates an interest in coordinating their reporting activities and in the institutions that carry out this coordination task. The admission of dynamics creates an interest in continuous management of that coordination function. Of course, this interest in coordination leads us to regulatory boards, such as the FASB, and their conceptual frameworks. These frameworks play an essential role in coordinating the activities of the regulatory board, but they are by nature fundamentally inconsistent with the information content perspective. The reason is that they shy away from close attention to the organization unit and how information might be used by whom.

Regulations and professional bodies are familiar institutional features in the world of accounting, yet our study to date has kept these and other institutional considerations at bay except for the occasional reference to reporting or auditing regulations. These institutions, however, have not been created for entertainment purposes. They provide an important coordination service and are an integral part of the accounting scene. It behooves us then to look more closely at the institutional side of our topic.

To develop this theme, we remind ourselves that accounting choices (e.g., recognition and aggregation) are deeply influenced by the way the reporting firm is organized, its technology, its environment including market structure and other sources of information, and so on. There is hardly any general notion of how to best "do the accounting." Rather, the best choice time after time depends on the *finer details* of the setting, the host of circumstances under which the firm operates. Just as with other forms of economic activity, we find no universal or nearly universal prescription. For that matter, we even find specialized regulatory agencies, such as the GASB[1] and the FASB.

We then expand the setting to include a number of reporting firms. Here we encounter the importance of coordinating the various firms' reporting policies. At the mundane level, this ensures the use of the same measurement scale just as a society uses the same scale for weights and measures (e.g., the metric system). More subtly, coordination both in terms of information content and scale eases the auditor's task just as it eases the task of an individual confronted with studying accounting reports from a variety of firms (and, for that matter, the task of those who enforce reporting and auditing regulations).

The final stop is the coordinating institutions themselves. Here we find accounting curricula, schools of accounting, accounting textbooks, auditors, standard-setting institutions, and enforcement agents along with competition among institutions. We also find competing "conceptual frameworks," which we interpret as competing attempts to achieve intertemporal coordination in the evolution of reporting standards.

MANAGED REPORTING PERSPECTIVE

To begin, reflect on the heavy stylization of our reporting firm, as in Chapters 17 and 18, for example. The setting was simple because all events took place within two periods at most, and no more than two products were produced. Reporting the cash outflows associated with labor acquisition and capital acquisition along with cash inflows from customers tends to reveal a great deal of whatever information the firm has acquired in such a streamlined setting. Of course, multiple products and aggregation, such as when we group revenues by broad product classes, tend to obscure the connection between the firm's information and its cash flows.[2]

Likewise, timing issues abound when we extend the horizon. Then payment is often separated from the real transaction, and inventories of various sorts are found at all stages of production. The flow in a prototypical production process is descriptive: Materials are acquired and suppliers are paid at a later date; materials are transformed into work in process and then into finished goods; other factors, such as labor and energy, are

---

[1] The Government Accounting Standards Board (GASB) is a companion body to the FASB that develops accounting and reporting standards for state and local governmental entities. For that matter, we also find agencies specialized on the audit side, such as the Auditing Standards Board.

[2] It is also important to recall that, even in this modest setting, valuation and evaluation uses of accounting reports are not perfectly aligned in terms of ranking various reporting alternatives.

paid for at a later date;[3] finished goods are (perhaps momentarily) inventoried and sold, and cash finally flows into the firm.[4] An even longer time span is found when investments in hopefully long-lived assets, such as R&D, are considered. Consequently, the cash flows report only part of the firm's story. What is the current status of the production process? What problematic liabilities (e.g., in the product warranty sphere) are emerging? How are the firm's longer-term prospects unfolding? With a serious gap between the firm's story as revealed by its cash transactions and what the firm knows, accrual reporting becomes a potentially important information channel, as we know. The cash flow series itself is simply too coarse or untimely.

Moreover, with contemporary technology and more globalized market structures, we see a growing demand for nearly continuous reporting throughout the life of the firm.[5] Likewise, evaluation of the management team takes place on a nearly continuous basis. Even allowing time for the audit process, this suggests that the periodicity of accounting reports is hardly inconsequential or fixed.

In turn, this complexity raises the question of when, how, and combined with what other information the firm should record its financial history and pass that recording or some summarization thereof into the public domain. After all, the firm itself best knows the exact nature of ongoing transactions and the long-term commitments and opportunities it faces. Recognition rules are essential in defining how the accounting database is maintained. They prescribe when and how various transactions are to be recorded, such as when a particular revenue item is reported and what related matching issues are associated with that recording. Given the massive number of transactions in which a typical firm engages, even in a short period of time, we look to some coherent recognition rule to guide its financial recording. Simply reporting the underlying details would be overwhelming.

The recognition rules must be carefully selected, just as the level of aggregation must be determined. Naturally, this places some discretion in management's hands. We approach this in terms of balancing various demands for financial information, usually partitioned into valuation and contracting or stewardship purposes, both internal and external to the firm. The valuation perspective emphasizes the valuation of the future cash flows whereas the contracting purpose emphasizes management's performance. Again we encounter a nonseparability issue because these two purposes are surely linked yet far from independent and far from

---

[3] Indeed, this payment may be both well into the future and uncertain, as is the case with long-term bonus arrangements and postretirement benefits.
[4] Here, too, the timing is not necessarily straightforward. Warranty issues as well as product liability issues may be involved.
[5] For that matter, continuous time valuation models are commonplace in modern finance.

coextensive. We know that information useful in one domain is not necessarily useful in the other, but we must also deal with a *pollution effect*. Once contracting issues and moral hazard issues are on the table, we must deal with whether and how management will take advantage of the discretion inherent in the accrual reporting process. It is naive to believe it is possible to disregard this discretion issue.

Finer Details Matter

The picture that emerges time and time again is one of an accounting system that is well matched to the task and circumstance at hand. For example, is the accounting system primarily aimed at the valuation domain or at the contracting domain? In answering this question, the particular circumstances of the setting matter. These include the incentive problem that rests within (and around) the organization, the information that is supposed to be conveyed via the accounting system to the financial markets, the information that is supplied by other means, and the possibility for auditing the accruals and the incentives that surround the firm's reporting.

This is not simple. The interrelation among various information sources and information uses is a delicate matter. Furthermore, some of the structure is hidden from view. The threat of what might be reported if off-equilibrium behavior is pursued is, after all, an important factor in supporting equilibrium behavior.

Also, these choices are far from benign as has been demonstrated in previous chapters. More important, this has been demonstrated through the centuries. How else do we explain the worldwide resources devoted to accounting, the contentious debates over accounting policy, and the ever-changing auditing and reporting regulations?

Choices Are Not Static

The point worth reinforcing is that the reporting choice is highly specific to the setting at hand. In all the examples explored, we have found that the optimal reporting choice depends on the specifics of the organization and its environment. We never once prescribed how to "do the accounting" without reference to a specific situation. The reporting choice is highly contextual. This is the inevitable conclusion of an information content perspective.

By implication then, we also should not expect the accounting choices to be stationary. Changes in the firm or its environment may well call for a change in accounting policy. Changes in manufacturing technology, for example, precipitated widespread interest in changing product costing methods to such an extent that designing and implementing ABC–type systems became an important consulting service. Likewise, the dramatic growth in financial instruments, such as hedges and swaps, led to new, still-evolving reporting regulations.

MULTIPLE REPORTING FIRMS

From here we extend the picture to include multiple, heterogeneous reporting firms. Finer details continue to matter, so working through each firm's reporting choices one at a time presumably would lead to a variety if not a hodgepodge of choices. Imagine the chaos!

By analogy, we are unaccustomed to total anarchy in various information spheres. Libraries are organized with a well-known cataloging device, which helps train individuals to use the library, to move easily among libraries, and even to become professional librarians. Standard documentation formats are used in SEC and IRS filings, not to mention police reports and building permits. English is the universal language in air-traffic control. (It is also the command and control language in NATO.) Latin is the universal language of the Catholic Church, and multiple acronyms are the universal language of management consulting. We have not previously mentioned the importance of using compatible if not the same software in a variety of work group and networked contexts.

Is accounting devoid of similar coordination issues? Hardly. At one level, we have repeatedly stressed the scaling issue, the fact that we typically find a variety of accrual procedures will convey the same information. This is, in turn, a largely academic point—and your authors freely admit to being academics—when we are dealing with a single firm. Admitting to multiple firms raises the question of coordinating the choice of scale. The analogy to physical measures is apt.

This is only the lead paragraph of the story. Network externalities abound. Consider the FASB's financial instruments reporting standards (e.g., FAS 133 and FAS 137). The variety and use of financial instruments exploded, which led to an interest in more information about what some particular firm was or was not doing in this sphere. Comparison with other firms' activities, so-called benchmarking, is also of interest. This means, among other things, that the usefulness of what one firm reports is affected by what other firms report.

So, we begin with widespread, growing interest in some type of disclosure. Coordinating these disclosure patterns in the guise of FAS 133 and 137, for example, has a number of advantages. It allows joint training of those who have to prepare the disclosures, of those who have to audit the disclosures, and of those who might use the disclosures. Coordination is hardly a perfect solution. After all, finer details matter, and these idiosyncratic details are somehow combined and compromised in designing and using the reporting standard. At the same time, though, coordination is a coordinated response, which in and of itself achieves certain efficiencies.

Network Externalities

Return briefly to our modeling of accounting procedures in Chapter 7. At time t, the firm observes its cash flow, denoted c_t, along with what other information is reflected in the accounting system, denoted y_t. The history of these (c_t, y_t) pairs was denoted h_t as of period t. The specified accounting procedures would then report an asset or stock measure of $A_t(h_t) = A_t(h_{t-1}; c_t, y_t)$ and an income or flow measure of $\hat{I}_t(h_{t-1}; c_t, y_t) = \hat{I}_t(h_t) = c_t + A_t(h_{t-1}; c_t, y_t) - A_{t-1}(h_{t-1})$, reflecting the historical accumulation from h_{t-1} to $(h_{t-1}; c_t, y_t)$. The receiver of the time t report then must know the procedures and the underlying stock and flow functions to decode the report.

Now imagine many such firms in a setting in which this information is important in valuation and contracting venues.[6] A receiver who deals with multiple firms must now be aware of an entire array of reporting functions, both in terms of the information they purport to convey (the underlying partition) and the scale with which that information is conveyed.

By analogy, suppose we want to collect average temperatures around the world to find the warmest spot. One issue in collecting these data concerns the measurement procedure itself such as the time of day the measure is taken and the accuracy of the instrument. A second issue is the scale that is used. Suppose half the world uses the Fahrenheit scale while the other half uses the Celsius scale. Merely reporting an average temperature of 20 degrees, not to mention indiscriminate averaging of the reported averages, is not very helpful.

Parallel issues abound in accounting. Merely comparing two nearly identical firms' accounting measures is hopelessly naive unless we understand the underlying procedures that are in place. If the firms are not using identical procedures—identical A_t functions in our model—the precise set of procedures and the precise reporting function must also be communicated. There is little reason to suspect the firms would naturally use the same reporting functions. Some relationships tilt the information choices toward control purposes while others tilt them toward valuation purposes. Moreover, if we do not see universal cooperation in something as straightforward as temperature measurement, it is unlikely we would find universal cooperation on scaling choices in the accounting arena.

Important coordination issues arise. Finer details matter, and there is little reason to suspect that one firm in sorting out its choices fully internalizes the effect that those choices will have on others in the larger financial reporting network.

Scale coordination is a transparent issue. We see standardization of this type across a variety of settings ranging from interchangeable parts in manufacturing to coordinated communication protocols. Less transparent is coordination on the information content dimension. This increases comparability (e.g., the earlier noted benchmarking theme); it reduces the overall communication problem in the sense that we have coordinated the

---

[6] Recall that importance in the valuation domain implies there is some demand for early resolution of uncertainty, which means we are outside our convenient setting of risk-neutral valuation.

choice of the reporting procedures, and this coordination eases the user's task of assimilating reports from a variety of firms. For example, imagine the task of forecasting earnings in a setting in which the procedures used to measure earnings are not well coordinated.[7]

This is where the auditor enters the story. Does the accounting report faithfully convey the firm's financial history at that point in time? Have the advertized, coordinated recognition rules and scaling choices been followed? Have misrepresentation temptations been kept at bay? In performing the audit, the auditor checks and attests to whether the mapping of the finer details of the firm's history into the proposed report is appropriate relative to the definitions, norms, and conventions that are encoded into the standards and, of course, the firm's history. Notice how the use of coordinated reporting procedures eases the auditor's task, just as by performing that task, the auditor helps enforce the coordinated choices. The implicit cost of this grand scheme is that micro management of the accounting systems is no longer perfectly adjusted to the specifics of the situation.

In sum, we have a playing field with a number of firms, a number of users, and a number of intermediaries (e.g., auditors, analysts, and compensation consultants). We also have enforcement agencies and specialists (e.g., the SEC and the legal profession). Each has a role to play, and interactions abound. The financial reports have consequences for the users' decisions. The users' use of the financial reports has implications for the information content of the reports. The presence of the auditors has an impact on the equilibrium that is reached in the reporting game, including the behavior of nonaccounting sources, as does the presence of enforcement agencies. Finally, the number of players affects the allowable reporting strategies. Coordination is everywhere.

Coordination Tools

It is often claimed that accounting is the "language of business." This colloquialism is actually the centerpiece of reporting coordination. The coordination tools contain a common language that defines the reporting conventions, the essential language for articulating recognition rules, the explicit disclosure and display requirements, and the aggregation methods. This adds content to our repeated contention that accounting uses the language and algebra of valuation to convey information.[8]

---

[7] Incentive issues also deserve some attention here. We are somewhat casual in describing the use of accounting information in terms of valuation and contracting. Compensation schemes often use market values in the form of stock options, for example. By implication, the use of accounting information for valuation purposes becomes infected by the evaluation use. Using the valuation measure in the compensation arrangement extends the concern for reporting incentives to the valuation sphere itself.

[8] Coordination activities are, in fact, widespread. Consider the interest in international "harmonization" or use of Extensible Business Reporting Language (XBRL) to provide a systematic set of data tags in the financial reporting sphere.

Moreover, this language is hardly static but evolves over time as new conventions are invented and gradually adopted in the language while others become obsolete and disappear. Crucial to this development is whether the conventions serve their purposes in helping the accounting system to convey information.

COORDINATING INSTITUTIONS

Naturally, it is the auditor who enforces coordinated behavior, but how is this efficiently extended to all firms? This is the role played by education, textbooks, and professional standards.

The centers that train accountants (and those who will use accounting products) provide the first level of coordinating institutions. These are the universities and colleges. Consider those who study auditing. In each school these students work through a program that includes the basics of economics, law, accounting, and auditing. The school clearly leaves its mark on these students. We also see competition among schools to provide the "best" education and accreditation to coordinate the programs offered.

Textbooks provide a second level of coordinating institutions. The big-selling textbook has an impact on generations of accounting students. At this level, competition also enters, sometimes based on subtle nuances and other times on different approaches to accounting education.

A third level is provided by the qualifying examination and the training programs that prepare candidates who sit for that exam. (Indeed, this particular aspect has taken on an added international flavor since the European Union (EU) has issued an eighth directive concerning the education of auditors.) Competition is also present; separate subject areas and qualifying examinations are offered by the AICPA and The Institute of Management Accountants, for example. Moreover, the examination itself is far from static, as witnessed by current changes in the Uniform CPA exam's structure and the growing interest in global certification.

Another level of coordinating institutions is formed by the standard-setting bodies. These include national and international institutions both in the reporting and auditing arenas. The most visible members of this club are the FASB and the IASB.[9] In addition to these two institutions, numerous national bodies formulate accounting standards.[10]

---

[9] The International Accounting Standards Board (IASB), recall, grew out of a restructuring of the IASC. At its initial meeting in 2001, the IASB adopted the existing body of International Accounting Standards, developed by the IASC. (IASB standards are termed International Financial Reporting Standards.) A similar tack was taken by the FASB when it replaced its predecessor organization, the Accounting Principles Board.

[10] From here, we quickly see a similar pattern on the legal side along with various enforcement agencies and governmental oversight. We also have highly focused regulatory agencies, such as the Nuclear Regulatory Agency, which imposes its own reporting requirements.

The mission statement of the FASB commits it "to establish and improve standards of financial accounting and reporting for the guidance and education of the public, including issuers, auditors, and users of financial information." Likewise, the objectives of the IASB, as stated in its constitution, are "to develop, in the public interest, a single set of high quality, understandable and enforceable accounting standards . . . ; to promote the use and rigorous application of those standards; and to bring about convergence of national accounting standards and International Accounting Standards."

These standard-setting institutions prescribe how to record and display various types of transactions, events, and balance sheet items.[11] They thus divide the set of accounting procedures into those that are allowed and not allowed for a specific type of accounting event. This amounts to specifying if not constraining the choice of partition and scale. Moreover, the FASB and IASB restrictions are not always consistent. For example, development costs are required to be accounted for as a long-lived asset according to the IASB whereas they are required to be written off as an expense according to the FASB. Because both require expenditures to be disclosed, the difference here is primarily one of scaling.[12] In a similar vein we note that the IASB approaches valuation with a fair value orientation while the FASB maintains a mixture of cost basis and fair value approaches.

Governance

Of course, this story is rather static. It portrays an interconnected setting in which coordination is desirable but ignores the fact that the world changes. However, changes in technology, global arrangements, and trading patterns all suggest changes in accounting. Modern information technology, for example, has created new tasks and new difficulties for auditors and has, in turn, led to new audit techniques and regulations. Likewise, the aforementioned explosion in financial instruments led to new reporting standards.[13]

---

[11] The reference to accounting as a language is also appropriate at this level. In Denmark there is a government institution called *Dansk Sprognævn*. The charter of this institution is to define and maintain the official Danish language. Naturally, the language evolves and new words enter it through international communication. Constantly Dansk Sprognævn monitors the development and decides if and when the "new" words should be adopted in the official Danish language.

[12] Notice, however, that the IASB approach retains the option to subsequently report that the original estimates were too optimistic. No optimism or its subsequent refinement is allowed in the FASB approach. Once expensed, so to speak, the matter is closed.

[13] Cost accounting standards provide another illustration. Originally, it was thought in some circles that the Cost Accounting Standards Board could issue a set of costing standards for use in cost-based contracting in the government arena and then close down after these standards were fully developed and articulated. Of course, that presumed a static world, and changes in technology and organization arrangements have kept these costing issues alive.

The larger picture is that coordination is a dynamic exercise. We therefore rely on various institutional arrangements to monitor, fine tune, and evolve the coordinated arrangements. That is, governance of the coordination becomes an issue. We now enter the world of designing and managing a governance structure that will reliably deal with the necessity of evolving the coordinated choices.[14]

Competition

Competition is also highly visible. Self-regulation competes with regulation just as textbook authors, schools, and certifying institutions compete with one another. The same holds for reporting standards themselves. Globalization has led to concern over which body will set standards on the global stage. At present, various national groups attempt to coordinate their activities, and the IASC, now the IASB, is undergoing a major change in structure. The FASB is also taking on more of an international flavor prodded, at times, it seems, by the SEC. Enforcement procedures remain an important element in the contest. There is fierce competition in the standard-setting market. Similarly, the FASB and GASB are far from independent and unaware of each other's activities.

Governance of the Governance Institutions

Who governs the governance institutions? Most of the institutions are run by a board with representatives from the auditing firms, industry, and academic institutions. At some level the trading exchanges and those who regulate the trading exchanges are also involved because they approve the set of reporting standards that must be followed in order to be quoted on that particular exchange.[15] Government institutions are heavily involved in the process. The same holds for professional bodies, such as the AICPA and the Financial Executives International.

For example, financial reporting in the EU is regulated by the fourth and seventh directives. These were subsequently adopted in the accounting laws of its member states. Financial reporting in the member states then must comply with these accounting laws. Consequently, financial accounting standards must comply with the national accounting laws. The EU, for that matter, now calls for compliance with the IASB's standards following a brief transition period.

In the United States the SEC has the power to issue accounting standards. It has delegated this power, however. The FASB's oversight and

---

[14] So-called standard overload is an often heard complaint based on the increasing number of regulations from a variety of sources.

[15] For example, all listed companies on the Toronto Stock Exchange must follow Canadian GAAP while foreign companies listed on the Montreal Exchange may use IASB or FASB standards (among others) and reconcile to Canadian GAAP. U.S. exchanges, following SEC regulations, allow foreign companies to use IASB standards provided they reconcile to U.S. GAAP. Domestic companies presently have no such option.

financial independence are provided by its trustees, who themselves represent a variety of organizations. The FASB is also officially advised by a separate advisory group. However, the trustees and advisors are not the only influential group surrounding the FASB. The SEC monitors the development of standards closely and interferes, explicitly or implicitly, whenever so motivated. Nor is congressional interference unheard of. Contact with the AICPA's Accounting Standards Executive Committee is routine. Furthermore, any proposed standard is approved only through an elaborate procedure involving extensive public hearings, deliberation, and redeliberation.

The other major player on the standard-setting scene is the IASB. It is governed in a manner roughly parallel to the FASB's governance except that its focus is explicitly global. The success of this venture naturally rests on various countries accepting and enforcing its promulgations.

SOCIAL WELFARE PERSPECTIVE

The picture that emerges is that accounting (and auditing) standards are more the product of a political than a technical, decision-oriented process. On closer reflection, this is natural and inevitable. After all, firms do not naturally adopt identical accounting systems, and aggregation over their diverse views is sure to be problematic. Moreover, circumstances change, each firm's accounting system changes, and the diversity among the various choices becomes dynamic as well. This invites additional regulation, but this is getting ahead of the story.

Conceptual Frameworks and Qualitative Characteristics

Both the FASB and IASB have developed and continue to evolve so-called conceptual frameworks. The FASB, for example, describes its quest as follows:

> Statements in the series are intended to set forth objectives and fundamentals that will be the basis for development of financial accounting and reporting standards. The objectives identify the goals and purposes of financial reporting. The fundamentals are the underlying concepts of financial accounting—concepts that guide the selection of transactions, events, and circumstances to be accounted for, their recognition and measurement, and the means of summarizing and communicating them to interested parties. Concepts of that type are fundamental in the sense that other concepts flow from them and repeated reference to them will be necessary in establishing, interpreting, and applying accounting and reporting standards.[16]

[16] FASB, 1980, Summary of Principal Conclusions.

The goal is to provide a framework or rationalizing basis for the development of reporting standards. The frameworks rely on three central features: Information is being provided;[17] this information is conveyed using the language and algebra of valuation;[18] and this information perspective can be well articulated with or by "qualitative characteristics" of that information. The information perspective and use of the language and algebra of valuation are, of course, the ever-present themes in our study, but the notion of qualitative characteristics has been studiously avoided.

The notion of *qualitative characteristics* is surely appealing. Suppose, for example, we are shopping for an automobile. Size, fuel economy, safety, acceleration, and price are all likely to matter. In searching for a house or an apartment, size, location, state of repair, and price are all likely to matter. In searching for a good information channel, design, relevance, reliability, and price are likely to matter. The common theme is to take a set of complex alternatives and project each along a list of dimensions or characteristics. From here, the choice in concept is made by scoring each in terms of the levels of their respective underlying characteristics.[19] Naturally, trade-offs among the characteristics are an essential part of the analysis.

---

[17] In the business enterprise sphere, the FASB states: "Financial reporting should *provide information* to help present and potential investors and creditors and other users in assessing the amounts, timing, and uncertainty of prospective cash receipts from dividends or interest and the proceeds from the sale, redemption, or maturity of securities or loans. . . . Financial reporting should *provide information* about the economic resources of an enterprise, the claims to those resources (obligations of the enterprise to transfer resources to other entities and owners' equity), and the effects of transactions, events, and circumstances that change resources and claims to those resources. Financial reporting should *provide information* about an enterprise's economic resources, obligations, and owners' equity" (FASB, 1978, paragraphs 37 through 41, emphasis added).

[18] "Elements of financial statements are the building blocks with which financial statements are constructed—the classes of items that financial statements comprise. Elements refers to broad classes, such as assets, liabilities, revenues, and expenses. . . . The items that are formally incorporated in financial statements are financial representations (depictions in words and numbers) of certain resources of an entity, claims to those resources, and the effects of transactions and other events and circumstances that result in changes in those resources and claims. That is, symbols (words and numbers) in financial statements stand for cash in a bank, buildings, wages due, sales, use of labor, earthquake damage to property, and a host of other economic things and events . . ." (FASB, 1985, paragraphs 5 and 6).

From here, the basic elements of assets, liabilities, and so on provide a screening function. Possessing the essential characteristics of one of the elements is necessary for formally recognizing that item in the firm's financial records. The next step brings issues of relevance and reliability into play. Reflecting on the material in Chapter 7, however, it is clear that commitment to these elements is a commitment to use the language and algebra of valuation to convey whatever underlying information is to be conveyed.

[19] Indeed, one can go further here and imagine all goods and services as providing some list of underlying characteristics, the individuals in the economy as having tastes defined over these characteristics, and so on.

The FASB stresses the overriding importance of providing useful information and views relevance and reliability as the characteristics that are essential for usefulness. *Relevance* is defined as the "capacity of information to make a difference in a decision by helping users to form predictions about the outcomes of past, present, and future events or to confirm or correct prior expectations." *Reliability* is defined as the "quality of information that assures that information is reasonably free from error and bias and faithfully represents what it purports to represent."[20] In turn, both characteristics are further identified via subcharacteristics:

> To be relevant, information must be timely and it must have predictive value or feedback value or both. To be reliable, information must have representational faithfulness and it must be verifiable and neutral. Comparability, which includes consistency, is a secondary quality that interacts with relevance and reliability to contribute to the usefulness of information. Two constraints are included in the hierarchy. . . . Information can be useful and yet be too costly to justify providing it. To be useful and worth providing, the benefits of information should exceed its cost. All of the qualities of information shown are [also] subject to a materiality threshold. . . .[21]

The IASB also relies on qualitative characteristics in its conceptual framework although it emphasizes understandability, relevance, reliability, and comparability. This leaves the grouping of characteristics slightly changed, although in philosophy and spirit the FASB and IASB listings are basically equivalent.

The idea, then, is that an information source's "value" can be conceptualized as depending on, for example, the relevance and reliability of what it reports: value = f(relevance, reliability), so to speak. Indeed, the argument extends to the view that the "user of accounting information will uniquely perceive the relative value to be attached to each quality of that information."[22] That is, the underlying information system choice problem can be well articulated by identifying each alternative's qualitative characteristics and proceeding from there.

We have insisted, however, on explicit identification of the setting, on something far more specific than qualitative characteristics. This is the foundation of an *information content perspective,* and there is no way to reconcile this insistence on finer details with the qualitative characteristics approach.

Although seemingly academic to a fault, it is important to understand the reasoning behind this fact. Return to the individual decision-making setup in Chapter 6 where we had a set of states, S, actions, A, and an

---

[20] FASB, 1980, (Glossary).
[21] FASB, 1980, Summary of Principal Conclusions.
[22] FASB, 1980, Summary of Principal Conclusions.

outcome function that associated outcomes, $x \in X$, with the state and act: $x = p(s, a)$. The probability measure was denoted $\pi(s)$, and the utility measure was denoted $U(x)$. So, fully describing the decision problem requires us to specify (the functions) p, U, and π, the problem setting itself (consisting of states, acts, and outcomes), the tastes, and the beliefs. From here we introduced information modeled as a partition of S. We then worked through the details of how the individual would best use the information provided, for example, by partition η and summarized this with the expected utility score, denoted $E[U \mid \eta]$. (See, for example, Exhibit 6.7.)

So, the fact that one information source, η_1, is superior to a second, η_2, in this setting is equivalent to the statement that $E[U \mid \eta_1] \geq E[U \mid \eta_2]$. This conclusion in general depends on the problem specifics, on the finer details, on the specification of p, U, and π. Of course, we also know we can avoid the tedium of laying this specification out if η_1 is a subpartition of η_2, but that is a special case and, in general, the finer details are controlling.

The qualitative characteristics approach, though, attempts to bypass this specification of finer details and concentrate on the characteristics of relevance and reliability, characteristics of the information itself. Think of this as specifying the states, S, and the partition, η, and, perhaps, the probability, π.[23] Now ask yourself, under what circumstances could this streamlined approach be consistent with the fundamentals. The answer is only when the finer details do not matter, only when the one information structure is a subpartition of the other.

Thus, if we are true to the information content perspective and if we are true to the idea of substituting qualitative characteristics for a specification of the finer details, we are reduced to subpartition-based comparisons. Taking this one step further leads to an inability to compare or choose from among numerous alternatives. The characteristics approach then by necessity provides a vague, an incomplete, representation of the underlying fundamentals.

This is the reason we say the qualitative characteristics approach, while appealing, simply cannot be reconciled with our information content perspective. It gives away the game. There is no easy way out, no quick answer.

Now you know why in Chapter 6 we were careful to stress the idea of comparing information sources and the fact this can be done at a general level, that is, by not being too concerned with the finer details of the setting, by relying on the subpartition idea. The subpartition structure is not

---

[23] Materiality rests on minor, or second-order issues, so not worrying about unusually small probability events would be introduced by carrying along a probability specification. Going concern is a case in point.

complete although it is transitive. Some information sources are simply noncomparable, absent the finer details of the setting.[24]

How, then, are we to interpret the conceptual frameworks? Remember that we are dealing with a regulatory institution, here the FASB or IASB. It behooves us to interpret the conceptual foundation as a document produced by and for a regulatory institution. These institutions perform an important, essential governance function. Their respective conceptual frameworks are not unassailable or complete policy guides. Rather, they provide attempts to signal, in broad brush terms, intertemporal coordination on the regulatory institution's part as it deals with the ever-present, ever-changing governance issues that arise. They provide a rhetorical guide to the policy business of the respective institution and a vehicle for "close-in" policy debate. At the same time, being less than definitive, they allow the regulatory institution slack in pursuing the evolution of their promulgations. In this sense, the frameworks provide a constitution, a commitment to proceed in some particular, albeit vague, fashion. They are rhetorical to a degree but also essential if society is to maintain relatively stable expectations about how they will manage regulatory issues in the future.[25]

Preference Aggregation and the Cost-Benefit Euphemism

This vagueness, in fact, is no accident. Even if the qualitative characteristics and information content themes were closely aligned, we would struggle over the issue of "balancing costs and benefits." At the regulatory level, these resolutions take on more a political than a logical or rational

---

[24] If you enjoy puns, the conceptual framework is not a representationally faithful depiction of the presumed task. To fully lay out the argument, "as fine as" or "subpartition of" provides only a partial though transitive ranking of the information alternatives. We know a measure exists, when confronted by a finite set of choices, if and only if the underlying ranking is complete and transitive (Note 2, Chapter 6). We are missing completeness; in general, information sources are not comparable; one tells us something the other does not and vice versa. So, the ability to move from the underlying characteristics, absent finer details, to a well-informed choice (e.g., an assessment of value) is simply not possible. Furthermore, notice that the argument is based on the easy case of a single user absent any (mis)reporting issues. The market-based valuation and evaluation cases are subject to the same line of argument, although the subpartition ranking does not necessarily hold in those fundamentally multiperson settings. Recall that information can destroy trading opportunities, for example, when it arrives before mutually beneficial insurance arrangements can be consummated.

[25] "The Board itself is likely to be the most direct beneficiary of the guidance provided by the Statements in this series. They will guide the Board in developing accounting and reporting standards by providing the Board with a common foundation and basic reasoning on which to consider merits of alternatives" (FASB, 1980 Summary of Principal Conclusions).

hue. Why, then, do we see political dimensions at this point? Intuitively, it seems, we should be able to aggregate individual preferences in a consistent fashion and proceed with the proverbial *cost-benefit orientation*.

This aggregation approach, however, leads us to social choice and Arrow's celebrated impossibility theorem. To set the stage, suppose we have some (finite) number of individuals who want to make a collective choice (such as set a definitive standard for reporting on the use of financial instruments). Each individual has well-defined preferences in terms of a complete and transitive ranking of the alternatives. Moreover, to stay with the easy case, these individual preferences are common knowledge; there is no concern for someone strategically misrepresenting their preferences.

Now, regardless of what the (complete and transitive) rankings are, we want some way to aggregate these individual preferences into a social preference. There are countless ways to do this, and Arrow imposes four conditions.

The first condition is that the aggregation process must always work in the sense that it leads to a complete and transitive social ranking of the alternatives given some specification of the individuals' complete and transitive rankings. No matter what the individual (complete and transitive) rankings are, the process should result in complete and transitive social rankings. This is called *universal domain*.

Second, no single individual should always get his way, no single individual should be all-powerful. This is called a *nondictatorship condition*.

Third, whatever the social ranking, it should respect Pareto optimality. This means under no circumstance should one option be socially preferred to another option if everyone has the opposite preference.

Finally, the movement from individual to social preferences should depend on the choices available, not unavailable or so-called irrelevant alternatives. This is called *independence of irrelevant alternatives*.

These four conditions are hardly assailable: The scheme should work in the sense of movement from individually rational preferences to social rationality; no dictator should be present; the system should not systematically deny the individuals what they want; and irrelevant alternatives should not be controlling.

The problem is that the four conditions are mutually incompatible. *Any* social choice mechanism, be it voting, market-based allocation, life in a family structure, or the FASB or IASB, violates at least one of the conditions.

Let's go a bit further. Suppose we cling to the last three conditions, meaning no dictator, no systematic silliness, and no irrelevant alternatives. Then we are stuck with the fact that aggregating individual preferences cannot lead to well-defined (i.e., complete and transitive) social preferences. Sometimes a choice will not be possible (i.e., incompleteness) or cyclic (i.e., intransitive). So, ask yourself: In the world of accounting regulation, have we ever seen reversals of regulations? Have we ever witnessed a seeming unwillingness to take a stand? This is the natural result. Get used to it!

At present we see this theme playing out in the international arena where the FASB and IASB offer competing views of "global GAAP." The IASB, recall, is more inclined toward fair value measurement while the FASB continues to place heavy weight on a mixture of historical cost and fair value measurement. So, at the margin, they offer different partitions, or different information content. The FASB standards also tend to be much more comprehensive and detailed. Can we say unequivocally which is preferred or better? Each represents an aggregation of diverse views and is the product of a politically laden process. We should expect no less. In addition, neither exists in a vacuum. Competing and complementary institutions are also present. Consider auditor training, licensing, and enforcement, for example.

Institutions matter.

Summary

The institutional side of accounting is rich, intriguing, and important. It reflects the fact that accounting is a specialized, sophisticated information source whose comparative advantage rests on its defense against manipulation; it also reflects the fact that this comparative advantage is heightened by coordination. It matters that most accounting systems are similar, in important ways, to one another, and it matters that changes in accounting practice are coordinated, at least to the degree that reporting standards and consulting products achieve coordination. All of this is made possible on the economywide level by the institutional fabric of accounting.

In reflecting on this institutional fabric, it is important to understand that this combination of training, indoctrination, and regulation does not prescribe or fully coordinate the practice of accounting; much is left to the individual firm. Finer details matter. It is likewise important to understand that these institutions have their own tensions to manage. The FASB and IASB and their respective conceptual frameworks represent a case in point. The end result of such a board's deliberations will have a political component; this is the essence of Arrow's theorem. Naturally, then, the board's organizing document, its constitution, its conceptual framework will be less than utterly coherent, less than tightly connected to the information content perspective. Its framework must accommodate the give and take of political life. This is not a cynical statement but an admission of reality. There is no unassailable way to aggregate individual preferences into a coherent, fully consistent social perspective. Why should accounting standards be exempt from such logic?

Selected References

Wilson (1983) is an important reference on the network externalities theme. Nurnberg (2001) illustrates the coordination theme, and Dye and Sunder (2001) stress competition among coordinating institutions. Reliance on qualitative characteristics is not unique to the noted conceptual frameworks; see, for example, AAA (1966). Similarly, Kinney (2000) emphasizes information "quality" as a function of relevance (where reporting standards reign), reliability (where auditing standards reign), and trustworthiness (where auditor independence, for example, is critical). The incongruity between the qualitative characteristics approach and the information content approach is laid out in Demski (1973). Our subsequent interpretation of the conceptual frameworks owes much to Sims (1996). Gjesdal (1981) and Kim (1995) explore the slippage between the subpartition ranking in a single-person setting as opposed to a contracting setting. Luce and Raiffa (1957) is a favorite reference for Arrow's theorem, as is Arrow (1990). Laffont and Tirole (1993), Sappington and Weisman (1995), and Sappington and Stiglitz (1987) are superb references on the subject of regulation. Watts and Zimmerman (1986) highlight the importance of "political cost" in a firm's choice of accounting method.

Key Terms

The information content theme stresses the **finer details** of the setting, meaning the firm, its environment, its technology, the market structure it operates in, its competing and complementary information sources, and so on. The **qualitative characteristics** theme stresses characteristics of the information per se, such as relevance and reliability, as a substitute for identifying and focusing on the finer details.

Exercises

19.1. The chapter makes constant reference to "finer details" of the setting. What does this mean, and why is it important in understanding the world of accounting?

19.2. Our approach to accounting theory began with and never strayed from the formal presence of uncertainty, yet the FASB's and IASB's conceptual frameworks barely acknowledge uncertainty. Explain.

19.3. Is it possible in theory to measure the quality or the quantity of information? (The answer is subtle, but all the details for it are present in this chapter.)

19.4. We have stressed information content as a nominal as opposed to an ordinal concept, for example. It was viewed as simply present or absent, and we shied away from claiming one system had "more" information content than another. Discuss this reticence, paying close attention to the subpartition (partial) ranking of information sources and to Arrow's theorem.

19.5. Our approach to accounting theory stresses information content in valuation and evaluation settings. In the former, the question is whether the information source is capable of altering the perception of future cash flows via systematic probability revision. In the latter, the question is whether the information source will be useful in the systematic crafting of a trading arrangement as defined by the optimal contracting exercise between the firm and the manager. How does this relate to the qualitative characteristics approach? Be specific.

19.6. Suppose we have three individuals ($i = 1, 2, 3$) and three recognition rules ($j = 1, 2, 3$). Simple majority rule determines the social ranking between each pair of recognition rules.

    a. Does this voting scheme satisfy Arrow's Pareto optimality condition?

    b. Does it satisfy his nondictatorship condition?

    c. What about independence of irrelevant alternatives?

19.7. This is a continuation of Exercise 19.6. Now suppose that the first individual strictly ranks the three rules 1 over 2 over 3, the second strictly ranks them 3 over 2 over 1, and the third strictly ranks them 2 over 3 over 1. Simple majority rule again defines the social ranking between any two recognition rules. What social ranking emerges? Is it complete? Is it transitive?

19.8. This is a continuation of Exercise 19.7. Change the second individual's ranking to 3 over 1 over 2. What social ranking emerges? Discuss.

19.9. In Chapter 6 we examined the subpartition idea summarized by the conclusion $E[U \mid \eta_1] \geq E[U \mid \eta_2]$ for all choice problems defined on S if and only if the partition induced by η_1 is a subpartition of the partition induced by η_2. How does this lead to the conclusion that the information content and qualitative characteristics approaches to information system choice are inconsistent?

Chapter 20

Professional Opportunity and Responsibility

It is time to bring our study of accounting theory to a close. One well trained in accounting is well trained in managing and using an accounting system, in dealing with and directing the evolution of the accounting system as the organization itself and its environment evolve. The organization might be a single firm, a government entity, an industry, or an entire economy. Regardless, the management task remains.

This management task is neither obvious nor benign. A poorly designed and managed accounting system can do enormous damage, just as a well-designed and managed system can well complement the other resources at the organization's disposal. As is the case with these other resources, it takes imagination, talent, insight, and effort to perform this management task in a high-quality, professionally responsible manner. The task is vastly more complex than adhering to regulations, textbook recipes, and a consultant's recommendations. In short, one well trained in accounting is by definition well equipped to deal with these opportunities in a responsible fashion.

Accounting theory, in turn, cannot make the irresponsible responsible, nor can it in and of itself deliver the blueprint for a well-designed system. Professional quality judgment is essential. Theory helps frame the issues, the very tensions, in this design and management exercise. Theory is a complement to but not a substitute for the responsible exercise of judgment.

With this in mind, we turn initially to a short reflection on the *information content theme* that is the center of our study. Following this, we return to the theme that theory is an attempt to compress the complex into a workable description or pattern without losing too much of the important details. As such, theory always has an error, which behooves us to identify what some of these errors might be, given the particular compression we have employed. Following this, we offer some guidelines to test your thinking about, your frame of, whatever accounting issue happens to be foremost at the time. These guidelines are not foolproof, of course, but they are useful in reminding us to concentrate on first-order effects and to give serious thought to whether our thinking in this regard has been sufficiently expansive and insightful. Beyond that, it is time to apply your own resources.

INFORMATION CONTENT

The basic premise in our work is that accounting is a source of information; it tells us something we do not know. This raises several issues. First, if there is something we do not know and want to know, we must admit to the presence of *uncertainty*. Stated differently, the starting point must be a resource allocation exercise in which uncertainty is a first-order effect. Thus, we have kept the prototypical firm with the K, L, and M factors front and center throughout our study. At every twist and turn, there was an element of uncertainty impacting some combination of the valuation of the claim to the firm's dividend or cash flow stream, the contracting arrangement with the firm's management team, and the firm's production plan itself. This, in turn, necessitated the constant presence of the mechanics of modeling resource allocation under uncertainty, our ever-present probabilities and risk preferences.

Second, if the accounting system is to be a source of information, we must equip it to observe, record, and communicate some set of events. We did this by envisioning the accounting system as a close cousin to present value–based valuation in mechanical terms but one that has access to an underlying event structure. Though obtuse on first encounter, the effect is that accounting uses a particular measurement scale to convey various events. It is important also to acknowledge that this recording is not done in unique fashion but that an entire class of equivalent measurement scales is present. For example, the firm might decide to capitalize and depreciate all capital expenditures on a straight-line basis over 5 or 10 years. Such a rigid rule identifies only the expenditures; the allocation rule, being rigid, conveys absolutely no additional information. Choice between 5 or 10 years here is simply the choice between two (equivalent) scales. At this level of abstraction, the information content school can distinguish among different event structures being reported but not among different scales being used to report some particular event structure. In a world in which different physical measurement scales are used (e.g., Fahrenheit versus

Celsius) and different languages are used (e.g., Danish versus English), it should come as no surprise that different accounting "treatments" are used (e.g., straight-line versus accelerated depreciation).

Third, accounting has been around a long time and shows no sign of declining in importance.[1] This suggests it has a comparative advantage relative to the vast array of alternate information sources. The accounting system, of course, deals in financial measures of events (which, if you think about it, is a scaling issue), but its strength is that it is designed to be difficult to manipulate. It is designed to be and generally is audited. As we have stressed, this strength has important implications for how we think about the accounting system and how we relate it, either abstractly or empirically, to surrounding events. For example, it is often a late-reporting information source. Most interesting, the well-designed and well-functioning accounting system that stresses its comparative advantage will, in equilibrium, routinely report a great deal of what is already known. In our formal language, its primary strength is its threat of what might be reported had the actors behaved differently.

The information content theme then is natural if not compelling, but giving it structure beyond that of a colloquialism requires a great deal of work. This alone should convince us that designing and maintaining an accounting system requires responsible, talented professional behavior.

THEORY AS STYLIZATION

Applying this responsible, talented professional judgment is no easy, routine task, and theory now enters as a guide for structuring or framing that task. Of course, pragmatic considerations weigh in at this point. A theory so inclusive that it covered every detail, every nuance (even if we knew how to construct it) would be overwhelming.[2] Instead, we take an approach that highlights what we hope are the important details, the first-order effects, and leave the rest to chance. This has the advantage of offering clarity (though we do not suggest you dwell too long on the clarity you found in this text on initial reading) but also compels us to admit that an error term is always present. Something has been left out. That is a guarantee.

What, then, have we left out? In the following sections we offer three categories of concern. These are surely not all inclusive, but they offer a starting point for reflecting on the strengths and weaknesses of the particular approach we have presented. Put differently, they offer insight into

---

[1] Some would argue that the importance of accounting in equity markets has declined in the presence of modern information technologies, but this ignores its importance in disciplining other sources of information.

[2] It also would not be a theory in the sense we emphasize. Theory is an organizing device that compresses what we know but with tolerable error.

the nature of the errors that are likely to be present in our focus on the information content theme.

Cognitive Issues

Rationality, indeed superrationality, is relied on in the formal modeling we have employed. We have relied on individual choice behavior that rests on tastes, which are encoded in a utility measure, and beliefs, which are encoded in a probability measure. Information is consistently processed via Bayes' rule. Mistakes are simply not made, and any information, once available, is instantly and costlessly assimilated. Which admissible scale to use in conveying the information is a matter of complete indifference. Moreover, when designing elaborate trading games, such as an auction with private information or a multiplay contracting game, the individuals fully recognize the game tree structure and well identify the equilibrium therein.

Surely this is fiction. People make mistakes all the time. People require time to read and digest a report. Moreover, when confronted with well-defined information processing and judgment tasks, individuals tend to exhibit consistent departures from the superrationality norm, although the precise source of these consistencies remains open to debate.[3] For example, individuals often exhibit a "representativeness heuristic" by basing a judgment on some hypothetical circumstance that is somehow representative of the setting at issue. We also know that when confronted with an information processing task, individuals can be influenced by the scale employed to convey the information, despite the fact that the scales are equivalent in a world of rationality.

Likewise, an important feature of organization design is the use of organization arrangements to improve the human side of decision making and judgment. Auditor and flight crew check lists are illustrative, as are various training sessions (e.g., repetition of team assignments in a variety of situations and the use of joint decision responsibilities). Additionally, one feature of security market regulation is the protection of the naive or amateur investor, hardly an issue in a world of superrational players.

Irrational behavior is considered to be of second-order importance in our analysis. After all, individuals have no urgent desire to consistently behave inconsistently, just as a firm that routinely leaves itself open to dominance in the market place invites removal from the industry. Importantly, then, our focus on rationality removes these types of concerns from our immediate focus. This has the advantage of directing attention to the

---

[3] For example, superrational behavior, when projected to a single decision embedded in a sequence of decisions, is unlikely to exhibit the appearance of superrationality simply because of interactions between the smaller and the larger set of tasks at hand. Similarly, behavioral finance is used to examine pricing anomalies, such as those with IPOs, although economic forces per se often speak to the same anomalies.

substance of the information, who possesses it, and the economic forces that are likely to influence its use and effect. The cost of this stress on information content, so to speak, is the suppression of important issues in the cognitive realm.

Transaction Cost Issues

Closely related is the notion of *transaction costs*. We see this when we hire a travel agent, an investment advisor, a real estate broker, or an attorney. In each case we are seeking help as we search for travel arrangements or investments, or engage in a real estate transaction. Brokerage fees are common, taxes are ever present, and rare is the individual who enjoys shopping for an automobile. Moreover, designing and negotiating a contract is no easy task, and contract enforcement (e.g., civil litigation) is far from invisible activity.

This leads us to incomplete and implicit contracts and the use of organization arrangements, reputation, trust, and formal governance procedures. The firm might employ a formal grievance structure to deal with personality conflicts between a supervisor and subordinate; it might establish an arbitration panel; it might construct seniority rules and other bureaucratic devices with the intent of balancing these types of frictions and temptations.[4] Similarly, residual decision rights come into play. For example, the purchase of a long-lived asset leaves the decision rights that pertain to that asset in the hands of the user, just as a lease of that asset leaves the residual decision rights in the hands of a different party.

The theme is much deeper, and eventually connects to the preceding cognitive theme. Here we encounter "bounded rationality," a limited form of rationality that stresses cognitive limitations.

Of course, our emphasis on information content treats contracting arrangements as costlessly designed with enormous foresight and unfailing identification of equilibrium behavior, just as it treats valuation as fully reflective of all available information.

Socialization Issues

Our emphasis also treats socialization and cultural issues as a second-order concern. Will the organization or group succeed in imbuing its new members with the company ethic or party line? Will this affect and be affected by the contracting arrangements? Do the structure and language of accounting with their emphasis on stocks and flows of "value" affect the perceptions and goals of the individuals involved? Do these individuals focus appropriately or inordinately on what the accounting system will or might report?

---

[4] For example, the employee might be tempted to spend too much time on "influence" rather than productive activities.

In a larger sense the firm's accounting system serves as a statement of what the firm values, just as it serves as a usable compression of a vast array of activities into a summary measure of accomplishment. No information source could do otherwise.

GUIDELINES

Given our theory is imperfect, we then ask what indicators might be useful to help ensure that we are using it with requisite sophistication. Here we offer some suggestions, six in number.

Exogenous Trap

First, do not fall for the exogenous issue trap! We all learned the basics of accounting by beginning with some transaction the entity had engaged in, such as the acquisition of a long-lived asset, and then pondering how to tell that story in the accounting records. This is an efficient way to learn mechanics but an inefficient way to move from mechanical alacrity to professional responsibility.

It is, in our view, important to begin with an identification of the setting that is sufficiently broad for the accounting issue to arise naturally, endogenously, if you will. If the issue concerns a problematic liability, make certain you frame the issue in a setting in which such a liability might arise. If the issue concerns derivative instruments, make certain you frame the issue in a setting in which the use of such instruments would arise. If the issue concerns inventory valuation, make certain you frame the issue in a setting in which holding inventory naturally arises.

The reason is simple. If you narrowly define the issue, you are reduced to looking for a rule or a parallel rule. You have moved the central issue to the side. The central issue is what information is to be conveyed, not what rule is to be followed. The key to responsibly addressing this issue is to understand what the firm is doing and why. Absent such a rich understanding, you have no basis for judgment other than pedantic use of a rule book.

Consider inventory valuation. Rather than simply ask how to value the inventory, it is important to begin with a broader frame that leads to it being rational for the firm to hold inventory in the first place. (This, in turn, reminds us that markets are less than perfect, so our infatuation with fully reliable, well-defined market-based valuation is likely to be just that, an infatuation. After all, the fact that the firm has powerful reasons to hold inventory suggests some type of market imperfection.) From here we move to address what information we want to convey via the inventory reporting. Conveying a sense of factor price volatility suggests that LIFO might be an interesting call. On the other hand, using relatively stable prices (or standard prices) puts more emphasis on conveying a sense of inventory magnitude, but the key to understanding what about this holding you want to convey via the accounting system is to understand why the firm is holding inventory in the first place.

Similarly, in dealing with a problematic potential liability, it is important to frame the reporting issue in a setting in which it is natural for that issue to arise. Otherwise, the subtle nuances are likely to go unnoticed. The potential liability might, for example, be associated with largely unanticipated environmental or product liability concerns, or with an anticipated but not yet contractually bound work force downsizing package of severance benefits. Originally, then, the firm chose to engage in some activity and is now confronted with a largely unanticipated, as yet poorly understood, and certainly unintended consequence of engaging in that activity. This suggests deciding whether to recognize a liability at some particular instant is a far more delicate issue than whether that liability is likely to materialize and can be well estimated at this time. The reporting issue, in fact, is part of the overall decision problem of whether the firm should engage in this activity in the first place. Focusing on this larger frame identifies a multiplay exercise that engages the firm, its employees, its customers, its neighbors, its competitors, and its auditor; it also exploits the fact that the firm has communication channels other than its accounting system.

Beginning with a larger view is no guarantee that the reporting issue is well identified, nor is it a guarantee the resolution of that issue will be straightforward. It has the advantage, however, of forcing context and structure into the analysis. This is the reason we continued to use the K (capital), L (labor), and M (management) firm throughout our study.

"Natural" Processing

Second, do not fall for the trap that whatever is reported will be processed in naive fashion or taken at face value. Do not presume the accounting report will be taken at face value with no attention paid to the accounting method or scale or to what has been reported by other information sources.

The board of directors' compensation committee is presumably well equipped to use a variety of information sources—in sophisticated fashion—when it comes to evaluating the management team. Aggressively expensing R&D is hardly an issue under these circumstances. The committee will be much more interested in what projects were supported and what success indicators have surfaced. Similar comments apply to equity market participants.

In other words, rely on "natural" processing of the information, here on economic forces, to extract the information content. Otherwise, you confine your analysis to a particularly sterile view of those who receive the accounting report. This is the reason we stressed endogenous information processing using all available information in a consistent, Bayesian revision fashion throughout our study.

Other Information

Third, do not fall for the trap that accounting is the only source of information. It is simply naive to treat accounting as the sole or primary source of information. This admonition comes in two forms. One is the fact that when the accounting system does not recognize some event, it does not follow outside observers are unaware of that event. Order books are a ready illustration. Another illustration is provided by a startup, that has not yet recorded earnings but has significant option value. That option value is estimated on the basis of a variety of information sources, far removed from what the accounting system is yet able to report.

Second is the fact that multiple sources of information do not simply "add together." They combine in a far from straightforward fashion. So, understanding the importance of conveying some particular informative event depends not only on whether others already know that event but also more broadly on what others know from other sources.

This concern for other information is, of course, easy, if not gratuitous, to point out in a theory text, but we want to underscore the point that the professionally responsible accountant is well aware of the firm's information environment in its broadest sense. Indeed, auditing relies heavily on nonaccounting sources of information, such as market share, analyst expectations, gossip in chat rooms, and so on.

The importance of some disclosure, then, varies with what else is being disclosed. The item under consideration may complement what the other sources are reporting or, at the opposite extreme, may be redundant in the presence of the other information. This is the reason we insisted on treating cash flow as a source of information and stressed the use of accruals to convey information over and above that conveyed by the cash flow itself as well as other sources.

Comparative Advantage

Fourth, in managing the accounting system, remember to play to its strengths, its comparative advantage. This strength is its credibility, the fact that it can be and usually has been audited. It is no accident that accounting systems shy away from recognizing revenue before production has taken place even if customers are standing in line. It is also no accident that we do not see finely honed, real-time internal reporting mechanisms that highlight the temporal option value of the firm's various resources. Nor is it an accident that the firm's external reporting is subject to reporting standards, auditing, and enforcement.

This comparative advantage theme suggests a degree of caution, if not moderation, when it comes to quickly expanding the accounting system's base. For example, a currently popular theme is to stress the reporting of fair value for the firm's assets and liabilities, including its intangible assets. Yet this calls for a dramatically larger information conveyance task and arguably runs counter to the system's comparative advantage.

The accounting system survives and thrives in a competitive environment. Economic actors have access to a myriad of information sources, but nevertheless we see concern for and anticipation of what the accounting system will report. This strongly suggests that the responsible professional understand and play to that system's comparative advantage.

Incremental Changes

Fifth, be wary of seemingly simple, straightforward solutions. One nearly ideological school of thought, mentioned earlier, is that accounting best serves its users when all resources are reported at fair value. By implication, every opportunity we have to move one more class of resources into the fair value net should be acted upon. From an information content point of view, we would analyze this expansion of fair value reporting in terms of whether gathering and communicating the underlying information that is essential for developing fair value estimates is a reasonable and useful addition to the accounting system's charge. Even if we were convinced of this, however, it does not follow that moving some resources onto the fair value plane is a good idea.

The reason is simple although often overlooked. Suppose we want to maximize a function of two variables, say $f(x, y)$. Also assume we know the function is maximized at $x = x^*$ and $y = y^*$. Now suppose y is at some value $\hat{y} \neq y^*$ and cannot be changed. Does it then follow that we are better off setting $x = x^*$ when we are unable to change the second variable from its value of $\hat{y}$? Not necessarily is the answer; it depends on the shape of the function. The best choice of x to mate with $\hat{y}$ is not necessarily x^*.

Thus, if some assets and liabilities are presently reported at fair value and others are not, it does not follow that progress is made by reporting a few more at fair value, even if we are convinced that the global, best solution is full bore fair value reporting. Theory is simply not very kind to easy solutions.

Dynamic Scoring

Finally, remember that every choice made in the accounting arena is, in an important sense, made in the middle of the firm's life. Being in the middle means there is more to come, and we should anticipate that some change in or some further refinement of the accounting system will not in general be a completely benign issue. Affected parties can be expected to react. Static scoring, so to speak, is hardly the road to exercising one's professional responsibility.

For example, if a manager balks at a particular accounting treatment, might we expect a search for an approach that would avoid the use of that treatment? Are many leases well designed to avoid capitalization under U.S. GAAP? Are intricate governance arrangements designed in part to take advantage of consolidation requirements? Are implicit contracts designed in part with an eye on what the accounting system will and will not report?

Accounting choices affect the economic life of the firm, and we should therefore expect and anticipate reactions to those choices.

Summary

Our study of accounting theory treats accounting as a source of information, a formal measurement system that uses the language and algebra of valuation to convey information. This focus on information requires us to admit to uncertainty and carry along an explicit reason for wanting to know something that is unknown, as well as some coherent description of how information is actually used. Otherwise, we are attempting to study something, information, while systematically underspecifying what this something is or how it might be used.

We use a probabilistic description of uncertainty coupled with systematic probability revision and optimal contracting to connect the parts of the puzzle. This treats cognitive issues, transaction costs, and socialization issues as second-order effects, in turn suggesting that we pause to consider the possible effect of such omissions, another example of uncertainty.

Here our advice is straightforward. Theory can be quite useful in structuring the task of sorting through an accounting issue, but in the end, judgment is essential. In exercising this judgment, we find it important to pay close attention to the setting in which the accounting issue arises. What has the firm done that leads to the issue? What portrayal of this activity, what information release, is appropriate, and how might this information be packaged? What other information is available? What is the accounting system's comparative advantage in carrying out this task? What larger issues are involved? What institutional reactions and adjustments might follow?

It makes little sense to tackle accounting issues in a vacuum in which the world is static, other information sources are absent, and the reporting firm's behavior is exogenous. Accounting is an important institutional fabric in our society. It deserves better than sloppy thinking.

Selected References

Admitting to less than superrationality and transaction costs opens the door to a variety of phenomena. Market efficiency and so-called anomalies are examined in Abarbanell and Bernard (2000), Bartov, Radhakrishnan, and Krinsky (2000), Fama (1998), Sloan (1996), and Loughran and Ritter (2000), for example. In turn, Feltham and Xie (1994) and Loughran and Ritter (2002) illustrate specific cognitive or contracting limitations in an exchange while Sargent (1999) uses them in a policy context, and Starmer (2000), Plous (1999), and Machina (1987) emphasize an individual setting. Hart (1995; 2001) and Williamson (1985) emphasize transaction costs in organization terms, Martin (1992) emphasizes culture, Dye (2002) examines dynamic scoring issues in an accounting context while Tirole (1999; 2001) emphasizes market frictions more broadly and LePine and Van Dyne (2001) stress organizational citizenship and helping peers perform.[5]

Exercises

20.1. What does it mean to say that accounting is a source of information?

20.2. What does it mean to claim that accounting uses the language and algebra of valuation to convey information?

20.3. Our study of accounting theory relied on two potential uses of that information, valuation and evaluation. Explain why it is important to identify uses, why these two uses were used in our study, and why we did not concentrate on a single use.

20.4. Once the fundamentals were in place, our study of accounting theory always began with a setting in which the firm found it rational to engage in behavior that created the accounting issue. Why is it important to treat the accounting issue as endogenous in this fashion?

20.5. What does it mean to claim that a great deal of the accounting system's strength or importance lies in what it might report off-equilibrium?

20.6. Why does theory concentrate on first-order effects, and why does our particular approach leave cognitive issues, transaction costs, and socialization outside its formal domain?

20.7. Let $f(x, y, z) = 9x - x^2 + 9y - y^2 + 5z - z^2 - xyz$.

   a. Determine the values of x, y, and z that maximize this function subject to $x, y, z \geq 0$. (You should find $x = y = 4.5$ and $z = 0$ rather appealing.)

   b. Now suppose that our initial position is $x = 3$, $y = 0$, and $z = 2.5$. Does moving x to its optimal setting of $x = 4.5$ improve performance? That is, is $f(x, y, z)$ higher under $x = 4.5$, $y = 0$, and $z = 2.5$ than $f(x, y, z)$ under $x = 3$, $y = 0$, and $z = 2.5$?

   c. Finally, hold $x = 4.5$ and $z = 2.5$ constant but try out $y = 0$ versus $y = 2$ versus $y = 2.5$. What do you observe? Does moving y to its optimal setting improve performance?

20.8. Repeat Exercise 20.7 for the case $f(x, y, z) = 9x - x^2 + 9y - y^2 + 4z - z^2$. Contrast what you find here with what you found in the original case.

20.9. What, if anything, does Exercise 20.7 tell you about our study of accounting?

[5] Likewise, Christensen and Feltham (2002) offer a wide-ranging, in depth treatment of the rationality approach.

References

AAA. *A Statement of Basic Accounting Theory.* American Accounting Association, 1966.

Abarbanell, J., and V. Bernard. "Is the U.S. Stock Market Myopic?" *Journal of Accounting Research* (Autumn 2000).

Abowd, J., and D. Kaplan. "Executive Compensation: Six Questions that Need Answering." *Journal of Economic Perspectives* (Fall 1999).

Aghion, P., and J. Tirole. "Formal and Real Authority in Organizations." *Journal of Political Economy* (February 1997).

Antle, R., and J. Demski. "The Controllability Principle in Responsibility Accounting." *Accounting Review* (October 1988).

Antle, R., and J. Demski. "Revenue Recognition." *Contemporary Accounting Research* (Spring 1989).

Antle, R., J. Demski, and S. Ryan. "Multiple Sources of Information, Valuation, and Accounting Earnings." *Journal of Accounting, Auditing & Finance* (Fall 1994).

Arrow, K. *Social Choice and Individual Values.* Yale University Press, 1990.

Arrow, K. *The Limits of Organization.* Norton, 1974.

Arya, A., J. Fellingham, J. Glover, D. Schroeder, and G. Strang. "Inferring Transactions from Financial Statements." *Contemporary Accounting Research* (Fall 2000).

Arya, A., J. Fellingham, and D. Schroeder. "Estimating Transactions Given Balance Sheets and an Income Statement." *Issues in Accounting Education* (August 2000).

Arya, A., and J. Glover. "Verification of Historical Cost Reports by an Economic Agent." *Accounting Review* (April 1996).

Arya, A., J. Glover, and K. Sivaramakrishnan. "The Interaction between Decision and Control Problems and the Value of Information." *Accounting Review* (October 1997).

Arya, A., J. Glover, and S. Sunder. "Earnings Management and the Revelation Principle." *Review of Accounting Studies* (1998).

Baiman, S., and J. Demski. "Economically Optimal Performance Evaluation and Control Systems." *Journal of Accounting Research Supplement* (1980).

Baiman, S., and R. Verrecchia. "Earnings and Price-Based Compensation Contracts in the Presence of Discretionary Trading and Incomplete Contracting." *Journal of Accounting & Economics* (July 1995).

Ball, R., and P. Brown. "An Empirical Evaluation of Accounting Income Numbers." *Journal of Accounting Research* (Autumn 1968).

Baron, J., and D. Kreps. *Strategic Human Resources.* Wiley, 1999.

Barth, M., D. Cram, and K. Nelson. "Accruals and the Prediction of Future Cash Flows." *Accounting Review* (January 2001).

Barton, J. "Does the Use of Financial Derivatives Affect Earnings Management Decisions?" *Accounting Review* (January 2001).

Bartov, E., S. Radhakrishnan, and I. Krinsky. "Investor Sophistication and Patterns in Stock Returns after Earnings Announcements." *Accounting Review* (January 2000).

Basu, S. "The Conservatism Principle and the Asymmetric Timeliness of Earnings." *Journal of Accounting & Economics* (December 1997).

Baye, M. *Managerial Economics and Business Strategy.* McGraw-Hill, 1999.

Bazerman, M. *Judgment in Managerial Decision Making.* Wiley, 1997.

Beaver, W. "The Information Content of Annual Earnings Announcements." *Journal of Accounting Research Supplement* (1968).

Beaver, W. *Financial Reporting: An Accounting Revolution.* Prentice-Hall, 1998.

Beaver, W., and J. Demski. "The Nature of Income Measurement." *Accounting Review* (January 1979).

Beaver, W., and R. Dukes. "Interperiod Tax Allocation and Delta Depreciation Methods: Some Empirical Results." *Accounting Review* (July 1973).

Beaver, W., R. Lambert, and S. Ryan. "The Information Content of Security Prices: A Second Look." *Journal of Accounting & Economics* (July 1987).

Bell, D., H. Raiffa, and A. Tversky. *Decision Making.* Cambridge University Press, 1988.

Bernard, V., and T. Stober. "The Nature and Amount of Information in Cash Flows and Accruals." *Accounting Review* (October 1989).

Boyes, W., and S. Happel. "Auctions as an Allocation Mechanism in Academia: The Case of Faculty Offices." *Journal of Economic Perspectives* (Summer 1989).

Brickley, J., C. Smith, and J. Zimmerman. *Managerial Economics and Organizational Architecture.* McGraw-Hill, 2000.

Burgstahler, D., and I. Dichev. "Earnings Management to Avoid Earnings Decreases and Losses." *Journal of Accounting & Economics* (December 1997).

Butterworth, J. "The Accounting System as an Information Function." *Journal of Accounting Research* (Spring 1972).

Canning, J. *The Economics of Accountancy.* Ronald Press, 1929.

Cavalluzzo, K., C. Ittner, and D. Larcker. "Competition, Efficiency, and Cost Allocation in Government Agencies: Evidence on the Federal Reserve System." *Journal of Accounting Research* (Spring 1998).

Chambers, R. *Applied Production Analysis: A Dual Approach.* Cambridge University Press, 1988.

Christensen, J. "Communication in Agencies." *Bell Journal of Economics* (Autumn 1981).

Christensen, J. "The Determination of Performance Standards and Participation." *Journal of Accounting Research* (Autumn 1982).

Christensen, J., and J. Demski. "Product Costing in the Presence of Endogenous Subcost Functions." *Review of Accounting Studies* (1997).

Christensen, J., and J. Demski. "Profit Allocation under Ancillary Trade." *Journal of Accounting Research* (Spring 1998).

Christensen, J., and J. Demski. "Conservative Accounting: A Contracting Perspective" (Working paper, University of Florida, 2001).

Christensen, P., and G. Feltham. "Communication in Multiperiod Agencies with Production and Financial Decisions." *Contemporary Accounting Research* (Spring 1993).

Christensen, P., and G. Feltham. "Sequential Communication in Agencies." *Review of Accounting Studies* (1997).

Christensen, P., and G. Feltham. *Economics of Accounting: Volumes I (Information in Markets) and II (Performance Evaluation)* (Kluwer, forthcoming, 2002).

Clark, J. *Studies in the Economics of Overhead Costs.* University of Chicago Press, 1923.

Collins, D., and P. Hribar. "Earnings-Based and Accrual-Based Market Anomalies: One Effect or Two?" *Journal of Accounting & Economics* (February 2000).

Collins, D., and P. Hribar. "Errors in Estimating Accruals: Implications for Empirical Research" (Working paper, University of Iowa, 2001).

Collins, D., E. Maydew, and I. Weiss. "Changes in the Value-Relevance of Earnings and Book Values over the Past Forty Years." *Journal of Accounting & Economics* (December 1997).

Das, S., C. Levine, and K. Sivaramakrishnan. "Earnings Predictability and Bias in Analysts' Earnings Forecasts." *Accounting Review* (April 1998).

Datar, S., G. Feltham, and J. Hughes. "The Role of Audits and Audit Quality in Valuing New Issues." *Journal of Accounting & Economics* (March 1991).

Dawes, R. *Rational Choice in an Uncertain World.* Harcourt Brace Jovanovich, 1988.

Debreu, G. *Theory of Value: An Axiomatic Analysis of Economic Equilibrium.* Yale University Press, 1959.

Dechow, P., A. Hutton, and R. Sloan. "An Empirical Assessment of the Residual Income Valuation Model." *Journal of Accounting & Economics* (January 1999).

Dechow, P., and D. Skinner. "Earnings Management: Reconciling the Views of Accounting Academics, Practioners, and Regulators," *Accounting Horizons* (June 2000).

Demski, J., "The General Impossibility of Normative Accounting Standards." *Accounting Review* (October 1973).

Demski, J. *Information Analysis.* Addison-Wesley, 1980.

Demski, J. *Managerial Uses of Accounting Information.* Kluwer, 1994.

Demski, J. "Performance Measure Manipulation." *Contemporary Accounting Research* (Fall 1998).

Demski, J., and G. Feltham. *Cost Determination: A Conceptual Approach.* Iowa State University Press, 1976.

Demski, J., and G. Feltham. "Economic Incentives in Budgetary Control Systems." *Accounting Review* (April 1978).

Demski, J., and G. Feltham. "Market Response to Financial Reports." *Journal of Accounting & Economics* (January 1994).

Demski, J., and H. Frimor. "Performance Measure Garbling under Renegotiation in Multi-Period

Agencies." *Journal of Accounting Research Supplement* (1999).

Demski, J., and D. Sappington. "On the Timing of Information Release." *Information Economics and Policy* (December 1986).

Demski, J., and D. Sappington. "Fully Revealing Income Measurement." *Accounting Review* (April 1990).

Demski, J., and D. Sappington. "Sourcing with Unverifiable Performance Information." *Journal of Accounting Research* (Spring 1993).

Demski, J., and D. Sappington. "Summarization with Errors: A Perspective on Empirical Investigation of Agency Relationships." *Management Accounting Research* (March 1999).

Dye, R. "Earnings Management in an Overlapping Generations Model." *Journal of Accounting Research* (Autumn 1988).

Dye, R. "An Evaluation of 'Essays on Disclosure' and the Disclosure Literature in Accounting." *Journal of Accounting & Economics* (December 2001).

Dye, R. "Classifications Manipulation and Nash Accounting Standards." (Working paper, Northwestern University, 2002).

Dye, R., and S. Sunder. "Why Not Allow the FASB and IASB Standards to Compete in the U.S.?" *Accounting Horizons* (September 2001).

Easton, P., G. Taylor, P. Shroff, and T. Sougiannis. "Empirical Estimation of the Expected Rate of Return on a Portfolio of Stocks" (Working paper, Ohio State University, 2001).

Edwards, E., and P. Bell. *The Theory and Measurement of Business Income.* University of California Press, 1961.

Eliashberg, J., and S. Shugan. "Film Critics: Influencers or Predictors?" *Journal of Marketing* (April 1997).

Fama, E. "Market Efficiency, Long-Term Returns, and Behavioral Finance." *Journal of Financial Economics* (September 1998).

Fare, R., and D. Primont. *Multi-Output Production and Duality: Theory and Applications.* Kluwer, 1995.

Farlee, M., J. Fellingham, and R. Young. "Properties of Economic Income in a Private Information Setting." *Contemporary Accounting Research* (Fall 1996).

FASB. *Statement of Financial Accounting Concepts No. 1,* "Objectives of Financial Reporting by Business Enterprises (Norwalk, CT: FASB, 1978).

FASB. *Statement of Financial Accounting Concepts No. 2,* "Qualitative Characteristics of Accounting Information" (Norwalk, CT: FASB, 1980).

FASB. *Statement of Financial Accounting Concepts No. 4,* "Objectives of Financial Reporting by Nonbusiness Organizations" (Norwalk, CT: FASB, 1980a).

FASB. *Statement of Financial Accounting Concepts No. 5,* "Recognition and Measurement in Financial Statements of Business Enterprises" (Norwalk, CT: FASB, 1984).

FASB. *Statement of Financial Accounting Concepts No. 6,* "Elements of Financial Statements" (Norwalk, CT: FASB, 1985).

Fellingham, J., and D. Newman. "Strategic Considerations in Auditing." *Accounting Review* (October 1985).

Fellingham, J., D. Newman, and Y. Suh. "Contracts without Memory in Multi-Period Agency Models." *Journal of Economic Theory* (December 1985).

Feltham, G. *Information Evaluation.* American Accounting Association, 1972.

Feltham, G., and J. Ohlson. "Valuation and Clean Surplus Accounting for Operating and Financial Activities." *Contemporary Accounting Research* (Spring 1995).

Feltham, G., and J. Ohlson. "Uncertainty Resolution and the Theory of Depreciation Measurement." *Journal of Accounting Research* (Autumn 1996).

Feltham, G., and J. Xie. "Performance Measure Congruity and Diversity in Multi-Task Principal-Agent Relations." *Accounting Review* (July 1994).

Fisher, I. *The Nature of Capital and Income.* Macmillan, 1906.

Frankel, R., and C. Lee. "Accounting Diversity and International Valuation." (Working paper, Cornell University, 1998).

Frankel, R., and C. Lee. "Accounting Valuation, Market Expectations, and Cross-Sectional Stock Returns." *Journal of Accounting & Economics* (June 1998a).

Freeman, R., and S. Tse. "A Nonlinear Model of Security Price Responses to Unexpected Earnings." *Journal of Accounting Research* (Autumn 1992).

Gibbons, R. *Game Theory for Applied Economists.* Princeton University Press, 1992.

Gietzmann, M., and J. Larsen. "Motivating Subcontractors to Perform Development and Design Tasks." *Management Accounting Research* (September 1998).

Gigler, F. "Self-Enforcing Voluntary Disclosures." *Journal of Accounting Research* (Autumn 1994).

Gjesdal, F. "Accounting for Stewardship." *Journal of Accounting Research* (Spring 1981).

Grossman, S., and O. Hart. "An Analysis of the Principal-Agent Problem." *Econometrica* (January 1983).

Grossman, S., and J. Stiglitz. "On the Impossibility of Informationally Efficient Markets." *American Economic Review* (June 1980).

Hakansson, N., J. Kunkel, and J. Ohlson. "Sufficient and Necessary Conditions for Information to Have Social Value in Pure Exchange." *Journal of Finance* (December 1982).

Harris, M., C. Kriebel, and A. Raviv. "Asymmetric Information, Incentives and Intrafirm Resource Allocation." *Management Science* (June 1982).

Harris, M., and A. Raviv. "Some Results on Incentive Contracts with Applications to Education and Employment, Health Insurance, and Law Enforcement." *American Economic Review* (March 1978).

Hart, O. *Firms, Contracts, and Financial Structure.* Oxford University Press, 1995.

Hart, O., "Financial Contracting." *Journal of Economic Literature* (December 2001).

Hendriksen, E., and M. Van Breda. *Accounting Theory.* McGraw-Hill, 1992.

Hicks, J. *Value and Capital.* Clarendon Press, 1946.

Hirshleifer, J. *Investment, Interest, and Capital.* Prentice-Hall, 1970.

Hirshleifer, J. "The Private and Social Value of Information and the Reward to Inventive Activity." *American Economic Review* (September 1971).

Holmstrom, B. "Moral Hazard and Observability." *Bell Journal of Economics* (Spring 1979).

Holmstrom, B., and P. Milgrom. "Aggregation and Linearity in the Provision of Intertemporal Incentives." *Econometrica* (March 1987).

Holthausen, R., and R. Watts. "The Relevance of the Value Relevance Literature for Financial Accounting Standard Setting." *Journal of Accounting & Economics* (September 2001).

Horngren, C., G. Foster, and S. Datar. *Cost Accounting: A Managerial Emphasis.* Prentice-Hall, 1999.

IASC. *Framework for the Preparation and Presentation of Financial Statements.* IASC, 1989.

Ijiri, Y. *Theory of Accounting Measurement.* American Accounting Association, 1975.

Indjejikian, R. "Performance Evaluation and Compensation Research: An Agency Perspective." *Accounting Horizons* (June 1999).

Ingersoll, J. *Theory of Financial Decision Making* (Rowman and Littlefield, 1987).

Jensen, M., and W. Meckling. "Theory of the Firm: Managerial Behavior, Agency Costs, and Ownership Structure." *Journal of Financial Economics* (October 1976).

Kim, S. "Efficiency of an Information System in an Agency Model." *Econometrica* (January 1995).

Kinney, W. *Information Quality Assurance and Internal Control for Management Decision Making.* McGraw-Hill, 2000.

Kraft, C., J. Pratt, and A. Seidenberg. "Intuitive Probability on Finite Sets." *Annals of Mathematical Statistics* (1959).

Kreps, D. *Notes on the Theory of Choice.* Westview Press, 1988.

Laffont, J., and J. Tirole. *A Theory of Incentives in Procurement and Regulation.* MIT Press, 1993.

Lambert, R. "Variance Investigation in Agency Settings." *Journal of Accounting Research* (Autumn 1985).

Lambert, R. "Contracting Theory and Accounting." *Journal of Accounting & Economics* (December 2001).

Lazear, E. "Performance Pay and Productivity." *American Economic Review* (December 2000).

LePine, J., and L. Van Dyne. "Peer Responses to Low Performers: An Attributional Model of Helping in the Context of Groups." *Academy of Management Review* (January 2001).

Lev, B. "On the Usefulness of Earnings and Earnings Research: Lessons and Directions from Two Decades of Empirical Research." *Journal of Accounting Research Supplement* (1989).

Lev, B., and T. Sougiannis. "The Capitalization, Amortization, and Value-Relevance of R&D." *Journal of Accounting & Economics* (February 1996).

Liang, P. "Accounting Recognition, Moral Hazard, and Communication." *Contemporary Accounting Research* (Fall 2000).

Liang, P. "Recognition: An Information Content Perspective." *Accounting Horizons* (September 2001).

Liu, C., S. Ryan, and J. Wahlen. "Differential Valuation Implications of Loan Loss Provisions across Banks and Fiscal Quarters." *Accounting Review* (January 1997).

Loughran, T., and J. Ritter. "Uniformly Least Powerful Tests of Market Efficiency." *Journal of Financial Economics* (March 2000).

Loughran, T., and J. Ritter. "Why Don't Issuers Get Upset about Leaving Money on the Table in IPOs?" *Review of Financial Studies* (2002).

Luce, D., and H. Raiffa. *Games and Decisions.* Wiley, 1957.

McMillan, J. "Selling Spectrum Rights." *Journal of Economic Perspectives* (Summer 1994).

Machina, M. "Choice under Uncertainty: Problems Solved and Unsolved." *Journal of Economic Perspectives* (Summer 1987).

Maor, E. *e: The Story of a Number.* Princeton University Press, 1994.

Marschak, J. "The Payoff-Relevant Description of States and Acts." *Econometrica* (October 1963).

Marschak, J., and K. Miyasawa. "Economic Comparability of Information Systems." *International Economic Review* (June 1968).

Martin, J. *Cultures in Organizations: Three Perspectives.* Oxford University Press, 1992.

Melumad, N., and S. Reichelstein. "Value of Communication in Agencies." *Journal of Economic Theory* (April 1989).

Milgrom, P. "Employment Contracts, Influence Activities, and Efficient Organization Design." *Journal of Political Economy* (February1988).

Milgrom, P. "Auctions and Bidding: A Primer." *Journal of Economic Perspectives* (Summer 1989).

Milgrom, P. "Game Theory and the Spectrum Auctions." *European Economic Review* (May 1998).

Milgrom, P., and J. Roberts. *Economics, Organization & Management.* Prentice Hall, 1992.

Milgrom, P., and N. Stokey. "Information, Trade and Common Knowledge." *Journal of Economic Theory* (February 1982).

Myers, J. "Implementing Residual Income Valuation with Linear Information Dynamics." *Accounting Review* (January 1999).

Myerson, R. "Incentive Compatibility and the Bargaining Problem." *Econometrica* (January 1979).

Myerson, R. *Game Theory: Analysis of Conflict.* Harvard University Press, 1991.

Nisbett, R., and L. Ross. *Human Inference: Strategies and Shortcomings of Social Judgment.* Prentice Hall, 1980.

Niskanen, J., and M. Keloharju. "Earnings Cosmetics in a Tax-Driven Accounting Environment: Evidence from Finnish Public Firms." *European Accounting Review* (September 2000).

Nurnberg, H. "Minority Interest in the Consolidated Retained Earnings Statement." *Accounting Horizons* (June 2001).

Ohlson, J. *The Theory of Financial Markets and Information.* Elsevier, 1987.

Parker, R., G. Harcourt, and G. Whittington. *Readings in the Concept and Measurement of Income.* Philip Allan, 1986.

Paton, W. *Accounting Theory* (1922; reissued in 1962 by Accounting Studies Press).

Paton, W., and A. Littleton. *An Introduction to Corporate Accounting Standards.* American Accounting Association, 1940.

Peasnell, K. "Some Formal Connections between Economic Values and Yields and Accounting Numbers." *Journal of Business Finance & Accounting* (Autumn 1982).

Penman, S. *Financial Statement Analysis and Security Valuation.* McGraw-Hill, 2000.

Penno, M. "Accounting Systems, Participation in Budgeting, and Performance Evaluation." *Accounting Review* (April 1990).

Plous, S. *The Psychology of Judgment and Decision Making*. McGraw-Hill, 1999.

Pratt, J. "Risk Aversion in the Small and in the Large." *Econometrica* (January 1964).

Preinreich, G. "Valuation and Amortization." *Accounting Review* (July 1937).

Prendergast, C. "The Provision of Incentives in Firms." *Journal of Economic Literature* (March 1999).

Radner, R. "Competitive Equilibrium under Uncertainty." *Econometrica* (January 1968).

Rasmusen, E. *Games and Information: An Introduction to Game Theory*. Blackwell, 2000.

Rogerson, W. "Overhead Allocation and Incentives for Cost Minimization in Defense Procurement." *Accounting Review* (October 1992).

Rogerson, W. "Economic Incentives and the Defense Procurement Process." *Journal of Economic Perspectives* (Fall 1994).

Ryan, S. "A Model of Accrual Measurement with Implications for the Evolution of the Book-to-Market Ratio." *Journal of Accounting Research* (Spring 1995).

Sappington, D. "Incentives in Principal-Agent Relationships." *Journal of Economic Perspectives* (Spring 1991).

Sappington, D., and J. Stiglitz. "Privatization, Information, and Incentives." *Journal of Policy Analysis and Management* (Summer 1987).

Sappington, D., and D. Weisman. *Designing Incentive Regulation for the Telecommunications Industry*. MIT Press, 1995.

Sargent, T. *The Conquest of American Inflation*. Princeton University Press, 1999.

Savage, L. *The Foundations of Statistics*. Wiley, 1954.

Schefter, J. *All Corvettes Are Red*. Simon & Schuster, 1997.

Schipper, K. "Commentary on Earnings Management." *Accounting Horizons* (December 1989).

Schlee, E. "The Value of Information in Efficient Risk-Sharing Arrangements." *American Economic Review* (June 2001).

Schrand, C., and B. Walther. "Strategic Benchmarks in Earnings Announcements: The Selective Disclosure of Prior-Period Earnings Components." *Accounting Review* (April 2000).

Scott, W. *Financial Accounting Theory*. Prentice-Hall, 1996.

Shavell, S. "Risk Sharing and Incentives in the Principal and Agent Relationship." *Bell Journal of Economics* (Spring 1979).

Sims, C. "Macroeconomics and Methodology." *Journal of Economic Perspectives* (Winter 1996).

Sloan, R. "Do Stock Prices Fully Reflect Information in Accruals and Cash Flows about Future Earnings?" *Accounting Review* (July 1996).

Solomons, D. *Divisional Performance: Measurement and Control* (Financial Executives Research Foundation, 1965; Irwin, 1968).

Sorter, G. "An 'Events' Approach to Basic Accounting Theory." *Accounting Review* (January 1969).

Starmer, C. "Developments in Non-Expected Utility Theory: The Hunt for a Descriptive Theory of Choice under Risk." *Journal of Economic Literature* (June 2000).

Sterling, R. "On Theory Construction and Verification." *Accounting Review* (July 1970).

Stiglitz, J. "Risk Sharing and Incentives in Sharecropping." *Review of Economic Studies* (April 1974).

Sundem, G., R. Dukes, and J. Elliot. *The Value of Information and Audits*. Coopers & Lybrand, 1996.

Sunder, S. *Theory of Accounting and Control*. South-Western, 1997.

Thomas, J. "Unusual Patterns in Reported Earnings." *Accounting Review* (October 1989).

Tirole, J. "Incomplete Contracts: Where Do We Stand?" *Econometrica* (July 1999).

Tirole, J. "Corporate Governance." *Econometrica* (January 2001).

Vatter, W. *The Fund Theory of Accounting and Its Implications for Financial Reports.* University of Chicago Press, 1947.

Verrecchia, R. "Essays on Disclosure." *Journal of Accounting & Economics* (December 2001).

Watts, R., and J. Zimmerman. *Positive Accounting Theory.* Prentice-Hall, 1986.

White, G., A. Sondhi, and D. Fried. *The Analysis and Use of Financial Statements.* Wiley, 1997.

Whittington, G. *The Elements of Accounting: An Introduction.* Cambridge University Press, 1992.

Williamson, O. *The Economic Institutions of Capitalism.* Free Press, 1985.

Wilson, G. "The Relative Information Content of Accruals and Cash Flows: Combined Evidence at the Earnings Announcement and Annual Report Release Date." *Journal of Accounting Research Supplement* (1986).

Wilson, R. "Auditing: Perspectives from Multiperson Decision Theory." *Accounting Review* (April 1983).

Wolk, H., and M. Tearney. *Accounting Theory: A Conceptual and Institutional Approach.* South-Western, 1996.

Zimmerman, J. "The Costs and Benefits of Cost Allocation." *Accounting Review* (July 1979).

Zimmerman, J. *Accounting for Decision Making and Control.* McGraw-Hill, 1999.

Name Index

Subject Index